1979
The first commercial cellular telephone system begins operation in Tokyo.

1991
A new Canadian Broadcasting Act replaces the 1968 Act, expanding the social and cultural goals of broadcasting and increasing the general purview of the legislation.

1991
CERN (European Organization for Nuclear Research) releases the World Wide Web (WWW).

2015 (Mar.)
CRTC relaxes Canadian-content regulations.

2015 (Feb.)
Sun News Network shuts down.

1973
The first call is made on a portable cellphone.

1993
The Canadian Telecommunications Act is legislated, affirming that "telecommunications performs an essential role in the maintenance of Canada's identity and sovereignty."

2014 (Oct.)
Postmedia buys 175 English-language newspapers from Quebecor.

1972
The first computer-to-computer chat takes place in California, at UCLA.

1993
Smartphones enter the market.

2014 (Jun.)
CBC unveils new digital-first strategy.

1995
The Canadian government comes online.

1971
The first email messages are sent.

1996
A United States patent is issued for MP3.

2014
Digital advertising becomes top source of media advertising revenues.

1971
The CRTC introduces Canadian content requirements in radio broadcasting.

1997
Larry Page and Sergey Brin register Google.com as a domain.

1998
The Canadian government amalgamates several funding bodies to create the Canadian Television Fund (CTF).

2006
Twitter is founded.

1970
VCRs (video cassette recorders) enter the market.

1999
Kitchener–Waterloo, Ontario, company Research In Motion introduces its first BlackBerry.

2006
Julian Assange founds WikiLeaks in Iceland.

1960	1970	1980	1990	2000	2005	2010	2015

1989
High-definition television is invented.

2010
Netflix video-streaming service arrives in Canada.

1969
The Canadian government creates Telesat Canada to oversee the development of a Canadian satellite system.

2010
The Canadian government creates the Canadian Media Fund.

1969
ARPANET is commissioned by the US Department of Defense for research into computer networking.

2010-2011
Social media play an important role in planning and communication during the Arab Spring protests, especially in Tunisia and Egypt.

1968
A new Canadian Broadcasting Act replaces the 1958 Act and brings cable under the jurisdiction of legislation, puts the social and cultural goals of broadcasting in legislation, and creates the Canadian Radio-Television Commission (now the Canadian Radio-Television and Telecommunications Commission).

2011
Canada officially switches from analog to digital television.

2013 (Jun.)
Edward Snowden leaks classified NSA files to the media.

1967
The Canadian government creates the Canadian Film Development Corporation to help spur the development of Canadian feature film.

2004
Facebook is launched from a Harvard dorm room.

2013
Alice Munro becomes the first Canadian woman—and the first lifelong Canadian—to win the Nobel Prize in Literature.

1964
Marshall McLuhan declares in *Understanding Media* that "the medium is the message."

2001
Jimmy Wales and Larry Sanger establish Wikipedia.

1961
CTV, Canada's first private television network, is established, along with the first Canadian-content regulations for television.

2001
Satellite-based digital radio is available.

2000
Napster popularizes free downloading/Internet piracy.

Eighth Edition

MASS COMMUNICATION IN CANADA

Mike Gasher
David Skinner
Rowland Lorimer

OXFORD
UNIVERSITY PRESS

OXFORD
UNIVERSITY PRESS

Oxford University Press is a department of the University of Oxford.
It furthers the University's objective of excellence in research, scholarship,
and education by publishing worldwide. Oxford is a registered trade mark of
Oxford University Press in the UK and in certain other countries.

Published in Canada by
Oxford University Press
8 Sampson Mews, Suite 204,
Don Mills, Ontario M3C 0H5 Canada

www.oupcanada.com

Copyright © Oxford University Press Canada 2016

The moral rights of the authors have been asserted

Database right Oxford University Press (maker)

Third Edition published in 1996
Fourth Edition published in 2001
Fifth Edition published in 2004
Sixth Edition published in 2008
Seventh Edition published in 2004

Second Edition published by McLelland & Stewart
@ 1991 Rowland Lorimer and Jean McNulty

Library and Archives Canada Cataloguing in Publication

Lorimer, Rowland, 1944-
[Mass communication in Canada]
Mass communication in Canada / Mike Gasher, David Skinner, and Rowland Lorimer. -- Eighth edition.

Revision of: Lorimer, Rowland, 1944–. Mass communication in Canada.
Includes bibliographical references and index.
ISBN 978-0-19-901315-9 (paperback)

1. Mass media--Canada--Textbooks.   2. Mass media--Textbooks.   I. Gasher, Mike, 1954–, author
II. Skinner, David, 1956–, author   III. Title.   IV. Title: Mass communication in Canada.

P92.C3L67 2016   302.230971   C2015-908301-X

Cover image: Nora Carol Photograph/Getty Images
Part- and Chapter-opening photos: Page 1: CP PHOTO; Page 2: THE CANADIAN PRESS/Paul Chiasson; Page 32:
Doug Schnurr/Shutterstock; Page 58: CBC Still Photo; Page 87: © Andrew Rubtsov/Alamy Stock Photo; Page 88: © Rick
Eglinton/ZUMA Press/Corbis; Page 119: AP Photo/Julio Cortez/CP; Page 149: Photopro123/Dreamstime.com/GetStock;
Page 179: Action Press/Canadian Press; Page 180: © Hero Images Inc./Alamy Stock Photo; Page 205: THE CANADIAN PRESS/
Graham Hughes; Page 239: © MARK BLINCH/Reuters/Corbis; Page 269: © European Union 2015—European Parliament;
Page 303: rmnoa357/Shutterstock; Page 304: Lucas Oleniuk/GetStock.com; Page 336: ValeStock/Shutterstock.
Page 150: From "We Used To Wait" by Arcade Fire. Words and Music by Win Butler, Regine Chassagne, Tim Kingsbury,
Richard R. Parry, William Butler and Jeremy Gara. Copyright (c) 2010 EMI Music Publishing Ltd. All Rights Administered
by Sony/ATV Music Publishing LLC, 424 Church Street, Suite 1200, Nashville, TN 37219. International Copyright Secured
All Rights Reserved. Reprinted by Permission of Hal Leonard Corporation.

Oxford University Press is committed to our environment.
Wherever possible, our books are printed on paper which comes from responsible sources.
Printed and bound in Canada

2 3 4 — 18 17 16

Contents at a Glance

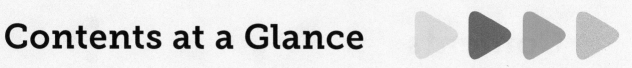

Contents

PART II Theoretical Perspectives 87

PART III The Communications Environment 179

PART IV   An Evolving Communications World   303

List of Boxes

Preface

Every new edition of *Mass Communication in Canada* begins as a minor revision and update, but ends up as a major overhaul. If digitization has altered our communication habits, redrawn the map of our communications world, changed how we engage with media, and shaken to the core the communications industries themselves, digitization has also had an impact on every chapter in this book. Think, for example, of how anachronistic some of our terminology has become. Is it meaningful any more to talk about media *consumers*, when each of us is also engaged in some form of media production, whether that entails posting and sharing content on social media sites, contributing reviews of movies and TV shows, submitting online comments about news stories, or developing our own blogs and websites? When we talk about radio, television, film, books, magazines or newspapers, do we mean the analog version, the online version, or the mobile version? What does watching TV or listening to music mean, when such media consumption can take place almost anywhere and anytime, using different devices? What, exactly, are we talking about? These questions preoccupied us at every stage of writing this book.

This is not to suggest that in this time of transition that everything is new. Certainly, one of the challenges in revising this textbook is separating what is fundamentally new and different from what only appears new. Yes, there are always new gadgets, new apps, or new services. But which of these truly alters how we communicate and which is simply old wine in a new bottle?

The increase in our access to information is typically celebrated, but one of the things we believe is fundamentally new is the extent to which we are under constant surveillance, as both state agencies and corporations exploit new media technologies to track, store, analyze, and act upon our communications and our behaviours.

Working conditions in the media industries have also changed fundamentally, in both the private and public sectors; secure and permanent positions are being replaced by precarious contract work, employers are demanding greater rights to sell and distribute that work across numerous platforms and through digital archiving, workers are being asked to produce their work for multiple platforms, while at the same time facing greater competition from the underpaid labour of freelancers and the free labour of interns and amateurs.

What is not new is the power media corporations exert in an increasingly commercialized communications sphere. If there remains considerable talk about the democratization of mass communication thanks to the accessibility of digital media, corporations continue to consolidate their power by growing larger, by integrating their operations across the full range of analog and digital media, by using their human and capital resources to produce and distribute content with high production values, and by employing their promotional and marketing power to grab the attention of audiences and advertising markets. In other words, the same tools available to citizens are available to corporations, governments, and other organizations with the resources to exploit these tools.

Another thing that is not new is the way in which this book is focused on communication in Canada. We recognize that globalization has broadened our world in many respects; has rendered all kinds of boundaries more porous than ever; and has altered the media landscape, and Canadians' conduct in it, in many ways. But globalization is always experienced from a particular perspective.

With the Canadian population being a relatively small one arranged thinly across a vast geography, the media in this country are fundamental to understanding our friends, neighbours, and fellow citizens. They are key to visualizing the circumstances that drive our problems, challenges, and ambitions. In other words, media sit at the heart of the forces that animate the Canadian polity. From this perspective, they are central to the democratic process, accommodating difference, and building common vision and goals. At the same time, Canadian governments at all levels draft laws, enforce regulations, fund institutions and enact policies that shape our mediascape in fundamental ways. This can include prohibitions of things ranging from hate speech and online bullying to state and corporate surveillance, as well as support instruments for particular media sectors and the production of certain kinds of content.

For all these reasons, having a Canadian focus, like the one we take in *Mass Communication in Canada*, Eighth Edition, is key to understanding the place and role of media in Canadian society.

Not only is this edition of *Mass Communication* fully updated with new examples, illustrations, and statistics, but it is also loaded with new content, reflecting both the shifting dimensions of the field of media and mass communication as well as the social and political implications of these shifts. Perhaps the biggest single challenge has been to document and analyze the growing influence that digitization and new media are having on our society. This is not to say that technology is the primary driver of social change, but media are certainly implicated in the shifting social, political, and economic dimensions of our society, and understanding their role in that regard is a key focus of this book.

Part I, "The Sociocultural Context," situates media and mass communication within this larger context and revisions in this section largely focus on how digitization and new media are implicated in the ways in which our daily lives and society are being restructured along social,

political, economic, and geographic dimensions. We have also revised the theoretical elements of these chapters, more fully integrating them with the historical context of their development.

In Chapter 1, we provide a broad introduction to the themes and ideas presented in the book, defining terms such as *communication*, *mass communication*, *media*, and *mass media*. Here, we introduce key models for understanding the social dimensions of communication, and we consider the ways in which communications systems are central to orienting us within the world.

Chapter 2 addresses the relationships between communication, society, and culture. Terms such as *culture*, *society*, *capitalism*, and *information and communications technology* (ICT) are defined and discussed, and the roles of media and communication in the political and cultural dimensions of society are further elaborated. Following the work of Canadian communication scholars Harold Innis and Marshall McLuhan, this chapter also explores the relationships between the ways in which people communicate and the structure of the society and culture in which they live.

In Chapter 3, we adopt an historical perspective and trace the roots of modern mass media in Western societies back to the Enlightenment and Gutenberg's development of printing by means of movable type. The ways in which media then developed as elements of industrial society are explored, as are some traditional theoretical perspectives on the social and political role of media in society. Libertarian and social responsibility perspectives on media are discussed here, as are the mass society thesis and political economy. In so doing, we underline in this chapter the close relationship between communication forms and economic and political systems.

Part II, "Theoretical Perspectives," surveys prominent theories pertaining to content, audiences, and technology. Chapter 4 provides an introduction to communication theory. The terms *representation* and *signification* are defined and social theory is introduced as a way of representing and understanding the world. The concept of agency is also introduced. The chapter goes on to review some of the main approaches to studying media content, particularly as they pertain to the creation of meaning and interpretation.

In Chapter 5, we further the theoretical discussion by considering the increasingly active interaction between media and audiences in the production of meaning. We discuss the differences between the way that communication scholars and industry researchers perceive audiences, and we explore various forms of media content, such as advertising. The ways in which new media are shifting the form, character, and dimensions of audience are given particular consideration.

We have revised Chapter 6 to emphasize the point that technology refers not merely to communications hardware and software, but as well to ways in which production practices are organized, and relatedly, to the point that all technologies are embedded within a social, cultural, political, and economic context.

Our discussion of technology serves as a nice bridge to Part III, "The Communications Environment," where we explore the structured context within which mass communication in Canada takes place today.

In Chapter 7, we review the history of cultural policy development in Canada. It has been updated to provide a better background to the challenges facing the various communications sectors today. Chapter 8 surveys the challenges and policy responses across the various communications sectors. The ongoing convergence of Canada's cultural industries is central to this discussion, as are its impacts on what were once the separate media silos of telecommunications, broadcasting, music recording, film, new media, publishing, and the postal service.

Chapter 9 addresses media ownership and the economics of mass communication in a period when new business models are being explored, changing the game for both media organizations and those who work for them. In Chapter 10, we bring together a number of themes in the book by providing a concrete discussion of journalism as a particular form of content production. Journalists practise in an evolving media environment that brings into play ideals, laws, settings, storytelling conventions, and economic imperatives.

Part IV, "An Evolving Communications World," is the last section of the book and situates Canadians' communications within a global context. In Chapter 11, we define what globalization means and survey a number of theoretical currents, while at the same time underscoring the point that the activities and institutions we have described throughout the book are not, and have never been, cut off from the rest of the world. Chapter 12 provides the conclusions and includes a concise summary of the ideas and perspectives covered in the book, while pointing the way to future study and directions of growth and development in the mass communication field.

While *Mass Communication in Canada* continues to evolve from the first edition published almost 30 years ago, it also continues to bear the stamp of the vision and foresight of its original authors: Rowland "Rowly" Lorimer and Jean McNulty. Their goal of providing a rigorous, theoretically informed introduction to the field of communication studies from a Canadian perspective continues to be the guiding force behind this book and we hope that we have been successful in continuing that tradition.

Acknowledgments

We would like to thank Dianne Arbuckle, Mircea Mandache, Jennefer Laidley, and Katrina Orlowski for their comments and contributions to this edition of *Mass Communication*. Our thanks also go to the anonymous reviewers of the text for their thoughtful observations and comments and, most particularly, the editorial, management, and sales teams at Oxford University Press Canada for their work and continued support of this book.

From the Publisher

The eighth edition of *Mass Communication in Canada* builds on the successful approach used in the previous editions that has served instructors and students well. It gives first-time students a comprehensive, engaging, and clear introduction to the study of mass communication, ensuring that they understand the subject matter in sociological, political, technological, and economic terms.

The coverage of the topics in the text retains the best features of the previous edition while adding new information on current trends and changes in mass media:

- Increased content on the social implications of new technologies, including their role in social change (Chapter 2, Chapter 6)
- New discussion of the shifting relationship between the Canadian government and the media (Chapter 3)
- A new section on feminist research in media studies (Chapter 5)
- Increased content on media convergence (Chapter 6)
- Discussion of government and business surveillance and individual privacy (Chapter 6)
- Content on issues and new policies in Canadian telecommunications and broadcasting (Chapter 8)
- Sections on the economics and current trends of media work and news production in Canada (Chapter 9, Chapter 10)

This completely revised and updated new edition combines substantive theory and history with contemporary issues, helping students grasp and relate to topics such as new media forms, historical and social contexts, privacy and surveillance, audiences and audience work, technologies, and global implications. Historically grounded discussions of fast-changing policy, law, and economics will be invaluable to Canadian students of mass communication.

Newly contributed boxes and appendices from Canadian communication scholars give students an in-depth yet accessible look into cutting-edge research and debates. These include the following:

Box 5.2	"Feminism and Media Studies," by Tamara Shepherd
Box 6.4	"Big Data," by Ganaele Langlois
Box 6.5	"What Are Algorithmic Media?" by Fenwick McKelvey
Box 8.3	"Over-the-Top Challenge to Broadcast Regulation," by Emilia Zboralska
Box 8.7	"The Video-Game Industry in Canada: A Snapshot," by Greig de Peuter
Box 12.5	"Data Literacy," by Jennifer Pybus
Appendix A	"Selling Soap: Is Dove's 'Campaign for Real Beauty' the Real Deal?" by Nicole Cohen
Appendix B	"Canada's Impact on the Global Children's Television Industry," by Natalie Coulter
Appendix C	"Two Opposing Views on Journalism Today": "Journalism Has Entered a Golden Age," by Henry Blodget and "The Golden Age of Journalism? You've Got to Be Kidding," by Paul Benedetti and James R. Compton

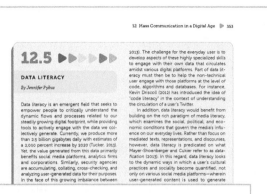

New text boxes appear throughout.

A contemporary design reflects the increasingly digital, quickly changing world of communication in which we live. We have striven for a look that is contemporary and a design that reflects the vibrancy and excitement of mass communication today without sacrificing content or authoritativeness.

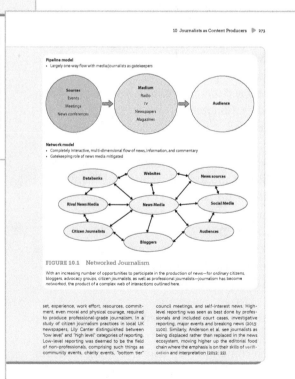

Aids to Student Learning

A textbook must fulfill a double duty: while meeting instructors' expectations for accuracy, currency, and comprehensiveness, it must also speak to the needs and interests of today's students, providing them with an accessible introduction to a body of knowledge. To that end, numerous features promoting student learning are incorporated throughout the book. They include the following:

Opening Questions help students focus their reading at the outset of each chapter by asking the questions that each chapter will explore and answer.

Lists of **Key Terms** at the end of each chapter highlight the important words that students might want to explore further.

Related Websites and **Further Readings** offer more resources for students who seek to expand their knowledge of mass communication.

Study Questions at the end of each chapter are a great tool for study and review.

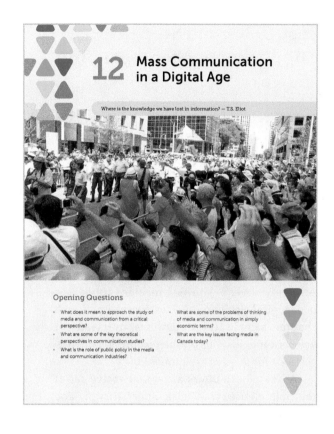

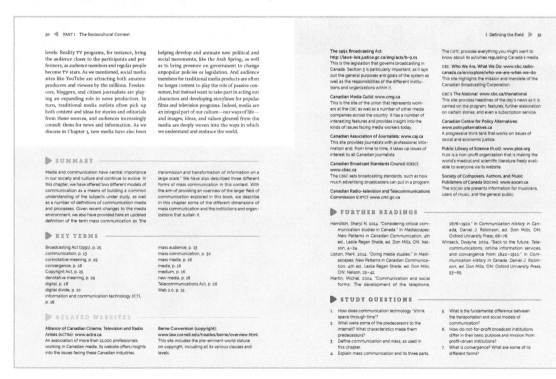

Instructor and Student Supplements Accompanying the Text

Today's textbook is no longer a volume that stands on its own—it is but the central element of a complete learning and teaching package. *Mass Communication in Canada* is no exception, as it is supported by an outstanding array of ancillary materials for both students and instructors, all available on the companion website: **www.oupcanada.com/MassComm8e**.

For the Instructor

An **Instructor's Manual** includes numerous pedagogical elements, such as overviews of each chapter, sample lecture outlines, overviews of key concepts, lists of online resources, and suggestions for student assignments.

A **Test Bank** offers a comprehensive set of multiple choice, true/false, short-answer, and discussion questions, with suggested answers, for every chapter.

PowerPoint® Slides summarizing key points from each chapter, and incorporating figures and tables from the textbook, are available to adopters of the text.

Instructors should contact their Oxford University Press sales representative for details on these supplements and for login and password information.

For the Student

The **Student Study Guide** offers chapter summaries, self-testing questions, lists of related websites, and much more.

Media Awareness Resources provide students with respected resources for news on the web, in print, and on television, as well as resources for commentary on media specifically.

To access these useful features, go to **www.oupcanada.com/MassComm8e** and follow the links!

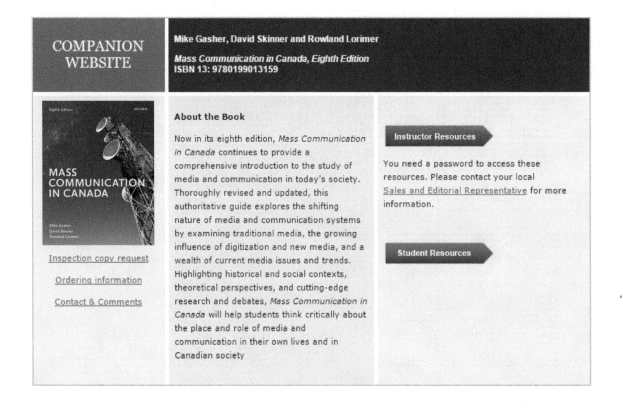

COMPANION WEBSITE

Mike Gasher, David Skinner and Rowland Lorimer

Mass Communication in Canada, Eighth Edition
ISBN 13: 9780199013159

Inspection copy request

Ordering information

Contact & Comments

About the Book

Now in its eighth edition, *Mass Communication in Canada* continues to provide a comprehensive introduction to the study of media and communication in today's society. Thoroughly revised and updated, this authoritative guide explores the shifting nature of media and communication systems by examining traditional media, the growing influence of digitization and new media, and a wealth of current media issues and trends. Highlighting historical and social contexts, theoretical perspectives, and cutting-edge research and debates, *Mass Communication in Canada* will help students think critically about the place and role of media and communication in their own lives and in Canadian society

Instructor Resources

You need a password to access these resources. Please contact your local Sales and Editorial Representative for more information.

Student Resources

The Sociocultural Context

I

1 Defining the Field

Without communication, what is there? — Anonymous

Opening Questions

- What is communication?
- What are communication media?
- How important are media to our knowledge and understanding of the world?

- How have shifts in communication media contributed to changing our understanding of the world?
- What are some of the larger social dimensions of mass communication and the institutions and organizations that sustain it?

Introduction

Media lie at the heart of our contemporary world. From cellphones to Facebook, television to blogs, newspapers to satellites, Twitter to Google, media and communication systems are central to our understanding of the world and how we coordinate our actions within it. In this textbook, we provide an introduction to the study of media and communication and their relationships to larger social institutions and processes. We examine their history, the ways in which they are woven into different elements and processes that form the dimensions of our lives, and various ways of interpreting how they shape and nuance our perspectives and experience of the world.

We introduce these themes and ideas in this chapter, illustrating the shifting nature of communication technology, considering how media and communication systems are central to the functioning and operation of our society, and examining the ways in which they orient us to the world. Traditional media, new media, and social media are all illustrated to be forms of **mass communication**. We give definitions for terms such as *communication*, *mass communication*, and *convergence*, and two models of the process of communication are examined. As you work through the text and our exploration of the field of communication, these definitions and models will provide the basis for building a common understanding of the subjects under study. Finally, in preparation for developing broader theoretical perspectives on media as social and cultural forms, the chapter goes on to outline and examine some of the main dimensions of mass media and communication.

Media in an Ever-Changing Communications Universe

Media are central to the ways in which, as individuals, we come to know and understand the world. As Isaiah Berlin puts it, they are "part of the 'general texture of experience,'" (Silverstone, 1999: 2). They are involved in almost all aspects of our lives—deciding on a career, getting an education, thinking about politics and government, finding the music we listen to, getting a job, purchasing clothes, planning a date, deciding what to eat and where to buy it, paying bills, and finding a place to live. Media help us decide what we need and want, why we care, and even who we are. They frame our focus on the world, draw us in, and entwine us in an artfully crafted patchwork of events and circumstances. From deep ocean trenches to inside volcanoes, and from local neighbourhoods to the surfaces of the moon and Mars, media carry us across space. They also play on how we experience time, providing windows on news and events unfolding currently in "real" time, as well as how we experience things that happened hours, days, or even years ago.

Statistics indicate how pervasive media are in people's lives. According to polls from 2013, Canadians spent approximately 36 hours per week either watching television or surfing online. We also spent 17.5 hours per week listening to the

radio; 8 out of 10 people read 1 or more newspapers in that time frame. We are connected to technology an average of 9.9 hours per day, using televisions, computers, tablets, mobile phones, and so on (Magazines Canada, 2013: 9). And the average Canadian spent 41.3 hours a month on the web, well ahead of the worldwide average of 24.6 hours (see Box 1.1).

1.1 ▶▶▶▶▶▶

CANADIANS ARE #2 IN INTERNET USAGE ON THE PLANET

This chart illustrates average internet usage in Canada and other countries. According to a 2013 report, we are number two in the world in internet usage, spending an average of 41.3 hours online per month. This is almost twice the world average of 23.1 hours. As we discuss in Chapter 11, however, what this average masks is how people living in urban centres, and those with higher incomes, have better access to the internet than those living in rural areas or those with lower incomes.

Average Hours Spent Online per Person per Month	
Country	Hours
United States	43.0
Canada	41.8
United Kingdom	38.9
France	27.9
Brazil	27.9
Germany	24.7
Japan	21.9
Russian Federation	25.0
China	17.6
Italy	19.0
World	24.6

Source: Based on comScore 2012 in *Magazines Canada,* 2013, p. 7.

But not only are communication media key to our individual lives, they are also central to the larger organization and functioning of our society. Media help bind Canadians together with common ideas and understandings of our culture. From maple leaves to hockey to health care and beyond, they create what Benedict Anderson (1983) calls an "imagined community" and help construct and feed our conceptions about Canada and what it means to be Canadian. Media are the major means through which governments—federal, provincial, and municipal—communicate with residents and citizens. (It may surprise you to know that government is the largest single advertiser in this country!) They are the primary way that businesses develop and communicate with customers. Media are also key agents in globalization. They are the central vehicle for controlling the world economy and the movement of goods and services around the globe—for example, coordinating centres of production in China with markets in Canada. And media also introduce people to different cultures and keep immigrants in touch with the countries from which they moved. Media as well work to generate a global cultural consciousness through blanket-coverage of political and economic news from around the world, mass sports events such as the Olympics and soccer's World Cup, and global tragedies such as the Malaysian Airlines Flight 370 and the earthquakes in Haiti and Japan. They also help raise our consciousness about our roles in impending environmental disasters, like global warming. In this heavily mediated world, where the implications of one person's or country's actions can span the globe, "think globally, act locally" has become the new universal mantra, and media are the vehicles through which such actions are coordinated.

Less than 25 years ago, the internet was largely the purview of scientists and researchers. Today, along with the more traditional media—such as television broadcasting, film, newspaper and book publishing, and sound recording (music)—the net is a major industry. But while some writers argue that new internet-based media are making old media obsolete, the internet isn't so much replacing traditional media industries as it is incorporating them and serving as another vehicle for their distribution. A decade ago, downloading music from sites such as Napster and Pirate Bay was thought to spell the death of the music industry; but that industry adapted and the popularity and revenues of sites like iTunes indicate the industry is still very much alive. While blogging and citizen journalism were once seen as displacing newspapers and traditional news sources, today's bloggers and people writing about news on social media develop much of the material they publish and circulate from those traditional media. Similarly, as services such as Netflix and Apple TV illustrate, television programs and networks, once seen as being displaced by internet programming, are finding a new means of distribution on the web.

The internet, however, does offer much more than traditional media. By joining computing power with transmission capacity, new media platforms and companies such as Google, Twitter, Facebook, Instagram, YouTube, and Wikipedia have opened up new ways of seeing and understanding the world, extended personal relationships and social networks, and enabled once-passive consumers of media to become producers of content. Yochai Benkler (2006: 2) points out that this new information environment holds a number of promises "as a dimension of individual freedom; as a platform for better democratic participation; as a medium to foster a more critical and self-reflective culture; and, in an increasingly information-dependent global economy, as a mechanism to achieve improvements in human development everywhere." As we shall see, while such promises are a long way from being fulfilled, the struggle to reshape the institutions and organizations that provide form and focus to this information environment, and the media it supports, is ongoing.

Back to the Future

It is easy for us to get caught up in the wave of new media and its propensity for expanding the reach and speed of communication and to forget the internet is only one of many major electronic media innovations introduced in the last two centuries. As these new media ushered in various forms of social change and, in some instances, made older media obsolete, they, too, were seen as revolutionary and world changing.

The telegraph, the world's first mode of electronic communication, was one of the most revolutionary of communications media. As James Carey (1989: 201) argues, "Perhaps the most important fact about the telegraph is [that it] permitted for the first time the effective separation of communication from transportation." No

Source: © Hans Laubel/iStockphoto.

By January 2014, there were more than 1.3 billion Facebook users and 645 million people registered on Twitter. In addition, numerous website chat lines and other social media, such as YouTube, Instagram, LinkedIn, and Skype, have changed the way many people interact. How many of these do you use? What others? What would your personal relationships be like without social media?

longer did letters and other forms of communication need to be transported physically by horse and rider, carrier pigeon, or ship. Instead, messages could be transported "at the speed of light"—the speed at which electricity travels—across vast distances. This innovation helped spur other changes, such as standard time zones and modern markets.

To be sure, the telegraph was a key technology in *shrinking space through time*—that is, reducing the time it took to accomplish particular tasks in space (see Figure 1.1). With the telegraph, transactions that might have previously taken weeks or even months to accomplish via mail could be completed in a few minutes. Rather than sending a written order by horseback, people could now transmit a short telegraphic message between Vancouver and Toronto and confirm the need for raw materials such as wood or iron ore to be shipped from the industrial periphery to factories in Canada's central core. Similarly, a telegram between Montreal and Halifax could initiate sending finished products such as stoves or furniture back out to the distant margins. Telegraph technology was also helpful in exerting political control over space. The news of uprisings and social discontent in distant colonies could be instantly communicated to central governments, and troops could be dispatched to effectively quell such disturbances. Just as the internet and social networking sites today seem to shrink the distance between friends and colleagues, the telegraph shortened the time to accomplish or coordinate action at a distance, thus making the world seem smaller.

But the telegraph was not invented in a vacuum. From semaphore towers to smoke signals, it had many predecessors, although due to their

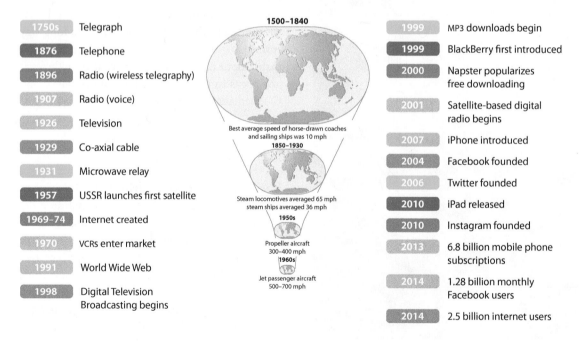

1750s	Telegraph
1876	Telephone
1896	Radio (wireless telegraphy)
1907	Radio (voice)
1926	Television
1929	Co-axial cable
1931	Microwave relay
1957	USSR launches first satellite
1969–74	Internet created
1970	VCRs enter market
1991	World Wide Web
1998	Digital Television Broadcasting begins

1500–1840
Best average speed of horse-drawn coaches and sailing ships was 10 mph

1850–1930
Steam locomotives averaged 65 mph
steam ships averaged 36 mph

1950s
Propeller aircraft 300–400 mph

1960s
Jet passenger aircraft 500–700 mph

1999	MP3 downloads begin
1999	BlackBerry first introduced
2000	Napster popularizes free downloading
2001	Satellite-based digital radio begins
2007	iPhone introduced
2004	Facebook founded
2006	Twitter founded
2010	iPad released
2010	Instagram founded
2013	6.8 billion mobile phone subscriptions
2014	1.28 billion monthly Facebook users
2014	2.5 billion internet users

FIGURE 1.1   The Shrinking Globe

With the invention of each of these new media, the world seemingly gets smaller. Whether we are buying or selling goods and services; keeping in touch with friends and family; or relaxing with film, video, or music, new media have increasingly helped make it easier to communicate with others and thereby made the distances between people and places seem smaller. In other words, these technologies "shrink space" by reducing the time it takes to coordinate action across distance.

Source: Adapted from David Harvey, *The Condition of Postmodernity*, 1989, Wiley-Blackwell, 241, plate 3.1.

vulnerability to bad weather and other natural hazards, none were as efficient (see Figure 1.2). But neither the invention of the telegraph nor its adoption as a major medium of communication happened overnight. Principles behind the technology were developed in the early eighteenth century and proposals for telegraph systems were being written by around 1750. While a number of attempts to establish telegraph lines began in 1800, it wasn't until the 1830s that the first successful telegraphs were established, and they didn't become relatively common until the 1850s—a century after the technology was first conceived.

The development and adoption of the telephone and radio followed a similar track. The idea of the telephone, for instance, leaned heavily on earlier inventions, such as the speaking tube (see Figure 1.3 on page 13). And patents for a range of electronic means of transmitting voice messages by wire or over the air were filed years before the telephone and radio that we know today were actually developed for widespread commercial use.

As they began to be used widely, both the telephone and the radio were seen as inventions that shrank space. The telephone initially was marketed as a business tool and used to help coordinate the sale of goods and services. Like the telegraph, it was seen as a means of closing the distance between businesses and their customers, as salespeople used the phone to contact customers, and customers were able to call suppliers to order products. It is worth remembering that prior to the telephone, people living on the prairie in Saskatchewan would have to write a letters to Eaton's department store in Toronto to order everything from clothes to pots and pans to houses and then wait weeks or even months for that order to be processed and delivered. With the widespread adoption of the telephone, much of that wait time was eliminated.

As we discuss in Chapter 3, "Media: History and the Canadian Context," radio, on the other hand—with its propensity for spreading ideas—was envisioned as creating common perspectives and understanding, or a common consciousness, between people. In a speech later that summer about the first Canadian national radio broadcast on 1 July 1927, Canada's sixtieth birthday, Prime Minister Mackenzie King talked about how the technology brought the people of Canada together through enabling them to hear speeches and other business of government in Ottawa. In doing so, he thought that people would become more interested and involved in the affairs of the country. As he said,

> On the morning, afternoon and evening of July 1, all Canada became, for the time being, a single assemblage, swayed by common emotion, within the sound of a single voice. . . . Hitherto to most

Source: HIP/Art Resource, NY.

Modern modes of communication build upon technologies of the past. The telegraph, for instance, was modelled on semaphore towers, like this one, which relied upon flags to communicate messages over distances. Invented in France in 1792, semaphore towers were a faster and cheaper form of communication than the mail. The rods on the top of the tower would move at various angles, creating shapes that were coded as letters or words.

Canadians, Ottawa seemed far off, a mere name to hundreds of thousands of our people, but henceforth all Canadians will stand within the sound of the carillon and within the speakers of Parliament Hill. May we not predict that as a result of this carrying of the living voice throughout the length and breadth of the Dominion, here will be aroused more general interest in public affairs, and an increased devotion of the individual citizen to the common weal. (Weir, 1965: 38)

From this point of view, we can see why Benedict Anderson (1983) considers communication technologies as central in helping create the "imagined community" of the nation-state.

Through the 1930s and '40s, radio became one of the major providers of news and entertainment. In living rooms across the country, families gathered around the radio after dinner to listen to radio plays, sporting events, and news. Whether broadcast from across town or across the country, radio brought people "closer" to distant events and circumstances while, at the same time, creating common points of reference for the population. Strangers meeting at school, work, on the bus, or at the coffee shop didn't seem so strange when it was discovered that they cheered on the same hockey team, laughed at the same jokes on the radio, and held similar concerns about the issues and events that gripped politics at city hall or Parliament in Ottawa.

Just like the telegraph and radio, television extended and deepened social ties, too. In 1969, TV showed images of humans' first footsteps on the moon, making history in connecting viewers to points beyond earth. But like all new communication technologies, there was some time between its invention and widespread adoption, and while television was first demonstrated in the mid-1920s, it wasn't until the 1950s that it began to elbow radio out of Canadian living rooms.

With the arrival of television, radio was seen by some as becoming obsolete and without any real future. With the development of new technology, however, radio receivers shrunk from the size of large boxes to small packages that could be installed in the dashboards of cars or stuffed in jacket pockets. In this guise, radio took on a new life as one of the first mobile electronic media. In the process, radio largely moved from the foreground to the background, as people began listening to it while performing other activities like driving from one place to another, working on the job, or doing chores at home.

Cable television, otherwise known as co-axial cable, was first introduced in US cities in the late 1940s and early '50s. Coaxial cables carry much more information than regular copper wire, so they were used to bring multiple television channels to places where over-the-air television signals were blocked by buildings or natural barriers.

By the late 1960s, people began to see the cable's carriage capacity as the gateway to a wide range of new information services similar to those available over the internet today. These new visions of a heavily connected way of life were heralded as the *wired city*. As we discuss in later chapters, cable-based interactive television was at the heart of these plans and through the 1970s, experiments in building communities where electronic communication was central to the fabric of everyday life took place in countries such as Canada, the United States, Japan, France, Germany, and Britain (refer also to the Telidon system on page 20). However, it wasn't until the 1990s and the widespread use of personal computers, digitized information, and the internet that the original vision of the wired city actually began to materialize.

From this brief history, we can see that media development and changes in communication are ongoing processes. Each advance in electronic communications technology was built upon previous technologies and, in many ways, continued to enhance the relationships established by the telegraph. Through helping extend people's reach and reducing the amount of time it takes to accomplish certain tasks and activities across space—such as ordering a book online rather than going to a bookstore, taking a course over the internet instead of commuting to a campus classroom, or skyping with friends and family in lieu of travelling distances to see them—media are said to shrink space through time. As media have changed, moreover, they have become increasingly pervasive in our lives, helping to shape how we see, understand, and act within the world. Whether the changes media have wrought in our lives are positive or negative is the subject of considerable debate.

Media and Technology: A Brave New World?

Promoters of new media and communication technologies often present a particularly optimistic or *utopian* view of media development. They claim that communication technology increasingly delivers more choice in information and entertainment. From news to entertainment programs, whether via film; music; video games; or websites like Hulu, Netflix, and iTunes, media offer more and more consumer choice and—as mobile technologies gain customers—services are increasingly available from any location. Google Books is working to make all of the books ever published available electronically for free. Digital communication systems also offer an increasingly available and convenient range of consumer products. From this perspective, access to education and government services is said to be better. And all of one's needs and desires can be met with a few clicks on a keyboard, as one can purchase food, clothes, shelter, pets, and sex online.

But wait, there's even more! New media are also often portrayed as ushering in truly participatory democracy on a global scale. With all the information available online, people are said to be able to inform themselves of the issues that affect their lives as never before. They can talk back to the institutions and people who hold power by telling governments and corporations what they think about issues and products. They can produce and circulate information that represents their point of view. The technology provides opportunities to vote on many issues. Supposedly, it offers true democracy where everybody knows and understands the issues that affect them, and has the ability to make their views known.

Others, however, are not so sanguine in their assessment of new media technology. They contend that communication systems designed on the basis of the profit motive or market principles primarily serve owners and investors, not citizens. For instance, because new (and old) commercial communications enterprises seek revenue from advertisers, they first serve the needs of those advertisers. Consequently only those media products that generate profits for advertisers are available. Owners of private media companies—radio or television stations, newspaper publishers, or internet service providers—are in business to make money for themselves and their shareholders, not to perform public service. All the better if they can perform some public service or provide some public good, but this is not their primary purpose.

As British media scholar and cultural critic Raymond Williams once noted, within such a media system people are free to say anything they want as long as they can say it profitably. Ideas and perspectives that fail to meet the logic of increasing profits—such as those calling attention to the drawbacks of consumer lifestyles or issues affecting the poor and cultural and ethnic minorities—are sidelined or left out altogether.

Media owners also want to attract the largest audiences for the least amount of money. In Canada, this has particular consequences. As you may have noticed, television broadcasters other than the CBC carry very little Canadian programming other than sports and news. Why is this? Is it because Canadians make bad television? If that were the case, why are so many American television programs filmed in Canada? No, as we shall see in later chapters, the problem isn't that Canadians make bad TV; rather, it is because American programming is sold to Canadian broadcasters at a fraction of its cost of production, and a fraction of the cost of producing or purchasing Canadian programming. In other words, American shows dominate Canadian programming not because Canadians want or prefer such media fare, but because media companies make much more money carrying US programming than Canadian shows.

Privacy is another key issue (see Chapter 6). In such a heavily mediated world, people are constantly sharing information about themselves. Whether it be on social networking sites or blogs, where we share ideas, pictures, and experiences with the friends and colleagues, or on web surveys, sign–ups, and applications, companies and governments are recording or following our online activities. Our actions and preferences are constantly being monitored and often accessed by advertisers, parents, schools, insurance companies, government spy agencies, and police departments. As a result, some people are finding themselves inundated with commercial spam, kicked out of school, denied medical insurance, fired from a job, and even charged with crimes.

Access is yet another problem (see Chapters 6 and 8). There is little doubt that media are becoming the lifeblood of our society and that access to media is important not only for satisfying individual needs and desires, but also for educational purposes and to exercise one's rights as a citizen. But not everyone has access to media systems. In our cities, large numbers of families and individuals cannot afford to own the latest computers and to have internet service. In some small towns, places in Canada's North, and rural areas across the country, even dial-up internet service is not available, let alone the high-speed access that many of us take for granted. And in many developing countries around the world even phone service is a luxury that many cannot afford. This **digital divide** is one of the key issues facing media policy-makers today.

So, do media serve public purposes or are they mere profit centres for investors? Is technology going to help in creating a better, more equitable world, or is it going to widen the digital divide? In a larger sense, will the gap between rich and poor get worse? Ultimately, what are the implications of the ongoing monumental changes in communications? Are we collapsing into a totally commercialized society that cannot differentiate between the worthwhile and the trivial, or are we evolving into a more equitable, free, informed, and just world?

As we shall see, there are no easy answers to these and other similar questions.

Our Approach

In this book, we approach the study of media and communications from a *critical* perspective. Here, the term *critical* does not refer to the many complaints that can be levelled at the media for being too commercial or making too much violent material available on television or the internet. Rather, taking a *critical perspective* means that we look analytically at the ways media are implicated in our knowledge and understanding of the world.

What role do media play in the construction of identity and the development of our tastes and desires? How do they inform our understanding of the places we live and work? What role do they have in political processes? Are television

With the motto, "Know the Media, Be the Media, Change the Media," Media Democracy Day strives to provide us with a critical perspective on media and the ways they shape and influence people's lives.

Source: Media Democracy Day.

sitcoms, shows promoting celebrities, and other seemingly innocuous programs simply "entertainment" or do they have other influences or impacts on our lives? Does it matter who owns the media? How does advertising influence what we see in the media? What role do the media play in the economy? In globalization? In other words, whose or what interests do media serve and what role do they play in creating and maintaining social relationships, particularly relations of wealth and power? These are the kinds of questions we address in this book—our aim is to explore the centrality of media and communication both in society and in our lives.

But to understand the way media and communication systems are implicated in our lives, we must first understand what it is we are investigating.

What Is Communication? Some Definitions and Models

As we start to examine the field of communication we need to consider what exactly it is that we are studying. In this section, we define terms and provide some models for helping to understand the process of communication.

At a basic level, *communication* is the act of making something common between two or more people. It is something people actually do. It is a form of social action, in that it implies the involvement of two or more people in a process of creating or sending and receiving or interpreting a message or idea. This process has been conceived in several different ways.

The Shannon–Weaver Model of Communication

One of the first models for thinking about the process of communication was proposed in 1949 by Claude Shannon and Warren Weaver, communication engineers working for Bell Laboratories in the United States. Shannon and Weaver's so-called mathematical or transmission model of communication makes reference to the basic technical characteristics of the process of sending and receiving messages.

In the Shannon–Weaver model, seen in Figure 1.2, a person—the encoder or *source*—formulates a message by putting an idea into words (e.g.: "What are you doing?"). The message is then sent through a particular channel or medium, such as email, voice mail, or text message. On the receiving end, the decoder receives and interprets the signals and on the basis of the symbols sent, formulates meaningful content. The decoder may then give the encoder *feedback* by letting the encoder know that she or he has received the message. By sending a message back, the decoder becomes an encoder (e.g.: replying, "Studying.").

Any interference in the transmission of the intended message (signified by the lightning bolts in the diagram) is referred to as *noise*. Noise may be loud background sounds that make it difficult for you to hear; a heavy, unfamiliar accent; static on the telephone line; or a typographical error in an email or text message.

This model's strength is its simplicity. It breaks the process of communication into a few very basic elements. In this way, it works well for engineers and technicians who speak in terms of the fidelity of messages and transmission technologies like cellphones and voice over internet protocol (VoIP). Because the model simplifies the process of communication so much, it works less well for researchers, social scientists, and others concerned with the social nature of communication, as we are here. In fact, except in terms of noise, it provides no consideration of the larger social context of communication.

Consequently, critics argue that while this model helps to identify the elements of the complex process of communication, it is much too simplistic. Communication is a social process and the ideas, symbols, and techniques that we draw on to construct messages are drawn from our larger social experience. Language, culture, media forms—the elements that form the social context within which messages are constructed and interpreted—all work to frame and determine not only the meaning we make of them, but also the kinds of messages that we create. For instance, no two languages approach the world the same way. Each language positions the speaker in sometimes

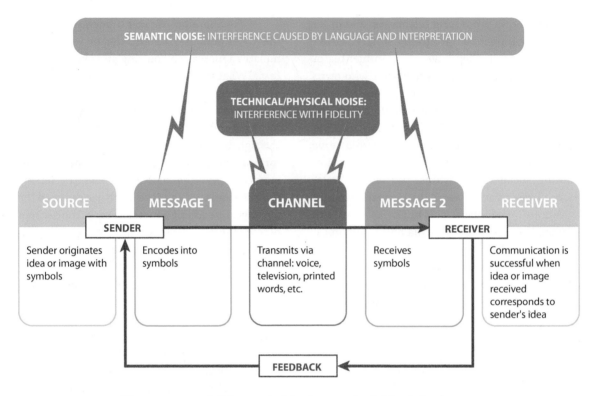

FIGURE 1.2 Shannon and Weaver's Mathematical Model of Communication (1949)

"The Communicative Process," adapted from Claude Shannon and Warren Weaver's *The Mathematical Theory of Communication*. A similar model based on verbal communication was proposed around the same time by Harold Lasswell: "Who says what to whom in what channel with what effect?"

Source: Copyright 1949/1998 by the Board of Trustees of the University of Illinois. Used with permission of the author and the University of Illinois Press.

subtly different ways of thinking about or being in the world. Similarly, there are differences in the way one's age, education, gender, race, or ethnicity nuance one's experience and understanding of the world. Not only can these kinds of social variables influence the way communication takes place, but they can also determine whether or not it takes place at all.

The Social Model of Communication

The social nature of communication can be seen in Figure 1.3. This model emphasizes social and media-related variables that inform the process of communication. The larger social environment or milieu within which message formulation takes place is termed the *encoding context*. At the other end, the *decoding context* represents the ideas

and understandings that the decoder brings to deciphering the encoded message. The nature of these larger frames of reference is the subject of theories of meaning generation and communicative interaction that we will explore in Chapters 4 and 5. From this perspective, successful communication is always contingent on the sender and receiver sharing some common idea or notion of the process and/or subject of communication, particularly in terms of language or experience.

As John Durham Peters (1999: 14) points out, "If meanings inhere not in words but in minds or references to objects, nothing can guarantee successful transit across the distance between two minds." For instance, if provided with the letters *a-p-p-l-e*, you would probably conjure the image of a juicy red (or green) fruit. However,

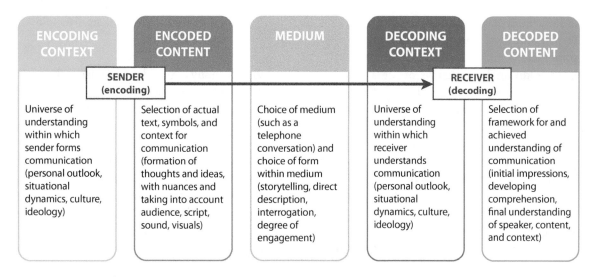

ENCODING CONTEXT	ENCODED CONTENT	MEDIUM	DECODING CONTEXT	DECODED CONTENT
SENDER (encoding)			RECEIVER (decoding)	
Universe of understanding within which sender forms communication (personal outlook, situational dynamics, culture, ideology)	Selection of actual text, symbols, and context for communication (formation of thoughts and ideas, with nuances and taking into account audience, script, sound, visuals)	Choice of medium (such as a telephone conversation) and choice of form within medium (storytelling, direct description, interrogation, degree of engagement)	Universe of understanding within which receiver understands communication (personal outlook, situational dynamics, culture, ideology)	Selection of framework for and achieved understanding of communication (initial impressions, developing comprehension, final understanding of speaker, content, and context)

FIGURE 1.3   A Social Model of Communication

the letters *p-o-m-a* would probably not have the same effect, unless you speak Catalan. So here we can see that sharing a common language is an important condition for effective communication. But even speaking the same language is no guarantee of common understanding. Words such as *love* and *happiness*, for example, can have very different meanings for different people.

However, from this perspective, not only is the process of communication structured by the social contexts of the sender and the receiver, it is nuanced by the medium of communication as well. Putting an idea into words, for instance, is not the same as painting a picture in an attempt to communicate the same idea. Nor is a television newscast item the same as a newspaper write-up of the same story. Each provides a different kind of information about the subject of the story. Similarly, a novel differs from its movie adaptation. The medium transforms the message by encouraging a certain structure in the encoding process, and further transforms it by making certain elements predominant for decoding. Television emphasizes the visual image. Writing emphasizes linearity and logic. Oral speech emphasizes social context, body language, and inflections of the voice.

The social model sees communication as both structured by and contingent on some shared social element or space. From this perspective,

communication is a cultural form, a social practice intimately woven into a larger set of ideas, values, and understandings of the world. Exactly how dependent communication is on the larger social context within which it takes place is an issue we take up in every chapter.

Based upon these considerations, we will define **communication** as *the action of making a message or idea common to two or more people*.

Of Mass, Mass Audiences, and Mass Communication

In reference to communication, dictionary definitions of the modifier *mass* tend to emphasize the meaning "large in scale," as in **mass audience**, mass action, or mass murder—so, *mass communication* means "communication on a large scale." It can also mean forms of communication addressed to large numbers of people or, perhaps, a large number of different messages being sent and received. Mass communication, however, can carry other meanings.

As we will see in Chapters 3 and 4, one common usage of the term *mass* sometimes is based on the perceived character of *audiences* for media as they emerged over time in the context of industrial society. As a consequence of industrialization in the eighteenth and nine-teenth centuries, many people in Europe and, to some extent, in North America, were uprooted from traditional, rural ways of life and moved to live in towns and cities where factories were located. This new way of life was fraught with problems. Removed from a traditional, essentially feudal and agricultural, way of life and the social values, customs, and bonds that gave that way of life form and function, people were viewed by some analysts in their new industrial context as a collection "of atomized, isolated individuals without traditional bonds of locality or kinship" (O'Sullivan et al., 1983: 131). According to these early social theorists, within this mass society, the supposed lack of commonly held traditional social values left these individuals particularly vulnerable to "(i) totalitarian ideologies and propaganda; and (ii) influence by the mass media (largely comprising, in this period, newspapers and the emergent cinema and radio)" (O'Sullivan et al., 1983: 131). Until the early twentieth century, this perspective had a strong impact on the development of communication theory, hence the term *mass communication* sometimes carries with it the idea that audiences for forms of large-scale communication are unsophisticated and vulnerable to manipulation. While, as O'Sullivan et al. go on to point out, "mass society theory has been refuted by historical evidence," this line of thinking still exists in many circles today.

John Thompson (1995: 24) points out that the notion of mass as large scale is problematic:

It conjures up the image of a vast audience comprising many thousands, even millions of individuals. This may be an accurate image in the case of some media products, such as the most popular modern day newspapers, films, and television programs; but it is hardly an accurate representation of the circumstance of most media products, past or present. . . . The important point about mass communication is not that a given number of individuals (or a specific portion of the population) receives the products, but rather products are available in principle to a plurality of recipients.

With literally hundreds of television channels available to the average household, as well as the many other forms of information and entertainment available over the internet, mass audiences numbering in the tens of millions for any particular scheduled program are becoming rare. Despite the fact that there still are mass audiences for some media events and programs, such as the Olympics, soccer's World Cup, and the Academy Awards, today's media fare is often tapered for much smaller audiences, such as programs on specialty channels devoted to sports, cooking, documentaries, or particular genre movies.

As discussed below, however, it is important to keep in mind that just because the audiences viewing some media products may be small does not mean those programs won't be seen by much larger aggregate mass audiences. People usually watch videos on YouTube, for instance, either by themselves or with one or two friends. Those single views, however, often add up to a mass audience of hundreds of thousands or even millions of people. Audiences for traditional media work the same way—for example, viewers might see a film in many different ways: at a theatre, through video rental, on a video-on-demand cable channel, downloaded from a website, on a smartphone or other mobile device, on a specialty channel, or on a regular television channel. Although each of these audiences may be relatively small, they often form a large, or mass, audience in the aggregate.

Mass Communication

Traditionally, the term *mass communication* has been used to describe the communication that happens by means of large traditional corporate media, such as mainstream movies, large daily newspapers, and broadcasting. O'Sullivan and his colleagues captured that meaning of mass communication:

Mass communication is the practice and product of providing leisure entertainment and information to an unknown audience by means of corporately financed, industrially produced, state regulated, high-technology, privately consumed commodities in the modern print, screen, audio, and broadcast media. (O'Sullivan et al., 1983: 131)

This definition was written prior to the development of the internet, smartphones, MP3 players, Google, Facebook, and blogs, but we, of course, know that times and technology have changed.

Beginning in the mid-1990s, when the internet began to be publicly embraced, the options for person-to-person communication on a mass scale expanded dramatically. Suddenly, it was possible to send an email to an address anywhere in the world that was connected with email. Transmission was instantaneous and generally free, obviating all the steps and costs in postal services, telegraph messages, and fax transmission. Gone were the constraints and pitfalls of sending traditional letters by post: there was no longer the need for writing paper; envelopes; postage stamps; mailboxes; mail pickup; sorting and handling by imperfect humans; travel by air, land, or sea; resorting; and delivery. Instead, dashing out a few lines on a keyboard and pressing "send" did the trick.

In quick succession, a number of technologies were added to early internet text-exchange protocols so that by the end of the 1990s, digital files of any type—text, sound, or image—could be exchanged between computers. By 2000, it had also become possible for any person, with a bit of effort and little more expense than a computer, some software, and internet access, to create a website that was accessible around the world. By 2005, blogs proliferated into the millions and wikis became common. By 2006, the term **Web 2.0** was being promoted to describe the invention of such interactive online applications. Today, online social media and networking services like Twitter, Facebook, LinkedIn, and many others engulf us in a complex web of networked relationships.

While the internet started off as a means for person-to-person communication, the success of the World Wide Web and digital technology and their increasing use by the business community and other organizations, the web has become both a mass person-to-person communication system and a decentralized broadcast or distribution system. It has quickly evolved into a large-scale interactive communication system that allows people in Canada, or in many other countries, to create content for next to nothing and make it available to the world, now facilitated by ubiquitous search engines. These many and continuing developments have fundamentally changed the nature of mass communication.

Consequently, from our current perspective, the traditional definition of mass communication is incomplete. Today, *mass communication* is better understood simply as *the transmission and transformation of information on a large scale* no matter what specific media may be involved. Such a definition involves three aspects or forms of organization (Lorimer, 2002):

1. *Mass communication is the production and dissemination of mass information and entertainment*—the production of entertainment and information to large audiences by means of print, screen, audio, broadcast, audiovisual, and internet technologies or public performance for both private and public consumption. In certain instances (e.g., broadcasting and, less often, print) it is state-regulated. Some examples are radio, television, newspapers, film, magazines, books, recorded and performed music, and advertising.

2. The second form allows for greater participation by many members of society as part of either their work or leisure. *Mass communication is the decentralized production and wide accessibility of information and entertainment.* Such communication is sometimes corporately financed, sometimes industrially produced, and often intended for small or niche audiences. It is rarely state-regulated and is undertaken by many individuals, organizations, and institutions. It includes websites, podcasts, blogs, print, film, audio, broadcast, and public performances.

3. The third form of mass communication accents interactivity as its defining attribute. *Mass communication is the interactive exchange*

of information (or messages or intelligence) to a number of recipients. Such interactivity encompasses the exchange of information that takes place among individuals and groups by means of public access to communication media and media outlets. This form of mass communication encompasses the increasing interactivity of interconnected, or *networked*, groups of people and includes applications such as Twitter and Facebook. It encompasses a wide range of technologies, such as telephones, computers, tablets, and an expanding range of mobile devices. As traditional media adopt more interactive relationships and features, differences between these types of media are breaking down.

Such a three-part definition of mass communication—within the overall definition: the transmission and transformation of meaning on a large scale—positions traditional media as just one form of mass communication rather than as the central and dominant form. It recognizes the importance of interactivity and decentralization in today's media and illustrates what Chadwick (2013) refers to as the "hybridity" of media and media systems: the blended and shifting nature of media and media systems as older media technologies and practices merge with new ones.

Media, Mass Media, and New Media

A **medium** is *any vehicle that conveys information.* Language is a medium, for instance, as are pictures, photographs, and musical instruments. Any vehicle or object that imparts meaning or information can be considered a communication medium. **Media** is the plural of *medium.*

We are particularly concerned with media involved in mass communication or **mass media**, *which are the vehicles through which mass communication takes place.* O'Sullivan et al. (1983: 130) define mass media by providing a list that is "usually understood as newspapers, magazines, cinema, television, radio and advertising; sometimes including book publishing (especially popular fiction) and music (the pop industry)." The focus here is on the large institutions and organizations that comprise traditional media. In the context of technological change and our three-part definition of mass communication, however, the different kinds of media involved in mass communication have become much greater than the traditional television, radio, and film and now comprise services and products such as the internet, websites, and cellphones.

It is also important to note that mass communication can involve a number of different types of media at the same time. If we watch a video on YouTube of someone singing a song, for instance, the media involved are the language in which the song is sung; the person's voice; the musical instruments, if used; the video itself; and the internet.

From this perspective, mass media can be seen as *any kind* of vehicle that conveys information on a large scale and so might include such things as buildings, statues, coins, banners, and stained-glass windows—any communication vehicle that comes in contact with a large number of people. These forms of mass media involve institutions communicating with many members of society. But while there are many such media of communication, we tend not to talk about them as media because their communicative role is secondary to housing people, commemorating history, serving as a medium of exchange, and so on (see Box 1.2).

The term *new media* came into prominence in the mid-1990s. New media differ from the traditional mass media in that they do not focus on centralized institutional production and mass dissemination. Instead, they decentralize opportunities to create and distribute media information. Any number of people, equipped with the right software applications, skills, and access to the internet, can produce new media content. But even though they are decentralized, these media still encourage wider participation and in some cases facilitate ongoing participation in

1.2 ▶▶▶▶▶▶

THE VARIOUS WAYS WE COMMUNICATE

Architecture, graffiti, memorial sculptures, public art, even clothing can be perceived as media of communication, even if their language isn't always accessible and their message isn't always clear. In some cases, these media evoke memories. The names of city streets—Papineau in Montreal, Granville in Vancouver, Yonge in Toronto—recall historical and political figures. Almost every town in Canada has some sort of war memorial serving as a symbol of personal remembrance and as a reminder to passersby of the sacrifice the town's citizens have made to Canada's past war efforts.

Building styles, too, can act as media or vehicles for communication of ideas and values. The number, size, and structural splendour of Montreal's churches, for instance, speak to the power and influence the Roman Catholic Church once wielded in Quebec. Christian churches are often built in the shape of the cross, and the stained-glass windows that adorn them usually relate stories from the Bible, both of these acting as communication media.

In New York, the twin towers of the World Trade Center soared over surrounding buildings providing a resounding symbol of America's power

Source: © Monilu/iStockphoto.

and primacy in the world economy, which is one of the reasons why al Qaeda targeted them on 11 September 2001. The CN Tower pictured below is a clear reminder that Toronto is the country's communications centre because it is a telecommunications tower serving 16 Canadian television and radio stations, as well as representing a major rail, air, and road transportation hub.

While these media draw much of their authority from being sanctioned, permanent community symbols, graffiti draws its communicative power from its ephemeral and rebellious qualities. Often dismissed simply as vandalism, graffiti nonetheless speaks to people. Sometimes, the message is a straightforward "I was here," as in the *tags*, or signatures, we see on city buildings, or in the names of people spray-painted on rock faces at various spots along Canadian highways. Other times, the message—often profane—may be one of protest or dissent. Whatever the case, graffiti serves very much as a "voice of the voiceless."

Source: © Jruffa/Dreamstime.com.

A church stained-glass window.

Source: © Bcbounders/Dreamstime.com.

Toronto's CN Tower.

the production and exchange of information. As Henry Jenkins (2006: 3) argues, new media are creating a "participatory culture" that is replacing more traditional "passive media spectatorship." In other words, **new media** are *technologies, practices, and institutions designed to facilitate broad participation—or interactivity—in information production and exchange (i.e., communication) on a mass scale.* Smartphone cameras, email, file sharing, text messaging, blogs, wikis, websites, social media—all these and more comprise new media.

But while new media bring fresh capabilities to media production and exchange, they are also broadening the reach and capabilities of traditional mass media. For instance, websites and online delivery are becoming more important for newspapers. Books are now often sold and distributed in electronic form online, and these e-books are read on tablets, computers, and smartphones. Music increasingly is marketed and distributed online in the form of MP3 technology as opposed to CDs, tapes, or vinyl records. Some traditional media are incorporating new media into their operations by having audience members contribute news and other media content. This bringing together, or *convergence*, of media forms is a characteristic feature of today's media environment.

Convergence

Over the last several decades, the mediascape has been very rapidly transformed, a product of technological innovation, fundamental policy shifts, and massive corporate mergers. The term **convergence**—the buzzword of the last decade or so—was initially coined to describe the merging, or bringing together, of a wide range of previously separate and distinct communication technologies and media.

At a very basic level, this has entailed the merging of computer and transmission technologies—that is technologies used to store, access, and transmit information—to create **information and communication technology** or **ICT**.

In the past, for instance, photographs were taken on film and circulated in hard copy. Video was recorded magnetically on tape. Music was distributed on tape or vinyl records. But in a few short decades, electronic **digital** technology has revolutionized all three of these things. What was recorded previously on distinct media forms now can be turned into the binary language of 1s and 0s and manipulated, transmitted, and read via the internet on computers. This *technological convergence* of voice, video, data, and other communication media is at the heart of new media and the changes that have gripped media industries over recent decades.

As we discuss in Parts III and IV of this book, changing media technology has been accompanied by changes in both government regulation and the structure of media industries, as companies that once operated in industries and fields held separate by technological and regulatory divides have restructured in an effort to gain competitive advantages in this shifting environment. In this context, *corporate convergence* has led to the growth of increasingly large media companies with investments in a range of different kinds of media. Whereas not so long ago, television, radio, cable systems, and newspapers were seen as quite different businesses, today's large companies, like Bell and Rogers, have interests in a range of media such as radio and television stations, magazines, cable systems, and wireless telephone and broadband companies. Similarly, Quebecor owns newspapers, television stations, cable systems, magazines, cable and wireless phone service, and music/video/book retail stores.

Convergence is also shifting the ways we understand and participate in media and media events. As the interactive features of new media converge with traditional media, audiences can participate directly in the outcomes of programs such as *Canada's Smartest Person* or *The Voice*, where they vote on which contestants get to continue on the show. On another front, program producers are also working to build audiences through *transmedia* storytelling techniques. Here,

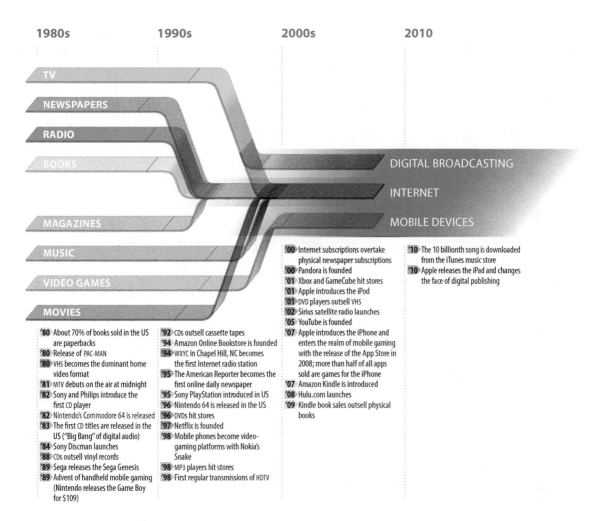

1980s **1990s** **2000s** **2010**

TV
NEWSPAPERS
RADIO
BOOKS
DIGITAL BROADCASTING
INTERNET
MAGAZINES
MOBILE DEVICES
MUSIC
VIDEO GAMES
MOVIES

'00 Internet subscriptions overtake physical newspaper subscriptions
'00 Pandora is founded
'01 Xbox and GameCube hit stores
'01 Apple introduces the iPod
'01 DVD players outsell VHS
'02 Sirius satellite radio launches
'05 YouTube is founded
'07 Apple introduces the iPhone and enters the realm of mobile gaming with the release of the App Store in 2008; more than half of all apps sold are games for the iPhone
'07 Amazon Kindle is introduced
'08 Hulu.com launches
'09 Kindle book sales outsell physical books

'10 The 10 billionth song is downloaded from the iTunes music store
'10 Apple releases the iPad and changes the face of digital publishing

'80 About 70% of books sold in the US are paperbacks
'80 Release of PAC-MAN
'80 VHS becomes the dominant home video format
'81 MTV debuts on the air at midnight
'82 Sony and Philips introduce the first CD player
'82 Nintendo's Commodore 64 is released
'83 The first CD titles are released in the US ("Big Bang" of digital audio)
'84 Sony Discman launches
'88 CDs outsell vinyl records
'89 Sega releases the Sega Genesis
'89 Advent of handheld mobile gaming (Nintendo releases the Game Boy for $109)

'92 CDs outsell cassette tapes
'94 Amazon Online Bookstore is founded
'94 WXYC in Chapel Hill, NC becomes the first Internet radio station
'95 The American Reporter becomes the first online daily newspaper
'95 Sony PlayStation introduced in US
'96 Nintendo 64 is released in the US
'96 DVDs hit stores
'97 Netflix is founded
'98 Mobile phones become video-gaming platforms with Nokia's Snake
'98 MP3 players hit stores
'98 First regular transmissions of HDTV

FIGURE 1.4 Convergence

Source: Rajan Dev and Oscar Villalon.

stories unfold across multiple platforms, with a second screen—such as a smartphone or tablet—providing clues or extra information about a plotline unfolding on television (CBC, 2013).

The convergence of new and traditional media also allows audience participation to extend directly into creating or remixing media products. In this regard, copyright critic Lawrence Lessig (2008: 29–33) argues that digital technologies have produced what he calls a more participatory read/write or "R/W culture." From this perspective, prior to interactive media, audiences necessarily had to assume a passive *read only* or RO

relationship with media content. Now, equipped with new digital media tools, they are empowered to have a read-and-write, or RW, relationship with media and to remix or create their own media products, whether that product is completely original or based on a product of popular culture.

Such participation is sometimes not welcomed by program producers. With shows such as *Survivor*, for instance, new media enable fans to track down and expose the outcome of programs before they run their course on network television, thereby spoiling the outcomes for the series producers. And for some fans of film series,

Telidon, from the Greek *tele* meaning "distant" and *idon* meaning "I see," was an early precursor to the personal computer developed by the Canadian Communications Research Centre in the late 1970s. It was Canada's version of the home-based link to the cable-based "wired world." A number of countries, including Britain and France, developed similar teletext systems. Unlike today's personal computers, however, these systems had poor computing power and stored very little information, depending instead on external, usually distant, databases. Pictured here is a Telidon trial conducted in 1976.

such as Star Wars and Harry Potter, co-opting the characters and settings of these films to write their own stories has landed such "grassroots artists . . . in conflict with commercial media producers who want to exert greater control over their intellectual property" (Jenkins, 2006: 21).

But fan-made media products that mimic the work of original content are not always frowned upon by the big media companies. As Joel Eastwood (2014) points out, "the recording industry is making more money from fan-made mash-ups, lip-syncs and tributes on YouTube than from official music videos. . . . Rather than order the video removed for copyright infringement, the record company can instead choose to run ads before and during the video, making money off the video's views." The money generated from these videos, however, goes to the companies holding the rights to the songs, not to the fans who made them.

The networked character of new media is also helping develop a new political culture. As we discuss in Chapters 2 and 3, working with email and social media platforms such as Facebook and Twitter, activists in countries around the world have been able to bring pressure on governments to change unpopular laws or regulations, and in some cases even bring about changes in government (Lievrouw, 2011).

On a number of different fronts, then, convergence and the interactive media technologies that it has spawned are key features of today's media environment.

Dimensions of Mass Media

As we will explore in later chapters, mass media are an integral part of our culture—our ways of life—and images, ideas, and values gleaned from the media are deeply woven into the ways in which we understand and embrace the world. By way of introduction to these ideas, and loosely building on the work of British media researcher Denis McQuail, we will now focus on the ways in which some dimensions of the media are informed by a larger set of social institutions, systems, and processes. One can understand mass and new media as being comprised of the following dimensions:

1. *a distinct set of activities*;
2. involving *particular technological configurations*;
3. structured by particular forms of ownership;
4. acting within *certain laws, rules, and understandings*;
5. carried out by *persons and organizations occupying certain roles*;
6. which, together, convey *information, entertainment, images,* and *words*;
7. to or among members of society.

We will examine each of these dimensions in turn.

A Distinct Set of Activities

From a technical perspective, such as Shannon and Weaver's mathematical model of communication (see Figure 1.2), mass media are indeed a distinct set of activities in terms of their communicative form and function. Take a news broadcast, for example: a news organization uses a device, such as a microphone, to turn a journalist's voice into a signal. The signal, travelling either as light in glass fibre or as an electrical impulse in a wire or coaxial cable, is connected to a carrier company, such as an internet service provider, telephone company, or cable company, that distributes a signal out into the world. On the receiving end, a device such as a computer, television, or radio decodes the signal and reconstitutes it as the announcer's voice. New media may involve a broader range of hardware and software in this process, but this transmission of content is, by and large, an activity that is distinct from other social activities.

The social model of communication, with its focus on social context, takes this idea of "a distinct set of activities" a few steps further. It stresses that the transmission function (moving meaning from one place or one person to another) accented by Shannon and Weaver is also integrated into a larger set of social ideas, values, and actions—and that the communicators themselves are active in creating messages that provide particular perspectives on, and understandings of, the world. News programs, for instance, not only inform us of particular events but they also tell us which of them are perceived as the most important events of the day. In focusing on accidents, celebrities, and violence associated with social protest, news programs can draw our attention away from other important issues that shape our lives, such as why tuition fees are rising or medical services are being cut back.

Source: © Jen Grantham/iStockphoto.

Focusing on this one person at a large protest draws our attention to that particular thing or event and away from the larger message that thousands of other peaceful protestors are trying to convey. And by concentrating on the action of a handful of individuals at the protest rather than the tens of thousands of other people who were there, the concerns of the many are overshadowed and lost.

Similarly, in highlighting the vandalism and violence sometimes associated with social protests, media distract us from the reasons people are protesting in the first place. Take the accompanying photo of a big protest, for instance—this image of an individual spray-painting graffiti on a police car draws attention away from the larger message that thousands of other, peaceful protestors are trying to convey.

Two early media theorists, Peter Berger and Thomas Luckmann (1966), described the way media work to create meaning in this regard. Through representing objects, events, and ideas in certain ways, the mass media "construct" images and encourage certain perceptions of reality. From this perspective, the social model stresses the role of both media producers and audiences as active, meaning-generating agents and the media as contributing to how we see and understand the world.

In summary, the mass media are distinct sets of activities because of the role they play in shaping our perceptions of the world. They are

1.3 ▶▶▶▶▶▶▶

TURNING THE WATCHERS INTO THE WATCHED

While television was originally designed for broadcasting signals from a single point of origin to many receivers/audience members, it has been adapted to a range of other uses over the years. In recent incarnations, closed-circuit television has been adapted to respond to increasing demand for surveillance and social control and is now used on a large scale to monitor activities on downtown city streets. During the 2010 meetings of the G20 in Toronto, for instance, police installed surveillance cameras on nearly every downtown corner of the city to keep an eye on protestors. After the G20, many of those cameras were not taken down.

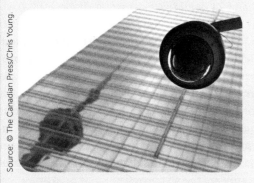

In George Orwell's *Nineteen Eighty-Four*, the ubiquitous secret surveillance of the populace by the dictator further permeates the consciousness of the citizens in the propaganda phrase, "Big Brother is watching you." Who is watching you today, and why?

Source: © The Canadian Press/Chris Young.

the primary tools used to make or manufacture meaning and to signify or construct reality.

Particular Technological Configurations

Media are found in particular technological configurations. Telephones, for instance, are part of

larger telephone systems; newspapers are produced by large newspaper companies that include large printing presses as well as online technologies; and internet service is configured within a network of computers, modems, servers, and telephone and cable transmission systems. Moreover, as we discussed earlier in this chapter, such systems are constantly being restructured or reconfigured, with an emphasis on convergence.

But, as Raymond Williams (1974) has pointed out, technologies are not invented outside of social context. Television, for example, emerged from the interests and conceptions of technical investigators and industrial entrepreneurs who foresaw an electronic medium of sound and visual communication for use in the family home. Similarly, inventors such as Marconi, Edison, and Bell were driven by the idea of inventing products that would have specific applications in the developing industrial and consumer-based societies. But just as the invention of new technology is shaped by societal forces, how it is used is also shaped by a larger set of forces.

Again, take television as an example. In its current form, it serves the interests of owners, advertisers, technicians, actors, and many others. Content is delivered to consumers at a fraction of its cost of production, subsidized by the price we pay for advertised products. TV also allows large, established companies that manufacture brand-name goods to keep their products at the forefront of people's minds. It provides jobs in the entertainment sector, and it also serves the interests of audiences by allowing diversion, entertainment, and a bit of education for people during their leisure time. In this way, television is well entrenched in society, but it took decades to develop these roles. And, as the increasing uses to which television screens are being put illustrates—such as gaming, surfing the web, and karaoke—it is currently being adapted to other purposes and interests.

Cellphones, too, have undergone rapid transformation. In 1990, a cellphone had the heft necessary to double as a weighty club and its only capability was to conduct telephone conversations.

Source: © BBC.

In a famous April Fool's Day joke from 1957, the British Broadcasting Corporation aired a report of a Swiss family harvesting spaghetti from a tree. Hundreds of people called the BBC, some asking how they might get their own such trees. As is sometimes the case with media reports, what the media presented here as "real," and some people thought was real, was a fabrication.

Today, however, smartphones slide easily into a pocket and allow users to not only carry on conversations but also take photographs, surf the internet, play music, exchange text messages, map their locations, and perform many other functions. We can see that in a short time, the development of the cellphone has been shaped by a wide range of influences on the part of hardware and software developers, marketers, and the public in general.

In summary, today's media are a set of technological configurations that facilitate the production, distribution, and consumption of information and entertainment in a variety of forms. But, set between a range of social interests influencing both their invention and development, those configurations are in an almost constant state of flux.

Particular Forms of Ownership

Technology is only one of the formative dimensions of media organizations. Another defining dimension is the form of ownership (see also Chapter 9).

Because we live in a capitalist society—a society based on private property and economic relations mediated through markets (see Box 2.3 in Chapter 2)—most media organizations are privately owned. As such, their primary purpose is to generate profits or income for their owners or shareholders, not to produce media content. First and foremost, if they are not profitable, they eventually go out of business.

Some privately owned new media, such as Facebook, YouTube, and Twitter, have struggled to turn what they do into profitable enterprises—that is, find a business model that can both financially cover the operation of the company and return a profit to its owners. With net profits of $642 million in the first three months of 2014, however, Facebook appears to have put that problem behind it (Trotman and Williams, 2014). In a few short years, YouTube also appears to have become a highly profitable operation, with $5.6 billion in revenue in 2013 (Spangler, 2013). On the other hand, although increasingly popular, Twitter was still struggling to break even in 2014. (We explore in later chapters the ways in which this drive to achieve profits affects both how these sites operate and issues such as the privacy of their users.)

Finding ways to make money from media is an old and familiar problem. In its early days, radio presented such a problem. As we discuss in Chapter 4, at the outset of radio broadcasting in the early 1920s, companies sent messages out over the air, without knowing who, if anybody, was listening. The only way to pay for the programs and other content they broadcast was with profits from the sale of radio receivers. Once those receivers left the store, getting money from their owners to pay for producing radio programs presented a difficult problem. In the beginning, one way of solving this problem was to charge people an annual radio licence fee and then use the money collected from that fee to pay for programming. While this model is still in operation in some countries, such as the United Kingdom, radio operations in Canada and the United States went on to adopt the telephone companies' business model, which involved charging companies to send broadcast messages through renting time on the air. This system proved quite popular with large corporations, which began creating radio programming to attract listeners to whom they could pitch their products and services. Over time, this system of *toll broadcasting* developed into the system of advertising-financed media programming that dominates radio and television today.

But this system is not without its problems. It means, for instance, that despite the fact we look to our media systems for news, information, and entertainment, their primary purpose is to sell us goods and services. Programming and other forms of content are designed to attract only certain kinds of audiences—those with the interest and money to purchase the goods and services advertised with that content. Ideas and programs that don't meet this commercial imperative are weeded out.

At the same time, producers are encouraged to spend as little money as possible on creating programs and content, as this expense negatively affects the bottom line. As a result, Canadian television is dominated by US television programs. Not because Canadians necessarily prefer American programs over Canadian ones, but because it is much cheaper to buy US programs that attract large audiences than it is to produce homegrown programs that will do the same. Having recovered much of their cost of production in the US market, American television producers sell their shows to Canadian networks at a fraction of their production cost—often 10 percent or less. Such an arrangement means that a Canadian network can buy the broadcast rights to a show like *The Simpsons* or *NCIS* that may have cost several million dollars to produce for several hundred thousand dollars or less. Obviously, it's very hard for Canadian producers to compete with this calibre of production.

Privately owned traditional media, such as newspapers, magazines, and radio and cable systems, are almost always subject to the same profit imperative and their content is shaped by this same concern. This is not to say, however, that privately owned media do not strive to serve some larger public interest, or that everything they do is driven solely by self-interest. As we discuss in the next section, Canadian private radio and television stations are licensed by the Canadian Radio-television and Telecommunications Commission (CRTC) and are specifically assigned public duties as a condition of licence. Similarly, many newspapers, websites, and other publications take their roles as important vehicles for public information seriously and strive to provide timely and accurate information important to public decision-making and debate. But the fact remains that for privately owned media organizations, the profit motive directly affects the character of the products they offer. How the business models adopted by profit-oriented new media will shape their content in the future remains to be seen, and with Facebook taking on video advertising in 2014, that process is well underway on that platform (Oreskovic, 2014).

Not-for-profit media are another part of the system. They are mandate-driven, rather than profit-driven. That doesn't mean that they don't have to make money or generate revenue to survive, but their primary purpose is something other than creating profits for their owners. Perhaps the best-known not-for-profit media corporation in Canada is the Canadian Broadcasting Corporation (CBC). The CBC's mandate is laid out in Section 3.1(m) of the 1991 Broadcasting Act and charges the corporation with a number of distinct responsibilities such as "being predominantly and distinctively Canadian" and contributing to a "shared national consciousness and identity." Because of the difficulties that broadcasting systems based on private ownership have had in generating programming that meets a wide range of homegrown interests and perspectives, many countries have long had a government-owned broadcaster like the CBC. Such organizations are said to be publicly owned in that, through the government, they are owned by the citizens of the country, or "the public." Such organizations generally operate at arms length from government and are often protected from day-to-day government interference through legislation.

Other not-for-profit media include provincial broadcasters, community radio, the Aboriginal

Peoples Television Network (APTN), Wikipedia, and Craigslist. As we shall see, generating the money necessary to meet their mandates is not always easy for such organizations.

Certain Laws, Rules, and Understandings

There are a number of laws and regulations directly related to media in Canada. These include several important federal statutes or acts that govern the structure and operation of the media, particularly in the fields of broadcasting and telecommunications. In the case of newspaper and magazine publishing, most industrialized countries, including Canada, exercise little direct control. No licences are required and media content is not restricted, except by broad laws directed at libel, sedition, hate, and pornography. There are various indirect supports and controls, however, such as taxation, business policies, and production and distribution subsidies. Canada has a number of federal production funds devoted to promoting the development of the broadcasting, film, music, and magazine industries, as well as new media.

In Canada, the **Broadcasting Act (1991)** is the pre-eminent statute controlling broadcasting (see Chapter 6). There are no equivalent statutes for Canadian print or recorded music, although Section 19 of the Income Act encourages

As a public broadcaster, the Canadian Broadcasting Corporation is mandate-driven, rather than profit-driven. The CBC's mandate is laid out in Section 3.1(m) of the 1991 Broadcasting Act.

Canadian ownership of newspapers and magazines (see Chapter 7). Broadcasting has received particular attention because there has been a long-standing concern that this field is important to nation building, particularly in the face of the dominance of US media in Canada. In addition to other formalities, such as defining broadcast undertakings, who can own media outlets, and technical matters, the Broadcasting Act outlines what broadcasting should do for society. In other words, it provides a framework for policy. It addresses the tacitly accepted values and ideals of Canadian society and the means by which broadcasting can contribute to their achievement.

The Broadcasting Act also provides for the existence of an agency to develop and administer regulations arising from the legislation. This organization, the aforementioned Ottawa-based Canadian Radio-television and Telecommunications Commission, administers the policies and provisions enunciated in the Broadcasting Act and the Telecommunications Act. The CRTC translates the principles of these acts into rules for industry players and other stakeholder groups.

A second key legal statute important to the field of communications is the **Copyright Act**. Copyright law transforms the expression of one's intellectual efforts—for example a poem, script, movie, story, newspaper/magazine article, or book—into a piece of property that can be owned. It is designed to help ensure that writers and artists are paid for their work and that their work is not used without their permission. These days, however, when technology makes it so easy to copy and/or change media products, how control over them should be exercised is a matter of great public debate (see Chapter 8). Under the terms of the Copyright Act, radio stations must pay musicians for the right to play their songs. To this end, each radio station contributes 3.2 percent of its gross advertising revenue to the Society of Composers, Authors, and Music Publishers of Canada (SOCAN; www.socan.ca/about).

Empowered by the Broadcasting Act, the CRTC determines content rules which, in turn, promote the development of the Canadian music industry.

For example, the CRTC requires AM and FM radio stations that specialize in popular music to devote at least 35 percent of their play time to Canadian selections. Prior to the enactment of radio content regulations, less than 5 percent of the music played on radio stations in Canada was by Canadian artists. As we illustrate in Chapter 8, the reasons for this were rooted in the structure of the industry itself, not because Canadians could not make decent music. This regulation has encouraged the development of a thriving Canadian

music industry and fuelled the careers of several generations of popular music artists, such as Drake, K'Naan, Arcade Fire, Diana Krall, Michael Bublé, The Tragically Hip, The Guess Who, Anne Murray, Céline Dion, and Gordon Lightfoot.

Another important communications statute is the **Telecommunications Act**. This legislation generally focuses on the infrastructure underlying the transmission of messages. The importance of telecommunications service becomes apparent when we consider new mass media and interactive media. Who owns and controls service provision, what kinds of services are offered, to whom they are sold, and on what terms all have an impact over the long term. In the past, telecommunications regulation was much more comprehensive and rigorous than it is today. There were strict rules governing the prices charged and the territories carrier companies could serve. Since the 1980s, however, regulations have been relaxed considerably and competition between different companies has been substituted for direct regulation as a means of controlling corporate behaviour. Moreover, for a number of reasons, the CRTC has decided not to regulate the internet in the same way that it does for broadcasting and telecommunications. Consequently, there are no specific laws addressing the content, structure, or operation of the internet in Canada. As we discuss in later chapters, this has been the source of controversy, as public interest groups have accused the large corporations that control the internet of operating in their own interest rather than serving the broader public interest.

The laws and rules that govern mass media have developed from a larger consideration of the social and economic value of media. Nevertheless, considerable debate remains over the public role media should play and the responsibilities they should shoulder. This debate is over what constitutes the public interest in the media realm and is explored in following chapters.

Organizational Dimensions of Media

The number of people and organizations involved in the media are vast. At one level, there are people both directly and indirectly employed

---

1.4 ▶▶▶▶▶▶

INTERPRETING THE BROADCASTING ACT (1991)

As time passes, societies change. Less frequently do statutes change; and so it is important to write statutes in such a way that they can be interpreted within the context of the time. For example, Section 3d(iii) of the Broadcasting Act declares that "the Canadian broadcasting system should through its programming and the employment opportunities arising out of its operations, serve the needs and interests and reflect the circumstances and aspirations of Canadian men, women and children, including equal rights, the linguistic duality and multicultural and multiracial nature of Canadian society and the special place of aboriginal people within that society." And Section 3i(i) notes that "the programming provided by the Canadian broadcasting system should be varied and comprehensive, providing a balance of information, enlightenment and entertainment for men, women and children of all ages, interests and tastes."

These two clauses address directly two basic differences in society, race and gender, and less directly a third: class. All three are often associated with inequality. The Broadcasting Act provides the framework and the impetus for the media to strive to address the changing norms and ideals of society with respect to race, gender, and class.

by media organizations. These include journalists, on-air announcers, editors, printers, studio technicians, technical support personnel, camera operators, designers, producers, directors, advertising sales staff, security, and cleaning crews. Media companies also engage a huge number of part-time and contract employees, as well independent producers. Employers find part-time and contract employees attractive for several reasons. First, they generally don't have to pay them as much as full-time employees in terms of wages or benefits. Second, they offer employers flexibility, in that they can hire people with particular skills for particular jobs and then let them go without worrying about having to keep on paying them until their skills are needed again. Much of the content in the magazine and television industries is created under contract by independent producers, and other media industries are trying to implement this model.

Another part of the larger institutional structure of media, but usually not directly employed by individual corporations, are industry organizations and lobby groups, such as the Canadian Newspaper Association. These organizations represent the collective interests of the owners of media companies and are generally involved with lobbying government and conducting other public relations campaigns, as well as collecting statistics and other information about the industry.

Playing a similar role, but for the employees of such organizations rather than their owners, are media unions and professional associations. Media unions in Canada, such as the Canadian Media Guild (CMG) and Unifor, play strong roles not only in representing their members' interests to employers, but also in forwarding those interests to local and national governments, as well as to national and international regulatory fora. The interests of media owners and media employees are not always the same, particularly in Canada where, as we have discussed, it is often much cheaper to import foreign media products than produce them at home. Performers in Canada also have their own professional organizations—in anglophone Canada, it is the 21,000-member Alliance of Canadian Cinema, Television and Radio Artists (ACTRA)—and film

and television producers have the Canadian Media Production Association (CMPA). These organizations represent the interests of their members with employers as well as conduct studies and keep statistics on the structure and health of their industries, and they represent their interests in government studies and enquiries.

Also on the production side are wire services that provide media content, particularly news (see Chapter 9). Founded in 1917, The Canadian Press (CP) is perhaps the best-known of these organizations. Until 2010, the company was run as a not-for-profit news cooperative that supplied both print and broadcast news from across the country to its newspaper, radio, and television members—coverage that the smaller newspapers and stations in particular would not otherwise have been able to provide. But with escalating concentration of media ownership, media chains began sharing stories among their own properties, rendering membership in CP redundant and leading to its being purchased by its three largest members: Torstar (which publishes the *Toronto Star*), Gesca (*La Presse*), and Bell Canada Enterprises (*The Globe and Mail,* though BCE sold its last stake in the *Globe* to Woodbridge in August 2015) (Iype, 2010).

CNW Group (formerly known as Canada NewsWire) also provides content to media outlets. But it operates as a public-relations service rather than as a news company. It primarily focuses on distributing event announcements and press releases from companies advertising new products and services. Instead of charging media outlets for using that content, CNW charges the organizations generating it. As media content is expensive to produce, the "free" content offered by this organization is quite popular with newspapers and other media outlets. CNW also specializes in posting and circulating client information on social media.

The advertising industry (see Chapter 5) forms another organizational dimension of the media. The industry is comprised of both Canadian and foreign companies and has both large anglophone and francophone components. Advertising agencies generally operate on a fee-for-service basis and receive a percentage of the fee their clients pay media outlets to run their ads. But many newspapers, radio and television stations, and new media outlets, such as large websites with heavy traffic, employ their own advertising people who sell and design ads. Similarly, many large companies have their own advertising departments.

Public-relations (PR) companies are somewhat similar to advertising agencies—sometimes companies offer both kinds of services—only they promote specific events and brands, or manage the larger public image of a company, rather than market-specific products or services.

Media-relations people also are employed by government, private corporations, not-for-profit companies, charitable organizations, industry lobby groups, and more. Many organizations employ communications people who specialize in engaging with media, as well as performing other communication functions. These people actively engage with media to try to ensure that the interests of their organizations are well represented in news stories and other media content, as well as to promote events they sponsor.

As we have seen, government regulators and policy people also play an important role in the operation of the media. In Canada, media largely come under federal jurisdiction; the departments of heritage and industry, as well as the CRTC, have considerable power and resources in developing and administering media regulations. Heritage Canada, for example, oversees a wide range of policies affecting books and magazines, film and video, broadcasting, and interactive media and music.

Still another set of organizations that actively engage and influence media coverage are think tanks and research institutes. The purpose of these not-for-profit organizations is generally to promote particular perspectives and understandings on issues of public importance and, where possible, to influence the development of public policy in ways that promote their mandate or interest. Among these, the Alberta-based Pembina Institute promotes sustainable energy solutions; the Canadian Centre for Policy Alternatives undertakes research and campaigns to promote

1.5 ▶▶▶▶▶▶

GOVERNMENT INFORMATION

In an attempt to increase access to information that governments want citizens to have, federal government departments have created their own websites. An interesting exercise in examining the impact of government information, and especially press releases, is to go to the section labelled "Newsroom," find one or two press releases, and then try to find stories built from those releases in the media. Start by googling a sentence or phrase from one of those releases. You may be surprised at how many media outlets simply republish them in part or in their entirety.

social, economic, and environmental justice; and the C.D. Howe Institute works on economic and social-policy issues. Over the last 30 years, conservative think tanks like the Fraser Institute and the MacDonald Laurier Institute and have been particularly successful in helping shift public policy in the direction of more market-oriented and individualist values (see Gutstein, 2009).

Information, Entertainment, Images, Sounds, and Words

The central element of media is, of course, content, which has traditionally been thought of in terms of information and entertainment, but it is delivered as images, sounds, and words. Theoretical perspectives on media content, or different ways of thinking about and analyzing it, are discussed in Chapters 4 and 5. For now, we simply wish to highlight the ways in which both classifying media content and trying to specify the meaning it contains can be somewhat slippery and arbitrary.

In television, distinctions are often drawn, for instance, between different types of programming, including information programs, such as news, documentaries, and editorials, and entertainment programs, such as films, situation comedies, and one-hour dramas. We must bear in mind, however, that entertainment is taken to be informative, just as information can be entertaining.

Meaning in media messages is not always clear or predetermined—images and words (and other media content) have at least two possible types or levels of meaning. The first is **denotative meaning**, which is the obvious, literal, or readily apparent meaning. The second is **connotative meaning**, which is the secondary, figurative meaning, or meanings, that might be associated with the image or word. The word *apple* might be read as having a denotative meaning as a kind of fruit and connotatively as representing knowledge or the Bible's story of Adam and Eve—or, perhaps, a particular computer company. Problems sometimes arise, however, in trying to develop agreement on exactly what are the denotative or connotative meanings associated with particular images or content. Take, for example, Japanese game shows, such as *Takeshi's Castle*, otherwise known as *MXC* or *Most Extreme Elimination Challenge*. In Japan, many of the colourfully dressed characters would be immediately recognized as specific cultural or folkloric characters—they would have immediate and specific denotative meaning. To Canadian audiences, however, such meaning is indecipherable. Similar problems arise in language use between generations. Words, like *dude*, *dope*, or *boss* have quite different denotative meanings depending on who is asked. The point here is that meaning is never predetermined. Just as media producers often go to great lengths to *encode* or put meaning into media content, audience members must also bring their own understandings of those words and images to *decode* that content.

Members of Society: The Mass Audience?

As we discussed earlier in this chapter, the **mass audience** is not to be

thought of as a mob or as an unthinking mass of individuals vulnerable to the intentional or unintentional manipulations of media practitioners. Rather, it is a convenient shorthand term for the great number of people who consume mass entertainment and information. Today, such audiences form around ongoing news stories (e.g., the protests in Ferguson, Missouri), large events, and international spectacles like the Olympics or soccer's World Cup, as well as popular books and films such as *The Hunger Games* novel and *Star Wars: The Force Awakens*. New media also attract mass audiences: in 2014, YouTube was getting over a billion unique visitors a month, and over 6 billion hours of video were being watched monthly. With over 2.4 billion views, Korean performer PSY's "Gangnam Style" was the most watched video on YouTube as of October 2015.

The ongoing growth of new media, however, and the ways in which it enables people to both produce media and network with large numbers of people, has changed traditional notions of audience. Today, audience members are themselves often media producers. To be sure, there is still a divide, and often a very big one, between professional and amateur media creators. But the lines between media content producers and not-so-passive audiences are blurring at a number of levels. Reality TV programs, for instance, bring the audience closer to the participants and performers, as audience members and regular people become TV stars. As we mentioned, social media sites like YouTube are attracting both

Source: Brian E. Benson/Earworm Music Group.

Mash-ups and remixes are a big part of new media culture. Every year, DJ Earworm creates a new mash-up of the year's most popular songs, but he's not the only one.

amateur producers and viewers by the millions. Freelancers, bloggers, and citizen journalists are playing an expanding role in news production. In turn, traditional media outlets often pick up both content and ideas for stories and editorials from these sources, and audiences increasingly consult them for news and information. As we discuss in Chapter 3, new media have also been helping develop and animate new political and social movements, like the Arab Spring, as well as to bring pressure on government to change unpopular policies or legislation. And audience members for traditional media products are often no longer content to play the role of passive consumer, but instead want to take part in acting out characters and developing storylines for popular films and television programs. Indeed, media are an integral part of our culture—our ways of life—and images, ideas, and values gleaned from the media are deeply woven into the ways in which we understand and embrace the world.

SUMMARY

Media and communication have central importance in our society and culture and continue to evolve. In this chapter, we have offered two different models of communication as a means of building a common understanding of the subjects under study, as well as a number of definitions of communication media and processes. Given recent changes to the media environment, we also have provided here an updated definition of the term *mass communication* as *"the transmission and transformation of information on a large scale."* We have also described three different forms of mass communication in this context. With the aim of providing an overview of the larger field of communication explored in this book, we describe in this chapter some of the different dimensions of mass communication and the institutions and organizations that sustain it.

KEY TERMS

Broadcasting Act (1991), p. 25
communication, p. 13
connotative meaning, p. 29
convergence, p. 18
Copyright Act, p. 25
denotative meaning, p. 29
digital, p. 18
digital divide, p. 10
information and communication technology (ICT), p. 18

mass audience, p. 13
mass communication, p. 30
mass media, p. 16
media, p. 16
medium, p. 16
new media, p. 18
Telecommunications Act, p. 26
Web 2.0, p. 15

RELATED WEBSITES

Alliance of Canadian Cinema, Television and Radio Artists (ACTRA): www.actra.ca
An association of more than 21,000 professionals working in Canadian media, its website offers insights into the issues facing these Canadian industries.

Berne Convention (copyright):
www.law.cornell.edu/treaties/berne/overview.html
This site includes the pre-eminent world statute on copyright, including all its various clauses and levels.

The 1991 Broadcasting Act:
http://laws-lois.justice.gc.ca/eng/acts/b-9.01
This is the legislation that governs broadcasting in Canada. Section 3 is particularly important, as it lays out the general purposes and goals of the system as well as the responsibilities of the different institutions and organizations within it.

Canadian Media Guild: www.cmg.ca
This is the site of the union that represents workers at the CBC as well as a number of other media companies across the country. It has a number of interesting features and provides insight into the kinds of issues facing media workers today.

Canadian Association of Journalists: www.caj.ca
This site provides journalists with professional information and, from time to time, it takes up issues of interest to all Canadian journalists.

Canadian Broadcast Standards Council (CBSC): www.cbsc.ca
The CBSC sets broadcasting standards, such as how much advertising broadcasters can put in a program.

Canadian Radio-television and Telecommunications Commission (CRTC): www.crtc.gc.ca

The CRTC provides everything you might want to know about its activities regulating Canada's media.

CBC: **Who We Are, What We Do**: www.cbc.radio-canada.ca/en/explore/who-we-are-what-we-do
This site highlights the mission and mandate of the Canadian Broadcasting Corporation.

CBC's *The National*: www.cbc.ca/thenational
This site provides headlines of the day's news as it is carried on the program, features, further elaboration on certain stories, and even a subscription service.

Canadian Centre for Policy Alternatives: www.policyalternatives.ca
A progressive think tank that works on issues of social and economic justice.

Public Library of Science (PLoS): www.plos.org
PLoS is a non-profit organization that is making the world's medical and scientific literature freely available to everyone via its website.

Society of Composers, Authors, and Music Publishers of Canada (SOCAN): www.socan.ca
The SOCAN site presents information for musicians, users of music, and the general public.

 FURTHER READINGS

Hamilton, Sheryl N. 2014. "Considering critical communication studies in Canada." In *Mediascapes: New Patterns in Canadian Communication*, 4th ed., Leslie Regan Shade, ed. Don Mills, ON: Nelson, 4–24.

Lipton, Mark. 2014. "Doing media studies." In *Mediascapes: New Patterns in Canadian Communication*, 4th ed., Leslie Regan Shade, ed. Don Mills, ON: Nelson, 25–42.

Martin, Michel. 2004. "Communication and social forms: The development of the telephone, 1876–1920." In *Communication History in Canada*, Daniel J. Robinson, ed. Don Mills, ON: Oxford University Press, 66–76.

Winseck, Dwayne. 2004. "Back to the future: Telecommunications, online information services, and convergence from 1840–1910." In *Communication History in Canada, Daniel J. Robinson, ed.* Don Mills, ON: Oxford University Press, 53–65.

 STUDY QUESTIONS

1. How does communication technology "shrink space through time"?
2. What were some of the predecessors to the internet? What characteristics made them predecessors?
3. Define *communication* and *mass*, as used in this chapter.
4. Explain *mass communication* and its three parts.
5. What is the fundamental difference between the transportation and social models of communication?
6. How do not-for-profit broadcast institutions differ in their basic purpose and mission from profit-driven institutions?
7. What is *convergence*? What are some of its different forms?

2 Communication: Social and Cultural Forms

The medium is the massage. — Marshall McLuhan

Opening Questions

- How might we define the terms *society* and *culture* in the study of communication?

- What are the roles of media in the public sphere?

- How have Harold Innis and Marshall McLuhan contributed to our understanding of the relationship between media and societal form?

- What roles do the media play in politics? In economics?

- What is technological determinism?

Introduction

In this chapter, we consider the nature of the relationships between communication, society, and culture. After defining key terms, we examine the ways in which communication and communication media are integral elements of the social and cultural fabric, as well as key dimensions of politics, economics, and processes of identity formation. Later in the chapter, we discuss Harold Innis's and Marshall McLuhan's work on how the ways in which people communicate shapes their society and culture. Oral, written, and electronic media are discussed in this light. The chapter concludes with our discussion of technological determinism, and consideration of how communication technology is only one of a number of influences on social structure and development.

Society, Culture, and Media

Set at the intersection between people and different social groups, organizations, and institutions, the media are vital elements of both society and culture. But while these terms are often used in the context of media and communication studies, what exactly do they mean? And what is their relationship to media and communication? Spending a little time thinking about this now will ease discussion later in the book.

Society is used in two main senses: (1) as a "general term for the body of institutions and relationships within which a relatively large group of people live" and (2) as an "abstract term for the conditions in which such relationships are formed" (Williams, 1976: 291). From this perspective, Canadian society is the product of a complex weave of institutions and relationships: Canada is comprised of particular cities and neighbourhoods; municipal, provincial, and federal levels of government; the legal system; educational institutions; transportation systems; the health-care system; businesses and corporations; sports teams, not-for-profit and voluntary organizations; religious organizations; and, of course, media. In other words, it is institutions and

organizations that we share—these connect and bind us together. Within the larger geographic dimensions of the country—and beyond—this complex weave of relationships and dependencies provides the common bonds that are the foundations of Canadian society.

Culture, on the other hand, "is one of the two or three most complicated words in the English language" (Williams, 1976: 87). One study found over 160 definitions circulating in the academic literature. We will do our best to sidestep this quagmire, limiting ourselves to three somewhat overlapping senses of the term.

An early English variant of the term *culture* was drawn from an agricultural usage, where it meant "the tending of something, basically crops or animals" (Williams, 1976:87). This notion of tending or growing or developing was transferred to people so that culture became thought of as developing one's mind; in particular, "a general process of intellectual, spiritual, and aesthetic development" (Williams, 1976:90). That's the first sense.

The second sense centres on the works and practices that are the focus of this process of development: intellectual and artistic works, such as music, painting, sculpture, and dramatic arts. Traditionally, however, this definition has been limited to classical or fine art forms, such as symphonies, ballet, classic literature, and Shakespeare's plays. These *high* cultural forms are sometimes contrasted against more everyday, and generally popular, forms of music, painting, writing, television programs, and so on, which are termed *popular culture* (see Chapter 7). *Folk culture* represents yet another kind or dimension of culture and generally refers to traditional or ethnic practices and arts, such as storytelling, singing, carving, weaving, dance, and traditional costumes. As we discuss in Chapters 3 and 4, one of the problems with this classification is that it sometimes carries elitist connotations whereby high culture is seen as superior, more intellectual, and more "refined" than popular or folk culture.

The third definition has its roots in anthropology and is generally used to indicate a "particular way of life, whether of a people, a group, or humanity in general." From this perspective, culture

Source: © Baytchev/Dreamstime.com.

Often, when we talk about "cultured" people, we mean those who know a lot about high culture like fine art, ballet, opera, or classical music. But we're all "cultured" people, sharing a way of life with others around us.

includes "knowledge, belief, art, morals, law, custom, and any other capabilities acquired by man as a member of society" (Thompson, 1990: 128). Canadian culture is multi-layered. At one level, we have a broad set of shared ideas and values regarding what it means to be Canadian, such as shared official languages, symbols (e.g., the Canadian flag), laws, games, customs, institutions, songs, and holidays. At another level, we have regional differences in culture and perspective: British Columbia, the Prairies, and Ontario all have distinctive ways of life. Quebec in particular, with its French language and histories, is particularly distinctive. Further, we have elements of Aboriginal cultures deeply woven into many common ideas and concepts, as well as contributions that various immigrant groups have made to Canadian ways of life. This third definition—"culture as a way or ways of life"—is the one we use in this book.

Media are a vital link in how we both see and understand our relationships to our society and culture. Canada is the second largest country in the world. Bounded by water on three sides, it is over 9,000 kilometres wide and has a total area of 9.9 million square kilometres. Given the vast scale of the country, many of our ideas and understandings of what makes up both our society and culture are created or reinforced through our interaction with media, and media content are both woven into, and from, the complex social and cultural fabric that blankets this geography. For instance, our understanding of international, national, regional, and local events and circumstances that shape our lives are drawn from the screens of smartphones, televisions, computers, and tablets, as well as the pages of newspapers and magazines. Both news and entertainment exploit stereotypical Canadian images and ideas like the Prairies, the Rocky Mountains, the Parliament buildings, moose, beavers, long winters, and universal health care to draw us into the narratives they create. Advertising often strives to link products like beer and coffee with Canadian symbols and icons—like maple leaves and hockey—to illustrate that they are key elements of our culture. And, at a more general level, film and television content employs a range of cultural figures and stereotypes we immediately recognize—such as the nuclear family, mischievous kids, dislike for school, greedy and cold-hearted bosses—to construct their stories and humour. In other words, media are a key vehicle through which we see, share, understand, and enjoy our relationships with our society and culture.

Because it is largely through media that we come to know our society and culture, there are many types of government policies and support programs to help ensure that media are Canadian-owned and that they reflect Canadian ideas and perspectives. Concerns in this regard are twofold. First is the threat that foreign media will simply eclipse or overrun local or national media. Such is the case with Canadian film and television products, where less than 5 percent of the films screened in Canadian theatres are Canadian, while the vast majority of television programs Canadians watch are produced elsewhere,

Both news and entertainment exploit stereotypical Canadian images and ideas like the Prairies, long winters, and universal health care to draw us into the narratives they create.

mainly in the United States. As we will see, the reasons for this state of affairs have very little to do with consumer choice; instead, because there is generally more money to be made from screening US films in Canadian theatres, Canadian films have very little access to theatres—especially outside Quebec. Similarly, because US sitcoms, reality TV, and one-hour dramas can be purchased from the States for a fraction of their production cost, most of this kind of programming on Canadian television—particularly on the private networks—is American, not Canadian. If Canadians want to see their society and culture reflected in their media, government regulation is necessary.

A second, related concern is that by consuming foreign media products, Canadians come to know more about foreign societies and cultures than their own. Polls often find, for instance, that despite the fact most people in Canada are proud to be Canadian and think of themselves as quite

distinct from Americans, Canadians often know more about US history than about Canadian history, and they know more about how the US government and law enforcement work than about their own (see Box 2.1). While it is difficult to link this phenomenon entirely to media consumption, it does raise questions about the effects of having Canadian media so heavily dominated by US content.

Some Social Roles of Media

As key elements of both society and culture, media play a number of other important social roles.

A Political Role

Most media theory sees the media as playing a central role in **politics** (see Chapters 3 and 4), and we know media and journalism are vital to

2.1 ▶▶ ▶▶ ▶▶

O CANADA: OUR HOME AND NAIVE LAND

Ipsos Reid/Dominion Institute History Quiz Reveals Canadians Know More about American History Than They Do about Canadian History

It appears that Canadians know more about the history and politics of their neighbours to the south than they do about their own country. According to a 2008 poll conducted in the format of a 20-question quiz by Ipsos Reid on behalf of the Dominion Institute, Canadians showed to have a higher average percentage of correct scores on questions about the United States (47 percent) than they did on questions about Canada (42 percent).

The quiz featured 10 questions about each country, and they ranged from questions about the founding of each nation to the decade that women's suffrage was granted in both countries.

Questions about Canada were paired with similar questions about US history, so that knowledge about the two countries could be compared. The largest discrepancy in knowledge had to do with heads of state. While 75 percent of Canadians knew that George W. Bush, US president at the time, was the American head of state, only 21 percent knew that the Canadian head of state was Queen Elizabeth II. On the other hand, Canadians were much more likely to know the first line of their own national anthem (53 percent) than the first line of the US anthem (25 percent). The best-answered Canadian questions dealt with John A. Macdonald being the first prime minister of Canada (61 percent answered correctly) and the year of Canadian Confederation being 1867 (61 percent). Canadians averaged 4.2 correct answers overall on the Canadian questions, and 4.7 correct answers overall on the US questions.

What might account for Canadians' poor knowledge about their own country? Could it result from the fact that much of the media content Canadians consume is made in the USA?

Source: Adapted from www.historicacanada.ca/sites/default/files/PDF/polls/canadaday.survey.dominioninstitute.1july08_en.pdf.

Canadian political life (see Chapters 7 and 8). Here, we will consider some of the more general aspects of media and information in politics.

While politics is sometimes thought of as voting or specific debates over policy, a broader, more inclusive way of thinking about the term is as "the process through which people make collective decisions." This definition includes formal processes of government, but it also includes a much wider range of activities that frame and animate formal government policies and activities, as well as informal discussions of social norms and values. From this perspective, politics is a key element in many aspects of social life. Whenever we are discussing or otherwise are engaged with issues of collective concern with other members of society, be it in a large or small group or simply with just one other person, we are engaging in politics.

Political activity takes place in the **public sphere** (Habermas, 1989), an abstract place where people are able to discuss and consider matters of common concern and interest. We say "abstract" because the public sphere is more of an idea than a specific place. In fact, any place where such discussion might take place can be considered part of the larger public sphere—whether that be media, coffee shops, auditoriums, public rallies and demonstrations, or parks.

Media are key elements of the public sphere because of the information they provide about public life (see Box 2.1). They are the central vehicle for the production and distribution of information about events taking place at different levels of government, and of information about other things such as wars, oil spills and other environmental disasters, natural disasters, visits of foreign dignitaries, and elections.

Indeed, our knowledge of almost all events of public concern is, in some way or another, drawn from media sources—in fact, any decisions that we make regarding our larger collective interests are, to some degree, related to media.

While television, radio, newspapers, and websites offer news and information about political issues and events, some media provide more interactive venues to debate and discuss political ideas and concerns. At any given time, for example, a number of videos on YouTube provide different perspectives on public issues. These are greatly varied and might range from issues concerning the environment, to gender issues, to media policy, and to social benefit regulations. Twitter and Facebook provide a similar, although more interactive, place for such discussions, and it is common practice for social activists and others to create Facebook pages addressing political issues. And, although controlled by the editors and owners, the editorial pages of newspapers provide a more traditional forum for discussing ideas and concerns about political issues of the day.

In Canada, media owners have a long history of using their products to influence political discussion and action. An early English-Canadian example of communication famously used as a political instrument is William Lyon Mackenzie politicizing Upper Canadians through his newspaper, the *Colonial Advocate*, and eventually leading some of them into rebellion in 1837. Pierre Bédard similarly spread his political ideas in *Le Canadien*, the newspaper he helped to establish. As the leader of the Parti canadien (later the Parti Patriote), Bédard used *Le Canadien* as a nationalist party organ to oppose the Château Clique, the ruling elite group of Lower Canada. Even earlier, in 1778, through *La Gazette littéraire* (precursor to *La Gazette de Montréal* [1785]), Fleury Mesplet, a colleague of Benjamin Franklin, spread the ideals of the American Revolution in French Canada.

Many contemporary media owners have admitted to controlling the range of perspectives available in their newspapers and other publications. Moreover, at election time, *The Globe and Mail* generally supports the federal and

2.2

THE TWO-STEP FLOW OF COMMUNICATION

In a classic study in the 1950s, Elihu Katz and Paul Lazarsfeld argued that information from the mass media is transmitted or channelled to the larger population by "opinion leaders"—that is, people with better access to the media and greater understanding of the news and topics covered there than most people have. Such people may be family or community members, teachers, or religious leaders and are then seen to be central in the larger diffusion or spread of ideas found in the media.

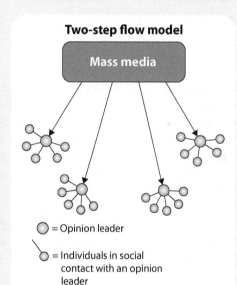

Two-step flow model

◯ = Opinion leader

◔ = Individuals in social contact with an opinion leader

FIGURE 2.1 Katz and Lazarsfeld's Two-Step Flow Theory of Mass Communication

Source: Katz and Lazarsfeld, 1955.

In September 2013, protestors took to Parliament Hill to protest the federal government's efforts to stop government scientists speaking out on their research and findings.

provincial Conservative parties, while the *Toronto Star* supports the Liberals. In Quebec, *Le Devoir* is a staunch supporter of Quebec independence whereas the Desmarais family's *La Presse* supports the federalist option and the federal Liberal party, in particular. When questioned about this, newspaper owners and management have defended their actions by arguing that control of editorial perspective is a privilege of ownership.

Governments, too, strive to control media coverage and thereby public opinion. Elected officials commonly refuse to grant interviews and try to withhold information on controversial topics. Stephen Harper's federal Conservatives have been well known for trying to control public opinion in this manner, such as with their efforts to muzzle scientists employed by the federal government (Chung, 2013). Similarly, when governments become dissatisfied with normal media coverage, they often create media events to orchestrate the release of significant information, or they advertise in order to speak directly to the public.

The political role of communication is generally constrained on one side by a concern with **freedom of information**, and on the other by people's right to **privacy**. Governments collect vast amounts of information through surveys, censuses, satellites, and mandatory reporting mechanisms, such as income-tax statements. Public access to some of that information, such as census data, is important because it is used by a great many organizations to plan and advocate for everything from social services to recreational programs to transit. Still, despite a great public outcry, the Harper federal government cut the more detailed long-form element of the Canadian census in 2010—some say to make it harder to gauge the impact of changing government policies. Such information is the lifeblood of informed policy discussions, and without the proper census data, it's almost impossible to make informed public-policy decisions (Grant, 2013). Similarly, access to government records and documents is important for journalists and others working to monitor the actions of government officials—these journalists need access to ensure that they can properly scrutinize the government and make sure those in public office are serving citizens' interests.

The US government in post-9/11 times, with very little resistance from the country's freedom-loving citizens, put in place vast schemes, exemplified by the Patriot Act, for the invasion of privacy of both Americans and those who have any dealings with the United States—ostensibly to help root out terrorists and related threats. Critics have warned that such a means of collecting information about the activities of citizens could lead to unwarranted charges of wrongdoing and the suspension of people's civil rights by the US government and its agencies. With the Conservatives' passage of Bill C-51 in June of 2015, such concerns were echoed in Canada (Watters, 2015). This legislation increased the power of police and security agencies and has raised the possibility of greater surveillance and control of environmental groups and others opposed to government policy (McCarthy, 2015).

In this regard, websites like WikiLeaks.org provide a controversial vehicle for government or industry insiders to leak or release secret information to the press. Such information might expose government or industry wrongdoing, or it might reveal activities or information being kept secret for national security reasons. As the

Edward Snowden worked for the US National Security Agency and leaked a series of documents that exposed massive spying by various governments, particularly his own, on the activities of their citizens.

Source: AP Photo/Marco Garcia.

media coverage surrounding National Security Agency whistle-blower Edward Snowden's release of thousands of classified documents illustrates, the question of whether or not such information should be kept secret, particularly if it is information held by the government, is a source of intense controversy.

In short, media and information are central to the political landscape and vital to the public sphere.

An Economic Role

Media play an important economic role in our society and culture. Not only are they important industries in their own right, but they are also key elements of our consumer culture, a growing information economy, and, according to some, an information society.

Traditional media, such as radio and television stations, newspapers, and related telecommunications companies, are big business. There are 1,000 community newspapers and 94 daily newspapers with paid circulation in this country, and daily newspapers posted $3 billion in revenue in 2013. Canada has more than 1,100 radio stations in Canada and over 700 television services. The Canadian broadcasting industry alone posted $17.1 billion in revenues in 2013. Combined, the telecommunications and broadcasting industries reported $60.7 billion in that year. If one adds new media, such as computer, software, and video game companies, they and related organizations together employ hundreds of thousands of Canadians.

Media are also central to the larger economy in a number of ways. As the major purveyor of advertising, they are the primary way that people are acquainted and connected with the many products they purchase. In other words, they are the main vehicles through which our consumer lifestyle is symbolically negotiated. Media are also a central means for businesses to find employees and, through business radio and television programs as well as business-related articles in web and hard-copy periodicals, they are one of the key vehicles through which people can better understand the economy and monitor the economic activities of both government and corporations. Corporations also conduct public-information and public-relations campaigns through media, raising their profile and attempting to promote positive public images.

Media generally also promote the larger interests of consumer culture. A good deal of the content is addressed directly to consumers, comparing or trumpeting the benefits of particular products. Similarly, much of the news is related to consumer issues, such as the price of gas and other commodities, or the effects of particular events on the economy. Other programs also valorize or aggrandize the benefits of consumer culture, illustrating the lavish lifestyles of the rich and famous and teasing the general public with luxuries to covet.

Perhaps most importantly, media and communication industries make up one of the fastest-growing sectors of the economy. For many, the recent rapid growth in information and communication technologies (ICTs) has signalled the rise of an **information society**, where the production, distribution, and consumption of information are the main drivers of the economy. As we discuss later in the chapter, this development goes hand in hand with **globalization** and the deindustrialization of the traditional industrialized countries in the northern hemisphere, such as the United States, Canada, the United Kingdom, and the countries of Western Europe. From this perspective, media and information industries have not only been pivotal for facilitating the transfer of manufacturing industries to places such as China, India, and a number of other countries, but they are also essential to creating new economic activity in the old industrialized countries.

Over the last 20 years, numerous federal governments and their agencies have invested considerable time and resources in attempting to better understand the role of ICTs in the economy and to develop policies that ensure Canada doesn't get left behind or become disadvantaged in this shifting information environment. Recent efforts in this direction include strengthening copyright legislation, establishing a fund to promote the development of new media content, and developing a policy to promote the growth of digital and broadband communication applications, products, and infrastructure—in short, the basis of an expanded Canadian information economy.

For all these reasons, media and ICTs are sometimes referred to as the "shock troops" of global **capitalism** (see Box 2.3). Both directly and indirectly, they spread, advertise, and promote the benefits of capitalist society in newly industrializing countries in terms that seem to promise steady jobs and income, an endless supply and wide array of products, and the opportunity to live a rich and comfortable life.

An Individual Role: Media and Identity

Our understanding of our place in society—who we are, along with our likes, dislikes, desires, fears, and loyalties—can be thought of as aspects of identity. Identity may be innate and genetic, wrapped up in the physical features of our being; but in other ways, it is a learned process, the product of our personal history, experience, and interactions with other people and institutions in the world. One might say that most of our identities are constructed through these social interactions, as we learn about the world and work to fit ourselves into it. In other words, much of our identity is socially constructed; we negotiate and interact with social and cultural processes and institutions. Elements in this process include family, work, social class, education, gender, race, ethnicity, and religion.

People have particular social roles—as adults, children, fathers, mothers, and so on. Culturally, we see ourselves as having unique traits in terms of race, ethnicity, habits, and customs. Politically, we are citizens and members of society. Economically, we are workers and consumers. As one of the principal vehicles through which we come to know and understand the world, media—particularly mass media—play a large role in helping develop these identities. As audience members, we are exposed to ideas, perspectives, and ways of thinking about and understanding the world.

2.3 ▶▶▶▶▶▶

WHAT IS CAPITALISM?

Capitalism is an economic system, or a system for the production, distribution, and consumption of goods and services. As Jim Stanford (2008: 34–5) points out in his book *Economics for Everyone*, "Two key features . . . make an economy capitalist":

1. Most production of goods and services is undertaken by privately owned companies, which produce and sell their output in the hopes of making a profit. This is called PRODUCTION FOR PROFIT.
2. Most work in the economy is performed by people who do not own their company or their output, but are hired by someone else to work in turn for a money wage or salary. This is called WAGE LABOUR.

Any economy driven by these two features—production for profit and wage labour—tends to replicate the following patterns, over and over again:

- Fierce competition between private companies over markets and profit.
- *Innovation*, as companies constantly experiment with new technologies, new products, and new forms of organization—in order to succeed in that competition.
- An inherent tendency to *growth*, resulting from the desire of each individual company to make more profit.
- Deep *inequality* (especially) between those who own successful companies and the rest of society who do not own companies.

- A general *conflict* of interest between those who work for wages, and the employers who hire them.
- Economic cycles or "roller coasters," with periods of strong growth followed by periods of stagnation or depression; sometimes these cycles even produce dramatic economic and social crises.

Some of these patterns and outcomes are positive and help to explain why capitalism has been so successful. But some of these patterns and outcomes are negative, and explain why capitalism tends to be economically—and sometimes politically—unstable. In part, capitalism has its origins in the enclosure movement in rural England in the sixteenth century, when peasants lost their direct access to the land—the means of production—and instead had to exchange their labour for wages (Wood, 2002). Capitalism subsequently spread throughout Europe in the seventeenth and eighteenth centuries. In pre-capitalist societies, most people worked for themselves, one way or another, and had direct access to the means of production (e.g., farmland). Where people worked for someone else, that relationship was based on something other than monetary payment (e.g., a sense of obligation or the power of brute force). And most production occurred to meet some direct need or desire (for an individual, a community, or a government), not to generate a money profit.

One of the key effects of private ownership of media is that profit is the primary goal of such organizations. Without a profit, the company will go out of business. Hence, much of the organization and its products are oriented toward this goal. As we shall see, this has powerful effects on the range and kinds of information found in the media, as well as how that information is presented.

Source: Stanford, 2008, 34–5.

Via news, films, music, cartoons, nature programs, and so on, media provide an environment in which to explore the world and how we connect with it. Through media, we enlarge our understanding of our place in the world. We can take political positions; develop a sense of national pride and patriotism; explore gender issues; develop ideas and interests around sexuality; and take a position on the environment. Any number of our understandings of the world and our place(s) within it may be negotiated and/or enhanced through the media.

Consumer culture underwent a dramatic expansion through the twentieth century (see

Source: © Megapress/Alamy.

Advertising strives to link specific products to how we feed, clothe, entertain ourselves, and make ourselves sexually and socially attractive. It encourages us to literally *purchase* who we are, or who we want to be.

Chapter 3). Media were in the forefront of spreading and developing that culture. Today, it is feels natural for people to satisfy their needs, wants, and desires through the marketplace. As Leiss and colleagues (2005: 4–5) argue, "Material objects produced for consumption in the marketplace not only satisfy needs, but also serve as markers and communicators for interpersonal distinctions and self-expression." Media generally encourage that view of the world, reflecting consumer culture back to us in many ways. Advertising in particular strives to link specific products to how we feed, clothe, entertain ourselves, and make ourselves sexually and socially attractive. It encourages us to literally purchase who we are, or who we want to be. As some writers argue, not only is this a growing trend, but it is also leading to deepening psychological crises and increasing social inequality, and is accelerating the destruction

of the planet (Coulter, 2014; Jhally, 1997). Consequently, understanding the ways in which media encourage us to understand ourselves is an important element in the study of mass media and mass communication.

Media and Social Form

So far, our discussion has generally built on the social model of communication outlined in Chapter 1 and has been focused on how media and communications processes and technologies are embedded in a larger social or cultural context. There are other ways of thinking about the relationship between forms of communication and society, however. Two Canadians, Harold Innis and Marshall McLuhan, were the first communication theorists to bring serious attention to the idea that the ways in which people communicate might actually shape a society and its culture.

Innis (1950), a political economy professor, was the first to articulate this perspective. He argued that each communication medium has a particular bias and thereby a particular influence on social structure and culture. In this regard, he claimed that oral communication and early hieroglyphic writing on clay tended to maintain cultural practices through time and emphasize a close-knit society that preserves outlooks, values, and understandings over long periods. In his words, Innis saw these media as having a **time bias**.

Written communication, on the other hand, favoured the establishment and maintenance of social relations through space, such as empires and power blocs spread over large geographic areas and across different cultures. Innis used the Roman Empire as his example. To conquer and then coordinate, administer, and police such a vast empire required a written system for recording and communicating messages on a portable medium that could be transported across vast distances. Laws were created, written down accurately, and then transported to the far reaches of the empire, where they were applied. In this way, Roman society spread "through space." Consequently, this latter medium displays what Innis called a **space bias**. Such biases of the dominant media in a society shapes the characteristics of that society. As Innis states,

> A medium of communication has an important influence on the dissemination of knowledge over space and over time and it becomes necessary to study its characteristics in order to appraise its influence in its cultural setting. According to its characteristics it may be better suited to the dissemination of knowledge over time than over space, particularly if the medium is heavy and durable and not suited to transportation, or to the dissemination of knowledge over space than over time, particularly if the medium is light and easily transported. The relative emphasis on time or space will imply a bias of significance to the culture in which it is imbedded. (Innis, 1951: 33)

McLuhan, a scholar of English literature, took up Innis's ideas and extended them to the modern period. McLuhan first studied the impact of printing, capturing its influence on society by coining the term *typographical man*, which referred to Western culture after the invention of printing with movable type (in Europe) by Johannes Gutenberg in 1454. The printed book was a tremendously powerful means of communicating ideas and knowledge in early modern Europe; McLuhan and others have argued that the printed book transformed Western societies so that working with this medium encouraged particular ways of thinking—namely, logical, linear thought, as well as individualism, conceptuality, science, and monotheism (McLuhan, 1962).

Next, McLuhan turned to an analysis of electronic society—characterized by inventors such as Guglielmo Marconi (radio transmission) as well as Canadians Reginald Fessenden (radio transmission) and Alexander Graham Bell (telephone)—and revealed its dynamics to a skeptical world. He was the first analyst of the impact of the new media of communication (radio, television, photography, film) on what we think of as modern societies, although certain British modernists, such as Wyndham Lewis, preceded him and had a parallel concern (Tiessen, 1993). McLuhan expressed his ideas in a distinctive, aphoristic way, referring to them as **probes**. And while many scholars dismissed them, his ideas had a great impact in the 1960s in North America and Europe, spreading to politics, the advertising world, and even the media.

Both Innis (1950) and McLuhan (1962), as well as many other academics in the **Toronto School (of communication theory)** who followed in their wake (e.g., Goody, 1977; de Kerckhove, 1995), placed their emphasis on the ways in which particular forms of media influenced the structure and development of societies. To better understand these ideas, it is useful to explore the dynamics of oral, literate, and electronic societies in some detail.

Oral Society

Innis claims that the means of communication set the basic parameters for the functioning of any society. In an oral society, knowledge is invested in the community and preserved by certain members of society—rather than in books, libraries, and other institutions, such as schools and universities. For instance, knowledge regarding medical treatment, how to build houses, where to fish, when to grow food, and how to do other activities for the maintenance and well-being of the community is held by particular individuals or family groupings. Similarly, a group's history and knowledge of the past—such as how they came to be in a particular place, patterns in weather, flooding, and other natural rhythms—as well as any other particularities of the time and space the community occupies, are held and shared by members of the community. As a result, the community is heavily dependent on each of its members for its well-being. Creating and storing knowledge in this way necessarily creates close-knit, interdependent communities, which must stick together through time to ensure their continued existence and prosperity. In

2.4 ▶▶▶▶▶▶

TIME BIAS

Societies have both history and geography—or, as Harold Innis would say, societies occupy both time and space. One way societies occupy time and space is through their communications media, which, Innis argued, have characteristic biases that make some media more conducive to carrying messages through time (e.g., heavy, durable materials like clay or the brick walls of buildings) and some media are more conducive to carrying messages through space (e.g., light, easily transportable materials like parchment or paper). Time-biased media are *time-binding* media, in that they connect us to the past through their enduring images and messages. Think of the stained-glass windows in churches that relate biblical tales, war memorials that ask us to remember fallen ancestors, or buildings that carry the names of their founders etched in stone or concrete. Similarly, historical murals, such as those in Chemainus, British Columbia, or Vankleek Hill, Ontario (see the accompanying photo), offer residents and visitors a sense of the town's past.

Source: Photograph by Mike Gasher. Reprinted with permission from the artists: Elisabeth Skelly and Odile Tétu.

Historical murals, such as this one in Vankleek Hill, Ontario, offer residents and visitors a sense of the town's past.

other words, dependence on an oral tradition or culture has a time bias that predisposes the community to stay together and maintain communication through time (see Box 2.4). Interruptions to close-knit ties can mean a loss of important knowledge for the community and can threaten its long-term existence.

In classical Greece, knowledge was maintained and transmitted through epic poems and what Innis (1951) called *epic technique*, which involved creating poems in rhythmic, six-beat lines—hexameters—that had certain rigidities and elasticities. The rigidities were the memorized parts. The elasticities were parts that permitted adaptation of certain elements according to time and place. Structural forms, words, stock expressions, and phrases acted as aids to memory, while the local language and situation provided the basis for ornamental gloss. The development of such techniques ensured that epic poetry would be undertaken by people with excellent memories and poetic and linguistic abilities. The techniques for memorizing and reciting epics were often passed on within families of professional storytellers and minstrels. According to Innis, such families probably built up a system of *mnemonic* or memory aids that were private and carefully guarded.

Providing a sense of the difference between oral and literate societies, anthropologist A.B. Lord explored the dynamics of a modern oral tradition in rural Yugoslavia, 1937–1959, in *The Singer of Tales* (1964). Lord notes that, for the oral bard, the recording of the words of a song is a totally foreign experience. A recording cannot represent the correct or best version because there is no correct or best version. Rather, each performance is unique in itself.

The dynamics of the oral tradition in a contemporary Canadian context are illustrated in

Source: Sandra Hunt.

Talking sticks have been used by many generations of North Pacific Coast First Nations peoples to record and commemorate important familial relationships and events. What is often taken as traditional or Aboriginal art is derived from symbols and techniques for preserving important cultural or historical information.

the *Delgamuukw* decision, a landmark ruling of the Supreme Court of Canada in which Aboriginal oral history has been accepted as a legally valid foundation for pursuing land claims. While such a decision may seem only right and proper, it has taken centuries for our literate culture to accept the veracity and authority of oral culture. In part, that acceptance has come about because of our relatively recent understanding of oral communication and oral culture (see *Globe and Mail*, 15 December 1997, A23).

The near destruction of the oral tradition among First Nations peoples in Canada was one of the tragedies of the residential schools. Through the late nineteenth and early twentieth centuries, the federal government and religious organizations worked together, particularly in the western provinces, to remove First Nations children from their families and place them in residential schools for their education. The effect of this move was to severely undermine the social structure of these cultures, which, to a large extent, depended on oral communication for passing on traditional knowledge and cultural understandings from one generation to the next. Removing the children from these communities broke the chain of learning and, as a result, knowledge of traditional languages and other cultural elements was severely weakened.

The ways in which oral societies preserve knowledge and cultural integrity are fundamentally different from those of literate society. But their capacity to preserve the past, to transform that past as necessary, and to base law in custom, illustrate their stability and their tendency to preserve, extend, and adapt culture.

It is important to note while many cultural communities may not have, or have had, a written dimension to their language as we understand that today, that doesn't mean that they do not have various technologies and techniques for recording and remembering important information. For instance the *quipu* was a system of knots used by the Incas in South America for recording and accounting purposes. Sand paintings have been used for a number of ritual and healing purposes. Dance has long been a way for many cultures to preserve and transmit information. And talking sticks and totem poles have been used by many generations of peoples of the North Pacific Coast to record and commemorate important familial relationships and events. What is often taken as traditional or Aboriginal art is derived from symbols and techniques for preserving important cultural or historical information.

Today, every community has its oral processes. Music often plays an especially strong catalytic role in the creation of communities, particularly for youth. Interestingly, where the values and ideas expressed in that music seemingly conflict with those seen as important by the larger society, steps are often taken by authority figures to suppress it. For instance, in some countries, forms of music that give voice to the excesses of youth culture, particularly with regard to sex and violence, are banned. In Western countries, restrictions against such anti-social music are less formal. Nevertheless, radio stations and television channels do not play certain songs and videos that are deemed salacious expressions of youth culture, although these may be available through the internet, record, and video stores. Some big-box stores, such as transnational giant Walmart, refuse to carry CDs with explicitly sexual content or material that they feel undermines "family values."

Literate Society

Greece, for Innis, represented an oral society, whereas Rome was a literate society. Greek history provides a record of the transition from an oral to a literate society, however, and so Innis cites Greek sources from the period when writing emerged that express the significance of the change from oral to written modes. In Plato's *Phaedrus*, for example, Socrates reports a conversation between the Egyptian god Thoth, the inventor of letters, and the god Amon. Amon says,

This discovery of yours will create forgetfulness in the learners' souls, because they will not use their memories; they will trust to the external written characters and not remember of themselves. The specific you have discovered is an aid not to memory, but to reminiscence, and you give your disciples not truth but only the semblance of truth; they will be bearers of many things and will have learned nothing; they will appear to be omniscient and will generally know nothing; they will be tiresome company, having the show of wisdom without the reality.

After relaying the conversation, Socrates states,

I cannot help feeling, Phaedrus, that writing is unfortunately like painting; for the creations of the painter have the attitude of life, and yet if you ask them a question, they preserve a solemn silence, and the same may be said of speeches. You would imagine that they had intelligence, but if you want to know anything and put a question to one of them, the speaker always gives one unvarying answer. (Plato, 1973: 84)

This conversation resembles discussions of television and the internet as they were introduced, especially those that focus on how those technologies would perhaps undermine traditional ways of thinking. This is not surprising, for the transformation from an oral to a literate society was as major a change as that from a literate to an electronic society. It marked a distinctive shift in the ways in which knowledge was developed, stored, and passed on. The passage also points out the degree to which knowledge and wisdom were negotiated in oral discourse—the product of two or more people discussing and applying concepts in a particular context—rather than derived from a singular, "silent," written perspective. One cannot question and reason with a written text in the way one can with a living person.

Rome and the Roman Empire represent the origin of literate society because many of the operating concepts and processes of Rome were based on the written rather than the spoken

2 Communication: Social and Cultural Forms ▶ 47

word. The development of contract law illustrates the Romans' ability to supplant oral practices with written ones. A written contract changes an oral pact into a legal obligation and permits a much more complex and contingent agreement. It is a precise written record of an agreed obligation between people or other legal entities. Such literate inventions allowed for an orderly and vast expansion of the Roman Empire.

Innis (1950, 1951) argues that writing and the portability of written media gave the Roman Empire a space bias—that is, a tendency to extend itself over a larger and larger territory. At its greatest extent in the third century AD, the Roman Empire maintained control of the lands and people around the entire perimeter of the Mediterranean, from Southern and Central Europe to the Middle East, North Africa, and the Iberian Peninsula, and on to the north and west through present-day France and Britain (see Figure 2.2). Crucial to the exercise of administrative power in the Roman Empire was the formation of abstract laws to apply uniformly in particular situations, which were then written down on a portable medium, such as parchment, so they could be consulted in any location.

The development of literate society in Western civilization reflected an attempt to replace spoken, poetic, and emotive language with clear, ordered, unambiguous, and logical written prose. This, in turn, laid the basis for extending particular ideas and concepts. For instance, in their writings, Cicero (106–43 BC) and other Stoic philosophers explained ideas that are now fundamental to modern thought, including the notions of a world state, natural law and justice,

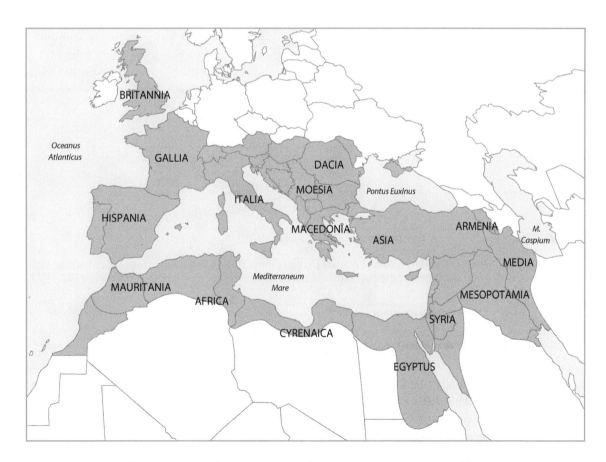

FIGURE 2.2   The Roman Empire at Its Greatest Extent in the Third Century AD

2.5 ▶▶▶▶▶▶

SPACE BIAS

The notion of space bias does not come easily to some, perhaps because the word *bias* most commonly has negative connotations. Innis used the word to mean "tendency" or "emphasis." The following footprint diagram in Figure 2.3 illustrates the space bias of satellite technology. By beaming down a signal to a particular area of the earth's surface, a satellite creates, at least to some degree, a community—of all those people receiving the same signal. People choose whether to watch and which channel to watch, of course, and different satellite footprints (the terrestrial areas covered by specific satellite signals) can carry the same content. The broadcast of a news program from a particular city to widespread geographic areas, however, creates an artificial spatial extension of that city. In some ways, CNN and the BBC are extensions of Atlanta and London, respectively, just as in the print medium *The Globe and Mail* is, to a degree, an extension of Central Canada. These are all instances of space bias.

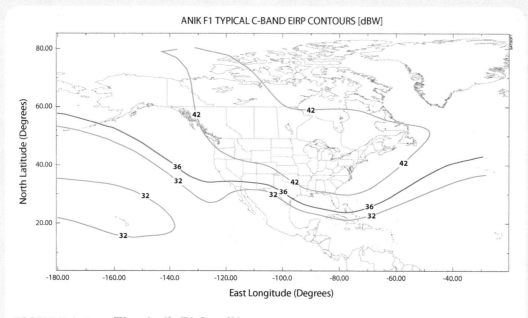

FIGURE 2.3 The Anik F1 Satellite

Telesat Canada's Anik F1 satellite creates a primary spatial community encompassing virtually all of Canada and much of the United States. As the map shows, weather signals extend that community to the rest of North America.

Source: Footprint courtesy of Telesat Canada.

and universal citizenship, as did libraries, which were scattered throughout the Roman Empire. During the Renaissance in Europe, these ideas gradually became more characteristic of literate societies. Such ideas and institutions were nurtured by writing—a technology for the static representation of ideas, which allows the eye to juxtapose and compare two ideas and to view many individual instances from which to abstract the general case.

But while print was important in the formation and administration of the Roman Empire, as that empire began to dissolve, print helped spur the emergence of the nation-states of Europe. The **lingua franca** or primary language of the Roman Empire was Latin, but places within the empire had their own languages and vernaculars. As the influence of Rome declined, these languages developed their own written forms and took on an important role in organizing the geography. In his book *Imagined Communities* (1983), Benedict Anderson considers the development of nation-states in regard to their languages. He argues that, in conjunction with the development of capitalism and a number of other factors, the creation of "print languages"—that is, commonly understood written languages—was essential to the process of developing independent countries because they provided a common medium within which people could develop an "imagined community." As Anderson states,

> These print languages . . . created unified fields of exchange and communication below Latin and above the spoken vernaculars. Speakers of the huge variety of Frenches, Englishes, or Spanishes, who might find it difficult or even impossible to understand one another in conversation, became capable of comprehending one another via print and paper. In the process, they gradually became aware of the hundreds of thousands, even millions, of people in their particular language-field. . . . These fellow-readers, to whom they were connected through print, formed, in their secular, particular, visible invisibility, the embryo of the nationally imagined community. (1983)

Most other writings about literate societies focus on the modern world. While they discuss the influence of writing, they do so within a context of an evolved technology and developed social, political, and legal institutions (e.g., McLuhan, 1962; Goody, 1977; Olson, 1980). The basic claim of these authors is that writing has favoured the development of a particular way of understanding the world: a logical, linear, sequential, and conceptual way of thinking. But just as writing has been seen as increasing the reach of ideas and particular ways of understanding and interacting with the world, so, too, have electronic forms of communication been envisioned as helping to remake social relations and the structure of society.

Electronic Society

McLuhan argued that the electronic media created, for the very first time in history, the possibility of instant communication between any two points on the globe: he referred to this reality as the *global village*.

While electronic communication is now heavily entrenched in our daily lives, in the early 1960s, when McLuhan introduced his notion of electronic society, it seemed both audacious and trivial to claim that somehow television, telephones, radio, and telex (the technologies that predominated in this period) were going to be as influential as writing and print had been. In trying to understand the early impacts of electronic communication on society, McLuhan introduced the idea of the **global village**. In using the term, he meant that electronic society has vast information-gathering and transmission capacities sufficient to make us intimately (perhaps too intimately) aware of the goings-on of people around the world. Though our electronic or virtual linkages with the whole world are always incomplete in the physical sense, they are becoming steadily more inclusive as technology as well as communications organizations and professionals extend their reach into our lives, thereby transforming our local and global environments.

McLuhan also referred to electronic communication as an "outered nervous system," and saw such media as extending our senses of sight, touch, vision, and hearing. Although now—in the age of the internet, remote sensing, and virtual reality—we can understand the significance of electronic media and instant worldwide communication in these terms, in the 1960s, when hardly a single computer existed and no non-military communications satellites flew above us, McLuhan's ideas were greeted skeptically.

A considerable literature argues that electronic forms of communication are bringing about the "end of geography." Until a short time ago, place and space were inseparable, but communications technologies, such as the telephone, email, and the internet, now allow two or more people in distant physical places to share the same communicative space and create a social linkage. Mosco (1998) summarizes this point of view:

> In the nineteenth century, spatial barriers meant that news took weeks by packet boat to get from New York to New Orleans. Now, distance is by and large insignificant and, particularly with the arrival of global mobile satellite systems, which will permit seamless wireless communication between any points on the globe, soon to be completely irrelevant.

Mosco's point is brought home by the fact that the most noted US victory of the War of 1812 occurred after the conflict was over. The 8 January 1815 Battle of New Orleans, in which American troops led by Andrew Jackson routed the British, with several hundred men killed and over a thousand wounded, took place more than two weeks after the Treaty of Ghent ending the war had been signed—but the combatants had not yet heard the news! As Mosco goes on to point out, however, while many contemporary writers and analysts are keen to trumpet this "triumph of technology over place," the reach of the virtual world extends only so far. A case in point: sunny real-time images of Caribbean beaches offer cold comfort to people enduring long Canadian winters with no travel plans.

Still, arguments regarding the influence of electronic media on social relations remain strong. From the 1964 publication of McLuhan's *Understanding Media* to the early 1990s, discussions of these relationships were focused on television because it was the dominant new medium of the period. Joshua Meyrowitz (1985), for instance, has argued that electronic media, above all TV, weakened the once strong divisions between children and adults, as well as eroded gender differences. Drawing heavily on the perspectives of McLuhan and Canadian sociologist Erving Goffman (1959), he claims that by exposing the "secrets" of the different social worlds inhabited by children and adults, or men and women, television affects the character of social relationships and breaks down the barriers between them. Television, for instance, undermines the innocence of childhood by providing them with a broader picture of world events; it also blurs the differences between children and adults by giving the former access to information about adult issues. In terms of gender, television programs offer all viewers insight into what were once treated as separate male and female cultures. From this perspective, electronic media's influence on social roles is not simply confined to industrial societies. In India, for instance, the social organization of domestic space in the household tended to keep men, women, and children apart for much of the time, thereby maintaining their distinct and traditional social roles and identities. But television's arrival in the households of rural India disturbed traditional relations between both the sexes and young and old by breaking segregation barriers in the family (Malik, 1989).

Other analysts make the point that television has shifted social modes of interaction and presentation. British theatre critic Martin Eslin (1980), for instance, has argued that, with the growth of television in people's lives, dramatization has become the predominant form of argumentation and presentation of "facts." The drama of spectacle has replaced reasoned analysis. Information is not collected, pondered, and transformed into televised information; rather, events may or may not be staged outside the ken of the viewer, and TV crews select short clips that they perceive as conforming to the "logic" of the medium, which is essentially dramatic. Televisually, the idea of newsworthiness shifts away from what may be logically or politically interesting to the visually fascinating or dramatically arresting. Indeed, this transformation is evident where television reporters are "embedded" with troops in war zones, such as they were in Iraq and Afghanistan. Under such conditions, reporters are constrained from having much communication with the people directly affected by the military action and so often present only a narrow, highly selective view of what is often in wartime a broad and politically complex crisis.

In such an atmosphere, those who can create good television are the ones who become newsworthy. Greenpeace (Dale, 1996), for instance, became very good at playing the logic of television through the 1980s and '90s so that now they usually are able to secure good media coverage for the issues they address. As the University of Toronto's Douglas Macdonald (CBC News, 2011) points out, "That is the genius that Greenpeace has always had, with scaling buildings and going out whaling and putting themselves between the harpoons and the whales—getting themselves into the news media. . . . We wouldn't see the kind of action by governments that we've had in the last 40 years if you hadn't had that kind of pressure applied by the environmental movement."

Large corporations and politicians pay particular attention to this televisual logic, carefully staging public announcements and other media events whenever possible. At the same time, since the 1950s TV has been a key vehicle for informing people of important events and introducing them to different ideas and cultures (see Box 2.6).

One consequence of living in this heavily mediated society is that it is increasingly difficult to discern the truthfulness of the images presented to viewers. We rarely know what happened the instant before the camera was turned on, or just after it was turned off. Nor do we know what is going on outside of the frame the camera lens provides on the images it presents. And while we do not usually know what has been omitted in any other mode of communication, such as print or radio, we are much more apt to feel with visual communication that we can "trust our own eyes." In short, the camera never presents the temporal or spatial frame, but tends to leave us convinced (see Box 2.7).

Trust in the visual image has been further undermined with the development of digital technology that allows anyone with a computer and the right software to alter, or even create, images in any number of ways. Thus, the old aphorism "seeing is believing" is quickly becoming obsolete.

With the development of, and widespread access to, personal computers and the internet, everyone, from communications scholars to government planners and members of the general public, are thinking about the social changes being brought about by electronic communication. The nature of education and commerce and the dynamics of cultures, political systems, and markets are all being changed by electronic communication.

For some, the more recent developments in electronic communication brought on by computers and the internet are shifting both the dimensions of human perception and the structure of society. Henry Jenkins (2006: 4) argues that such electronic media are enabling a new "collective intelligence." "None of us knows everything; each of us knows something; and we can put the pieces together if we pool our resources and combine our skills." Commonly offered examples of such collective intelligence include Google and Wikipedia.

For others, electronic communication networks have become central to the ways in which society is organized and in which we experience the world. Manuel Castells (1996) argues that such networks are shifting the basic structure of society and driving globalization. For Castells, these networks are the new locus of social power, replacing geographic centres such as cities and countries in this regard. In his more recent works, he says that these networks are fundamental to both how people understand the world and the ways in which social power is exercised. From this perspective, those interests that control the

2.6 ▶▶ ▷ ▷ ▶▶ ▷

TV AS CULTURAL ANIMATEUR

The following historical anecdotes, based on a set of columns by John Doyle, *The Globe and Mail*'s television critic, are meant to underline that just like newspapers and books, television is an important medium that signals key events and brings valuable information and perspectives to members of society. Some of those events are presented here:

May 1939: RCA broadcasts the first live sports event, a baseball game. The broadcast laid the foundation of sports television and the new sports economy.

Fall 1951: *I Love Lucy* establishes a whole new pop culture comedy genre.

March 1954: Television cameras capture the bullying of Senator Joseph McCarthy with contemptuous narration by Edward R. Murrow, thereby hastening an end to the senator's witch-hunting tactics and political career.

Fall 1960: Television watchers are convinced that John F. Kennedy wins his television debate against Richard Nixon. Radio listeners hold the opposite opinion. For the first time, the television image assumes a key position in political campaigning.

May 1961: In the United States, the chair of the Federal Communications Commission—similar to Canada's CRTC—declares television a "vast wasteland."

Fall 1966: *W5* is launched by CTV as an investigative-style public affairs show exposing corruption in politics and business.

July 1969: The first person walks on the moon and the event is linked to earth via a live broadcast.

November 1969: *Sesame Street* is created and is enormously popular for its role in helping children to learn.

September 1972: Paul Henderson scores the TV-captured winning goal in the Canada–Soviet Union Summit Series of Hockey.

June 1985: Live Aid is a massive television event linking two rock concerts in London and Philadelphia, and it raises millions of dollars for famine relief in Africa.

Fall 1996: CBC airs *The Newsroom*, created by Winnipegger Ken Finkleman, which satirizes the network broadcasting the show. Finkleman becomes a television auteur.

11 September 2001: The destruction of the twin towers of the World Trade Center in New York, witnessed by viewers on live television, marks a radical shift in how social freedoms are perceived.

December 2004: Television coverage of the Indian Ocean tsunami helped generate an unprecedented outpouring of $7 billion in humanitarian aid from individuals.

Summer 2008: Coverage on television of the Beijing Summer Olympics attracts 4.7 billion or 70 percent of the world's population.

Summer 2014: Including internet streaming, television coverage of the World Cup of men's soccer is watched by billions who enjoy the global sporting event.

---

networks also control society—with large corporations and conservative-minded business interests currently holding the reins of power.

Similarly, electronic communication networks are also seen as shifting the ways in which interest groups and social movements operate. Such networks allow much more flexibility in the ways groups and movements are formed and a more effective means for social dissent and effecting progressive social change (Dyer-Witheford, 1999; Day, 2005; Lievrouw, 2011).

The increasing mobility of electronic forms of communication adds yet another dimension to the shifting influence of media technology. While land-based wireless services cover less than 25 percent of the country's area, they are within reach of 99 percent of Canadians. Although penetration rates are low in Canada by international standards, approximately 80 percent of Canadians subscribe to such services (CRTC, 2013). Today's smartphones, tablets, and other mobile devices promise real-time voice, data, and

2.7 ▶▶▷▷▶▶▷

THE CAMERA NEVER TELLS THE WHOLE TRUTH

In a famous incident from the Iraq War of the 2000s, the media reported on a large crowd toppling a statue of Saddam Hussein as troops moved into Baghdad, "spontaneously" expressing their joy at being "liberated" by US forces. Later, it was revealed that the statue toppling was a staged event. American soldiers had orchestrated it and there were only a few dozen people in the square where the statue was. The video footage was tightly shot, making it look like there were many more people on hand than there actually were.

Source: AP Photo/APTN.

One of the photos distributed by mainstream media outlets, this image is closely cropped, making the size of the crowd difficult to determine.

high-quality multimedia capabilities anytime and anywhere service is available.

Not only does this technology allow people to accomplish many tasks from a multitude of locations, but it also raises a host of new privacy concerns—particularly issues of surveillance, as corporations and governments use it to locate and track whom they perceive to be prospective customers (corporations) or potential criminals (governments). As we discuss in Chapter 6, as information about all of our purchases and activities is amassed in huge databases, it is all too easy for these institutions to use the information against us. Whether it is techies tracking our drug, alcohol, and grocery purchases to formulate the "risks" we might present automobile, health, and life insurance companies; police forces and other government officials reviewing our email and participation in rallies and marches to assess our political affiliations and possible threats we could pose to law and order; or potential employers checking social media pictures and posts in an effort to gauge our reliability as possible employees, new technology poses unprecedented threats to personal privacy and freedom.

At the same time, technology also presents a wide range of opportunities for challenging dominant political, economic, and cultural interests. As Leah Lievrouw (2011: 3) points out,

> Websites; mobile telephones, digital photography, video, and audio; blogs; wikis; file sharing systems; social media and open-source software all permit social groups with diverse interests to build and sustain communities, gain visibility and voice, present alternative or marginal views, produce and share their own do-it-yourself information sources, and resist, talk back, or otherwise confront dominant media culture and power.

These perspectives illustrate the communications technology dichotomy—it can both threaten and facilitate citizens' abilities to protect their personal and collective well-being. So, it is more important than ever for the public to know who controls communication technology. Many people are determined to preserve the internet as a place for public discourse because keeping the channels of communication open and accessible to everyone gives us more input and control over our public and private lives.

Technology and Social Change

Marshall McLuhan used his famous phrase "The medium is the message" (and later, his play on that aphorism, "The medium is the massage") to emphasize the effects that media have on the ways in which we understand the world and act within it. And, indeed, it would seem that communication media, and the technology that gives it form, do have a profound effect upon how we see and understand the world. Following Innis's and Mcluhan's approaches, Elizabeth Eisenstein argues (1983) that the printing press and the books it provided led to an "unacknowledged revolution" in human thinking and organization, and that print media and the knowledge they provided opened a wide range of new horizons for public knowledge and individual possibility.

Other viewpoints, however, such as the social model of communication that we described in Chapter 1, take a more nuanced approach to the role of technology, and particularly communication technology, in society. Raymond Williams (1974), for example, notes that rather than instigate and lead social change, communications technologies are the product of broad forces that shape and form societies. Working along these lines, David Ze (1995) and others have challenged Elizabeth Eisenstein's thesis, arguing that printing with movable type had no parallel effect in Korea and China, where it was invented several hundred years earlier than in Europe. Ze in particular argues that in China, where it was controlled by emperors, printing was an agent of social stability rather than of change and it was used to transmit official versions of a limited number of texts. Printers had everything to lose and nothing to gain in printing original material. Consequently, he concludes, the existence of a technology by itself does not necessarily affect society significantly.

Similar debates continue today around the role of information and communication technologies (ICTs) in society. Through the 1950s and '60s, advances and reliance on technology fuelled research and speculation on the growing role of technology in both the economy and social organization in general. Technology and technological systems were increasingly seen as heralding the development of an **information society**; that is, a society where ICTs are key to the creation of wealth and defining the direction of social development. It was in this context that McLuhan pondered the ways in which electronic media extended the human senses and shattered the barriers of space and time to provide the experience of living in a global village.

Drawing on these themes, Daniel Bell published his book *The Coming of Post-Industrial Society* (1976) and set the stage for a debate on the changing structure of the economy. Through the late 1960s and early '70s, Bell and others following his lead posited that the economy was shifting from a dependence on large-scale industry to a post-industrial phase, where knowledge and information work would predominate. Industrial jobs wouldn't disappear entirely, but be transferred to other places as companies closed factories in traditional manufacturing centres and moved their production to newly industrializing regions with lower wages and fewer labour and environmental regulations, such as the American Sunbelt, Mexico, India, and China.

Through facilitating the movement of capital and goods, ICTs played a key role in this shift in labour processes. They provided a vital link between the newly industrialized countries where these goods are now produced, and the markets in old industrialized centres—such as North America and Western Europe—where they are consumed. At the same time, ICTs have also been central to the reorganization of industry in these old industrial centres, as well as the creation of new jobs and work opportunities in computer hardware and software, telecommunications, and related fields. Similarly, as we have discussed, the impact of new ICTs has not been confined to the workplace, as social media and other new media technologies have increasingly shifted the ways we practise politics, socialize, and spend our leisure time.

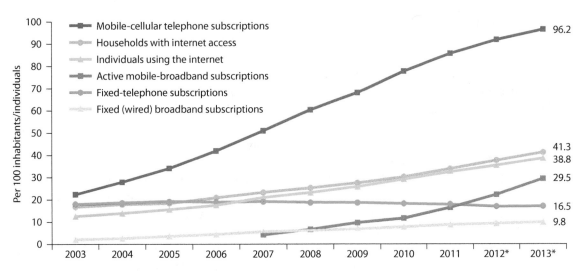

FIGURE 2.4   Global ICT Developments, 2003–2013

This chart illustrates the dramatic growth of ICTs around the globe. Does such growth signal the development of an information economy?

Note: *Estimate

Source: ITU World Telecommunication/ICT Indicators database.

But we must be careful not to put too much emphasis on the role of technology in this restructuring of society. While technology can play an important role in the form and direction development might take, it is not the only variable in this process. The shift in location of manufacturing jobs, for instance, was not simply the product of new ICTs. The main driver of the change was the end of an economic boom that had started after the Second World War and ran into the late 1960s and early '70s. At that time, a series of events such as rising inflation, stagnant economic growth, and the 1970s Arab oil crisis, signalled the onslaught of a deep and stubborn economic recession.

New technology, and particularly ICTs, offered industry and policy-makers one way to try and get the economy moving again. Through transferring manufacturing to places with low wages and less stringent labour and environmental regulations, it was hoped that lower prices for consumer goods would spur consumers to once again start buying products. But that shift in the location of

manufacturing might have taken place without new ICTs. Either that or industry and policy-makers might have chosen another strategy to jumpstart the economy. Indeed, this strategy has had deep and lasting impacts on the economy, one of which is a general lack of well-paying jobs for the middle class and high unemployment among young people today. In other words, utilizing ICTs in this manner has had clear benefits for some social interests, such as large corporations and their shareholders, but for others, however, the economic benefits have not been so clear-cut.

If we overemphasize the transformative effects of communication media and technology, this can lead toward the snakepit of technological determinism. In other words, it tends to frame technology as the primary force shaping society (a phenomenon that we explore in greater detail in Chapter 6). While neither Innis nor McLuhan was an avowed technological determinist, we must be careful when studying their insights on technology. While their work can help us shape the ways in which we see and understand the world, it is paramount that we not see technological development and its effects on our society as inevitable and out of people's control. Without taking into account how human agency and social interaction shape both technology and the uses made of it, analysts neglect to account for how technology is employed to advance particular interests and slide into technologically derived descriptions of the social process. For instance, in our capitalist society (refer to Box 2.3), corporations like Microsoft, Apple, and Google develop and implement new technologies primarily because they are profitable, not simply because they are socially useful or further the public good. While, as we shall see, there can be good reasons for societies to invest in activities and technologies that are financially unprofitable, if new technologies fail to make a profit for privately owned companies and their shareholders, they are soon consigned to scrap heap of history without public or government support.

This critique, however, does not mean that analyzing the role of ICTs is not useful, or that such analyses don't tell us important things about the ways media and communications affect social action and organization. Rather, it alerts us to the complexities of the social world and reminds us that a thorough understanding of a social phenomenon necessitates employing several theoretical and methodological perspectives.

 SUMMARY

In this chapter, we have conveyed the complex relationship between communication, society, and culture and have considered some of the social impacts of media and mass communication. We discovered how two Canadians, Harold Innis and Marshall McLuhan, were the first scholars to draw serious attention to the idea that ways people communicate might actually shape a society and its culture. In this context, we examined how oral, literate, and the various modes of electronic communication can affect social development, processes, and structures. In the current context, however, we must be careful about putting too much emphasis on technology as the primary force shaping society. As we discuss in Chapter 6, other factors, such as politics and economics, are key to the process of technological development.

The relationships between communication media and social form are one of the key subjects of communication studies. Human affairs cannot be divorced from the communication system used to represent or discuss them and the design of our communication systems frames and animates the ways in which we see and understand the world. But how new forms of electronic communication will work together with larger political, economic, and cultural forces—particularly contemporary capitalism—to reconfigure our society remains to be seen.

 KEY TERMS

capitalism, p. 40
culture, p. 33
freedom of information, p. 38
globalization, p. 40
global village, p. 49
information society, p. 54
lingua franca, p. 49
politics, p. 35

privacy, p. 38
probes, p. 43
public sphere, p. 54
satellite footprint, p. 48
society, p. 33
space bias, p. 43
time bias, p. 42
Toronto School (of communication theory), p. 43

RELATED WEBSITES

Canadian Journal of Communication:
www.cjc-online.ca
The *Canadian Journal of Communication* is Canada's principal communication periodical. Students can make good use of it by accessing the site and searching for essay topics. The *CJC* is a leading proponent of online journal publishing and makes its back issues accessible online.

Council of Canadians: www.canadians.org
The Council of Canadians involves itself in a wide range of issues where it feels that Canadians have a distinct set of interests.

Harold Innis Research Foundation:
www.utoronto.ca/hirf
The Harold Innis Research Foundation at the University of Toronto fosters scholarly work, including a research bulletin that focuses on Innis's theories.

International Telecommunications Union (ITU):
www.itu.int/en/Pages/default.aspx
The ITU is the United Nations agency focusing on telecommunications and information and communication technologies (ICTs).

McLuhan Program in Culture and Technology: The Coach House Institute:
mcluhan.ischool.utoronto.ca
For years, the McLuhan Program has been referred to simply as the Coach House by many who have spent time on the University of Toronto campus. The Mcluhan Program carries on research and courses in the spirit of Marshall McLuhan's revolutionary media studies work.

Wikileaks: wikileaks.org
A controversial website that specializes in exposing government secrets.

 FURTHER READINGS

Castells, Manuel. 1996. *The Rise of the Network Society*. New York: Blackwell. The first in Castell's trilogy outlining his influential theory of network society.

Coulter, Natalie. 2014. "From the top drawer to the bottom line: The commodification of children's cultures." In *Mediascapes: New Patterns in Canadian Communication*, Leslie Regan, ed. Don Mills, ON: Nelson, 409–26.

Eisenstein, Elizabeth. 1983. *The Printing Revolution in Early Modern Europe*. Cambridge: Cambridge University Press. Eisenstein examines the role of the printing press and movable type.

Innis, Harold. 2009. "From empire and communications." In *Communication in Canadian History*, Daniel Robinson, ed. Don Mills, ON: Oxford University Press, 35–9.

International Telecommunications Union. 2013. *Measuring the Information Society*. Available at www.itu.int/en/ITU-D/Statistics/Documents/publications/mis2013/MIS2013_without_Annex_4.pdf.

McLuhan, Marshall. 1964. *Understanding Media: The Extensions of Man*. Toronto: McGraw-Hill. In this book, McLuhan focuses on the influence of the media on the modern world. The various essays that make up the text explore the implications of (largely) electronic information systems. The book is interesting both for its insight and its foresight.

STUDY QUESTIONS

1. Define the terms society and culture. What are the key differences between them?
2. What is the *public sphere*? What role or roles do media play in it?
3. What did Harold Innis mean when he described societies dependent on oral forms of communication as having a *time bias* and those dependent on written forms as having a *space bias*?
4. What did Marshall McLuhan mean by the aphorism, "The medium is the message"?
5. Would Innis argue that electronic media have a time bias or a space bias? Explain.
6. What is technological determinism? Why is it a concern when we are analyzing the possible social effects of communications technology?

3 Media: History and the Canadian Context

> The greatest power of the mass media is the power to ignore.
> — American essayist Sam Smith

Opening Questions

- What were Renaissance and the Enlightenment? Why are they important to contemporary notions of citizenship and democracy?

- What were the roles and purposes of media as they developed in industrial society?

- How do libertarian theory, the social responsibility theory of the press, the mass society thesis, and critical political economy each conceive of the role(s) of the media in society?

- What are the distinctive characteristics of the Canadian state that have helped shape its communication systems?

- Describe four different dimensions of the relationship between government and the media today.

Introduction

As we have seen, the mass media are far more than sources of information and entertainment. They are essential social, political, and cultural institutions. Building on Chapter 2, we shift the focus here from communication technology to the larger social and historical contexts that give that technology form and function. We open the chapter by tracing the historical roots of media development and illustrate that today's media are the product of dramatic shifts in the ways in which people understood the world and their relationships to it. This change in worldview—and the institutions of science, industry, and government that it gave rise to—is the fertile ground within which the media developed. We examine different theories of the political role of media in this context, and we go on to consider the ways in which the distinctive elements of the social, political, and physical geography of the Canadian state have nuanced the form and structure of the Canadian media. We finish the chapter by considering some of the distinctive characteristics of the relationship between media and politics in Canada.

The European Roots of Media and Western Society

While papermaking and movable type were first developed in Asia, it might be said that the modern mass media began to emerge in mid-fifteenth-century Europe with Johannes Gutenberg's development of the printing press in Mainz, Germany, in 1454. This advance in technology is often used to designate the end of the Middle Ages and the beginning of the Renaissance—a transition from a social order where people were subservient to the powerful Church and monarch to one that was more sympathetic to the freedom of individuals and ideas. The **Renaissance** and the movements and conceptual developments that followed it—humanism, the Reformation, the Counter-Reformation, the **Enlightenment**, and the **Industrial Revolution**—paved the way for liberal-democratic industrial societies and modern forms of mass media.

A major aspect of the Renaissance was the rediscovery and revival of learning and literature from antiquity, especially the Greek and Roman empires, which had been lost and suppressed during the Middle Ages. This recovered knowledge helped to reorient social perspectives concerning the place of humankind and nature in the cosmic order. Led by Italian thinkers and artists, the Renaissance was the beginning of a reassertion of reason and the senses that had characterized classical Greece. Emerging from the Renaissance was *humanism*, a broad philosophy that celebrated human achievement and capacity. Although often couched in religious contexts, in art, sculpture, and architecture, humanism celebrated the human form and encouraged an empirical understanding of the world—*empirical*, meaning this perspective allowed that people might come to understand the world through individual observation and experience rather than religious texts and emissaries of the Church. The great works of art and architecture that characterize the period were grounded in these ideas, and they led to Western culture's knowledge of such things as mathematics, mechanics, and geometry, an awareness of perspective, and a theory of light and colour. In the practice of this empirical knowledge, humanism emphasized people's abilities to

Much of Renaissance (*re-naissance*, meaning "born again") architecture and design was taken from Greek and Roman designs. In what other ways have the Greeks and Romans influenced our culture?

Source: © rusm/iStockphoto.

know and understand the world beyond what had been the teachings of the Church.

At this point in European history, the dominant **ideology** (see Chapter 4) held that the world was ordered by a divine hand and that true knowledge of the world came from God or through his emissaries on earth: the Pope and the priests of the Church. In the feudal system of production that dominated the period, social position and responsibilities were inherited by birth—royalty and aristocrats held their stations and governed according to a doctrine of divine right (see Figure 3.1). By demonstrating the abilities of individuals to understand and shape the world, humanism

The Feudal System

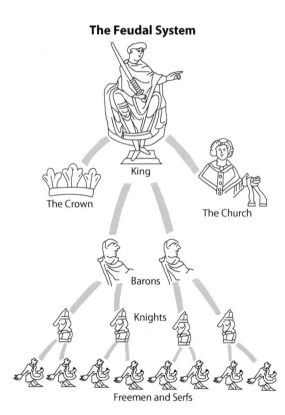

FIGURE 3.1   Feudal System

Feudal society had a well-defined class structure and social position, and responsibilities were inherited by birth. In what ways do you think this differs from the way our society is structured today? In what ways do you think it's similar?

sowed the seeds of a secularized society within this traditional order.

The dissemination of humanist ideas was facilitated by the technologies of writing and printing, which allowed individuals to develop and record their ideas and communicate them in a manner understandable by many. Printing presses were established throughout Europe over the next centuries and encouraged the spread of literacy. As literacy spread, so, too, did the thirst for ideas. With printing, ideas rejected by the ruling elite in one regime could be exported into others, leading to a destabilization in these states. As American historian Robert Darnton (1982) has demonstrated, a regular business of printing books in Switzerland and smuggling them into France was an important precursor to the French Revolution.

The transposition of Renaissance ideas to Germany found fertile ground in the religious reform movement. The German Reformation followed Renaissance principles with a freedom of conscience from institutionalization (the Roman Catholic Church)—arguing that each individual could come to know God directly—and attempted to redefine religion and morality on a more individual basis. The Reformation began in earnest with Martin Luther reportedly nailing his 95 theses to the door of Wittenberg's Castle Church in 1517 to protest against the selling of *indulgences*—remissions, granted by the pope, from temporal punishment for sins confessed and forgiven. Luther's theses, written in Latin, were quickly translated into German, printed, and circulated throughout Germany. He also translated the Bible into German. By making the Bible more accessible, printing undermined the power of the Catholic Church and its priests to act as intermediaries in delivering religion to the people and led to mounting support for a restructuring or "reformation" of Church doctrine and to the development of Protestantism.

Both the Reformation and the Renaissance were brought to a close in Europe during the sixteenth and seventeenth centuries by the Counter-Reformation, a **conservative** backlash that re-established monarchical absolutism in church and state, the most extreme manifestation of this being the Spanish Inquisition. During the Counter-Reformation, European states, recognizing the powerful role of ideas, writing, printing, and communication in general, placed severe controls on printing to limit the dissemination of humanist ideas. Particular printers and writers were branded as heretics and were tortured and executed.

The backlash against humanism that characterized the Counter-Reformation did not last, and in the early eighteenth century a new attempt at humanism that combined logic and empiricism introduced the Age of Reason, otherwise known as the **Enlightenment**. The Enlightenment was distinguished by an intellectual approach based on a scientific and rational perspective on the world. It heralded a fundamental shift in worldview that championed science over religion and justice over the abuse of power, and a social contract that specified individual rights and freedoms over the absolutist rule of monarchs and popes.

The writings of Enlightenment philosophers, such as John Locke (1632–1704), Voltaire (1694–1778), Jean-Jacques Rousseau (1712–1788), and Adam Smith (1723–1790), worked to undermine the inherited right of monarchs and the Church to control government. They argued that people possessed natural, inalienable social rights, and they upheld the market over feudal forms of production and exchange.

These shifts in social ideas that characterized the Enlightenment were fuelled by an emerging elite competing with the aristocracy for power. This prosperous and educated **bourgeoisie**— or new land-owning class—had been working to build a market economy and colonial trade from about the sixteenth century onwards. Through the eighteenth and early nineteenth centuries, the Enlightenment's legacy of scientific reason combined with the growing wealth of the bourgeoisie to fuel change in social and political structure. First with the American War of Independence (1775–1783), and later with the French Revolution (1789–1799), Europe and North America were gripped in conflict as a new social order took shape. The result was a massive upheaval in European society that laid the groundwork for yet another change in social structure, the shift from an agrarian to an industrial society—a transformation that, again, was fertilized by communication.

Beginning with the invention of the printing press and onward, the spread of knowledge based on a humanist understanding of the world prepared Western society for profound political and social change, from feudalism to capitalism, from farming to industry, from medieval to Renaissance and then to an Enlightenment worldview. In the realm of politics, the acquisition of such knowledge allowed a new class of citizens to emerge and gain enough education to compete with the aristocracy for the right to govern. Similarly, in culture, talented and knowledgeable creative artists brought forward secular literary, musical, and artistic works that were appreciated by the viewer for their visions and understandings of the world rather than their religious significance.

It was in this context that what Jürgen Habermas called the *public sphere* took form (refer to Chapters 2 and 10). And, because they inform the

A nineteenth century drawing of Johannes Gutenberg (1398–1468), the inventor of the European movable-type printing press, inspecting a page produced by his printing press. Why is the printing press so important in Western history? What kinds of changes did the invention of the printing press bring about?

Source: © jpa1999/iStockphoto.

public about the important issues of the day, it was under these circumstances that knowledge- and information-based institutions—or, in other words, the media—became, and have remained, essential to the larger process of government.

The Industrial Revolution, Communication, and Social Form

Paralleling the Enlightenment giving rise to new ways of thinking about people's relations to each other and to the world, the **Industrial Revolution** introduced a major change in social organization. With the application of growing scientific knowledge to production, industry began to dominate in the late eighteenth century in Western Europe.

As landlords moved to turn their lands to commercial agriculture, serfs, tenant farmers, and others dependent on those lands for their livelihoods were forced to migrate, either into the swelling cities and towns where the new "manufactories" were being built or across the oceans to developing colonies, which increasingly served as sources for raw materials in industrial production. New forms of transportation, such as railways and steamships, provided means for moving people, raw materials, and finished goods, while new forms of communication, such as the telegraph and newspapers, provided vehicles for coordinating buyers and sellers, workers and employers, and governments and citizens.

The growth of industry complicated social relationships as urbanization and migration stamped the landscape with the spatial and temporal edifices and rhythms of industrial production. This production demanded the coordination of social action across increasing physical distances, as both raw materials for factory processes and foodstuffs for rising populations converged on burgeoning urban centres.

Industrial life also redrew the dimensions of family life. The traditional extended family, whereby mother and father, children, grandparents, and aunts and uncles might live in close proximity—even in the same home—gave way to the more streamlined family unit we know today (sometimes called the *nuclear family*), a more flexible form of social organization that was more easily moved from place to place in pursuit of work opportunities.

Industrial production also shifted the temporal dimensions of social life. Work in a rural, agricultural setting is ongoing, requiring a paced way of life in which the work and daily living must adjust to daily and seasonal cycles, structured by the necessary tasks of caring for livestock, raising crops, and sustaining and maintaining the family and the household. Industrial production demanded a different temporal division of the day so that a new distinction arose between work and leisure time.

It was in this context that modern communications media took form. In the face of the changes wrought by the new industrial way of life, the media developed what Raymond Williams has called "specialized means" to close the geographical and social distances created

Source: © Lingbeek/iStockphoto.

During the Industrial Revolution, young men started leaving the farms of their families to work in urban factories or on infrastructure like the Firth of Forth Road Bridge near Edinburgh. Life changed dramatically during this time, and people looked to different forms of media to close the geographical and social distances created by these new workspaces and serve new social interests and needs. In what ways are media responding to social change today?

by industrial production and to serve new social interests and needs. As Williams (1974: 22–3) illustrates, "the press [developed] for political and economic information; the photograph for community, family and personal life; the motion picture for curiosity and entertainment; [and] telegraphy and telephony for business information and some important personal messages." Let's consider the forces behind the development of each of these media.

As we discussed in Chapter 1, in the context of developing industrial society, the telegraph greatly enhanced the coordination of people and goods across vast distances. It was a key advance in what Karl Marx described as people's abilities to "shrink space through time." It forestalled the necessity of physically sending messages from one place to another and enabled communication literally at the speed of light. Both government and industry could respond much more quickly to developing events, accomplishing so much more in shorter periods of time that it seemed as though space—or the distances between places and things—had actually shrunk. Governments more quickly learned of revolts in far-flung parts of their territories and responded with troops, thereby securing more readily the supply of resources and markets. Manufacturers could order raw materials from suppliers a continent away, while orders for goods could be taken from cities and towns scattered across the country. The telephone built upon and enhanced the economic relations created by the telegraph, and although today we think of the telephone as primarily for personal communication, it was first and foremost, and generally remains, a business tool.

On the face of it, the photograph was a simple technique for capturing images on light-sensitive glass or paper. But as the new emerging economic system tore traditional kin and friendship ties apart, it became a way of constructing and remembering family and community. As Susan Sontag (1999: 177) points out,

Photography becomes a rite of family life just when, in the industrializing countries

of Europe and America, the very institution of the family starts undergoing radical change. . . . Those ghostly traces, photographs, supply the token presence of dispersed relatives. A family's photograph album is generally about the extended family—and often it is all that remains of it.

With the rise of large commercial newspapers in the late nineteenth century, the photograph also becomes a way of familiarizing readers with political and business leaders—of "putting a face to the name"—as well as, through images, linking them with far-off events. In these ways

Source: © marlenka/iStockphoto.

Two young sisters pose in an early photograph most likely taken by a studio camera. Large plates coated with light-sensitive chemicals were replaced at the back of the camera for each succeeding photograph. Most photographers developed their own plates and images until John Eastman in 1888 developed the Kodak camera with celluloid film that could be returned to the manufacturer for developing. This, in turn, led to cameras being bought and used by an increasing number of individuals.

photography helped sew the seams of the emerging industrial-based social fabric.

Motion pictures—an extension of the photographic image—were given cultural freedom to grow by the new rhythm of the industrial day that divided time between work and leisure. As people moved into cities and towns and took up industrial ways of life, an increasing number of urban dwellers had free time and disposable income. Entrepreneurs worked to find ways to capitalize on these circumstances, and new products or **commodities** (see Box 3.1) were created to sell to this growing body of consumers. Through the early twentieth century, among these new commodities was the motion picture. The motion picture was also the product of the economies of scale engendered through industrial production (see Box 3.3). Many copies or prints of the same film could be shown simultaneously in widely scattered cities and towns, thereby spreading the cost of production among many audience members.

Of all the modern media given both form and function by the development of industrial society, however, the newspaper or "the press"—named after the printing press—was both the earliest to develop, and it was the most pervasive.

The Beginnings of the Modern Media: The Newspaper or "Press"

In the eighteenth and early nineteenth centuries, some degree of organization was brought to the cacophony of publishing voices created by the printing press, as newspapers began to

---

3.1 ▶▶▶▶▶▶

THE COMMODITY AND COMMUNICATION

One of the most dynamic features of capitalism as an economic system is the way it works to convert things for which we find need and uses in our lives into products for which we must pay market prices. Critical commentators call this *the commodification of everyday life*—that is, what Karl Marx highlighted as the process of turning "use value" into "exchange value" (see Mosco, 2009). Others celebrate this process as the entrepreneurial spirit of capitalism.

Think of all the different elements of the process of communication that have been commodified over the last few years. Television and radio used to arrive free over the air. Now the monthly cable or satellite bill can eat up a day's pay. Time spent in movie theatres—particularly the interval between people taking their seats and the feature film starting—has been commodified, as the theatre owners have used advertising to turn that time into a product they can sell to advertisers. Internet access is purchased by the month or by the byte. Telephone service has evolved into an ever-increasing array of products, such as voice mail, text messaging, and various web-based telecom services. Even the ring tones for cellphones have become products for sale. And, increasingly, information itself—such as news, government reports and statistics, and course readings—is becoming a product for sale.

As we shall see in the following chapters, this ongoing commodification of communication products and processes lies at the heart of what people call the *communication economy* or the *communication revolution* and is seen as a key factor in economic growth. It creates a growing divide between the communication haves and have-nots, however, between the information-rich and the information-poor. And, given that communication products and processes play key roles in our knowledge and understanding of the world, the commodification of communication and information—or turning both information and access to it into products we have to pay for—can't help but undermine people's abilities to exercise their full rights and responsibilities as citizens.

be aligned with (and sometimes even owned by) political parties. This pattern—the emergence of many newspapers, then their reduction to a few, often politically aligned, publications—has been repeated in many Western countries at various points in their histories. And just as this pattern has repeated itself, so has the subsequent transition of control of newspapers from political parties to business interests. In book and magazine publishing, a variation on the same pattern can be seen, with control first being established in the hands of wealthy patrons; then to some liberal members of the elite; and, finally, passing—sometimes first through political hands—to business enterprises.

In Canada, newspapers in the early and mid-nineteenth century were generally under the control of partisan political interests. As Robert Hackett and Yuezhi Zhao (1998: 20) observe in *Sustaining Democracy? Journalism and the Politics of Objectivity,*

> Often owned by a group of wealthy partisans . . . papers had the explicit purpose of representing a political party. Overall, they tended to serve the ruling political and business elites. . . . Newspapers often counted on financial support from government patronage or direct party subsidies. Shaped by party affiliations, the journalism of the time was replete not only with special pleading for the politicians who financially supported each paper, but also with vicious personal attacks on political foes.

By the early twentieth century, however, the cost of producing newspapers drove them into the control of business. Perhaps the largest influence on this shift in ownership was the development of industrial society. Around the end of the nineteenth century, the growth in industry and urban populations led to developments in both mass production and mass marketing.

The modern newspaper in Canada is rooted in the "1890–1920 [period], when, among other things, a rapidly expanding urban population, increased literacy, the economic boom of the Laurier era, and a growing national market of consumer markets contributed to the profitability of new newspaper ventures" (Sotiron 1997: 4). Newspaper publishers found that providing marketers with a vehicle to reach the increasing numbers of consumers was more profitable than direct alliances with political parties, and advertising soon became their major source of revenue. As modern newspapers evolved within industrial society, they crossed the boundary between the public life of work and community and the private home. In this configuration, papers began to serve multiple roles.

Not only were they the source of political and community news, but they also provided a wide range of other information important to people confronted with an increasingly complex society. Want ads linked job seekers and employers, merchandise and service ads linked the swelling ranks of workers with a growing number of products, and personal ads helped people locate partners and friends in the increasingly impersonal urban environment.

New technologies animated these changes. Cheap newsprint and faster printing presses lowered the cost of producing newspapers, while the telegraph and later the telephone were plentiful conduits for the information needed to fill pages and attract readers. Thus, just as the photograph, the motion picture, the telegraph, and the telephone took form and function in the emerging structure of industrial society, so, too, did newspapers (Schudson, 1978).

Journalism also changed to meet the new industrial regime. In news, *objectivity* replaced partisan reporting as papers sought to reach a wider readership and increase circulation and profits (see Hackett and Zhao, 1998; Schudson, 1978). The use of headlines and photographs to capture the attention of potential readers became popular, as did partitioning newspapers into different sections and offering a range of different features—such as serialized novels—to attract a diverse readership.

As the press became more a business than a service, publishers also promoted their own interests, emphasizing the freedom to pursue profitability in the marketplace unencumbered by state restrictions (see Chapter 8). Journalists developed a complementary ethic by stressing their need for independence from the state for reportage and analysis. This dual business and journalistic thrust has allowed the press to establish some distance from the politicians of the day. This is not to say that in claiming their independence, newspapers, and the media as a whole, represent the interests of all citizens. On the contrary, as we will see in the following chapters, the media generally represent the interests of the power elites in society—mostly business types, but also the agendas of the political and intellectual elites.

While newspaper readership has been declining in recent years, the electronic media that dominate our lives today are very much a product of this history. Controlled by corporate interests, the profit motive plays a strong role in shaping media form and content. Still, however, just as they have since the early days of industrial society, media continue to provide a key link between people, governments, and the larger society within which they live.

Perspectives on the Media

From the beginning, the media have played a key role in the shifting relations of social power. In Martin Luther's day, the printing press was used to undermine the traditional power of the Catholic Church. As newspapers developed through the seventeenth and eighteenth centuries, governments in Britain and Europe used a range of measures to censor and control the circulation of news in order to maintain social and political control. Through the late eighteenth and early nineteenth centuries, liberal writers such as Jeremy Bentham, James Mill, and John Stuart Mill advocated that a press independent from government regulation (a "free press") was central to good government and democracy.

It was in this context that in a speech to the British House of Commons, Edmund Burke referred to the press as "the fourth estate," meaning that alongside the other "estates" or institutions of social governance—the clergy, the nobility, and the commons—the press played an important role as a kind of political watchdog, guarding the rights of citizens through publicly reporting on affairs of state. Over the last few centuries, consequently, freedom of the press from government interference became an important political ideal, and it is reflected in the Constitution of the United States, the United Nations' Universal Declaration of Human Rights, and the Canadian Charter of Rights and Freedoms. While it is indeed true that newspaper readership has been declining in recent years, newspaper and television news organizations remain the largest producers of news and public affairs content, and the bulk of the news available on the internet originates from these sources. So, the term *press* is taken to represent the media as a whole, rather than just newspapers. And while the term may conjure up old-fashioned images of huge metal printing presses hammering out reams of ink-stained paper, it is important to remember that the media still play important social and political roles in society.

While newspaper readership has been declining in recent years, newspaper and television news organizations remain the largest producers of news and public affairs content, and the bulk of the news available on the internet originates from these sources.

Source: © PhotoTalk/iStockphoto.

While newspapers have historically contributed to political freedoms, they have over time come to be operated as commercial enterprises and there has been a growing concern that corporate interests—namely, the pursuit of private profit—have dominated over the public interest in their operation. Press barons of the late nineteenth century were known to sensationalize news, and sometimes even to make it up, in their efforts to attract readers. And today there are many examples of how news production and, sometimes, perspectives in news media are tilted toward the interests of the shareholders of media companies rather than to the general public.

Still, defining the exact social role of the press, and subsequently that of the media, is a matter of some debate and depends largely on one's theoretical perspective, and different theories of society take different approaches to understanding the role of the media in that context. In this section, we consider four perspectives on media and society.

The first two—the libertarian theory of the press and social responsibility theory—draw on liberal theories of society to consider what they believe to be the ideal role that media should play in social and political life, as well the social conditions necessary to realize that role. Drawing from early Enlightenment philosophers, they emphasize the freedom of the individual, and the idea that the media, too, should enjoy relative freedom from both government and commercial interests so that it might provide unbiased perspectives on events and circumstances. Rather than privilege individual freedom, the second two perspectives—the mass society thesis and political economic theory—emphasize the ways in which larger social forces have an impact on both the way in which people understand society and how the media represent it.

Although quite different in character, these theories or perspectives underpin the ways in which many people think of the social and political roles of the media today. As you may recognize, liberal theory, and particularly the social responsibility theory of the press, is the dominant

way of thinking about the media and its role in society. The point to consider here, however, is not which of these theories is the correct or "true" perspective on the media and society, but rather the insight that each brings to the analysis.

Libertarian Theory

Such philosophers as John Locke, David Hume (1711–1776), and John Stuart Mill (1806–1873) nourished the liberal concepts of agency and the free will of individuals. Modern libertarian theory derived its fundamental assumption that individual freedom is the first and foremost social goal to be sought. Libertarians are highly suspicious of the state; they maintain that limiting the powers of the state and other impediments to individual action will create the most advantageous situation for all.

Libertarian theorists tend to see the mass media as an extension of the individual's right to freedom of expression and, hence, as independent voices that help to make government responsible to the people. The media do so by supplying information to people such that they might judge government's performance and, come election time, vote accordingly. Apart from this watchdog role, libertarians also see the mass media as assiduous pursuers of free speech. From this perspective, freedom of speech is considered one of the most important of all freedoms; and while it may result in problems and difficulties in the short term, as in the case of pornography and of hate speech, libertarians maintain it is the best way to preserve freedom and the rights of all citizens. In striving to ensure distance between the government and the mass media, the libertarians place media in the hands of private citizens. The rights to publish and to free expression are fundamental rights of citizenship and must not be tampered with, particularly by government.

One of the main problems with this perspective, however, is that in the face of the overarching importance placed on freedom of speech or expression, there is little concern for the fact that in the course of media production and operation, the corporate sector promotes its own interests—those of developing markets and of accruing profits—which are placed above the interests of the people, society, and the government of the day. Consequently, rather than allowing journalists to dedicate themselves to "serving the people," privately controlled media tend to maximize their own interests as private, profit-oriented corporations, thereby undermining the libertarian ideal they often claim to uphold.

Social Responsibility Theory

The social responsibility theory of the press was originally put forward in the United States in 1947 by the Commission on the Freedom of the Press (or Hutchins Commission)—a nongovernmental enquiry into the state of the US media. The study was motivated by a concern that left to their own devices, the media companies were not upholding the broad public principles that libertarian theory claimed they would and that a new vision or understanding of the role of the media in society had to be formulated. While also drawing on liberal theories of society and the libertarian theory of the press, the study concluded that the libertarian arrangement often fails to produce media that are generally

FIGURE 3.2 Reporters Without Borders: Press Freedom Index

Reporters Without Borders is a non-profit organization based in France that monitors attacks on the media and freedom of information. Every year, it produces a "Press Freedom Index" that strives to track the freedom of information in countries around the world. As Christophe Deloire, the organization's secretary general points out, the index "is a reference tool that is based on seven criteria: the level of abuses, the extent of pluralism, media independence, the environment and self-censorship, the legislative framework, transparency and infrastructure."

Source: Reporters Without Borders World Press Freedom Index 2015.

of benefit to society. Hence, they put together a broad set of civic-minded principles to guide newspaper operations. They stopped short, however, of recommending government enforcement of those principles, instead allowing that media should be self-regulating.

In Canada, there has been a long-standing concern that corporate interests might be superseding the public interest in the press and, as we discuss in Chapter 7, there have been a number of government-sponsored inquiries in this regard. In taking up this concern, the 1981 Kent Royal Commission on Newspapers (Canada, 1981: 235) explained the social responsibility theory well, pointing out that as newspaper publishing began to be taken over by big business, the notion of social responsibility was born of a need to fight against the potential of a new authoritarianism by big-business ownership of the press. The Kent Commission defined the concept of social responsibility as follows:

> The conjoined requirements of the press, for freedom and for legitimacy, derive from the same basic right: the right of citizens to information about their affairs. In order that people be informed, the press has a critical responsibility. In order to fulfill that responsibility it is essential that the press be free, in the traditional sense, free to report and free to publish as it thinks; it is equally essential that the press's discharge of its responsibility to inform should be untainted by other interests, that it should not be dominated by the powerful or be subverted by people with concerns other than those proper to a newspaper serving a democracy. "Comment is free," as C.P. Snow, one of the greatest English-speaking editors, wrote, "but facts are sacred." The right of information in a free society requires, in short, not only freedom of comment generally but, for its news media, the freedom of a legitimate press, doing its utmost to inform, open to all opinions and dominated by none. [C.P. Snow was, for years, editor of *The Manchester Guardian*—a British newspaper (called *The Guardian* today) known for its rigorous reporting and social conscience.]

While, as we shall see, there are no formal laws laying out the exact role of the media in Canadian society, this is perhaps the most common way of thinking about it. Ironically, although a US commission coined the term *social responsibility*, the concept is better accepted in Canada and Europe than the United States. This is because in the States, the First Amendment to the Constitution states that "Congress shall make no law . . . abridging the freedom of speech, or of the press." Being the first of the constitutional amendments, it sits at the top of the hierarchy of rights. The Canadian Constitution does not allow for such a hierarchy of rights, whereby one right takes precedence over another (for instance, the freedom of the press versus the right to a fair trial). In Canada and Europe, then, it is possible to limit free speech based on a consideration of its consequences—for instance, reporters must be careful not to discuss a crime in such detail as to jeopardize a person's right to a fair trial (see Chapter 9). Despite the fact that the social responsibility theory of the press might be seen as the dominant theory of the media in Canada (see Chapter 8), however, exactly what the dimensions of media responsibility are in this country and how they might be either taken up by or imposed on the private corporations that own a large part of Canada's media remain the subject of public debate.

The Mass Society Thesis

For many writers during the Industrial Revolution, the new way of life was without cultural foundation. As they saw it, cut free from a traditional feudal agricultural way of life and the social values, customs, and bonds that gave that life form and function, people in the new industrial context became a collection of isolated individuals—an undifferentiated "mass" society within which no assumptions about social order and people's place and function in it were held in common.

In this state of social atomization and potential moral disorder, the masses were regarded by the social elite of the day as somewhat threatening, as though through their new-found political and economic power these people posed a severe threat to the existing cultural order and the abilities of the wealthy and other elites to sustain their way of life. The nature of the perceived threat to the establishment varied from writer to writer. For some, it was viewed as a potential state of anarchy, a breakdown of social order. Others expressed concern that these people were commonly subject to manipulation and easy targets for totalitarian social and political movements. In this way, media are seen as a unifying force in society, a means of conjoining minds in common cause and action, although not necessarily toward positive ends.

Through the early twentieth century, this perspective wound its way into a range of academic disciplines and had a strong impact on early communication theory. To a large extent, it framed new media, such as radio and film, as part of a new "commercial" or **mass culture** where media content is simply an unsophisticated commercial product designed to placate the masses with cheap entertainment and, through advertising, incorporate them into a more consumer-oriented way of life. The major problem with this perspective is that it is elitist—privileging the idea that the high-cultural values held by the more educated and affluent members of society are superior to those of poorer and less educated citizens. At the same time, it also assumes that the more affluent are better able to see through and resist the slick sales pitches of advertisers and the propaganda of authoritarian governments. As we shall see in Chapter 5, underlying these conceptions of the purpose of mass media was an unsophisticated vision of the relationship between media and audiences—one that assumes the media have a direct effect on

people's behaviour—and a perspective that has been firmly proven to be untrue.

Political Economy and Marx

In the early to mid-nineteenth century, as capitalist industry was introducing massive social change in Europe, Karl Marx argued that the capitalist system was built on a set of social relations in which politics and economics were inextricably linked. Modern Western societies, Marx argued, were characterized by a new and revolutionary mode of production—industrial capitalism—in which scientific techniques, applied to the mass production of an ever-increasing range of goods (or *commodities*, in Marx's terms), created wealth for the owners of capital (see Box 3.1). In Marx's analysis, industrial society is organized around the reproduction of capital—that is, the creation of surplus or profits from productive activities. This tends to create two main classes: capitalists, the owners of the means of production (factories, commercial property, and so on), and workers, who, because they don't own productive property, must sell their labour power to capitalists. Marx argued that this system of production generally serves the interests of the capitalists (a tiny fraction of the population), while workers (the vast majority of people) are exploited by the capitalists. They can be fired at any time and for whatever reason, and they have to fight to squeeze a living wage out of industrialists.

As Marx saw it, modern capitalism transformed all aspects of life, particularly at the political level, as government and the structure of the state increasingly came to represent the interests of capital. New laws were enacted to protect private property, particularly the productive property of capitalists. Labour legislation laid the legal framework for relations between capital and labour. Taxation raised funds for creating infrastructure—roads, railways, canals, harbours, and communication systems—that kept the wheels of commerce moving. Schooling was redefined along industrial models in order to teach people the skills necessary to become productive workers. And when workers rebelled through strikes or some other form of civil disobedience, the police force could be called upon to restore order.

At the heart of a Marxist analysis of modern society is a belief in the possibility of a better life that could be shared by all—a life that is blocked by the private appropriation of wealth. Material abundance could be available to all if the techniques of modern manufacturing were somehow regulated with everyone's interests in mind.

Marx's ideas shaped the political life of the twentieth century throughout the world. In most European democracies, political parties tended to develop in one of two directions: those who represent the interests of the owners of productive property and those who represent the interests of workers. Although the Russian system of authoritarian state socialism clearly failed, communist and socialist parties still command strong showings in elections in European countries and elsewhere in the world. Marx's emphasis on the fundamental importance of economic life on the structure and other elements of social life remains a substantial and important contribution to social theory.

Writers working from Marx's analytic legacy are critical of the ways in which the structure of society affords benefits—wealth and power—to some groups of people over others; hence the term *critical political economy*. In particular, critical political economy focuses on the ways in which the allocation, production, distribution, and consumption of social resources enable and constrain social action. That is, it is concerned with the way the ownership and control of society's resources—especially productive resources—give owners a larger say in the form and direction society takes than to those lacking such controls.

In terms of media, critical political economy is concerned with the ways in which the media support dominant interests in society, helping them maintain power and control (see Chapter 5). In contrast to the libertarian and social responsibility theories of the press, which argue that the

Source: © traveler1116/iStockphoto.

Drawing from the work of Karl Marx (pictured here on an East German stamp), critical political economy argues that in capitalist societies, the media are a key institution in promoting capitalism and in helping maintain social inequality. How do you see this at work in the media today? In what ways do the media challenge social inequality?

media can and should have a relatively independent place in the political and economic processes that govern society, critical political economy argues that in capitalist societies, the media are a key institution in promoting capitalism and in helping maintain social inequality (Mosco, 2009).

From this perspective, media support the capitalist system and the inequalities it perpetuates in a number of ways—first, and perhaps most obviously, by promoting the sale of commodities (see Box 3.1). Advertising is pervasive in the media and provides a constant barrage of messages that encourage people to purchase goods/services and support the capitalist system. Second, more generally, the media promote a consumer lifestyle. Woven throughout media content, be it news, entertainment, or advertising, is a constant refrain that the consumer lifestyle—that is, satisfying one's wants, needs, and desires through the market—is the best and perhaps only way to be happy. And third, news, information, and entertainment programming generally assume the existing economic system and the institutions and social relations it entails are the best and most legitimate way of doing things. Social problems, such as unemployment, poverty, and corruption, are seen as the fault of particular events or individuals—not the system itself. Consequently, in all these ways, the media and media content are seen as one of the main vehicles in helping to legitimate and support our political and economic systems.

Which of these perspectives is the true or correct one? The short answer is that there is no single true perspective. As we saw in Chapters 1 and 2, the social roles and structure of the media are complex. To some extent, social responsibility theory—with its belief that the media play an important role in democratic societies in terms of and informing the public—is the dominant way of thinking about the media and its role in society in Canada. But all four continue to influence the ways in which people think about the media today. To understand what role media play in any particular instance, we need to examine the specific relations of power in which they are implicated.

Mass Media and Canadian Realities: History and Structure

Just as larger social, political, and economic events, such as the Enlightenment and the Industrial Revolution, have shaped communications media in general, so, too, have the development and structure of the Canadian state, as well as a distinctive Canadian culture, nuanced the structure and operation of media in Canada.

In the early nineteenth century, European settlement of the geography that is now Canada took the form of a collection of colonies scattered across the vast northern half of North America. Industry at that point was largely devoted to the export of staples or raw materials for manufacturing in Britain and the United States. In this context, the lines of communication followed the lines of commerce and ran either overseas to Britain or north–south into the United States. But by the mid-nineteenth century, both Britain and the United States had enacted trade restrictions on the colonies, forcing them to look to themselves for development. In the face of these pressures, Canadian Confederation in 1867 was the first step to building an economic unit out of these colonies.

In 1879, Prime Minister John A. Macdonald introduced Canada's National Policy, a set of initiatives designed to turn the idea of an east–west economy into a reality. The National Policy had three particularly important components:

1. the building of a transcontinental railway;
2. a tariff designed to limit the entry of manufactured goods from the United States and Britain; and
3. efforts to entice immigrants to settle the prairies.

The railway was to provide a reliable line of transportation for people and goods across the country, and particularly to move raw materials from the margins of the country to the industrial heartland in Central Canada where they would be manufactured into goods and shipped back out to market. In other words, the railway was to bind the country into a cohesive political economic unit with a "ribbon of steel." The tariff was used to tax materials and manufactured goods entering the country. Its purpose was to protect Canadian industries in their infancy by keeping cheap competitive goods outside the country. At the same time, it encouraged foreign investment, as non-Canadian companies wishing to tap into the expanding Canadian market were encouraged to build factories and produce goods here in order to avoid the tariff. The tariff was necessary because Canada had a much smaller population than either Britain or the United States and did not have the **economies of scale** (see Box 3.3) necessary to produce goods at a price that could compete with similar goods produced in those countries. Finally, immigration policy actively sought settlers from Central and Eastern Europe to populate the Prairie provinces, both to develop the land and raise grain for the central Canadian market and to serve as a market for the manufactured goods of Ontario and Quebec (See Box 3.2: "A Dark Side of Canadian History").

Despite these measures, because of the large size of the country and the small population, it was often difficult to wring profits from business in Canada, so the government often had to step in to encourage private investment. For instance, the Canadian Pacific Railway (CPR) was issued a wide range of government payments and subsidies to encourage the building of the transcontinental railway. Similarly, because of the large investment necessary, Bell Telephone was given a monopoly on long-distance telephone service in Central Canada so that it might exploit economies of scale when building that system.

3.2 ▶▶▶▶▶▶

A DARK SIDE OF CANADIAN HISTORY

As James Daschuk illustrates in his book *Clearing the Plains: Disease, Politics of Starvation and the Loss of Aboriginal Life*, John A. Macdonald's efforts to drive the railway across the country and encourage European settlement of the prairies came at great cost to the indigenous peoples who lived there. As he points out,

A key aspect of preparing the land was the subjugation and forced removal of indigenous communities from their traditional territories, essentially clearing the plains of aboriginal people to make way for railway construction and settlement. Despite guarantees of food aid in times of famine in Treaty No. 6, Canadian officials used food, or rather denied food, as a means to ethnically cleanse a vast region from Regina to the Alberta border as the Canadian Pacific Railway took shape. (Daschuk [quoted in *The Globe and Mail*], 2013)

Source: University of Toronto/Thomas Fisher Rare Book Library.

3.3 ▶▶▶▶▶▶

ECONOMIES OF SCALE

Economies of scale reflect the fact that the greater the quantity of a particular product is made, the less each one costs to produce. Much of the cost of an industrial product is in setting up the factory that will produce it. Whether one is producing cars, stoves, or matches, buying the real estate on which the factory is located, building the building in which it will be housed, and then designing and creating the machinery that will make the product represent a much greater investment than the raw materials that go into the product. For instance, if putting together a factory for making stoves, if it costs $1 million and the labour and raw materials that go into each stove cost $100, then the cost of manufacturing one stove will be $1,000,100. If 10,000 stoves are produced, then the cost of each stove would be $200 ($1,000,000 divided by 10,000 equals $100 + $100 in raw materials). If 1,000,000 stoves are produced, however, the cost falls to $101 each ($1,000,000 divided by 1,000,000 equals $1 + $100 in raw materials). Consequently, because the United States over the years has had a population roughly 10 times the size of Canada's, manufactured goods coming out of the United States have been cheaper than those made in Canada. As we shall see, these economics also apply to media products.

Still, it was all but impossible for the government to attract private investment in some areas. When private investment could not be found, both the federal and provincial governments frequently undertook some businesses themselves, often in the form of Crown—or government-owned—corporations. Canada's second national railroad, for example, the Canadian National Railway (CNR), bolstered service to some areas and brought a railway option to others not served by the CPR. Canada's first transcontinental airline, now Air Canada, was a Crown corporation, as was the first national broadcaster, the CBC. Later, the country's first satellite company, Telesat Canada, was also a government initiative. In short, historically, because of the unique features of the Canadian state, the government has often taken a strong hand in shaping the economy. At the federal level, these efforts have been motivated by a strong nationalist sentiment.

This tradition of nation building is reflected in the structure of Canada's media industries. Just as the railway was seen as binding Canada physically, so in the 1930s broadcasting was envisioned as bringing the country together through a common Canadian consciousness or perspective on the world (see Box 3.4). Consequently, the government set up the Canadian Radio Broadcasting Commission, which later became the Canadian Broadcasting Corporation, to create a national broadcasting network and Canadian programming—two activities that the private sector was unable to undertake profitably at the time.

Later, various policy measures in the magazine, newspaper, publishing, music, film, and telecommunications industries—including online media—were undertaken with similar objectives in mind: to help build and strengthen a common Canadian culture. In other words, they were enacted with nationalist purposes in mind. As we shall see, however, the government record in building and strengthening Canadian culture is spotty at best, and while government policy has often been framed by strong language that claims concern for Canadian culture, it has not always been backed with strong action.

Distinctive Characteristics of the Canadian State

Before considering some of the larger political principles and cultural concerns that underpin the Canadian media, we need to understand the distinctive characteristics of the Canadian state that have shaped the development of its communication systems. We have already looked at two of these characteristics: the *vastness of the*

3.4 ▶▶▶▶▶▶

BROADCASTING AND NATION BUILDING

In the face of an overwhelming spillover of US programming into Canada, the federal government set up the Canadian Radio Broadcasting Commission (CRBC), and later the Canadian Broadcasting Corporation (CBC), to build a national broadcasting network and create Canadian programming. In introducing the 1932 Broadcasting Act to the House of Commons—the legislation that created the CRBC—Prime Minister R.B. Bennett outlined what the government saw as the purposes of that legislation:

> This country must be assured of complete Canadian control of broadcasting from Canadian sources, free from foreign interference or influence. Without such control radio broadcasting can never become a great agency for communication of matters of national concern and for the diffusion of national thought and ideals, and without such control it can never be the agency by which consciousness may be fostered and sustained and national

Source: © HultonArchive/iStockphoto.

Early on, Canadian legislators recognized radio's ability to operate on the principle of free speech and its potential to create a national community.

> unity still further strengthened. . . . No other scheme than that of public ownership can ensure to the people of this country, without regard to class or place, equal enjoyment of the benefits and pleasures of radio broadcasting.

country and the *small size of Canada's population*. These geographic and demographic facts have pressed governments to invest in expensive national transmission systems so that Canadians can stay in touch with each other.

A third significant characteristic, derived in part from the size of the country, is Canada's *regionalism*. Canada is not just a country of physical geographic variety; it is a vast country of regional cultures. From the disparate French and British colonies scattered throughout what is now Canada grew a "confederation." This nation required means of internal communication, but not those in which messages would be generated only from a central point and fed to outlying regions. Each region needed to generate its own

information such that the region's particularities might be reflected to the whole. This would help bring the country together—or such has been the ideal.

Canada is also a nation of *two official languages* (English and French), which is now enshrined in the country's Constitution Act, 1982. But Canadians have committed themselves to more than a freedom of language choice for individuals. They have committed themselves to providing federal government services, including broadcasting, in both official languages. Bilingual government services and bilingual broadcasting channels (not just programs) are a testament to the right of any Canadian to live and work wherever she or he may wish. They are also a continual reminder to all that we are officially a bilingual country.

In 1971, during Pierre Trudeau's first term as prime minister, Canada also officially became a *multicultural country* and, although it was long in coming, an increasing number of media programming services are tailored to various ethnic communities.

A final, never-to-be-forgotten characteristic of Canada's communications environment is its proximity to the United States. Economies of scale in media production (see Box 3.5), coupled with our acceptance, particularly in anglophone Canada, of some similar basic political and economic philosophies and this proximity, have led to a massive penetration of US products and ideas into Canada. More US television programming is available to the vast majority of Canadians than is Canadian programming. On most Canadian commercial radio stations, more US than Canadian music is available to listeners. On virtually all magazine racks in Canada, more US magazines are available to the reader than Canadian magazines, this despite the fact that more than 2,300 magazines are published in Canada. Over 95 percent of the films screened in Canadian theatres are foreign productions, mainly American ones. More US authors than Canadian authors are read by the average Canadian schoolchild. Our proximity to the United States and the resultant spillover of US cultural products comprise a major factor to be considered when assessing Canada's communications environment. Because, unlike many Canadian media outfits, US media companies for economic reasons, favour distributing homemade products over imported ones, the United States has less tolerance for products that are not recognizably American, and so the counter-flow—Canadian ideas/products moving stateside—has been very limited.

In the face of the challenges posed by these characteristics of Canadian media markets, Canada has a fairly strong record of achievement in forging a national communications system. Table 3.1 provides a chronology of dates of important communications achievements, including many Canadian firsts.

3.5 ▶▶▶▶▶▶

THE ECONOMICS OF MEDIA REPRESENTATION

As in other industries, economies of scale underlie media production. Much of the cost of producing a magazine or book, for instance, is in paying the writers, editors, photographers, and typesetters to create the "first copy." After that, these initial expenses are spread across the number of copies produced. So, if the cost of gathering and putting together all of the material that goes into a particular magazine is $50,000, if 50,000 copies of that magazine are printed, the editorial cost of each magazine is $1.00. But if 500,000 magazines are printed, the cost falls to only 10 cents per copy. Similar economics apply to film and television, where the "cost per viewer" is spread over the number of audience members.

Because the market for media products in the United States is roughly 10 times the size of the market in Canada, the cost per reader or audience member for those products is often significantly less in the States than it is for Canadian production aimed primarily at a Canadian audience. Consequently, it is often much more profitable for Canadian distributors of media products to sell US books, magazines, TV shows, and films than those made specifically for the Canadian market. As a result, US media products are often more commonly available in Canada than home-grown versions. It is not because Americans make better media products than Canadians that our markets are overrun with US fare; it's simply because more money can be made from selling them in Canada than from producing our own.

Each of these developments was cause for some celebration and some sense of pride. Each in its own way strengthened east–west links from the Atlantic to the Pacific and was a factor in nation building and cohesion. Just as important as the

TABLE 3.1
Some Important Achievements in Canadian Communication History

Year	Achievement
1885	A transcontinental railway
1901	A transatlantic radio link
1927	A trans-Canada radio network
1932	A trans-Canada telephone network
	First Broadcasting Act is passed
1948	World's first commercial microwave link
1956	World's first tropospheric scatter transmission system
1958	A transcontinental television service
	A transcontinental microwave network
1959	First Canadian communications satellite experiment, including use of the moon as reflector
1968	Founding of the Canadian Film Development Corporation
1970	Beginning of fibre optic research
1972	A domestic geostationary communications satellite
1973	First nationwide digital data system
	World's first digital transmission network (Dataroute)
1976	Bill C-58: legislation to help Canadian magazine industry
1990	Completion of a 7,000-kilometre coast-to-coast fibre optic network, the longest terrestrial fibre network in the world
1991	Canadian Broadcasting Act is passed
1993	Canadian Telecommunications Act is passed
1996	Launch of the first North American commercial digital radio service
1999	Aboriginal Peoples Television Network is launched
2005	Canadian Television Fund is founded
2010	Canadian Media Fund is set up
2014	98% of Canadians have access to broadband coverage

the 1960s and '70s, television temporarily stalled indigenous self-development by introducing yet another Southern medium devoid of First People's images, voices, and cultural activities."

But while privately owned media organizations have generally welcomed government support through various forms of regulation, they have not always been enthusiastic about assuming particular responsibilities in return for that support. In the broadcasting field, for instance, support for private broadcasters and Canadian ownership of broadcast outlets has been a constant theme of successive Broadcasting Acts and media regulation. But with the exception of the CBC, broadcasters and the large media corporations of which many are now a part have been more interested in importing and distributing US programs than in producing Canadian content because that is where the profits lie. Similarly, while the government has played a strong role in helping build the telecommunications system that supports the internet, the private companies that own much of that infrastructure have not always been cooperative in terms of working to balance the public interest against their own private interest (see, for example: Moll and Shade, 2008, 2011; Vipond, 2011; Armstrong, 2010; Raboy, 1990; Weir, 1965; Babe, 1990; Rutherford, 1990; Peers, 1969, 1979).

These realities continue to present challenges to government, business, and other social groups for creating communication systems that serve all Canadians in a fair, equitable, and comprehensive manner.

The Mass Media and Canadian Culture

We can now turn to examining the relationship between Canadian culture and Canada's mass media—including government's administration and regulation of them. This relationship is interesting and complex.

Recall from Chapter 2 that, set at the intersection between people and the different social

technological achievements in building the system are the legislative achievements behind that technological expansion, the 1932 Broadcasting Act and the 1993 Telecommunications Act. These statutes gave voice to the public interest in the development of these communication systems and set in law the public goals and ambitions that underlie them. Still, addressing the needs of all the different regions and peoples of the country has been difficult, particularly in the North, where, as Lorna Roth (2005: 221) notes, "When first introduced in

Source: © garett_mosher/iStockphoto.

The media are central to how we come to understand and share culture. For this reason, media industries, such as television broadcasting, are often called *cultural industries*.

groups, organizations, and institutions that make up our society, the media are primary vehicles in communicating the depth and breadth of the ways of life—or culture—of Canadians. The federal government notes that culture "includes the knowledge, beliefs, art, morals, customs and all other capabilities acquired by a particular society" (from a report on Canada's cultural industries titled *Vital Links* [Canada, 1987: 11]). To this schema we might add the laws, institutions, and organizations that give society form, making culture a way, or ways, of life. In Canada, we have a distinctive set of institutions—such as governments, schools, universities, media, the healthcare system—that give Canadian cultural form, as well as the distinctive ideas, values, and beliefs that exist within that larger framework of social institutions.

Media are central to how we come to understand and share culture, and, in a large industrial nation such as Canada, the media are intricately woven into the social fabric. They are the means through which the exchange of ideas, experience, images, and interpretations and perspectives on the world takes place. Indeed, it is generally through the media that we come to know our society, its institutions and organizations, and the other people with whom we

share our national culture. For this reason, the media industries—such as those involved in radio and television broadcasting, digital media, film, music, newspapers, magazine and book publishing, and more—are often called *cultural industries*. As we discuss in Chapter 8, Canada's cultural industries provide an information base around which various communities and other social groups that make up our society can coalesce and interact, at the best of times contributing to social cohesion and a sense of belonging on the part of all members of society.

Canada's modern communications system is historically rooted in transportation. While it is true that Sir John A. Macdonald and his government had the CPR built primarily to ensure the flow of goods and immigrants, with the influx of both came the flow of information—through the mail and the telegraph. The post office instituted inexpensive second-class mail rates to encourage the circulation of newspapers and magazines, which helped knit the country together. These, and other commercial communications—like the Eaton's department store catalogue—gave Canadians a sense of connection with their compatriots elsewhere in the country. For instance, people on the prairies or the West Coast, ordering a pump organ from Clinton, Ontario, or a wood stove from Sackville, New Brunswick, gave Western Canada an economic link and a social connection to Eastern Canada.

From these humble beginnings, over the years successive federal governments have implemented a range of policies to encourage the development of Canadian media and a media system operating on an east–west axis. Today, many of the laws and regulations that address the cultural industries are administered by Heritage Canada (see Figure 3.3), the federal government department responsible for this field of legislation.

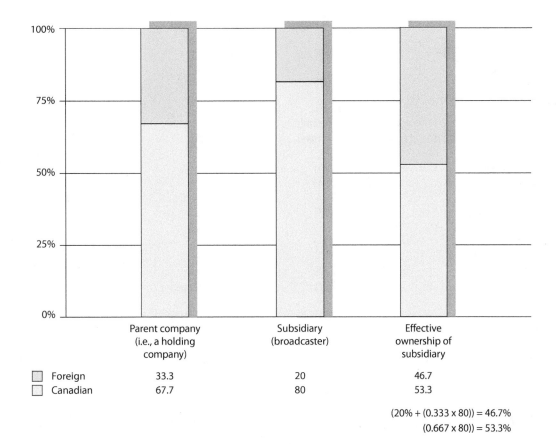

	Parent company (i.e., a holding company)	Subsidiary (broadcaster)	Effective ownership of subsidiary
☐ Foreign	33.3	20	46.7
☐ Canadian	67.7	80	53.3

$$(20\% + (0.333 \times 80)) = 46.7\%$$
$$(0.667 \times 80)) = 53.3\%$$

FIGURE 3.3   Maximum Allowable Foreign Ownership of a Canadian Broadcaster

As free trade between nations continues to increase, so does foreign ownership. This figure illustrates how Canadian law allows effective ownership of a broadcaster up to as much as 46.7 percent through indirect ownership (of a holding company) and direct ownership of a broadcaster that is a subsidiary of the holding company. An uptick in the allowable percentage of foreign ownership would potentially give majority control to a foreign interest. Because it is more difficult to hold companies that are headquartered outside of the country accountable to domestic laws and regulations, rules requiring that Canadian media companies have majority Canadian ownership have been common in Canadian media regulation. Foreign ownership is often seen as a key problem in maintaining cultural sovereignty and many other countries, including the United States, have similar regulations.

While Canadian governments have nodded to the importance of media and cultural products in the life of the nation, they have not been consistent protectors and supporters of Canada's cultural industries. One of the main points of concern has been competition from US media products (Grant and Wood, 2004; Babe, 1990). Foreign content has always been a part of the flow of information within the Canadian nation, but it has also been the subject of controversy. Tables 3.2 and 3.3 list the top programs in the English and French television markets for the period of 2–8 March 2015. The figures provide a sense of the size of the audiences for each program. Quebec-made television dominates the schedule in that province. But in the rest of Canada, US shows dominate overwhelmingly— so much so that if we were to take Table 3.2 as an indication of what English Canadians know about themselves and others through television, we would have to conclude that anglophone Canadians must be suffering from an identity crisis

TABLE 3.2
Top English-Language Programs, Canada, 2–8 March 2015

Rank	Program	Broadcast Outlet	Day	Total (thousands of viewers)
1	Big Bang Theory	CTV	T	4,491
2	CSI: Cyber	CTV	W	2,644
3	Criminal Minds	CTV	W	2,370
4	Survivor: Worlds Apart	Global	W	2,273
5	The Odd Couple	CTV	T	2,239
6	Marvel's Agents of S.H.I.E.L.D.	CTV	T	2,119
7	Blue Bloods	CTV	F	2,109
8	Gotham	CTV	M	2,075
9	Amazing Race 26	CTV	F	2,046
10	Once Upon a Time	CTV	S	1,817
11	Hawaii Five-O	Global	F	1,791
12	Big Bang Theory	CTV	T	1,770
13	Forever	CTV	M	1,754
14	CTV Evening News	CTV	MTWTF	1,706
15	MasterChef Canada	CTV	S	1,684
16	The Blacklist	Global	T	1,624
17	Grey's Anatomy	CTV	T	1,577
18	Elementary	Global	T	1,565
19	American Crime	CTV	T	1,500
20	Chicago Fire	Global	T	1,491
21	Madam Secretary	Global	S	1,452
22	Big Bang Theory	CTV	MTWF	1,338
23	Motive	CTV	S	1,278
24	Secrets and Lies	CTV	S	1,190
25	Modern Family	City	W	1,171
26	Hell's Kitchen	City	T	1,139
27	CTV Evening News (wkd)	CTV	SS	1,136
28	The Good Wife	Global	S	1,128
29	The Voice	CTV Two	M	1,116
30	Battle Creek	Global	S	1,098

*Based on confirmed program schedules and preliminary audience data. Demographic: All persons 2+.

Source: © 2015 Numeris.

TABLE 3.3
Top French-Language Programs, Quebec, 2–8 March 2015

Rank	Program	Broadcast Outlet	Day	Total (thousands of viewers)
1	Voix, La	TVA	S	2,749
2	Unité 9	SRC	T	2,131
3	Beaux malaises, Les	TVA	W	2,075
4	LOL :-)	TVA	S	1,495
5	Yamaska	TVA	M	1,400
6	19–2	SRC	W	1,291
7	0'	TVA	T	1,288
8	Accès illimité	TVA	S	1,266
9	Lance et compte	TVA	M.	1,246
10	Vlog	TVA	S	1,194
11	Enfants de la télé	SRC	W	1,192
12	Au secours de Béatrice	TVA	W	1,186
13	Voix, La	TVA	M	1,093
14	Un sur 2	TVA	W	1,073
15	Mémoires vives	SRC	T	1,053
16	Nouvelle adresse	SRC	M	1,028
17	Auberge chien noir	SRC	M	1,022
18	Poule aux oeufs d'or, La	TVA	W	1,002
19	Voix, La	TVA	W	975
20	Facture	SRC	T	972
21	Parent, Les	SRC	M	918
22	Tout le monde en . . .	SRC	S	911
23	Tricheur, Le	TVA	MTWTF	909
24	Gags, Les	TVA	M	808
25	TVA Nouvelles (18h–LV)	TVA	MTWTF	803
26	En direct . . . univers	SRC	S	791
27	Liste noire, La	TVA	T	776
28	30 vies	SRC	MTWT	751
29	Ciné-Extra	TVA	S	748
30	Prière de ne pas . . .	SRC	T	740

Source: © 2015 Numeris.

because of the profusion of US-made programming. Economically, this large-scale presence of mainly American media products has drawn criticism for taking away jobs from Canadian media workers and undermining Canadian industry in general. Culturally, as we discussed in Chapter 2, such foreign media products have worked to make Canadians and their public institutions strangers in their own land.

Canadian government investment in communications has traditionally stressed telecommunications transmission and technology. In the

1990s, amid budget cuts to public broadcasting, the federal government spent millions upgrading transmission networks. More recently, the federal government's focus has been on developing a Canadian digital policy—in 2014, the feds announced their Digital Canada 150 program (Canada, 2014e). While the accompanying document offered little in the way of new initiatives, it did promise a policy "underscored by five key pillars: connecting Canadians, protecting Canadians, economic opportunities, digital government, and Canadian content" and it illustrated that the federal government has a focus on the country's digital environment (Canada, 2014e: 3).

Historically, the federal government's commitment to current technology and effective, rapid transmission has been a mixed blessing (Charland, 1986). In spite of the rhetoric used to justify each new major expenditure, the technology has provided a conduit for foreign media to reach Canadian audiences that has not necessarily served the cultural needs of Canada and its citizens. Within Canada, the telecommunications infrastructure has served private-sector growth, including the formation of national newspapers such as *The Globe and Mail* and the *National Post*, which have taken advantage of satellite and other communications technologies to print regional editions of their newspapers simultaneously in different parts of the country. In the case of broadcasters and the large telecommunications companies that now own them, through the insistence of the CRTC, some cultural benefits have emerged from private-sector growth. But, by and large, in the private sector the electronic media have been reluctant contributors to national cultural goals.

The usual rationale for government investment in communication infrastructure is that technological development creates jobs—that numerous spin-off technologies lead to the creation of new industries, products, and jobs. In the language of economists, there are significant **multiplier effects**, meaning that such investment leads directly and indirectly to job creation. It is certainly the case that a ready infrastructure has assisted Canadian business to embrace the internet as a business tool. New internet businesses have been founded and traditional businesses have been able to take advantage of Canada's robust technological infrastructure.

Canadians have never been in a position, however, to produce enough programs and other content to fill the transmission capacity that has been developed in electronic media. Even if Canadian producers could somehow produce the programs, there would not be enough money in the pockets of advertisers, the public, and governments to pay for the range of choice available in the infrastructure. In other words, we have created an information environment that keeps us abreast industrially of the most advanced nations but that opens us to inundation by foreign cultural products. We neglected to design a system that would guarantee the development of Canadian culture and cultural production. The reason, it would seem, is a belief on the part of policy-makers in the liberal doctrine of free enterprise—an extension of the idea of liberal individualism. This idea has overshadowed our abilities to represent the distinctive elements of a Canadian culture in our media venues.

The adjacently situated Americans, who happen to be the world's most successful entertainment and information producers, have no trouble stepping into Canada's cultural vacuum. The selection—and, perhaps most importantly, the price—they offer in such areas as television and film is too attractive for private business to refuse. For as little as one-tenth the cost of producing a season of half-hour television dramas in Canada, US producers can provide a high-quality program with high ratings and ever-so-attractive stars, complete with press attention and magazine commentary that spill over the border in US media products.

While Canadian governments have sometimes provided subsidies and enacted legislation to protect Canadian media products and support producers, they have been reluctant to impose heavy restrictions on private enterprise or to restrict the ability of foreigners to do business in Canada. Consequently, only in Quebec is the regional culture thoroughly reflected in the media (see Table 3.3). In the rest of the country, the result of this focus on technology, liberal market principles, and lack of determination to ensure a dominance of Canadian media products has been, for decades, a cultural low road.

As the internet continues to provide an expanding choice of largely foreign news and entertainment products, such as MSNBC, Netflix, and Apple TV, the proportion of Canadian alternatives continues to shrink. Exactly what impact this situation might have on the ways in which we see and understand our country and its place in the world is yet to be determined.

Politics and the Canadian Media Today

As we have seen, the media traditionally are portrayed as playing an important role in the governance of society. In Chapters 9 and 10, we examine the structure of the media and the role of journalists and other content producers in the system. In this section, we build on the brief discussion in Chapter 2 to more closely consider the distinctive role of the media in Canadian politics.

As we have seen, in terms of liberal theory, the media are often portrayed as a counteractive force to potential abuse of power by the state. Similarly, the social responsibility theory is perhaps the most common way of understanding the political role of the Canadian media and, to a degree, that relationship is enshrined in law. For instance, under Section 2 (b) of the 1982 Canadian Charter of Rights and Freedoms, everyone is guaranteed "freedom of thought, belief, opinion and expression, including freedom of the press and other media of communication." At the same time, legislation allows journalists and others to access information generated by government and its agencies, including things like drug analyses, departmental budgets, and internal reports on government activities and reviews. Journalists generally take their responsibilities as guardians

of the public interest quite seriously and deliver unbiased reports and perspectives in this regard.

In practice, though, things are not always so clear-cut. While the media's freedom of expression is guaranteed in law, it is difficult to muster the resources necessary to consistently produce and distribute quality media content. Despite claims by some that new media provide the opportunity for everyone to become a journalist (as we discuss in Chapter 8), producing quality journalism requires highly trained people and other resources, and media organizations with such assets are expensive to operate. Similarly, journalists and critics often claim that Canadian access-to-information legislation is weak and full of loopholes, making it easy for government and industry to avoid serious scrutiny. And media owners and managers can also play a strong role in both the types of stories reporters produce and the perspectives they take in them. Consequently, as critical political economy suggests, the media generally tend to support existing social relations of political and economic power.

Moreover, the relationship between the media and government is much more nuanced than the watchdog metaphor allows. The news media depend on the government for information and for advertising, and the government depends on the news media to disseminate that information. But the government's desire to keep certain information from the media, such as information that might undermine the popularity or priorities of the party holding the reins of power, imbues that relationship with ambivalence. At the same time, the desire of the media to maintain their independence from government transforms that ambivalence into a love–hate relationship for both sides (see, for example, Kozolanka, 2014; Nesbitt-Larking, 2007; Rose and Kiss, 2006).

As Catherine Murray (2007: 527–44) illustrates, the media's engagement with public policy process is often seen to have four dimensions: *reporting and framing policy*; *interrogation and whistle-blowing*; *investigation and policy analysis*; and *interpretation, policy evaluation and advocacy*.

Source: Vince Talotta/*Toronto Star* via Getty Images.

Acting as watchdogs on government, on 16 May 2013, the *Toronto Star* and the US news site Gawker reported on a video that showed Mayor Rob Ford of Toronto smoking what appeared to be crack cocaine and making homophobic and racist remarks. Ford initially denied the allegations, but several months later, after a judge released a description of the video, the mayor admitted to having a substance problem and checked himself into a rehabilitation centre.

Reporting and framing involves the media selectively reporting on "press releases, policy statements, reports," what they hear from elected officials and their staff, "as well as what interested parties outside of government say" (Murray, 2007: 527). In this guise, the media generally act to simply inform the public of government activities. Interrogation, or whistle-blowing, focuses directly on the watchdog function of the media. From simply asking questions to doggedly working to uncover illegal or unethical activity, it involves journalists taking a more adversarial relation to government activity than simply reporting. Investigation and policy analysis leads to the social responsibility element of the media–government–society equation and extends factual reportage to ensure that media "provide citizens with sufficient quality and scope of information to exercise their democratic rights" (Murray, 2007: 535). Potentially more partisan forms of media content, such as "commentary, editorials, documentaries or point-of-view public

affairs shows . . . op-ed pages, and call-in shows, which provide a clear evaluative position" make up the last category (Murray, 2007: 542).

At the same time, individual politicians can put their stamp on relations between the government and media. Pierre Trudeau, for instance, was continually engaged in matching wits with the press. During Jean Chrétien's time as prime minister, he was known for his waffling on issues with the press, often leaving reporters and pundits unsure of where he stood on issues of the day.

Stephen Harper and his government have been particularly noted (some say infamous) for attempting to control their relationship with the media using an iron fist. A June 2010 news story in the *Toronto Star*, for example, revealed that the Harper government was taking extraordinary steps to manage all government dealings with the media (Blanchfield and Bronskill, 2010). At any event where members of the media would be present, both Conservative MPs and their staff members, as well as non-elected public servants, were subject to a Message Event Proposal (MEP). As the *Star* article states, "An MEP template typically includes the following subtitles: Event, Event type, Desired headline, Key messages, Media lines, Strategic objectives, Desired soundbite, Ideal speaking backdrop, Ideal event photograph, Tone, Attire, Rollout materials, Background, and Strategic considerations." Not only does the use of MEPs demonstrate an unprecedented degree of control used by the Harper government over media–government relations, but, as Blanchfield and Bronskill point out, it has "also blurred the time-honoured separation of non-partisan public servants and political staffers and sidelined seasoned government communicators."

Government advertising can also be used as a political tool. Such advertising can take many forms: from simple notices of government contracts, public hearings, and job vacancies; to announcements of changes in policy and important holidays or celebrations; to self-serving partisan advertising that trumpets the achievements of the party in power. As Rose (2014) illustrates, however, there is evidence that governments commonly use such advertising for partisan political gain and this kind of use of public funds is ripe for political reform.

With its many sources of information and capacity for information-sharing, the internet appears to be shifting the relationship between government and the media, as well as the way governments reach their constituents and supporters. As Elmer et al. (2014) illustrate, social media platforms and sites are changing the ways political parties and supporters conduct campaigns, get their messages out to supporters, and attract new supporters. While recent political uprisings in places like Egypt, Libya, and Tunisia have been linked to social media, at the same time, there has been a "rise of a whole industry of political campaigning online that is aimed at helping professional political actors manage their campaign(s) through mobilizing users, spread their messages, and fundraise" (Elmer et al., 2014: 240). Moreover, as we discuss in Chapter 12, citizen groups such as Lead Now and Open Media are using new media to press their interests on government, sometimes with success. While at this point it is difficult to say exactly what the impact of web-based media will be on traditional media in the political sphere, online media are playing an increasingly important and expanding role in the political process.

When placed in the context of the history of the media outlined earlier in this chapter, contemporary tensions, shifts, and changes in the relations among the government, the media, and the public illustrate one thing with certainty: the relationship between government and the media is one of ongoing negotiation and change.

▶ SUMMARY

The evolution of the modern mass media began in the mid-fifteenth century with Gutenberg's development of printing by means of movable type. Printing with movable type was an important element of a social shift that saw the eclipse of feudalism and the dawning of the Renaissance, followed by the Reformation, the Enlightenment, and the Industrial Revolution. Government by divine right of monarchs was replaced with the notion of the *consent of the governed*. From the fifteenth century onward, the printing press and other media have served an important social role in gathering information and informing citizens. As we have seen, however, different theories of society have envisioned this communication role and function in different ways.

In the course of their development, the press and, subsequently, other communication media have been influenced by their social and historical location; that is, they have been given form and function by a larger set of social circumstances and events. The rise of industrial society, along with urbanization, increased literacy, and the eight-hour workday all provided the context within which contemporary media took form. In Canada, the development of modern media was further shaped by basic geographical and social realities, such as our vast, sparsely populated, bilingual, multicultural, and regional country, situated next to the United States—the world's largest economy and most aggressive exporter of entertainment and information products.

As we shall see in Chapter 8, after years of subsidies and support, magazine and book publishers, filmmakers, and sound-recording artists are, to a degree, increasing their domestic market share and making a mark on the world stage. These successes are fragile, however, and require the ongoing support of governments. Canadians must remind themselves that they are not alone in taking action to regulate the mass media and to stimulate cultural industries. While efforts to define and protect cultural industries have weakened in the face of growing transnational business and trade agreements, the struggle still continues for many countries to maintain control over their own cultural development.

 KEY TERMS

bourgeoisie, p. 85
commodities, p. 64
conservative, p. 60
economies of scale, p. 72
Enlightenment, p. 61

ideology, p. 60
Industrial Revolution, p. 62
mass culture, p. 70
multiplier effects, p. 81

 RELATED WEBSITES

Access to Information and Privacy Acts:
www.tbs-sct.gc.ca/atip-aiprp/index-eng.asp
These two acts provide a sense of Canada's legislation in the areas of privacy and access to information.

The Canadian Encyclopedia:
www.thecanadianencyclopedia.ca/en
An encyclopedia focused specifically on the history and peoples of Canada. Something quite unique, particularly in a country that is awash in foreign media products.

Canadian Heritage: www.pch.gc.ca
Every Canadian student concerned with culture, the media, and heritage should visit the federal government's Canadian Heritage website.

The Canadian Journalism Project: j-source.ca
A website devoted to Canadian journalism and journalism issues.

**Gutenberg Press: www.youtube.com/
watch?v=7XLWleZgU3s**
A video demonstrating the use of a Gutenberg press.

**Milton's *Areopagitica*: www.buddycom.com/
reviews/areopag/index.html**
An important work on censorship by the English poet John Milton.

Rabble.ca
A vibrant Canadian site of alternative news and views.

 FURTHER READINGS

Armstrong, Robert. 2010. *Broadcasting Policy in Canada*. Toronto: University of Toronto Press. A comprehensive account of the history and dimensions of broadcasting policy in Canada.

Canada. 1981. *Report of the Royal Commission on Newspapers* (Kent Commission). Ottawa: Minister of Supply and Services. This dated but most recent royal commission on the press brings forward many issues that are still important today. Its background papers are also very informative.

——. 2003. *Our Cultural Sovereignty: The Second Century of Canadian Broadcasting*. Report of the Standing Committee on Canadian Heritage, June. Ottawa: Communication Canada Publishing.

Available at www.parl.gc.ca/InfoComDoc/ 37/2/HERI/Studies/Reports/herirp02-e.htm. This report provides good background on the history, structure, and problems facing Canadian broadcasting.

Kozolanka, Kirsten, ed. 2014. *Publicity and the Canadian State*. Toronto: University of Toronto Press.

Starr, Paul. 2004. *The Creation of the Media: Political Origins of Modern Communications*. New York: Basic Books. This Pulitzer Prize–winning book explores the weave of politics, economics, and technology in the making of the US media.

Vipond, Mary. 2011. *The Mass Media in Canada*, 4th ed. Toronto: James Lorimer. This book provides a historical perspective on the development of the Canadian mass media.

Wagman, Ira, and Peter Urquhart. 2012. *Cultural Industries.ca: Making Sense of Canadian Media in the Digital Age*. Toronto: James Lorimer.

Weir, Ernest Austin. 1965. *The Struggle for National Broadcasting in Canada*. Toronto: McClelland & Stewart. As the title suggests, the author presents an account of the development of public broadcasting in Canada and of the political and cultural milieu out of which this regime was established.

Williams, Raymond. 1974. *Television, Technology and Cultural Form*. Glasgow: Fontana Collins. Focusing on the development of television, Williams illustrates how technological development is the product of a broad set of social forces.

 ## STUDY QUESTIONS

1. How did Enlightenment ideals influence the development and role(s) of the mass media?
2. Describe how modern media took form during the development of industrial society.
3. Describe some of the ways in which the federal government has played a central role in developing both the economy and the media in Canada.
4. Provide some examples of economies of scale in media organizations.
5. Describe four perspectives on the role of the media in society and their connections to larger theories of society.
6. Describe four dimensions of the media's engagement with the Canadian public policy process.

II

Theoretical Perspectives

4 Media Content: Studying the Making of Meaning

> The philosophers have only interpreted the world, in various ways; the point is to change it. — Karl Marx

Opening Questions

- How do the terms *representation* and *signification* apply in the study of communication?

- What is meant by the phrase the indeterminacy of communication?

- What is *social theory* and what is its purpose?

- What is an *encoding/decoding* model?

- What is human agency and what does it mean to say that social structures and process can be both "enabling" and "constraining"?

- What are some of the main theoretical perspectives on media content?

- Do the media provide a full, unbiased perspective on the world?

Introduction

In Chapters 4 and 5, we build on earlier discussions of communication theory to offer rigorous definitions of terms such as *social theory* and illustrate some of the main approaches to the study of media content and audiences. In this chapter, we begin by introducing terms that describe some basic characteristics of the process of communication and media content. Building on a model that describes communication as a process of encoding and decoding, we introduce a number of common theoretical and methodological perspectives that communication theorists use when studying content and illustrate how these theories relate to the larger social practice of communication. We examine several key content genres, such as news, soap operas, and reality TV, with particular attention given to advertising.

Representation and Signification

When we study communication, and particularly communication content, we are generally studying practices or processes of **representation**. What is representation? It's the act of putting or *encoding* ideas into words, paintings, sculpture, film, plays, television programs, or any other medium of communication. A picture of a plane crash is not the crash itself, obviously, but a *representation* of that crash. A map is not an actual place but a drawing or a picture that *represents* that place. An advertisement for an SUV (sports utility vehicle) is not the vehicle but a representation of a way of looking at or thinking about such a vehicle. Even a live telecast of a hockey game or some other sporting event is not the game itself but a series of carefully chosen and constructed images, camera angles,

A map is *representation* of a place that it seeks to describe.

and commentary that represent the event in an audiovisual package.

Using any medium of communication, a person selects certain elements of reality to describe the object, event, person, or situation he or she wishes to represent. Representations are, to a large extent, simplifications and interpretations of the objects and events they describe. (The accompanying map, for instance, doesn't describe every rock, valley, and tree in the actual landscape it represents. Rather, it illustrates broad features and landmarks and distances between them.) The person receiving or *decoding* that communication then uses what he or she knows of what is described and what that person knows of the system of representation—most often, language—to come to an understanding of what was encoded by the sender.

A more rigorous way of thinking about representation is as a process of signification. Signification is using signs to make meaning. What's a **sign**? Anything with meaning: a word, an image, a sound, a painting, even things themselves like dark clouds on the horizon. The Swiss linguist Ferdinand de Saussure—sometimes considered the founder of **semiotics** or the science of signs—posited that signs are composed of two elements: the signifier and the signified. The **signifier** is the thing that we see, hear, or feel: the image on a screen, sounds, or small bumps on paper. The **signified** is the idea or mental concept we draw from those signifiers: the ideas in a blog, in music, or in Braille words. The process of signification is a process of making meaning. Indeed, from this perspective the whole of our experience of the world is a process of signification as we translate the signs we encounter into meaning: dark clouds mean rain, a short chapter means less homework, an angry parent means trouble.

C.S. Peirce categorized signs into three different types: icon, index, and symbol. An **icon** looks like the object it describes. For instance, maps and photographs both are icons. An **index** is related to the object it represents. Smoke is an index of fire and a sneeze is an index of a cold, allergy, or irritant. A **symbol** is a sign that bears no direct resemblance to what it signifies. Words are symbols, as is the image of an apple when it is used to represent something other than fruit, such as knowledge or a particular brand of electronic products.

Intertextuality, Polysemy, and the Indeterminacy of Representation

The idea that a sign can represent or signify more than one thing raises the indeterminacy of representation (defined more fully below). To some, the image of a sporty SUV might signify or represent luxury, adventure, or sex appeal; to others, environmental disaster. The sound of falling rain might signify or represent a soothing summer's evening or an impending flood. The meaning of any particular sign is not guaranteed but is dependent on the context of its use and interpretation.

In other words, signs do not exist in isolation—they are either explicitly or implicitly part of larger "texts" or sets of signs and symbols. Images of SUVs are often found in advertisements that portray them as part of mountain adventures or happy family outings. The melodic splash of rain is often used to establish a mood

Source: oksana.perkins/Shutterstock.

▮ What does the image in this ad signify to you? What do you think it was intended to signify to audiences?

in music, film, or television programs. In other words, the meaning of these signs is itself given form by its relation to other signs in the context of a larger symbolic system. If we are confronted by images and sounds without this kind of grounding, to make meaning out of them we often supply our own context, drawn from memory and imagination.

The idea that meaning is made in the context of larger symbolic systems draws our attention to two other important elements of the process of signification. The first is the **intertextuality** of the process of making meaning. Intertextuality refers to the meaning we make of one text depending on the meanings we have drawn from other sets of signs we have encountered (Kristeva, 1969; Barthes, 1968). That is, meaning is grounded in the relationships we find between different texts. Our understanding of the picture of the SUV as a family vehicle is dependent on our combining knowledge of the SUV as a mode of transportation and the representation of the people in the image as a family. Folding the two signifiers together—SUV and happy family—creates the signified "family vehicle." Similarly, our understanding of the ways automobile exhaust emissions are related to global warming might also lead us to interpret the SUV as an instrument of environmental degradation. Thus, our past experience—our individual histories—provides the backdrop for interpreting the signs and symbols we encounter in everyday life.

The second important point to note here is that making meaning is an active process. Making the connection between signifier and signified, joining past and present experience, requires active participation. When the meaning of things appears obvious, even natural, it still requires active work. We make or create meaning. Even when it seems the meaning of a television program, web post, or film scene is obvious and that everyone should "get it," making meaning from that representation requires effort or work on the part of the person viewing it.

Because signs can be open to a variety of interpretations, they are said to be **polysemic**—that

is, having "many meanings" (Jensen, 1990). Depending on the context, an image of an apple might be interpreted as knowledge, as a computer company, or simply as fruit. The different types or levels of meaning drawn from such an image may be denotative and connotative, where **denotative meaning** refers to the literal or most obvious interpretation of the sign and **connotative meaning** refers to the range of other less obvious or more subjective meanings that may be drawn.

Advertisements exemplify the purposive use of signs to create different levels of meaning. For instance, by using seemingly ordinary women in its ads instead of the professional models who generally represent the standards of beauty in soap and cosmetic advertising, Dove's Real Beauty Campaign (see Appendix A in this book) attempted to resignify the usual advertising meaning of beauty.

The fact that signs are polysemic highlights the importance of context for the creation and interpretation of meaning. The social and cultural conditions surrounding the production of media texts, as well as those involved in their consumption, play into the meaning generated from them. Similarly, the fact that any given sign can have many meanings illustrates the *indeterminacy of*

Source: Dove/PA Wire URN: 8069588: Press Association via AP Images.

In what ways do these women differ from conventional models? What does this presentation mean to you? How do you think other viewers interpret it? What are the denotative and connotative dimensions of these images?

representation (see Figure 4.1). On the one hand, the meaning of signs and the messages of which they are a part is indeterminate because there is a multiplicity of ways of representing an object, action, or event—another representation can always be made. On the other hand, they are indeterminate because there is no *necessary* correspondence between the meaning encoded in a particular message by the sender and that decoded by the receiver. Because decoding messages requires active participation on the part of the person or people receiving the message, there is no guarantee that the receiver will actually get or understand the intended meaning. Nevertheless, each representation is grounded in a specific context as the person and/or medium doing the representing works to guide the audience or receiver of the message toward a specific or preferred meaning.

There are many factors determining polysemy, or the indeterminacy of representation. Different media provide different systems for making meaning, and one system of representation cannot encompass the full spectrum of the meaning of another. For instance, a painting cannot be fully translated into a prose essay, or even poetry. Nor can a sculpture be completely transformed into a photograph or a hologram. Inevitably, something is lost.

Polysemy and the indeterminacy of representation tend to lead the study of communication away from the foundations of science and social science toward the foundations of interpretation we find in the humanities. It is concerned more with **rhetoric** (how things are said) and hermeneutics (how things are interpreted) than with "truth" (see Box 4.1, "Media/Culture Binding" on page 96).

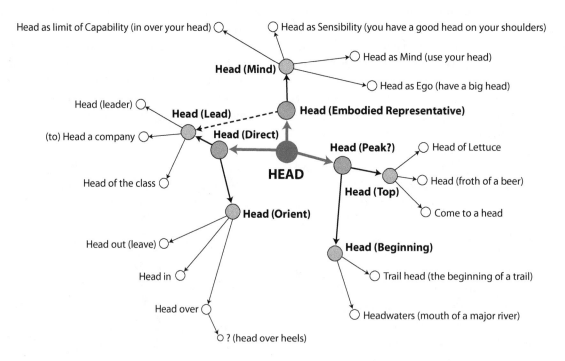

FIGURE 4.1   Polysemy and the Indeterminacy of Representation

This diagram illustrates some of the many meanings of the word *head*. When you see the word, how do you decide which meaning is being used?

Source: Ryan Dewey. HEAD: Polysemous Network for an Open Class Lexical Item. 2010. Used by permission. RyanDewey.org.

In the study of communication, the importance of a statement is not limited to whether it predicts events, can be refuted by others, or generates interesting hypotheses—all standards used in science. What is important also entails how an act of communication selects and *represents* or *reconstructs* something, and what gives a particular representation its force, its ability to persuade, or its attractiveness. Whatever makes a particular novel, painting, or film more popular or revered than another, or even a novel more "powerful" than a film, cannot be satisfactorily discussed by reference to the relative "truth" of each communication. Such media and individual works are discussed by communication scholars in terms of their rhetorical force or the nature or style of their representation.

If we compare media in this way, the visual dimension of film and television quite consistently adds a specific sense of reality that another medium, such as print, cannot provide. What film and television gain in that dimension, however, they often lose in subtlety, character development, and room for imaginative play when compared to print. Similarly, the discussion of abstract ideas changes when one moves from books to the popular press or to television. Television invites a pluralism of sight, sound, and personage that is partially present in radio and absent in print—more than a few minutes of the same person talking on television, no matter what the visuals, tend to undermine the speaker's credibility or, at least, the viewers' interest. Just the opposite seems to hold for print—a single authorial voice will more readily elicit a reader's attention and understanding. The characteristics of different media tend to nuance the crafting of content in particular ways.

Communication Theory as Social Theory

In studying the process of communication we often draw on social theory, and particularly communication theory, for helping us to understand how processes of communication are nuanced and operate. What is **social theory**? Generally, it is a representation of the social world; a set of ideas about how the world is organized and functions. We all have ideas about how the world works, but our assumptions are often fragmentary and contradictory. Take, for instance, common-sense proverbs such as "many hands make light work" and "too many cooks spoil the broth." While they both purport to provide a way of understanding and approaching work, they offer contradictory perspectives on how to do so. In contrast, social theory strives to offer rigorous, logical explanations of elements of the social world. It is a representation of the world that attempts to provide a systematic and comprehensive explanation of the relationships between individuals, social groups, and the world around them.

What is the purpose of social theory? At one level, it provides explanations of how things work and why things are the way they are. At another level, such explanations guide action: to alleviate social problems and improve the quality of life or to construct social policy. To paraphrase Karl Marx, "The purpose of social theory is not simply to understand the world but to change it," and change it in a progressive manner that makes things more egalitarian and provides more equal access to the fruits of our society for all citizens.

As a kind of social theory, communication theory is a way of representing the complex process of communication. It is a way of trying to understand the different forces that contextualize and give form to human communication and, particularly for our purposes, mass communication.

There are, however, a wide variety of communication theories. Some are elements of larger theories of society, such as the libertarian, social responsibility, mass society, and Marxist political economy we examined in the previous chapter. Others offer only partial explanations of the process of communication, such as the semiotic explanation of the process of signification discussed above. Some provide simple, highly abstract perspectives, such as Shannon and Weaver's model of communication that we outlined in Chapter 1 (see Figure 1.2), which asserts that communication both begins and ends with individuals. Others, such as the social model of communication (see Figure 1.3), illustrate the process of communication as given form by a great many factors and variables.

To provide a better understanding of the variety of ways different theories approach and envision the process of communication, we will now turn our attention to another model of communication.

The Encoding/ Decoding Model

As we have seen, mass communication is a process that involves both **encoding**, or creating media messages, and **decoding**, or interpreting them. While these are active processes, in each of these moments a range of social institutions and forces serve to frame or contextualize the ways in which messages are constituted and the ways in which people make meaning from them.

Drawing from Stuart Hall's (1993) discussion of this process, Figure 4.2 illustrates some of the key elements involved in it. Please note, however, that although the diagram displays these pieces of the process as individual parts, all of these parts are interrelated in reality. As we saw in Chapter 3, communication media are integral to the societies of which they are a part, not separate or distinct technical systems. Similarly, the professional values of media workers are woven between organizational and technical imperatives, not ideas separated or distinct from social

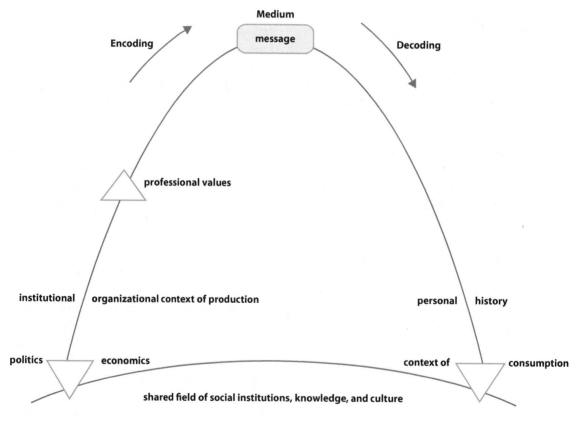

FIGURE 4.2 Encoding and Decoding

Source: Adapted from Hall, 1993.

context. For purposes of illustration, however, we have abstracted the process of communication from this larger social context and exploded its pieces to highlight the different roles that each plays. Each of these pieces is described below.

First is the shared field of social institutions and knowledge, or culture, within which the media system operates—the general social milieu in which we live. It comprises language and social customs: ideas we hold about gender, family, and work as well as the laws, regulations, and other social processes and structures that frame and animate society and the ways we think and act in the world. To a large part these are the elements of what we referred to as industrial society in Chapter 3. Or, they might be thought of as culture, or the ways of life that make up our society. Certainly, the ways that each media producer and consumer experiences and draws on this larger social milieu are not the same; they are often quite different. For instance, a fashion magazine draws upon a very different set of ideas and circumstances to create its product than the producers of a television program like *The Simpsons*. This larger social milieu, however, does provide a common field of referents for people to draw on and to make meaning from.

Second, broad political and economic processes contextualize how the process of media production is undertaken. On the political side, we would include specific laws and regulations that frame the way media organizations operate and what media professionals do: libel laws, copyright, and media ownership regulations. In the case of broadcasting, we would include the Broadcasting Act and the regulations promulgated by the CRTC; for film, distribution regulations; and for newspapers, ownership regulations. As we saw in Chapter 3, each medium operates in a specific legal and regulatory context that informs the way its products are created. On the economic side, we are concerned with the ways in which the drive for profits, or commercial forces, can impinge on production. As we have seen, the economies of scale enjoyed by US producers help flood Canadian markets with their media

products. All of these political and economic circumstances influence the media content or, in other words, the ways in which media products represent the world.

Third is the institutional or organizational context within which media messages are created. Here, we might consider the ways in which organizational mandates or imperatives frame what media organizations do and the products they create. The National Film Board (NFB), for example, is guided by its mandate to "represent Canada to Canadians." This purpose underlies all of the work the NFB produces. Similarly, as laid out in the Broadcasting Act, the CBC's mandate guides the public broadcaster's actions. Private broadcasters and other media have profits as their motive. Hence, both the ways their resources are organized and the media products they produce reflect that imperative.

A fourth dimension of influence on the way media represent the world is the professional values that guide media producers. Media professionals are guided in their practices by specific ideas about the characteristics of the products they create. Journalists go to journalism school to learn how to identify newsworthy events and produce news reports. Similarly, television writers working on situation comedies, soap operas, and other program genres are governed by assumptions and guidelines as to how those programs are structured.

Fifth, as we have discussed, the medium through which representations are communicated can have great influence on the form and structure of ideas and information. Telling a story in a novel is quite different from telling it in a film. Radio addresses audiences quite differently from television or newspapers. News is often presented on the web in a different way than in traditional media.

Finally, at the level of decoding, the context of consumption, where and by whom media products are consumed, influences the meaning that is made from them. Age, education, family background, religion, gender, race, and ethnicity are all elements of one's background or history that can play on how media messages are decoded. Moreover, much of this personal history is social experience—that is, experience drawn from the larger field of social institutions, knowledge, and culture. For Stuart Hall, these factors could result in interpretations or "readings" of messages that range from "dominant," such as those that are in complete agreement with the ideas/perspectives contained in the message, to "oppositional," such as those that are in total disagreement with those ideas.

Again, while the encoder's and decoder's experiences of this field may be vastly different, it does provide a common set of *referents*—ideas, situations, and circumstances that can be referred to or represented in media products. Consider again *The Simpsons*, which is broadcast in many countries and a number of different languages around the world. The culture and institutions found in these countries are often quite different, yet people in these different places are able to decode the meaning from this program and share in its humour. How so? To a large extent, this is because the show's writers draw on a set of characters and circumstances familiar to all those people. The program focuses on a typical nuclear family—father, mother, and three children—who live in a typical American town and lead a typical life that includes homemaking, working, going to school, spending time with friends, and getting into trouble. In other words, both the characters and the situations they encounter are stereotypes of lives in an industrial society that many recognize and to a degree understand, even though they may not live like that or approve of the stereotyping. In creating the program, *Simpsons* writers draw on ideas familiar to a very diverse group of people. And, in large part, the wide appeal of that program depends on their ability to find common points of knowledge and understanding in the midst of that diversity.

4.1 ▶▶▶ ▶ ▶▶ ▶

MEDIA/CULTURE BINDING

The media interact with everyday life in various ways. They inform us about politics, life in other cultures and places, how people kiss, how people smoke, how people rob banks, how children and others play with toys, how people dance. The list of human behaviours modelled in media is endless. But the interaction is not a one-way process. The media draw their content from the real lives of particular individuals and groups. In an example that captures this relation well, renowned writer and semiologist Umberto Eco looked at it this way:

1. A firm produces polo shirts with an alligator on them and it advertises them.
2. A generation begins to wear polo shirts.
3. Each consumer of the polo shirt advertises, via the alligator on his or her chest, this brand of polo shirt.
4. A TV broadcast (program), to be faithful to reality, shows some young people wearing the alligator polo shirt.
5. The young (and the old) see the TV broadcast and buy more alligator polo shirts because they have "the young look."

- *Which is the mass medium?* The ad? The broadcast? The shirt?
- *Who is sending the message?* The manufacturer? The wearer? The TV director? The analyst of this phenomenon?
- *Who is the producer of ideology?* Again, the manufacturer? The wearer (including the celebrity who may wear it in public for a fee)? The TV director who portrays the generation?
- *Where does the (marketing) plan come from?* This is not to imply that there is no plan, but rather that it does not emanate from one central source.

Source: Eco, 1986, 148–50.

As a social model of communication, the encoding/decoding model draws our attention to the fact that the process of communication is given form by social factors. Individuals who work in a particular institutional and organizational context employ professional values to construct media messages that draw on social knowledge supposedly shared by their intended audience; then, the messages are delivered through particular technical systems to audience members with particular social backgrounds. In turn, these individuals draw upon social knowledge accrued through their personal histories to decode the messages and deploy that information in their lives.

This model is useful for understanding how certain theories envision the process of communication. Few theories claim to explain the influence of all of these different dimensions on that process. Rather, they focus on how a number of those elements work to determine how the media operate and the influence they have.

Agency and Structure: A Key Concern in the Study of Communication

A central consideration of social theory in general, and media and communication theory in particular, is the relationship between *agency* and *structure*. To put this another way, can people generally undertake whatever actions they choose? Or do the structures and processes in which people live and work determine the range and character of the actions they can undertake? This is a pivotal question for trying to explain how society operates.

Take the economic system, for example. The economy enables people to earn money, which, in turn, can help increase the number things they can do. Go to university, take a trip, buy a house—money can increase the range of action one might undertake or, in other words, it can increase a person's *agency*. The education system can act in a similar way, with a good education,

people can better understand how the world works and their place within it. Well-educated people can understand how the political system works and who or what interests benefit from its current structure; understand how the media system works and who or what interests it supports; and understand how the economic system works and use that knowledge to get money. Education, too, can increase one's agency. As a number of researchers have pointed out, however, social institutions, processes, and structures are both *enabling* and *constraining* (see Giddens, 1984). In our economic system, for example, those with money are enabled to access a wide range of goods and services. Those without money are not as capable. So, our economic system constrains those who are, for one reason or another, unable to access money. The education system functions in much the same way. Those who have access to education generally have better access to wealth and power in our society than those who don't.

The issue of agency/structure is also a key question for trying to understand and explain how media systems operate. In terms of media and communication, it might be summarized like this: can people generally encode whatever ideas and meanings they want into media messages and programs? Or, do the structures and processes in which people live and work determine the range and character of the messages and ideas they can produce?

Language itself provides a structure for communication, a set of words and rules for communicating. While that structure is enabling because it allows the communication of a vast range of ideas, it is also constraining in that we can communicate in that language only if we correctly enact its vocabulary. Similarly, while the job of being a reporter at a large newspaper is constraining in that one has to adhere to editorial policies and professional values regarding what kinds of events constitute news, how to write a news story, and organizational rules and deadlines, it also is enabling because it allows one to write about changing events and circumstances on a daily basis from a range of perspectives, and because the material one writes will be read regularly by thousands of people.

Understanding the relationship between agency and structure, the ways in which communication processes and institutions work to enable and constrain the ways in which communication takes place and the ideas that can be communicated is one of the central concerns of communication theory.

Perspectives on the Study of Content

Over the years, a number of perspectives have been developed and used to study media content. A few of the more historically important perspectives are discussed in this section—literary criticism, structuralism, semiotics, and post-structuralism; discourse analysis; critical political economy; content analysis; and media form or genre analysis. Some of these perspectives are drawn from larger theories of society and communication. Others are better understood as methods or approaches for examining media content and might be used in concert with larger theories. Here, our purpose is to simply introduce these ideas and provide some understanding of the history of their development. In particular, we consider how they address the encoding of media messages and the larger set of social and linguistic forces that they see as coming to bear on the production process. Rather than provide a comprehensive review of the different theories of content at play in the field of communication studies, this section is meant to help introduce the range of perspectives brought to bear on that study. Should analysis focus on the author/writer? On the text/content itself? Or on the larger set of social circumstances that influence the author/writer? There is no easy answer to these questions and the multiplicity of perspectives underscores the importance of the notion that it is not which one of them is the correct perspective, but rather what useful insight each brings to the analysis of media content.

Literary Criticism

Literary criticism is the study and interpretation of texts. It explores the different ways that texts can be analyzed and understood. Its roots reach back to when written records first emerged. As soon as something is recorded, it becomes open to interpretation and discussion. Major movements and changes in world history have focused on examinations and re-examinations of particular texts. Martin Luther, for example, challenged the interpretation of the Bible by the Roman Catholic Church and the right of the Catholic Church to control access to and to be the sole interpreter of the scriptures. Similarly, from the Sung dynasty (AD 900) and thereafter in China, official interpretations of classic Confucian texts were promoted and unofficial versions were banned.

Debates in literary criticism have been particularly important for communication studies and for the study of content because they draw our attention to the various ways meaning might be drawn from texts. Should texts be read simply in terms of the intentions of the author? Or might meanings decoded by readers other than what the author intended be considered legitimate "meanings" of the text? Might texts be viewed as the product of forces that impinge on the author, like language and culture?

One of the traditional modes of criticism is to view texts in terms of the presumed intention of the author. From this perspective, interpretation tries to uncover what the author consciously had in mind, as expressed in the text. Freudian analysis purports to explain, furthermore, what the author had subconsciously in mind. The text is treated only as the specific product or vehicle of an individual author-creator whose other works may be cross-compared in the same light (e.g., the novels of Jane Austen, the plays of Shakespeare). This approach spread to film studies, with the director carrying the authorship mantle (e.g., one can make a cross-comparison of the films of Alfred Hitchcock). Such an approach in film analysis became known as *auteur theory*, which focuses on the personal vision of the director and

Source: Courtesy of adbusters.org.

Adbusters often employs semiotics to create *sub-vertisements*: ads slightly changed, or subverted, to expose the negative effects of the products they promote. Here, the signifier—the vodka bottle—has been modified to shift its signified from the usual party atmosphere depicted in liquor ads to something less alluring.

treats that person as the creative originator of the film.

In the early twentieth century, a variant of literary criticism, New Criticism, gained prominence. From this perspective, analysis is confined to the texts per se and both authorial intention and reader response are disregarded in favour of a close reading aimed at revealing ambiguities and multiplicities of meanings within the work itself. More recently, emerging schools of literary criticism have incorporated concepts from linguistics, sociology, and anthropology to extend debates into a wide range of factors (including language and culture) that can be drawn into the interpretation of content. However, while this perspective acknowledges the indeterminacy of representation and the polysemic nature of signs and texts, analysis is confined to the text itself and does not consider relationships between the text and external factors like the personal history of the author or larger social or cultural factors that may have influenced its production.

Structuralism, Semiotics, and Post-Structuralism

In the 1950s and '60s, a perspective known as *structuralism* became dominant in the social sciences and humanities, especially in the fields of linguistics, anthropology, sociology, psychology, and literature. In the analysis of media content, the aim of **structuralism** is to discover underlying patterns or structures that shape both texts and genres; to try to uncover common linguistic or thematic patterns that give them form—a quite different perspective from the one about New Criticism described above. Here, the author is viewed primarily as a vehicle who enacts the extant rules of language and culture in the creation of her/his work (or life). To put it another way, from a structuralist perspective, to a large extent, we do not speak language so much as *language speaks us*. In other words, the agency of the author, reader, or audience member is not seen by structuralists as a key factor in how meaning is created.

An early and seminal work exemplifying structuralist principles was that of the Russian folklorist Vladimir Propp. In the 1920s, Propp collected over 400 traditional tales from different parts of Europe and showed how they all had a similar narrative structure. First, he identified a set of basic (lexical) elements (all stories have certain similar items): a hero or heroine, a villain, a helper. Second, he described the motifs that propel the narrative from beginning to end. Thus, something must happen to set the hero (usually male) in motion: at some point, the villain will disrupt the hero's plans, and at another juncture, the hero will receive aid from a helper (who may or may not be female) to overcome the obstacles in his way. Propp was able to reduce the apparent complexity of a great number of different stories to a simple set of underlying narrative elements that could be combined in a strictly limited number of ways (see Propp, 1970). The structural analysis of narrative has subsequently been applied to all manner of stories, including James Bond novels and films (Eco, 1982; Bennett and Woollacott, 1987), romantic novels (Radway, 1984), and soap operas (Geraghty, 1991). Figure 4.3 illustrates structuralism at work in the romance genre.

Once narrative structures and surface elements were identified, Propp and other structuralists were able to identify common themes that recurred in stories from all over the world. The magical union of strength and beauty, power in two forms, is a good example of a myth to be found in virtually all cultures. In this instance, the male embodiment of spiritual and bodily strength (usually a prince) grows up in his kingdom. The female embodiment of beauty and perceptiveness (a princess) grows up in her kingdom. One or both may be disguised in a certain way (a frog prince, a pig princess) or confined (Sleeping Beauty, Cinderella), sometimes as a result of immature vulnerability (plotting by unworthy usurpers, innocence). An event, story, or intervention of some sort induces one (usually the male in a patriarchal society or the female in a matriarchal society) to set out on a quest, sometimes purposeful, sometimes not. The seeker finds the sought (the object of his or

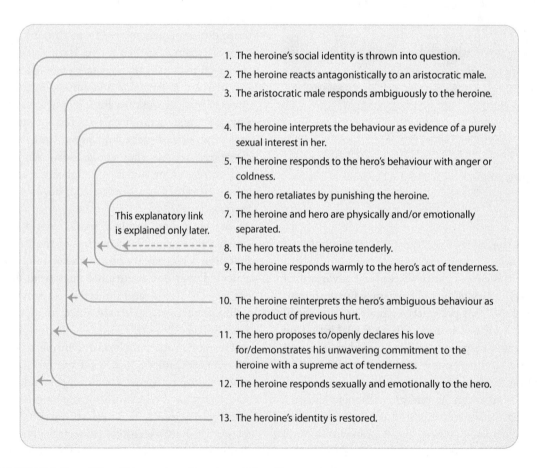

FIGURE 4.3   The Narrative Logic of the Romance

Source: From Janice A. Radway. *Reading the Romance: Women, Patriarchy, and Popular Literature.* Copyright © 1984, new introduction © 1991 by the University of North Carolina Press. Used by permission of the publisher, www.uncpress.unc.edu.

her dreams, again evidence of divine blessing) and recognizes her/him by virtue of her/his or both of their inner senses, inherent kindness, or nobility. This something not only confirms the union, but it also confirms the special qualities of both seeker and sought, which befits them to rule others (divine right of kings). The children of the union are, of course, very special, since they inherit the qualities of both.

Such myths live on. In Canada, perhaps the most obvious twentieth-century example of the myth of the prince/princess ascending the throne would be the courtship and marriage of Charles, Prince of Wales, and Diana, a commoner who became Princess of Wales. As with so many myths, however, the story ended tragically. So powerful are such myths that US film stars have handlers who build up their mythological identity (or public persona) by counselling them to accept only certain roles. Some pursue a particular type of character (e.g., Arnold Schwarzenegger, Melissa McCarthy), while others pursue versatility (e.g., Meryl Streep, Christian Bale).

Another influential scholar in the field of structuralism was the Swiss linguist Ferdinand de Saussure, mentioned earlier. Saussure developed what was later seen as the structural analysis of language (1974). Saussure proposed that language could be scientifically studied in the abstract as an underlying set of linguistic structures (*langue*, in his terms) and combined together by any native speaker to produce an utterance (*parole*). As he argued, "Language is a system of signs that express ideas, and is therefore comparable to a system of writing, the alphabet of deaf-mutes, symbolic rites, polite formulas, military signals, etc. But it is the most important of all these systems" (Saussure, in Silverman, 1983: 4–5). To better understand this system, he proposed a science of signs—*semiotics*.

For Saussure, meaning is made in the difference between signs. Given that symbols bear no necessary relation to what they represent, the only way to identify the symbol is by knowing what it is not. A red light at a traffic intersection, for example, is not a green light (see Silverman, 1983).

Anthropologist Claude Lévi-Strauss extended the structuralist formula into social interaction and claimed to show in his work "not how men think in myths, but how myths operate in men's minds without their being aware of the fact" (Lévi-Strauss, 1969: 12). The point is that words carry preconceived ideas, or *signifieds*, about things and thereby provide a frame or screen for interpreting the world. From this perspective, one can begin to see why structuralism sometimes claims that people are "spoken" by the language they use rather than the other way around.

As we have seen, based on the sign (signifier/signified), a semiotic analysis distinguishes between two levels of meaning: the denotative and the connotative. Using this schema, Roland Barthes (1972) famously decoded ideological meanings in everything from wrestling and striptease to the paintings in the Louvre, television shows, popular novels, and advertisements. By making connections between the images found in everyday media and the ideologies of bourgeois capitalist society, Barthes strove to uncover the ways that popular culture promotes dominant ideas and values.

Consider a picture or ad portraying an SUV as a family vehicle that can be used for city transportation and country adventure. From Barthes's perspective, the ad not only represents the SUV as a part of family life, but also draws on a deeper more subtle set of assumptions and values— another order of connotations. Based on the notion that the meaning of the ad is found in the differences between the images that it contains and possible alternatives, underlying the ad are ideas such as the following: the nuclear family is the natural and dominant social unit; private vehicles are a preferred mode of transportation; and people's domination of nature is both a legitimate and pleasurable leisure activity. Social issues such as what comprises a family in this day and age and the forms of environmental damage caused by the use of gas-powered vehicles are ignored, buried under these more dominant contemporary social myths. In other words, the text positions the reader in reference to the objects

Can we do more and use less?

Our answer is Yes.

We're all part of something bigger. In the next 20 years the global demand for energy is expected to grow by more than one-third. So how do we find better ways to responsibly provide the energy we need so everyone can benefit from a healthy environment today and tomorrow?

We're Canada's largest energy company. Come and see how our breakthroughs in technology are improving environmental performance as we take on the essential questions around energy in the world we share.

Come and see whatyescando.com

SUNCOR

Source: Used with permission of Suncor.

What are the assumptions and values present in this picture? How do those relate to Suncor as a company?

in the ad in particular ways and encourages a very specific reading, or understanding, of those objects. From this perspective, by accepting the idea that the SUV is the perfect family vehicle, not only are you accepting the obvious premise of the ad, but you are absorbing the baggage of these underlying ideas as well. Through the 1970s and '80s, Barthes-style semiotic analysis became the preferred way of reading cultural texts (e.g., see Williamson, 1978, for an analysis of advertisements).

While both structuralism and semiotics provide useful insights into the ways in which language structures the form and content of communication, perhaps their biggest shortcoming as modes of analysis is how they underplay the importance of the particular in favour of the general—of langue in contrast to parole. Hence, the way in which they underplay human agency and the roles of the individual speaker and listener (or producer and consumer) of communication

and the context of the message in the process of communication became a key source of criticism.

Beginning in the 1960s, post-structuralism emerged as a critique of the idea that a consistent structure to texts exists and that the process of encoding somehow fixes or solidifies meaning for the decoder. A number of the main proponents of post-structuralism had been structuralists earlier, among them Roland Barthes.

For post-structuralists, "meaning" is made in the act of decoding, and thereby is the purview of the reader or audience member. Whatever sense is to be made of any particular word, image, or sound is the product of the people interpreting those signs and depends on the perspective(s) they bring to the task. Women may interpret content differently from men, homosexuals differently from heterosexuals, children differently from adults, and so on. Understanding texts involves *deconstructing* them to uncover the possible play on differences they contain. Meaning is never fixed in content. It remains as fluid as the next reader makes it. In semiotic terms, post-structuralism argues that signs have come undone and that signifiers can no longer be said to have specific signifieds. Take, again, the SUV ad. Who cares about the happy-heterosexual-family symbolism seemingly bestowed on the vehicle by the advertising company? With one look at the ad's description of its spacious interior and stylish appointments, perhaps an LGBT environmentalist group will decide that this is the perfect mode of transportation for getting its members to their latest waterfowl habitat recuperation project in the mountains.

This is the point made by Barthes in his famous essay, "The Death of the Author" (1977b). Since the text becomes meaningful only in the act of being read and understood, the source of meaning, Barthes argued, is the reader—not the author, as auteur theory would propose. One effect of this startling reversal in approach was the empowerment of the reader or audience. No longer chained to the dull task of trying to find out what Shakespeare "had in mind" when he wrote *Hamlet* (an impossible task anyway, argued

Barthes), the reader or audience member was now drawing from her/his own experience, free to create his/her own meanings and open up rather than close down the meaning of a text. Gone was any notion of a "true" or "authentic" meaning of the text, or that meaning was somehow locked into the text itself. Set against the multiplicity of possible interpretations by readers or audience members, texts were polysemic and had any number of different possible meanings. The conception of reading also changed from the passive absorption of the text's imposed meaning to an active exploration of its possibilities.

As we illustrate in Chapter 5, this shift in interpretation parallels a shift in the ways audiences are viewed in terms of their relation to media content.

Discourse Analysis

Discourse analysis is another perspective with a long history, dating back more than two millennia to the discipline of *rhetorica*, or rhetoric. The study of rhetoric was focused on making speeches more effective, and generally addressed the planning, organization, specific operations, and performance of speech in political and legal settings (van Dijk, 1985, vol. 1: 1; cf. Murray, 2012). From this perspective, it sought to understand how language engaged audiences.

Combining elements of rhetorical theory and structuralism, discourse analysis focuses on how language, as a system of representation, provides us with a particular perspective or "position" in the social world. It posits that language is a kind of structure, and that by being inside that structure, language gives us a particular view of the world. Today, there are many strands of discourse analysis at play in communication studies (see Fairclough, 2010; van Dijk, 1997). A major stream focuses on specific instances of language use and their relationship to social power. Another, following the work of Michel Foucault, considers how specific modes of language use bind our ways of thinking and become "sedimented" into specific institutions and relations of social power.

The first of these modes of analysis points to how particular patterns and conventions of language usage become taken for granted and considers how these patterns serve as larger frames of reference to shape our experience and understanding of the world. Discourse analysis has, for example, been used to illustrate the gendered character of language—the long-standing prevalence of words like chair*man*, fire*man*, fish-er*man*, and so on—and to demonstrate through historical referents how this kind of language has supported patriarchal forms of domination in society. Hence, today, to promote more egalitarian relationships, we use gender-neutral language: *chair, chairperson, firefighter, fisher.*

This type of analysis also provides a way of understanding how particular elements of media content work together to create a larger perspective on, or way of seeing, social events and circumstances. A discourse analysis of federal election coverage, for example, might look at all of the different kinds of media content focusing on the election—coverage of debates, polls, editorials, news stories—and analyze the ways in which different leaders and parties are treated in that coverage. Were they given equal time/space? Were the views of one party or leader given more favourable or sympathetic treatment than others?

Similarly, discourse analysis might explore the ways in which texts position different discourses and the power relations inherent in that positioning. In their article, "'It's Not Easy Being Green': The Greenwashing of Environmental Discourses in Advertising," Jennifer Budinsky and Susan Bryant illustrate how some companies borrow from the language of environmentalism to frame their still environmentally destructive products as "friendly" to the environment (Budinsky and Bryant, 2013). For instance, Clorox, a company heavily involved in the sale of environmentally damaging chemicals, promotes a "green" line of such products. And despite the fact that automobiles remain one of the main contributors to global warming, carmakers such as Ford and Toyota promote seemingly environmentally friendly cars. As the authors point out, the language of environmentalism is often used in advertising to hide or smooth over the connection between consumers' continued purchase of damaging products and the ongoing deterioration of the environment.

The second type of discourse analysis has a more structuralist character and argues that, in the form of ideas or sets of ideas, discourse (language) becomes a way of knowing the world and, in turn, a way of controlling it. In a series of studies that includes histories of madness, prisons, and sexuality, Michel Foucault (1980, 1988, 1995) illustrates how, through making crime, madness, and sex into objects of scientific inquiry and discipline, the "knowledge" or ideas generated from these inquiries become a vehicle to control action and behaviour.

As ways of thinking and being in the world, discourses become "sedimented," or structured, into institutions and organizations. They become rules and regulations that govern our lives and our ways of thinking, seeing, and being in the world. In this way, words move from being simply ideas to becoming disciplining social practices. Consider how the idea of education, for instance, has become sedimented or structured into particular practices, objects, and institutions, such as classes, textbooks, and schools or universities. In other words, the idea of education has taken form in very specific physical spaces (classrooms), activities (attending lectures), and practices (writing exams and essays).

By this account, we live immersed in discourse, like fish in water, with its invisible currents shaping and determining much if not all of our lives as language, in the form of ideas, takes on a life of its own. At the personal level, larger social discourses frame our ideas, hopes, and desires. Our identities are given form by the discourses of which we are a part: what it means to be male, female, Canadian, and so on. From this perspective, media content can be seen as part of these larger discursive formations, part of the social mechanism through which norms, values, and other ideas about how the world "is" and "should be" are circulated and reproduced.

Critical Political Economy

Working from the Marxist perspective that the media generally support private capital and the dominant interests in society (see Chapter 3), writers in the field of critical political economy have approached the media from a number of directions (see Mosco, 2009). In the 1970s, for instance, Dallas Smythe noted that in contrast to the seeming fact that the purpose of the media is to serve the interests and tastes of audiences—that is, to inform and entertain people—the product from which private broadcasters and newspapers draw the balance of their income is audiences and that the real business of commercial media companies is selling audiences to advertisers. From this perspective, media serve the interests of owners, not the public at large. As he argues,

> The capitalist system cultivates the illusion that the three streams of information and things are independent: the advertising merely "supports"' or "makes possible" the news, information, and entertainment, which in turn are *separate* from the consumer goods and services we buy. This is untrue. The commercial mass media *are* advertising in their entirety . . . both advertising and the "program material" reflect, mystify, and are essential to the sale of goods and services. The program material is produced and distributed in order to attract and hold the attention of the audience so that its members may be counted (by audience survey organizations which then certify the size and character of the audience produced) and sold to the advertiser. (Smythe, 1994: 9)

Taking a somewhat broader perspective in their book *Manufacturing Consent: The Political Economy of the Mass Media*, Edward Herman and Noam Chomsky (2002: 2) argue that there are five political, economic, and organizational "filters" screening the US news media to ensure that the news works in favour of political and economic elites:

1. the concentration of ownership of the media in the hands of a few large private corporations;
2. the media's dependence on advertising as their principal source of revenue;
3. the media's reliance on government and business elites as sources of news and opinion;
4. "flak," or negative feedback from powerful established interests when the news plays against their interests;
5. strong belief in the "miracle of the market" as a means to satisfy social needs and desires. As they argue, the model "traces the routes by which money and power are able to filter out the news fit to print, marginalize dissent, and allow the government and dominant private interests to get their messages across to the public."

Taken together, these conditions under which media operate work to ensure that news content generally works to support the status quo and help maintain the legitimacy of both our form of government and economy.

The political economy of communication has been employed to illustrate how new media technologies are being used to reshape global media industries (Winseck and Jin, 2012); how corporate interest generally overrides the public interest in Canadian telecommunications policy (Moll and Shade, 2011, 2008; Winseck, 1998; Babe, 1990); why the Canadian media are generally dominated by US products (Pendakur, 1990; Smythe 1981); how corporate media generally represent a narrow range of perspectives and opinions (Hackett and Gruneau, 2000); and how political economic factors shape Canadian television production (Druick and Kostopoulos, 2008).

In sum, the main point made by critical political economy is that the larger political and economic relationships that govern society reach down to structure not only the ways in which the media operate but also the ways they represent the world to us. With practice, it is relatively easy

Source: F-61-1-2-0-17 of F-61, the Media and Public Relations Office fonds, Simon Fraser University Archives.

Dallas Walker Smythe (1907–1992) was a groundbreaking Canadian political activist and researcher; his field was the political economy of communication.

to see the "truth" of this perspective. If a privately owned media outlet fails to make a profit, for example, eventually it will likely go out of business, taking whatever ideas or perspectives it circulates with it. Hence, only those television programs that are profitable, or most profitable, get shown. Similarly, as we have discussed, because there is much more money to be made from running US television and film products than there is from screening similar Canadian fare, both the small and large screens in Canada are overrun with Hollywood content. In the face of these factors, governments have taken a number of steps to help ensure that a wide range of ideas and perspectives find voice in this country, including the creation of our publicly funded broadcaster: the CBC/Radio Canada.

It should be noted here that the degree to which media production is actually limited by political economic factors, and how the influence of such factors should be weighed against that of other social variables such as race, gender, and ethnicity, is the subject of much debate.

The Cultural Critique

One of the key strengths of both structuralism and political economy is the way they provide a means of understanding how media content is the product of a larger set of material social circumstances. Indeed, as the encoding/decoding model illustrates, media producers can't just create whatever content they want. The agency of media producers in the production process is guided by a whole set of factors, such as the available budget, professional values or norms, and a host of other social and cultural factors. But while political economy points to economics as the key or overriding determinant in production and the way content is created, other perspectives, such as cultural studies, take a broader perspective (see Chapter 5).

Why, for example, are there more male media executives than female ones? And as we discuss below, why are minorities consistently under-represented or misrepresented in television advertising? How is it that racial stereotypes—often negative (Hirji, 2014)—can be found in news coverage? These are not questions that a political economic analysis can easily answer. Instead, we need to look to perspectives that foreground the way other social factors or determinants, such as gender, ethnicity, and race, influence the ways in which the media and media content represent the world to us. Understanding the ways in which these issues play out in the production of media content and the larger impact that this misrepresentation may have on people's lives is an important element of communications research.

Content Analysis

While it merits our attention here because it is often employed as a method for analyzing media content, *content analysis* is not a theory. Rather, it is used in conjunction with such approaches as

discourse analysis or critical political economy to identify the specific characteristics of media content, such as how particular people, social groups, or places are framed or treated in news stories and what is either included or left out of particular stories or television programs (Richter et al., 2011; Krippendorf, 2004).

Content analysis emphasizes the quantitative aspects of media content, specifically, the number of occurrences of a particular category of phenomenon. For instance, what places (cities, provinces, or countries) are covered in news stories? What kinds of subjects are covered? What sources do reporters quote or draw on in writing a story? Are some politicians quoted more than others? Are some think tanks called on more than others? How often are minorities covered in news stories? How are they covered?

The system of analysis works this way. First, the analyst determines the variables to be measured. Variables may include things like the general subject or theme of a story; the particular people, places, or events represented; whether these things are framed or treated in a positive or negative light; and the sources or experts quoted. The researcher then sets up units of analysis—phrases, sentences, paragraphs, column inches, and so on—and counts these variables and perhaps their relation to other aspects of content, such as pictures or long pieces with prominent placement. On the basis of frequency of occurrence in one or more media products (e.g., newspapers, TV news programs), the analyst can provide a reading of the media treatment of an issue over time.

If you are using a content-analysis approach, then, what has been left out of a story might be just as important to you as what is included. A study by NewsWatch Canada, for example, illustrated that over a six-month period on CBC and CTV television newscasts, "right-wing think-tanks received 68 per cent of all references while left-wing think-tanks received 19.5 per cent" (Hackett and Gruneau, 2000: 204). While these statistics don't tell us what the news stories were about, they illustrate that during the specified

4.2 ▶▶▶▶▶▶

RACIAL BIAS FOUND IN CANADIAN TV ADVERTISING

A study undertaken by Shyon Baumann and Loretta Ho from the University of Toronto–Mississauga found that visible minorities were consistently under-represented and misrepresented in Canadian television advertisements. As Elaine Smith explains,

> Baumann and Ho reviewed 244 commercials to see how frequently and in what way various visible minorities were portrayed. They found that blacks were not underrepresented, based on the percentage of the Canadian population that is black, but the same was not true for South Asians or East Asians. People of Middle Eastern ethnicity and Aboriginal peoples were basically invisible in prime-time advertising.
>
> Meanwhile, whites were disproportionately represented in TV commercials, appearing in 87 percent of commercials although they make up only 80 percent of the population.
>
> In terms of content, the researchers found that blacks, South Asians and East Asians were portrayed using narrow cultural schemas: the blacks as blue collar; the Asians as technocrats. By contrast, Caucasians were represented by four different schemanostalgic, highbrow, nuclear family and natural (outdoorsy, health-conscious), allowing for much more varied expectations of their behaviours and characteristics.

Source: Smith, 2014. Available at news.utoronto.ca/racial-bias-canadian-advertising. University of Toronto Mississuaga

period, right-wing sources were consulted or referred to more than three times to one. Similarly, a content analysis of the online editions of Canada's self-described national newspapers—*The Globe and Mail*, the *National Post*, and *Le Devoir*—showed that their coverage was not national at all, but largely confined to the cities and provinces in which they were based and the activities of federal government institutions (Gasher, 2007). And, in a comparison of their coverage of climate change, Gunster (2011) found that mainstream and independent or alternative media in British Columbia took quite different perspectives.

Other studies illustrate both a general lack of representation of people of colour in mainstream Canadian media, and that when they are represented, it is often in the form of stereotypes (Hirji, 2014; Jiwani, 2010). Similarly, a study of advertising in Canadian television commercials (see Box 4.2) found that visible minorities were consistently underrepresented and misrepresented (Smith, 2014).

In another instance, a content-analysis focusing on the coverage of Latin America in the US press over time revealed that the dominant definition of news—what was most often reported about Latin America—was natural disasters, such as earthquakes and volcanoes. During the 1970s, there was a gradual shift toward a focus on dictators and banana republics. Such analyses are revealing not only in terms of the trivialization of the definition of *news* for an entire region of the world but also in terms of the significant absences—the failure to offer any serious account of the economic, political, or social developments of that region of the world.

As can be seen from these examples, content analysis can be a valuable tool for helping to uncover systematic biases or problems in the ways in which the media represent particular social groups or perspectives.

Genre or Media Form

Another type of analysis that can be used as a complement to any of the above frameworks is derived from McLuhan's notion that "the medium is the message." The presentation of meaning is constrained by both how the medium itself structures and carries content and the genre or content type, of which any particular piece of content is a part.

In terms of the medium, Heyer (2003) illustrates analysis focuses "on a consideration of the properties embodied in the carriers of that content and the influence those properties have on production, transmission, and reception." Genre analysis looks to the way artistic or professional conventions structure or dictate the production and consumption of content. But when examining particular types of content, there is not always agreement on how to distinguish conventions from the influence of the medium (cf. Meyrowitz, 1994).

Take, for instance, the differences between the presentation of news on television and in the newspaper. Although they belong to the same broad content genre—news—the way in which television and newspapers present their content is quite different. On television, the news team focuses on creating compelling visuals and a story that can be told quickly and simply. On the other hand, a newspaper story depends for its strength on elements such as a logical presentation of the facts and thorough analysis. Is this difference a product of the medium (television versus newspaper) or convention (the way in which the journalists choose to present the story)?

A television anchor could present the written text of a newspaper story on television, although the full reading may seem time-consuming and boring for the viewer, compared to the fast-paced visuals of a regular TV news clip. Indeed, online media do often present news in textual form on screen. On the other hand, there are obviously considerable differences between paper and an electronic screen and these differences can have important influences on how information is presented (cf. Heyer, 2003; see also Box 4.3).

In any event, apart from the influence that the medium may have on content, understanding the larger cultural and economic histories of media genres and forms provides important

4.3 ▶▶▶▶▶▶

ON ORSON WELLES'S *WAR OF THE WORLDS*

Paul Heyer has created an interesting text/audio analysis of Orson Welles's *War of the Worlds* controversy. In October 1938, Welles broadcast a radio program that was seemingly a live report of a Martian invasion of earth. Thousands of people mistook the report as real and a degree of public panic ensued. Heyer's work is a media form analysis that discusses the intuitive understanding Welles had of radio as a medium. Heyer's 2003 article covering this, "America under attack 1: *The War of the Worlds*, Orson Welles, and 'media sense,'" is in *Canadian Journal of Communication* 28, 2: 149–65. Or you can access it online at www.cjc-online.ca/index.php/journal/article/view/1356/1421.

insights on both the character of their content and their larger cultural significance.

Soap Operas

Developed at the beginning of the 1930s in the early days of commercial radio, soap operas were a popular cultural form designed to socialize a home-confined female audience with disposable income into the art of consuming, especially household cleaning products (Williams, 1992; LaGuardia, 1977). Today, televised French- and Spanish-language versions—téléromans or telenovelas—are particularly popular in Quebec and Central and South America.

Soaps are one of the most analyzed of all the narrative genres on television. They have been of particular interest to feminist scholars because they are a preferred form of entertainment for female viewers in many countries. Analysis has concentrated on the form and content of soaps and on the pleasures they offer viewers.

Over time, academic perceptions of soaps have changed. At first, they were considered the epitome of that commonly criticized aspect of television that echoes the mass society thesis: trivial, mindless entertainment. Gradually, however, just as the pleasures offered by other forms of popular culture, such as films, magazines, sports, and other television fare were legitimized as valid pastimes, so, too, were soaps viewed in a more positive light (Geraghty, 1991; Radway, 1984).

Music Videos

In a fashion similar to the soaps, music videos emerged because producers wanted to socialize an audience into purchasing their product. The difference between the soaps and music videos is that, with videos, the product to be purchased is part of the promotional vehicle used to bring it to the attention of the audience. Music videos are visually enhanced versions of the recorded music that audiences are intended to purchase. They provide a visual track to the sound recording and sometimes, as in the case of Michael Jackson's groundbreaking song "Thriller," or, more contemporarily, some rap and hip-hop videos, they are highly crafted works of art in their own right.

As media content, music videos give viewers an entry point to popular culture. They provide examples of clothes and accessories to buy, how to behave, what expressions to use, and so forth. In highlighting material for imaginative creation, music videos complement fashion photographs and magazines. Viewers make individual interpretations and inject a dynamism built on popular music, enhancing fashion photographs' frozen-in-time quality (see Goffman, 1959; Fornas et al., 1988). As James Curran (1990: 154) has remarked, "[popular] music is viewed as a laboratory for the intensive production of identity by adolescents seeking to define an independent self." In this vein, researchers often examine these videos to see what subcultural trends they appear to be following or animating, and to assess their role in shaping individual and cultural values (cf. Jhally, 2007).

Reality TV

A genre that has enjoyed increasing popularity over the last 15 years is reality-based television. As a category of content, reality TV encompasses a range of different types of programming,

HOCKEY WIVES

Source: © Bristow Global Media Inc/Mark O'Neill.

Reality TV shows like *Hockey Wives* shrinks the distance between program and audience as seemingly ordinary people (or, in the case of *Hockey Wives*, non-professional performers) become television stars and videos and other material created by non-professionals are used in television programs.

including game shows, talent searches, cooking and food programs, sports, lives of celebrities, talk shows, hidden cameras, hoaxes, and a "day or week in the life" of prominent personalities.

Reality TV sometimes has the patina of a documentary style and focuses on "real-life," unscripted situations. Other times, plot and narrative structure are achieved through editing and/or having subjects participate in contrived scenarios. Other traditional narrative techniques, such as characterization, are achieved through focusing on people with outlandish personalities and jobs or by careful screening and casting of participants.

For producers and television networks, a prime attraction of reality TV is its low cost. With neither expensive actors to pay nor high-priced sets and special effects to create, reality-based television is one antidote to the difficulties presented by today's fragmenting television market, one that has shrinking audiences and ad dollars accruing for individual broadcast stations in the sea of choices now available. Most of the cast members of these programs work for nothing, and the sets or locations require little preparation. Meanwhile, on the decoding side of the equation, reality TV shrinks the distance between program and audience as ordinary people become television stars, and videos and other material created by non-professionals are used in television programs. The relatively recent emergence of this new television genre sparked a range of research into its political economic origins and cultural significance (Baltruschat, 2009; Murray and Oulette, 2004).

Advertising

Perhaps the most dominant and pervasive media genre is advertising. It has profound significance in our market-based, consumer society and animates much of the economy, linking producers and consumers by creating awareness and demand for products and services. Advertising lies at the very foundation of the commercial mass media, financing the production and distribution of most information and entertainment.

For a surcharge paid on consumer products (the cost of ads is built into the cost of products), advertising has become the central means for financing the media. With media like newspapers, television, radio, and websites, as well as cable, satellite, and mobile delivery systems, consumers pay only a small portion, if any, of the cost of content. Rather, the bulk is paid by advertisers, who hope that audiences *pay attention* to the content they sponsor and, more particularly, to the advertising messages that content includes.

Media's dependence on advertising has a profound impact on the content and design of their products. For instance, products are designed to attract audiences from particular demographics or with certain characteristics. Whether we consider a newspaper like *The Globe and Mail* that is tailored to catch the interest of high-income professionals; a magazine such as *Chatelaine,* designed to attract young urban women; or a television station such as *Spike*, geared specifically to young men, the main consideration of publishers and producers is who exactly will read or watch their content. And, by extension, will advertisers pay for the attention of that audience? Consequently, content is tailored to attract particular people.

Similar questions underlie social media. In their quest to monetize, or make money from, their services, companies like Facebook, YouTube, Google, and Twitter have been feverishly working to find ways to generate advertising revenue from their services. In fact, as we shall see in later chapters, the sometimes surreptitious means through which new media organizations are collecting and selling information about users has given new life to the old adage, "If you are not paying for the product (or service), the product is you."

The design of media products also reflects this commercial imperative. Episodic network television programs, which generally have a climax or plot conflict just before a cut to commercial, are written to pull audiences through the ad breaks. After a reader moves past the front page of a hard-copy newspaper, the spreads are generally designed so that the first place readers' eyes fall is on advertising. Online content, too, is increasingly designed to ensure that a viewer's eyes meet with the sponsoring advertisers.

Modern advertising developed over time in conjunction with the growth of mass media, and as Johnston (2010) notes, "the first newspaper published in Canada, the *Halifax Gazette* (1752), contained ads for a grocer, a job printer, and a tutor located in Halifax itself." Advertising as we know it today, however, took form with the rise of contemporary industrial society. From about 1880 through the 1920s, as industry was expanding, workers' wages were increasing, literacy rates were rising, and a consumer society was emerging. It was during this time that advertising agencies were founded and began to

supply industry with creative services and market research. Together, these services helped propel the industry to new heights (see Boxes 4.4 and 4.5).

Because it stimulates demand, advertising is sometimes celebrated as essential to the affluence of consumer society. But it is also criticized as the major impetus behind environmental degradation and shrinking natural resources. The continuous bombardment of flashy and seductive ads is seen as fuelling an increasing array of **false needs**—goods and services that people do not really require—and driving a lifestyle characterized by an escalating frenzy of consumption (Leiss et al., 2005: 83–7). In a world where shopping is celebrated as a form of recreation—sometimes described as "retail therapy"—the

4.4 ▶▶▶▶▶▶

ADVERTISING AND CONSUMER SOCIETY

In a 1930 address to the Association of National Advertisers, US president Herbert Hoover captured the key importance of advertising to consumer society:

> Advertising is one of the vital organs of our entire economic and social system. It certainly is the vocal organ by which industry sings its songs of beguilement. The purpose of advertising is to create desire, and from the torments of desire there at once emerges additional demand and from demand you pull upon increasing production and distribution. By the stimulants of advertising which you administer you have stirred the lethargy of the old law of supply and demand until you have transformed cottage industries into mass production. From enlarged diffusion of articles and services

> you cheapen costs and thereby you are a part of the dynamic force which creates higher standards of living.

> You also contribute to hurry up the general use of every discovery in science and every invention in industry. It probably required a thousand years to spread the knowledge and application of that great human invention, the wheeled cart, and it has taken you only 20 years to make the automobile the universal tool of man. Moreover, your constant exploitation of every improvement in every article and service spreads a restless pillow for every competitor and drives the producer to feverish exertions in new invention, new service, and still more improvement. Incidentally, you make possible the vast distribution of information, of good cheer and tribulation which comes with the morning paper, the periodical, and the radio. And your contributions to them aids to sustain a great army of authors and artists who could not otherwise join in the standards of living you create.

Source: John T. Woolley and Gerhard Peters, *The American Presidency Project* [online]. Santa Barbara, CA. Available at www.presidency.ucsb.edu/ws/?pid=22428.

4.5 ▶▶ ▶ ▷ ▷ ▷ ▶▷

WORLD WAR I AND THE BIRTH OF PUBLIC RELATIONS

As Ira Basen points out, modern marketing has roots in selling participation in World War I to the American public:

> In April 1917, the First World War had been raging for almost three years, but the United States had remained outside the fray. Although supportive of the Allied Powers, President Woodrow Wilson urged Americans to be neutral in thought and action. Public opinion in the U.S. was solidly behind him—Wilson had been re-elected in November 1916 on the slogan, "He kept us out of war."
>
> Five months later, the president had a change of heart.
>
> Persuading Americans to support the war would be a more challenging task.
>
> Within days of the declaration, the president authorized the creation of the Committee on Public Information.
>
> The CPI brought together many of the brightest minds in advertising, journalism,

Source: Library and Archives Canada, Acc. No. 1983-28-826.

Propaganda for World War I in Canada originated in Britain, but by World War II, Canada had established the Bureau of Public Information and the National Film Board to do PR for the war effort.

inevitable outcome is depleted forests, diminishing oil supplies, and global warming.

Today, advertising is a multi-billion-dollar industry. In 2009, advertisers spent more than $12.5 billion advertising their wares in Canadian newspapers and magazines, on television and radio, and in online media. Online advertising is very quickly taking on increasing importance, with revenues rising from $98 million in 2000 to $3.5 billion in 2014. But while online advertising is on the rise, much of it is coming at the expense of newspaper and conventional television advertising, as these media struggle to reinvent themselves in the digital age. In any event, all this expenditure adds up to an environment where we are bombarded with commercial messages. Some writers claim that people living in cities see up to 5,000 ads per day—in the media, on billboards, on posters, and even on personal clothing.

While in its early incarnations, advertising was a way to increase sales by supplementing or making known consumer satisfaction, it has become the means whereby producers create needs, launch products, and maintain sales. Industry has a great capacity to produce, and the health of those industries—and, by extension, our market economy—becomes dependent on consumption keeping pace. Because so much graphic design, academia, and a relatively new industry called public relations.

Within months, Americans had shed their initial war reluctance. Young men were flocking to recruiting offices, and millions were giving money to support the "Liberty Loan" program to help finance the war effort.

The CPI was the largest propaganda machine the world had ever seen. And while its title stressed "information," the Committee's publicists understood that electrifying American public opinion would take an appeal to the emotions, not the intellect.

The CPI's Division of Advertising churned out posters and ads that depicted German atrocities that never happened, played up threats to American homes and families that were wildly exaggerated, and generally appealed to the fears and anxieties that lurked beneath the surface of public consciousness.

All of this was observed with great interest by a young member of the CPI team named Edward Bernays.

Bernays was the nephew of Sigmund Freud and he shared his uncle's fascination with the unconscious mind. But while Freud sought to liberate people from their subconscious drives and desires, Bernays wanted to harness those passions for commercial ends.

His work with the CPI had convinced him that if you could sell war by appealing to images and symbols, then you could do the same thing to sell just about anything.

Bernays returned to New York after the war and set himself up as a "counsel on public relations," determined to put his theories into action.

One of his earliest successes was for the American Tobacco Company. It had hired Bernays to figure out a way to get American women to feel comfortable about smoking in public.

After consulting a colleague of his uncle's, Bernays concluded that women needed to see cigarettes as "torches of freedom" that would help emancipate them from the social taboos imposed on them by men.

He arranged for several young women to walk down 5th Ave. in New York during the Easter parade, smoking.

As Bernays expected, the story made front-page news across the country, and the rest, unfortunately, is history.

Source: Ira Basen, CBC News. Available at www.cbc.ca/news/world/how-ww-i-helped-entrench-the-art-of-mass-persuasion-1.2684519. © CBC

Source: © itchySan/iStockphoto.

Today, advertising is everywhere—even on our clothing.

is at stake, and the constraints of space or time are so great, an astonishingly high investment is involved in the making of advertisements. It is not uncommon for a 30-second television spot to cost more to produce than a 30-minute program. Millions of dollars of production investment in the advertised product hang in the balance. And, of course, there are the residual costs paid to media outlets and actors to have the advertisement seen or heard again and again.

Advertising attempts to create a relationship between particular products and potential consumers. This is particularly important when the products are essentially identical in their basic defining characteristics, such as taste and alcohol content for beer or cleaning capacity for detergent. In their book *Social Communication in Advertising*, Leiss et al. illustrate that over the years, advertisers and marketers have used five basic cultural frames or strategies or to try to build this relationship (2005: 566–8). In the first few decades of the twentieth century, as modern advertising began in earnest, ads were simply a source of information describing the specific characteristics of goods. In the second period (1920–1950), advertising became more symbolic, equating products with "status and social authority." Between 1950 and 1970, the discourse moved to become more "personalized in terms of feelings such as romance, sensuality, and self-transformation." In the 1970s and '80s, advertising began to incorporate lifestyle imagery and "products form the emblems of various group consumption practices." Most recently, although goods themselves remain mass produced, representations of their use have been "de-massified" and consumers are encouraged to use products to promote and enhance their own individualism. Today, one can find all five frames operating in advertising.

There are also different types of advertising. Apart from straightforward broadcast, display and classified ads that market specific products to consumers, four other types are significant. The first includes advertisements for a company rather than its products. Usually called institutional advertising, these ads are designed to propagate a favourable corporate image and promote the virtues of a corporation rather than a particular product or product line. Because environmental concerns are high on the public agenda, today such ads often focus on how environmentally friendly corporations are. Think about how many companies try to portray themselves today as "green," for example.

The second type of advertisement includes those that masquerade as reporting. They have been called a variety of names, including infomercials, advertorials, custom or sponsored content, or *native advertising*. These are stories, photos, and other materials that promote particular products, corporations, or corporate activity. For

4.6 ▶▶▶▶▶▶

LOOKING FOR AD SPACE

As if the space over urinals were not enough, *Time* magazine used escalator handrails in the Metro Toronto Convention Centre to remind people of its existence. ING bank (now known as Tangerine) used the floor of a major walkway serving all three of Vancouver's Seabus, Skytrain, and West Coast Express public transit systems. Some enterprising entrepreneurs, operating seemingly on the wrong side of the law, scattered ads for fake photo IDs on the streets and sidewalks in the nightclub district of Vancouver, and boxers and other athletes sometimes temporarily tattoo their backs and chests with ads that will reach audiences while they are under the camera's gaze.

print publications, they are sometimes written by journalists, but they also may be supplied by companies specializing in this kind of content or written by an employee or agent of the company that is the subject of the article. Television infomercials, programs, and sometimes even news items, which push particular products, are similar to advertorials. As advertising revenue shrinks in newspapers, magazines, and conventional television in the face of competition from the internet and specialty channels, this kind of content is becoming more popular with such media. And as its popularity with publishers and other media producers grows, so, too, does the difficulty in telling it apart from other forms of content (Krashinsky, 2014).

Another type of advertising is **product placement**. Hollywood movies have long had plugs for products written into their scripts. In the 1932 Marx brothers comedy *Horse Feathers*, for instance, there is a famous scene (in bad taste) where Groucho Marx's character, Professor Wagstaff, tosses another character a roll of Life Savers candies when she falls out of a canoe and calls for help. Even though product placement has been happening for a very long time, it is now ubiquitous in movies. Car manufacturers pay big bucks to have their vehicles showcased in action adventure films, such as the James Bond series, and cereal and liquor manufacturers pay to have both visual and oral references to their products woven into film and television scripts.

Finally, a growing form of advertising production is sourced from audience members as companies call on audiences to craft commercials themselves. Frito-Lay, for instance, has run consumer-produced ads on the Super Bowl broadcast for several years and companies such as Starbucks and General Motors have also tried to capitalize on this trend. If nothing else, the hype around such contests itself generates an excitement for the brand and strengthens audience attention to those ads.

The expansion of advertorials, infomercials, product placement, and other forms of promotional content illustrates how the relationship between content and advertising has shifted over the years. Advertising used to be seen as distinct from other forms of content, but as creeping commercialism has become more and more a part of our culture, and competition between media outlets more fierce, the line between advertising and other forms of content has blurred. Now it is increasingly difficult to tell them apart.

At the heart of this promotional culture is the *brand*. As Asquith and Hearn (2012: 246) illustrate,

> The term "brand" is most commonly understood to stand for a distinct form of marketing practice, intended to link products and services to resonant cultural meanings through the use of narratives and images. In recent years, the practices of branding have moved from attempting to directly discipline consumer taste to working more indirectly by constructing a particular ambience for consumption, comprised of sensibilities and values, which may then condition consumer behaviour. A brand no longer refers to a simple commodity but to an entire "virtual context" for consumption. . . . While the object of the logo or trademark was initially to guarantee quality, it has now become the sign of a definite type of social identity, which summons consumers into relationship with it.

In this way, brands can be seen as part of the "de-massification frame" identified by Leiss et al., as consumers are encouraged to assemble a set of signifiers (or brands) to construct their own identity.

Because of its cultural significance, advertising is one of the most heavily studied forms of media content and researchers have approached it from a wide variety of perspectives. Critical researchers like Leiss et al. or Asquith and Hearn look to see the ways in which it is both woven into and animates the broader social and cultural currents of our lives. Others, drawing on the theoretical legacies of literary criticism and semiotics examine the ads themselves to see how they portray race, ethnicity, and gender relations. Still others read through the ads to illustrate how they work to legitimize the capitalist system and maintain the status quo. But, no matter how one reads them, advertisements offer a rich field for social analysis.

4.7

MEDIA CREATING MEANING: POSSIBILITIES AND LIMITATIONS

In drawing on the larger field of social knowledge and events the media are constantly influencing us: they select certain events to bring forward; they create an image of those events; and they create a discourse within which events and issues are defined (see Coulter, 2014; Mills, 2004; Mitchell, 1988). But beyond influencing our view of reality, do the media have the ability to create a reality quite at odds with the facts?

Following the 9/11 attacks on the World Trade Center and the Pentagon and the US invasion of Iraq in 2003, a series of polls conducted in the summer of 2003 in the States found that 48 percent of respondents incorrectly believed that links between Iraq and al Qaeda had been found, "22 per cent that weapons of mass destruction had been found in Iraq, and 25 per cent that world opinion favoured the US going to war with Iraq" (PIPA/Knowledge Network, 2003). No evidence has ever been found, however, to support any of these assertions. In other words, the poll illustrated that the American people were badly misinformed as to the circumstances surrounding the invasion of Iraq. The poll also found that people's misconceptions varied significantly depending on their source of news, with 80 percent of those reporting Fox News as their major source having one or more of these misconceptions, while only 23 percent of those depending on public broadcasting networks (e.g., PBS, NPR) had one or more. More than half of the respondents were found to believe also that Iraq was at some level involved in the attacks—a perception that US intelligence agencies have said is unfounded. Moreover, people holding these misconceptions were more likely to support the war in Iraq. Can the US media be held directly responsible for promoting these misconceptions? The poll provides no direct evidence that they have done so. But it does suggest that the media have done a very poor job of informing the American public on a matter of global political importance.

▶ SUMMARY

In this chapter, we have examined the creation and interpretation of media content, or, as the semioticians say, the process of signification. We considered the use of social theory in this context, and how it provides important insights into how symbols, such as the words and ideas contained in language, are constructed and used to interpret the world of objects, events, persons, and even representations.

The study of representation involves understanding the nature of polysemy, intertextuality, and grounded indeterminate systems. In less technical words, it involves understanding how messages are open to a variety of interpretations, how interpretations depend on other representations, and how there are bound to be a finite but unpredictable number of interpretations of the object, event, or phenomenon being represented.

We examined a number of approaches used to understand and analyze media content. These included theoretical perspectives—such as literary criticism; structuralism, semiotics, and post-structuralism; discourse analysis; and critical political economy—and methodological orientations, such as content analysis and genre/media form analysis. We illustrated theory to show it contains assumptions people make about the relationships between media texts and larger social relationships and forces, whereas the methods were seen as ways of differentiating between or analyzing different kinds of content. Each has particular strengths and draws out various forces playing on content.

Understanding the relationships between media content and different individuals, social groups, and larger social forces is key to understanding the role of communication in our society.

KEY TERMS

connotative meaning, p. 91

content analysis, p. 106

decoding, p. 94

denotative meaning, p. 91

discourse analysis, p. 103

encoding, p. 94

false needs, p. 111

icon, p. 90

index, p. 90

intertextuality, p. 91

polysemic, p. 91

product placement, p. 115

representation, p. 89

rhetoric, p. 92

semiotics, p. 117

sign, p. 89

signified, p. 90

signifier, p. 89

social theory, p. 93

structuralism, p. 99

symbol, p. 117

 RELATED WEBSITES

Advertising Standards Canada:
www.adstandards.com/en
A listing of Canadian advertising codes and guidelines, as well as information and reports on public complaints, can be found at this site.

Media Smarts: www.mediasmarts.ca
Media Smarts provides information and insightful analysis of various media issues, including violence in the media.

Media Education Foundation: www.mediaed.org
This organization specializes in videos about media, culture, and society.

The Semiotics of Media: www.uvm.edu/~tstreete/
semiotics_and_ads/contents.html
A website on semiotics created by Professor Tom Streeter of the University of Vermont.

Theory.org: www.theory.org.uk/lego-hall.htm
Who says that academics don't have a sense of humour? This site offers a respectful play on social theory.

FURTHER READINGS

Hirji, Faiza. 2014. "The colour of difference: Race diversity and journalism in Canada." In *Mediascapes: New Patterns in Canadian Communication*, 4th ed., Leslie Regan Shade, ed. Don Mills, ON: Nelson, 390–408. A good discussion of the representation of race in Canadian journalism.

Hall, Stuart, Jessica Evans, and Sean Nixon. 2013. *Representation*, 2nd ed. Los Angeles: Sage Publications. An excellent introduction to theories of representation and meaning.

Johnston, Russell. 2014. "Advertising in Canada." In *Mediascapes: New Patterns in Canadian Communication*, 4th ed., Leslie Regan Shade, ed. Don Mills, ON: Nelson, 104–20. A good, brief history of the development of the advertising industry in Canada.

Leiss, William, Stephen Kline, Sut Jhally, and Jacqueline Botterill. 2005. *Social Communication in Advertising*, 3rd ed. New York: Routledge. This is an excellent history of advertising and the different ways advertising constructs relationships between people and products.

Media, Culture and Society. This is the pre-eminent British media studies journal, founded in the 1970s by five young media scholars.

Mosco, Vincent. 2009. *The Political Economy of Communication*, 2nd ed. Thousand Oaks, CA: Sage. A good overview of the history and application of the political economy of communication.

▶ STUDY QUESTIONS

1. Use the encoding/decoding model to analyze a popular TV program such as *The Simpsons*. What kinds of shared ideas and social values do the programs' writers draw on to tell the story? Why do you think the writers picked these to include in the program? How do the scheduling and structure of the program reflect the fact that it is a commercial television show?

2. Perform a semiotic analysis of a magazine advertisement for a product (e.g., automobile, cologne) or a company. What are the signifiers used in constructing the ad? What are the signifieds? How do these work together to construct meaning? How many different meanings can be taken from the ad?

3. How do the different elements of the encoding/decoding model work to enable and constrain human agency in the process of communication?

4. Undertake a content analysis of a major news story (the story may be covered over a number of days in a variety of articles across many publications). Who are the major sources quoted in the story? What perspectives appear to have been left out?

5. Find examples of the five advertising *cultural frames* identified by Leiss et al.

6. Do companies like American Apparel exploit young women in their advertising? Be sure to include a consideration of polysemy.

Perspectives on Media and Audiences

What the media are selling, in a capitalist society, is an audience.
— 1970 Special Senate of Canada Committee on the Mass Media

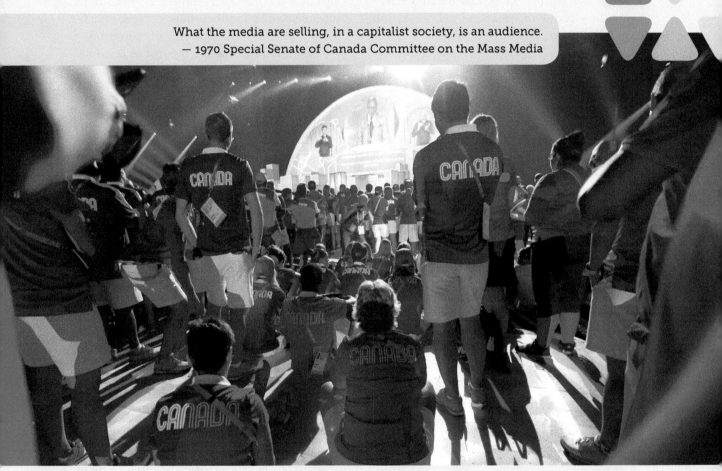

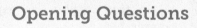

Opening Questions

- How do media relate to their audiences?
- What theoretical perspectives are used to study audiences?
- How are audiences researched?

- What are some of the shortcomings of the media industry's audience research?
- What are some of the concerns associated with social media tracking their users?

Introduction

As we have seen, media weave through our lives at many levels. At the political level, they help frame and animate our understanding of the events and circumstances that define citizenship, how society is organized politically, and our role and purpose in that organization. At the level of culture, media play on our knowledge of particular ways of life, social groups, gender, and racial and ethnic distinctions. They also collude in our understanding of social roles (e.g., mother, father, child, teacher), organizations, and institutions. They address us as fans and devotees of particular media personalities and types of programs. And economically, they position us as consumers. In all these ways, media frame and animate our sense of identity and provide an understanding of ourselves in relation to others and the world. By and large, however, the media address us as audiences—that is, as sets or groups of individuals for whom their content is designed. Media seek audiences: sometimes to inform, other times to enlighten, still other times to entertain, and usually to sell to advertisers or pay a fee for the receipt of content.

With the explosion of new, often interactive media choices, people are gaining more control over the terms of their participation as audience members and able to contribute to media production. In both traditional and new media, user-generated content is providing an expanding part of our media choice. Still, the overarching relation is one where content is designed for consumption by specific groups or types of individuals, generally with a profit motive in mind.

Media audiences are of interest to academic and industry researchers. Scholars and social scientists seek to understand the nature of the interaction between the media and their audiences; what audiences do with media content; how they engage with television, books, magazines, and music; how media influence perceptions and understandings of the world; and how they guide or influence social action.

Members of the industry have a different agenda. They want to know the size and the demographic characteristics (e.g., age, gender, ethnicity) as well as other attributes of particular audiences, such as education, income level, and purchasing patterns, so they can pinpoint the characteristics of the audience or "product" they are selling to advertisers and marketers. Industry members also want to know how audiences respond to audience-building techniques so they can understand how to attract larger audiences or audiences with specific characteristics. Similarly, new media companies such as Facebook and Google want to develop profiles of their users so they can better target advertising to those persons' interests, needs, and desires.

In this chapter, we explore approaches to the audience. It begins with a brief overview of the different ways that audiences have been understood through history, and goes on to consider some of the complexities of the relationships between audiences, media, and culture. We then examine several different academic perspectives on the audience, as well as contemporary industry perspectives. We close the

Ever since the television became a common household item, researchers have been interested in studying how audiences interact with this medium

Source: © LifesizeImages/iStockphoto.

chapter with a critical discussion of some of the shortcomings of industry conceptions of audiences and a consideration of some of the different dimensions of current shifts in the relationships between audiences and media content.

Shifting Perspectives on Audience

Notions of what comprises an audience and the relationships between audiences and different kinds of performances, spectacles, media, and media content have shifted radically over time and can vary dramatically between cultures. Theatre in early Greece, for instance, was both political and intellectual in content, and "'the public was an active partner, free to comment, to be commented upon, to assist, or to intervene' with the on-stage production" (Sullivan, 2013: 11). At the same time, these audiences were also sometimes "'talkative and unruly . . . [sometimes]

disrupting performances by shouting, jeering, throwing fruit, and worse," (Arnott, 1989: 6). By comparison, "Roman theatre was designed for non-political spectatorship" (Sullivan, 2013: 10). And in the declining years of the Roman empire, "Instead of encouraging citizen participation, the goal was to stave off popular rebellion by refocusing the attention of the masses on ritualized violence and entertainment" (Sullivan, 2013: 11). In Shakesepeare's sixteenth-century England, theatre audiences were also noisy and unruly as well as divided by class, with the wealthier patrons seated well above the poorer folks who stood on the ground in front of the stage. On another front, traditional theatre performances in Japan and China might last for hours or even days.

By vastly increasing the number of books in circulation, Gutenberg's printing press helped create a new kind of audience (Sullivan, 2013: 9). With printing, the act of communication between the originator of a message and its recipient(s) became increasingly *mediated*. In other words, it

Source: © koratmember/iStockphoto.

Are cave paintings like this one in Issan, Thailand, a form of mediated communication meant for a specific audience?

was unhinged or disconnected from specific time and place such that "the writer addressed him- or herself to an invisible collectivity of readers who may exist in different locales, historical time periods, and cultural contexts" (Sullivan, 2013: 12).

As we have seen, with the development of industrial society and mass media, such as newspapers, radio, and television, an increasing number of these new kinds of audiences took form. Within the context of the mass society thesis that we discussed in Chapter 3, these audiences were envisioned as large, anonymous, and generally undifferentiated groups or masses (*mass audiences*). They were generally much larger than public gatherings for performances or political events had been previously and, as McQuail (2010: 58) points out, they were seen as having some particular characteristics:

> (The mass audience) was very widely dispersed, and its members were usually unknown to each other or to whoever brought the audience into existence. It lacked self-awareness or self-identity and was incapable of acting together in an organized way to secure objectives. . . . It did not act for itself but was, rather, "acted upon" (and thus an object of manipulation). It was heterogeneous in consisting of large numbers from all social strata and demographic groups, but also homogenous in its choice of some particular object of interest and according to the perception of those that would like to manipulate it.

As advertisers and marketers struggled to better target customers for their products through the mid-twentieth century, however, a more nuanced vision of audiences took shape and they were segmented into particular demographics: groups of a particular age, sex, education, or income level. Industry research focused on finding ways to appeal to these market niches. And, in an attempt to capitalize on the information gathered from this research, through the 1980s and early '90s, marketing combined with technological innovation to create an increasing number of media outlets—from magazines, to newspapers, to cable and satellite channels—devoted to appealing to particular demographics.

At the same time, as illustrated in our discussion later in this chapter of the different academic perspectives on audiences, communication researchers began to take a closer look at the ways in which audiences interacted with media products. In the process, they discovered that media consumption was much more nuanced than had been previously thought. As we illustrated in Chapter 4, advertisers moved to incorporate these findings into their appeals to consumers and, in recent years, a growing number of ads have invited audience members—as individuals—to weave products into their own unique lifestyles (Leiss et al, 2005: 566–78).

Over the last twenty years, digitization and media convergence have been used to increasingly break down the distance between media production and consumption. On television, game shows, such as the CBC's *Canada's Smartest Person*, invite audience members to play along and then post and discuss audience scores on the program. Talent competitions like *The Voice* employ

Jenna Marbles is an extremely popular YouTube sensation. Her channel has over 15 million subscribers.

Source: © ZUMA Press, Inc./Alamy Stock Photo.

audience members to pick winners. Television dramas have enrolled audiences to help pick endings and plot lines. And, of course, internet sites like YouTube allow all members of what was once thought of as the "passive" audience to become media producers themselves. As Napoli (2011: 12) points out, what is particularly interesting about this shift in audience relations is that

> it represents in some ways a return to a conceptualization of the audience that was predominant in the pre-mass media era . . . [when] early manifestations of the audience were very much participatory and interactive. . . . Theatre audiences, for example, once engaged in a wide variety of activities, ranging from singing songs to yelling instructions and insults at performers to yelling at (and fighting with) each other. . . . It was only with the development of electronic mass media . . . that the dynamic between content provider and audience became increasingly unidirectional.

But while new technology has offered audiences increasing choice and participation, as we have discussed in previous chapters, it has also served to fragment audiences. People now watch programs on an increasing range of screens—from laptops to tablets to phones—and, when watching TV, they are often multi-tasking, using their laptops or other devices at the same time. One US study found that 77 percent of people watching TV were also using their computers (Reuters, 2013). **Audience fragmentation** presents a serious challenge to broadcasters, as fragmentation leads to a lowering of the advertising rates they can charge for any one program. To combat this issue, they are working to *reaggregate* audiences across different platforms. For instance, after paying $5.2 billion in 2013 for the rights to broadcast *Hockey Night in Canada*, Rogers announced that in order to maximize the size of the broadcast audience, they would begin streaming games, thereby allowing fans to catch

them on any device that could access the internet. Similarly, to help keep audience attention riveted to particular television programs, producers are increasingly offering online components to their broadcast programs, such as backstories for lead characters, series-themed games, and videos on the making of the program.

But just as interactive media technologies have given audience members more control over the range and character of their media consumption, so, too, have those technologies allowed companies and governments to track the movements and interests of media consumers. Privacy experts warn that this information can make us vulnerable in a number of ways. For example, present and future employers might search out information on our media preferences and online activities to help judge our suitability for particular jobs. Insurance companies might look for clues as to the potential risk we might pose in terms health-care and life insurance. Police forces and governments might examine our purchases and activities to consider the potential threats we might pose to what they define as the public good. This latter concern is particularly chilling in an era when Canada's federal government has taken aim at environmentalists as a possible terrorist threat (McCarthy, 2012).

The character of audiences will continue to shift as new media technologies alter the relationships between the production and consumption of media products. But as we discuss in the next section, how audiences interpret media is not simply a matter of technology.

Making Meaning in Context: Culture, Media, Audience

As they *decode* media content, audience members do not accept all of what they see or hear—regardless of whether that content is the facts of a news story or the general portrayal of society and its values in a film, television show, or novel. Watching television, reading books or magazines, listening to music, and so on are largely casual or leisure activities, and no research has ever shown that the media have the power to induce audience members to act against or outside their will.

Media–audience interaction is probably best thought of as a sometimes energetic, sometimes passive engagement between audience members and the media. Insofar as decoding media content requires audiences to have some understanding of a larger set of social values and institutions, this interaction also takes place at a social or cultural level. From this perspective, audience members, the media, and cultures can be conceived of as a closely woven meaning-generating system.

Let us consider the example of a young woman, home early from classes, who tunes into WWE on TV to find Undertaker and Sting throwing each other around the wrestling ring. No one is home, least of all her brother, who left the television on this channel the day before. Though normally not a fan of wrestling, she is captivated by the spectacle for several minutes. But she quickly finds that the bout is nothing special. "Boring," she thinks, and reaches for the remote.

This example illustrates many of the elements of meaning generation. As our protagonist is confronted with this wrestling program, she immediately recognizes the scene and the characters and can sense if anything appeals to her in this action soap opera directed at young men. She analyzes the material on the screen by interpreting the events in her terms and then reacting accordingly.

Is this interaction complex and multidimensional? Yes. After some consideration, our viewer finds little in the scene that appeals to her. The fact that none of the advertising accompanying the program is relevant to her illustrates that advertisers don't expect it to. The interaction is also mediated by the context, and the choices found in the moment. Were she at a friend's house and the friend wanted to watch, she might stay with the program a while longer. But here at home by herself, she wonders what the other channels have to offer. What's happening on Facebook? Twitter? What is in the fridge? When is her next assignment due? In assessing whether or not to watch, her perspective is framed by her

understanding of the other activities available to her at the time, her knowledge of wrestling, and her interest in the spectacle. The young woman considering her other options, her sighs of boredom, her flopping down on the couch in the first place all are part of the meaning she is making of the situation she is in.

Given these media–audience dynamics, where does culture as an active, meaning-generating system figure in this scenario? Cultural dynamics play themselves out in the young person's vision of herself and the relevance of the program to her. Also, the fact that the program is aired and commands vast audiences is part of a cultural dynamic. Finally, the very scene of these modern gymnasts/gladiators, dressed as stereotypical heroes and villains, heaving each other around in a sensational action theatre, draws on a wide range of cultural ideas and values.

Because the relation between media, audiences, and cultures is based on interaction and is not predetermined, any consideration of the interaction of audience behaviour, media content, and cultural form must take place within a very broad framework—one that has the potential to encompass any and all elements of the interaction. Building on our discussion of the encoding/decoding model in the previous chapter, we can see that audience interpretations of media content derive from at least the following factors: (a) the social background or history of the audience member; (b) her/his current state of mind; (c) the social situation, or context, within which the media consumption is taking place; and (d) the text or content, including the range and character of media options available. Given these criteria, we are able to understand the possible roots of our viewer's behaviour. Nevertheless, a particular part of her individual personality or attitude in that moment might have caused her to behave differently. We cannot know exactly how she will react. (In fact, a quick Google search will quickly illustrate that, although they make up a minority of the fan base, there are many female wrestling fans.) The point of analyzing media–audience relations, however, is not to predict audience behaviour but rather to understand it.

Culture is a key element in this meaning-generating system. The individual's cultural milieu works to help create identity through acting as the reference point to a host of factors. As we have discussed, culture is a set of ideas and values, or way of life, through which people understand and relate to the larger set of organizations, institutions, and relationships among which they live. It is a dynamic derived from the wealth, history, and present-day attitudes and actions of groups and individuals in their respective social milieux. By conducting daily interactions in their social milieu, people generate meaning through a constant process of selection, restylization (or appropriation), and transformation.

The study of audiences can be approached in many different ways. We will examine six academic approaches to the audience: (1) effects research; (2) uses and gratification research (U&G); (3) Marxist analysis and the Frankfurt School; (4) British cultural studies; (5) feminist research; and (6) reception analysis (see also Sullivan, 2013; Napoli, 2011; Murray, 2010; McQuail, 2010; Ruddock, 2007). As with the perspectives on content we examined in the last chapter, the point here is to provide an overview of some of the main ways audiences have been approached by researchers, as well as to illustrate some of the key issues audience research has raised—not to present a comprehensive review of these perspectives.

Effects, Agenda-Setting, and Cultivation Analysis

Early studies of the media following World War I (1914–1918) presupposed media to have direct **effects** on human behaviour and attitudes. Fuelled by the success of propaganda campaigns during the war, which seemed to indicate that the masses would believe almost anything they were told, researchers posited the "magic bullet," "hypodermic needle," or "inoculation" theory of communication, built on the idea that media could inject ideas into people's heads.

This perspective was supported by the social science of the day, which, on the one hand, subscribed to the mass society thesis—which, as we have seen, characterized people, particularly the lower classes, as easily manipulated—and, on the other hand, embraced early behaviourist conceptions of psychology that saw human behaviour as a simple response to external stimuli. The early success of newspaper and radio advertising, which stimulated demand for the growing range of products generated by industry during the interwar period, added credence to this idea.

But while the success of war propagandists and early advertisers seemed to demonstrate that people were easily swayed by media suggestion, studies conducted after World War II (1939–1945) found that the impact of media messages on individuals was weak and, if anything, acted to reinforce existing ideas and beliefs rather than to alter opinions. In a review of effects research published in 1960, Joseph Klapper, a respected media researcher of the day, concluded that "mass communication does not ordinarily serve as a necessary or sufficient cause of audience effects, but rather functions through a nexus of mediating factors" (cited in McQuail, 2010: 457).

Having found weaker effects than anticipated, researchers undertook the task of reanalyzing the relations between media and audiences and began to look for more diffuse, indirect effects. Working in this vein in the early 1960s, Bernard Cohen argued that news "may not be successful in telling people what to think, but it is stunningly successful in telling its readers what to think about" (cited in Croteau and Hoynes, 2003: 242). For example, the front-page headlines of *The Globe and Mail* (and presumably, to some extent, the *National Post* and the *Ottawa Citizen as well*) play a significant role in what questions are asked the next day in the House of Commons, as do the lead stories on the national television news networks. This idea that the media serve an **agenda-setting function**, that they work, selectively, to draw the public's attention to particular events and circumstances, has gained a measure of credibility among media researchers.

Source: © Gruffyddthomas/Dreamstime.com.

▌ What effect do you think large-scale advertising has on the things we buy?

Beginning with George Gerbner in the late 1960s and 1970s (1969, 1977), researchers have also examined the effects of viewing behaviour on people's conception of social reality—a perspective that has evolved into what is called **cultivation analysis**, wherein content is studied for its ability to encourage or cultivate particular attitudes in viewers toward particular people or perspectives (see Sullivan, 2013; Signorielli and Morgan, 1990). For instance, Gerbner's work illustrated that people who watch a great deal of television overestimate the amount of violence in society and tend to have a "bunker mentality" to protect themselves from what they perceive to be a violent world. In spite of the broad acceptance of Gerbner's work, however, certain British studies (e.g., Wober and Gunter, 1986) have not been able to replicate his findings.

Effects analysis, which abstracts the process of communication from its social context and tries to draw a straight line between sender and receiver, has been greatly criticized, essentially because researchers have not been able to identify clear, strong effects from media exposure. Just as the Shannon and Weaver model of communication discussed in Chapter 1 was shown to be too simplistic to account for the many influences on the ways media messages are constructed, so, too, is the effects model not able to illustrate the many influences on decoding. From this perspective, human agency is reduced to a simple reaction to content without consideration of how a larger set of social characteristics and forces (e.g., age, gender, education, mental condition) bear on media reception.

Research on agenda-setting suffers from similar defects. It offers no explanation for how or why the media select what they will cover or what forces might be at play to help sensitize audience receptivity to messages. As the encoding/decoding model outlined in Chapter 4 illustrates, the media draw their material from a larger set of social circumstances. Perhaps the news agenda is set in this context by local, national, and world events. On the other hand, perhaps the agenda is set by public or audience demand, or possibly it is an interaction of media institutions, audiences, and this larger set of social circumstances. In short, the effects tradition of media research raises more questions than it answers.

Moreover, when concerns over media effects are raised, it is interesting who is or is not condemned for putting forward certain media constructions. German film director Leni Riefenstahl, who died at the age of 101 in 2003, was never forgiven for her movies *Triumph of the Will* (1935) and *Olympia* (1938), which portrayed Hitler's Nazis in a heroic and superior light. In contrast, D.W. Griffith, whose *The Birth of a Nation* (1915) portrays African Americans as ignorant and crude, is revered as a film-industry pioneer. Oliver Stone mostly escaped condemnation for his movie *Natural Born Killers* (1994), even though copycat crimes were committed in its wake. Stanley Kubrick, on the other hand, withdrew *A Clockwork Orange* (1971) from circulation in Britain after some of its violence was re-enacted in real life. The debate around such controversial movies, however, often reproduces effects theory simplistically. Little attention is paid to the social circumstances—such as poverty, inequality, racial discrimination, alcoholism, child and sexual abuse, or extreme misogyny—that animate real-life violence.

Uses and Gratification Research

Uses and gratification research (U&G) began both as a response to findings of limited effects and as a reaction to the growing concern, rooted in the mass society debates, that popular culture—the wide variety of new television, radio, and musical content that started to gain

---

5.1 ▶▶▶▶▶▶

THE LANGUAGE OF MOVIES AND TELEVISION

Part of the structuring process of each media form is that it develops a language the audience comes to understand. The following are examples of "languages" that North American audiences have come to learn from watching many hours of film and television content.

- All police investigations require at least one visit to a strip club.
- All beds have L-shaped sheets to allow the man to bare his chest and the woman to hide hers.
- Ventilation systems are perfect hiding places. They reach every part of a building, are noiseless to enter and easy to move along both horizontally and vertically, and no one thinks to look there.

- German accents are sufficient should you wish to pass for a German military officer.
- When alone, foreigners speak English to one another.
- All women staying in haunted houses are compelled to investigate strange noises in their most revealing underwear.
- Cars that crash almost always burst into flames.
- Any person waking from a nightmare sits bolt upright.
- All bombs are fitted with large time displays that indicate exactly when they are to go off.
- You can always find a chainsaw if you need one.
- Having a job of any kind ensures that a father will forget his son's eighth birthday.
- Any lock can be picked easily unless it is on a door to a burning building in which a child is imprisoned.
- The more a man and woman hate each other initially the greater the chance they will fall in love in the end.

Source: Adaptation of "A Sampler of One-Liners and True Facts," by Gary Borders, *The Daily Sentinel* (Nacodoches; Gary B. Borders).

popularity in the 1950s—was undermining or debasing audience tastes (Sullivan, 2013; Blumler and Katz, 1974). Based in social psychology, instead of focusing on the question *What do media do to audiences?* the central question of the U&G approach is *What do audiences do with the media?* The underlying premise was to focus on the agency of audience members and explore their motivations in the active selection of media content. Take, for example, two university students who decide to see an action movie after their last exam of the semester. They are not yet at the theatre to see the film, but a U&G approach already sees the students' activities as relevant. Going to a movie provides a good chance to relax, get together with friends, enjoy whatever is of interest in the movie, and go out for a coffee afterwards to socialize. Movies give people a chance to talk about other, related interests.

In contrast to effects research, the uses and gratification approach is more attentive to audience variables—that is, the orientations and approaches audience members bring to their selection and interpretation of media content. Given its roots in social psychology, U&G has concentrated on the micro (personal) and meso (group or institutional) levels of social existence, with little attention paid to the macro level: the social, ideological, cultural, or political orientations of the audience. Work during the 1980s discussed never-ending spirals of uses and effects in which audience members look to the media for certain kinds of information (Rosengren and Windahl, 1989). Having gained this information, audience members behave in a particular way and then return to the media for further information, and so on. In fact, the two fields—effects research and uses and gratification research—have been growing closer together and are, to a degree, complementary.

But while U&G theory puts more emphasis on agency than does effects theory, it still focuses on abstracting media consumption from the larger social context. Media consumption is reduced to an individual desire, process, or relationship. The influences of larger social factors are not fully explored. Moreover, U&G theory is **functionalist**: that is, it is based on the assumption that media function to serve some kind of audience need, and then researchers set out to discover what that need is. No account is taken of the larger social origins of this supposed need or of how the process of media consumption plays into a larger set of social forces and institutions. For instance, the facts that the leisure time within which media are consumed is a product of industrial society; or that much media content is focused on working to sell products to consumers, are not considered. To put it another way, the larger social purposes of media and how audience uses and understandings of media are shaped by other social conditions are outside the frame of analysis.

Marxist Analysis and the Frankfurt School

Marxism sees society as animated by a set of social forces based on capitalist forms of production (see Chapter 4). Working from this larger frame, Marxist perspectives generally focus on how the media support dominant interests in society, helping them maintain power and control over time. Consequently, Marxist perspectives don't focus on media–audience relations per se and/or on the ways media interact with, or impinge on, the agency of individual audience members. Instead, Marxist critics consider the ways in which media integrate audiences into the larger capitalist system.

One of the most far-reaching and influential Marxist critiques of twentieth-century media and culture comes from a group known as the **Frankfurt School**. The leading members of this group of intellectuals were Max Horkheimer, Theodor Adorno, and Herbert Marcuse; their ideas were formed in the 1920–1940 interwar period (Jay, 1974). At first, they worked at the Institute for Social Research attached to the University of Frankfurt, but when Hitler came to power, because they were Jews and their ideas were fundamentally out of step with fascism, they had to leave Germany, eventually settling in the United States. Adorno and Horkheimer found faculty positions at Columbia University, where they remained until after World War II. In the late 1940s, Adorno and Horkheimer returned, with great honour, to Frankfurt, where they continued to work in the university until the 1970s. Marcuse (1963 [1954], 1964) settled in San Francisco, where he made his major contributions and became an intellectual hero of the counterculture there in the 1960s.

These theorists argued that capitalist methods of mass production had profound impacts on cultural life. Capitalist methods had been applied, in the nineteenth century, to the manufacture of the necessities of life; that is, to material goods like machinery and clothing. As we have seen, beginning in the 1920s—although interrupted by the Great Depression and World War II—capitalist forms of mass production yielded an increasing range of cheap commodities, coupled with reasonably well-paid factory jobs that enabled people to purchase these goods. With the help of advertising, families were persuaded that the acquisition of cars, household appliances, and fashionable clothing and accessories was essential to modern life. New forms of mass communication such as cinema, radio, and photography (in newspapers and magazines), complete with formulaic and commercial content, became woven into this way of life, celebrating and helping integrate people into it. At the same time, these new mass-produced cultural products displaced older, high-cultural forms of leisure and entertainment, such as symphonies, ballet, theatre, poetry, and great literature. Adorno and Horkheimer pooled these developments together under an umbrella term: "the culture industry" (Adorno and Horkheimer, 1977 [1947]).

The Frankfurt School argued that, through such developments, industrial capitalism penetrated deeper into cultural life and began creating a ready-made way of life. Thus, people's wants and desires were both created and satisfied through the marketplace. Building on the concerns of the mass society theorists that industrial society heralded a loss of social and cultural values, Adorno and Horkheimer saw marketers rushing to fill this void with an endless parade of commodities.

But for these theorists, this new way of life was devoid of any deeper meaning or understanding of the world. The pleasures derived from consumption of these commodities lasted only as long as it took for them to come to market. They argued that the distinctions between different makes, models, and brands of everything from cars to toasters are largely illusory and based on quickly shifting styles rather than on substantive differences in their qualities or characteristics. Popular films and music were seen to be simple and formulaic, their plots and rhythms easily recognized and understood. And in the ongoing churn of the market, no lasting relationships or deeper understandings of the world might be made.

From this perspective, culture and the media serve only one master: capital. All culture becomes a product of industrial capitalism and the guiding logic is one of corporate profit. Audiences are fed meanings by advertisers and manufacturers and the possibility of the media acting as a venue for democratic discussion of issues of public concern disappears. Audience members are seen as little more than cultural dupes, or as Smythe (1994: 9) puts it, unpaid "workers" for the capitalist "consciousness industry" who are inexorably drawn, via the media, into a prepackaged world where choice is simply an illusion that supports this domination. (For a critique of this reading of Adorno and Horkheimer, see Gunster, 2004.)

The Frankfurt School members have been accused of cultural elitism and of pessimism. Perhaps most importantly, because they see people as easily manipulated by media, their perspective provides little room for human agency. The audience is simply a tool of the capitalist economy. Today, very few people would suggest that the *culture industry* (a useful term) has the entirely negative effects that the Frankfurt School claimed it did. Nevertheless, the members of the Frankfurt School rightly pointed out the importance of analyzing cultural industry as integral to capitalism and critically questioned its impact and effect on contemporary cultural life.

The issues they addressed have continuing relevance. Since they first developed their analysis, the expansion of elements of the cultural industry has spread the influence of consumer culture throughout the world; from blue jeans to films to Disney-style theme parks, particular cultural icons and narrow cultural expressions are the currency of global culture. The Lord of the Rings movie trilogy, for instance, was an international marketing extravaganza. Indeed, it was so successful that it spawned a sequel trilogy based on *The Hobbit*.

Thanks to TV and the internet, much of the world and the popular adventures it offers seem familiar to us. Because we can all stay in the same hotels, frequent the same theme parks, and buy the same things in the same shops in the same shopping malls at locations around the world, we've all "been there and done that." The trends the Frankfurt School identified years ago pepper the globe today and conjoin us in one grand commercial culture.

British Cultural Studies

British cultural studies began as a reaction to Marxist and other media theories that downplayed the role of human agency and discounted the apparent pleasures of popular culture. The impact of the growing mass culture in postwar Britain, particularly on the working class, was of interest to a number of intellectuals in the 1950s, including Richard Hoggart (1992 [1957]) and Raymond Williams (1958). To advance his concerns, Hoggart established the small post-graduate Centre for Contemporary Cultural Studies at the University of Birmingham, which his colleague Stuart Hall took over in the late 1960s. Hall's work in the 1970s with graduate students in what came to be called the **Birmingham School** of cultural studies was increasingly influential and largely defines what is today known as cultural studies.

Two main lines of development can be identified in the short history of British cultural studies from the 1950s to the present: the analysis of working-class culture, particularly the culture of young working-class males, and then, in response to feminist critiques at the centre, the analysis of young working-class females (Women's Studies

Group, 1978; see also Turner, 1990; McGuigan, 1992; Storey, 1993; Schulman, 1993). A central concern was the use of mass culture, by both sexes, to create and define gendered identities. What clothing you chose to wear, the kind of music you listened to, whether you had a motorcycle or a scooter—these things helped create your image and define your personality.

Instead of individuals being manipulated by the products of mass culture—as the Frankfurt School had argued—cultural studies turned the relationship around. Individuals could take these products and manipulate them, subvert them, to create new self-definitions. The classic study of this process is Dick Hebdige's *Subculture: The Meaning of Style* (1979), which looked at how young, white working-class males created identities for themselves through music: from mods and rockers in the 1950s and '60s through to punk and beyond in the 1970s.

Cultural studies paid particular attention to the ambiguous relationship between musical styles and social identities and to the embrace of black music and the culture of young, black males by young, white working-class males. This trend is captured beautifully in the 1991 film *The Commitments*, based on the Roddy Doyle novel, when the protagonist, Jimmy Rabbitte, assembles a group of working-class Dublin youth in an R&B band and asks them to repeat after him, "I'm black and I'm proud." While cultural studies illustrated that the appropriation of meaning was much more complex than previously thought, it also demonstrated that social forces and institutions worked in complex ways to help reproduce the dominant order. For instance, in his classic study of an English high school, Paul Willis (1977) shows how rebellion against established authority leads working-class youth to working-class jobs.

An important strand in the study of contemporary culture has been analysis of film and television. In the 1970s, the British Film Institute's journal *Screen* put forward a structuralist-inspired analysis of film, arguing that how a story is told (through techniques of editing, visual images, and so forth) controls and defines how it might be viewed. In other words, they argued that the narrative techniques of cinema—often called *film language*—subtly but powerfully imposed their meanings on the viewer, who cannot avoid being "positioned" to see the film in a particular way. The notion of **position** refers particularly to the point of view constructed for the viewer through filmic techniques—that is, how the viewer is "put in the picture." In a classic analysis of Hollywood movies, Laura Mulvey (1975) argued that the pleasures of this kind of cinema were organized for a male viewer and that women (both in the storyline and as objects to be looked at) were merely instruments of male pleasure—objects of a male gaze.

Stuart Hall and his students, undertaking an analysis of how television and other media work, developed a more open kind of analysis. They argued that media content is structured to relay particular meanings—preferred readings—to audiences, but that it is quite possible for audiences to refuse that meaning and develop their own interpretation of what they hear and see (Glasgow Media Group, 1976).

Ideology, Primary Definers, and Negotiated Meanings
The key concept in such analyses is **ideology**. Ideology is one of those words that has had a number of definitions over the years (see Eagleton, 2007; Larrain, 1979, 1983; Thompson, 1980 [1963]). The term is generally taken to mean "a coherent set of social values, beliefs, and meanings that people use to decode the world—for example, neo-liberalism or socialism." There are number of variations on this definition, however, each with its own nuances.

A Marxist interpretation of the term *ideology* takes into account a particular set of ideas, values, and beliefs that support the dominant or ruling class. From the Marxist viewpoint, capitalism promulgates such ideas as "the poor are lazy," "unions and strikes are bad for society," and "capitalism is the only viable economic system." In reality, these ideas can be proven to be not true. There are many people who work very hard for minimum wage, but are by definition still poor. The eight-hour workday and forty-hour workweek were hard-won concessions from industry, largely as a result of union activity. And, there are indeed many ways to organize an economy other than around capitalist relations of production. Still, ideas like this persist and manage to augment the inequality problem in our society. For instance, why is there a growing gap between lower- and higher-income people in our society today? Why have people allowed the average income to stagnate for the last 20 years while high-income earners continue to make more? Why don't the poorer people stand up for themselves and demand better wages, a fairer tax system, and vote for politicians who will deliver these things? The answer, in a Marxist analysis, is ideology—that despite growing inequality, people, particularly those who are poorer, believe that society is fair and/or there is nothing to be done about this state of affairs.

Through accepting these kinds of ideological misrepresentations of social reality, Marxists argue that the working class is prevented from understanding how they are exploited or oppressed and come to accept the values of the ruling class. In other words, through accepting the above assertions as true, people have been lured into a *false consciousness* regarding how capitalist society works. From this point of view, ideology is a way of representing the world to oneself, a set of ideas that one uses to impose order on society and to decide what place different people and groups should occupy in the social order. By presenting versions of social reality that represent the existing order as natural, obvious, right, and just—in short, as the way things are and ought to be—the effect of ideology is to maintain the status quo, or to accept the domination of the powerful over the powerless. Just as accepting the idea that "the poor are lazy" serves to make it appear that people who are poor are deservedly so.

In the face of the social unrest of the 1960s and '70s—the civil rights movement in the United States, the rise of feminism throughout the Western world, and the student movement in

Source: Chris So/*Toronto Star* via Getty Images.

Can talent and other reality-TV competition shows like *Dragons' Den* challenge the status quo? In what ways do they uphold the dominant ideology?

North America and several European countries—some social scientists began to argue that there was more than one form of ideological oppression at play. Not only did ideology keep the workers in a subordinate position but, given these protests, it had also been doing the same for women, people of colour, and other social groups. Through their acts of protest, these groups illustrated that they had started to see through the ideology that had kept them in subordinate social positions and now had their own ideas about how the social world should be structured, and what their positions in that world should be. In other words, they had their own ideologies.

While these protests did have some positive impact on changing the unfair structure of society, to a large part, the existing order, or status quo, has been maintained. Hence, with an eye on this struggle for social power, the question for researchers became *Amid all of these possible competing ideologies, why is it that the one that generally helps keep wealthy white males in positions of power seems to prevail?*

Exploring this question in the British context, cultural-studies researchers argued that British television was a key vehicle in helping reproduce the dominant ideological or value system—loosely understood as a paternalistic, class-based consensus that believed in the monarchy, the Anglican Church, Parliament, and the rule of law, among other things (Hall, S. 1980; Hall et al., 1978). For these researchers, television news and current-affairs programs are major vehicles for reproducing dominant values: powerful **primary definers** (interviewed politicians, experts, military figures) are routinely allowed to frame the issues, express their opinions, and offer interpretations of events and circumstances (Hall et al., 1978). Alternative or oppositional interpretations of events are seldom, if ever, allowed expression. An extreme example of this in Britain was the banning of members of Sinn Fein (the political wing of the Irish Republican Army [IRA]) from British television (see Curtis, 1984; Schlesinger, 1983).

Working from this idea, we can see that news isn't the only culprit here. Television dramas, films, song lyrics, popular novels, and so on can be seen as a set of morality tales from which we are to take lessons in what constitutes desirable and undesirable behaviour. Think about police shows and dramas that underscore that certain kinds of behaviours are bad or immoral. Talent and other reality-TV competition shows tend to perpetuate the idea that hard work and dedication to training or selling a start-up business idea will pay off in stardom and/or big contracts—even though the fact that the number of star-quality or business-wizard contestants those programs recruit demonstrates that hard work and talent doesn't guarantee success.

Moreover, when viewed from the perspective of the dominant ideology, media products and ideas that fail to conform to the values inherent to that set of ideas are often seen to be dangerous and cause negatives effects. Consider, for instance, the range of things that Walmart has reportedly banned from their shelves, including albums by Kanye West, Sheryl Crow, and Marilyn Manson (Kleinman, 2012). It would appear that the work of these musicians doesn't meet with what Walmart executives consider should be the dominant set of social values, or what they see as the dominant ideology.

Despite the fact that media products may reflect the dominant ideology, Stuart Hall (1978) and the cultural studies perspective argue that different people may decode them in very different ways. Indeed, as protesters from the 1960s to today demonstrate, not all people decode either the media or social life in the same way. Depending on their social background (e.g., gender, class, race, ethnicity, culture), they often hold different and/or competing ideas about how the world should be ordered and their place within it. In other words, they articulate meaning differently—although the dominant ideology may be reflected in media products, it doesn't mean that people receiving and interpreting those products must accept that perspective as their own way of looking at the world. (Indeed, just because Walmart executives see some popular musicians as subversive, doesn't mean other people are reading them that way.)

A study by David Morley (1980)—a graduate of the school—was an important step in establishing the Birmingham School perspective. Morley looked at how viewers of a BBC news and current-affairs program called *Nationwide* interpreted or decoded the program. He found, as Hall had suggested, three different responses: *dominant*, *negotiated*, and *oppositional*. Some viewers accepted what was presented in the program at face value, which accented national unity; strong family values; and suggested that Britain was essentially a nation of white, middle-class families living in suburbia. In other words, they accepted the program's preferred meaning. Other viewers, however, took a more critical or negotiated view of the program and did not see it as wholly representing British society; a few groups of viewers (notably young blacks) rejected the *Nationwide* premise altogether.

Spurred by the work of the Birmingham School, from the 1980s to the present day, the cultural-studies approach to media analysis has helped foreground research on how audiences make sense of media products (Barker, 2012; Lee, 2003). Embracing a broad definition of ideology, the approach rejects the strongly deterministic view of the Frankfurt School and the journal *Screen*, instead stressing that media consumption is an active process. It also illustrates how culture is more than simply a range of prepackaged ideas and experiences spoonfed to us by industry and advertisers—it is actually a rich and dynamic field, filled with a complex range of social meanings.

Feminist Research

Like Marxism, feminism is deeply critical of the character of modern societies, which, it argues, are based on fundamental inequalities (de Beauvoir, 1957 [1949]; Friedan, 1963). But where Marxism locates the root of inequality in capital ownership and class division, feminism points to the male domination of society (patriarchy) as the root of profound inequalities and injustices in the world. And, in fact, such inequalities are pervasive aspects of modern life. For instance, a 2010 study found that Canadian women on average are paid about 25 percent less than men (Cool, 2010). Only 3 percent of Canada's CEOs are women, and women graduating with MBAs on average earn $8,167 per year less than their male colleagues in their first year of work (McInturff, 2014). In 2014, only 72 of 370 members of Canada's federal Parliament were women. And men committing violence against women is much more prevalent than the reverse scenario.

Despite the fact that such inequalities have been known and documented for many decades, how is it that patriarchal values continue to hold sway? Communication researchers have studied how media and cultural products can contribute to normalizing the oppression of women and perpetuating these differences. As Kimmel and Holler (2011: 241) point out in their book *The Gendered Society*, the "media are part of a gigantic cultural apparatus that reproduces gender inequality by making it appear that such inequality is the natural result of existing gender differences. First the media create the differences; then

5.2 ▶▶ ▶ ▶ ▶▶

FEMINISM AND MEDIA STUDIES

By Tamara Shepherd

Broadly speaking, feminism describes a range of theories and modes of advocacy that share a concern with the equal rights and treatment of women. Historically, feminism tends to be seen as a series of movements or waves, which describe critical moments of ideological and political struggle. Within these waves, diverse forms of media have played a central role both as tools for furthering feminist advocacy and as battlegrounds for conflicts over gendered representation.

The first wave describes a period around the late nineteenth and early twentieth centuries, when women famously fought for and eventually won the right to vote. Women's suffrage, which can be traced to earlier proto-feminist texts in literature and philosophy, was the issue that served to crystallize concerns about women's status in education, property ownership, and marriage. Correspondingly, it was print media that played a key role in translating feminist ideas into protest activities, with feminist periodicals and pamphlets serving to articulate the political agenda of suffragettes in a largely male public sphere. Print, along with some early silent films, contributed to the media framing

Source: © Philip Scalia/Alamy.

of feminism as a collective identity, thereby facilitating collective action.

For media studies, feminism's second wave becomes even more salient, as it coincides with other political struggles around representation and rights between the 1960s and mid-1970s. Ideologically, second-wave feminist thought drew from contemporary philosophical currents in psychoanalysis and Marxism to critique the imaginary "ideal woman." This ideal woman was represented widely across popular media forms, especially in advertising, magazines, cinema, and television. Critiques of such representations helped form the basis for activism, where feminist protest took shape around issues such as pay discrimination and reproductive rights.

Starting around the 1980s, the more radical strains of the second wave helped plant the

the media tell us that the inequality is the natural result of those differences."

As Tamara Shepherd details in Box 5.2, feminism is often seen as a series of waves or movements, each with its own relationship to media and media studies. This section provides a very short review of some of this work as it relates to the second and third waves. For instance, as part of what Shepherd describes as the second wave of feminism, Judith Williamson's (1978) groundbreaking work, *Decoding Advertisements: Ideology and Meaning in Advertising*, examines how advertising plays a central role in promoting ideological perspectives that perpetuate gender stereotypes. And, following in this vein,

Jean Kilbourne's Killing Us Softly video series documents how television and print advertising provides distorted perspectives on femininity (Media Education Foundation, 2010).

In later work, feminist researchers developed the idea of gendered narratives, exploring how some types of stories (narrative genres) appeal or speak to male readers or viewers while other types appeal to female readers and viewers (Radway, 1984, is the key text). David Morley (1986) studied TV viewers in family settings and discovered a consistent profile of male and female preferences. One principal program category was television soap operas, with their largely female viewing audiences, and many studies have since seeds for the third wave. Here, feminists worked to extend the critique of patriarchy to consider how it oppressed other social groups based on race, ethnicity, ability, and sexual orientation. Taking cues from postmodern and post-structural theory, the third wave sees identity as a more multiple and fluid concept, meaning that stereotypical media representations of race and gender needed to also be critiqued in terms of how they help perpetuate forms of discrimination under white capitalist patriarchy.

Yet at the same time that the third wave expanded considerations of gendered discrimination, popular news media mounted a conservative backlash against the radicalism of the second wave. Sensational depictions of second-wave feminists as "bra burners" and "man haters" were common as conservatives attempted to reverse women's flight away from the home and into the workforce. Simultaneously, some strains of media studies shifted their focus toward lowbrow culture and domestic audiences, offering feminist analyses of previously vilified cultural forms, such as television talk shows and romance novels. Rather than critiquing the producers of stereotypical media texts, feminist studies of popular audiences identified moments of pleasure, community formation, and identity construction within women's domestic consumption of popular media, arguing that these everyday experiences were politically empowering. This latter strand of third-wave feminism is still dominant today.

From this vantage point, the current *post-feminist* movement is seen as incorporating feminism into dominant power structures of patriarchal capitalism. Coinciding with a neo-liberal focus on the individual (rather than the collective) as the primary unit of political agency, post-feminism champions a woman's individual choice as ultimate empowerment. Consolidated in popular music through acts like the Spice Girls and television programs like *Sex and the City*, the late-1990s post-feminist boom saw feminism as a taken-for-granted position that no longer needed to be fought over since women were now fully "equal," at least in Western society.

Yet, women and other marginalized groups are, of course, not treated equally. Patriarchy still dominates most places in the world, and so the message of earlier waves of feminism continues to be crucial for creating new representations and new forms of political action. What appears to be an impending fourth wave of feminism has not yet manifested into a coherent movement, but related theoretical perspectives such as queer, disability, and postcolonial studies point toward the ways in which feminist media studies have helped sustain the critique of structures of dominance in the production and consumption of print and electronic media, moving images, and new media technologies.

Tamara Shepherd teaches on politics and communication in the Department of Media and Communications at the London School of Economics and Political Science.

examined what women enjoy in such programs (Seiter et al., 1989). As Kimmel and Holler (2011: 241) illustrate, today's media markets reflect these differences: "There are women's and men's magazines, chick flicks and action movies, chick lit and lad lit, pornography and romance novels, soap operas and crime procedurals, guy video games and girl video games. Blogs and zines—and, of course, advertising that is inextricably connected to each of these formats."

As Andrea Press (2000: 28–9) observes, **feminist research** approaches the media from at least three, sometimes overlapping, dimensions. The first looks at "feminism, difference and identity" and "highlights the experiences of those

who have remained unheard and gives voice to that which has remained unspoken." Here, analysis focuses on how media representation and social discourse override or frame out particular perspectives and voices. A second strand of research, "feminism and the public sphere," emphasizes the "role of the media in facilitating—or hindering—public debate," particularly in terms of "giving voice to those previously unheard, such as women, under-represented groups, and others whose ideas have not previously entered public debate." For instance, in the new media field, Shade (in Grossberg et al., 2006: 291) points out, "There are tensions in gender differences, whereby women are using the Internet to reinforce their private lives and men are using the Internet for engaging in the public sphere." The third dimension, "new technologies and the body," considers "broader questions about media, technology, and the relationship of both to the body" (Press, 2000: 29). Recent research has also focused on *cyberfeminism*, which, as Gajjala and Oh (2012: 1) point out, covers "how power plays out not only in different locations on line but also in institutions that shape cyberspace."

At a more general level, contemporary feminist media scholarship examines how media consumption is woven into the fabric of everyday life, how media products and institutions are both shaped by and give form to particular perspectives and ideas on gender and sexuality, and how women and other social groups deploy media, along with other facets of their experience, to make meaning of their lives (cf. Gajjala and Oh, 2012; Sarikakis and Shade, 2008; Hermes, 2006). As Sawchuk (2014: 73) illustrates, feminism has proven itself over the years to be "not simply an extraneous add-on to the media agenda, but intrinsic to the study of communication." Moreover, as she also points out, with its attention to the ways social relations spin unequal relations of power, it has also been key in

helping develop other important critical perspectives on communication such as queer theory and critical race studies (2014: 72–3).

Reception Analysis

In the 1980s, cultural and feminist studies of the mass media increasingly looked at how audiences made sense of cultural products, how they interpreted what they read, saw, and heard. But it became apparent that to do this, it was necessary to attend not simply to the product itself (the novel, the film, the TV drama), but also, more generally, to the context in which the consumption of the cultural product took place. **Reception analysis** thus takes into account the social setting in which audiences respond to the products of contemporary popular culture. In this way, it is somewhat similar to uses and gratification theory. However, rather than emphasizing what use or gratification an audience member gains from media exposure, reception analysis focuses on how he or she actively interprets what the media text has to offer and how media consumption is reintegrated into the personal dimensions of her or his life. As Gray (1999: 31) puts it, this work "place[s] media readings and use within complex webs of determinations, not only of the texts, but also those deeper structural determinants, such as class, gender, and . . . race and ethnicity. These studies have also shed light on the ways in which public and private discourses intersect and are lived out within the intimate and routine practices of everyday life."

Reception analysis has been of particular interest to feminist scholars in a number of ways. For instance, when US researcher Janice Radway studied American women readers of romantic fiction, she found that they emphasized how the activity of reading became a special, personal time when they left behind domestic chores and responsibilities to husbands and children, and

Source: © Lise Gagne/iStockphoto.

Reception analysis looks at the social setting in which audiences respond to the products of contemporary popular culture. The dynamics of power relations between males and females, parents and children, and older and younger siblings have been studied in relation to, for example, who has access to the remote control.

5.3 ▶▶▶▶▶▶

FAN STUDIES

By Steve Bailey

One important recent development in the study of media audiences has been the development of the distinct field of "fan studies" that emerged in the 1980s and '90s. Fan studies has roots in a number of earlier scholarly perspectives in the study of communication and culture, most notably work in the British cultural studies tradition. Scholars such as Paul Willis and Dick Hebdige became interested in the role that passionate attachments to forms of media culture played in the composition of a social identity and in the behaviour of individuals with such deep interests in particular performers, programs, and other cultural objects. Hebdige, for example, looked at the ways that subcultures formed around appreciation for certain styles of clothing or genres of music. Another important influence was the work of literary scholar Janice Radway, author of *Reading the Romance*, who studied avid female readers of romance novels, a genre considered to be of low quality and little interest by mainstream work in literary studies. The recognition that this mode of consuming mediated messages required specific forms of research and had distinct characteristics was then extended into a recognized field of fan studies. Part of this effort was designed to move the study of fandom way from one that view fans as pathological or stereotypically obsessive in their interests and study them as manifestations of one segment of a larger audience community.

Scholars of media fandom, or "fanthropologists" as they are sometimes jokingly called, tend to rely on research methods associated with anthropology and qualitative sociological approaches, especially ethnography. They often study fans in natural social situations, such as concerts, fan conventions, or other social gatherings and tend to favour methods such as interviews and detailed questionnaires to gather data on fan behaviour. Increasingly, scholars of fandom have examined a range of "secondary texts" produced by fans, such as fan fiction, artwork inspired by a particular cultural object or performer, and other forms of cultural production. The crucial work in the development of fan studies was Henry Jenkins's 1992 book *Textual Poachers*, which explored these types of activities in considerable detail. The creative work of fans

Dressed as Stormtroopers from the Star Wars movies, a man and his son attend Fan Expo, a three-day conference for sci-fi, anime, and horror show lovers held in Toronto.

Source: The Canadian Press/*Toronto Star*—Tara Walton.

is analyzed to help understand how they relate to the objects of their interest and passion and to make better sense of the importance of fandom in the development of worldviews, forms of identity, and social behaviour. This area of fan research has become increasingly intertwined with scholarship examining "participatory culture," which involves the examination of a variety of forms of cultural consumption that involve productive activities on the part of consumers, such as recording comical "filke" songs that parody mainstream culture or performing unauthorized modifications of commercial video games.

Most recently, scholars of media fan cultures have focused a great deal of attention on the impact of the internet on fan communities. The rise of virtual culture has allowed for the formation of large international fan communities connected through websites, email lists, and other forms of new media communication. This technological shift has greatly expanded the number of individuals who participate in some form of fan culture and has also allowed for the development of a wide range of cultural practices, such as the making and distribution of video and audio mash-ups of popular culture, works by fans. An important early work in this area was Nancy Baym's 2000 book *Tune In, Log On: Soaps, Fandom, and Online Community*, which examined the use of the internet by soap opera fans, and has continued in the work of a number of contemporary researchers.

Steve Bailey is author of 2005's *Media Audiences and Identity: Self-Construction in the Fan Experience*. New York: Palgrave Macmillan. Reproduced with permission of Palgrave Macmillan.

created a time and space for themselves and their own pleasure. They saw it as a moment of self-affirmation (Radway, 1984). This discovery points to the importance of attending to what lies outside the cultural products themselves. The meaning of romance fiction for Radway's readers was something more than the form and content of the stories themselves. Instead, meaning was found in the ways that the act of reading resonated with other important elements of their lives.

In the same way that Radway examined romance reading, work was undertaken on how family members use radio, TV, newspapers, magazines, video players, and satellite dishes. It showed that these media can be used for a range of purposes that have little to do with their content. Parents may watch a TV program with a child to nourish their relationship rather than to learn what the program is about. The dynamics of power relations between males and females, parents and children, and older and younger siblings have been studied in relation to, for instance, who has access to the remote control for the TV or who can record programs (Morley, 1986). Here, the attention is directed toward what the audience brings to a viewing or decoding, the social context, and the act of viewing. Women, for instance, often juggle television watching with domestic chores. Children often play while watching TV and look up only when their ears tell them that the plot is thickening. Men often watch programs not of their own choosing. In some families and at some times, a switched-on television functions as a conversation stopper or mediator, rather than as a source of watched programming (cf. Bryce, 1987; Modleski, 1984)

British media scholar Paddy Scannell (1988) has analyzed the manner in which broadcasting works at the level of individual audience members to sustain the lives and routines of whole populations, while researchers Roger Silverstone (1981) and John Hartley (1987) have discussed how television provides the basis for symbolic participation in a national community, or sometimes, as in the cases of Belgium, Switzerland, and Canada, an international linguistic community.

More recently, researchers have begun to explore how new media are changing people's perception of themselves, offering new avenues for identity formation. For instance, through a series of case studies, Sherry Turkle (1995) illustrates how computers, with their access to chat rooms, online games, and other web offerings, are providing what Andrea Press and Sonia Livingstone (2006: 189) describe as "a more malleable notion of 'self.'" Similarly, as Sullivan (2013: 182) points out,

> technologies such as computers, iPods, mobile phones, and portable media players have enabled children and parents to carve out personalized media environments for themselves within the same physical space, often to the detriment of family time and face to face relationships. Instead of engaging with one another, we are increasingly engaged with people, events and ideas outside the four walls of the home. Sociologist Anthony Giddens argues that this effective collapse between the public and private realms is one of the hallmarks of our modern way of living. However it also poses new challenges to traditional notions of privacy, safety, and security offered by the very notion of "home."

Thus, from the perspective of reception analysis, an "audience" is not so much an identifiable group transfixed on a particular text or program as it is a variable set of individuals, whose lives (and conceptions of the meaning of media consumption) are structured between media texts and the shifting dimensions and determinants of their own lives (see Box 5.4). In other words, from this perspective media are seen as one element in a larger set of institutions, technologies, and discourses that provide the means through which people live their lives.

As media become increasingly mobile, and both places and forms of reception increasingly diverse, it will be interesting to see how these shifting contexts of reception influence how we understand both media and our relationship to it.

Industry Audience Research

While academics have had their own reasons for studying mass media audiences, media institutions themselves have long been keenly interested in finding out what people read, listen to, and watch. This information has obvious economic value: the more precise the information they have about their audiences, the greater the possibilities to sell these audiences to advertisers.

Traditionally, such research concentrated on audience size: the bigger the audience for a television program, the more attractive it would be to advertisers. But since the 1970s, industry researchers have tried to provide more accurate information about what kinds of viewers are attracted to which programs. Such information can be particularly valuable. For instance, a program may not reach a mass prime-time audience, yet it may have a strong viewership among young, affluent professionals. That program may then command premium prices on advertisements—more than the ads on the program with the larger audience.

Audience attributes other than simple purchasing power can also be attractive to advertisers. For instance, for the makers of Barbie, an audience of prepubescent girls and their mothers is of great value. As Sullivan (2013: 98) notes, increasing pressure to target-specific people has led to even more refined techniques for segmenting audiences, such as *psychographics* and *lifestyle measurements*. Psychographics "refers to the general association of personality or psychological traits with groups of consumers" (Sullivan, 2013: 98). Lifestyle measurements "define a group of individuals according to their product and media consumption habits. . . . Individuals might be classified as 'frequent travelers,' [for example] if they make more than four airline trips per year" (Sullivan, 2013: 98).

Such segmentation has been given impetus by the explosion of new broadcast channels.

(Targeting broadcast audiences with very specific demographics is called **narrowcasting**.) Over the last 30 years, the number of television channels available to Canadian audiences has mushroomed from less than 20 to hundreds. This has led to severe **audience fragmentation**, as viewers have been scattered across this expanding television landscape; the increasing draw of the internet has also further fragmented the audience. In 1969, 35 percent of the English-speaking television audience watched the CBC while 25 per cent watched CTV. By 2011–2012, the CBC share had fallen to 5.5 percent, and, together, CTV, Global, and other non-specialty channels garnered about 25 percent of the viewing audience. This increasingly fragmented audience has given rise to increasingly innovative techniques for tracking and targeting potential customers.

As we discussed at the beginning of this chapter, the reality of fragmented audiences has put also pressure on broadcast companies to find innovative ways to reach large numbers of people. This has led to concentration of media ownership as companies work to reach or re-aggregate audiences by owning a number of different television channels or media outlets. We will examine this phenomenon more closely in Chapter 9. But for now you should note that in Canada, audience fragmentation has also led to vertical integration among media corporations, as cable and satellite distributors have been purchasing television networks and specialty channels in an attempt to help distribute the cost of programming across different broadcast outlets. Similarly, the proliferation of mobile media has also motivated telecommunications companies to acquire broadcast properties, as they strive to obtain content for the new mobile services they are offering. These are some of the reasons behind both Rogers' and Bell's acquisitions of broadcast properties in recent years.

Three concepts or measures are commonly used to gather data on how many people are watching or listening to particular programs:

1. **reach**: the number of audience members available during a particular program period;

2. **share**: the percentage of the audience *reach* who are watching a particular program during a specific time period; and

3. **viewing time**: the number of hours spent viewing during a day, week, or longer period of time.

Share is generally the most important statistic, as it describes what percentage of the available audience is tuned in to a particular program.

But while such ratings measure the number of people watching or listening, they don't provide information as to why people tune in particular programs. As Savage (2014: 137) illustrates, this information is usually gathered through three methods: *surveys*, *focus groups*, and *program tests*. All three methods can be used either before or after programs have been broadcast. Research undertaken before or during production is sometimes termed **formative research** and can provide insight into how to tailor scripts, staging, or other program elements to increase audience appeal. **Summative research** is done after a program's completion and provides some measure of effectiveness at meeting audience interests and concerns (Withers and Brown, 1995).

Diaries and Meters

Traditionally, media consumption was measured by means of diaries kept by audience members, in which people made notes about the TV or radio programs they followed. In 1993, BBM Canada (formerly the Bureau of Broadcast Measurement) introduced the *people meter*, an electronic device that sat on top of televisions and measured audience viewing habits. The meters showed that audience members were spending less time with media than they reported in the diaries. Because of this, ad rates needed to be readjusted. In 2009, BBM introduced portable people meters that track audience members through recording inaudible codes embedded in broadcast programming.

While audience research measurement techniques for broadcast programming are growing more sophisticated, it is also becoming increasingly difficult to track people as they move between different media, and particularly to online program distributors such as Netflix, YouTube, and Apple TV. Without such information, neither industry nor government agencies like the CRTC can rigorously measure or understand the impact these services are having on Canada's mediascape.

Patterns of Consumption: Audience Choice or Industry Economics?

Understanding television consumption is important if policy-makers are to ensure there is an ongoing presence of homegrown television products available to Canadians in the current shifting technological environment. Research illustrates that despite the growing presence of computers and the web, per-person television viewing actually increased on average from about 22 hours per week in 1994–1995 to 28.2 hours per week in 2011–2012 (CRTC, 2013). As Figure 5.1 shows, however, foreign programming dominates English-language television. On mainstream privately owned television networks, only 38.5 percent of the programming watched by audiences is Canadian in origin. Over 60 percent of

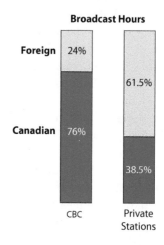

FIGURE 5.1 English-Language Conventional TV and Canadian Programming: Percentages

Source: © 2009 Numeris.

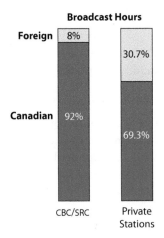

FIGURE 5.2 French-Language Conventional TV and Canadian Programming: Percentages

Source: © 2009 Numeris.

the programming viewed is foreign. On the CBC, on the other hand, 76 percent of the programming viewed is Canadian. Alternatively, Canadian programming is by far the dominant form on French-language television, taking up 92 percent of viewing time on SRC and 69.3 percent on private stations.

As we've seen in previous chapters, this disparity is at least in part the product of the economics of the Canadian market. Because US producers recover much of their cost in their home market, Canadian rights to popular US programs can be purchased for approximately one-third of the cost of rights to Canadian programs (CBC, 2003: 2). Partly because they are more aggressively marketed than their Canadian counterparts, the most popular US programs also attract larger audiences and fetch higher advertising rates than Canadian shows. It isn't surprising to know, then, that US programming in English Canada is much more profitable for broadcasters than original Canadian programs. Consequently, private broadcasters much prefer scheduling US programs over Canadian programs. It is important to note that this is not because US programs are necessarily better quality, or because anglophone Canadians

prefer US programs over Canadian ones. Instead, the preponderance of US programs is simply due to the fact that it is much cheaper for broadcasters to use US programming over Canadian product to build audiences to sell to advertisers.

The CBC also exploits this disparity in cost and sometimes schedules popular Hollywood films and US comedy series. Rather than putting the profits from foreign programs in the pockets of private shareholders, however, all of that revenue is spent in the public interest for programming and running the public broadcaster's operations. Because of linguistic and cultural differences, audiences in French-speaking Canada are less interested in, or tolerant of, US programs, and they generally prefer content that reflects local perspectives on the world.

Some Limits of Industry Audience Research

Conducting traditional audience research that focuses on measuring the size and demographic character of viewer groups has its limitations, particularly when it comes to understanding the needs and desires of target viewerships. While it tells producers how successful they have been in reaching particular types of people, it offers little understanding of the ways media engage audiences with their social and political environments. True, their demographic characteristics may be known and their degree of attentiveness estimated, but because audience members are not conceived as citizens who might benefit from, or even require certain information to help them make informed social and political decisions, the range of media content offered is limited. For instance, some of the kinds of questions industry audience research does not address in this regard include the following: *Do the media in general impart values that reflect the ideals of society and contribute to its improvement and survival? Do they adequately inform citizens about domestic and international affairs? Do they allow us to see our own achievements or to know about ourselves so that we understand how we can make a contribution to society?*

Such questions are important because the greater use that society and individuals make of the media, the greater are the media's responsibilities in informing people of the larger political, economic, social, and environmental forces that contextualize their lives. If audiences are seen only within limited frameworks (e.g., to be entertained but not enlightened), then the media's contribution to society is limited. Moreover, access to the media—particularly television—is increasingly costly, leaving many people with reduced access, particularly in terms of Canadian programming. As we illustrate in Chapter 8 with our discussion of the cultural industries, such questions are particularly relevant in Canada, where media have been traditionally viewed as performing important public functions. Reducing

media to a simple calculus of the marketplace serves to undermine our knowledge and understanding of the many dimensions of public life, as well as our abilities to participate in it.

Public Broadcasters

Both commercial media outlets and public media institutions conduct audience research. However, while private media are primarily in business to make money for their shareholders, public broadcasters, such as those in Canada, Britain, and Australia, carry a much broader set of responsibilities. Under the terms of the 1991 Broadcasting Act (Section 3m), for example, the CBC is mandated to offer a range of "predominantly and distinctively Canadian" programming that "informs, enlightens, and entertains," while

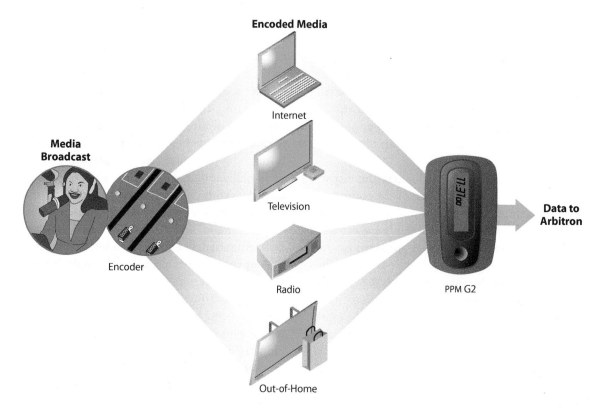

FIGURE 5.3 How PPMs Work

The portable people meter (PPM) can determine what consumers listen to on the radio; what they watch on broadcast, cable, and satellite television; what media they stream on the internet; and what they hear in stores and entertainment venues.

Source: © Arbitron, Inc.

"actively contribut[ing] to the flow and exchange of cultural expression." In order to meet such responsibilities, public broadcasters need to better understand their audiences than their privately owned cousins. Consequently, they have often had to do their own audience research.

In Britain, for instance, the BBC had set up its own listener research department by 1936 to answer questions about listener habits and preferences, such as when people get up, go to work, return from work, and go to bed. The same department took responsibility for television once it was established.

In Canada, the CBC attempted to use commercial audience research services for years, although it realized their shortcomings (Eaman, 1994). The most obvious example of their failings came in the form of the ratings of a CBC radio station operating out of Watrous, Saskatchewan. Even though it was well-known that this station had a listenership throughout the Prairies, and even into British Columbia, surveys carried out by Elliott-Haynes showed the audience share to be almost zero. The main reason for this inaccuracy seemed to be that only urban areas were surveyed, and within a limited time period via telephone. Later work showed that the CBC in Watrous was the most listened-to station in Saskatchewan. By 1954, the need for high-quality audience research for public broadcasting had become increasingly urgent. Moreover, the conceptualization of what information was needed had advanced beyond audience share to qualitative information. So, following the lead of the BBC, the CBC set up its own research department.

5.4 ▶▶▷▷▷▶▶

MEASURING MUSICAL TASTES

Industry research employs program categories to help measure the popularity of different types of music. Such categories allow for greater precision in assessing the success of particular genres of music in attracting listeners and fans. They also demand that music programmers conform to the categories that are measured, however, making it difficult for artists who mix or cross these genres to get airplay. For example, even though she was very successful in selling records, because her music did not fit neatly into industry program categories Canadian music legend k.d. lang found it very difficult to get her songs played on the radio early in her career (Seigenthaler, 1989).

Popular music is divided into the following categories on commercial radio (those listed here are categories revised in 2010, and are contained and elaborated on in CRTC Broadcasting Regulatory Policy 2010-819):

Content Category 2—Popular Music

This encompasses musical selections in the genres or groups of genres set out below:

Content Subcategory 21: pop, rock, and dance
Content Subcategory 22: country and country-oriented
Content Subcategory 23: acoustic
Content Subcategory 24: easy listening
Content Category 3—special interest music
Content Subcategory 31: concert
Content Subcategory 32: folk and folk-oriented
Content Subcategory 33: world beat and international
Content Subcategory 34: jazz and blues
Content Subcategory 35: non-classic religious
Content Subcategory 36: experimental music

Today, video-sharing sites like YouTube help some artists break through such barriers, although they do little to help them overcome the economic disparities between the Canadian and US media markets (see Chapter 8 for more about this).

Eaman has summarized the types of research undertaken by the CBC over the years. These include

- the impact of cable on television viewing;
- critiques of other studies;
- indirect indicators of audience demand;
- program balance analysis;
- analysis of Canadian content and gender roles;
- research on audience maximization;
- audience composition;
- special broadcasts audiences;
- audience behaviour, or how often people listen to and/or watch what and when;
- habits and interests of certain age groups;
- comparisons of certain audiences to the general population;
- audiences' opinions of programs;
- opinions of what programs should be broadcast.

The Transforming and Vanishing Audience: Opportunities and Risks

Because people today have more and more choice between different types of media, and they also find growing degrees of interactivity in these media, conceptions are changing of both media and audiences. As we have seen, television is becoming interactive, as game shows allow audiences to play along with onstage contestants, and dramas provide apps that extend and develop characters and storylines. Audiences increasingly access sports programs from a range of devices. In some cases, they can even choose the camera angles they watch games from. And adding yet another dimension to the experience, social media sites like Facebook and Twitter provide venues for kibitzing about particular plays, players, and statistics.

On the web, the distinction between producer and audience is particularly blurry now that it's commonplace for people to upload video and create blogs, podcasts, games, webcam sites, and other material for public consumption. With these interactive forms of media, the audience "vanishes," drawn up into the content itself. This is, of course, particularly true on social media such as Facebook, Pinterest, and Twitter, where the content is mostly created by users. (While still a popular place to upload video, YouTube is looking increasingly like traditional television, as both individuals and large corporations stock the site with their own *channels*, complete with commercials and audience research that draws upon traditional forms of measuring broadcast audiences. See Box 5.6, "Monetizing the Web: Turning the Audience into Media Professionals.")

One of the most striking features of this transformation of the audience from a passive content receiver to an active content creator is how the business models of many of these companies have come to depend on the material that audiences create. As Cohen (2008: 8) puts it, "the business models of Web 2.0 ventures depend on the performance of free labour; without it there would be no content and therefore no profit." Indeed, much of the information or content that one puts into the web—whether a Facebook post, a Google search, or pictures of one's favourite things—is what drives these businesses. Computer programs pore over these entries, developing profiles of peoples' interest, hopes, and desires which, in turn, are sold to advertisers, marketers, and almost anyone else who will pay for it.

For instance, based upon users' posts on Facebook, the organization sells a service called "lookalike audiences" that allows companies or other organizations to locate people who have similar characteristics to their existing customers, audiences, or other groups of people they want to reach or know about. As Facebook notes, "Lookalike audiences let you reach new people who are likely to be interested in your business because they're similar to a customer list you care about" (Facebook, 2014).

Users, however, have little or no control over how the information they post to the internet is used, as one woman found out when she became

5.5 ▶▶▶▶▶▶

THE AUDIENCE COMMODITY

When Dallas Smythe wrote about the "audience commodity" in 1977, he was referring to the way which audiences were packaged for sale to advertisers. His contention was that the time audiences spent watching television, reading newspapers, and consuming other media was, in reality, unpaid labour time and that it was this unpaid labour that media companies exploited when they sold audiences to advertisers.

Whether or not watching television, listening to the radio, or reading a newspaper could be counted as unpaid labour quickly became a hot topic of debate in critical media studies circles and continues to be a contentious issue today. With the rise of the internet and social media, however, Smythe's ideas have taken on new significance. On sites like Facebook, Twitter, Pinterest, and Google, it is precisely the unpaid labour of people posting and searching for material that yields the information these companies sell to advertisers and other interested parties. Computer programs pore over these entries, looking for information on these users' interests, hopes, and desires, which, in turn, is sold to advertisers, marketers, and almost anyone else who will pay for it. As a number of researchers have pointed out, users are performing unpaid labour in this way—labour that is directly translated into an information commodity that is sold to these companies' customers (see McGuigan and Manzerolle, 2014).

Source: © Petar Chernaev/iStockphoto.

Because the posts you make on sites like Facebook and Twitter form the basis of information products they sell to advertisers and others, that activity can be seen as performing unpaid labour for those corporations.

pregnant and began searching for information on babies. She soon found herself confronted by pop-up ads on her computer from companies that wanted to sell her baby clothes, toys, and other things related to child-rearing. But when she suffered a miscarriage and lost the baby, the ads didn't stop and became a cruel reminder of what had happened to her (Anderssen, 2014). As we discuss both in this chapter and in Chapter 6, information given up on the internet can also be used for more nefarious purposes, as insurance companies, employers, and law-enforcement

5.6

MONETIZING THE WEB: TURNING THE AUDIENCE INTO MEDIA PROFESSIONALS

In October 2006, Google announced that it had agreed to buy YouTube for $1.65 billion. At the time, YouTube was delivering over 100 million video views per day and had 65,000 new videos being uploaded daily. Finding ways to "create value"—or make money—from those people and the videos they contribute to the site was the main impetus to the acquisition.

Today, YouTube is still a favourite place for people to upload videos they have made of their pets or antics with their friends and family, but it is also becoming increasingly commercialized, as

Google has mounted a big push to have the site compete with traditional TV. According to a report in *Bloomberg Businessweek*, in 2012–2013, Google opened "new studios in Los Angeles, London, and Tokyo, launched more than 100 new original content channels, and made advances totaling more than $300 million to some of its top video makers" (Hamilton, 2013). The article goes on to state that

the ensuing rush of fresh talent, including stunt master Devin Super Tramp, singer Sam Tsui, and science geek Emily Graslie, has been good for YouTube, which says more than 1 billion people worldwide visit the site on a monthly basis, up 25 percent from the previous year. Advertisers paid an estimated $4 billion for YouTube ads in 2012, up 60 percent from 2011, according to RBC Capital Markets stock analyst Mark Mahaney. He expects the site to attract $5 billion in ad dollars this year. (Hamilton, 2013)

agencies scour information scraped from the internet for clues individuals may pose to profitability or public safety. While, years ago, being an anonymous member of the mass audience may have seemed boring because nobody was paying any attention to you, drawing attention as an active audience member on the internet today comes with risks.

▶ SUMMARY

The interaction between media and audiences is a dynamic interaction in which audience members actively and selectively interpret media content based on frameworks of understanding they bring to that content. Such a perspective provides a means for explaining how media, audiences, and culture interact in a non-deterministic fashion and, particularly, how audiences engage with media.

Generally, academic research on audiences is framed by precepts and ideas drawn from larger social theories. The theoretical approaches reviewed in this chapter reflect this orientation. Set in the context of theories of mass society, effects research highlights the direct impact of the media on the behaviour of

audience members. Uses and gratification research focuses on what audience members tend to do with media content. Marxist research and the Frankfurt School draw attention to the ways the production of media and cultural products influences the ways in which they represent the world and the relations of power they help engender. Cultural studies accents the agency of individuals and the multiplicity of social factors that come to bear on how audiences interpret media and incorporate them in to their lives. Feminist research brings forward the gendered nature of narratives and, like cultural studies, explores how the audience member is positioned by the narrative. And against the backdrop of contemporary social theories that accent human agency, reception analysis tends to consider the many ways media and media content are woven into the lives of audience members. Industry research largely generates quantitative measures on the nature of audiences, their size, age, location, education, family income, use of certain products, use of leisure time, and so on.

All these approaches to the audience offer information and insight for explaining and understanding, but not predicting, audience behaviour, which depends not only on what audience members bring to the text, but also on the culturally specific character of that material.

Understanding internet users and usage is a growing area of inquiry. It is clear that new communications technologies and the growing convergence between broadcasting and the web are having dramatic impacts on how audiences are constructed, as well as the role of media in forms of communication and citizenship. In this context, the role and purposes of new media are ongoing sites of struggle among industry, audiences, public-interest groups, and policy-makers (see, e.g., McGuigan and Manzeroll, 2014; Gajjala and Oh, 2012; Ruggles, 2005; Moll and Shade, 2004). How this struggle will play out remains to be seen.

 KEY TERMS

agenda-setting function, p. 125
audience fragmentation, p. 139
Birmingham School, p. 130
British cultural studies, p. 130
cultivation analysis, p. 126
demographic, p. 120
effects, p. 125
feminist research, p. 135
formative research, p. 140
Frankfurt School, p. 128

functionalist, p. 128
ideology, p. 131
position, p. 131
primary definers, p. 132
reach, p. 139
reception analysis, p. 136
share, p. 140
summative research, p. 140
uses and gratification research (U&G), p. 127
viewing time, p. 140

 RELATED WEBSITES

Audience Dialogue: audiencedialogue.net
As the website says, it "exists to provide useful information for communicators of all kinds—broadcasters, publishers, aid agencies, arts organizations, webmasters, and anybody else who's interested in using research-based techniques to make their organizations more effective."

Numeris: en.numeris.ca
Formerly BBM, this is the website for the largest broadcast audience research company in Canada.

Cultural Theory—British Cultural Studies:
www.youtube.com/watch?v=zyUYG1J3tKI
This short lecture by Professor Ron Strickland of Illinois State University provides a good introduction to British cultural studies.

The Frankfurt School: www.marxists.org/
subject/frankfurt-school/index.htm
This website provides a history of the Frankfurt School and discusses some contemporary theorists carrying on the school's legacy. See particularly the entries for Theodor Adorno and Max Horkheimer.

Vividata: www.vividata.ca
A not-for-profit organization representing the interests of Canadian publishers, advertising agencies and advertisers, this company helps facilitate advertising sales for magazines and newspapers through surveying audiences for these media across the country. As their website states, "Vividata surveys approximately 36,000 Canadians, aged 12+, annually to capture their news and magazine readership." Visit their website to get a better understanding of how they accomplish this task.

FURTHER READINGS ──────────────────────────

Barker, Chris. 2012. *Cultural Studies: Theory and Practice*. Thousand Oaks, CA: Sage Publications.

McInturff, Kate. 2014 (1 May). "Where are all the women on Canada's 100 top CEOs list?" Canadian Centre for Policy Alternatives. Retrieved 3 October 2014 from www.huffingtonpost.ca/kate-mcinturff/canada-100-top-ceos_b_454681.

Napoli, Philip. 2011. *Audience Evolution*. New York: Columbia University Press. A detailed analysis of the shifting nature of audiences.

Radway, Janice. 1984. *Reading the Romance*. Chapel Hill, NC: University of North Carolina Press. Radway's book is a classic analysis of how women readers use romantic fiction and demonstrates the contribution scholars can make to understanding the interaction between the media and people's lives.

Savage, Philip. 2014. "Audiences are key." In *Mediascapes: New Patterns in Canadian Communication*, 4th ed., Leslie Regan Shade, ed. Don Mills, ON: Nelson, 127–49.

Sullivan, John L. 2013. *Media Audiences: Effects, Users, Institutions, and Power*. Thousand Oaks, CA: Sage Publications. A good introduction to the study of audiences.

 STUDY QUESTIONS ──────────────────────────

1. Describe how each of these perspectives approaches the audience in fewer than 50 words:
   - effects research
   - Frankfurt School
   - cultural studies
   - feminist studies

2. "Some reception studies (e.g., Radway, 1984) appear to describe the interaction between audiences and content as secondary to the tangential actions surrounding the interpretation of content. The act of reading counts more than what the person derives from the content itself." Comment on this observation in relation to other methods of analysis.

3. Which of the perspectives on audiences would you use for writing an essay about the role of television in family life? Why?

4. Which of the perspectives on audiences corresponds most closely to your own views, and why?

5. Are you concerned about social media companies monitoring your activities on their sites? Why or why not? Discuss.

Communication Technology and Society: Theory and Practice

6

I used to write
I used to write letters
I used to sign my name
— Arcade Fire

Opening Questions

- How do we define *technology*?
- What does it mean to say technology is socially embedded?
- What is technological determinism?
- Why does a constructivist approach prevail today in studies of technology?
- What does *media convergence* mean?

- In what ways do digital media differ from analog media?
- What is the relationship between technology and public policy?
- What challenges do the surveillance capacities of new media technologies present?

Introduction

A discussion of technology is essential to a book about mass communication because mass communication as we defined it in Chapter 1 is mediated communication. What we typically refer to by the generic term *the media* are technologies: devices connected to social, political, and economic structures, enabling communication across time, across space, and with an unlimited number of interlocutors. When we think about communications technology, especially in this day and age, the tendency is to conjure exciting new gadgets and cool software applications, to think about constant upgrades, relentless innovation, even revolutionary change. It is without doubt an exciting time for students of communication, who can monitor daily the transitions underway in how we communicate, reflect on the challenges all cultural industries face in the shift from fixed and wired analog systems to mobile and wireless digital forms, and participate first-hand in the existential experiments media organizations are undertaking to find new ways to conduct business. There is a lot to think about.

In this chapter, we seek to address the question "What's going on?" But in doing so, we want to provide some much-needed perspective on the subject of communications technology, by broadening the view of what we mean by "technology" and by situating technological change within a context informed not simply by science and engineering, but also by politics, economics, culture, and history. As compelling as the digital age may be, it is not the first time that seismic shifts have occurred in the communications field, nor is it necessarily the most consequential period—the jury is still deliberating on that, given the need to think about how the changes we are witnessing today compare to the invention of the printing press in the middle of the fifteenth century and its subsequent role in the Enlightenment, or the developments in rapid succession of photography, telegraphy, telephony, cinema, and radio in the nineteenth century, which altered profoundly and permanently our senses of time and space. One of the most difficult parts of this exercise is to distinguish between what is fundamentally new—even revolutionary—and what is merely novel: new in a more superficial or cosmetic sense. Here, it is important to consider the broad context in which new technologies emerge and how they come to be used and structured within institutional systems. What we need to resist is the idea of the "technological sublime," what Jennifer Daryl Slack and J. Macgregor Wise define as "the almost religious-like reverence paid to machines" (2007: 17).

We begin this chapter by defining what we mean by technology, situating technological devices within socially constructed systems. We then assess five theoretical perspectives to understand technology's place in society. The topic of media **convergence** is addressed as part of a larger discussion of the distinctive characteristics of the digital media in general and the internet in particular, relating these distinctions to the policy challenges they raise. We conclude the chapter with our own version of a cost–benefit analysis of recent technological changes, especially the tension between new-found surveillance capabilities and citizens' right to privacy.

Perspectives on Technology

The word *technology* is from the Greek *techne*, meaning "art, craft, or skill." This etymology reminds us we can see that technology refers to much more than tools, gadgets, machines, or devices. Rather, the term encompasses both the devices *as well as* a knowledge or understanding of their use or operation, an understanding of how they fit into a larger set of social circumstances

The authors wish to thank John Maxwell for his work on previous iterations of this chapter. John is an associate professor in the Master of Publishing Program at Simon Fraser University.

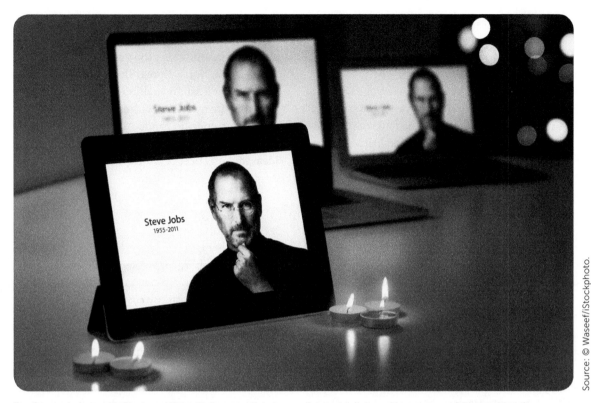

▮ Do you agree with Slack and Wise that our society has an "almost religious-like reverence" for machines?

or way of life. Technology should be seen as complexly woven into the circumstances and rhythms of social life.

Slack and Wise (2007: 72) remind us that technologies are inherently social and cultural—it is people who create and use technologies, activities that reflect values and choices. The creators may be scientists, engineers, or backyard inventors, but the context in which their creation occurs will inform what they are trying to create and the purposes they envision their technology serving.

Creation requires time, skills, money and often infrastructural support, investments that demand some kind of compensation. Clearly, the research and development that corporations fund is aimed at either saving money through resulting efficiencies or generating revenues by bringing new products or services to market. But even the research of public-sector scientists is aimed at serving some institutional demands, typically that of funding agencies, either public

or private, who have identified particular needs and encourage investigation in specific directions (e.g., finding a cure for cancer, understanding the social impact of screen violence). Users, too, whether individuals or organizations, shape technological development, both through the demands or needs they express and, ultimately, how they adapt the technology to their daily lives. Communication technologies, for example, are often envisioned and promoted as serving idealistic purposes like public education or democracy, but wind up being employed just as frequently for entertainment, amusement, or commerce. As the Canadian physicist Ursula M. Franklin puts it,

What needs to be emphasized is that technologies are developed and used within a particular, social, economic, and political context. They arise out of a social structure, they are grafted on to it, and they may reinforce it or destroy it, often in ways that are neither foreseen nor foreseeable. (1996: 57)

Here, technology belongs to a larger social system, and as we discussed initially in Chapter 2 when we introduced the ideas of Canadian communication theorists Harold Innis and Marshall McLuhan, our predominant means of communication can tell us a lot about our culture. Slack and Wise (2007: 127–29) encourage us to think about technology as "articulation," getting past the idea of technologies as mere things. Technologies instead are products and practices that assume their specific form thanks to their particular connections, their place in a network of related activities. They are, in other words, embedded—socially, culturally, politically, and economically. The **cyborg** metaphor emphasizes how humans and human activity articulate with technologies (see Box. 6.1).

In his classic work *Television: Technology and Cultural Form* (1974), Raymond Williams makes a similar point, arguing that technology reflects the overall organization of society (see Chapter 3). In and of itself, for instance, the telegraph is simply a wire with an electric current running through it. But, in the context of developing industrial society, it is a means of coordinating the movement of people and goods across vast distances. Similarly, television, by offering programs to fill our leisure time and advertising to drive the consumption of a vast range of goods and services, feeds and maintains the mass society that industrialization created.

This also means that specific devices change their purpose and function depending on the context in which they are embedded. A laptop computer, for example, may be perceived and used as a word processor and research tool in the workplace, and a games console and video platform at home. On a larger scale, the same medium can assume a very different form and purpose depending on the country and/or political system in which it operates. If television, for example, is a medium of general information (e.g., news programs, documentaries) and

entertainment (e.g., movies, sitcoms, sports events) in Western democracies like Canada, it is strictly a medium of propaganda in totalitarian regimes like North Korea. The same device, but a different context and a different outcome.

These perspectives on technology are clearly not about specific kinds of tools or electronic devices, but rather about the complex network of ideas and practices of which they are a part. (1996)

Thinking about Technology

In *Questioning Technology* (1999), philosopher Andrew Feenberg provides an account of the major conceptual frameworks and orientations social scientists and philosophers have used to think about technology. His analysis provides four main ways to think about and understand technology: instrumentalism, determinism, substantivism and critical theory. A fifth perspective, constructivism, is closely related to critical theory.

Instrumentalism is a relatively naive position, which views technology as a value-neutral tool that can shorten the path to natural ends or, alternatively, social goals; technology here is simply a means to an end and can be used for whatever purpose we choose. If we need a drink of water, for example, a cup works better than either our hand or putting our face in a pool of water. If we need to get from Vancouver to Toronto, a plane gets us there faster and more easily than a bus or a train. Technology from an instrumentalist perspective is above all a tool for our use.

Conversely, **technological determinism** holds that technology operates according to an inexorable logic inherent in the technology itself, that the technology has "an autonomous functional logic that can be explained without reference to society" (Feenberg, 1999: 77; see also Croteau and Hoynes, 2014: 299–300). Technology here is associated with notions of progress, perceived as a straightforward track toward improvement, and the effects of technology are attributed by determinists to the technology itself, rather than to human decisions about how

6.1 ▶▶▶▶▶▶

CYBORGS

We typically associate cyborgs—or cybernetic organisms—with science-fiction characters in movies or video games: Alex Murphy (*RoboCop*); Max Da Costa (*Elysium*); Ava (*The Machine*); Jax, Kano, and Sub-Zero (*Mortal Kombat*); Master Chief (*Halo*); Matthew Kane (*Quake 4*), and so on.

One of the reasons these characters resonate so powerfully with audiences and gamers is that it is not much of a stretch to see ourselves as part human, part machine, particularly in a technologically advanced and affluent society such as Canada. In a well-known essay, Donna Haraway (1991) insists that we are cyborgs. The cyborg is "a creature of social reality as well as a creature of fiction," she writes, arguing that "we are all chimeras, theorized and fabricated hybrids of machine and organism; in short, we are cyborgs" (149–50). Haraway celebrates the cyborg as a model for challenging standard divisions of identity, overcoming what Slack and Wise term "the technologies of categorization" (2007: 169). Haraway writes,

> Late-twentieth-century machines have made thoroughly ambiguous the difference between natural and artificial, mind and body, self-developing and externally designed, and many other distinctions that used to apply to organisms and machines. (1991: 152)

The cyborg metaphor is a clear manifestation of the idea that technology comprises much more than machinery, but is tied as well into techniques or ways of performing tasks, and

reflects the larger sociocultural environment in which machines and ways of doing things are embedded. To take a simple but far-reaching example, the priority society places on health care and lifespan longevity can be seen in the efforts expended on developing technologies to improve life (e.g., eyeglasses, hearing aids, prosthetics), extend life (e.g., pacemakers, immunization, antibiotics, organ transplants), and even create life (e.g., fertility treatments, cloning).

If technological systems can enhance personal comfort, and make it easier to communicate and to travel, there is a flip side. In the workplace, we can very much feel like the proverbial cogs in the machine, especially if our job is one in a series of repetitive, mechanical steps and does not require thinking, judgment, or creativity—or, if our job is made redundant by technology, as happened in the newspaper industry when computerization displaced many printers' jobs (see McKercher, 2002).

This is what Harry Braverman (1974) famously described as **deskilling**, the process by which previously skilled jobs are broken into a series of tasks that can be performed by semi-skilled or unskilled workers.

Braverman attributed this process largely to the **scientific management** movement in the late nineteenth century, which he defined as "a science of the management of others' work under capitalist conditions" (1974: 90). Scientific management is sometimes called *Taylorism*, after Frederick Winslow Taylor, who sought to improve economic efficiency through increases in labour productivity. In the early twentieth century, Taylor conducted a series of time and motion studies to break down work-related tasks into their component parts and determine the most efficient means of organizing such tasks (see Taylor, 1997 [1911]). Taylorism was ideally suited to industrialized, mass-production processes that combined workers and machinery in various forms of assembly line.

it is developed and employed. It is easy to see examples of determinist thinking in the trends toward miniaturization and mobility: the mobile phone you carry today will inevitably be replaced by one that is smaller or lighter and allows you to do more with it, an assertion that ignores the myriad choices producers, marketers and end

users will make concerning the phone's future development. From the determinist perspective, human control over the exact direction of technological development is minimal—the technology, in a sense, has a life of its own.

In a stance related to technological determinism, **substantivism** claims that technology operates according to its own inherent logic, but this logic does not necessarily represent progress or improvement. The harsh social realities of the Industrial Revolution, the development of nuclear weapons, and more recently the threat of environmental disaster have given substantivists much to think and write about to bolster their perspective. Take the automobile, for example: the availability of mass-produced cars in the early twentieth century led to the development of large-scale infrastructure (roads, highways, suburbs, shopping malls) designed with cars and car travel in mind. We now live in a world where the urban sprawl (not to mention air pollution and dependency on fossil fuels) brought on by a car-oriented culture is difficult to escape; more efficient and more environmentally friendly modes of mass transit are notoriously difficult

Source: © apolloicdag/iStockphoto.

How might we think about cellphones using the five perspectives on technology explained here?

to design, build, implement, and finance, in part because population density is so low in the suburbs. The structure has become self-reinforcing: the only way to live in what has become a car culture is to drive a car.

Taking their position to a logical conclusion, Feenberg reports that substantivists view the modern condition as reflective of the essence of modern technology—its rationality, its efficiency, its priority on control and calculability (1999: 4–7). The more pessimistic or dystopian of the substantivists argue that technological thought and action threaten non-technological values as they extend ever deeper into social life. We become, in a sense, slaves to the machine. Thus, it is not uncommon for organizations to adopt rules suited to the capacity of the technological system rather than to the needs of users. Consider, for example, the online forms with their opaque instructions we are increasingly required to complete, or the automated telephone answering services we reach when our inquiry isn't on the limited menu of selections offered. As Jacques Ellul (1964), one of the foremost theorists working from this perspective, expressed it, technique has become autonomous.

Wilson Dizard has summarized Ellul's position, best expressed in Ellul's *The Technological Society* (1964), as follows:

1. All technological progress exacts a price— while it adds something, it subtracts something else.
2. All technological progress raises more problems than it solves, tempts us to see the consequent problems as technical in nature, and prods us to seek technical solutions to them.
3. The negative effects of technological innovation are inseparable from the positive. It is naive to say that technology is neutral, that it may be used for good or bad ends; the good and bad effects are, in fact, simultaneous and inseparable.
4. All technological innovations have unforeseen effects. (Dizard, 1985: 11)

Ellul's points about technology are exemplified in current concerns about our dependency on oil and how best to transport it and refine it.

A complementary viewpoint to Ellul's can be found in the classic work of Canadian philosopher George Grant. In *Technology and Empire* (1969), Grant argued that the foundation of all modern, liberal, industrial, and post-industrial societies is to be found in technique and technology. He claimed that the dominant doctrine of modern liberalism was "the belief that human excellence is promoted by the homogenizing and universalizing power of technology" (Grant, 1969: 69). While these points have a ring of truth, they also express an inevitability and a pessimism that have been challenged.

None of instrumentalism, determinism, or substantivism is adequate to fully explain technology. Proponents of **critical theory** insist we have choices about how we develop technology, shape its development, use it, incorporate it within larger systems, and engage with it to a greater or lesser extent. Feenberg (1999) argues that theorists Herbert Marcuse and Michel Foucault—scholars who were part of the New Left movement of the 1960s and '70s—opened up the opportunity to think about technology and technological development as something other than an external force. Rather, they made it possible to conceive of technology as existing within society, as integral to society in the same way as religion, education, culture, economics, and political systems; technology is thus subject to the same kinds of criticism and reform.

This twofold notion—that technology exists within society and that social forces and political decision-making can control both the nature of the machines that emerge and their usage—means that technology develops in a **socially contingent** manner. In other words, technology arises and takes a particular form depending on the dynamics of the society in which it emerges—which may include rejection, as happened with fax machines when they were first invented, and with movable type in China (prior to Gutenberg). Critical theory sees technology as offering possibilities from which society chooses a course of action. Such sites of struggle raise issues of power, control, and freedom that society must address. As we discuss in Chapter 7, for example, Canada was compelled to make choices about how to perceive and organize the new technology of radio in the 1920s—whether it would function as a medium of local or national broadcasting, as an industry or as a public service, and so on. And we as a society continue to make such choices.

Constructivism has emerged from the shortcomings of instrumentalism, determinism, and substantivism. Today, a constructivist framework largely prevails in studies of technology. Constructivists argue that technology is socially constructed and shaped by social forces (as Slack and Wise emphasized in our discussion in the previous section). There are always viable alternatives to our research and development priorities, the form technology will take, and the uses to which it will be put. Constructivists argue that to

Green energy technologies like wind turbines and solar panels are a response to concerns about the world's dependency on fossil fuels. How do technologies like this relate to society? Does technology shape social forces, or do social forces shape technology?

Source: © stephenmeese/iStockphoto.

succeed, any given technology must have a technical and a social logic; in other words, new tools or systems succeed where they work properly and find support in the social environment. We can see this today in the example of technologies employing alternative energy sources, intended to respond to environmental concerns. Governments can encourage wind and solar-power projects (e.g., Ontario's 2009 Green Energy Act) and automotive manufacturers can produce vehicles powered by alternative fuels (e.g., hydrogen, ethanol, electricity), but it is society at large that will determine their viability and their precise uses.

This social construction can be hard to recognize because once a new device or system finds a supportive environment, it can undergo a process of closure. Closure refers to the fixing of the device or system into a socially recognized object, producing a kind of *black box*, an artifact or way of doing things that comes to be seen as natural, inevitable, or most logical. Once this occurs, the technology's social origins and possible alternatives are forgotten, leading to what Feenberg terms a "determinist illusion." Terry Flew and Richard Smith (2014) cite the example of the QWERTY keyboard; designed for typewriters to prevent the keys of frequently combined letters from sticking together, it survived the transition to computer keyboards even though there was no longer a sticking problem and research has demonstrated that the QWERTY keyboard is not the most efficient arrangement of letters (Flew and Smith, 2014: 64).

The constructivist perspective seeks to undermine closure and recover a sense of history when regarding any technology. The telephone, for example, was once conceived as a broadcast receiver (see Box 6.3 below), and after a long history as a point-to-point oral communications device, it now serves as a point-to-point written communications device, camera, sound recorder, video screen, notepad, agenda, GPS, and computer tablet. Radio broadcasting was initially perceived as a means of point-to-point communication, and the internet was conceived as a military communications system. Given this history, David Croteau and William Hoynes argue that "the development and application of new media technologies is neither fixed nor fully predictable." While a new medium's inherent technical capacities provide constraints and parameters, these technologies are ultimately defined by social forces, including legislation, policy, social norms, and market pressures (2014: 300; see also, Goggin, 2011).

Wiebe Bijker claims that what we call a machine is better understood as a **socio-technical ensemble** (Bijker, 1993: 125). This means that any machine—from a chainsaw or hair dryer to a space station or the Hubble Space Telescope—arises from a socially defined intention of its developers, who are able to create a particular technical device for intended and sometimes unintended uses: a socio-technical ensemble.

The assembly line is an example of a socio-technical ensemble, bringing together machinery and workers to organize the mass production of goods from start, as raw materials, to finish, as completed products ready for sale. How do you think the creation of new technologies in an assembly-line process affects technological innovation?

Felczak (2006) makes two further points. If machines are socio-technical ensembles, then it follows that engineers are social activists. They design machines with the intention of reconfiguring social relations and, hence, changing society. And, in the context of information technology, social scientific investigation can embrace an activist element. There is considerable work devoted to the study of the changes—actual and potential—we are seeing in the so-called digital age; some of it is critical of the appropriation of cyberspace by commercial forces, other work is more hopeful that new media forms can help constitute a more democratic communications system (e.g., McChesney, 2013; Patel et al., 2012; Gleick, 2011; Kidd and Chen, 2008).

Technology and Western Society

Is Western society uniquely placed in its relationship with technology? Probably not—all cultures and societies can be seen as being based on tightly integrated technologies. Sociologist of science Bruno Latour suggests that what distinguishes modern society from so-called traditional societies may be the size and scope of our socio-technical ensembles, rather than any qualitative difference in the way people think or how cultures act (see Blok and Jensen, 2011).

As successive layers of technology have taken root in Western society and successive layers of infrastructure have been laid down, we should not be surprised to find that our dependency on these systems has grown. So enthusiastic is the acceptance of technology by Western, especially North American, society that some would argue the world is increasingly in the clutches of the technological imperative—that is, we have convinced ourselves that we should continuously develop new technologies and apply them broadly for a better life. Rather than change our ways, we tend to assume that technological solutions will be found to problems like climate change or the degradation of the oceans. Furthermore,

6.2 ▶▶▶▶▶

OLD MEDIA, NEW MEDIA

We often hear references to "old media" and "new media" without being clear about what these terms refer to or what differentiates them. All media, of course, were at one time new, and all new media will someday be old. The internet, for example, is not particularly new to us.

The term *old media*—or *legacy media*—refers to analog media like hard-copy newspapers, magazines, and books; film on celluloid; radio; and conventional television. Analog media are those media with distinct physical properties, produced and distributed through medium-specific facilities. Hard-copy books, for example, are texts printed with ink on paper, produced by large presses, and delivered to bookstores and libraries in large trucks. Analog films consist of reels of celluloid containing thousands of cells, each of which features a photographic image. Copies are made and transported to cinemas, where they are displayed by projectors that unreel the film while projecting light through the photographic cells at a rate of 24 frames per second. Analog media have a physical or material presence.

The term *new media* refers to digital media, computer-based technologies like the internet. All digital media employ a common electronic language of 0s and 1s and are produced using computers with purpose-specific software. Content produced digitally can be read, viewed, and/or listened to on a range of digital players. The contents of digital media are produced and distributed electronically.

Further confusion between these terms, of course, stems from the fact that old media are increasingly digitized, so that there are digital versions of newspapers, magazines, books, films, and radio and television programs.

development of technology in Western society is usually a deliberate attempt to create material objects, interventions, or systems that allow the developer to reap financial reward. In this sense, technological development is a business—and the economies of Western nations are wrapped up intimately with the innovation, development, and promotion of new technologies. One result is that the technological distance between countries of the Global North and Global South in communication has been increasing. This gap is often called the **digital divide**. We cover this concept in more detail in our discussion of globalization in Chapter 11, but the term refers to the disparities between technological *haves* and *have-nots*, the differences between people who have access to technologies and the skills to use them, and those who do not. These gaps can be measured between countries, but also within domestic populations (see van Dijk, 2012).

We can see that technologically oriented societies affirm and embrace machinery, the social organization necessary to adopt that machinery, and the acquisition of the requisite skills and techniques needed for its operation for private financial benefit, largely without social or political interference. The enthusiastic acceptance of technology is sometimes so complete that both analysts and the general public accept the projections about the future of society based on technological capacity. This is a straightforward example of technological determinism; if technological development can do something, society will take full advantage of its technological capacity and will be shaped fundamentally by it, and in predictable ways.

Technological determinists, for instance, have argued that the internet leads to greater democratization (e.g., Shirky, 2008, 2010; Bruns, 2008); in fact, this assertion is hotly disputed (Grofman et al., 2014; McChesney, 2013; Dahlberg and Siapera, 2007). Greater amounts of information do not equate automatically with a better-informed citizenry or a healthier democracy. We can identify in a general sense what new technologies enable—for example, the internet enables the collection and rapid dissemination of information—but precisely how those enabling capacities will be employed or how far they extend is unpredictable. We need to ask, *What kind of information will be collected and disseminated, and who will undertake these tasks, and for what intent?* As we discuss later in this chapter, there is growing concern today about governments' access to information about citizens and corporations' exchange of personal data about consumers.

Determinism fails to consider that technology does not drop out of the clear blue sky or from the head of some genius. Rather, it is derived from specific and typically collective efforts to solve problems or find opportunities. Technological determinism also ignores the role of state and institutional control over the industrialized application of technology. As is apparent, the internet can as easily be used for dictatorship or terrorism as for democracy; it can further bigotry as easily as it can enable enlightened debate. In the early days of the internet, users fought against its commercialization; today, it is a powerful conduit for all kinds of e-commerce. If politicians wish, they can enact policy so that a certain technology (e.g., the internet) can be used only in certain ways (e.g., for legal forms of communication), and hence, with certain consequences (e.g., clamping down on child pornography or organized crime). Such control is not just in the hands of governments—often, corporate interests exercise their power to shape technological systems in order to preserve market influence. But users, too, play a role.

The Dangers of Technology and Technological Hubris

Implicit in our everyday perspective on technology is the notion that technology can transform society for the good—that it inherently contributes to progress. But as Ellul (1964) points out, the consequences of the transformative dynamic of a given technology usually go unrealized in its initial application. Antibiotics serve as a good example. While antibiotics have been a godsend to public health, we now understand that strains of antibiotic-resistant bacteria have emerged precisely because of our overuse of these drugs. Each winter, health officials worry that a drug-resistant strain of flu may cause a world pandemic. Similarly, the development of monocultures—single varieties of plants that are most productive and generate the most economically harvestable crop—makes food supplies vulnerable to failure. The 1912 sinking of the *Titanic* is perhaps the most famous symbol of **technological hubris**—the massive ship was viewed by many so-called experts as unsinkable because it was the latest and greatest product of human ingenuity. This example of hubris cost more than 1,500 lives.

In communication, similar issues surround the limitations of technology. While more people are able to access vast amounts of information, economies of scale come to influence what information is available; thus, information attracting only a limited audience tends to disappear, or is not gathered and stored in the first place. Specialty magazines disappear from newsstands, and scholarly works that focus on narrow, even if important, subjects—such as the influence of ethnicity on modern farming communities—can have a difficult time getting published because they address a small, highly specialized audience.

The control systems of the large producers tell them that they can make more money elsewhere, especially as more and more segments of society are subjected to a commercial logic (see Chapter 9). Some kinds of national, provincial, and regional news, as well as information about our neighbours down the street, become harder to find as the news media shift their focus to what will sell. Finally, elements as mundane as the number of hours one might spend sitting in front of a computer or TV screen, or the lack of socialization involved in working from home, may have considerable unanticipated health consequences when multiplied throughout society. Again, this is what Ellul meant by the inseparability of the good and bad effects of technology.

Media Convergence

For much of the history of media, communications technologies operated in distinct fields, organized as discrete industries, owned and controlled by industry-specific organizations, and governed by particular sets of laws and policies (which we discuss at greater length in Chapters 7 and 8). This history gives the impression that

Source: © Manakin/iStockphoto.

The *Titanic*, which sunk after hitting an iceberg in the North Atlantic in 1912, remains a potent symbol of technological hubris. The arrogant belief that it was unsinkable resulted in the loss of more than 1,500 lives. Do arrogant beliefs about technology still exist? What kinds of "unsinkable" technologies still exist in our world?

these so-called silos were products of the technologies themselves, that the technical specifications of analog media determined their application and their organization. But if their technical composition was not irrelevant, it was not determining. Technology did not prevent newspaper publishers from using their printing presses to publish magazines or books, or from moving into other media spheres. In fact, newspaper publishers were some of the first to get into the radio broadcasting business in the 1920s and '30s. As we note in Box 6.3, in the earliest days of the telephone, people experimented with broadcasting theatrical performances and concerts over telephone lines. Similarly, there were two visions for radio in its earliest years: point-to-point communications and broadcasting. If broadcasting became the predominant industry form, point-to-point was used for things like marine communications as well as police, fire, and ambulance services. Even the internet was first devised as a system for military communications. The history of convergence demonstrates that these media silos were social constructs.

In common parlance, *convergence* means coming together, such as two rivers converging to form one larger river. Media convergence refers to either the merging of previously distinct media technologies and media forms through digitalization and computer networking, or a business strategy by which the media properties of a communications conglomerate work together (Gasher, 2013). Media convergence has a longer history than is generally acknowledged. Some newspaper publishers did engage in other kinds of printing and, as mentioned above, newspaper companies were among the first organizations to invest in radio stations. Radio broadcasters later entered the television business (e.g., CBC/Radio-Canada). Hand in hand with these developments, we have seen a long-term trend toward corporate convergence. If, early in the twentieth century, independent newspapers became part of chains and independent radio stations became part of networks, it became common in the latter part of the century for companies like Quebecor

and Bell—originally the Bell Telephone Company of Canada, now Bell Canada Enterprises—to expand into other communications industries and even into unrelated fields. Quebecor, for example, which began as the publisher of a single community newspaper in Montreal in 1950, evolved into a communications conglomerate with subsidiaries in newspaper, magazine, and book publishing; television broadcasting; cable television distribution; and music retailing (see Chapter 9).

Digitization and computer networking facilitated this transition. Digitization is the process by which all forms of information—textual, visual, aural—are translated into a common language of 0s and 1s, so that content produced originally for one digital platform can be used on all other platforms. Computer networking ties all of these digital platforms together on our various screens. The result is what we are witnessing today: the breaking down of meaningful distinctions between media forms. We listen to music on our smartphones, we watch television on our laptops, and we read books on our e-readers.

As we will discuss in greater detail in Chapters 7 and 8, governments are significant players in the convergence game. Historically, public policy—laws, regulations, conventions—has supported media silo distinctions between, for example, broadcasting and telecommunications, between publishing and broadcasting, and government agencies continue to patrol these boundaries where cross-media ownership and corporate concentration are concerned. Currently, public policy can be seen as both asserting and responding to pressures for technological and corporate convergence, seeking to strike a balance between social and economic demands.

While convergence has obvious implications for media economics, policy formation and the specific cultural industries, Henry Jenkins (2006) perceives a cultural transformation as well. What he terms "convergence culture" entails "a shift in the way we think about our relations to media" and "may have implications for how we learn, work, participate in the political process, and

6.3 ▶▶▶▶▶▶

FIRST BROADCASTERS USED THE TELEPHONE

Source: From *Popular Science*, September 1933. 39.

Who were the earliest broadcasters? Ten years before the first radio programs were put on the air, a group people in Chicago regularly delivered musical programs and news bulletins over the telephone lines of many subscribers. This rare old photograph shows these pioneers broadcasting from their studio. Each singer is holding a microphone, while other individual microphones are attached to the instruments. To listen to the music, a subscriber had merely to sit beside the telephone and hold the receiver to one ear. If a phone call came in while the subscriber was listening, the musical program was automatically disconnected.

connect with other people around the world" (2006: 22–3).

Technology and Policy

Policy decisions in the communications sphere are guided by three central issues: (1) ensuring that the needs of the public and of cultural and national groups are met, (2) ensuring that Canada has viable cultural industries; and at the same time (3) ensuring that certain businesses do not become too powerful and thwart the participation of others and prevent further social and technological development. The attempt by Microsoft to dominate in nearly every software market is a case in point. Some feel that the success of Google is equally threatening.

While allowing for both convergence and competition sounds like a good idea, regulatory agencies like the CRTC cannot easily forge appropriate policy. Telephone and cable companies, for example, provide internet access to consumers and are known as **backbone providers**. They also provide connectivity to small internet service providers (ISPs), who in turn sell internet access to the public. Similarly, the cable companies own some of the specialty TV channels and provide access to these not only to the public but also to their competitors. Clearly, there are conflicts here: first, between the large and small ISPs; and second, between the cable companies and the independent specialty channels. Government policy sets the rules of the game, determining whether, for instance, cable companies can own specialty channels. But the CRTC's powers are limited by many factors, including the number of corporations willing to create products for sale (see also Chapters 7 and 8).

Netflix is a good example of a new service creating headaches for policy-makers and the television broadcast industry. Providing online video streaming of popular television programs and films, Netflix is not subject to the same regulatory requirements as Canadian television broadcasters, such as fees to support Canadian audiovisual production, Canadian-content regulations, closed-captioning and other regulated programming standards. As Netflix has gained in popularity—it was adopted by 2.5 million Canadian households in 2012—the television industry complains of unfair competition, and the CRTC is compelled to rethink a regulatory regime designed for a pre-digital era (see Geist, 2014; Ladurantaye, 2010).

Policy issues can have a significant international component and getting a foreign company, particularly one running a monopoly service, to adhere to the regulations in all the different countries in which it operates can be a difficult task. Yet more challenging to policy-making is the internet; while different countries have different laws on free speech, privacy, access to information, and so forth, the internet undermines those laws by being available everywhere and based nowhere.

The Internet and Digitization

The internet presents challenges for traditional conceptions of communication technology and industries, in its starting assumptions, its structure, and the ways in which people are using it. The sheer size of the internet today means that how it differs from older communication models represents a major shift in the way we must think about communication media. For instance, according to Internet World Stats in 2012, more than one-third of the world's population now uses the internet (www.internetworldstats.com/stats.htmInternet), and it is structured as an international, rather than national, communications system (see Figure 6.1).

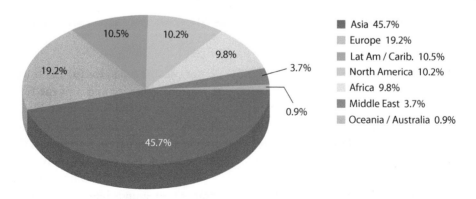

FIGURE 6.1 Internet Users in the World, Distribution by World Regions, 2014

The foundations of the internet were laid in the United States in the 1960s, when large amounts of Cold War–era government funding were poured into the new computer-science departments at universities. Researchers at the time were interested in developing an interactive computer network. The original **ARPANET** project (circa 1969) connected computer systems at five US universities, enabling information and message exchange between them (see Figure 6.2). One of the key ideas behind the network was that if, in the event of a nuclear attack, one or more of its nodes were destroyed, the network could still function. ARPANET grew into what we now know as the internet—the international network of computer networks—through the 1970s and early '80s, by which time most of the underlying technological infrastructure in use today had been worked out.

Demonstrating a particular socio-technical ensemble, a number of interesting features of the early internet shaped how it works today. First, the internet was developed as a **peer-to-peer system**; there is no central control point in the network. The internet is arranged like a web, in which points on the network are redundantly interconnected; the route by which any particular piece of information travels is guided by software rather than by the physical connections, and all points on the internet are equals or peers—at least in theory. The internet trades information units called *packets*, which are something like envelopes with "To:" and "From:" labels on them. Network software reads these address labels and makes decisions about how to transfer packets along the web. Furthermore, these packets are like sealed envelopes; the contents are important only to the computer systems at

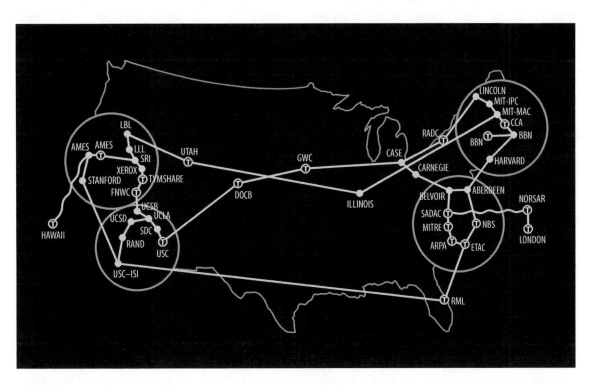

FIGURE 6.2 ARPA Geographic Map, September 1973

The original ARPANET project connected computer systems at five US universities, enabling information and message exchange between them. One of the key ideas behind the network was that if, in the event of a nuclear attack, one or more of its nodes were destroyed, the network could still function.

Source: Courtesy of the Computer History Museum.

either end of a transmission. The internet is thus described as an end-to-end architecture, with the network itself remaining ignorant or, at least, neutral about what is being transferred. This feature is called *network neutrality* and ensures that all data being transferred receive equal treatment by the network. The concept of net neutrality is at the heart of how the internet is to be defined, whether as a public good supporting democracy or as a commodity belonging to the market economy (Schulte, 2011: 48).

An interesting feature of the internet is that it has existed for much of its life as a publicly funded system, first in the United States, and today in most other countries as well. Since the mid-1990s, however, more and more of the internet is made up of corporate, for-profit components, while substantial chunks worldwide still are run by governments and/or academic institutions. This has given the internet a different character from large-scale corporate media such as in the television industry, and effective corporate control of the internet is still limited, although this status is in flux as corporate interests make larger and larger investments in internet infrastructure. The internet certainly is not free from significant corporate involvement. The strongest areas of economic growth so far have to do with network provision—that is, the companies that own the connections and charge for access—and web search engines. In 2005, Google became the largest media company in the world by market valuation (the total value of all shares held); at US $80 billion, it was larger than Time Warner, Disney, and Viacom. It is interesting to consider that this value resides in a company whose service most of us use every day without paying a cent.

A second significant feature of the internet is that its underlying technologies have for the most part been developed and released non-commercially as open systems and more recently as open-source software. This means that the software, standards, and protocols making the internet run are not owned or controlled by any one party, but, rather, are publicly available. The major internet engineering process has for

decades revolved around a system of requests for comments or RFCs. The RFC is effectively a peer-review system where contributions of software and system design are openly circulated, reviewed, and improved on by a community of engineers in much the way Wikipedia is open to participation in its content. The result is that anyone wanting to contribute to the process can do so. Over the past two decades, RFCs have grown into a general strategy for software development, with a rich variety of components available as **open source**—that is, free for examination, modification, use, and distribution, without typical commercial trappings such as licence fees, trade secrets, or usage restrictions.

This model of systems development has proved enormously successful for the internet itself, but it also has cultural implications. In a world in which works—text, music, video, and so on—are stored and transferred digitally, and consequently can be copied and distributed globally in an instant and for almost no cost, traditional conceptions of copyright and intellectual property have become increasingly problematic, especially for century-old industries that have grown up around a more traditional copyright landscape, treating content as a form of private property. Into the legal battles that result from technological change comes the open-source movement, bringing with it a completely different sensibility about how and by what terms works should be circulated and exchanged. We discuss copyright in greater detail in Chapter 8.

With regard to internet usage by the general public, the World Wide Web emerged as an internet application in the early 1990s and quickly grew to be the largest user of internet bandwidth—the capacity of a network for carrying information. The web, which provides a friendly interface to the internet, grew in its first decade to the point where it allowed for an almost infinite number of niche audiences to access content of interest to them. For much of the web's first decade, its basic model was a simple page-delivery system. However, its increasingly interactive capability has transformed users into veritable webmasters. The biggest trend in recent years has been the rise of social networking (see Chapter 1).

The web's status as a new, interactive mass medium—often called Web 2.0—comes to the fore when we consider the extent to which it enables consumers of media content to become producers as well. Some have termed this trend "prosumption" or "produsage" and celebrate it as an important step toward the democratization of communication and the erosion of corporate media power (see Lessig, 2008; Bruns, 2008; Jenkins, 2006). Examples of sites and applications that enable individuals to produce their own content abound: Wikipedia, YouTube, Facebook, Twitter, Instagram, 8Tracks, Strava, as well as countless websites, blogs, and citizen journalism sites. Bruns's four key principles of produsage are (1) inclusive rather than exclusive production; (2) a "heterarchical" network structure rather than a hierarchical, top-down structure; (3) always unfinished and continuing production; and (4) freely available, community-held content in an information commons (Bruns, 2008).

While there is no doubt we enjoy increased capacity to participate in the production, distribution, and sharing of media content, the extent to which this represents democratization, threatens corporate power, or provides us with an information commons—a space open to all—is highly debatable. David Croteau and William Hoynes (2014) note, first of all, that the extent of content production by users is vastly overstated. They remind us of the 1 percent Rule, which claims that "for every person who creates content, there are 99 who do not" (2014: 307). For his part, Christian Fuchs (2009) maintains that user interactivity actually extends corporate power in what he calls "the Internet gift economy." Fuchs explains that in exchange for free access to these commercially owned sites and web applications, users contribute free content, which enhances the sites' commercial value. So, users' content helps popularize and legitimize these sites among other users, allowing the sites' owners to charge more for advertising and/or exchange users' personal data for profit. Fuchs writes, "The

more users make of advertisement-based free online platforms and the more time they spend online producing, consuming, and exchanging content, communicating with others, the higher the value of the prosumer commodity they produce will become, the higher the advertisement prices will rise, and the higher the profits of the specific Internet corporations will be" (2009: 82; see also Elmer, 2004). Fernando Bermejo (2011) sees in this a "double articulation" of audience labour, in that "users are producers of content that attracts other users while, at the same time, generating data about themselves that is used to turn them into consumers." So, users provide both content and data and this audience labour is appropriated by media companies through the terms of use of websites and internet service providers (Bermejo, 2011: 273–4).

That said, interactivity is a defining feature of digital media, and it is clear that some industries (e.g., book and newspaper publishing, sound recording) have been shaken to the core by our new-found capacity to bypass traditional production and distribution channels. We discuss this further in Chapters 8 and 9, and we also address in Chapter 10 the impact of social media, blogging, and citizen journalism in particular on both the practice of journalism and its structuring as a commercial news industry. But interactivity serves for the moment as an example of the unforeseen and unforeseeable consequences of technological development in the communications sphere, and how specific devices and applications are socially embedded, tied into larger cultural, political, and economic matrices.

Another defining feature of digital media is mobility. The ongoing transition from wired to wireless has implications for the form and content of communications media, and how we engage with them. As a highly connected society, we are still coming to terms with what it means to be able to carry our devices wherever we go and access wireless networks in an increasing number of places. For one thing, mobility alters fundamentally the spatial and temporal bounds of our communications (see Crow et al., 2010: 10). We

6.4 ▶▶▶▶▶▶

BIG DATA

By Ganaele Langlois

The term *big data* refers to the automated collection, storage and analysis of vast amounts of information in order to produce new knowledge about scientific, environmental, economic, and social issues. The term came into being in 1997 in a NASA article (Cox and Ellsworth, 1997) that highlighted the limits of existing technology to analyze and visualize ever-growing and complex sets of information. Since then, big data has turned from a problem about how to deal with too much information to a new frontier of opportunities in scientific, economic, and social development (Mayer-Schönberger and Cukier, 2013). The development of automated information storing and processing systems was key in this transformation, as it made possible the comparison among large and varied data sets.

We currently see big data used in three different sectors: science, business, and government (Bryant et al., 2008). In the hard sciences, big data helps understand climate change and trends over long periods of time. For instance, big data can help visualize not only changes in temperature due to global warming, but also how rising sea levels, droughts, and other recurring events due to climate change will provoke forced migrations and where those migrations will take place. Such knowledge can be used to predict zones of future conflicts over resources and habitable settings (IPCC, 2014).

Big data is used in the business environment to create valuable knowledge about consumer habits. Data itself refers to informational facts about an object, such as age, gender, residence location, friendship networks, consumption habits, and so on. Correlated with the data from other individuals, personal data become valuable as they help define specific populations of people with similar characteristics. Furthermore, detailed knowledge accumulated over time provides in-depth social and psychological profiles. Such knowledge can be used to create instantaneous targeted and personalized advertising and recommendations when surfing online, for instance.

Governments make use of big data to gain knowledge and guidance with respect to policy-making. However, the more noticeable and problematic use of vast amounts of data has been in relation to the widespread and constant surveillance of individuals by various state agencies, such as the Communications Security Establishment of Canada and the National Security Agency in the United States (Greenwald, 2014). Such tactics are being defended as ways to prevent terrorism and crime, but have ushered in a new set of concerns about privacy and government control over citizens' lives. Such concerns can be expanded to private corporations that make a business out of personal data collection, such as Google, Facebook, and Apple. That one's health, financial, and work data could be accessible for a price raises important issues about how employers, government, and businesses like insurance companies might deny services to users deemed unworthy or unprofitable. Thus, there is a pressing need for regulation and legislation about the use of data.

We are currently seeing local civic uses of big data for purposes other than control or profitability (see, for instance, Occupy Data: occupy-dat.org). The main issues encountered with civic uses of big data are limited resources and access to hardware and software, as well as limited access to data sets, particularly those that are privately owned.

Ganaele Langlois is an assistant professor in the Department of Communication Studies at York University in Toronto.

can work at home and play while at work, and we are confined less and less to the schedules set by others, whether that means watching our favourite TV series when we want—through time-shifting or binge viewing—or responding to texts or email messages either as they arrive or during a set time in the day. The flip side, of course, is that we are increasingly contactable, whether by employers on our time off or by telemarketers. Mobility also encourages further technological convergence. Rather than carry separate devices for specific purposes, each of our mobile devices offers multiple functions. As we noted earlier in the chapter, the hand-held smartphone allows us to read an e-book, watch television, make a short video, surf the web, play games, or, yes, talk to someone.

A third defining characteristic of digital media is individualization. If the legacy media—especially cinema, radio, television, home music systems, but also hard-copy newspapers—were typically experienced collectively, digital media are much more personal. This trend began in the 1980s with the personal computer, but it gradually included cellphones (phone numbers belong to individuals rather than households), MP3 players (with their personalized playlists), and the screens—either cellphone or computer—on which TV shows, sports events, and movies are increasingly viewed, and on which games are played. A significant part of the attraction of these devices is their personalization; we can adapt them to our own particular needs and use them as we see fit (see Goggin, 2011; Crow et al., 2010).

Technological Change: A Cost–Benefit Analysis

If there has been a note of caution in our discussion of technology so far in this chapter, it is for good reason. As much as we marvel at the scope and pace of technological change in the communications sphere—none of the authors would wish to return to the days when a textbook such as this would be researched within the physical confines of libraries and archives and written on a typewriter. History teaches us that benefits always come with some kind of cost. There are always trade-offs to what we consider advancements in our ability to communicate, and a full picture of the pros and cons to technological change emerges only with time. We provide a number of examples in this section of the chapter.

Increased Communication Capacity, Speed, and Flexibility

For many of us, it is easier to communicate and to find information than ever before. With satellites, optical fibres, sophisticated switching technologies, and data communication engineering, rather than merely having an ability to get a message from A to B, we now speak in terms of bandwidth and nanoseconds, how quickly and globally we can communicate.

Canada is and always has been at the forefront of communication technology, beginning with the first phone call made in the world by Alexander Graham Bell from Brantford, Ontario, to Paris, Ontario, on 10 March 1876; the first transatlantic telegraph message from Poldhu, England, to Signal Hill in St. John's, Newfoundland, at noon on 12 December 1901; and the first radio broadcast, by Canadian Reginald Fessenden, on Christmas Eve in 1906. Canada was the first nation to launch a domestic communication satellite and the federal government has maintained a commitment to both speed and capacity in the country's communications. For instance, broadband services were available to 99 percent of Canadian households in 2012, and slightly more than 85 percent of households subscribed. There remain, however, notable differences in broadband access between the country's urban centres and its rural areas and the North (CRTC, 2013, 177–78).

The digital divide that van Dijk (2012) analyzes pertains not only to the different nations of the world, but also between populations—even within countries like Canada that boast advanced communications infrastructure. We discuss the digital divide further in Chapter 11, but it is worth noting here that when it comes to internet access and usage, which many of us take for granted, there remain discrepancies among Canadians depending on income and educational levels, age, and community size. If Statistics Canada determined that 83 percent of Canadian households had internet access in 2012, only 58 percent of households with incomes of $30,000 or less enjoyed access. Similarly, only 28 percent of Canadians 65 and over in the lowest income quartile used the internet, compared to 95 percent aged 16 to 24 in the same income category (Statistics Canada, 2013). These data become

6.5 ▶▶▷▶▶▶

WHAT ARE ALGORITHMIC MEDIA?

By Fenwick McKelvey

YouTube receives 72 hours of uploaded video every minute, but copyright law requires YouTube to prevent the uploading of infringing content. How can YouTube monitor this deluge? Algorithms, of course. Its ContentID system monitors every upload and compares it to a database of known copyrighted works (or references files). A match causes ContentID either to block, keep up, or redirect the video's ad revenue to the copyright holder (Dayal, 2012; Google, 2014). The copyright cops have become copyright bots.

YouTube is one example, as ContentID demonstrates how contemporary media and information technologies depend on algorithms. If software "is the set of instructions that direct a computer to do a specific task" (Ceruzzi, 1998: 80), then algorithms are the specific instructions to complete that task (Goffey, 2008). The advertisements on your website, your search returns, and what status updates you read on Facebook NewsFeed depend on algorithms.

Calling media algorithmic offers another perspective to emphasize the perpetual work of algorithms running in the background to control our communication systems. Algorithms work to control all sorts of media, including YouTube. They find and recommend results, thereby influencing content consumption. The internet itself functions as an algorithmic medium because all information transmitted depends on internet routing algorithms.

Algorithms have been part of major debates on media policy in Canada. When Bell and Rogers installed new software in their internet infrastructure, it set off a major debate over network neutrality (see "Net Neutrality: Twenty-First-Century Common Carriage?"—Box 8.2 in Chapter 8). Should the internet treat all applications equally, or should network providers be able to discriminate or throttle (i.e., slow down) certain applications? The CRTC eventually held a review of the internet traffic management practices of ISPs. The decision led to the CRTC prohibiting network providers from using their algorithms to

1. block the delivery of content to customers;
2. noticeably degrade time-sensitive internet traffic; and
3. delay traffic "to the extent that it amounts to blocking the content."

The CRTC continues to enforce these rules.

Algorithms pose a problem to media policy because they usually operate in the background and lack systems of representation. How do you regulate forces you cannot observe? Their running code is often imperceptible and hardly ever known to its users. A packet does not arrive with an explanation of what decisions it took along its journey, nor does a suggested app in the Google Play Store (Ananny, 2011). "Insights into the inner workings of information algorithms is a form of power," writes Tarleton Gillespie, "vital to participating in public discourse, essential to achieving visibility online, constitutive of credibility and the opportunities that follow" (Gillespie, 2014: 185).

Algorithmic media are systems composed of algorithms. There is no cheat sheet or lone algorithm that will explain how the system works. Algorithms—at least at the level of internet routing—compete with each other as much as cooperate (McKelvey, 2010; Van Schewick, 2010). Even when a software's code is open, algorithms are not entirely predictable. Developers would never run tests or betas if they were.

To study algorithmic media, we have to be even more observant about their everyday operations. The concept then encourages looking at these many processes and how they interact. Do your search results change when you use a different account or location? How many of your posts do your friends see? Why were those apps recommended to you? Does your internet service seem slow? If we interact with algorithms every day, then just like a fish in water, we have to be more aware of our algorithmic media.

—Fenwick McKelvey is an assistant professor in the Department of Communication Studies at Concordia University in Montreal.

especially meaningful as government service outlets, schools, banks, insurance companies, and retailers presume access and disadvantage those without it.

Increased Flexibility in Production and Distribution

Over the last 25 to 30 years, the traditional, centralized, capital-intensive model of communication media has been eroded by digital media. In the late 1980s, desktop publishing brought layout and the design of books and magazines to anyone with a computer, a laser printer, and some basic skills. In the mid-1990s, the web brought a new form of global distribution online at minimal cost. In the late 1990s and early 2000s, inexpensive digital tools transformed music and video production and independent producers were increasingly able to reach audiences directly via social networking sites such as MySpace and Facebook. YouTube, Twitter, and Instagram have furthered this trend, complemented by the proliferation of hand-held mobile devices.

But the emergence and growth of these corporate aggregators has resulted in the reintroduction of intermediaries, countering the initial trend. Some call it **re-intermediation**, prompted by the filtering capacities of these services. A good example is Apple's iTunes music store, which presents a new mechanism for filtering, sorting, and—more importantly—promoting music available online. YouTube provides another example, whereby hundreds of millions of video clips are available for free. These re-intermediators have established their own brand identity and presence. With the burgeoning of content, the traditional challenges of producing, manufacturing, and distributing product are being replaced by the provision of a wide range of content filtered, organized, and capable of being sampled and remixed in new ways. What makes this possible is not just a wealth of content but an enormous increase in the amount of readily available information about the content, through blogs, reviews, tags, comments, and cataloguing data. As Chris Anderson points out in his 2006 book, *The Long Tail: Why the Future of Business Is Selling Less of More*,

> Consumers act as guides individually when they post user reviews or blog about their likes and dislikes. Because it's now so easy to tap this grassroots information when you're looking for something new, you're more likely to find what you want faster than ever. That has the economic effect of encouraging you to search farther outside the world you already know, which drives demand down into the niches. (Anderson, 2006: 56)

But if these services make available vast quantities of both professional and user-generated content, they nonetheless reassert their power to determine the terms for access to their services. This includes whether or not we can download content and at what price, whether and how much they will compensate content producers, and, ultimately, whether or not they will prohibit certain materials on, for example, moral or political grounds. (See our discussion of walled gardens in Chapter 11.) They have reasserted themselves as gatekeepers, even if that role has been modified. Martin Hirst, John Harrison, and Patricia Mazepa (2014) argue that these practices result in the organization of information

YouTube and iTunes are good examples of re-intermediation: the reintroduction of online intermediaries who specialize in aggregating or packaging content.

Source: © photojournalis/iStockphoto.

according to economic priorities, place information under private control and/or management, and assume for their own commercial purposes the role of public information repositories—a role traditionally held by true public institutions such as libraries and archives—by providing "free" content. "While Google, like other companies, can decide what advertising it accepts, or not, it can also decide what words and sites it will list and you can access, or not; and what information is available, or not" (Hirst et al., 2014: 312).

Models and Databases: Controlling Things and Processes

Computers are and always have been about models; the earliest computers were used to construct a model to allow projections of reality. Today, the mother of all information technologies is the database—most commonly, the relational database that structures information as collections of rows and columns and the web of interrelations between them. By collecting a large amount of real-world data as they are produced, and placing this material in a database, one can develop a sophisticated model with an immense amount of power to analyze what has gone before, understand what is happening currently, and predict what will happen next. Google's statistically improbable phrases (SIPs) allow discourse communities to be identified and publications of interest to be brought to the attention of consumers. (Perhaps the best explanation of statistically improbable phrases is to cite some examples. Terms such as *content analysis* and *mass communication* are highly probable in communication-analysis documents and, although occasionally used, are highly improbable in everyday discourse.) No doubt, law-enforcement agencies use the same techniques to try to identify criminal activity. Each time an individual goes on a deadly rampage—for example, the June 2014 killing of three RCMP officers in Moncton—some wonder whether analysis of websites might allow prior identification of potential murderers.

Developing and analyzing databases of information in an effort to create new systems and processes of control is a growing field of study. Manufacturing relies on computer modelling and feedback. The emerging field of bioinformatics merges computer science with genetics, as researchers populate vast databases with genetic information, seeking to understand genetics through constructing computer-based models of the human (and many other species') genome. The combination of anthropological techniques (ethnography) with biological data into ethnobiology is allowing two different realms of information to be merged.

Such activities are sometimes referred to as **topsight**, and the pursuit of topsight is one of the major thrusts of high technology today. Every electronic transaction is recorded and the sum total of transactions creates a body of data, which, in turn, can be mined for valuable information. This information can then be used by the person who collects it or it can be sold to another party. The direct recording of information also results in a net decrease in the costs of the transactions. No longer is paying for an item one function, assessing the store's stock levels another, counting cash yet another—with electronic transactions, all this and more are rolled into one. Yet, effectively, such activities represent a scaling up of processes normal to small business. The small business often knows its customers intimately: "The usual, Mr. Wodehouse?" Computerization of information allows the intimacy of such interactions to be synthesized. Some feel uncomfortable with such machine synthesis, and many would claim it makes a poor (possibly an alienating) attempt at knowing the customer or, for that matter, of knowing its product. For example, people who have ever purchased anything online from Amazon have probably recognized the odd sidebar suggestions of what else they might be interested in buying.

System Vulnerability

The storage capacity of today's computers, whether we are talking about the hard drive on our laptops or remote, cloud-based servers, can make life easier in many ways, as can such services as online shopping and electronic banking. But our move to a digital world introduces certain vulnerabilities. There is always the possibility of a major cosmic event involving substantial electromagnetic disturbances, as Canada experienced in 1994 when two of its communication satellites were disabled by cosmic particles (Lam et al., 2012). More common, however, is concern about the theft of data and the spread of malicious software, commonly known as malware, which can contaminate computer systems. Systems exist to protect sensitive data like credit card numbers (as well as passwords and other identity tokens). Usually, such tokens are encrypted before being transmitted over the network. But, as with locks on doors, whatever can be encrypted can also be cracked, given enough effort. Practical, real-world data security—as with physical locks—is concerned with making things secure enough to make it not worth an attacker's while. Nothing is ever 100 percent secure, however. The Canada Revenue Agency, for example, was the victim of the so-called Heartbleed security bug in 2014, resulting in the theft of 900 social insurance numbers from its servers (Leblanc and Ha, 2014). Social insurance numbers, normally kept confidential, can be used in identify theft and other forms of fraud.

As if attempts to disrupt normal internet activity by technically defeating a system via spam, viruses, and encryption cracking were not enough, we must also consider the role of human beings in the techno-social internet ensemble and examine the vulnerabilities of millions of online users. One of the most common examples of online fraud is **phishing**. You receive an email message seemingly from your bank or preferred email service in which you are asked to update information or renew your account. All you need to do, the message tells you, is click on the provided link and log in with your username and password. The problem is that the site you are asked to connect to is not the bank or your email service, and so when you type in your username and password, you are unwittingly providing this information to the people behind the scam. For very *little* investment, even a small percentage of people who respond by following the link and logging in can pay off for these crooks.

Extreme fraud involves stealing the identity of another. Identity theft entails collecting enough information on someone so that the fraud artist can begin to assume that person's identity. Knowing this to be a possibility, people who make extensive use of the internet routinely provide false information in response to the requirement by certain sites and internet services to provide a user identity—they give the false identity in order to protect themselves. The relative instability of identity and authentication schemes on the internet leads to opportunities for fraud on both small and large scales.

Surveillance versus Privacy

Digital technologies permit sophisticated and pervasive monitoring of both public and private spaces, as well as the tracking of individuals' behaviour. Minna Tarkka (2011) describes "a totalizing grid and mesh of surveillance" comprising geographic information systems, Global Positioning Systems (well-known by drivers as GPS), radio frequency identification, and closed-circuit television systems (Tarkka, 2011: 131). This surveillance grid has some obvious social benefits when it comes to things like personal, home, and national security, or crime prevention and law enforcement. Images from closed-circuit video cameras, TV news footage and individuals' smartphone cameras, for example, helped police identify the perpetrators of the bombings at the 2013 Boston Marathon, just as they helped Vancouver police identify and charge close to 300 rioters during the 2011 Stanley Cup final, even though research indicates the overall effectiveness of surveillance for crime prevention is unsubstantiated (Hirst et al., 2014: 286–9).

Surveillance tools and practices also benefit governments, which rely on statistical data for policy formation, and government agencies interested in tracking long-term social, economic, health, or environmental trends. They also help meteorologists warn of threatening weather systems and assist air-traffic controllers in doing their jobs. One of the reasons the disappearance of Malaysian Airlines flight MH370 was such a compelling news story in 2014 was the fact that it defied all of these surveillance systems; it was the exception that proved the rule.

There is a fine line, however, between these benefits and more invasive strategies that compromise our right to privacy. We are learning more and more about the extent to which government agencies and corporations are encroaching on this right, legally and illegally. Privacy is interpreted in the most general terms as the right to be left alone and is considered a basic human right, included in Section 8 of Canada's Charter of Rights and Freedoms as well as Article 12 of the Universal Declaration of Human Rights.

Canadians' privacy is governed by two specific pieces of legislation: the 1983 Privacy Act, which permits individuals access to personal information held about them by the federal government, and imposes fair information obligations on the government in terms of how it collects, maintains, uses, and discloses personal information under its control; and the 2001 Personal Information Protection and Electronic Documents Act, which seeks to balance individuals' privacy rights with organizations' needs to collect and use information for economic purposes (Holmes, 2008: 4–5).

In a study of Canada's privacy laws, Nancy Holmes writes, "To experts in this area, privacy is equated with the right to enjoy private space, to conduct private communications, to be free from surveillance and to have the sanctity of one's body respected. To most people, it is about control—what is known about them and by whom" (2008: 1).

All laws and policy documents are subject to interpretation, of course, and Canadians share with citizens around the world an increasing concern about the protection of their privacy. The Communications Security Establishment of Canada (CSEC) was little known to most Canadians until it made the news in 2013 when the extent of its electronic spying activities was revealed. The

CSEC is a security and intelligence agency mandated by the National Defence Act to

> acquire and use information from the global information infrastructure for the purpose of providing foreign intelligence, in accordance with Government of Canada intelligence priorities; to provide advice, guidance and services to help ensure the protection of electronic information and of information infrastructures of importance to the Government of Canada; to provide technical and operational assistance to federal law enforcement and security agencies in the performance of their lawful duties. (CSEC, 2014)

Even though the CSEC is prohibited by law from spying on Canadians, documents leaked by former US National Security Agency (NSA) contractor Edward Snowden revealed that the CSEC had used the free Wi-Fi system at an unidentified Canadian airport to track the metadata of randomly selected Canadians as a way of identifying foreign security threats, something to which the CSEC later admitted. Metadata is the electronic equivalent of the "To" and "From" addresses on a letter envelope. The Snowden documents alleged further that Stephen Harper's government allowed the NSA in coordination with the CSEC to spy on delegates to the 2010 G8 and G20 summits in Toronto, and that the CSEC conducted industrial espionage against the Brazilian ministry of mines and energy (Fekete, 2013; McDiarmid, 2013; Greenwald, 2014).

This news was a revelation to Canadians, most of whom neither were aware that such an agency existed nor understood the scope of its activities. There was particular concern about oversight. The CSEC is subject to review by the Office of the Communications Security Establishment's commissioner, but it is not subject to legislative or judicial review from elected parliamentarians (Brean, 2014).

Context here is important. Canadian governments have a long history of opening mail;

6.6 ▶▶▶▶▶▶

EDWARD SNOWDEN: HERO OR TRAITOR?

In November 2013, a *Globe and Mail* editorial asked whether Edward Snowden should be considered a hero. Snowden is the former US National Security Agency subcontractor who leaked top-secret information about the NSA's domestic surveillance activities to *The Guardian* and *The Washington Post* in 2013. Snowden was charged by the US government under the Espionage Act, but he has been living in Russia seeking to avoid extradition (see Greenwald, 2014).

Among the revelations contained in the Snowden leaks was the fact that Communications Security Establishment of Canada had monitored internal communications within Brazil's Mines and Energy Ministry and that it had tracked communications through the Wi-Fi network at an unidentified Canadian airport.

People like Snowden, journalist Glenn Greenwald, and WikiLeaks founder Julian Assange have turned the tables on these powerful and secretive state agencies by exposing details about their activities and sharing publicly some of the data they would prefer to keep secret. They defend their actions in the name of democracy and citizens' right to privacy. The states and the state agencies they are surveilling, however, accuse them of traitorous behaviour, undermining their efforts to maintain national security. Do you think Edward Snowden is a hero or a traitor?

Source: Sarah Lynn Mayhew, SLM Art.

By blowing the whistle on surveillance activities by the NSA and the CSEC, Edward Snowden became both a hero and a controversial figure around the globe.

eavesdropping on telegraph and telephone conversations; monitoring programs and personnel at Crown corporations like the CBC and the NFB; reading and collecting publications; and sending covert representatives to political, labour, and cultural meetings, public demonstrations, and protests (Hirst et al., 2014: 275). And in the aftermath of the 9/11 attacks on New York City and Washington, such surveillance has been intensified in the so-called War on Terrorism. For example, Canada passed its Anti-Terrorism Act in December 2011, enlarging and extending

6.7 ▶▶ ▶▶ ▶▶

A PANOPTIC SOCIETY?

It is worth asking whether the surveillance technologies available to governments, border-control agents, military and police forces, and private corporations, constitute a form of panopticism.

The English philosopher of utilitarianism Jeremy Bentham developed the Panopticon in the late eighteenth century as a model form of prison. The prison would feature a central guard tower surrounded by an annular building of prisoners' cells. The cells would have windows front and back, allowing light to shine through. The idea was that the prisoners would be visible at all times to the guards, but the guards could not be seen by the prisoners. Because the prisoners would not know when they were being observed, they had to assume they were being watched constantly, and thus would discipline themselves.

In his classic work, *Discipline and Punish*, Michael Foucault (1995 [1979]) posits Bentham's Panopticon as "the diagram of a mechanism of power reduced to its ideal form" (Foucault, 1995 [1979]: 205). The major effect of the Panopticon, Foucault writes, is "to induce in the inmate a state of conscious and permanent visibility that assumes the automatic functioning of power" (201). The Panopticon, though, was more than a prison; it was also a laboratory that "could be used as a machine to carry out experiments, to alter behaviour, to train or correct individuals" (203). Foucault adds, "It is polyvalent in its applications; it serves to reform prisoners, but also to treat patients, to instruct schoolchildren, to confine the insane, to supervise workers, to put beggars and idlers to work" (205).

Applied to the surveillance techniques of society at large, panopticism implies that citizens will assume they are constantly being watched and will therefore behave accordingly, internalizing the state's regulatory power. We have to ask whether we want this, especially in a democratic society, because it could impede citizens' sense of freedom, inhibit their lawful right to express criticism and dissent, and their right to peaceful protest, and provide law-enforcement agencies grounds to infringe upon these freedoms.

Source: Courtesy the artist and David Zwirner, New York.

Canadian Artist Stan Douglas's "Panopticon, Isla de Pinos" shows Presidio Modelo, a now-abandoned Cuban prison, modelled on Bentham's Panopticon. How is Bentham's Panopticon like the surveillance state? What are the advantages and disadvantages of surveillance for society?

the surveillance powers of the Canadian Security Intelligence Service (CSIS) (Hirst et al., 2014: 278–9).

Innocent Canadians can pay the price when they get caught up in this web. Canadian Liberal senator David Smith was flagged as a "potential terrorist" on a no-fly list in 2012 when, ironically, he attempted to board a flight from Toronto to Ottawa to attend a meeting of the Special Anti-Terrorism Committee, of which he is the former chair (Hirst et al., 2014: 287). The most notorious case, however, is that of Maher Arar, a Canadian software engineer who was taken into custody by US authorities as he passed through a New York airport on a flight to Montreal following a 2002 vacation in Tunisia. Accused of having links to terrorism, he was held incommunicado in the United States for 12 days before being shipped off to Syria where he was tortured over a period of 10 months. A subsequent commission of inquiry exonerated Arar, but it was unable to verify reports that the RCMP and unidentified Canadian officials were implicated in his rendition by passing information about Arar to US authorities and, subsequently, damaging his reputation by leaking information to Canadian journalists. Nevertheless, both the RCMP and the Canadian government issued public apologies to Arar, and the Canadian government awarded him more than $10 million in compensation for his ordeal.

Canadian government departments and police forces remain active in monitoring Canadians' activities in cyberspace. Canada's Supreme Court ruled unanimously in June 2014 that internet users have a reasonable expectation of privacy and that government and police officials were violating Canadians' constitutional privacy rights by obtaining information about telecom subscribers' identities without a warrant (MacCharles, 2014). The ruling followed a report by Rogers Communications that it had received 175,000 requests for subscriber information in 2013, a figure that represented 1.75 percent of its 10 million subscribers (Greenwood, 2014).

Gavin John David Smith (2009) describes the paradox in which society's response to security

concerns "is as much the problem as the solution," a situation in which "technologies of security produce ontologies of insecurity" (145). Hirst et al. argue that this climate of insecurity is a product of, among other things, the increasing presence of security guards (in private and public spaces), security checkpoints (at airports, concert venues), security cameras, radar cameras, gated communities and both news coverage and TV crime dramas that can feed into a sense of moral panic (2014: 286–91).

As we discussed earlier in this chapter, corporations are also collecting information on users of digital networks, primarily for marketing purposes, turning users into commodities. *The Wall Street Journal* reported in 2010 that each of the top 50 websites in the United States installed, on average, 64 different pieces of tracking technology on visitors' computers, usually without notice (Croteau and Hoynes, 2014: 326). The two standard practices in collecting information are *tracking* and *scraping*. Tracking involves the use of sophisticated statistical analysis and algorithms to create a user profile, identifying such characteristics as sex, age, income, residence, marital status, parental status, likes, dislikes, and health conditions, among other things. This profile is sold to advertisers to more precisely target potential customers. Scraping entails copying

In recent years, there has been an increasing presence of a wide-ranging security apparatus: security guards, security checkpoints, security cameras, and radar cameras at roadway intersections. Does the increase of security make you feel more or less safe?

Source: © Alija/iStockphoto.

online conversations and personal information from social networking and job-posting sites. These data can then either be sold to employers or advertisers or packaged as endorsements for a particular product or service (Croteau and Hoynes, 2014: 327).

What we typically think of as digital services provided to us for free (e.g., search engines, social media, Wi-Fi access in cafés and airports) actually come at a cost; we divulge personal information in exchange for access in what Greg Elmer et al. (2004) terms "a digitized and networked information economy" (4–5).

Aside from Canada's courts and the news media, researchers and activists specializing in privacy issues are hoping to draw the general public into the surveillance versus privacy debate. The University of Ottawa hosted a Politics of Surveillance Workshop in May 2014, at which the *Ottawa Statement on Mass Surveillance in Canada* was presented. It was subsequently published on the website OpenMedia.ca (read the statement at openmedia.ca/statement) asking people to sign on. The statement expresses concern about "big data" and "ubiquitous surveillance," and asks that all governments respect the Canadian Charter's privacy provisions; clarify and strengthen privacy laws; extend the powers of federal and provincial privacy commissioners; and publicly acknowledge secret international security treaties. Finally, the statement asserts that "a full, transparent and participatory public process must begin to create a comprehensive legal framework for information and privacy rights and freedoms, built on the Canadian Charter of Rights and Freedoms and acknowledging the United Nations' reaffirmation of privacy as a fundamental human right."

Social networking sites like Facebook, LinkedIn, Twitter, Instagram, and Pinterest are among the most popular digital media applications and texting has replaced telephone calls and emails for many kinds of interpersonal communication. If these sites and applications have become indispensable tools for keeping abreast of what's happening in all aspects of daily life, from our circles of family and friends to the worlds of news, sports, entertainment, celebrity gossip, and related diversions, they leave us vulnerable to people who are not our friends.

Recent and highly publicized cases of cyberbullying have led to a public outcry and proposed legislation by the federal government. Rehteah Parsons of Dartmouth, Nova Scotia, hanged herself and died in hospital in 2013 after photos of her alleged gang rape at age 15 were distributed online. In 2012, Amanda Todd of Port Coquitlam, British Columbia, killed herself at age 15 after repeated instances of cyberbullying, including being blackmailed into exposing her breasts during a video chat session with a stranger, photos of which were posted to Facebook. If these are particularly extreme cases of online harassment, they demonstrate the extent to which digital interactivity can be used for ill as well as good.

▶ SUMMARY ────────────────────

We live in an age when technology—and communications technology especially—occupies a very central place in our lives, and it is important to understand what we mean by technology and the relationship between technology and human activity.

We began this chapter with some theoretical perspectives that emphasize the practical, social, situated nature of technology. We reviewed several theoretical perspectives of technology, including instrumentalism, determinism, substantivism, critical theory, and constructivism. We discussed the limitations of the first three in particular, and how theorists increasingly see technology as a phenomenon that, like other areas of social practice, is best understood as socially constructed. We noted how machines can be seen as socio-technical ensembles, as phenomena that have technical elements but are social in their application or manifestation. We emphasized how technology changes things rather than solves problems; positive and negative consequences of technology are always intertwined and, to some extent, unpredictable. We examined closure and how closure on a particular socio-technical ensemble leads to a determinist illusion that the machine/system/black box could only have developed in the way it finally did.

Communication technology is closely linked to control, and public policy in the past century has had a major impact on the particular socio-technical ensembles and the resulting industries with which we now live. Media convergence is breaking down media silos and generating new policy challenges that require twenty-first-century approaches.

The social rationales most often used in favour of technological development highlight democracy and education. But the realities of technological communication systems, once they are introduced, involve various forms of commercial exploitation. History is repeating itself in this regard; in spite of the democratic potential of new media forms, corporations—some new, some old—remain key players in shaping cyberspace.

This is not to suggest that the game is over, or that opportunities for exploiting digital technologies for more progressive goals have been foreclosed, but it is a reminder to think about what is "new" about new media. We concluded the chapter by demonstrating that new media forms entail both new possibilities and new problems. There has been very little consideration of the macro implications of the development of the information sector. This lack of prior consideration is part of the technological imperative, which assumes that any unforeseen problems can be solved in time by still newer technological solutions. Today, for example, we hear such arguments in regard to climate change and environmental degradation. The blithe acceptance by society of technology because it means economic gain, at least for some, blinds us to considering the desirability of technological developments for society as a whole, whether those developments involve health, entertainment, war, fashion, or life itself.

 KEY TERMS

ARPANET, p. 163
backbone provider, p. 162
closure, p. 156
convergence, p. 150
critical theory, p. 155
cyborg, p. 152
deskilling, p. 153
digitization, p. 160
digital divide, p. 158
instrumentalism, p. 152

media silo, p. 160
open source, p. 164
phishing, p. 171
re-intermediation, p. 169
scientific management, p. 153
socio-technical ensemble, p. 156
substantivism, p. 153
technological hubris, p. 159
topsight, p. 170

 RELATED WEBSITES

Canarie: www.canarie.ca/en/home
The Canarie website carries a wealth of information on Canada's data network.

Internet World Stats: www.internetworldstats.com/stats.htm
A useful source of current data on internet usage worldwide.

Office of the Privacy Commissioner of Canada: www.priv.gc.ca/index_e.asp
An information-rich site pertaining to privacy issues and initiatives affecting Canadians, including tips on protecting your privacy.

Wikileaks: wikileaks.org
A non-profit organization that provides an online platform for the publication of leaked documents and other original source material, accompanied by news stories providing the data with context.

Wired **magazine: www.wired.com**
Wired is an influential source of news and commentary on new media. The magazine's masthead touts Marshall McLuhan as its patron saint.

 ## FURTHER READINGS

Crow, Barbara, Michael Longford, and Kim Sawchuk, eds. 2010. *The Wireless Spectrum: The Politics, Practices and Poetics of Mobile Media*. Toronto: University of Toronto Press. A collection of essays examining what wireless, mobile technologies mean for the day-to-day lives of individuals and the public at large.

Feenberg, Andrew. 1999. *Questioning Technology*. New York: Routledge. An analysis of the nature of technology, including a review of various theories that attempt to explain technology.

Flew, Terry, and Richard Smith. 2014. *New Media: An Introduction*, 2nd Canadian Edition. Don Mills, ON: Oxford University Press. An introduction to the social, political, and economic impacts of new media through the years.

Hirst, Martin, John Harrison, and Patricia Mazepa. 2014. *Communication and New Media: From Broadcast to Narrowcast*, Canadian Edition. Don Mills, ON: Oxford University Press. An assessment of the implications of media convergence through the lens of political economy.

Jenkins, Henry. 2006. *Convergence Culture: Where Old and New Media Collide*. New York and London: New York University Press. An analysis of contemporary sociocultural transformations resulting from media convergence.

McChesney, Robert W. 2013. *Digital Disconnect: How Capitalism Is Turning the Internet Against Democracy*. New York: The New Press. A critical view of what the internet's commercialization means to its democratic potential.

Slack, Jennifer Daryl, and J. Macgregor Wise. 2007. *Culture and Technology: A Primer*. New York: Peter Lang. An accessible discussion of current debates that demonstrate the interplay between technology and culture.

 ## STUDY QUESTIONS

1. What is determinism and why is it inadequate to our theoretical understanding of technology's place in society?
2. How do we define technology and what does it mean to say technology is socially, cultural, politically and economically embedded?
3. We cited the sinking of the *Titanic* in 1912 as an example of technological hubris. What is technological hubris? Cite a more contemporary example.
4. What are the trade-offs we make when we access free websites and other digital applications?
5. What is constructivism and why is it the prevailing theory of technology today?
6. What are the pros and cons of society's increased surveillance capacities?

III

The Communications Environment

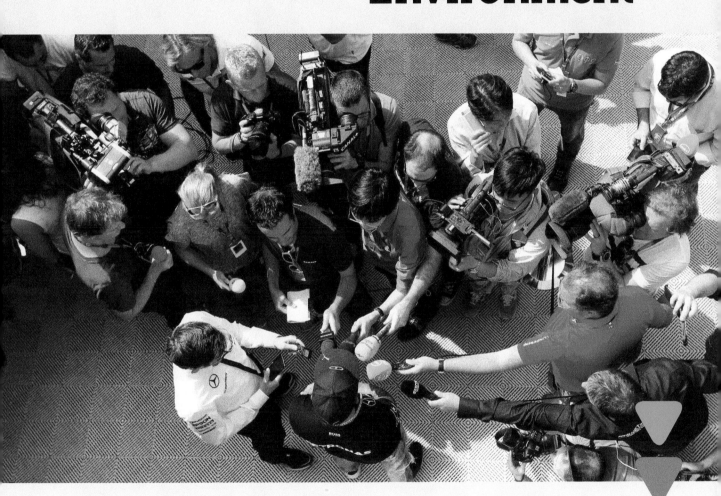

7 The Formation of Public Policy

The cornerstone of Canada's approach . . . is the premise that culture is a way of life and an essential element of a community's survival. — Sarah Armstrong

Opening Questions

- What does it mean to say that mass communication is a highly structured activity?

- What is communications policy?

- How is communications policy developed?

- What role does the public play in policy development?

- What ideas guided communications policy development in Canada for most of the twentieth century?

- What has changed in terms of the way the Canadian government develops communications policy?

- Why is policy now developed in a global context?

Introduction

Mass communication takes place in a constructed environment, informed by communication technologies (as we discussed in the preceding chapter), but also by laws, policies, conventions, economic imperatives, guiding ideals, and public pressures. Communications policy is established by international regulatory bodies and national and regional governments to ensure that media serve not only their owners and content creators, but individual citizens and society as a whole. These policies establish rights and responsibilities individually and collectively. If media workers have the right to freedom of expression, they also have a responsibility to respect individuals' privacy and laws pertaining to libel, copyright, hate speech, and so on. If media owners have the right to a reasonable return on their investment, they also have an obligation to exert responsibly their market power and to respect the larger social and cultural goals of their community.

Policy development in any one jurisdiction is always part of a larger, international policy context because mass communication takes place across borders— increasingly so today. Copyright laws are believed to have been introduced in the late fifteenth century, and international telephony has been regulated since the early twentieth century. Policy is particularly germane today when digital technologies enable media content to penetrate every region of the globe in an instant.

The policy discourse in Canada, articulated through a series of royal commissions, task forces, public hearings, and committee reports, serves as the country's collective response to the question, *What is communication for in Canada?* The answers to this question help us understand the logic behind policy decisions, laws and regulations.

In Canada, communications policies can be developed by governments in committee, subject to usual parliamentary procedures, or by public agencies like the CRTC. Depending on their impact, they may or may not generate

7.1 ▶▶▶▶▶▶

DEFINING TERMS: LEGISLATION, REGULATION, POLICY

The term legislation refers to acts, statutes, or laws that have been passed by Parliament or a provincial legislature. The Broadcasting Act and Telecommunications Act are examples of legislation.

Regulations are "the rules that address the details and practical applications of the law. The authority to make regulations related to an Act is assigned within that Act. Just like statutes, regulations have the full force of law" (Law Central Alberta). For instance, the structure of the CRTC and its powers to make regulation are described within the Broadcasting Act, and it uses those powers to make regulations derived from terms and ideas laid out in that legislation.

The term policy refers to the set of rules, laws, and practices that govern a particular activity. For instance, the rules, laws, and practices governing broadcasting are called broadcasting policy.

An order-in-council is an order typically formulated by the federal cabinet and authorized by the Governor General. Orders-in-council are commonly used to make appointments, such as appointments to a royal commission (Forsey, 2006).

much media or public attention. More significant policy initiatives, the emergence of new problems in the communications field, or the advent of new media technologies typically prompt federal and provincial governments to call for public hearings, either through royal commissions, task forces, or parliamentary committees. This allows governments to collect information, to gauge opinion from the public, from the business community, from the research community, and from people directly involved, and to receive specific recommendations.

These consultative exercises inform, but do not determine, communications policy in any simple way. Typically, the resulting reports contain background information, valuable data, arguments from various perspectives, and pertinent recommendations to governments and government departments that emerge from months—often years—of study. The recommendations tend to range from the pragmatic to the idealistic, from those that represent mere tinkering with the status quo to much more radical propositions. The government of the day weighs the political, economic, legal, and sociocultural implications of these recommendations and decides if and how to act. Many of our most prominent cultural institutions—the NFB, the

Canada Council, Telefilm Canada, the CRTC, the CBC—emerged from such recommendations.

Canadian government interventions in the communications field have been guided for most of the past century by a logic that frames the media, culture, and society in terms of the nation-state. While these interventions, and this logic, have never gone unchallenged, they have faced particularly strong opposition in recent years on three fronts: the fiscal, the technological, and the philosophical. First, can Canada afford to promote and protect indigenous cultural activity? In an era of deficit reduction at all levels of government, the cultural sector has not been spared budget cuts. The severity of these cuts means some cultural programs have disappeared and those that survive strain to fulfill their mandates. Increasingly, too, governments are looking to the private sector to fulfill Canadians' communications needs. The flip side of this question is, of course, can Canadian governments afford not to intervene? Second, with the rise of new, powerful, pervasive, and global communication networks, is it technologically feasible, even possible, for governments to intervene in communicative activities that stretch beyond their borders? For the time being at least, Ottawa has answered affirmatively, but the question becomes more pertinent daily. Finally, should Canadian governments be involved in cultural production in the first place, given the costs, the private-sector alternatives, the global climate of liberalized trade, and concerns about what state intervention means for the independence of cultural producers?

In order to address these questions properly, we need to understand how and why Canada's communications policy structure emerged. In this chapter, we situate the Canadian policy discussion within a global context, then address public involvement in Canadian policy development. Next, we trace the historical trajectory of communications policy in Canada through four defining twentieth-century policy documents. This section reveals the bases on which communications policy was forged until the 1980s: the

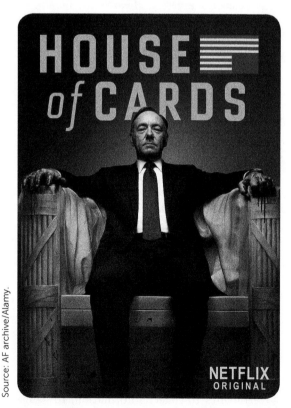

Source: AF archive/Alamy.

The CRTC heard arguments from Netflix and other organizations in September 2014 discussing the future of television regulations in Canada. How do services like Netflix challenge policies promoting Canadian content?

project of building a nation and a national culture, and the concern that a strict market approach to communications would lead to further dominance of the Canadian mediascape by the United States. We conclude the chapter with a discussion of how those themes, while they remain pertinent, no longer resonate as they once did with the public, cultural producers, or governments. If they're still part of the discussion, new policy challenges, such as globalization, and Canada's increasingly diverse population, have arisen. In Chapter 8, we will look at the policy picture from the perspective of each of the communication sectors in turn, particularly as digitization and the emergence of the internet are breaking down the clear distinctions between sectors.

Back to the Future

The instantaneous global communication enabled today by ubiquitous digital technologies resurrects communication policy themes that have been played out for more than 500 years, since the invention of the printing press in the mid-fifteenth century. We hear regular news reports that countries like Iran, North Korea, Myanmar (Burma), China, and Cuba seek to prevent or strictly control cross-border communication flows (e.g., banning foreign journalists, shutting down wireless networks, blocking access to certain websites, conducting surveillance on private email correspondence), particularly when those communications concern political subjects. It is important to understand, however, that all countries patrol their communications borders: to protect national security, to prevent the illegal circulation of certain materials (e.g., child pornography), to ensure the integrity of financial data, to protect national cultural industries, and so on.

International communications scholar Cees Hamelink (1994) describes communications policy as a by-product of global contact between peoples, companies, and governments. Most of this contact prior to 1800 came about through meetings of individual traders, merchants, and diplomats. But following the expansion of trade markets during the Industrial Revolution (which led to the expansion of trade markets within and beyond Europe) and the French Revolution (which fostered nationalism throughout Europe and reinforced the sovereignty of nation-states), greater need arose for multilateral state governance (Hamelink, 1994: 5–6).

Each of the communications sectors required its own forms of international governance. As early as the sixteenth century, the postal system in Europe was regulated by bilateral agreements to facilitate and standardize the circulation of letters across borders. Expanding shipping and railway networks necessitated a more formal, multilateral agreement. A first meeting in Paris in 1863 and a subsequent meeting in Berne, Switzerland, led to the Berne Convention and the founding of the General Postal Union in 1874 (renamed the Universal Postal Union in 1878) and "introduced basic norms and rules that still hold today" (Hamelink, 1994: 7). These include the freedom of postal transport within countries belonging to the union and the standardization of charges collected by each country for mail service between members.

Similarly, the development of telegraphy in the early nineteenth century required standardization and cooperation across borders. Again, this began with bilateral agreements, and the agreements between European countries in the 1850s provided the template for the 1865 International Telegraph Convention. Telephony was incorporated into the agreement in 1903 and in 1932, the International Telegraph Union and the International Radio-Telegraph Union merged to become what we know today as the International Telecommunications Union (Hamelink, 1994: 8–9).

The first international conference to discuss radio communication ("wireless radio-telegraphy"), held in Berlin in 1903, led to the 1906 Berlin Radio Convention, adopted by 29 countries. The convention allocated frequency bands within the earth's electromagnetic spectrum for use by specific services (e.g., marine communication, emergency communication) at a time when radio was used for two-way, point-to-point communication rather than the broadcasting we are familiar with today. A subsequent radio conference in Washington in 1927 drafted a new Radio Convention and Radio Regulations to address a range of issues raised by radio broadcasting, from **frequency allocation** to station ownership and state control (Hamelink, 1994: 9–10).

The printing press prompted the notion of **intellectual property**, and it is believed that the first copyright laws emerged in Vienna in the late fifteenth century. Most of the earliest copyright laws protected only national citizens' works. The US Copyright Act of 1790, for example, did not protect foreign authors' works, which led to the rampant pirating of books by best-selling English authors, most famously Charles Dickens, as Box 7.2 explains (Hamelink, 1994: 11). A series of bilateral agreements on intellectual property rights were signed between 1840 and 1866, when the First International Convention on Copyright in Berne—the Berne Convention—granted protection to foreign-published works. Further discussions produced the Berne Treaty on copyright in 1886, which states,

> In the development of authors' rights the basic principles have been to ensure remuneration for an author by protecting his work against reproduction (for 50 years after the author's lifetime), to demand respect for the individual integrity of the creator, to encourage the development of the arts, literature and science, and to promote a wider dissemination of literary, artistic and scientific works. (Hamelink, 1994: 13)

Included within the definition of intellectual property is industrial property; national patent protections emerged in the late eighteenth and early nineteenth centuries. The first multilateral negotiations took place in Vienna in 1873 and led in 1883 to the Convention for the Creation of the Union for the Protection of Industrial Property (Hamelink, 1994: 14–16).

The founding of these international governing institutions was fraught with struggles over questions of political and economic sovereignty, and over questions of communicative power, as they continue to be today. As cultural production became large-scale cultural industry in the twentieth century, there were both cultural and economic concerns about media imperialism; already by the last half of the nineteenth century, three news agencies dominated the production and circulation of international news around the world, dividing global territories among themselves and thus monopolizing the framing and definition of current events. By 1914, the major Hollywood film companies had captured 85 per cent of the world film audience (McChesney, 1997: 12–14). The United Nations Educational, Scientific and Cultural Organization (UNESCO) became the principal forum for discussion about how to resolve political tensions produced by the expansion of the world communications system, particularly between east and west during the Cold War and between the Global North and Global South that persist today. The World Trade Organization has become the venue for discussions of the economic implications of communicative exchange.

It should be noted that provincial governments also develop policy particular to their needs, Quebec being the most obvious example. If governments privilege the collective concerns of their jurisdictions—sovereignty, identity, the economy—**non-governmental organizations** like Amnesty International and Reporters Without Borders foreground basic individual human rights, including the **right to communicate**, privileging the universal application of such rights according to such conventions as the **Universal Declaration of Human Rights** (see Box 7.3).

7.2 ▶▶▶▶▶▶

CHARLES DICKENS

Mass pirating of English-language books by foreign, especially English, authors persisted throughout the nineteenth century, despite the urgings of British (and some American) authors and politicians for the US Congress to recognize international copyright. Charles Dickens's *A Christmas Carol*, for example, sold for $2.50 in England and for six cents in the United States (Vaidhyanathan, 2001: 50). In January 1837, 55 British writers petitioned US Congress, but a proposed bill to protect their intellectual property on US soil was opposed by publishing houses in the States and went nowhere (Vaidhyanathan, 2001: 51).

In 1842, Dickens himself toured the United States. "At many stops, Dickens pleaded for international copyright. Yet his audiences were filled with fans who had happily paid very low prices for American-printed, leather-bound copies of his work, from which Dickens earned nothing. Dickens was asking his readers to pay more money for his product, and they were in no mood to do so" (Vaidhyanathan, 2001: 51). Dickens's account of his US tour, *American Notes* (1842), sold 50,000 pirated copies in the United States in three days.

The historical American recalcitrance with respect to international copyright seems ironic today when the States, one of the world's largest producers of cultural materials, chastises, and pursues legal remedies against countries like China that flaunt intellectual property agreements.

Source: © Jaume Ribera/iStockphoto.

Pirated movies like these are sold around the world for a fraction of their retail price, none of the profits going to the people who produced them.

7.3 ▶▶▶▷▷▶▶

UNIVERSAL DECLARATION OF HUMAN RIGHTS

The Universal Declaration of Human Rights was the first global statement outlining the basic elements of non-negotiable human rights and the foundation for international human rights law. Its first draft was written by a Canadian, John Peters Humphrey, a legal scholar who served as the director of the Human Rights Division of the United Nations Secretariat. The 30-article document was adopted by the United Nations General Assembly on 10 December 1948. Canada was one of 48 countries voting in favour of the declaration.

Article 19 of the declaration speaks most directly to communication: "Everyone has the right to freedom of opinion and expression; this right includes freedom to hold opinions without interference and to seek, receive, and impart information and ideas through any media and regardless of frontiers." The full document can

While Canada supports universal free speech, this does not include speech that promotes violence or hatred toward identifiable groups.

Source: © Richard Levine/Alamy.

be found at www.ohchr.org/EN/UDHR/Pages/Introduction.aspx.

It is useful to remember, though, that in spite of its title, the declaration's various articles are far from universally accepted. United Nations membership in 1948 was one quarter of what it is today, as most of the Global South was unrepresented and only four African countries were members (Fowler, 2014).

The Canadian Public in Public Policy Formation

The formation of communication policy necessitates a tricky balancing act between individual and collective needs, and between universal principles and national and regional exigencies. Increasingly, too, policy formation is governed by international trade agreements. For a country as diverse as Canada, it is especially perilous. How do you accommodate the individual and collective communications needs of a relatively small yet extremely diverse population occupying the world's second-largest country, most of whom live close to the border with the United States, the world's richest and most powerful media empire? How do you balance the needs of individuals with the collective needs of francophone and Aboriginal Canadians and other minority

groups? How do you ensure Canadian voices are heard without foreclosing Canadians' access to the international mediascape? And how do you ensure Canadians' voices are heard on all of these questions in the policy-development process?

The issue of whether public opinion matters to policy formation is an important one in a country that has gone to considerable effort and expense establishing **task forces** and **royal commissions** to study issues ranging from foreign investment to national cultural development. The CRTC, for example, is legally required to conduct public consultations (Raboy and Shtern, 2010: 88). While most analysts would agree that public opinion is important, how it matters is not clear. Is public consultation merely a public relations exercise, or does it play a part in policy decisions?

A consideration of who constitutes "the public" participating in such inquiries must be central to any discussion of this policy institution.

While hearings are open to anyone wishing to participate, they most often attract interested parties—industry stakeholders, labour leaders, researchers, organized pressure groups—rather than the general public. The reasons for this are many. First, members of the general public may not know when such hearings are taking place, or be aware of their significance. Intervening in public-policy processes for fields such as broadcasting, telecommunications, hydro rates, or many other matters of civic importance requires specialized knowledge and most people simply don't have the time or energy to keep up with such issues. Second, even if they are up to speed with such issues and concerns, members of the public must take time off work and pay their own way to testify or appear at such hearings. Obviously, this is a heavy burden for most people. On the other hand, because they directly benefit financially from regulation, many large corporations employ public-relations or regulatory-affairs staff whose job it is to lobby government and attend regulatory hearings. The costs associated with this activity are then added to the corporate cost of doing business and built into the rates or fees these companies charge their customers. While these observations do not negate the importance of public consultation to policy formation, they substantially qualify the extent to which such inquiries can be seen as impartial surveys.

As we will see in the reading of four key twentieth-century policy documents that follows, answers to the question *What is communication for?* are both important and subject to change. These documents, and the hearings that produced them, give us a sense of the particular social, political, and economic contexts in which policy debates took place, and give us a taste of the policy discourse and how it evolves over time.

The Aird Commission, 1929

The Aird Commission—officially, the Royal Commission on Radio Broadcasting—represents a watershed moment in communications policy history because it was the first public consultation of its kind and it resulted in the recommendation that a national and publicly owned broadcasting network be introduced into a field that up until then was dominated by local and privately owned radio stations (Vipond, 1992). As Marc Raboy (1990) has noted, after the Aird Commission, broadcasting policy in Canada became national policy. But the Aird Commission has significance beyond broadcasting. Besides proposing the initial blueprint for a Canadian radio network, Aird recommended, and helped to initiate, a particular pattern of cultural governance. Historian Mary Vipond (1992: 219) comments, "A new view of the role of the government vis-à-vis culture and the media was thereby implied. Never before had the state been assigned such control over a cultural field."

Through the 1920s, the airwaves became increasingly crowded as signals from much more powerful US radio stations interfered with those of their weaker Canadian counterparts. At the same time, the content of some religious broadcasts became a growing political concern. As a result of these issues, the Canadian government recognized the need for a more comprehensive approach to broadcast policy. The minister of marine and fisheries, P.J. Arthur Cardin, asked ministry officials to prepare a report with recommendations for federal broadcasting policy. That departmental report, submitted 15 November 1928, recommended the establishment of a royal commission (Bird, 1988: 37). Less than a month later, Sir John Aird, president of the Canadian Bank of Commerce, was appointed chair, and was joined by two other commissioners: Charles A. Bowman, editor of the *Ottawa Citizen*; and Augustin Frigon, an electrical engineer who was director of Montreal's École Polytechnique and director-general of technical education for the province of Quebec (Canada, 1929a: 2). The royal commission held public sessions in 25 Canadian cities between April and July 1929, during which time it received 164 oral statements, 124 written submissions, and held conferences and received written statements from all nine provinces (Canada, 1929b: 5–6, 18–21).

7.4 ▶▶ ▷ ▷ ▷ ▶ ▷

MAJOR COMMUNICATIONS POLICY DOCUMENTS

The following are key communications policy documents that have informed governments for the past 80 plus years. The reports, available through most public and university libraries, are written in a clear and accessible style and are valuable to researchers for the data and analysis they contain, but also for the language they use to talk about the respective roles of the public and private sectors in producing and delivering communications services to Canadians.

1929   Report of the Royal Commission on Radio Broadcasting

1951   Report of the Royal Commission on National Development in the Arts, Letters and Sciences

1957   Report of the Royal Commission on Broadcasting

1961   Report of the Royal Commission on Publications

1968   Report on Book Publishing

1969   Report of the Task Force on Government Information

1971   Mass Media: The Uncertain Mirror: Report of the Special Senate Committee on Mass Media

1971   Instant World: A Report on Telecommunications in Canada

1977   The Publishing Industry in Canada

1977   The Film Industry in Canada

1977   Disney Report on Federal Tax Issues of Concern to the Arts Community in Canada

1978   English Educational Publishing in Canada

1978   French Educational Publishing in Canada

1981   Report of the Royal Commission on Newspapers

1982   Report of the Federal Cultural Policy Review Committee

1983   Towards a New Broadcasting Policy

1984   The National Film and Video Policy

1984   Report on the Taxation of Visual and Performing Artists and Writers

1985   Report of the Film Industry Task Force

1986   Report of the Task Force on Broadcasting Policy

1986   Report of the Task Force on the Status of the Artist

1986   Report on Funding the Arts in Canada to the Year 2000

1986   Report of the Task Force on the Non-theatrical Film Industry

The Aird Commission remained faithful to the agenda that had been established in its mandate. Most significantly, the commission rendered radio a government institution. The commission's order-in-council proposed three options for action, all of which required state intervention in some form: private enterprise with government subsidy; a federally owned and operated system; or, a provincially owned and operated system. Citing public support for placing broadcasting "on a basis of public service," the commissioners argued that only some form of public ownership could satisfy "both the interests of the listening public and of the nation" (Canada, 1929b: 5–6). Not only would radio broadcasting in Canada be a public service national in scope, but it would also be federally owned and operated with "provincial authorities" exercising full control over programming (Canada, 1929b: 6–7).

A national company would own and operate all stations in Canada, and each province would have a provincial radio broadcasting director "who will have full control of the programs broadcast by the station or stations located within the boundaries of the province for which he is responsible," as well as a provincial advisory council. The national company—the Canadian Radio Broadcasting Commission—would have a 12-member board of directors, 3 directors representing the Dominion and 1 from each province (Canada, 1929b: 7). The proposed CRBC would also have the capacity for chain broadcasting to permit national broadcasts (Canada, 1929b: 8). In addition to the existing licence fees on radio receivers—a user-pay system—the CRBC would be financed by a federal subsidy, a proposed $1 million for five years (Canada, 1929b: 10).

The conclusions of the Aird Commission were in some ways predetermined by its formation (Vipond, 1992: 213). First, the Aird Commission's agenda was largely set by the radio branch of the federal Department of Marine and Fisheries when it established the terms for the royal commission in 1928. Second, the Aird commissioners had biases, especially commissioner Charles Bowman, who had previously written a series of editorials in the *Ottawa Citizen* advocating a public-service model for Canadian broadcasting, and commission secretary Donald Manson, the chief inspector of the radio branch, who was dissatisfied with radio's status quo. Third, before the

public hearings began, the commissioners—John Aird especially—were perturbed by the US network NBC's assumption that Canada was part of its market. Finally, Vipond (1992: 207) notes that the social context of the late 1920s was conducive to the federal government's intervention in radio broadcasting. Nationalists in both English and French Canada had throughout the decade remarked (Vipond, 1992: 207–8; see also Raboy, 1990: 18–19, 29) on the threat posed to Canadian identity by "the flood of American popular culture pouring over the border" (Vipond, 1992: 207).

Marc Raboy (1990: 7) has argued that the significance of the Aird Commission is that it "infused broadcasting with a national purpose." The Aird commissioners described the purpose of their inquiry as "to determine how radio

Members of the Aird Commission, from left to right: Charles Bowman, Sir John Aird, Donald Manson, Dr Augustin Frigon.

Programming, too, was categorized in the terms of the nation-state. It would be predominantly Canadian and would have a considerable educational component, unlike the local and regional programming that had characterized private radio in Canada up to that point. Aird determined that the primary purpose of the CRBC "would be to give Canadian programs through Canadian stations" (Canada, 1929b: 10). Closely tied to the issue of Canadian programming was Aird's call for an emphasis on educational programming, meaning "education in the broad sense, not only as it is conducted in the schools and colleges, but in providing entertainment and of informing the public on questions of national interest." Educational broadcasts would include exchanges of programs with other parts of the country, but also foreign programming. Aird recommended that specified time slots be set aside for "educational work" (Canada, 1929b: 6–11).

The Aird report attributed its findings to "the people" and thus asserted that the report spoke for the people of Canada. Aird posits the people as constituents and the royal commission as their representative body, even though the consultation process was limited in scope and attracted primarily interest groups (e.g., radio station owners and managers, broadcasting equipment manufacturers, radio club spokespeople). The report is full of attributions to public opinion. Through their public consultation process, the Aird commissioners felt confident they could represent the interests of the Canadian public, in the same manner that politicians represent and speak for their constituents.

Besides its recommendation to nationalize radio, the Aird Commission raised two themes that would surface in subsequent reports and which inform Canadian communications policy to the present day: the relationship between communications media and commerce; and the cultural menace represented by close proximity to the United States.

Aird detected two problems with the structure of radio as a local, private enterprise. First,

broadcasting in Canada could be most effectively carried on in the interests of Canadian listeners and in the national interests of Canada" (Canada, 1929b: 5), thereby invoking the order-in-council that established their mandate. The Aird report, in other words, was neither the Canadian government's first word on radio broadcasting, nor were the commissioners starting with an entirely blank slate in their attempts to develop Canada's first comprehensive broadcasting policy.

The medium of radio was also perceived as an instrument of national purpose. "In a country of the vast geographical dimensions of Canada, broadcasting will undoubtedly become a great force in fostering a national spirit and interpreting national citizenship" (Canada, 1929b: 6). Radio's potential to promote national unity was cited as one of the reasons radio should be subsidized by Ottawa (Canada, 1929b: 10).

7.5 ▶▶▶▶▶▶

CANADIAN RADIO LEAGUE

The release of the Aird report in October 1929 coincided with the beginning of the Great Depression, which delayed serious consideration of its recommendations. The Canadian Radio League, founded in 1930 by Graham Spry and Alan Plaunt, led a campaign to support the Aird Commission's central recommendation of a national public radio system under Spry's famous slogan, "The State or the United States." Spry (1931) illustrated the nationalist purpose he foresaw for the technology of broadcasting:

> Here is an agency which may be the final means of giving Canada a national public opinion, of providing a basis for public thought on a national basis. . . . There is no agency of human communication which could so effectively unite Canadian

to Canadian and realize the aspiration of Confederation as radio broadcasting. It is the greatest Canadianizing instrument in our hands and its cultural influence . . . is equally important.

The Canadian Radio League lobbied politicians and government officials and mustered support for public broadcasting in the face of counter-arguments by the private broadcasting industry. R.B. Bennett's Conservative government passed the Canadian Radio Broadcasting Act in 1932, establishing the Canadian Radio Broadcasting Commission, which took over the radio facilities of the Canadian National Railway and established a rudimentary network of private and public stations broadcasting in French and English. The CRBC, however, struggled from a lack of funding, a weak mandate, and administrative problems. A new Canadian Radio Broadcasting Act was passed in 1936, establishing a restructured Canadian Broadcasting Corporation as a Crown corporation and ensuring its financial stability through a $2.50 radio licence fee.

---

the private stations suffered from a lack of revenue, which "tended more and more to force too much advertising upon the listener." Second, stations were crowded into urban areas, where the revenue potential was greatest, resulting in the duplication of service in some areas and other, less-populous areas being "ineffectively served" (Canada, 1929b: 6). Aird was especially critical of the commercialization of the radio airwaves through advertising, and the report recommended the elimination of "direct advertising," though it was more tolerant of indirect advertising, or sponsored programs. But, the "ideal program should have advertising, both direct and indirect, entirely eliminated" (Canada, 1929b: 10).

The distaste of the Aird Commission for advertising was matched by its displeasure that the majority of programs heard by Canadians originated in the United States. "It has been

emphasized to us that the continued reception of these has a tendency to mould the minds of young people in the home to ideals and opinions that are not Canadian" (Canada, 1929b: 6). By international agreement, Canada had in 1929 only 6 exclusive and 11 shared broadcast wavelengths, and Aird recommended a more equitable division of the broadcast spectrum with the United States (Canada, 1929b: 11).

In sum, Aird took a huge step in advocating state intervention in the cultural sphere. By endorsing the idea that radio broadcasting should be established on the basis of a national public service and governed by a national institution, the Aird report proposed a framework patterned after that of the nation-state itself and dramatically extended the state's power into cultural affairs. Aird also introduced into the policy discourse two recurrent topics: commercialization and Americanization. These themes would form the central tenets of communications policy formation in Canada up to the present day.

The Massey–Lévesque Commission, 1949–1951

In the wake of World War II, Louis St Laurent's federal government commissioned in 1949 the most sweeping study of the cultural field in Canadian history, a study that was to include within its scope museums, libraries, archives, historical sites, monuments, scholarship, voluntary societies, crafts guilds, and the mass media. The study was struck at a time when, after the devastation and expense incurred by the war, both government and industry were reorganizing and the foundations of what would become today's consumer and popular culture were being formed. The co-chairs of what was officially named the Royal Commission on National Development in the Arts, Letters and Sciences, 1949–1951, were Vincent Massey, chancellor of the University of Toronto, and Georges-Henri Lévesque, dean of the Faculty of Social Science at Laval University in Quebec City. The Massey–Lévesque Commission held 224 meetings, 114 of them public; received 462 briefs; and heard 1,200 speakers. The briefs included submissions from 13 federal government institutions, 7 provincial governments, 87 national organizations, 262 local bodies, and 35 private commercial radio stations and drew on a series of background research studies (Canada, 1951: 8).

The order-in-council establishing the Massey–Lévesque Commission, like the Aird Commission two decades earlier, gave it an agenda that situated the broad spectrum of cultural activity within the national interest. The commissioners were asked to examine and make recommendations upon six areas: the operation and future development of such federal agencies as the National Film Board, the National Gallery, the National Museum, the Public Archives and Library of Parliament; Canada's relations with UNESCO and other international bodies; relations between the government and national voluntary associations; methods to make people in foreign countries more aware of Canada; measures to preserve historical monuments; and "the principles upon which the policy of Canada should be based, in the fields of radio and television broadcasting" (Canada, 1951: xxi; see also Shea, 1952: 10–11).

The Massey–Lévesque Commission took for granted the state's governance of the cultural sphere in the national interest. At one point, in fact, the report questioned whether culture and citizenship could even be distinguished as separate realms (Canada, 1951: 31). Consistent with the order-in-council from which it received its mandate, the commission perceived cultural activity as a clear state responsibility.

Massey–Lévesque restated the principles on which national public radio had been established; it even recommended that the new broadcast medium, television, follow radio's model (Canada, 1951: 301–2). The commission not only reinforced the cultural policies that had turned radio and, subsequently cinema (the National Film Board was established in 1939) into governmental realms of activity, but greatly broadened state jurisdiction in the cultural sphere. One recommendation, for example, was the establishment of a new federal institution, the Canada Council for the Arts, to lend funding support to the arts, humanities, and social sciences (Canada, 1951: 377–8). As the Canada Council's proposed mandate suggested, Massey–Lévesque brought a number of activities within the purview of the national interest. Universities, for example, were assigned "special responsibility for certain national problems" and were seen as "recruiting grounds for the national services." Massey–Lévesque further recommended the establishment of a national botanical garden, a national zoological garden, and a national aquarium (Canada, 1951: 326). Even voluntary associations were cast as national institutions.

Culture, the report emphasized, is also part of what it means to be a self-respecting nation-state; it is a manifestation of civilization attained. Cultural activities, the report stated, "lie at the roots of our life as a nation" and they are "the foundations of national unity" (Canada, 1951: 284). For the Massey–Lévesque Commission, however, the idea of culture was somewhat different from the one that we have been using in much of this book. Rather than seeing culture as a general "way or ways of life," the commissioners saw activities like classical music, painting, sculpture, and dramatic arts as the epitome of cultural achievement. Cast from an elitist cultural perspective, cultural expression in the Massey–Lévesque report (Canada, 1951: 271) is the search for essence, the search for a "Canadian spirit," a bond that defines as Canadian in their soul the constituents of the nation-state, no matter what their language, ethnicity, race, and so on.

The report refers to national cultural institutions as part of our "national equipment as a civilized country" (Canada, 1951: 380) and lamented the lack of two essential institutions: a national library and a national historical museum (Canada, 1951: 323). "It has been suggested to us that one measure of the degree of civilization attained by a nation might fairly be the extent to which the nation's creative artists are supported,

The Canada Council for the Arts, one of the recommendations of the Massey–Lévesque Commission, continues to promote arts in Canada. In addition to other activities, the council shows off new works of art on its Flickr account.

Source: Detail of Paul Robles's *My Beautiful War*. Used with permission of Paul Robles/Art Bank.

encouraged and esteemed by the nation as a whole" (Canada, 1951: 182).

Cultural phenomena and institutions that were not under state control, and particularly emerging popular cultural forms, were portrayed by Massey–Lévesque as potentially harmful influences. Here, most of the commission's angst was reserved for feature films, which it described as "not only the most potent but also the most alien of the influences shaping our Canadian life" (Canada, 1951: 50). What is not explained in the report is why it recommended no action in the feature-film sector, given the Canadian industry's domination by Hollywood.

Massey–Lévesque accepted uncritically the concept of a national culture and that cultural production should be perceived in national terms. "Canada became a national entity because of certain habits of mind and convictions which its people shared and would not surrender. Our country was sustained through difficult times by the power of this spiritual legacy." Tradition is always in the making, the report noted, "and individuals interested in the arts, letters and sciences throughout our country are now forming the national tradition of the future" (Canada, 1951: 4–5). Such institutions as archaeological, art, and historical museums "help to develop a Canadian spirit without raising questions of race, religion, or political convictions" the commissioners averred (Canada, 1951: 94).

The commission acknowledged differences within Canada, but it was divided as to their significance. Canada's demographic and geographical diversity inspired creativity; but difference was perceived as a potential threat to national unity. Regional difference should contribute to national unity rather than "sectionalism":

> Canadian sectionalism is not yet a thing of the past, but it is certain that the energetic efforts of the Canadian Broadcasting Corporation in providing special regional programmes and informative talks, and in introducing a great variety of Canadians to their fellow citizens, have done much

to bring us nearer together. From Vancouver Island to Newfoundland and from the Mackenzie River to the border, Canadians have been given a new consciousness of their unity and their diversity. (Canada, 1951: 280)

Massey–Lévesque confessed an interest in First Nations arts and crafts "for its own sake and because it affects the well-being of an important group of people" (Canada, 1951: 239), but endorsed the suggestion that "the Indian can best be integrated into Canadian life if his fellow Canadians learn to know and understand him through his creative work" (Canada, 1951: 243). In this formulation, First Nations culture becomes a force for national unity.

As Aird had done, Massey–Lévesque placed the educational dimension in the foreground of cultural activity, and assumed responsibility for it. The

commission's explicit intention was that Ottawa support and promote cultural work of "merit." For example, the report discussed film "chiefly as a means of furthering national unity and popular education" (Canada, 1951: 50), which may partly explain its neglect of the feature-film sector. The commission expected a higher standard of programming from public radio than from private radio (Canada, 1951: 286). One of the dangers the commission perceived in private commercial broadcasting was that such a system may produce "many programs which are trivial and commonplace and which debase public taste" (Canada, 1951: 280–1).

Also like Aird, Massey–Lévesque purported to speak for the people; many of its comments were attributed to the oral and written submissions it received. "We believe we have heard the voice of Canada. We should like to think that we have recorded and reproduced this voice as clearly and as honestly as it came to us throughout our country and from so many of our fellow-citizens." Despite this enthusiasm, the report notes, on the same page, that most of the evidence came from organized groups and "we heard very little from the citizen who represented no one but himself" (Canada, 1951: 268).

Massey–Lévesque also spoke to the issues of commercialization and Americanization. Faced with complaints from the private sector about government monopolizing film production and radio and television broadcasting, the report responded that the NFB and the CBC were protecting the nation "from excessive commercialization and Americanization" (Canada, 1951: 58). "Broadcasting in Canada, in our view, is a public service directed and controlled in the public interest by a body responsible to Parliament" (Canada, 1951: 282–3).

The commission shared Aird's distaste for broadcast advertising,

Source: Library and Archives Canada/PA-191984.

The Massey–Levesque Commission desired to help Canadians create a national identity through cultural institutions for the arts and sciences, much like the Trans-Canada Highway made transportation and travel easier across the country. In what ways have national cultural institutions helped form a Canadian identity?

while acknowledging its importance as a source of revenue, particularly with the recommended introduction of the more costly medium of television to the CBC's portfolio. Massey–Lévesque, for instance, recognized that complete elimination of advertising from the national radio network was "impracticable," depriving Canadian companies of a national audience for their advertisements and the CBC of more than $2 million in advertising revenue. To ban commercial advertising from the national radio network, the commissioners argued, risked lowering the standard of programming and might divert listeners to US stations (Canada, 1951: 290–1). These comments were echoed with regard to television.

With the exception of feature film, Massey–Lévesque was apprehensive about the US cultural presence in Canada. The report argued that Canada is culturally dependent in its "uncritical use of American educational philosophy" (Canada, 1951: 16–17), in reading more foreign than domestic periodicals (17–18), and in the reliance of Canadian newspapers on foreign, principally American, news services for their international news coverage (62–3). The ultimate danger of such dependence was cultural annexation.

Massey–Lévesque introduced financing to the cultural debate, a topic that has become central to policy discussions in our time. Unlike today, however, the financial bind was confined to the cultural institutions themselves and wasn't a reflection of the government's fiscal health. The commission referred to a "financial crisis" affecting both the CBC and Canadian universities; it recommended stable, long-term state funding to address the CBC's problem and to maintain its independence from government (Canada, 1951: 293–4). Similarly, the commission recommended Ottawa assist the universities through annual contributions based on provincial population figures (Canada, 1951: 355).

In sum, Massey–Lévesque endorsed the federal government's initial cultural interventions and recommended Ottawa expand its responsibility in this field, framing the arts, letters, and sciences in terms of Canada's national interest.

Not only specific media like radio, television, and documentary film were deemed part of the state's cultural dominion, but cultural activity in general was also appropriated within the federal government purview. The commission defined cultural production as a requisite element of nationhood, and thus perceived the cultural sphere as state jurisdiction. Even the sciences were given a countrywide cast, as evidenced by the report's call for a national aquarium, botanical garden, and zoological garden.

Cast from a culturally elitist perspective, Massey–Lévesque posited private enterprise as antagonistic to the nation-building project in Canada and counterproductive to its framing of culture as national culture. The commission cited as proof the contrast between the meritorious and educational programming of the CBC and the "trivial and commonplace" output of private radio. More importantly for the commission, the commercialization of culture would mean its Americanization, casting the very project of nationhood itself in peril.

The Fowler Commission, 1956–1957

The Fowler Commission—officially, the 1957 Royal Commission on Broadcasting—resulted from a Massey–Lévesque recommendation that the subject of television broadcasting be reconsidered by an independent investigating body within three years of the beginnings of television broadcasting in Canada. Again, the commission's agenda was largely set; the December 1955 order-in-council establishing the Fowler Commission insisted that "the broadcasting and distribution of Canadian programmes by a public agency shall continue to be the central feature of Canadian broadcasting policy" (Canada, 1957: 293).

Chaired by Robert Fowler, the commission held 47 days of hearings in 1956 in 9 of the 10 provinces (bad weather cancelled the hearings in Newfoundland). It heard 276 briefs from individuals and organizations and received an additional

600 submissions by letter. Fowler was asked to make recommendations on seven points, including CBC television policy, the provision of adequate programming for both public and private television, financing (how much and from what sources), and the licensing and control of private television and radio "in the public interest" (Canada, 1957: 293–4).

Fowler's initial question was: Is there a need for the state regulation of broadcasting in Canada? The Commission responded in the affirmative and cited public support for this conclusion. "We are satisfied that for Canada this is a legitimate and proper function of the state, and under our constitution it is a function of Parliament" (Canada, 1957: 81).

Fowler explained its conclusion in four ways. The first was technological imperative. Rejecting the "freedom of the press" analogy, which the Canadian Association of Radio and Television Broadcasters (CARTB) had used to push for a devolution of state control of broadcasting, Fowler noted that the limited number of available radio and television frequencies necessitated allocation and a state licensing system (Canada, 1957: 100–2).

Second, Fowler portrayed broadcasting as too powerful a medium to permit a laissez-faire approach. "Broadcasting is too important and its influence too great, to have the basic decisions as to those persons who shall be in charge of broadcasting removed from the control of those who are directly responsible to the Canadian people" (Canada, 1957: 100–2). On this basis, Fowler rejected CARTB's proposal to delegate broadcast regulation to an independent board of broadcast governors (Canada, 1957: 133).

A third justification for state regulation was "to restrain commercial forces from the excesses to which they may go" (Canada, 1957: 84–5). This meant prohibiting too much advertising and encouraging a stronger commitment on the part of private broadcasters to "the public interest"—encouraging them to produce Canadian programming rather than just import cheaper US fare. Reasserting the primacy of the public

interest, the commission argued that "it is not the freedom of the private station operator or the commercial sponsors that is important; it is the freedom of the public to enjoy a broadcasting system which provides the largest possible outlet for the widest possible range of information, entertainment and ideas" (Canada, 1957: 86).

Finally, Fowler argued that state-regulated broadcasting was the only way to ensure Canadian broadcasting:

> If we want to have radio and television contribute to a Canadian consciousness and sense of identity, if we wish to make some part of the trade in ideas and culture move east and west across the country, if we seek to avoid engulfment by American cultural forces, we must regulate such matters as importation of programmes, advertising content and Canadian production of programmes. (Canada, 1957: 110)

There was, in other words, "no choice" for Canada:

> We cannot choose between a Canadian broadcasting system controlled by the state and a Canadian competitive system in private hands. The choice is between a Canadian state-controlled system with some flow of programmes east and west across Canada, with some Canadian content and the development of a sense of Canadian identity, at a substantial public cost, and a privately owned system which the forces of economics will necessarily make predominantly dependent on imported American radio and television programs. (Canada, 1957: 109)

While defending the national public service structure of broadcasting, the Fowler Commission nevertheless revealed some cracks in its foundation: the growing hostility of private broadcasters; complaints about the CBC's centralization in Montreal and Toronto; and the subsumption of difference—regional, French–English, ethnic—within the national whole. Fowler gave little weight to criticisms of the CBC's concentration in Central Canada, describing Montreal and Toronto as "necessarily" being "the two principal programme production centres in Canada" (Canada, 1957: 71). Conceding that ideas programs could more easily be decentralized, Fowler maintained that arts programs benefited from Central Canadian concentration. "From the purely artistic point of view, the national audience deserves the best and in almost every case the best will be found in the larger centres." A policy of "indiscriminate decentralization" would mean "the Canadian public will have to pay more money for less quality" (Canada, 1957: 70).

The Fowler report acknowledged that Canadian broadcasting had to be representative. Regional needs had to be met and the commission emphasized the need for programming "as diversified and designed to satisfy as many different tastes (minority as well as majority) as economics and practicability may allow" (Canada, 1957: 75). Consistent with this, Fowler proposed a board of broadcast governors that would be representative, with at least one of the 15 members from each of Canada's five regions: the Maritimes, Quebec, Ontario, the Prairies, and British Columbia (Canada, 1957: 94).

The broadcasting system Fowler envisaged was not without cost, and the commission saw that its primary duty was "to deal with problems of business administration and finance" (Canada, 1957: 1–2), particularly as television service meant substantially higher costs. The commission portrayed national public broadcasting as a necessity for Canada, and similarly deemed the broadcasting system it favoured as worth the expense, especially in the context of a prosperous economy. "It is . . . clear that we could have had cheaper radio and television service if Canadian stations became outlets of American networks. However, if the less costly method is always chosen, is it possible to have a Canadian nation at all?" (Canada, 1957: 9). Fowler's major recommendation was increased and stable multi-year

Source: © Sarah Affleck.

The Fowler Commission gave little weight to criticisms of the CBC's concentration in Montreal and Toronto, saying that decentralization would result in lower quality. In what ways does the internet change this conversation?

financing, based on 10-year forecasts of cost estimates (Canada, 1957: 265–6).

The Fowler Commission adopted a pragmatic, yet condescending, view of the commercialization of Canadian broadcasting. By the mid-1950s, selling goods had become one of the "four principal functions" of the broadcasting system (Canada, 1957: 44), yet the alliance of these four functions clearly was uneasy. Fowler described as "a conflict of interest and motives" the private broadcaster's "uncomfortable conflict between his desire to render a public service and his sound business instincts" (Canada, 1957: 85).

Fowler maintained the rhetoric of Aird and Massey–Lévesque in portraying the United States as a threat to Canadian culture, "No other country is similarly helped and embarrassed by the close proximity of the United States" (Canada, 1957: 7–8). Like Aird and Massey–Lévesque,

Fowler posited the privatization of broadcasting as the Americanization of Canadian radio and television (Canada, 1957: 230–3).

In sum, the Fowler Commission further reinforced the three themes that had legitimized state intervention in the cultural sphere in Aird and Massey–Lévesque. Fowler insisted that broadcasting remain a national service governed by the state and rejected the private-enterprise alternative by casting the full-scale commercialization of Canadian broadcasting as its Americanization. Fowler also hinted at a new force in the communications policy debate: economics. With television, the costs of state governance had risen dramatically and, thus, state intervention in the cultural field was meeting increased resistance.

The Applebaum–Hébert Committee, 1981–1982

The Federal Cultural Policy Review Committee was established in August 1980 by Minister of Communications and Secretary of State Francis Fox. He insisted the scope of Applebaum–Hébert be "broad and include all the main programmes of the Federal Government" (Canada, 1982a: 369). Its mandate was to pick up where Massey–Lévesque had left off three decades earlier (Canada, 1982a: 3–5).

Like the commissions discussed above, however, Applebaum–Hébert was not without an agenda. Rising out of the recession of the late 1970s, the committee was a product of the end of the post–World War II economic boom; underneath it lay a concern for finding ways to reduce the cost of cultural subsidies. At the same time, the interests in maintaining the elite cultural activities championed by Massey–Levesque had been dulled by the rise of a new popular culture that championed and celebrated commercial cultural forms.

The committee published and distributed 50,000 copies of a discussion guide in December 1980 in order to stimulate public participation in its hearings. The guide introduced the 18-member committee, "defined the field

of inquiry," provided an historical overview of federal cultural policy, "outlined challenges and options facing Canadian cultural policy in the years ahead," and invited submissions (Canada, 1982a: 370). Applebaum–Hébert held public hearings in 18 cities in every province and territory in 1981 (Canada, 1982a: 370).

The Applebaum–Hébert report represents a significant shift in thinking about the state's cultural role in general, and in attitudes toward the specific guiding principles by which state intervention had to this point been motivated and justified. While Applebaum–Hébert endorsed a role for the state, it redirected it. Conspicuously absent from the report was the anti-commercial and anti-American rhetoric characteristic of the Aird, Massey–Lévesque, and Fowler reports.

The Applebaum–Hébert report sought to balance what it perceived as a continuing need for an active state role in the cultural sphere with a concern for cultural producers' independence from state influence and control. The committee insisted that federal agencies such as the Canada Council for the Arts, the CBC, the National Arts Centre, the NFB, and the Canadian Film Development Corporation should be exempt "from political direction in the form of ministerial directives of either a general or a specific nature" (Canada, 1982a: 35–8). The committee also insisted on the independence of cultural producers related to funding. "If cultural life is to be autonomous and self-directed, it is important that it not become excessively dependent on one source of support—and especially on one government source" (Canada, 1982a: 57). In the performing arts, for example, Applebaum–Hébert envisaged the following income sources: "box office receipts, governments at all levels, and private donations from individuals, corporations and foundations" (Canada, 1982a: 174).

Yet, the committee was not completely consistent on the autonomy question. Applebaum–Hébert endorsed collaboration between cultural affairs and international trade promotion, and between travelling performing artists and Canadian business interests abroad. The committee proposed a Canadian International Cultural Relations Agency to administer international cultural relations under the secretary of state for external affairs (Canada, 1982a: 334–7).

Looking at Applebaum–Hébert now, it is striking for the absence of a national identity or a national unity discourse, though the report did tie the preservation of heritage properties to Canadians' "sense of place and continuity with their past" (Canada, 1982a: 110), and the committee regretted the absence of Canadian materials in the country's cultural institutions.

Nevertheless, Applebaum–Hébert maintained state governance as a central tenet. The committee was not deterred by the current economic recession that created pressure on governments to curtail spending. Reflecting its support of a cultural role for the state, it recommended the creation of a federal ministry of culture (Canada, 1982a: 46–7), the establishment of a Contemporary Arts Centre (148), the introduction of a depreciation allowance and purchasing incentives to stimulate private demand for contemporary visual art (151), and greater support for Canadian magazines (225–6).

With regard to two central cultural institutions, however, the Applebaum–Hébert report advocated a retreat by the state. The committee recommended that the NFB be transformed into a research and training centre, delegating the bulk of its production activities to independent producers (Canada, 1982a: 256–5); and it recommended that the CBC relinquish all of its television production activities, with the exception of its news programs, in favour of acquiring shows from independent producers (292–4).

The Applebaum–Hébert report is particularly noteworthy for the break it made with the neat equation between the state's interests and those of the Canadian public in the cultural domain.

Source: www.thelightcone.com.

The Applebaum–Hébert Committee emphasized that in order for cultural life to be autonomous, it needs funding from places other than the government, like box-office receipts or investments from private donors. How does changing where funding comes from change the arts and what it communicates?

Besides divorcing cultural producers from the nation-building project, Applebaum–Hébert acknowledged, and portrayed positively, **regionalism** and multi-ethnicity, referring in its opening chapter to "the different cultural traditions that Canadians so cherish" (Canada, 1982a: 8).

Applebaum–Hébert also signalled an important shift in attitudes concerning the private sector's place in cultural production. The report placed new emphasis on building audiences and markets for Canadian cultural products. Applebaum–Hébert was less interested in resisting commercialism's encroachment than in devising means by which to create space for Canadian voices. Building audiences was proposed as a strategy to increase public support for both culture and federal cultural policy.

Finally, Applebaum–Hébert demonstrated none of the anti-American sentiment of previous commissions. The report lamented the dominance of US cultural products in the Canadian marketplace, not because of any pernicious American influence, but because Canadian cultural works were correspondingly underrepresented—in publishing (Canada, 1982a: 224), in sound recording (240), in television broadcasting (249–50), and in cinema (252–8). In spite of this, Applebaum–Hébert refused a protectionist stance, preferring to recommend pro-active strategies by which Canadian cultural products could capitalize on the US-dominated industrial infrastructure, which the committee accepted as part of the cultural landscape.

Applebaum–Hébert maintained to a considerable extent the logic of state governance of the cultural sphere, but it did not do so unquestioningly. It shifted the state's role away from that of proprietor and regulator of culture toward the more comfortable roles of custodian, patron, and, especially, catalyst. Applebaum–Hébert is also remarkable for the extent to which it abandoned the three motivating themes that had been the basis of Canadian cultural policy for the preceding half-century. The committee discarded the schema that equated state governance of culture with its Canadianization, and the market governance of culture with its Americanization.

Re-evaluating Canadian Communications Policy

What we have seen through the evolution of Canada's communications policy discourse is a broad and fundamental re-evaluation of state involvement in the cultural sphere. There has been a shift in social values that applies specifically to three of the ideological pillars on which Canada's cultural policies have been based. The first of these pillars equated the interests of the state with the interests of the Canadian public. The second rejected the wholesale commercialization of cultural production in Canada. The third conceived of the United States as a force of cultural imperialism to be resisted. In this formulation, Canadian state intervention ensured Canadian sovereignty over cultural expression in the belief that the commercialization of culture would result in its Americanization and threaten Canadian culture and the bonds of nationhood.

The first signs of a shift could be detected in the Fowler Commission's report, which noted the rise of private-sector opposition to state intervention, concerns about the centralization of Canada's principal cultural institutions, and the problem of satisfying regional and minority cultures within a larger national communications policy apparatus. The Applebaum–Hébert report may have best encapsulated the policy shift in its credo that "the essential task of government in cultural matters is to remove obstacles and enlarge opportunities" (Canada, 1982a: 75). This became the prevailing theme of approaches to policy development since the 1980s.

In part, this shift was the product of the commercialization of culture in the post–World War II era, but additionally, Canadian nationalism also underwent change during this time. The immediate postwar period and the years leading up to centennial celebrations in 1967 could be described as a period of strong Canadian nationalism, but that sentiment was rivalled in the 1960s and '70s by a growing regionalism. The 1960s saw the emergence of a strong Quebec nationalist movement that had both militant and progressive elements. The sense of Quebec's distinctiveness grew through the 1980 referendum on sovereignty, the repatriation of the Canadian constitution in 1982, and the Meech Lake (1987) and Charlottetown (1992) constitutional accords. Quebecers' sense of themselves as a distinct people was fuelled, too, by early successes at finding a French-speaking voice in popular music (Robert Charlebois, Beau Dommage, Offenbach), film (Claude Jutra, Pierre Perrault, Gilles Carle), literature (Hubert Aquin, Anne Hébert, Réjean Ducharme, Marie-Claire Blaise), theatre (Michel Tremblay, Robert Lepage), and television (*La Famille Plouffe*). Protected by language and promoted by a star system that English Canada has never been able to emulate, Quebec's communications sector is another mark of the province's distinct status.

This period, too, marked the rise of Western regionalism, particularly in Alberta. The Trudeau government's National Energy Program of 1980—a unilateral attempt by Ottawa to assert federal control over an industry under provincial jurisdiction—confirmed the view that the resource-based industries of the Western and Atlantic provinces were economically subservient to Central Canada's manufacturing sector, producing intense resentment especially in provinces like Alberta and British Columbia, which were seeking to assert their growing economic and political power.

As so many of Canadians' communication needs became served by commercial media through the 1970s and '80s, the argument that commercialization threatens Canadian culture became harder and harder to sustain. Even Canada's public television broadcaster, the CBC, has come to resemble a commercial service, with its menu of professional sports, Hollywood movies and game shows, and derivative reality-TV programs. Recessions in the mid-1970s and the early 1980s compelled governments to rethink their spending on cultural programs and organizations. As both the Fowler and Applebaum–Hébert reports signalled, economics had become a significant factor in policy discussions, and fiscal restraint has been a predominant theme of every government since the 1980s.

In this context, political ideologies have become much more fiscally conservative. After years of state intervention under Pierre Trudeau's Liberals, Brian Mulroney's Progressive Conservatives declared Canada open for business, embracing free trade with the United States and less state intervention—what is misleadingly termed **deregulation** (see Box 7.6)—in all sectors of the economy. International agreements liberalizing trade in this period had significant implications for government communications policy, because national policies were subject to scrutiny by international trade bodies such as the **World Trade Organization**. Communications policy can now be seen as being formulated in a global context.

Comedians Joël Legendre, Pierre Brassard, Hélène Bourgeois Leclerc, Véronique Claveau, Laurent Paquin, and Michel Courtemanche say goodbye to the year 2014 for the Quebec television viewers, showcasing current events and the distinct culture of French-speaking Canada.

While, as we shall see in Chapter 8, concern over the influence of US giants on the Canadian mediascape remains strong, "communication policy in Canada has always been heavily influenced by proximity to the United States, now that proximity has become global" (Abramson and Raboy, 1999: 776). The 1995 G7 meeting in Brussels was "a point where the governance of markets and [communications] technologies intersected" (Abramson and Raboy, 1999: 781). This "post-Brussels shift" is significant because Canadian communications policy is "increasingly formulated in multilateral international fora," which results in "the globalization of Canadian communication policy."

Related to this is the dispersal of policy-making among different ministries within the Canadian government (Abramson and Raboy, 1999: 787). The federal government's recent

7.6

DEREGULATION OR REREGULATION?

The term used most commonly to describe governments' retreat from intervening in the marketplace—whether in communications, health care, education, or anywhere else—is deregulation. The term *deregulation* implies that these sectors of the economy are gradually being freed from regulation because governments are withdrawing their powers of surveillance and control to allow market forces to hold sway.

But market forces are also a form of regulation, producing simply an alternative form of governance. Some commentators prefer to use the term *reregulation*, because it more accurately and precisely captures the process that is taking place. Reregulation suggests that these sectors continue to be regulated, but market regulation is being substituted for state regulation.

digital media policy, Digital Canada 150 (Canada, 2014e), for example, was developed by Industry Canada. The policy primarily addresses access and economic opportunity concerns. Its five priorities are connecting 98 percent of Canadians with high-speed (i.e., 5 Mbps) access by 2017; providing protection against cyberbullying and malware; creating economic opportunity for Canadian businesses; providing greater access to government materials and data online; and giving Canadians greater online access to Canadian cultural materials (Canada 2014a–d).

The other dimension to globalization, of course, is the global circulation of digitized communications, which will be a central theme in our discussion of the cultural industries in Chapter 8. During the CRTC's Let's Talk TV hearings in September 2014, for example, the popular online movie and TV streaming service Netflix was posited as a threat to Canada's commercial television industry and emerged as a challenge to the CRTC's regulatory authority (*The Globe and Mail*, 2014).

A further challenge to Canadian policymakers is addressing the increasing diversity of the country's population, if the communications media are to serve as a vehicle for social cohesion. As we discuss further in Chapter 11, Canada is a country of immigrants in which one fifth of the population self-identifies as visible minority, and where there are great distinctions between urban and rural populations. In the 1950s, 95 percent of immigrants came from Europe and the United States; since the 1990s, 60 percent come from Asia. More than half of Canada's youngest people (under age 20) have ethnic origins other than British, French, Canadian, or Aboriginal (see Baeker, 2002: 181). As policy researcher Greg Baeker notes, "For ethno-racial and visible minorities with diasporic links to other nations, the privileging of the historical (time) and territorial (space) claims of Aboriginal and English- and French-speaking Canadians fails to reflect the reality of Canada today" (Baeker, 2002: 183).

▶ SUMMARY

We may wonder why communication policies, regulations and laws are necessary. We have provided in this chapter a historical explanation, tracing the origins of, and rationale behind, state involvement in the communications sphere.

Communication takes place within an environment constructed by laws, policies, conventions, economic imperatives, guiding ideals, and public pressures. Communications policy establishes the rules by which mediated communication occurs, and dates back to the first days of the printing press in the fifteenth century, when books began to be produced on a large scale and were traded across borders. Policy is developed at both the local and global levels, as governments need to respect international covenants dealing with the circulation of cultural products while addressing their own particular exigencies.

Communications policy in Canada has historically framed the media, culture, and society in terms of the nation-state, so that communications policy is always also national policy. Priorities, though, can shift through time and we have in this chapter traced policy development through four pivotal moments of the twentieth century. If policy was driven initially by the need to develop within Canadians a strong sense of nation and national culture, which treated commercialization and Americanization as threats to those aims, the thematic rationale began to shift in the 1960s and '70s. The financial burdens of state intervention became much more of an issue, regionalism became a rival sentiment to nationalism, and Canadians became accustomed to the commercialization and the Americanization of media. By the 1970s, most US commercial popular culture was less foreign to Canadians than the products of their own culture in many areas.

While US domination of the Canadian communications marketplace continues to be defined as a problem by policy analysts, it no longer resonates the same way with Canadian governments or with the Canadian people. The context of policy formation has shifted significantly since the 1980s. The greater integration of world markets has resulted in an increasing tendency to perceive and regulate communication products and services as commodities like any other good or service, undermining preferred treatment of domestic communications industries. Canadian governments have been advocates of liberalized trade and have spread the responsibility for policy development to ministries, such as Industry Canada, that are primarily concerned with international trade and economic development. Digitization, too, has drawn all communications activity into a global sphere. A further shift has occurred in the make-up of the Canadian population; our increased diversity requires much more flexible and inclusive policies to serve Canadians' communication and cultural needs.

 KEY TERMS

Berne Convention, p. 183
Canadian Radio League, p. 191
copyright, p. 181
deregulation, p. 201
frequency allocation, p. 184
globalization, p. 183
intellectual property, p. 184
International Telecommunications Union, p. 183

legislation, p. 181
non-governmental organizations, p. 184
regionalism, p. 199
right to communicate, p. 203
royal commission, p. 186
task force, p. 186
Universal Declaration of Human Rights, p. 184
World Trade Organization, p. 201

 RELATED WEBSITES

Canadian Radio-television and Telecommunications Commission: www.crtc.gc.ca
The CRTC governs broadcasting and telecommunications in Canada and its website is an excellent source of information about recent decisions and upcoming hearings.

Department of Canadian Heritage: www.pch.gc.ca
Heritage is the government ministry responsible for communications and culture. Its website contains information on all of the cultural industry sectors as well as information on the ministry's funding programs.

Industry Canada: www.ic.gc.ca
This is the government ministry responsible for economic activity in Canada, a portfolio that includes economic aspects of culture and communication, such as intellectual property and the internet. Its website is a good source of information about the ministry's programs and policies.

Friends of Canadian Broadcasting: www.friends.ca
Friends is a lobby group dedicated to the preservation and promotion of Canadian identity and culture on radio and television. Its website is a good guide to current broadcast policy changes and the issues raised by those changes.

Canadian Centre for Policy Alternatives: www.policyalternatives.ca
This is an independent research centre advocating policies for social and economic justice. Its series of policy papers includes studies touching on communication and culture.

 FURTHER READINGS

Hamelink, Cees J. 1994. *The Politics of World Communication*. London: Sage. This book provides a comprehensive summary of global communications policy development from its earliest manifestations to the late twentieth century.

Raboy, Marc. 1992. *Missed Opportunities: The Story of Canada's Broadcasting Policy*. Montreal and Kingston: McGill-Queen's University Press. Here is a history of broadcast policy development in Canada and a critique of its framing as national policy.

——, and Jeremy Shtern, eds. 2010. *Media Divides: Communication Rights and the Right to Communicate in Canada*. Vancouver: University of British Columbia Press. This book situates Canadian communications policy within the larger movement dedicated to the democratization of communication and establishing the concept of communication rights.

Abramson, Bram Dov, and Marc Raboy. 1999. "Policy globalization and the 'information society': A view from Canada." *Telecommunication Policy*, 23. This article situates Canadian communications policy formation within a new global context.

Vipond, Mary. 1992. *Listening In: The First Decade of Canadian Broadcasting, 1922–1932*. Montreal and Kingston: McGill-Queen's University Press. The brief but fascinating history of Canadian radio prior to the establishment of a national broadcaster is detailed in this work.

 STUDY QUESTIONS

1. What purpose(s) does communications policy serve?
2. Why is governance of mass communication not simply left to market forces?
3. What were the predominant themes motivating communications policy development through the first half of the twentieth century? Why were these themes predominant?
4. To what extent do these themes remain pertinent today?
5. How has the policy development context changed since the 1990s?
6. What has led to the increasing commodification of cultural products and communications services?

Communications Policy: Sector by Sector

8

> The central objective, then as now, centres on how to reconcile economic and socio-cultural objectives in view of technological innovations. — Daniel J. Paré

Opening Questions

- What new challenges confront Canada's policy-makers?

- What does it mean to say that media technologies, media forms, and media industries have converged?

- How do international trade agreements affect communications policy formation?

- How does the increasing diversity of Canada's population inform communications policy?

Introduction

If, as we discussed in Chapter 7, the development of communications policy must always take into account the constructed environment in which a particular form of mass communication takes place—technologies, laws, existing policies, conventions, economic imperatives, guiding ideals, public pressures—policy formulation must also adapt to change. One of the most significant changes of the past two decades has been **convergence**, which in the context of communication means the digital merging of previously distinct analog technologies, media forms and media industries (see Chapter 6). A second dramatic change has been pressure for countries like Canada to revise and formulate communications policy in conformity with new international trade covenants. Finally, the makeup of the Canadian population has changed with new global migration patterns, further diversifying Canadian communities and their communicative needs. What has not changed, though, is a central policy aim: ensuring that Canadians have the full citizenship, cultural, and economic opportunities mass communication affords.

As we have discussed in earlier chapters, digitization is the translation of information from various analog formats into patterns of 1s and 0s that can be transmitted along cables, fibre optic networks, telephone lines, and over the air, then reconstructed by various kinds of electronic receivers, such as computers, cellular phones, DVD players, MP3 players, and so on. In the past, it made sense to talk about distinct media forms—magazines, radio, television, cinema— as completely separate industries. But these media silos are breaking down rapidly. Almost all media content today is produced digitally, with the result that it can be distributed both in its conventional form (e.g., hard-copy magazines, over-the-air radio and television, celluloid film) and digitally, typically via the internet. The internet, though, is not simply an alternative delivery mechanism; it has become our central medium, transforming and bundling media content of every type and from every source, serving as the feeder system to all our digital devices. It is common now to hear people say they no longer read newspapers or watch television; they *do*, in fact, but the newspaper articles they read are retrieved through social media sites and read on their laptops or tablets or phones, just as the television shows they watch might be streamed through YouTube or Netflix.

As Figure 8.1 illustrates, this convergence of media forms has been aided and abetted by the convergence of media companies themselves, which are no longer in the newspaper or television business exclusively, but are producing content for audiences on a variety of media platforms. The CBC, for example, which for 70 years was a broadcasting company, transformed itself into a multimedia company in 2009 with the greater integration of its radio, television, and online operations, and in 2014 announced its intention to prioritize its digital platforms. The Montreal media company Quebecor, which began as a newspaper publisher, owns magazines, newspapers, a book publisher, a web portal, a cable distributor, and a television network (among other media properties); it uses its portal—http://fr.canoe.ca—to showcase content from a range of its media holdings.

One of the most attractive features of digital technology is its capacity for **interactivity**. As users of these communication services, we are quickly adapting to a mediascape in which we have increasing choice about how—and when and where—we listen to music or watch television or read a book. If there has always been a participatory element to audiences' consumption of media products, digital technology allows more and more people to become producers, whether in creating their own videos, music compilations, websites, or blogs, or in manipulating the output of media professionals (e.g., creating mash-ups, using recorded music as a soundtrack for a home video). In a similar vein, it has lowered the barriers to entry for more sustained communications projects like citizen journalism and other alternative media formulations (see Lessig, 2008).

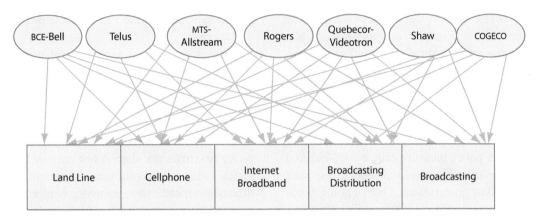

FIGURE 8.1   Competition Landscape in the Era of Convergence

Communications companies that began as broadcasters, publishers, or cable or telephone companies have become multi-platform media conglomerates, creating a much more complicated—and concentrated—picture of media ownership in Canada today.

Source: Canada. House of Commons, "Canada's Foreign Ownership Rules and Regulations in the Telecommunications Sector," June 2010. At www.parl.gc.ca/HousePublications/Publication.aspx?DocId=4618793&Language=E&Mode=1&Parl=40&Ses=3&File=123.

If communications policy is to be relevant and effective, it must take these changes to what is called the *media ecology* into account. A second significant change to the policy environment since the 1980s has been pressure to liberalize international trade and to eliminate protectionist legislation, including rules and regulations pertaining to the fields of communication and culture. Canada signed a free-trade agreement with the United States in 1987, and then endorsed the North American Free Trade Agreement (NAFTA) with the States and Mexico in 1994. Canada is also a member of the World Trade Organization (WTO), which has its own international framework for multilateral trade dating from 2007. These agreements seek to encourage international trade in goods and services across all sectors, and in so doing, create an open market by abolishing national policies perceived as discriminatory. One of the most contentious areas in these trade deliberations is cultural policy, which is designed precisely to discriminate on the basis of nationality in order to protect and promote indigenous cultural activities and industries.

The United States is not only Canada's largest trade partner and closest neighbour, but also the world's foremost advocate for breaking down trade barriers, particularly in industries like television, film, music, and publishing, where it has dramatic economies-of-scale advantages, and is a net exporter. (The United States is less enthusiastic about free trade in areas in which it is a net importer, such as softwood lumber.) The enormous quantity of cultural materials US companies produce and their ability to recover their costs of production in their own domestic market—the world's richest—provide US **cultural industries** with tremendous advantages in the global marketplace. For example, it is generally 10 times cheaper for Canadian television networks to buy and broadcast US programs than it is to produce their own; the star power and promotional heft behind those American productions only compound this structural advantage. If there were no measures to promote the production and distribution of Canadian cultural products, there would be little room for Canadian creators in their own mediascape; we would, in a sense, be back where we started in the early to mid-twentieth century.

For this reason, Canadian negotiators insisted on a cultural exemption in the original 1987 free-trade agreement with the United States and in NAFTA. This exemption, however, is highly qualified and not really an exemption at all. Not only do the agreements allow several exceptions, but the exemption itself comes with a key proviso that allows for one of the signatories to take a form of retaliation "of equivalent commercial effect" in response to protectionist measures. In other words, the United States could argue that a Canadian policy measure causes a US cultural industry financial damage, and seek redress from the Canadian government. One ongoing trade irritant between the two countries is Canada's subsidization through tax credits of US film and television producers shooting on location in Canada (see Armstrong, 2010: 227–8).

There is no general exemption for cultural industries under the WTO either, although this sector has been subject to discussions. The United Nations Educational, Scientific and Cultural Organization (UNESCO) has adopted a Convention on the Protection and Promotion of the Diversity of Cultural Expressions, and Canada was the first country to ratify it in 2005. But this convention has not been signed by the United States and to date has no bearing on international trade law. There will continue to be pressure on countries like Canada to conform to strict market regulation of the cultural industries, rather than adhering to a regulatory regime that sees in these industries both economic and cultural dimensions.

Serving Canadians' communicative needs has also become more challenging, both for media producers and governments, due to the increasing diversity of our population. Canadians come from every part of the world and there are great differences among Canadian communities: between rural, suburban, and urban communities; between our major cities; and between our provinces and regions. If this complicates the task of forging an actively national mediascape, of, in the words of Dwayne Winseck (2010), maintaining spaces for "civil discourse and the mutual understanding that democracies depend on to survive" (Winseck, 2010: 377), it is further complicated by our increasingly ready

access to international communications goods and services.

In this chapter, we provide brief profiles of the major communications sectors and examine sector-specific policy challenges in full recognition of the convergence of media forms and media industries well underway. But we also pick up where Chapter 7 left off, recognizing, too, that policy priorities are shaped not only by technological and industrial exigencies, but are ultimately driven by our collective response generated by one persistent question: *What is communication for?*

Telecommunications

The historical core of the telecommunications sector is the telephone industry, but the telecommunications sector has become the veritable backbone to a growing range of applications, from conventional and wireless telephony to the provision of internet services. There is no better illustration of media convergence, and how telecommunications has evolved, than the new generations of smartphones, which act as telephones, cameras, video and audio players, and personal computers all in one small, hand-held device, linked into networks owned and controlled by communications conglomerates. Telecommunications is a $44-billion industry with six subsectors: local wireline telephone service, long-distance wireline telephone service, internet services, data transmission, private line, and wireless services (CRTC, 2013: iv). The five largest companies—Bell, MTS, Rogers, Shaw, and Telus—generate 85 percent of telecommunications revenues. Wireless services form the largest and fastest-growing sector, accounting for almost half (46 percent) of Canadians' spending on telecommunications (CRTC, 2013). Eighty-six percent of Canadian households have cable or satellite television service, 81 percent subscribe to a wireless service, and 78 percent have high-speed internet. The number of households with landline wireline telephone service is declining, but remains at 86.5 percent (CRTC, 2013: ii). In

2012, Canadians reported an average of 4.5 communications connections per household (e.g., local phone service, internet access, wireless service, cable or satellite television) and household spending on communication averaged $185 per month. Canadians are spending more each year on wireless and internet services, accounting for more than one-third of household spending on communications (CRTC, 2013: 23, 29–30).

As an indication of the changing ways in which Canadians are accessing media content, one-third of Canadians watch internet television at least some of the time and 60 percent read news online. The top five internet uses are online video (72 percent), online audio (61 percent), YouTube video (61 percent), reading news (60 percent), and social networking (59 percent) (CRTC, 2013: 185–6). English-speaking Canadians spent an average of 20.1 hours per week online in 2012, compared to 13 hours per week for French-speaking Canadians (CRTC, 2013: 186).

Telecommunications is governed in Canada by the 1993 Telecommunications Act. Under the terms of the Act, *telecommunications* is defined as "the emission, transmission or reception of intelligence by any wire, cable, radio, optical or other electromagnetic system, or by any similar technical system." Consequently, in formal terms, *broadcasting* is a kind of telecommunication, although the Telecommunications Act pertains to matters of technology, infrastructure, and distribution networks rather than the content of the communications they deliver.

As with broadcasting, the **Canadian Radio-television and Telecommunications Commission (CRTC)** is charged with enforcing the rules laid out in the Telecommunications Act. However, the Telecommunications Act requires the CRTC to rely on market forces "to the maximum extent feasible" and to regulate "where there is a need to do so, in a manner that interferes with market forces to the minimum extent necessary" (CRTC, 2010c: 5). At the same time, the federal government also retains the right to vary, rescind or refer back for reconsideration all CRTC decisions (Paré, 2012: 115).

The telecommunications sector began as the telephone industry. What other applications does it have now?

Telecommunication companies are service providers, offering transmission services for a fee. There are two types of telecommunications carriers. Common carriers are obliged to carry any message (content) that a company or individual wishes to send at equitable cost. Telephone companies, for example, are common carriers, merely transmitting our voice messages. Contract carriers, on the other hand, provide transmission services to specific companies or individuals, but are not obliged to provide those same services to other individuals or companies. The banks, for example, contract for telephone and data communication services and obtain bulk rates unavailable to the average citizen. The internet is not subject to **common-carriage** rules.

The major telecommunications issue of the last decades of the twentieth century was the transition from monopoly services to competing services. As communications scholar Daniel J. Paré writes, "A defining feature of this period was the notable shift in policy discourse away from viewing communications and information as public goods toward perceiving them as largely technological phenomena that predominantly fell under the auspices of private sector considerations" (2012: 116). Through to the 1980s, private telephone companies were granted monopoly status in designated Canadian territories, with the understanding that they would provide

TELECOMMUNICATIONS ACT, SECTION 7*

The foundation for Canadian telecommunications policy is contained in Section 7 of the 1993 Telecommunications Act. It states,

7. It is hereby affirmed that telecommunications performs an essential role in the maintenance of Canada's identity and sovereignty and that the Canadian telecommunications policy has as its objectives

(a) to facilitate the orderly development throughout Canada of a telecommunications system that serves to safeguard, enrich and strengthen the social and economic fabric of Canada and its regions;

(b) to render reliable and affordable telecommunications services of high quality accessible to Canadians in both urban and rural areas in all regions of Canada;

(c) to enhance the efficiency and competitiveness, at the national and international levels, of Canadian telecommunications;

(d) to promote the ownership and control of Canadian carriers by Canadians;

(e) to promote the use of Canadian transmission facilities for telecommunications within Canada and between Canada and points outside Canada;

(f) to foster increased reliance on market forces for the provision of telecommunications services and to ensure regulation, where required, is efficient and effective;

(g) to stimulate research and development in Canada in the field of telecommunications and to encourage innovation in the provision of telecommunications services;

(h) to respond to the economic and social requirements of users of telecommunications services; and

(i) to contribute to the protection of the privacy of persons.

* Notes omitted.

Source: Government of Canada Telecommunications Act, section 7; http://lois.justice.gc.ca/PDF/T-3.4.pdf 2010. Reproduced with the permission of the Minister of Public Works and Government Services Canada, 2011.

equitable telephone service at reasonable rates to both urban and rural markets, subsidizing toll-free local calling with the long-distance rates they charged. That system was gradually transformed, however, and in September 1994, in what has come to be known as Telecom Decision 94–19, the CRTC ruled that competition must be the basis for the provision of all telecommunication services, including local telephone service. This decision required companies to separate the costs of providing any single service (e.g., local phone service) from those for any other service (e.g., long-distance phone service), meaning that companies would no longer be allowed to cross-subsidize services.

Telecommunications Policy Issues

The key policy issues in telecommunications today concern market regulation, as discussed above; convergence; net neutrality; competition in wireless service provision; and foreign investment.

Regarding convergence, communications policy historically has segregated carriage services (telecommunications, governed by the Telecommunications Act) from content services (broadcasting, governed by the Broadcasting Act). In 1996, however, the Canadian government introduced a policy that allowed competition between telecom and broadcast companies (Paré, 2012: 116). This policy led to convergence between

8.2 ▶▶▶▶▶▶

NET NEUTRALITY: TWENTY-FIRST-CENTURY COMMON CARRIAGE?

Building on regulatory concerns of common carriage, net neutrality refers to internet service providers (ISPs) treating all content and applications equally, without degrading or prioritizing service based on their source, ownership, or destination (see Milberry, 2012). Concern over a non-neutral network rises from fears that internet service providers have a financial interest in discriminating against competitors or different classes of users. Indeed, this is what early telecommunications policy surrounding common carriage sought to prevent: imbalanced power relations stemming from control over communication resting with those who own the networks of communication.

As it stands, existing laws may not prevent wholesale ISPs from offering new services that prioritize some content (either that of their subscribers or of particular applications) over other content. This would authorize a two-tier internet with a "fast lane" for those willing or able to pay higher fees—namely corporate clientele—and a "slow lane" for the public: small content providers (e.g., alternative media outlets), content creators (e.g., bloggers, artists), and regular users. While this creates a more profitable system for incumbent ISPs, it also has the effect of creating a closed, non-neutral network requiring additional fees for priority access.

A related issue is that of *throttling* or *traffic shaping*. Here, ISPs control the speed over which particular types of traffic travel the internet. Some have already begun to slow traffic originating from peer-to-peer (P2P) applications, creating a de facto two-tiered internet. Using deep packet inspection (DPI) technology, P2P downloads are identified and slowed down, ostensibly to make space for other traffic on a congested network, while those transmitting "approved" content remain in the fast lane. P2P traffic uses similar amounts of bandwidth as the proprietary services, such as iTunes or Bell Video Store. However, no punitive measures against "bandwidth hogging" have been undertaken against these services (Mezei, 2009). For more information, see http://saveournet.ca.

Source: Milberry. 2012.

---

some of the country's largest telecommunication and broadcasting companies and today these companies (e.g., BCE, Rogers, Shaw, Quebecor) are in direct competition with each other in both the creation and purchasing of content and the delivery of that content to media platforms. As we discuss in Chapter 9, this vertical integration between content and carriage raises another set of issues, including the ability of independently owned TV networks and stations to access distribution networks (cf. Paré, 2012: 117).

Building on regulatory concerns of common carriage, net neutrality refers to internet service providers (ISPs) treating all content and applications equally, without degrading or prioritizing service based on their source, ownership, or destination (see Box 8.2). Concern over a non-neutral network rises from fears that internet service providers have a financial interest in discriminating against corporate competitors or different classes of users. Indeed, this is what early telecommunications policy surrounding common carriage sought to prevent: imbalanced power relations stemming from control over communication resting with those who own the networks of communication.

In the face of concerns that Canadians pay too much for cellphone service, the federal government has been trying to introduce more competition in the provision of wireless services. Bell, Rogers, and Telus bought up the majority of the wireless spectrum used for personal communication services in 2001, and continued to expand their holdings in subsequent spectrum auctions. These three companies continue to dominate wireless service provision—Bell and Rogers alone accounted for two thirds of wireless subscribers in 2012 (CRTC, 2013: 207). Efforts to introduce greater competition to the wireless market, however, have not been particularly successful, and whether or not introducing a so-called fourth entrant into the national market will result in lower prices and improved service is a controversial issue (Faguy, 2014a, b; Lewis, 2014; Skinner, 2013).

Another nagging issue in the telecommunications industry is foreign ownership. The Telecommunications Act stipulates that telecom companies must be Canadian-owned and controlled. This is a recognition of the increasing importance of telecommunications services, and the sensitive data these services carry as Canadian citizens, governments, and businesses conduct more and more of their affairs online. The CRTC has argued that Canadians consider communication services "essential," and that it is difficult to separate concerns about telecommunications network infrastructure from concerns about the content that infrastructure carries. "The requirement to maintain Canadian content assets in domestic hands . . . requires that existing foreign ownership restrictions be maintained" (CRTC, 2010c: 214–5). This will continue to be a policy issue worth monitoring in the coming years. Daniel J. Paré argues that the issue raises the question of how the public interest is to be interpreted. Will the definition of *public interest* privilege "commercial- and consumer-oriented considerations (e.g., increased competition, improved services, greater innovation, lower prices, harmonizing Canadian policy with that of Canada's trading partners)"? Or perhaps the understanding of public interest will favour "socio-cultural considerations . . . which maintain that the carriage of communication signals cannot be separated from cultural identity, national sovereignty, and a democratic public sphere" (Paré, 2012: 124–5).

Broadcasting

Broadcasting in Canada is a $17-billion industry that includes radio and television, as well as the distribution services of cable and satellite (CRTC, 2013: iii). Distribution is the largest sector of the industry, accounting for 52 percent of revenues, followed by television (39 percent) and radio (10 percent). Five large companies—Astral, Bell, Quebecor, Rogers, Shaw—dominate the industry, generating 81 percent of total revenues (CRTC, 2013: 48). Eighty-six percent of Canadian households subscribed to cable- or satellite-TV services in 2012, the latest year for which statistics are available, but internet TV is clearly growing as a rival delivery service: more than 20 percent of Canadians watched television on computer screens and mobile devices in 2012 (CRTC, 2013: ii).

If radio is the smallest broadcasting subsector in terms of revenues, it remains popular and profitable. There are more than 1,200 audio services in Canada, 99 percent of which still broadcast over the airwaves: 878 services in English, 246 in French, and 32 broadcasting in a third language (CRTC, 2013: 55). Canadians listened to radio an

Source: Route66/Dreamstime.com.

In what ways has satellite technology played an important role in closing the gaps between Canada's regions?

average of 19.6 hours per week in 2012 (CRTC, 2013: 59), a number that remains relatively stable. Radio in Canada comprises private commercial, national public, community, campus, Aboriginal, and religious broadcasters. Private commercial radio accounts for 77 percent of the audience in an average week, with the public broadcaster, CBC/Radio-Canada, accounting for 13.4 percent (CRTC, 2013: 60). The average profit margin for private radio companies in 2013 was 20.3 percent (8.5 percent for AM stations, 22.9 percent for FM stations). The radio industry in Canada employs more than 14,000 full-time workers (Statistics Canada, 2014a).

Canadian television offers more than 700 domestic and international services across conventional, pay, pay-per-view, video-on-demand and specialty TV options. The average viewer watched 28.2 hours of television per week in 2012 (Statistics Canada, 2014b: 75–7). Specialty services in English accounted for 35.7 percent of the Canadian television audience in 2012, followed by private conventional services (25.6 percent), pay-TV (6.2 percent) and the CBC (5.5 percent). Non-Canadian television services accounted for 13.9 percent of viewing (Statistics Canada, 2014b: 78–9), but it is important to remember that a great deal of US television programming is carried, and viewed, on Canadian channels, meaning Canadians watch more US programming than this figure suggests. The most lucrative television sectors are the pay and specialty services, with an average profit margin of 26.5 percent in 2013, the highest yet; conventional television reported a 0.6 percent loss. Canada's television industry employs more than 19,000 full-time workers (Statistics Canada, 2014b).

As we noted in our discussion of telecommunications, broadcast services are migrating online and an increasing number of Canadians are listening to radio and watching television via these over-the-top services (see Box 8.3). One of the most popular services for streaming film and television programming is Netflix, and while the company won't release its exact subscription numbers, an estimated 29 percent of English-speaking Canadians were subscribing to the service in 2013 (Bradshaw, 2014b). If convenience and affordability are two reasons for Netflix's growing popularity, perhaps the biggest reason has to do with programming choice, and this raises a number of policy issues that the CRTC is currently wrestling with (see Faguy, 2014c; Taylor, 2013; Bradshaw, 2014b).

Television broadcasting in Canada is subject to the Broadcasting Act. However, in 1998, the CRTC decided not to regulate new media activities on the internet, following up with an "exemption order" in 1999 that exempted online broadcasting services from licensing (Paré, 2012: 116–17). Consequently, streaming video services like the California-based Netflix are not subject to broadcast regulation. In specific terms this means: TV broadcasters have to respect Canadian-content regulations, whereas streaming services do not; TV broadcast distributors, whether cable or satellite companies, are mandated to include in their packages select Canadian channels (e.g., CBC, Radio-Canada, CTV, TVA, APTN) whereas streaming services can offer programming à la carte; and broadcasting distributors are required to contribute 6 percent of their revenues to the production of Canadian content via the Canadian Media Fund (CRTC, 2013: i). In 2011–2012, for example, Canadian broadcasting companies contributed $3.4 billion to the production of Canadian programming (CRTC, 2013: i). *Globe and Mail* media writer Simon Houpt (2014) has described Netflix as "an economically and culturally parasitic foreign entity." He writes, "Netflix is currently pocketing an estimated $300 million a year from Canadian consumers. Its total investment in Canadian programming so far? One season of *Trailer Park Boys*: 10 half-hour episodes of cheaply made TV." The CRTC conducted public hearings on these and other issues in 2013 and 2014; two of the key discussion topics were the possibility of regulating streaming video services like Netflix and forcing broadcast distributors to offer subscribers greater choice in the channels they are required to pay for (see CRTC, 2014a, b; Faguy, 2014c; Bradshaw, 2014b).

8.3

OVER-THE-TOP CHALLENGE TO BROADCAST REGULATION

By Emilia Zboralska

The term *over-the-top* (OTT) service generally refers to any online service or application that delivers content over the top of traditional distribution methods such as cable and satellite. These services also operate over the top in the sense that they utilize open internet networks, which they do not manage or control to distribute their content. OTTs include services such as Netflix, Hulu, and Amazon Prime, among a growing list of others. These services first began as content aggregators, but now produce original programming as well. They tend to turn a passive viewer into an active user—and they allow users to "pull" content whenever they want it, instead of waiting for the content to be "pushed" to them by way of a broadcaster's pre-determined schedule.

Over the top is sometimes also applied to the TV Everywhere (TVE) services launched by traditional content distributors. Most of the current TVE services are hybrid services rather than true OTTs, however; although they operate over the internet, most are based on authentication models, which require users to provide proof of their subscription to a traditional television distributor before they are permitted access.

An estimated one-third of anglophone Canadians now subscribe to the US-owned streaming service Netflix, making it the most popular OTT in the country (Media Technology Monitor, 2014). OTTs are currently exempt from regulation in Canada. This means that unlike the regulated system, OTTs are not confined to the rules and regulations that govern the traditional media. OTTs present significant challenges to the regulation of broadcasting in Canada. Current broadcasting policy has been designed for the push era. Scheduling requirements, such as the rule requiring that 50 percent of prime-time programming be Canadian, make no sense in an on-demand environment. Furthermore, while it is possible to extend content quotas to the OTT environment, there is no guarantee that this programming will be accessed. This severely challenges the social and cultural goals of Canadian broadcasting policy. Foreign-ownership restrictions are also being bypassed by foreign OTTs that have direct access to Canadian consumers through the internet. Restricting access to these companies could be interpreted as censorship, and would not be favourable from a political perspective.

OTTs also present significant challenges to the economic stability of the broadcasting system. The presence of OTTs in Canada has been associated with both "cord shaving" and "cord cutting" behaviours, whereby consumers reduce the number of TV services they subscribe to, or cancel their subscriptions completely, leading to a reduction in broadcast distribution revenues. Distribution revenues are a significant source of funding for original Canadian content, since cable and satellite distributors are required to contribute a portion of their revenues to original production funds, including the Canadian Media Fund (CMF). A reduction in these revenues means a reduction in funding available for original content. As viewership becomes increasingly fragmented across a sea of platforms, broadcasters are also likely to experience a decrease in advertising revenues.

Because of their dependence on inexpensively imported US content, Canadian broadcasters and distributors are also at significant risk of becoming irrelevant. Instead of going through these intermediaries, content creators can decide to stream directly to the Canadian consumer through their own websites or OTT services.

Every country in the world regulates broadcasting, in part because the over-the-air broadcast spectrum is finite and requires management of assigned airwaves, not only for standard radio and television services but also for emergency services used by such agencies as police, fire, ambulance, and the military. As we discussed in Chapter 7, however, the Canadian government, like many others around the world, regulates broadcasting as well because it serves national, cultural, and political goals. Section 3 of the 1991 Broadcasting Act lays out those goals—it is reprinted in Box 8.4.

Over-the-top services like Shomi and Netflix are creating new challenges for broadcast regulations in Canada.

OTTs also compete with Canadian broadcasters for exclusive rights to top-tier American programming. If Canadian broadcasters lose out on these major deals, audiences are likely to follow where the hits go.

Because OTTs straddle both broadcasting and telecommunications, they also introduce increased complexities with respect to how they should be managed. Broadcasting and telecommunications represent separate policy silos, and are governed by distinct legal documents. The vertically integrated industry in Canada means that the incumbent broadcasters are also ISPs. This leads to a complicated nexus of interests, whereby the consolidated companies have the opportunity to provide their own programming with preferential treatment, or to make OTTs less attractive by discouraging streaming behaviour through the imposition of internet caps, and by charging higher prices for internet access. New policies that take into consideration the converged nature of OTTs are required.

The future status of foreign OTTs in Canada and the matter of their regulation are far from clear. While this was one of the issues considered at the CRTC's fall 2014 Let's Talk TV hearing on Canadian broadcasting policy, no decision on the issue has been rendered at the time of writing.

—Emilia Zboralska is a doctoral candidate in the Joint Graduate Program in Communication and Culture run by Ryerson University and York University.

Access to content produced by Canadians is "the underlying principle of the broadcasting objectives." The CRTC states, "Canadian content must not only exist, it should also be available to all Canadians both as participants in the industry and as members of the audience" (CRTC, 2013).

The commission ensures that content produced by Canadians is broadcast through a number of policies, including Canadian-content regulations for radio and television broadcasters, the carriage of Canadian services by cable and satellite providers, and minimum Canadian ownership of

8.4

BROADCASTING ACT, SECTION 3: "BROADCASTING POLICY FOR CANADA"

3. (1) It is hereby declared as the broadcasting policy for Canada that

(a) the Canadian broadcasting system shall be effectively owned and controlled by Canadians;

(b) the Canadian broadcasting system, operating primarily in the English and French languages and comprising public, private and community elements, makes use of radio frequencies that are public property and provides, through its programming, a public service essential to the maintenance and enhancement of national identity and cultural sovereignty;

(c) English and French language broadcasting, while sharing common aspects, operate under different conditions and may have different requirements;

(d) the Canadian broadcasting system should
 (i) serve to safeguard, enrich and strengthen the cultural, political, social and economic fabric of Canada,
 (ii) encourage the development of Canadian expression by providing a wide range of programming that reflects Canadian attitudes, opinions, ideas, values and artistic creativity, by displaying Canadian talent in entertainment programming and by offering information and analysis concerning Canada and other countries from a Canadian point of view,
 (iii) through its programming and the employment opportunities arising out of its operations, serve the needs and interests, and reflect the circumstances and aspirations, of Canadian men, women and children, including equal rights, the linguistic duality and multicultural and multiracial nature of Canadian society and the special place of aboriginal peoples within that society, and
 (iv) be readily adaptable to scientific and technological change;

(e) each element of the Canadian broadcasting system shall contribute in an appropriate manner to the creation and presentation of Canadian programming;

(f) each broadcasting undertaking shall make maximum use, and in no case less than predominant use, of Canadian creative and other resources in the creation and presentation of programming, unless the nature of the service provided by the undertaking, such as specialized content or format or the use of languages other than French and English, renders that use impracticable, in which case the undertaking shall make the greatest practicable use of those resources;

(g) the programming originated by broadcasting undertakings should be of high standard;

(h) all persons who are licensed to carry on broadcasting undertakings have a responsibility for the programs they broadcast;
 (i) the programming provided by the Canadian broadcasting system should be varied and comprehensive, providing a balance of information, enlightenment and entertainment for men, women and children of all ages, interests and tastes,
 (ii) be drawn from local, regional, national and international sources,
 (iii) include educational and community programs,
 (iv) provide a reasonable opportunity for the public to be exposed to the expression of differing views on matters of public concern, and
 (v) include a significant contribution from the Canadian independent production sector;

(j) educational programming, particularly where provided through the facilities of an independent educational authority, is an integral part of the Canadian broadcasting system;

(k) a range of broadcasting services in English and in French shall be extended to all Canadians as resources become available;

(l) the Canadian Broadcasting Corporation, as the national public broadcaster, should provide radio and television services incorporating a wide range of programming that informs, enlightens and entertains;

(m) the programming provided by the Corporation should
 (i) be predominantly and distinctively Canadian,
 (ii) reflect Canada and its regions to national and regional audiences, while serving the special needs of those regions,

(iii) actively contribute to the flow and exchange of cultural expression,

(iv) be in English and in French, reflecting the different needs and circumstances of each official language community, including the particular needs and circumstances of English and French linguistic minorities,

(v) strive to be of equivalent quality in English and in French,

(vi) contribute to shared national consciousness and identity,

(vii) be made available throughout Canada by the most appropriate and efficient means and as resources become available for the purpose, and

(viii) reflect the multicultural and multiracial nature of Canada;

(n) where any conflict arises between the objectives of the Corporation set out in paragraphs (l) and (m) and the interests of any other broadcasting undertaking of the Canadian broadcasting system, it shall be resolved in the public interest, and where the public interest would be equally served by resolving the conflict in favour of either, it shall be resolved in favour of the objectives set out in paragraphs (l) and (m);

(o) programming that reflects the aboriginal cultures of Canada should be provided within the Canadian broadcasting system as resources become available for the purpose;

(p) programming accessible by disabled persons should be provided within the Canadian broadcasting system as resources become available for the purpose;

(q) without limiting any obligation of a broadcasting undertaking to provide the programming contemplated by paragraph (i), alternative television programming services in English and in French should be provided where necessary to ensure that the full range of programming contemplated by that paragraph is made available through the Canadian broadcasting system;

(r) the programming provided by alternative television programming services should

(i) be innovative and be complementary to the programming provided for mass audiences,

(ii) cater to tastes and interests not adequately provided for by the programming provided for mass audiences, and include programming devoted to culture and the arts,

(iii) reflect Canada's regions and multicultural nature,

(iv) as far as possible, be acquired rather than produced by those services, and

(v) be made available throughout Canada by the most cost-efficient means;

(s) private networks and programming undertakings should, to an extent consistent with the financial and other resources available to them,

(i) contribute significantly to the creation and presentation of Canadian programming, and

(ii) be responsive to the evolving demands of the public; and

(t) distribution undertakings

(i) should give priority to the carriage of Canadian programming services and, in particular, to the carriage of local Canadian stations,

(ii) should provide efficient delivery of programming at affordable rates, using the most effective technologies available at reasonable cost,

(iii) should, where programming services are supplied to them by broadcasting undertakings pursuant to contractual arrangements, provide reasonable terms for the carriage, packaging and retailing of those programming services, and

(iv) may, where the Commission considers it appropriate, originate programming, including local programming, on such terms as are conducive to the achievement of the objectives of the broadcasting policy set out in this subsection, and in particular provide access for underserved linguistic and cultural minority communities.

(2) It is further declared that the Canadian broadcasting system constitutes a single system and that the objectives of the broadcasting policy set out in subsection (1) can best be achieved by providing for the regulation and supervision of the Canadian broadcasting system by a single independent public authority.

Source: Government of Canada Broadcasting Act, Section 3, http://laws.justice.gc.ca/PDF/B-9.01.pdf 2010. Reproduced with the permission of the Minister of Public Works and Government Services Canada, 2011.

broadcast networks. The CRTC's regulatory duties derive from Section 5(2) of the Broadcasting Act, requiring the commission "to regulate and supervise the broadcasting system in a flexible manner that, among other things, takes into account regional concerns, is adaptable to technological developments, and facilitates the provisioning of broadcasting programs to Canadians" (CRTC, 2010c: 5). These duties include

- defining categories of broadcasting licences;
- issuing and renewing licences, up to a maximum of seven years;
- modifying existing licence conditions;
- suspending or revoking licences (the CBC licence excepted);
- licensing cable distributors and satellite delivery systems;
- hearing complaints about the broadcasting system; and
- reviewing mergers of media companies.

The CRTC is not simply a rubber-stamp agency. In 1999, the commission reduced the length of the licence of Montreal AM radio station CKVL from seven years to three, punishing the station for the insulting and vulgar remarks of "shock jock" André Arthur and the failure of the station's owner, Metromedia CMR Montreal Inc., to take seriously numerous public complaints about Arthur (Canadian Press, 1999). In 2004, the CRTC denied the licence-renewal application of Quebec radio station CHOI-FM, arguing that the station, and radio host Jeff Fillion in particular, repeatedly aired derogatory comments about women, people of colour, and psychiatric patients, a decision that was subsequently affirmed by the Federal Court of Appeal (Thorne, 2005; Armstrong, 2010: 89–92).

But to say that the CRTC merely regulates the broadcasting system to achieve policy objectives set by Parliament understates the extent to which the CRTC has been obliged to interpret policy. It also understates the extent to which the CRTC has established policies of its own in areas such as cable, specialty TV, and new media.

In March 2010, for example, the CRTC ruled that private television networks have the right to negotiate **fee-for-carriage** compensation, a fee for the use of their signals by cable and satellite distributors. This ruling came with the proviso that if the networks opt to negotiate such a fee, they forgo the regulatory protection that requires all cable and satellite distributors to carry conventional networks, as well as forgoing their guarantee of a preferred location on the dial. The TV networks were seeking this new revenue stream after having posted an operating loss ($118 million) for the first time since the CRTC began tracking the industry's finances in 1996 (Krashinsky, 2010a).

In recent years, a major shift in broadcasting policy has occurred pertaining to the issue of access, from an original emphasis on signal coverage to an emphasis on participation. From as early as 1936, one of the fundamental principles of Canadian broadcasting policy has been the extension of service to all Canadians, and private broadcasters' place in the national broadcasting system has been to help in providing Canadians in all areas of the country access to the reception of radio, and later television, broadcast signals (Canada, 1986: 5–14).

The notion of "access to broadcasting" began to assume another dimension in the 1960s, once extensive territorial coverage of radio and television had been achieved and a private television network (CTV) had been established. Access came to mean the inclusion of all Canadians in the content and production of programming. While the issue of Canadian content has been significant since the first decade of radio, the idea of requiring a minimum percentage of broadcast time to be used for transmitting Canadian television productions was instituted by the board of broadcast governors in 1959.

Today, Canadian content regulations stem from the CRTC's obligation under the Broadcasting Act to ensure that each licence-holder makes "maximum use . . . of Canadian creative and other resources in the creation and presentation of programming." The CBC's programming, according

TABLE 8.1
Canadian Content

The commonly used phrase *Canadian content* is an unfortunate misnomer because, for regulatory purposes, it refers not to the content of a song or film or television program, but to the people who produce it. In other words, the content itself can touch on any subject, and does not have to concern Canada at all. For music or audiovisual programming to qualify as Canadian content, it must be produced by Canadian citizens according to specific requirements by the Canadian Audio Visual Certification Office (CAVCO), for film and television content, and the CRTC's MAPL criteria for musical content.

For instance, as outlined below, under CAVCO regulations, for a creative series to be recognized as a Canadian production, a total of at least six points must be allotted according to the following scale. Points are awarded for each Canadian who rendered the services.

Non-animated Productions (Live Action)	Points Awarded
Director	2
Screenwriter	2
Lead performer for whose services the highest remuneration was payable	1
Lead performer for whose services the second highest remuneration was payable	1
Director of photography	1
Art director	1
Music composer	1
Picture editor	1

Animated Productions	
Director	1
Design supervisor (art director)	1
Lead voice for which the highest or second highest remuneration was payable	1
Camera operator where the camera operation is done in Canada	1
Music composer	1
Picture editor	1
Layout and background where the work is performed in Canada	1
Key animation where the work is performed in Canada	1
Assistant animation and in-betweening where work is performed in Canada	1

Source: Report of the Auditor General of Canada, November 2005, Office of the Auditor General of Canada. Reproduced with the permission of the Minister of Public Works and Government Services, 2015.

to the Act, should also be "predominantly and distinctively Canadian."

The Canadian-content quota has never been well received by the private broadcasters, who have protested each requirement vigorously and sought to minimize their carriage of Canadian-produced materials (see Babe, 1979). In March 2015, the CRTC removed content regulations on daytime television for conventional stations and relaxed them for some specialty services in the hope that requiring fewer hours of Canadian programming would spur broadcasters to spend more money on "big-budget" productions that

might be sold internationally (CRTC, 2015). Consequently, conventional television licensees are no longer required to air Canadian content during the daytime, but they must carry at least 50 percent Canadian programming in the evening hours. Specialty- and pay-TV channels will typically require 35 percent. What impact these changes will have on news and local programming is not clear. If investment patterns within the system shift, however, there are bound to be changes in the range and types of content available.

The principal battleground for disputes over Canadian content quotas has been English-language television, where Hollywood productions are readily available, cheap to buy, and popular with audiences and advertisers. Over the years, the federal government has engineered a number of programs to help boost production of Canadian content (cf. Armstrong, 2010: 126–42). The most recent iteration of these efforts is the Canada Media Fund (CMF), which had a funding budget of approximately $368 million in 2014–2015. These funds are derived from contributions from both cable and satellite broadcasters—which must contribute 5 percent of their revenues to the fund—and the federal government. The CMF has two funding streams: the Convergent Stream, which supports the creation of convergent television and digital media content for consumption by Canadians anytime, anywhere; and the Experimental Stream, which "encourages the development of innovative, interactive digital media content and software applications" (CMF, n/d).

Over the years, the range of Canadian programming has undergone considerable refinement. In the 1970s and '80s, there was an increasing recognition of Canada's multicultural makeup and demands were made that the broadcasting system should reflect this reality. As Lorna Roth (1998: 493–502) notes, by the early 1980s, one in three Canadians was of non-British, non-French, and non-Aboriginal descent, and the federal government began to enshrine guarantees of cultural and racial pluralism in the Constitution, in Sections 15 and 27 of the Canadian Charter of Rights and Freedoms (1982), and in legislation (e.g., the 1998 Multiculturalism Act).

Inclusion was one of the central themes informing discussions leading up to the adoption of a revised Broadcasting Act in 1991, as evidenced in Section 3 (1) (d) (iii) (cf. Raboy, 1995b). The Canadian broadcasting system should

> through its programming and the employment opportunities arising out of its operations, serve the needs and interests, and reflect the circumstances and aspirations, of Canadian men, women and children, including equal rights, the linguistic duality and multicultural and multiracial nature of Canadian society and the special place of aboriginal peoples within that society. (Canada, 1991)

A signal achievement in the diversification of Canadian broadcasting was the establishment of the Aboriginal Peoples Television Network, which was licensed as a national network in 1999, a world first. APTN provides a range of news, variety, and dramatic programming, and broadcasts in English, French, and a variety of Aboriginal languages: Inuktitut, Cree, Inuinaqtuun, Ojibway, Inuvialuktun, Mohawk, Dene, Gwich'in, Mi'kmaq, Slavey, Dogrib, Chipewyan, Tlingit, and Michif. More than 80 percent of its programming originates from Canadian producers (APTN, 2014; see also, Roth, 2005).

The CRTC is not broadcasting's only regulator. The Canadian Broadcast Standards Council (CBSC) and Advertising Standards Canada (ASC) are industry associations providing a measure of self-regulation. The CBSC, for example, has policies on equitable portrayal, violence, ethics, and journalistic independence, although it investigates only when complaints are made (CBSC, 2014). The ASC administers the Canadian Code of Advertising Standards, which includes the Broadcasting Code for Advertising to Children. This children's code contains guidelines pertaining to the factual presentation of products and services, product prohibition, sales pressure, comparison claims, as well as limits on the amount of advertising per program (Advertising Standards Canada, 2014). In Quebec, television advertising on children's programming is prohibited under the Quebec Consumer Protection Act (Armstrong, 2010: 153–4).

Recorded Music

A great proportion of radio broadcasting is, of course, recorded music. There has been a significant symbiosis between radio broadcast policy and policies designed to encourage the production

Source: Paul Patterson.

The Broadcasting Code for Advertising to Children contains guidelines pertaining to the factual presentation of products and services, product prohibition, sales pressure, comparison claims, as well as limits on the amount of advertising per program. Do you think books like these should be classified as advertising?

and dissemination of Canadian music. Historically, the most important policy development for Canadian recorded music was the CRTC's establishment in 1971 of Canadian content quotas for radio, recognizing the link between radio airplay and record sales. The quotas were a response to the under-representation of Canadian recording artists on Canadian radio stations at the time. In 1968, for example, Canadian music accounted for between 4 and 7 percent of all music played on Canadian radio, in a period when the popular music scene was exploding and Canadian musicians like Gordon Lightfoot, Leonard Cohen, Neil Young, Joni Mitchell, and The Guess Who were part of the explosion (Filion, 1996: 132). A points system known as MAPL was devised to determine whether or not recordings qualify as Canadian, based not on their actual content, but on who produces them (see Box 8.5).

Radio's primacy as a promotional vehicle has been waning since the 1980s, as, initially, music video stations (MuchMusic and MusiquePlus in Canada) became popular television hubs for music fans, and, more recently, a combination of MP3 players, social media sites, online radio, and streaming audio services have gained prominence. Websites permitting bands to upload and promote their music provide a much more diverse spectrum than conventional radio can muster, with its limited, mainstream genres. CBC Radio 3 (music.cbc.ca/radio3), for example, streams music from independent Canadian musicians, many of whom receive little or no mainstream radio airplay. And download sites like Apple's iTunes make available a tremendous array of music, both old and new, an inventory that no bricks-and-mortar record shop can match.

8.5 ▶▶▶▶▶▶

THE MAPL SYSTEM— DEFINING A CANADIAN SONG

Canadian content regulations focus on the factors of production and work to ensure that Canadians have the opportunity to participate in media production.

The CRTC defines a Canadian musical selection in its radio regulations. Within these regulations, four elements are used to qualify songs as being Canadian: *music, artist, performance,* and *lyrics* (MAPL).

To qualify as Canadian content, a musical selection must generally fulfill at least two of the following conditions:

- **M** (music): the music is composed entirely by a Canadian
- **A** (artist): the music is performed, or the lyrics are sung, principally by a Canadian
- **P** (performance): the musical selection consists of a live performance that is recorded wholly in Canada, or performed wholly in Canada and broadcast live in Canada
- **L** (lyrics): the lyrics are written entirely by a Canadian

There are several other special considerations where a piece of music may qualify as being Canadian, including the following: an instrumental composition is written by a Canadian, or a performance of an instrumental composition is written by a Canadian.

Source: Adapted from www.crtc.gc.ca/eng/info_ sht/r1.htm.

The growing popularity of digital music is reflected in the sales of music recordings. If in 2007, digital sales—primarily downloads— accounted for just 10 percent of the Canadian industry's sales revenues (totals include physical sales, digital sales, and live-performance rights),

by 2013, digital sales represented 49 percent of industry revenues (Music Canada, 2012, 2013). Still, this figure understates digital music sourcing; digital music sales, whether as downloads or streaming, don't match the revenues lost from declining physical sales (Music Canada, 2014) and the industry estimates that about one-third of all internet users access unlicensed music sites on a regular basis (Music Canada, 2013: 9). By 2014, the prevalence of audio streaming meant that even downloads were decreasing in number.

Streaming is a two-sided coin; while it is a boon to listeners, who can access a tremendous variety of music on the digital platform they deem most convenient whenever they choose, there is little money in it for those who produce the music: musicians and recording companies. In a 2013 report, Music Canada cited the following royalty rates: $0.001 per stream on Pandora, $0.002 per stream on Sirius XM, and $0.004 per stream on Spotify. The report stated, "To put this in perspective, 10,250 streams per hour on Pandora would be needed to provide the minimum hourly wage in Canada for just one band member" (Music Canada, 2013: 8). Music Canada and Re:Sound, the non-profit agency responsible for collecting and distributing these payments, argue that these payments are too low (Music Canada, 2014; Re:Sound, 2014). With the importance of radio airplay diminishing and the paltry payments coming from digital royalties, Music Canada contends live performance is becoming a more important means of reaching audiences, building a fan base, and earning a living, particularly for those musicians who are not nationally or internationally known (Music Canada, 2013: 10).

The financial impact of the music business in Canada has shrunk considerably. The industry generated $765 million in revenues from the sales of recorded music and live performance in 2001, compared to just $437 million in 2013 (Music Canada, 2013). Four major recording companies— Sony Music Entertainment Canada, EMI Music Canada, Warner Music Canada, and Universal Music Canada—account for 70 percent of sales (Music Canada, 2012: 2).

8.6 ▶▶ ▶ ▶ ▶▶

COPYRIGHT

Digital technology, which allows for easy, inexpensive, and almost perfect copying and distribution of digital content over the internet, has prompted new copyright legislation. Copyright law vests in the creator, not outright ownership, but the right to control copying of a work. It is a temporary monopoly property right: the right to benefit financially from the sale of copies of a created work (e.g., writing, music, photography, film)—and a more long-lasting moral right: the right to be associated with the work as its creator. Copyright law also establishes public or user rights as a way of balancing the rights of society with the rights of the creator. This balance is based on the notion that ideas emanate from the social whole and the individual gives expression to them through the intellectual work of articulating these ideas.

Copyright is a central issue today because the protections it affords creators are the foundation of the creative economy. It provides both financial protection and financial incentive to the creators of original works; the work belongs to them and gives them control over its dissemination. Relatedly, it provides both financial protection and financial incentive to media companies who seek to market media works.

But copyright legislation stipulates users' rights as well. First, copyright law limits the term of the monopoly property right. Second, it circumscribes creators' rights by protecting only the expression of the idea, not the idea itself. Third, it includes a user right called *fair dealing*. This creates categories in which copyrighted materials can be used without seeking their creators' permission.

In 2012, the federal government introduced new copyright legislation, Bill C-11, a.k.a. the Copyright Act, and a number of its new provisions pertained specifically to digitization. The legislation permits time shifting (e.g., the recording of television programming for later viewing), format shifting (the conversion of digital files to other formats for use on other digital platforms), the creation of backup copies of digital files, the remixing of music, mash-up videos, and the use of commercial music as background in home movies (see Geist, 2012). Bill C-11 also expanded the categories of fair dealing to include education, satire and parody (Geist, 2012).

The full text of Canada's Copyright Act can be found here: http://laws-lois.justice.gc.ca/eng/acts/C-42/Index.html.

Besides Canadian-content regulations, a second significant policy measure was the establishment in 1982 of the Fund to Assist Canadian Talent on Record, which became known as FACTOR/MusicAction when a French-language component was added (www.factor.ca, http://musicaction.ca). With the encouragement of the CRTC, the fund was created by several radio broadcasters (CHUM, Moffatt Communications, Rogers Broadcasting) in partnership with two major industry associations (what are now known as the Canadian Independent Music Association—www.cimamusic.ca—and the Canadian Musical Reproduction Rights Agency—www.cmrra.ca) to channel money into the Canadian music industry. Together, FACTOR and MusicAction contributed almost $27 million to the industry in 2010 (Music Canada, 2012: 14). The funds provided are used, for example, to produce demo tapes and promotional video clips and to organize promotional tours by musicians.

In May 2001, the federal Department of Canadian Heritage announced a new Canadian Sound Recording Policy, entitled *From Creators to Audience*. Its goal is to provide support at the every level of the sound-recording process—from the development of creators to the building of audiences, as its title suggests. The policy established the Canada Music Fund, which absorbed the pre-existing Sound Recording Development Program and promised to

- build community support and skills development of creators;

Source: Isaiah Trickey/Getty Images.

British Columbian band Hedley at the 2014 MuchMusic Video Awards. The band has yet to break into the US market, but it is wildly popular in Canada. What are some of the reasons for this?

- support the production and distribution of "specialized music recordings reflective of the diversity of Canadian voices";
- provide project-based support to new emerging artists;
- develop the business skills of Canadian music entrepreneurs;
- ensure the preservation of Canadian musical works;
- support recording-industry associations, conferences, and awards programs; and
- and monitor industry performance.

The government renewed and restructured the Canada Music Fund in 2009 and by 2014, it was operating several programs in support of Canadian music (Canada, 2014d).

Cinema

The film industry has enjoyed the same kind of symbiotic relationship with television as the music industry has had with radio. Given the long-standing difficulty Canadian-made feature films have had in penetrating Canadian movie theatres, television has been their most reliable means of distribution. And yet, like music, digital platforms—online and wireless mobile— are becoming more and more significant outlets

for all forms of audiovisual production. To what extent Canadian films will succeed in reaching audiences this way, and whether their creators and producers will be adequately compensated, remain open questions.

The Canadian theatrical film industry is relatively small, generating just $351 million in spending during the 2012–2013 fiscal year, producing 93 feature films (59 in English, 34 in French). The average budget for English-language features was $4.6 million, and $3 million for French-language features. Most of this production took place in Ontario (46 percent) and Quebec (42 percent) (CMPA and AQPM, 2013: 68–9).

Governments' principal policy contributions have come in the production sector of the film industry, rather than in the distribution or exhibition ends. More than half (59 percent) of the financing of Canadian feature films comes from government-funding programs: provincial tax credits (21 percent), the Canadian Feature Film Fund (19 percent), federal tax credits (6 percent), and other public-funding sources (13 percent). The Canadian Feature Film Fund, established in 2000, is administered by Telefilm Canada and contributes more than $90 million annually to film development, production, distribution, and marketing (CMPA and AQPM, 2013: 75–6).

Federal and provincial governments in Canada have been sponsoring motion-picture production in one form or another since the earliest years of the twentieth century, and Ottawa has operated a national film-production organization continuously since 1918. Canada, however, has been much more successful in the spheres of industrial and documentary film production— for example, films produced by the NFB, founded in 1939, have won 12 Academy Awards (see Table 8.2)—than in the higher-profile domain of dramatic, feature-length film production: the kinds of movies we see in our theatres. In this latter area, Hollywood is the dominant player in the Canadian market, accounting for 82.4 percent of box-office receipts in 2012–2013, compared to Canadian films' 2.5 percent share (CMPA and AQPM, 2013: 82). Even though directors like

Deepa Mehta, Bruce McDonald, Léa Pool, Atom Egoyan, François Girard, Denis Villeneuve, Sarah Polley, Mina Shum, Denys Arcand, Jean-Marc Vallée, and Xavier Dolan have given renewed vigour to Canadian feature filmmaking since the early 1980s, domestic films have averaged only between 2 and 6 percent of box-office revenues, and less than 5 percent of screen time in Canadian cinemas.

In a sense, our own domestic cinema is foreign to Canadian audiences. For most of its history, the Canadian film market has been treated as an extension of the US market. The industry has been characterized by vertical integration, in which the same Hollywood studios that produce feature films also own film-distribution companies and movie theatres. Vertical integration ensures the distribution and exhibition of Hollywood studio films, making it very difficult for independent film producers to compete. Until 2004–2005, the same companies that owned major Hollywood studios also owned Canada's principal theatre chains—Famous Players and Cineplex Odeon—and the distribution companies that supplied those theatre chains with films.

Today, Cineplex Entertainment (www.cineplex.com) is Canada's only significant chain, with

Source: ZUMA Press, Inc./Alamy.

Nancy Grant, Suzanne Clement, Anne Dorval, director Xavier Dolan, and Olivier Pilon attend the *Mommy* premiere during the 2014 Cannes Film Festival, where the movie won the Jury Prize and was nominated for the Palme d'Or. What are some of the reasons domestic films have averaged only between 2 and 6 percent of box-office revenues and less than 5 percent of screen time in Canadian cinemas?

TABLE 8.2
The National Film Board's Academy Awards

National Film Board filmmakers have won 12 Academy Awards (and 1 honorary Oscar) to date, in addition to 73 nominations. You can watch many of the following films on the NFB website: www.nfb.ca.

FILMS

Year	Title (Director)
1941	*Churchill's Island* (Stuart Legg) Best Documentary Short Subject
1952	*Neighbours* (Norman McLaren) Best Documentary Short Subject
1977	*Le Château de sable* (Co Hoedeman) Best Animated Short Film
1977	*I'll Find a Way* (Beverly Shaffer) Best Live Action Short Film
1978	*Special Delivery* (John Weldon, Eunice Macaulay) Best Animated Short Film
1979	*Every Child/Chaque enfant* (Eugene Fedorenko) Best Animated Short Film
1982	*If You Love This Planet* (Terre Nash) Best Documentary Short Subject
1983	*Flamenco at 5:15* (Cynthia Scott) Best Documentary Short Subject
1994	*Bob's Birthday* (Alison Snowden, David Fine) Best Animated Short Film
2004	*Ryan* (Chris Landreth) Best Animated Short Film
2006	*The Danish Poet* (Torril Kove) Best Animated Short Film

OTHER CATEGORIES

Year	Award
1989	Honorary Oscar in recognition of NFB's fiftieth anniversary
1999	Technical achievement to NFB scientists Ed H. Zwaneveld and Frederick Gasoi and two industry colleagues for the design and development of the Film Keykode Reader

Source: www.nfb.ca.

163 theatres and 1,643 screens across the country. The company purchased the 24 theatres belonging to Canada's second-largest chain, Empire Theatres, in 2013, while AMC Entertainment Inc. has been divesting its international holdings to focus on the US market. The way Canadians watch movies is clearly changing, but theatre-going remains popular among Canadians; box-office revenues increased every year from 2007 ($1.4 billion) to 2012 ($1.8 billion) (CMPA and AQPM, 2013: 84).

After decades of Hollywood dominance on our theatre screens, Canadians have come to associate cinema with Hollywood cinema, rendering "foreign" all those films made by other countries, including Canadian-made films. In 2012–2013, the most recent year for which figures are available, Canadian films accounted for almost one fifth of the movies playing in Canadian theatres, but a meagre 2.5 percent of the box office: 1.5 percent in the English-language market, where competition with Hollywood films is heaviest, and 9 percent in the French-language market (CMPA and AQPM, 2013: 81–3). No Canadian film penetrated the top 10 in box-office receipts in 2012–2013, but seven films topped $1 million in box-office earnings (CMPA and AQPM, 2013: 85).

Although the primary federal policy concern in the postwar period has been increasing the production and distribution of Canadian feature films for theatrical, home video/DVD, and television release, provincial governments—most notably in Quebec, Ontario, and British Columbia—have instituted programs to encourage Hollywood producers to locate their film and television productions in such cities as Montreal, Toronto, and Vancouver (see Gasher, 2002; Elmer and Gasher, 2005). These foreign location service productions accounted for $1.74 billion in spending in 2012–2013, close to two-thirds of it in British Columbia alone. US producers were responsible for 78 percent of the 220 foreign location service productions that year (CMPA and AQPM, 2013: 89).

History

In the early years of the last century, Ottawa perceived cinema as a medium of nation building.

The first state-sponsored films in Canada were tools to promote immigration from Britain to settle the Prairies; motion pictures are believed to have played a key role in Canada attracting three million immigrants between 1900 and 1914. Early films were also used to lure industry and investment capital (Morris, 1978: 133–5). The use of film as a medium of propaganda during World War I led governments to play an increasing role in film production, and Canada became the first country in the world with government film-production units, although Ottawa consistently rejected calls to curtail US monopolization of the commercial film sector. A distinction was made by state officials between the purposeful films of government production and entertainment films (Magder, 1985: 86). The establishment of the National Film Board of Canada under the direction of John Grierson in 1939 entrenched the state as a producer of films for nation-building purposes.

Increasingly since the end of World War II in 1945, the federal government has been called upon to address the commercial film sector. The first serious attempt by the Canadian government to stimulate indigenous feature-film production was the establishment of the Canadian Film Development Corporation (CFDC, now Telefilm Canada) in 1967. The CFDC was mandated to invest in Canadian feature-film projects; loan money to producers; present awards for outstanding production; support the development of film craft through grants to filmmakers and technicians; and "advise and assist" producers in distributing their films (Magder, 1985: 148).

Canadian governments have been reluctant to impose protectionist measures on the film industry, even though Ottawa heard repeated calls for screen quotas in Canadian movie theatres throughout the twentieth century. Part of the problem, certainly, is that the operation of movie theatres falls under provincial jurisdiction, and a nationwide screen quota would demand coordination among the 10 provinces. But there really is no public appetite for reducing in any way Hollywood's stranglehold on the Canadian market. Most Canadians—including francophones in Quebec—believe that attending the movies means going to Hollywood films. And this has been exacerbated by the reality that until at least the late 1980s, there was probably not a large enough stock of quality Canadian features to warrant a quota. While the Mulroney government in the 1980s talked tough about taking back control of Canada's commercial film industry, it was also negotiating a **trade liberalization** agreement with the United States. At the end of the day, it was decided that restructuring the Canadian film industry ran contrary to the spirit and the letter of the free-trade agreement that was in the works (see Gasher, 1988).

As a result of Canadian cinema's difficulty in penetrating Canadian movie theatres, television has become since the 1980s the largest source of revenue for private Canadian film and video companies. Television has been a friendlier platform for Canadian movies, thanks to Canadian ownership and Canadian-content regulations, the CBC's inherent interest in Canadian content, and the licensing in the 1980s of pay-TV and specialty channels devoted to broadcasting feature-length films. In recognition of the promise television held, the federal government in 1983 altered the mandate of the Canadian Film Development Corporation. The federal Department of Communications introduced the $35-million Canadian Broadcast Development Fund, to be administered by the CFDC, which later that year changed its name to Telefilm Canada to reflect its new emphasis on television. While the sum of money in the broadcast fund may not appear significant, it increased considerably the ability of production companies to access other sources of investment and it encouraged Canadian film producers to look more and more to television production.

Since the early 1980s, Ottawa has been gradually ceding its leadership role in the film policy field to the private sector and the provinces. Even though Telefilm remains the single most important source of film funding, no film can be made with Telefilm money alone. Filmmakers find themselves tapping half a dozen sources of funding to get their films made. Canada's major banks

and broadcasters have become important sources of financing for both project development and film and television production. These funding sources include the Harold Greenberg Fund, Bell Broadcast and New Media Fund, Bravo!Fact, the Cogeco Program Development Fund, the Rogers Group of Funds, the Independent Production Fund, the Shaw Rocket Fund, and the Quebecor Fund.

Canada's provincial governments have adopted a two-track film strategy. Every province in the country has a film office to promote it as a location for film and television production, primarily to Hollywood producers. In addition, the provinces provide development, production, and/or post-production support to indigenous producers through such funding vehicles as grants, loans, direct investment, and tax credits on labour costs. The Canadian Media Production Association provides current listings of public-sector and private commercial funding sources and programs (see www.cmpa.ca/business-affairs-production-tools/funding-opportunities).

Digitization is compelling theatre companies to convert their projection systems from 35 mm film to digital, which allows for closed-captioning and language choice, and 3-D. Their business includes online ticket and DVD sales, in-house media (pre-show advertising, film magazines), and merchandising.

Reminiscent of the late 1940s and early 1950s when television arrived, movie theatres

In what ways are filmmakers attempting to make the cinema experience different from home viewing? In your opinion, do these methods work?

Source: © Pamela Moore/iStockphoto.

8.7 ▶▶ ▶ ▶ ▶▶

THE VIDEO-GAME INDUSTRY IN CANADA: A SNAPSHOT

By Greig de Peuter

From *Angry Birds* on the smartphone to *Call of Duty* on the Xbox, video games and gaming platforms are not only increasingly pervasive but also seriously lucrative. Globally, annual game-industry revenue is predicted to surpass $80 billion in 2017. Games can be hugely expensive to make, and game development is a notoriously risky business. Profits, however, are potentially massive. Take, for example, *Grand Theft Auto V*. Released in 2013, *GTA V* cost an astounding $266 million to produce, but it raked in $800 million in sales during its first *day* on the market: "That was the biggest launch day ever for any piece of entertainment—any movie, any record, anything at all," reported *Fast Company* (Kamenetz, 2013). So whereas "crisis" is a common theme in coverage of the movie and music industries, the video-game sector appears to be thriving. As game-based movies and music-based games demonstrate, however, video games mix and merge with other media in an ever-more-convergent entertainment complex. And while the video-game industry is heterogeneous, its corporate titans and micro-start-ups alike are driven to extract financial value from our digitally mediated ludic diversions.

The video-game industry is multi-layered. The big moneymaker is the console side of the business, an oligopoly currently dominated by Microsoft (Xbox), Nintendo (Wii), and Sony (PS4). Console makers have tended to price their hardware below cost in an effort to build market share and in turn generate profit from game software licensed to play on their proprietary systems. The creative fuel of the business is game development, an industrial subset that includes the console makers' in-house game studios, a multitude of third-party studios that produce games under contract to publishers, and a mushrooming population of indie developers that distribute games online through app stores or console network services (e.g., Xbox Live). There is a long-standing power imbalance between most developers and publishers, since the latter finance game production (and, thus, influence the games that get made) and market games (which can affect a developer's commercial fate). Game development also displays a high level of ownership concentration, with large developer-publisher conglomerates frequently dominating the bestsellers list. Game development tends to favour companies with deep pockets; budgets for developing a console title average $8.7 million (Maimona, 2013), and a rule of thumb is that 10 percent of the games earn 90 percent of the money.

Canada is a significant node in the globalizing game industry, particularly in game development. According to a Nordicity (2013: 45) report funded by the Entertainment Software Association of Canada, the games industry contributed $2.3 billion to the Canadian economy in 2012. Nordicity reports that there are 329 game companies in Canada (2013: 7): 54 percent are micro-enterprises with no more than 4 staff; 34 percent are small operations with 99 or fewer employees; 9 percent are medium-sized firms with between 100 and 499 staff; and the remaining 4 percent are vast entities, most of which are satellites of developer-publisher behemoths such as Ubisoft, which employs approximately 3,000 people in Canada (Nordicity, 2013: 15). Even though there is a large pool of game companies in Canada, a small fraction of them account for a disproportionate share of the revenue and jobs.

The game business may be booming in Canada, but in key aspects the seat of economic power is elsewhere. Many of the industry's largest developer-publishers, such as Electronic Arts (US), Activision Blizzard (France), and Capcom (Japan), have Canadian outposts. Although more than three-quarters of game businesses in the country are Canadian-owned (Nordicity, 2013: 16), the biggest ones tend to be foreign-owned. Electronic Arts, Disney (US), Nexon (South Korea), and many additional mega-publishers have extended their presence in Canada by buying up smaller homegrown studios. This is part and parcel of ownership concentration, a process that has been especially pronounced in the console-game-development sector.

Although the technology industry has a pull-yourself-up-by-your-bootstraps reputation, the multinational firms that dominate game development in Canada are supported by significant state subsidies. In the late 1990s, Quebec's promise of tax breaks enticed the France-based Ubisoft to set up in Montreal what has grown into one of the largest studios in the world. And in 2010, Ubisoft opened a studio in Toronto after the province of Ontario offered the company incentives valued at $263 million on the condition that Ubisoft create 800 jobs by 2020. Government assistance, said one Ubisoft executive, is simply "part of the equation" when deciding where to expand (cited in Ebner, 2009).

Canada's digital play business directly employed 16,500 people in 2012 (Nordicity, 2013: 3). Nordicity's profile suggests that the nation's game workforce is decently paid (average salary: $72,500), relatively young (average age: early thirties), and has high levels of formal education (2013: 4). By all accounts, working in game development is challenging and rewarding. Still, the industry doesn't entirely live up to its work-as-play image; one Canadian studio owner acknowledges that game companies have a "reputation for treating people badly" (cited in Gooderham, 2010). Especially controversial is overwork, a problem publicized a decade ago by an infamous blog post by the anonymous "EA Spouse" that detailed endemic excessive hours at game-industry giant Electronic Arts (EA). The game workforce is also profoundly gendered: merely 16 percent of the games workforce in Canada is female, and women hold a narrow 5 percent of technical roles (Nordicity, 2013: 32). Redressing this imbalance in game production is essential to respond to sexism in game culture, an enduring problem most recently exposed in the so-called Gamergate controversy in 2014, whereby a number of women in the industry were subjected to misogynist attacks (see Wingfield, 2014).

A burgeoning game market does not guarantee employment security. A game that flops in the market can result in huge job losses. Studio closures and job cuts at major market–listed developers have been familiar industry news stories since the economic crisis of 2008. The game-development workforce is also stratified: at one end of the hierarchy are celebrity designers; at the other are those who play-test games for bugs—the workers most likely to earn the lowest company wage, to be hired on a temporary basis, and to be excluded from benefits programs. Lower production costs for mobile games hold promise for a renaissance in independent games, but indie game development remains a "precarious business" (Gouglas et al., 2010: 17). Risk is acute for rookie studios whose fate hangs on a single project. What's more, the average salary at a micro-size studio is $28,900, which is less than half the industry average (Nordicity, 2013: 10).

While game-production activity dots the country, nearly 80 percent of game companies in Canada are in British Columbia, Quebec, and Ontario (Nordicity, 2013: 23). Within these provinces, the sector is primarily clustered in three cities: Vancouver, Montreal, and Toronto. In British Columbia, there are some 5,150 game workers at 67 studios (Nordicity, 2013: 30, 23). The more than 8,750-strong game-labour force in Quebec, the country's largest, is concentrated in Montreal—and its nucleus is Ubisoft. Ontario hosts a large number of studios (95) but the employment base (1,850) is significantly smaller compared to BC and Quebec (Nordicity, 2013: 23, 30). Lacking access to a major employer like EA in the Vancouver area, developers in Toronto struck out on their own in droves, launching studios specializing in lower-cost platforms such as mobiles.

Ultimately, however, the geography of video-game production is international; a new game concept might be conceived of in Canada, based on intellectual property owned by an entertainment company headquartered elsewhere, funded from another country, developed with inputs from multiple far-flung locales, and marketed to a global audience. Virtual games, in turn, depend on actual hardware, most of which is manufactured in lower-wage regions—and, when discarded, game-machine components eventually snake their way to e-waste villages in the Global South. So although it has a strong Canadian presence, the video-game industry spreads around the planet—and its pleasures and its pains are very unevenly distributed.

—*Greig de Peuter is an assistant professor in the Department of Communication Studies at Wilfrid Laurier University.*

today compete with increasingly sophisticated, high-definition and wide-screen home theatres, as well as a growing number of online movie services. For example, iTunes has been offering movie downloads since 2008, and as we discussed in the section on television broadcasting, Netflix is becoming a threat to cable and satellite TV providers with its attractive and inexpensive television and movie offerings. As they did at the dawn of television, filmmakers are seeking ways to make the cinema experience distinct from rival viewing platforms (e.g., by experimenting with 3-D, huge screens, digital sound).

New Media

While for many people, "new media" today may not seem so new, since the 1990s, the media landscape has changed considerably. Many new features adorn the current media landscape. We are referring in broad terms here to new media technologies, new media forms, and new media applications that are associated with the production of digitized information and its distribution through converged computerized communications networks. Such technologies include the internet, CD-ROMs, DVDs, hand-held mobile devices, and portable computers of all kinds. New media applications also include interactive gaming, text messaging, video conferencing, mash-ups, and social networking (Burkell, 2010: 314–17). Because new media are digital, they allow for a converged and networked architecture, and they permit—even encourage—interactivity and content manipulation. According to Statistics Canada (2013a), 83 percent of Canadian households had internet access in 2012, logging on to the internet via desktop and laptop computers, netbooks, smartphones, mobile phones, MP3/MP4 players, and video-game consoles. The federal government hopes to increase this number through its Connecting Canadians program, launched in July 2014. Through an initiative that subsidizes internet service providers, Connecting

Canadians seeks to bring high-speed internet access to an additional 280,000 homes in rural and remote areas (Industry Canada, 2014).

Industry Canada (2014) groups 33,000 companies within a $155-billion information and communication technologies sector, employing 522,000 people. Eighty-seven percent of these companies are involved in the software and computer-services industry, which includes software publishing, computer systems design, data processing, telecommunications services, and program distribution. The sector is characterized by small companies (most have fewer than 10 employees), a well-educated workforce (more than 45 percent have university degrees), and considerable private-sector spending on research and development (Industry Canada, 2013).

As we discussed above, digital technologies pose new regulatory challenges for the CRTC, and it continues to make rulings in the telecommunications and broadcast sectors in an effort to keep pace. The CRTC, however, has to date decided not to regulate Canadians' internet activity. In the face of challenges to regulation, such as the rise of OTT services, whether or not the commission continues to forgo regulation in this area remains to be seen.

The internet, of course, is not entirely beyond government regulation; online activity remains subject to the Criminal Code of Canada and as police forces become more sophisticated in their use of digital technologies, criminal charges increase, particularly in the areas of corporate espionage, organized crime, and child pornography. In 2014, for example, an ex-soldier in Edmonton was convicted of internet-based sex crimes, and the RCMP filed charges against a Dutch man in the case of Amanda Todd, the British Columbia teen who killed herself after being harassed online (Cormier, 2014; Hager, 2014). The Montreal teenaged hacker Michael Calce (known as "Mafiaboy") pleaded guilty to 56 charges and served eight months in a group home for his February 2000 denial-of-service attacks on five major websites, including Yahoo!, eBay, and CNN

(CBC News, 2008). Officials are also patrolling the web for fraud and privacy violations, including identity theft.

Further, as Vanda Rideout and Andrew Reddick (2001: 265) point out, new media are subject to the regulation of the market economy, effectively depriving Canadian citizens of policy input. One of their central concerns is the corporate power that converged media corporations can exert in the digital marketplace. "What is somewhat different is that whereas particular firms may have dominated one or a few parts of the communications sector [in the past], now, with corporate, technical and content convergence, a handful of firms are dominating the whole communications marketplace" (Rideout and Reddick, 2001: 273).

Publishing

The book, magazine, and newspaper publishing industries face numerous challenges, especially in the transition from analog to digital production and distribution. For more than 500 years, publishing has meant the printing, transportation, and storage of physical and relatively bulky reading materials, and a substantial portion of the costs associated with publishing are contained in the physical production and distribution of these materials: printing presses, paper, ink, transport, and the skilled tradespeople who carry out these processes. These costs are compounded in a country like Canada, with a huge land mass and a relatively small and widely dispersed population. As more and more people access reading materials electronically—via the internet, tablets, smartphones, and e-readers—there is great potential for publishers to reduce production costs and, at the same time, expand their audiences. In this transitional period, though, most publishers are having to produce both hard-copy and electronic editions with no assurance that the burgeoning market for electronic publications will generate the revenues that hard-copy publishing has provided, at least any time soon. The newspaper

industry is discussed in considerable detail in the next two chapters, so our focus here is on book and magazine publishing.

Book Publishing

Book publishing is a $1.8-billion industry in Canada, with 1,500 publishing houses employing approximately 9,000 workers. But revenues and profit margins are in decline, and vary greatly between publishing houses that produce original, Canadian works and those that import foreign titles (Statistics Canada, 2014c: 4; Boggs, 2012: 95). The industry is heavily concentrated in Toronto and Montreal; publishers in Ontario and Quebec accounted for 94 percent of industry revenues in 2012 (the most recent statistics available). Publishers earned three quarters of their revenues from domestic sales of their own titles and the titles to which they had exclusive rights. Canadian-controlled publishers earned 70 percent of their revenues from sales of their own titles. Textbooks account for 45 percent of the Canadian market, adult trade titles represent 36 percent, and children's books occupy 15 percent (Statistics Canada, 2014c: 9).

Like all of the communications industries described in this chapter, the book industry is confronting digitization and its implications.

Source: © Yuri_Arcurs/iStockphoto.

An increasing number of people have put their printed books on a shelf and turned to e-readers. What does this mean for the publishing industry? And what effect does this have on the way we read and learn to read?

Digitization is a promising development in many respects; whether through online book sales, electronic publishing, on-demand publishing, self-publishing, direct orders, or supply-chain management programs, digitization holds out the promise to reduce printing, storage, and transportation costs; facilitate book promotion; increase author–reader interaction; and make more books available to more Canadians (Lorimer, 2012: 260–86). One of digitization's immediate benefits to publishers and retailers has been the creation of databases to track the circulation of books through the system. Book-Net Canada, created in 2002, makes available data on warehouse holdings of individual titles, bookstore stock levels, and weekly sales (Lorimer, 2012: 171). This is critical in an industry coping with bulky items, and when retailers maintain the unique right to return unsold books within a specified time period.

Digitization also entails significant challenges for bricks-and-mortar booksellers, however, and it affects the author–publisher relationship. Online retailers like Amazon and AbeBooks are convenient for buyers, but they reduce customer traffic to local bookstores, which specialize in customer service—and online retailers can demand from publishers greater discounts than are typically available to smaller sellers (Lorimer, 2012: 226). Smaller independent bookstores in Canada are already competing with a national monopoly bookseller in Chapters/Indigo, as well as increasingly popular newcomers like the big-box retailers Walmart and Costco. While online retailers can attract increased attention paid to authors and facilitate the sale of their books, they can also reduce royalty rates through direct negotiation with authors and increase the availability of second-hand books, for which authors receive no royalties (see Boggs, 2012: 98–9). On the book-production side, researcher Jeff Boggs (2012) argues that the emergence of online-only publishers can have a detrimental impact on the Canadian industry because they operate beyond Canadian copyright law, which governs the physical importation and distribution of books

in the Canadian market. "Digital books can be bought from websites in other jurisdictions, reducing demand for titles in Canada's copyright space" (Boggs, 2012: 98).

The most vulnerable sector of the business pertains to the publishing of original Canadian titles, and this is the principal role of Canadian-owned publishers. Industry scholar Rowland Lorimer (2012) insists that a number of *market distortions* hamper the viability of a domestic industry for Canadian works, necessitating government programs offering both industrial and cultural support. The first market distortion he cites is the importation of *run-on copies* of foreign-published book titles; because these books are priced based on their large sales volumes, they create downward pressure on the price of Canadian books destined for a much smaller domestic market. The second market distortion is the frequent inclusion of the Canadian market when US companies purchase the North American publishing rights to popular international book titles; this represents a lost opportunity for Canadian publishers in their own market. Third, Canada has only one national bookstore chain, and the business model of Chapters/Indigo privileges high-volume sales, leaving little shelf space for the non-mainstream and mid-list titles in which Canadian publishers tend to specialize (Lorimer, 2012: 48–9). Lorimer describes the organization of Canadian book production as "essentially feudal": "With or without publishers' approval, authors toil away without a wage to complete books for a small share of the return—often, for unestablished authors, as little as 5 per cent of retail price." Given that the average sales for indigenous Canadian titles range between $14,000 and $20,000, this can mean authors earning between $700 and $1,000 in royalties (Lorimer, 2012: 316). This is why many Canadian authors need day jobs.

French-language publishers have been far more successful in getting their books to readerships; better than 90 percent have access to national distribution and close to 90 percent of Canadian French-language titles are distributed across the country (Ėdinova, 2008: 8). This advantage is due in part to the fact that they do not face the same head-to-head competition from the United States as English-language publishers do. But there are two other factors. One is Quebec's Bill 51, passed in 1981, to protect Canadian-owned booksellers. Bill 51 establishes an accreditation system whereby public institutions like schools and libraries are required to order their books from accredited local retailers (rather than directly from publishers or through wholesalers). Accredited publishers, distributors, and retailers are also eligible for Quebec government assistance programs (Ėdinova, 2008: 20–2; see also Canada, 2014a, b). The French-language publishing industry also uses an efficient book-ordering system, called the *système d'offre*. Based on agreements between distributors and retailers, newly published books are automatically shipped to bookstores in predetermined numbers. The distributors assume the shipping costs and the retailers assume the costs of returning unsold books (Ėdinova, 2008: 19). This system ensures the timely and consistent diffusion of new French-language books by Canadian authors.

The federal government supports book publishing through both legislation and funding programs. Lorimer describes the Copyright Act as "the main structural support for the industry" (2012: 166). Revised in 2012, the Act grants "sole supplier status" to Canadian importers and distributors, giving them exclusive rights to provide books to wholesalers and retailers. The government's principal support program is the Canada Book Fund (formerly the Publishing Industry Development Program), which was granted $39.5 million in ongoing annual funding in the 2014 federal budget. The Canada Book Fund has two components: Support for Publishers, which aids the production and promotion of Canadian-authored books through financial assistance to Canadian-owned and controlled publishers; and Support for Organizations, which assists the promotion of Canadian-authored books by industry organizations and associations through programs for marketing, professional development, strategic planning, internships, and technology projects (Canada, 2014a, b). The Canada Council for the Arts, a Crown corporation founded in 1957, provides grants each year to Canadian writers in a variety of genres. The National Translation Program for Book Publishing is a fund to support the translation of Canadian-authored works: between English and French in Canada, and from English and French to other languages in international markets. The Public Lending Right provides annual payments to Canadian authors based on the presence of their books in libraries (Canada Council, 2014).

The federal government also protects the Canadian book industry through ownership restrictions with policy dating from 1974. The current investment policy restricts foreign investment in new businesses to Canadian-controlled joint ventures, prohibits the direct acquisition of a Canadian-controlled business by a non-Canadian, reviews indirect acquisitions based on the net benefit to Canada, and requires non-Canadians wishing to sell an existing book-industry venture to ensure that Canadian investors have full and fair opportunity to bid (Canada, 2010b: 8). The review committee for foreign investment policy affirmed that "Canadian control of Canadian book publishing is a key and long-standing tenet of the Government's policy in this area given the demonstrated commitment of Canadian-owned firms to the identification, development, and support of a wide range of Canadian writers' (Canada, 2010b: 9). This policy came into play in the 2010 decision to approve the establishment of a Canadian distribution centre by the US-based company Amazon, one of the largest online booksellers, judging it to be in the best interests of Canada (Canada, 2010b: 11–12).

As in other communications spheres, the provinces have their own support systems for book publishing. Ontario, for example, has the Ontario Arts Council, which offers grants to publishers and writers; the Ontario Book Publishing Tax Credit; the Trillium Award to reward excellence among Ontario writers; and the Ontario Media Development Corporation's Book Fund,

Export Fund, and a fund to assist screen adaptations of Ontario publications (see Ontario Arts Council, 2014; Ontario Media Development Corporation, 2014).

Revenu Québec offers a tax credit for book publishers and does not impose provincial income tax on writers' royalty payments. Quebec's Société de développement des entreprises culturelles (SODEC) has funding programs for book exports, publishing, the production of special editions, book fairs, libraries, book transportation, and digitization—and it supports collectives and associations in the book-publishing sector (SODEC, 2014).

Magazines

Magazine publishing in Canada is a $2-billion industry, producing more than 2,000 titles. As in book publishing, Ontario and Quebec house most of the industry's activity, together accounting for almost 80 percent of revenues in 2011—the latest statistics available (Statistics Canada, 2014d). And as with Canadian books, Canadian magazines compete with US periodicals, but Canadian magazines' share of the market has risen over the past 30 years; American magazines tend to dominate the newsstands, while Canadian magazines lead in subscription sales. Similar to what is happening in the newspaper industry, magazines are increasing their audiences online while their hard-copy circulation numbers fall; a study of 30 magazine websites by the Print Measurement Bureau showed an incremental audience increase of 25 percent, while their print readership dropped. Eight of the top 10 magazines in the Canadian market reported readership losses of between 1.8 and 14.8 percent between 2013 and 2014; only *Cineplex Magazine* (5.1 percent) and *CAA Magazine* (2.3 percent) experienced readership upticks. The top 3 French-language magazines—*Touring*, *Qu'est-ce qui mijote*, and *Coup de pouce*—maintained their readership numbers over the same period (Digital Readership, 2014).

Faced with significant competition and high distribution costs, the magazine industry is one of Canada's most volatile and diverse media sectors. Some magazines are published by large media corporations like Transcontinental, Quebecor, and Rogers, while others are produced by foundations, associations, and artists' collectives. New magazine titles appear each year, but many of these titles don't last long. More than 100 new magazines were launched between 2007 and 2012, and almost 60 percent of Canadian magazines available today were launched after the internet became widely available in 1989 (Magazines Canada, 2013b). Canadian magazines earn about 75 percent of their revenue from advertising and roughly 25 percent from circulation, although this varies greatly from magazine to magazine.

The precariousness of the Canadian magazine industry is reflected in its labour practices. Magazines tend to have much smaller editorial staffs than newspapers, and so depend for a considerable amount of their content on freelance writers, photographers, and illustrators. Freelancers are typically contracted article by article, meaning they are constantly pitching story ideas in the quest for the next assignment. And the rates they are paid—from 30 cents per word at smaller magazines, to $1 or $2 per word at larger-circulation publications (Professional Writers Association of Canada, 2014)—have remained roughly the same since the 1980s (Cohen, 2012). In April 2014, the Ontario's Ministry of Labour served notice that unpaid magazine internships were in contravention of the Employment Standards Act, prompting the cancellation of gratis internships at a number of magazines, including *Toronto Life*, *The Walrus*, and *Canadian Geographic* (Masthead, 2014b). Unpaid internships are common at Canadian magazines and newspapers; on the one hand, they provide students and other aspiring journalists and writers an opportunity to gain experience and contacts that might not otherwise be available to them, but on the other hand, they can be exploitive, using interns' free labour instead of paying them, or others, for the same work.

Magazine policy is driven by the same logic as policy in book publishing: first, the need to create space in a relatively small and dispersed market for Canadian voices on a range of topics, from current affairs to popular culture, from the arts to sports and leisure activities; and second, the desire to support a domestic industry. The most important policy instrument for magazine publishers is Section 19 of the Income Tax Act.

The key source of government funding comes from the Department of Canadian Heritage's Canada Periodical Fund, which replaced both the Canadian Magazine Fund and the Publications Assistance Program in 2010. The fund contains three elements: Aid to Publishers, which supports content creation, production, distribution, online activities, and business development for Canadian magazines (print and online) and non-daily newspapers; Business Innovation, which provides monies for small and mid-sized magazines (print and online); and Collective Initiatives, which funds organizations' efforts to increase the overall sustainability of the Canadian magazine and non-daily newspaper industries (Canada, 2014c).

The biggest change, however, was the cancellation in 2009 of the $15-million annual subsidy that Canada Post used to provide to support the Publications Assistance Program (PAP). Given the magazine industry's reliance on subscriptions mailed to readers, Magazines Canada had described the Canada Post–subsidized PAP as "the most successful cultural industry policy of the Government of Canada" (Magazines Canada, 2005: 10). Distribution has become the fastest-rising cost for magazine publishers.

Postal Service

The postal system typically is overlooked by communications scholars, even though it is our oldest mass medium and it continues to move close to 10 billion pieces of correspondence—letters, notices, invoices, parcels—each year (Canada

In 2014, Canada Post announced that it would be discontinuing door-to-door services; instead, Canadians would receive their mail at community mailboxes like this one. What are the advantages and disadvantages of the new system?

Source: Francis Labbé/Radio-Canada.

Post, 2014: 1). Its history remains closely bound to the history of transportation in Canada (see Gendreau, 2000). The post office was one of the first federal government departments established after Confederation in 1867, but both the French and British colonial regimes had postal service in the earliest days of the colony. The French relied on ships to transport mail across the Atlantic Ocean from France and along the St Lawrence River valley in the seventeenth and eighteenth centuries. Mail was carried overland by travellers and fur traders forming a "human network of communication" (Willis, 2000: 36–7). The British established a formal postal system along the St Lawrence River valley in 1763 under the governance of a deputy postmaster general. Service was introduced to Nova Scotia in 1785 (Willis, 2000: 39–40). Canada Post was created as a Crown corporation in 1981 after having been run directly as a department of the federal government since 1868. Governed today by the Canada Post Corporation Act (1985), it has the exclusive right to collect and deliver letters up to 500 grams in Canada (Canada Post, 2014: 18). Canada Post, however, competes with other private direct-marketing and courier companies in these growing industry sectors (see McKenna, 2014).

Not surprisingly, the physical delivery of such items as letters, documents, greeting cards, invoices, and bank statements has been in decline since 2006, largely replaced by electronic mail, and Canada Post suffers for it (Canada Post, 2014). The Crown corporation reported a loss of $269 million for 2013, with its volume of deliveries dropping for a fifth straight year. The growth areas for the company are its parcel service—with deliveries up 6.9 percent in 2013, thanks to the increasing popularity of online shopping—and its digital services: epost, as well as canadapost.ca and its mobile app (Canada Post, 2014: 1–4).

Under pressure to demonstrate its continuing viability, Canada Post introduced a five-point plan to reduce costs and implement efficiencies in December 2013. The plan includes abandoning by 2018 door-to-door mail delivery to households—to be replaced by community mailboxes—adopting a tiered pricing system for letter delivery, and increasing its number of franchised post offices (Canada Post, 2014: 19).

Canada Post is part of a global network of national postal services operating on the basis of equitable, universal service to citizens. An international agreement established the General Post Union in 1874 (later renamed the Universal Postal Union), ensuring the free transportation of mail within member countries and the standardization of charges collected by each country for mail service between members (Hamelink, 1994: 7). As a Crown corporation providing what is considered to be a key communications service, Canada Post is required by the federal government to undertake special obligations. These include the provision of free mail service between Canadian citizens and designated members of government; reduced postal rates for the shipping of books between libraries; the transportation of nutritious, perishable foods and other essential items to isolated northern communities; and the free mailing of materials for the blind (Canada Post, 2014: 21). Given the fiscal challenges Canada Post faces—decreasing amounts of mail, an increasing number of Canadian addresses, regular annual deficits, free electronic mail alternatives, increasing competition from private courier services—it will be interesting to monitor in coming years the results of its efficiency plan and the extent to which the federal government continues to support the policy principle of equitable and universal service in a communications network that ties together every Canadian community.

▶ SUMMARY

Through this examination of specific policy sectors, we can see that the task of providing Canadians with a range of opportunities to produce and receive communications, while ensuring the viability of Canadian cultural industries, presents governments with constant challenges.

We began the chapter by outlining three significant changes affecting the media landscape in recent years, changes that have far-reaching implications for Canadian communications policy: the convergence or merging of previously distinct technologies, media forms, and media industries; trade liberalization, which puts pressure on Canada to make its policies, laws, and regulations conform to international trade agreements; and changes in immigration patterns which have further diversified the Canadian population and its communications needs. What has not changed is Canada's central policy priority of ensuring that Canadians benefit from the opportunities that mass communication affords.

We have provided here a profile of each of the major communications sectors—telecommunications, broadcasting, recorded music, cinema, new media, publishing, and postal service—and have outlined their respective policy challenges, providing current information about these industries and policy responses by governments. Each of the sectors had things in common (e.g., new services, digitization) as well as distinctions particular to their field.

It is clear that each of these sectors remains in a transitional phase between analog or hard-copy platforms and new, digital platforms. This transition implicates communications companies seeking emergent revenue streams while still reliant on traditional income sources; it implicates individuals transitioning to new ways of communicating; and it affects policy-makers striving to serve the interests of Canadian communications industries and Canadian citizens in an environment characterized by an increasing amount of global governance.

 KEY TERMS

Canadian content, p. 213
Canadian Radio-television and Telecommunications Commission (CRTC), p. 209
common carriage, p. 209
convergence, p. 206
cultural industries, p. 207
cultural sovereignty, p. 216

fee-for-carriage, p. 218
interactivity, p. 206
net neutrality, p. 211
streaming, p. 213
trade liberalization, p. 227
wireless spectrum, p. 211

 RELATED WEBSITES

Canadian Radio-television and Telecommunications Commission: www.crtc.gc.ca
The CRTC website contains a wealth of information about the broadcasting and telecommunications industries, as well as industry studies, press releases, and current decisions rendered.

Department of Canadian Heritage: www.pch.gc.ca
This site is that of the government ministry responsible for the arts and cultural industries. It contains information on a number of cultural industry sectors as well as news releases and speeches pertaining to the ministry.

Industry Canada: www.ic.gc.ca
This site belongs to the federal ministry responsible for industry, which includes some of the cultural industries such as telecommunications and new media. The site contains industry profiles as well as research reports and statistical data.

Music Canada: www.musiccanada.com
This site belongs to a non-profit trade organization serving the music industry and musicians in Canada. Music Canada contains news and research material pertaining to all aspects of the sound recording industry in Canada.

Masthead Online: www.mastheadonline.com
Masthead provides news and information about all aspects of the publishing industry in Canada.

 FURTHER READINGS

Armstrong, Robert. 2010. *Broadcasting Policy in Canada*. Toronto: University of Toronto Press. This is an accessible, comprehensive, and current portrait of the policy picture for broadcasting in Canada. It covers every aspect of broadcast regulation in detail, and situates Canadian policies with respect to international trade and cultural agreements.

Canadian Journal of Communication. Canada's premier source for current research on communication issues in all areas. Current and back issues can be accessed online at www.cjc-online.ca/index.php/journal.

Kozolanka, Kirsten, Patricia Mazepa, and David Skinner. 2012. *Alternative Media in Canada*. Vancouver: UBC Press. This edited collection documents recent developments and the issues involved around media reform and alternative media initiatives.

Lorimer, Rowland. 2012. *Ultra Libris: Policy, Technology, and the Creative Economy of Book Publishing in Canada*. Toronto: ECW Press. This is a comprehensive study of book publishing in Canada, with an emphasis on policy instruments that have been developed to support the Canadian publishing industry.

Wagman, Ira, and Peter Urquhart, eds. 2012. *Cultural Industries.ca: Making Sense of Canadian Media* *in the Digital Age*. Toronto: James Lorimer. This book consists of chapters on each of the cultural industries in their transition to digital, as well as a section pertaining to questions of media research.

▶ STUDY QUESTIONS

1. What prevents Canada's media companies from moving more aggressively into digital platforms?
2. What is net neutrality and why has it become an important issue?
3. While online services have increased choices for media consumers, they are hurting some producers of music, television programming, and published materials. Why is this the case?
4. The CRTC has decided not to regulate the internet. Does this mean that the internet is not subject to any form of regulation?
5. How have your media usage habits changed in recent years?
6. What are the most important communications concerns facing Canadians? What can be done about those concerns?

Ownership and the Economics of Media

9

> You can say that at times freedom in our kind of society amounts to the freedom to say anything you wish, provided you can say it profitably. — Raymond Williams

Opening Questions

- How has the context of media economics changed in recent years?
- How do media organizations participate in the economy?
- What resources do media organizations require?

- What role(s) does advertising play in mass communication?
- What fundamental distinctions are there between publicly owned and privately owned media?
- What do we mean by the democratization of media?

Introduction

The economics behind the production, distribution, and consumption of media content is one of the central preoccupations of our time. The basic principles haven't changed; media economics is about ensuring that the communications needs and desires of society are met through a system that remains accessible and affordable to citizens while at the same time ensuring producers and distributors at all levels are adequately compensated.

But the context of media economics has changed dramatically in recent times, owing to a number of interrelated factors. Mainstream media companies are increasingly part of concentrated conglomerates, placing renewed emphasis on revenue generation. Those companies face vastly increased competition, not only from other commercial producers large and small distributing media content across a global network of digital platforms, but also from every kind of DIY producer with an internet connection. A tremendous amount of this content is distributed without any direct cost to consumers, disrupting the conventional revenue streams of subscription and **advertising**. At the same time, budget-conscious governments are withdrawing subsidies and other supports, increasingly allowing **market** regulation of the communications sector to prevail. Communications workers face a more competitive and precarious **labour** market as media companies rely increasingly on flexible contract work, and the demand for skilled labour is influenced by so-called *prosumers*: consumers of media content who have become producers as well. Digitization threatens to render all analog forms of media obsolete, but does not—yet, at least—generate sustainable revenue flows to commercial producers. And consumers insist on increased choice of what content is available to them—as well as how, when, and where—combined with a reluctance to pay for it. The ground is shifting dramatically, as we signalled in the preceding chapters, and the search for new and sustainable economic models is on. In this chapter, we address the economic structuring, and restructuring, of mass communications.

All forms of mass communication require resources. Producing media products requires resources of time, money, labour, and materials, and what economists seek to understand is how these resources interact to meet peoples' communicative needs and desires.

The media economist Robert G. Picard identifies four groups served by the media: owners, audiences, advertisers, and workers (1989: 8–9)—to which we would add a fifth: governments. Each of these groups is multi-layered and requires some elaboration. The category of media owners, for instance, can range from the complex management groups of large, converged, and publicly traded corporations—such as Quebecor or BCE—to community groups or individuals with their own websites. Some of these groups are motivated primarily by profit; others by some kind of public service or social purpose. Media owners include governments (e.g., the CBC/Radio-Canada, the NFB), political groups (e.g., the Communist Party of Canada's newspaper *The People's Voice*), non-profit foundations (e.g., *The Walrus*, published by The Walrus Foundation), non-governmental organizations (*Greenpeace Magazine*), cooperatives (e.g., the Atlantic Filmmakers Cooperative), and individual business people (e.g., Brunswick News). Regardless of who they are or what their motivation is, media owners participate in some way in the economy.

We used to think of audiences as passive consumers of media products and services. But as we discussed earlier, research has demonstrated that audiences are much more active in the ways they choose, receive, draw meaning from, and make use of media than was previously understood or appreciated. These audiences have become even more active in the era of digital media, which allow media consumers to also become media producers, whether by engaging in online discussion groups, putting together music compilations for their MP3 players, sharing commercial TV or film on YouTube, alerting followers to breaking news via Twitter, or going much further in producing mash-ups or blogs, sampling music, or documenting their own daily lives on Facebook. Regardless of the nature of their media use, members of the audience are crucial to the economic vitality of the media.

Advertisers use media not only to promote the goods and services they want to sell, but as well to project a certain kind of brand identification. Think of the number of companies using advertising to foster a "green" image. From an economic standpoint, advertisers generate revenue for media organizations in their quest to speak to audiences about the products and services they want to sell; what they are buying when they advertise is access to media audiences (see Box 9.1).

Media workers comprise a heterogeneous group, ranging from the star directors and actors of a Hollywood blockbuster to those who make their living in the film industry as carpenters, electricians, drivers, and hairdressers. Some

media workers, in other words, have a central and direct role to play in the creation of the content we see on our screens, while many others play indispensable roles in media support networks—running printing presses, entering data, selling advertising, applying makeup, maintaining servers. Some of these workers are paid royalties or have an ownership stake and, therefore, have a clear and direct financial interest in the welfare of the enterprise. Others are hired project by project and are paid an hourly wage for a contract of limited duration. So, workers can have very different stakes in the operation, the mission, and the overall welfare of the media organization.

Through their cultural-policy apparatus, governments adopt guidelines and laws that compel media organizations to serve the needs and wants of national or regional constituencies, as we saw in Chapters 7 and 8. This has meant ensuring Canadians have access to the cultural and economic opportunities that participation in the media affords. And Canadian governments

Source: © KathrynHatashitaLee/iStockphoto.

The role of media workers varies widely. What work would have gone into these billboards at Toronto's Yonge-Dundas Square?

9.1 ▶▶▶▶▶▶

ADVERTISING

Advertising is a medium of communication in and of itself, and serves a number of purposes. Its most obvious purpose is to provide consumers with information about goods and services available in the marketplace. Advertisements can also be used to provide information of general public interest; governments, for example, are among the biggest media advertisers and use advertising both to inform citizens—about new programs, changes in laws or regulations, public health warnings, and so on—and to persuade citizens about government policy. They can also be read for what they say about predominant social and cultural values (e.g., gender roles, notions of beauty, health, happiness, success).

Less obvious, perhaps, is the role of advertising in the overall economy. A capitalist economy requires perpetual and ever-increasing consumer spending. Advertising, in this way, is an important driver of the economy, acting as a catalyst for consumer spending. Economists believe it creates demand for products and services (Leiss et al., 2005: 32–3), and without "a mechanism for mass distribution of information about products," the economies of scale of mass marketing may be unattainable (Leiss et al., 2005: 16). Companies, as actors within the larger economy, advertise in order to maintain and expand revenue flows, to generate new and repeat business, to create new markets by informing consumers about new products and services, and to compete with rival companies and brands.

The media are advertising's principal vehicles of delivery. As communications theorist Dallas Smythe (1977) observed in his classic article, "Communications: Blindspot of Western Marxism," the media's principal commodity is the audience, which is sold to advertisers. If advertising first appeared in newspapers, magazines, and catalogues, and on flyers, posters, and billboards in the last half of the nineteenth century, all media serve advertisers today and "the business of advertising structures media operations in a capitalist economy" (Johnston, 2010: 104). Russell Johnston argues that "every media outlet tries to produce an audience sought by advertisers" (2010: 105).

For media companies, advertising is a critical revenue source. In the case of commercial over-the-air radio and television, free newspapers and magazines, and many websites, it is their sole revenue source. Other media combine subscription fees with advertising. Most daily newspapers and monthly magazines derive 60 to 80 percent of their revenues from advertising, which greatly subsidizes the newsstand or home-delivery price.

Digital advertising has been the biggest growth sector in media advertising over the past two decades, and it finally surpassed television in 2013 to become Canada's top advertising platform (Interactive Advertising Bureau of Canada, 2014). Digital advertising accounted for $3.5 billion in spending in 2013, up 14 percent from 2012, and almost twice as much as in 2009. The largest amount of growth in digital advertising was accounted for by mobile and tablet devices, with spending up 177 percent from 2012. Television advertising was second at $3.47 billion, followed by daily newspapers at $1.68 billion, radio at $1.6 billion, magazines at $558 million and "out-of-home" advertising (e.g., billboards) at $514 million. While the number of media advertising platforms increases, the total amount of ad spending in Canada remains relatively stable—it was $11.26 billion in 2013. If these figures make it appear that new media are putting old media out of business, it is important to note that the legacy media companies in broadcasting and print publishing all have digital platforms and are participating in the digital economy.

Advertising has been moving beyond conventional media spaces as well. The previews that are screened prior to the feature attraction in Canadian movie theatres can be seen as a form of advertising, and it is now common today for audiences to be subjected to paid advertisements prior to those previews. Companies often pay film producers a fee for *product placement* within the movies: the use of a recognizable brand by the characters or as a visible element of the backdrop.

And advertising is turning all public spaces into vehicles for ads: bathroom walls, handles of self-serve gas pumps, the floors in subway systems, you name it. Even the logo on your sweater, your jeans, or your running shoes is an advertisement of sorts.

recognized early the media's role in fostering a sense of national identity; Benedict Anderson (1983) has highlighted the role of media in creating "imagined communities," and this continues to be a central driver in cultural policy today.

Particularities of Media Economics

Resources are the ingredients media producers require in order to generate and disseminate communicative content; media economics studies how these resources are acquired, allocated and paid for. Typically, these resources fall into five categories: *time*; *labour*; *technology*; *capital*; and *material resources*. Some media forms are more resource-intensive than others and therefore demand greater investment. Motion-picture production, for example, typically requires large crews encompassing a diverse collection of highly skilled workers, elaborate costumes and sets, considerable amounts of advanced technology, and significant levels of capital investment. The major film companies also have their own distribution networks. Few have access to such resources. While low-budget films do get made and distributed, film production remains a resource-intensive form of art. Other media forms have much lower barriers to entry; a novel can be produced primarily through the time and labour of a lone individual and a simple website can be produced single-handedly with a personal computer.

The matter of what resources are required for media production is significant because it speaks directly to the questions of how mass media are organized, who owns the media, and whether they are owned for profit, for public service, for advocacy, for prestige, or some combination of these. Questions about resources have a direct bearing on the kinds of books, music recordings, video games, films, and magazines that are produced and made available to us.

We may not normally think of time as a resource, but, of course, it takes an investment of time to produce media content. This is particularly significant in the case of content that is produced on a speculative basis, such as the time invested in writing a book with no assurance of publication, and content that is produced by amateurs in their spare time, such as videos or music posted to YouTube. But it applies as well to the production of waged or salaried workers.

The category of labour includes all of the human resources required. This can range from a single individual writing and uploading a daily blog, to the dozens of people required to produce a weekly TV drama series, to the hundreds involved in the production of a big-budget feature film. The number of people and their skill level will have a noticeable impact on the quality of the production. The mass media bring together people specialized in particular creative processes with those skilled in the business side of the operation. The larger the media company, the greater the divide between these groups tends to be.

Technology refers partly to the equipment and, increasingly, to the specific software applications media organizations require. Clearly, some mass media (e.g., film, television, sound recording, computer games) require more investment in hardware and software than others. But, as we noted in Chapter 6, technology also refers to the particular step-by-step processes by which production and dissemination are organized, and how, or whether, labour is divided among the various production tasks. Typically, large media organizations divide the production process into a series of specialized tasks—like an assembly line—while smaller organizations commonly require workers to perform several separate tasks. Digitization has made multi-tasking easier, allowing large media companies to cut staff and either outsource production tasks or combine them in-house as a cost-saving measure. Computerization, for example, allowed newspaper companies in the 1970s and '80s to eliminate some of their production departments (e.g., inputting and coding data, sizing photographs, page design and layout) and turn those production tasks over to journalists working with user-friendly software applications (see McKercher, 2002).

Capital refers not simply to money, but to money that is invested in media enterprises with the expectation of a return on investment. Most commonly, the return is financial, but there are other kinds of returns. In the case of commercial media, investors are seeking a financial return at least comparable to what they would receive for investing in any other enterprise. But they may also be interested in the prestige that accrues from owning a media company or from being involved in a media project. Power and influence are other forms of return for commercial investors. Governments that own, or invest in, mass media have a primary interest in returns, such as cultural development, regional industrial development, nation building, job creation, or the expansion of the variety of cultural products and the range of voices within their jurisdictions. Governments may also turn their media into avenues for promoting their platforms and showcasing their achievements, especially prior to elections. Non-profit societies, cooperatives, and interest groups may participate in media to fill what they perceive to be gaps in media content or for the sole purpose of advocacy.

The media use material resources, too: paper to print books, magazines, and newspapers; plastics to produce CDs, DVDs, video games, and cellphones; metals to produce TV sets, computers, DVD players, and sound systems; chemicals to produce ink and to fuel delivery vehicles. These materials not only cost money, but they also link media economies to other economies and to the rules, regulations, and challenges affecting those economies. The attraction of electronic publishing is that it avoids the significant costs of paper, ink, and fuel for delivery vehicles, and it also allows publishers to sidestep the environmental implications of using paper, ink, and fuel.

Much of the excitement about digital media, in fact, is that they are much less resource-intensive than their old-media cousins. This translates into significant cost savings for old-media producers, but they also lower what economists call the barriers to entry for new participants in media production. Establishing a website, for instance, requires relatively few technological and capital resources, although it can require human resources comparable in number and skill level to old media if the site is to maintain standards of quality for content and thereby compete with all the other similar websites to generate an audience.

There are two aspects to economic markets. The first is the good or service offered, and the second is the boundaries within which this offer takes place. Media economist Robert G. Picard explains: "A market consists of sellers that provide the same good or service, or closely substitutable goods or services, to the same group of consumers" (Picard, 1989: 17). The Canadian market has a number of distinguishing features that must always be taken into account in considering the economics of mass communication in Canada, as Box 9.2 explains. There have been significant changes to both aspects of media markets in recent years. Convergence, first of all, means that there are more and more sellers of comparable communications products and services. Second, the global reach of digital communications networks means market boundaries have shifted, bringing still more competitors into media markets. We discuss this in more detail below.

Media markets are distinguished from other kinds of markets in that they serve two markets at the same time: the audience market and the advertising market (see Picard, 1989: 17). Audiences pay for access to media content with money and/or with their time. Advertisers pay media producers for access to audiences whose demographic characteristics fit with the customers they seek to attract.

Satisfying Needs and Wants

Each society makes decisions about how to structure its economy to satisfy its needs and wants. Western democracies are founded on a number of fundamental freedoms, including freedom of the individual, both as a political actor and as a participant in the economy. They have predominantly free-market or capitalist economies, in which

9.2 ▶▶▷▶▷▶▶

THE CANADIAN MARKET

The very particular characteristics of the Canadian media market inform all of the economic decisions made by media companies, governments, and labour organizations. Although Canada constitutes an attractive market based on its affluence and technological sophistication, we have a relatively small population—33 million—dispersed across a huge land mass, with most of us clustered within 100 kilometres of a border shared with the world's most productive and lucrative media market: the United States. If most Canadians share a common language with Americans, we also have a significant French-language population concentrated in Quebec, which constitutes a media market of its own. Canada has a diverse population, based on race, ethnicity, and religion, as well on the regions in which people live. These characteristics of the Canadian market speak to our limited market power.

As users and consumers of media, we want access to the best the world has to offer, and in that sense we belong to a world market for popular culture. We want our artists, musicians, writers, and performers to be able to participate in that world market. And a great number—among them Rachel McAdams, Justin Bieber, Margaret Atwood, Drake, Alice Munro, Douglas Coupland, Atom Egoyan, David Cronenberg, Samantha Bee, Jean-Marc Vallée, Jim Carrey, Sarah Polley, Ryan Gosling, Kiefer Sutherland, Kim Cattrall, and Robert Lepage—have succeeded internationally.

But we also need a distinct and viable market for Canadian media products and services, those which may not have much reach beyond Canada's borders, but remain invaluable. As all peoples do, we want books and films and songs that speak to, teach us about, and keep a lasting record of, our unique experiences. We want news and information that keeps us abreast of what is happening here—locally, regionally, nationally—and that reflects our own views and interests. We want to be able to see ourselves—literally, figuratively—in poems and plays and in the visual arts.

When we look at how mass communication in Canada is structured, we need to consider these particularities of the Canadian market.

individuals are at liberty to engage in private enterprise, producing and consuming according to their own interests. But no economy is completely free; governments at all levels participate in the economy, in some instances providing the infrastructure that allows private enterprise to thrive—for example, building roads, delivering water and hydroelectricity, funding public education, providing subsidies, establishing favourable tax rates—and at other times tempering market forces when they feel it is in the public interest, however that interest may be defined. Typically, governments temper market forces both through restrictions and via incentives.

For most of the twentieth century, the Canadian state took an interventionist stance toward the cultural industries. But, since the early 1980s, governments have become much more willing to let markets dictate prices and costs of production, not only in the communications realm, but also in the fields of health care and education. Free-market economics is becoming more popular worldwide and even former communist countries are keen to become part of international organizations devoted to freer trade. The crumbling of international trade barriers and advancements in technology have increased the global flow of communication services across borders, resulting in the availability of many more cultural choices from abroad than we've ever had before. And the globalization process, which we discuss in detail in Chapter 11, calls into question conventional notions of community and place; people's sense of how they belong to the national community has changed. All in all, it is becoming more and more difficult for governments to assume control of cultural production on behalf of their constituents.

These changes pertain to matters of how mass communication is structured, and for what purpose. Some media organizations are privately owned—by individuals and companies—and respond to the profit motive, negotiating a compromise between the most profitable products and consumer demand. Others are publicly owned—by governments, non-profit societies, and cooperatives—and respond to what they perceive to be collective needs and wants, mostly in areas of the economy, where private enterprise cannot satisfactorily meet collective needs and wants. Media products, that is, have value, both to individuals and to societies, serving us at different times in different ways. Sometimes, they serve us as citizens, and their value derives from the extent to which they inform and enlighten. Other times, they serve us as consumers, and their value derives from their ability to generate an audience. Still other times, media industries serve our career aspirations, serving us as places to earn a living or to satisfy our need for expression. In Canada, historically, we have attempted to strike a balance among these values, although there is an increasing tendency to perceive the most popular media products as the best, and to devalue those products that serve minority or fringe audiences. As Box 9.3 explains, success in the marketplace is not a reliable gauge of value.

A fundamental problem is the tendency of many people, especially economists, to apply the free-market perspective to sectors of the economy in which it may not be entirely appropriate. Economists often argue that if films, books, TV programs, magazines, and sound recordings cannot survive in the marketplace, then they do not deserve to survive. To intervene to support what large audiences are not interested in, the argument goes, is to use the state to subsidize the tastes of an elite. While the merits of economism—the perception of cultural production as commercial enterprise—can certainly be debated, further consideration takes us back to our earlier discussion of returns on economic investment. Not all returns are financial. Not all returns are immediate. For that matter, not

all costs are financial. This point is important because it goes to the heart of how we perceive cultural production and what role we assign the mass media in society.

Economists talk about market externalities. Market externalities are the costs and benefits of economic activity that are not accounted for by—that are external to—the immediate economic transaction between buyer and seller. For example, critics of graphically violent films and video games claim that such films and games exact social costs—in law enforcement, in health care, in social welfare—that are not part of the production cost or sale price of these items. Instead, those costs are assumed by society at large. On the flip side, externalities can be positive: the benefits of a good public education—literacy, numeracy, critical-thinking skills, specialized knowledge, and so on—spread beyond the tuition-paying student and the school to society at large.

Market economies have a number of other limitations. In its comprehensive survey of state involvement in cultural activity in Canada, the Applebaum–Hébert Committee (Canada, 1982a: 64–71) noted that governments often intervene in the cultural sphere in cases of market failure, when the market does not or cannot serve adequately the cultural needs of society. Markets, for example, typically do not recognize the longevity of cultural products, which may be produced by one generation and maintain their value through subsequent generations. Think of the number of artists—Van Gogh, Rembrandt, or our own Emily Carr—who are today recognized for their genius, but who were not adequately compensated for their creations in their own lifetimes. Markets may also fail to accommodate infant industries: new, domestic industries that cannot compete right away with well-established and large-scale transnational industries. Canadian feature film and dramatic television are good examples of industries that continue to struggle to find markets in the context of Hollywood's long-standing dominance of this country's commercial theatre and television screens. Cultural production also confounds market

9.3 ▶▶ ▷▶ ▷ ▶▶

THE MYTH OF MERITOCRACY

Myths are stories we tell ourselves to help us understand the way the world works. The myth of meritocracy is a story about the egalitarian nature of the media marketplace, whereby consumers discriminate among cultural products solely on the basis of universally accepted conceptions of worth. It asserts, in essence, that those books or records or movies that deserve to be made will be made and find an appreciative audience in the marketplace. While we might all like to believe that the media marketplace works without bias, the myth of meritocracy discounts completely the political economy of cultural production.

Merit, of course, is not completely irrelevant; audiences don't simply watch happily everything that's put in front of them, and we can all point to fine works that we've read, watched, or listened to that have proved to be immensely popular. But the notion of merit is greatly overstated. For one thing, consumer demand is a product of industry supply. When we choose a television program or a movie to watch, our choice is restricted to what's available. When we browse the magazine racks, our choices are limited to what's being displayed. Most often, we have no say in what is produced.

Second, the myth of meritocracy denies the market power behind certain cultural producers. The major Hollywood film companies, for example, are tied into international distribution networks and theatre chains, ensuring themselves screen time in movie theatres around the world and narrowing the field of competition considerably by erecting significant barriers to entry. Their market power also allows them to hire the greatest star actors and directors to create, produce, and publicize the film.

Finally, the myth of meritocracy ignores the question of whose tastes determine the qualitative norm against which all other productions are measured, and how those tastes are determined.

Commercial radio, for instance, sets constraints pertaining to the length of songs, the language used in lyrics and the subject matter, which clearly favour easy listening over more challenging or provocative selections. We tend to buy the music we hear on the radio. Similarly, commercial television favours 30- or 60-minute dramatic programs with recognizable personalities and formats as well as accessible, non-threatening storylines. Programming that doesn't fit these broadcast parameters usually isn't aired, and certainly not during prime time. The sites offering us digital content typically promote the "most popular" or the "most shared," whether they are YouTube videos, book selections on Amazon, or stories on Yahoo News.

The World Wide Web has vastly increased the size of the marketplace and created at least some room for alternatives (see Anderson, 2006). This innovation addresses, in part, our first point about audience choice, but it does nothing to address either the question of market power or of qualitative norms.

The media market most certainly has a commercial bias—the greater the size of the audience a book, movie, or song is likely to appeal to, the better the chance it will be produced and benefit from its producer's market power. But commercialism is only one particular kind of worth, rendering cultural production as commodity production and appealing to the tastes of the majority. Other values (e.g., cultural worth, educational worth, minority taste, intellectual challenge) are largely excluded from this equation.

There can be other kinds of biases, too, when, for instance, decision-makers determine that audiences aren't interested in works about women, or about people of colour, or stories that address explicitly people in exotic places like . . . Canada. Canadian popular music and literature fought such biases half a century ago; today, we don't think twice now when a Canadian musician/performer wins a Grammy or a Canadian writer wins the Booker or Nobel Prize. But Canadian dramatic television and, especially, Canadian feature films still face hurdles in screen markets, at home and abroad, in large part because they tend to be distinctly Canadian and they don't always subscribe to Hollywood's production formulas.

economics because it entails a large element of risk and requires a substantial investment of a society's resources, and because the public has a "limitless variability of tastes." The most common instance of market failure in the cultural sphere, however, involves the market failing "to register the full benefits conferred" by cultural activity (Canada, 1982a: 64–71).

Free-market or laissez-faire economics reduces all goods and services to the status of commodities, objects that attain their value through marketplace exchange. While we often believe a market economy to be responsive to consumer demand for choice, the cultural theorist Raymond Williams (1989: 88) reminds us that the organization of communication within a capitalist economy imposes "commercial constraints," so that "you can say that at times freedom in our kind of society amounts to the freedom to say anything you wish, provided you can say it profitably." Commodities, by definition,

are "validated" strictly through sale (see Chapter 3). If we perceive books as, first and foremost, commodities of exchange, then their value is measured in retail sales.

Economism also casts individuals as consumers playing a narrow role in the economy, rather than as citizens with a larger role to play in democratic society. Television programs, theatrical performances, and museum exhibits are not simply goods or services that we buy and sell, but opportunities for the kind of communication that is fundamental to the understanding of culture. They are expressions of a way of life and of a system of beliefs and values. They are expressions of ideas and perceptions that help people to imagine themselves within the culture and to articulate their personal contributions to its priorities.

There is no denying the tensions between the public good and the private commercial interest. Canada's Broadcasting Act recognizes these tensions by assigning social responsibilities to

If we perceive books as, first and foremost, commodities of exchange, then their value is measured in retail sales, making *Fifty Shades of Grey* more valuable than a book on reducing environmental waste in Canada.

all radio and television licence holders, including minimum Canadian-content regulations and special additional responsibilities for the public sector. Section 19 of the Income Tax Act provides recognition in the form of effectively restricting majority ownership of Canadian newspapers, magazines, and broadcasting stations (i.e., any medium that accepts advertising) to Canadians; this requirement, however, has been diluted considerably and there is pressure on the federal government to ease this restriction further to increase the pool of potential buyers and thereby decrease the number of Canadian properties owned by concentrated media companies. The public goals of communication are also recognized in the support policies of the Department of Canadian Heritage for cultural industries, even if these programs are under review by a federal government committed to balancing its books and under pressure from the United States through World Trade Organization challenges.

Historically, cultural production is associated with *both* Enlightenment values and the emergence of a capitalist economy. As we noted in Chapter 3, the Enlightenment was distinguished by an intellectual approach based on a scientific and rational perspective of the world, a fundamental shift in worldview that championed science over religion, justice over the abuse of power, and a social contract that specified individual rights and freedoms over the absolutist rule of kings and clerics. Capitalism, which traces its roots to the late fifteenth century, is an economic system based on exchange relations, the private ownership of the means of production (see Box 9.4), and the clear separation of capital (owners of the means of production engaged in the pursuit of profit) and labour (workers who satisfy their material needs—food, shelter, clothing—by exchanging their labour for a wage).

Organizing Structures

No media industry in Canada is governed exclusively by free-market economics. Governments, both provincial and federal, are implicated in one form or another in the structure of every media industry: as proprietors (CBC, NFB); custodians (museums, galleries, theatres); patrons (commissions, grants, sponsorships); catalysts (tax incentives, subsidies); or regulators (CRTC). The result is that our mass media are organized as a complex mixture of public and private enterprise.

Newspaper publishing comes closest to an exclusively private enterprise, but even here, Section 19 of the Income Tax Act ensures that Canadian newspapers remain Canadian-owned; the newspaper industry is protected by the state from foreign takeover and foreign competition. Newspapers are considered by the state to be relatively untouchable because they are so closely associated with the historical struggle for freedom of the press (and, subsequently, other mediated forms of expression). In the post–World War II period, governments in Canada, the United Kingdom, and the United States all have ignored reasoned calls to intervene in the newspaper industry to ensure a better balance between the press's freedom to publish and its responsibility to keep citizens properly informed. Both the Davey Committee (Canada, 1971: 255–6) and the Kent Commission (Canada, 1981: 237) raised concerns about ownership concentration in Canada's newspaper industry and proposed legislative mechanisms to address the problem. The Standing Senate Committee on Transport and Communications (Canada, 2006a) revisited this question in 2003 and, besides echoing previous commissions on the topic of corporate concentration, added corporate consolidation and cross-media ownership to the list of concerns about conglomerate ownership. The Kent Commission proposed a Canada Newspaper Act to balance the rights and responsibilities of a free press and recommended legislation both to correct the worst cases of corporate concentration and to prohibit the further concentration of ownership. Magazine publishing in Canada is distinguished from the newspaper business in this regard by its dependence on both government subsidies (e.g., direct grants) and protectionist

9.4 ▶▶▶▶▶▶

THE MEANS OF PRODUCTION

When economists refer to the means of production, they are talking about the mechanism or process by which we satisfy our material needs for food, clothing, and shelter, and thus ensure our survival and the survival of our dependents. The means of production are, bluntly, the means of life.

In older, agrarian societies, peasants had direct access to the means of production; by working the land they could literally live off the land, eating what they grew and gathered, slaughtering livestock for food, leather, fur, and other necessities; felling trees for fuel and collecting stones to use with wood to construct shelters. By controlling the means of production, they had direct access to, and control of, the means of their own survival. Most of us today would regard this means of survival as meagre and not particularly appealing. But the point we want to make is that peasants' relation to the means of production was fundamentally different from our own living today. Capitalism is a very specific economic and political system. A capitalist economy is an exchange economy mediated always by market relations.

Capitalism separates workers from the means of production. Instead of having direct access to the means by which to produce our life needs, we exchange our labour for wages and, in turn, exchange those wages for food, clothing, and shelter. If we cannot sell our labour (i.e., we are unemployed), we are cut off from this exchange economy. As the historian Ellen Meiksins Wood (2002: 7) explains, "Material life and social reproduction in capitalism are universally mediated by the market, so that all individuals must in one way or another enter into market relations in order to gain access to the means of life." When we apply for a job, for instance, we are entering the job market, offering our labour in exchange for wages. In turn, we take those wages and enter the housing market, the food market, and the clothing market, exchanging our wages for our life needs. This is the sense in which we mean the market mediates between individuals and the necessities of life.

If our access to the means of production is governed by market relations, so is our access to the products of our own and of others' labour. Even when our work is devoted to the production of food, clothing, or home-building supplies, we don't own those products, but must purchase them as we would any other commodity.

Why is this important?

Some people today argue that digital communication technologies return ownership of the means of production to ordinary people. The inference is that those who wish to engage in media production themselves no longer need to work for the corporate media conglomerates, but can set up shop themselves. The further inference is that corporations no longer wield the economic power they once did, that **corporate concentration** in the media industries is no longer the concern it once was.

But this is where an important distinction must be made between the means of production and workplace tools. A carpenter who owns her own set of tools, no matter how extensive, does not own the means of production. That person must engage in the capitalist economy by exchanging her specialized labour for a wage. Only when the carpenter establishes her own business—which requires all of the infrastructure necessary to secure and fulfill contracts, and ultimately to make a living—can she be said to own the means of production, to own the means of satisfying her material needs. Even then, all of the carpenter's business relations are conducted through the market, where she must compete with all of the other woodworking businesses for customers.

Similarly, someone with a website or a blog does not own the means of production—he owns only the tools with which to produce his website or blog. Those tools do not constitute the means of production in and of themselves, nor do they necessarily constitute the means with which to satisfy the blogger's material needs of survival.

Yes, personal computing grants individuals unprecedented access to the mediascape, as the millions of personal blogs, Facebook pages, Twitter accounts, and small websites attest. But a distinction must be made between communicating as a hobby, a pastime, or some other kind of personal project and communicating to make a living.

legislation (the Income Tax Act) for its survival in a marketplace dominated by US publications (see Dubinsky, 1996).

Table 9.1 summarizes the Canadian daily newspaper ownership groups, testifying to the high level of corporate concentration in this segment of the economy (up-to-date statistics can be found at www.newspaperscanada.ca). Postmedia's 43 newspapers account for more than a third of the national weekly circulation in Canada, while the top six companies together—Postmedia, Quebecor, Torstar, *The Globe and Mail*, Groupe Capitales Médias, Power Corp. (Gesca)—account for about 84 percent of weekly circulation. A new column added to this table is digital readership, recognizing the increasing importance of the digital editions of newspapers.

The state presence is much more apparent in the broadcasting sector. Radio, for example, has private, commercial stations operating alongside publicly owned broadcasters (i.e., CBC and the French-language Radio-Canada) and community stations. CBC and Radio-Canada compete with the commercial broadcasters for audiences, but for the most part they do not compete for advertising. Public radio in Canada had been completely commercial-free since 1974, leaving the public broadcaster wholly dependent on federal government funding for its operations. But given its financial pressures, the CBC received permission from the CRTC in 2013 to run four minutes of national advertising per hour on its secondary services: CBC Radio 2 in English and Espace Musique in French (Infantry, 2013). CBC's

TABLE 9.1

Daily Newspaper Ownership Groups, 2015

Owner	Number of Paid Dailies	Daily Average (Print/ Digital)	Share of Canadian Dailies (%)	Weekly Total (Print/ Digital)	Share of Total Weekly Circulation (%)	Total Weekly Digital only*	Share of Total Weekly Digital (%)
ALTA Newspaper Group/Glacier	3	31,856	0.62	203,575	0.65	3,831	0.06
Black Press	7	31,975	0.63	157,895	0.51	336	0.006
Brunswick News Inc.	3	36,751	0.72	220,506	0.71	0	0.00
Continental Newspapers Canada Ltd.	3	39,747	0.78	278,228	0.89	1,424	0.02
F.P. Canadian Newspapers LP	2	124,834	2.44	759,303	2.44	164,626	2.81
Glacier Media	7	117,663	2.30	667,960	2.15	12,283	0.21
Globe and Mail Inc.	1	356,561	6.98	2,139,363	6.88	730,142	12.45
Groupe Capitales Médias	6	233,018	4.56	1,505,337	4.84	154,096	2.63
Halifax Herald Ltd.	1	82,483	1.61	577,382	1.86	79,855	1.36
Independent	6	72,800	1.42	427,597	1.37	42,987	0.73
Postmedia Network Inc.	43	1,786,475	34.95	11,036,796	35.49	2,656,471	45.31
Power Corp. (Gesca)	1	250,045	4.89	1,500,260	4.82	535,782	9.14
Quebecor	2	437,439	8.56	3,062,075	9.85	947,432	16.16
TC Media	11	313,933	6.14	1,692,295	5.44	78,010	1.33
Torstar Corp.	13	1,195,202	23.39	6,871,846	22.09	455,445	7.77
Sing Tao Newspapers	1	NA	0.00	NA	0.00	NA	0.00
Total	110	5,110,781	100.00	31,100,424	100.00	5,862,720	100.00

*Circulation data from 2013

Source: Newspapers Canada.

principal radio services remain ad-free. Community radio stations are run by non-profit societies with a democratic management structure, and raise money from a combination of advertising, government subsidies, and fundraising activities such as radio bingo. As we discussed in Chapter 8, all radio stations are regulated by the CRTC; they are required to meet the specific conditions of their broadcast licence as well as Canadian-content quotas. The domestic sound recording industry, though owned by private interests, has been the principal beneficiary of Canadian-content regulations on radio.

Whether publicly or privately owned, all media need to generate, maintain, and grow their audiences, as we discuss in Box 9.5 on marketing.

Television, too, is a mix of private, public, and community broadcasting stations. A significant difference is that the stations of CBC and Radio-Canada, including the CBC News Network and Le réseau de l'information, compete with the commercial broadcasters for both audiences and advertising. This competition for advertising has long been a sore point with the private broadcasters, who feel the CBC encroaches on their business, specifically when the public broadcaster goes after programming particularly attractive to audiences and advertisers (e.g., professional sports, US game shows, blockbuster Hollywood films) but seemingly unrelated to the CBC/Radio-Canada's public-service mandate. Even supporters of public broadcasting sometimes argue that advertising competition distorts the public broadcaster's mission. However, the CBC contends that, due to cuts in government funding, it needs this revenue to make ends meet while producing quality Canadian programming. Besides, as Leonard Brockington, the first chair of the CBC, argued in the 1930s, the CBC is the only broadcaster that delivers 100 percent of the revenues it earns from advertising back to taxpayers in the form of Canadian programming. The profits of private broadcasters go to shareholders, not to the public.

Both private and public television in Canada are regulated (e.g., licensing, Canadian-content quotas, advertising limits) and both private and public broadcasters benefit from federal and provincial subsidies for the creation of Canadian film and television programming. Specialty channels form the sector of the ownership picture that will bear closest scrutiny in the years ahead; as audiences fragment, these services have become particularly attractive properties and a growth area for both public and private broadcasters and for cable and satellite distribution companies. As we discussed in Chapter 8, the CRTC conducted public hearings in 2014 aimed at offering Canadians more choice in the TV channels they receive than the standard packages on offer from distributors.

The film industry in Canada is a special case because it has both public and private production houses, but the distribution and exhibition sectors of the industry are organized along principles of private enterprise. Governments in Canada have been involved in film production—as patrons, catalysts, and regulators—since early in the twentieth century, as we noted in Chapter 8. Hollywood began to dominate the burgeoning commercial film industry in the 1920s, which did not sit well with Canadians in the period of strong Canadian nationalism following World War I. The federal government established the National Film Board of Canada in 1939 as a means of asserting a greater Canadian presence on cinema screens. The NFB, though, has largely been confined to producing the kinds of films that tend not to be shown in commercial theatres—documentary, experimental, animation, and sponsored films—leaving the production of dramatic feature-length films to the (mostly American) private sector. If there has been competitive tension between the NFB and private-sector producers, it has been over contracts for sponsored films, which are films commissioned by governmental departments and corporations for educational and marketing purposes. Even the private producers of feature films in Canada rely heavily on government subsidies and tax breaks for production, distribution, and marketing, and public television has been one of Canadian cinema's most dependable exhibition venues.

9.5 ▶▶ ▶ ▷ ▷ ▶ ▷

MARKETING

Whether or not media organizations are structured as commercial enterprises, great effort is expended in identifying audiences, determining their needs and consumption habits, maximizing their numbers, maintaining their loyalty, and, in the case of media that carry advertising, matching audiences to appropriate advertisers. Audiences, in other words, are not already pre-assembled, simply waiting for the show to start—they need to be built through a number of activities that fall under the general category of marketing. Marketing includes surveys of actual and potential customers, analysis of ratings, circulation and/or attendance data, advertising of all kinds, other forms of publicity, and promotional campaigns.

Media organizations conduct regular surveys to determine who their audiences are (their age, sex, income bracket, education level, media usage, and so on), what their needs are, and to what extent they are satisfied with the services they're receiving, as we touched on in Chapter 5.

Television and radio stations subscribe to ratings services, newspapers and magazines subscribe to circulation auditing services, movie companies follow box-office receipts closely, and websites use a number of means to track audience behaviour, all in an effort to measure their connection to audiences and users, and who exactly they are connecting with. These data form a feedback mechanism by which audiences communicate to media organizations through their consumption activities.

Media organizations don't have exclusive audiences, but they must constantly compete for attention with all the other media products and services vying for peoples' eyes and ears. Advertising is one way of doing this. A second is promotion, and the two often work hand in hand. If you look at the entertainment section of any daily newspaper, you will see advertisements for CDs, DVDs, films, and upcoming concerts and shows, with related review articles and celebrity interviews. The advertisements are paid for, but the articles result from promotional activities that encourage arts journalists to report on their products and interview their stars. Film festivals, for example, provide an opportunity for moviemakers to create buzz around a film; journalists play along by reviewing the films and interviewing and photographing the stars. Concert tours, similarly, give both fans and journalists live access to musicians while promoting their latest recording.

Maintaining audiences has become increasingly difficult with the explosion of communicative activities now competing for people's time and attention because such products and services are what media economists call "experience goods"; we can measure the true worth of a movie or a book or a magazine only after we have consumed it. The recommendations of friends, colleagues, or opinion leaders in a given community can go a long way in promoting a media product or service, which is why many websites incorporate users' comments and/or reviews.

Besides advertising and promotion, media companies have devised a number of strategies to maintain audience allegiance. The most benign means is through branding, which is the creation of an identity for a company or a specific product that generates clear and positive associations among consumers. Through branding, a media company is depending on its reputation to ensure repeat, and growing, business. Media companies use their brand identifications to differentiate themselves from competitors. The CBC, for example, through its slogan "Canada lives here," reminds people that its services are produced by Canadians for Canadians.

There are more assertive means as well. One way to keep people coming back is through so-called loyalty programs. The bookstore chain Chapters/Indigo, for example, asks customers to register for rewards programs that lead to discounts on their purchases. Once you've signed up, it's in your financial interest to keep buying books at the chain stores rather than shop elsewhere.

If such loyalty programs encourage repeat customers, a second, more devious, means is to wall people in, to compel them to keep using your products and services. Wireless phone companies, for example, typically offer customers free or discounted phones only if they sign an exclusive, set-term service contract with that provider. E-book producers similarly restrict the sources from which e-books can be purchased and downloaded. This is the strategy employed by Apple (see Lyons, 2010); iPads, for example, will play videos downloaded from the iTunes Store only.

Until recently, telephone service was defined by Ottawa as a "natural monopoly" and Canada had both private (e.g., BC Telephone, Bell Canada) and provincial state monopolies (e.g., Sasktel, Manitoba Telecom Services) operating side by side. The CRTC, however, began to deregulate the industry in the 1980s, first opening up long-distance telephony to competition and in 1994 opening all telephone services to competition. Similarly, the Crown corporation Canada Post monopolized mail service until the 1980s when private companies created a market for specialized courier services.

Even art galleries, theatres, concert halls, and museums, insofar as they can be seen as mass media, are characterized by a mix of public and private ownership, with content generated by both public- and private-sector sources. The international web of computer networks we call the internet has no single owner, but it, too, counts on both public- and private-sector initiatives for its operation and its content. Cyberspace is a medium of exchange for all kinds of communication and defies any simple structural category.

The goals of creating and maintaining a Canadian national identity and stimulating economic growth remain in perpetual tension in the communication sphere, and the various ownership

structures of the media in Canada speak to Ottawa's ongoing struggle to keep both objectives in view. Where the Canadian people fit into this picture is an important question. Canadians are, at the same time, citizens, audience members, workers, consumers, and taxpayers with diverse interests, and their support for both private enterprise and public service contributes to the tension around ownership structures.

Public Ownership

The central difference between public and private forms of ownership relates to the question of return on investment. If private enterprises are interested primarily in a financial return, public enterprises seek other kinds of return: cultural development, industrial development, job creation, national identity formation, and so on. **Public ownership** is devoted to providing communication as some kind of public service based upon public goals: to enable citizenship, to foster a sense of community on regional and national scales, and to promote regional and national cultures. (It's also worth noting here that we discuss another more complicated aspect of public ownership in Box 9.6.) Private ownership is devoted to providing communication for profit. Regardless of the mix of private and public enterprise described above, this distinction is fundamental and needs always to be kept in view if we are to make the link between the ownership structure of a medium and the purpose of the communication it provides.

The idea of public service is to employ the mass media for social goals. This can mean the provision of universal and equitable service to all Canadians, as in the telecommunication, postal, radio, and television industries. It can mean foregrounding the educational component of communication, which informs all cultural policy to some extent. Or it can mean ensuring a Canadian voice in film, radio, TV, publishing, and popular music, where there has been, and remains, a clear risk of being drowned out by American voices. Communication as public service is inherently

Source: © AlbanyPictures/iStockphoto.

While taxi companies certainly don't have a monopoly like Bell or Canada Post, they are running into trouble with the growing popularity of the ride-share app Uber. Meanwhile, Uber has had its own trouble with the legal aspects of its business in Canada and in the United States.

9.6 ▶▶ ▶ ▶ ▶ ▶

PUBLIC OWNERSHIP

Public ownership is a slippery term used in two contradictory ways by economists: sometimes to mean ownership by the state on behalf of its citizens—*the public*—and at other times to mean ownership by a group of self-interested shareholders. These are very different kinds of ownership.

The first sense of public ownership refers to Crown corporations like Canada Post or the Canadian Broadcasting Corporation, which are owned by the state on behalf of the Canadian people.

The second sense of public ownership refers to corporations whose shares are publicly traded through the stock exchange. They are "public" in the sense that shares in these companies can be bought and sold by anyone with the means to do so. Rogers Communications is an example of a publicly traded company; anyone can buy an ownership share.

Economists use the term *public* to mean "publicly traded" because there are also *private* companies owned privately—typically by a family or a small group of owners—and shares in the company are not for sale through stock exchanges. Brunswick News, for example, is a private media company owned by J.K. Irving of New Brunswick.

In this book, we use *public ownership* to mean "state-owned," and *private ownership* to mean "either shareholder-owned or privately held."

also meant the concentration of film, radio, and television services in Central Canada, creating a hierarchical distinction between the "national" preoccupations of Ontario and Quebec and the "regional" concerns of the other provinces and territories.

The central ethic of the public corporation, though, is connected to the democratic ideal. More specifically, it is to provide a public service to both the users of the service and to the population as a whole. If private enterprise operates on a simple user-pay basis, public enterprise employs a much more complex cost structure, in which the users of the public service do not pay the full cost of providing that service. The costs are shared by all taxpayers. For example, visitors to the National Gallery in Ottawa pay an admission fee, but the fees collectively do not recover the full costs of operating the gallery or of purchasing and maintaining the art collection contained therein. The remaining costs are covered by the federal government via tax revenues—money collected from every Canadian, most of whom have never visited and are unlikely ever to visit the National Gallery. The rationale for such a cost structure is the need to promote national culture and the conviction that a strict user-pay system would not meet this objective. The government-owned mail system, Canada Post, has a slightly different cost structure, but the same principle applies: we all share in the costs of maintaining a basic and essential communications service. In the case of Canada Post, rather than determine the cost of posting a letter on the basis of the costs of delivery (e.g., it costs less to send a letter across town than across the country), Canada Post charges us the same rate for the same stamp whether our letter is mailed three blocks away or across three time zones within Canada. The rationale for this cost structure is the need to provide equitable mail service to all Canadians, whether they live in concentrated urban centres or remote northern communities.

Public enterprise has a long and distinguished tradition in every Western country. Canada has made extensive use of public enterprise throughout its history, with the most common form being

inclusive, addressing audiences as *citizens* rather than as *consumers*, and asserting citizens' rights to communicate and to be informed.

The public service ideal, of course, is not without shortcomings when it comes to putting principles into practice. In Canada, public service has often meant national service (i.e., communication in the service of nation building). It has the Crown corporation. But it is not without its drawbacks. As noted by Marc Raboy in his classic study of Canadian broadcast policy, *Missed Opportunities: The Story of Canada's Broadcasting Policy (1990), national* communications services can become *nationalist* services, catering to the goals of the nation rather than to the divergent and possibly contrary goals of the various regions of the country. The CBC, for example, struggles constantly to accommodate the great diversity of perspectives that constitute our national culture. Similarly, the production headquarters of these services tend to be centralized—in Toronto for English Canada, in Montreal for French Canada—distancing them from the communities they are mandated to serve. In a country as large and diverse as Canada, this can have repercussions for access to these institutions—as audiences, as cultural producers—as well as for the interests and concerns they serve. That said, privately owned media operating on a national stage face similar challenges (e.g., the national newspapers *The Globe and Mail* and the *National Post* and the private TV networks CTV, Global, and TVA).

Public ownership removes the element of choice from our decisions about media consumption, and can cause resentment among those who have to pay for services through their tax dollars but don't use the services. We all pay for CBC radio and television broadcasts, NFB documentaries, and performances at the National Arts Centre, but not all of us are faithful consumers and some of us may very well object to their programming choices.

Public ownership grants a tremendous amount of responsibility and power to governments in deciding when, where, and how to intervene in the communications economy. As governments change, so can the state's cultural priorities. More importantly, public ownership creates an opportunity for political interference. Even though public media companies are managed at arm's length from the government of the day, they nonetheless depend upon governments for their mandates and their operating budgets. The CBC, for example, has seen its annual appropriation from Parliament—its largest revenue source—shrink dramatically over the past 20 years, from about $1.5 billion in the early 1990s to $1.16 billion in 2011–2012, while at the same time being made responsible for more services. The 2012 federal budget announced a further reduction to CBC funding of $115 million over three years (CBC, 2012).

Though direct political interference is rare—and can also be brought to bear on privately owned media companies—a number of high-profile incidents serve as a reminder that the state retains this power to pressure public institutions. In 1990, the National Gallery drew heavy criticism for its $1.8-million purchase of a modernist painting by the New York artist Barnett Newman called *Voice of Fire*, which had hung in the US pavilion at Montreal's Expo 67. Among the critics was Progressive Conservative MP Felix Holtmann, the chair of the House Communications and Culture Committee (Geddes, 2010). In 1992, CBC Television attracted the ire of Canadian war veterans and Senator

We all pay for CBC radio and television broadcasts, National Film Board documentaries, and performances at the National Arts Centre, like this performance of Celebrity Chefs of Canada at the NAC. What are some of the advantages and disadvantages of public ownership?

Source: Celebrity Chef Canada.

Jack Marshall, the chair of the Senate Subcommittee on Veterans Affairs, for its three-part World War II series *The Valour and the Horror*, produced by the Montreal documentary filmmakers Terence and Brian McKenna (Nash, 1994: 526–33). Parts two and three of the series were particularly critical of Canadians' participation in the blanket bombing of German cities and in the Normandy invasion. During Senate subcommittee hearings, the CBC was condemned for airing the series, and the CBC ombudsman produced a report concluding that the series was "flawed and fails to measure up to CBC's demanding policies and standards" (Nash, 1994: 531). In 2008, Stephen Harper's Conservative government adopted Bill C-10, an amendment to the Income Tax Act, allowing the federal government to deny tax credits to film and television projects considered offensive for reasons of violence, hatred, or sexuality. The bill was reportedly prompted by the release in 2007 of a Canadian film comedy entitled *Young People Fucking*.

Prime Minister Stephen Harper announces $5 million in cuts to arts and culture funding.

Source: © Terry Mosher.

Private Ownership

Private-sector ownership assumes two basic forms. The ownership of a company can be closely held, either by an individual or by a very small group (often family members). Or the ownership of a company can be widely held by a large group of shareholders, who buy and sell their interest in the company through the stock market. In the latter case, a company will form a board of directors answerable to its shareholders.

The general ethic of the private or commercial media outlet is survival and growth in a marketplace driven by profit. This ethic does not derive merely from the personality traits of private-sector owners—it is structural. Commercial corporations are organized for the purpose of earning returns for their owners, based on their ability to find a market for a product or service and their ability to meet, and ultimately expand, that market. If publicly owned media have an obligation to serve all Canadians, private media serve only those who constitute their target market: those audiences most attractive to advertisers.

Because the bottom line in the private sector is profit, private media companies have considerable latitude in changing course to maximize their economic returns. In radio broadcasting, this can mean a repositioning in the market, either through the introduction of new program segments, or through a complete change in format, from, say, all-news to golden-oldies music. A book publisher might decide to stop signing contracts for poetry or avant-garde fiction and focus on how-to books or celebrity biographies. More radically, a communications company can move into other industries altogether, whether those markets are in the sphere of communications or not. Consider the example of Thomson Corporation. Now known as Thomson Reuters, the company started as a small newspaper publisher in Timmins, Ontario, in the 1930s, and it became one of Canada's two largest newspaper owners by the 1980s, boasting significant newspaper holdings in the United States and the United Kingdom by the 1990s. The company that was primarily a newspaper publisher for half a century had completely abandoned the newspaper industry by 2003 for what its directors perceived as greener pastures in other industries: financial, legal, scientific, and health-care publishing, as well as medical and travel publishing. Thomson returned to journalism only when it merged with Reuters, one of the world's largest news services, in 2008 (Thomson Reuters, 2009). The Thomson family returned to the newspaper business in 2010 when its Woodbridge subsidiary reacquired an 85 percent stake in *The Globe and Mail* (Ladurantaye, 2010)—and it assumed full ownership of the *Globe* in August 2015.

Within the private sector exists a considerable variety of ownership structures. The single enterprise is, as its name suggests, a business form in which owners confine themselves to one business with no connections to other companies. It is a single, independent firm that usually operates on a small scale. Some examples persist, particularly among magazines, community weekly newspapers, and small-town radio stations, but single enterprises are fewer and fewer as chains both large and small gobble them up or force them out of business.

Chain ownership, a common form of media organization in Canada, is the linking, or horizontal integration, of a number of companies in the same business—typically, newspapers, radio stations, or television stations—occupying different markets. Chains are usually geographically dispersed, but sometimes members of the chain will occupy the same location and aim for distinct audiences. Vancouver's two daily newspapers, the *Sun* and *Province*, for example, are both part of the larger Postmedia Network, but they seek different readers and advertisers within the Lower Mainland of British Columbia. Member companies in a chain may have agreements to buy and sell services from each other. Postmedia newspapers, for instance, share editorial content (stories and pictures) among member papers and have their own wire services. In addition, chains often consolidate administrative resources, so that accounting and marketing services or departments responsible for technological innovation will be able to serve all members in the chain. Television networks are also chains; CTV, for example, has affiliate stations in eight provinces, co-ordinating programming through its Toronto headquarters (CTV, 2014a). Such sharing of resources offers chain operations tremendous cost advantages over single enterprises. Typically, chain ownership provides the advantages of reducing competition and creates economies of scale.

Vertical integration is the concentration of firms within a specific business that extends a company's control over the entire process of production. A vertically integrated company, for instance, will have subsidiary companies involved in every aspect of an industry. The most common example of vertical integration is the commercial film industry, in which the major Hollywood companies not only own production studios and distribution companies, but they also have subsidiaries involved in theatrical exhibition, television, and video/DVD rental to ensure their films reach audiences and generate revenues. The advantages inherent in vertical integration are substantial. A vertically integrated company ensures itself of resource supplies and sales markets, and it minimizes other uncertainties, such as competition, related to the circuit of production.

Conglomerate ownership is characterized by large companies with a number of subsidiary firms in related and unrelated businesses. Besides the advantages of scale, shareholder risk is reduced because the conglomerate is not dependent for its profits on any one industry. **Convergence** is the name given to the economic strategy media conglomerates employ in an attempt to create synergies among their media properties. One of Canada's most converged conglomerates is Quebecor Inc. Through its various subsidiaries, Quebecor owns two leading daily newspapers and more than 75 magazines. Quebecor is also in the business of television (TVA), telecommunications and cable distribution (Videotron), new media (Canoe), publishing (TVA Publishing), video-game development (BlooBuzz Studio) and retailing (Archambault)—and the company is also behind the bid for the return of a National Hockey League franchise to Quebec City. See Table 9.2 for more about converged conglomerates.

TABLE 9.2
Converged Conglomerates in Canada

Quebecor Inc.

Publishing

- *Newspapers: Sun Media Corporation (2 major dailies, plus commuter daily *24 Heures Montréal*, almost 200 community newspapers, shopping guides, and other specialty publications)
- Magazines: TVA Publishing- publishes more than 75 magazines

Televison

- Videotron: As of 31 March 2014, Videotron was serving 1,811,100 cable television customers, including 1,532,700 subscribers to Digital TV
- TVA: the largest French-language television network plus 8 speciality services: LCN, addikTV, MOI&cie, Argent, Prise 2, CASA, YOOPA and TVA Sports. TVA Group also has an interest in Canal Évasion and Sun News

Telephony

- Videotron: 521,600 subscriber connections to its mobile telephone service and cable telephone service to 1,280,400 Quebec households and organizations

New Media

- Canoe Inc.: 9.4 million unique visitors per month in Canada, including more than 4.2 million in Quebec
- Videotron: the Quebec leader in high-speed internet access, with 1,419,200 subscribers to its cable service as of 31 March 2014

Retail

- Archambault is a major player in Quebec's book retail business—hard copy and digital; 14 shops and one e-store offer one of the broadest arrays of titles in the province; on archambault.ca, there are over 64,000 titles in French—the largest catalogue of French-language e-books in North America

Shaw Communications Inc.

Television

- Shaw Cablesystems G.P.—3.4 million customers
- Shaw Direct—more than 900,000 customers
- Shaw Broadcast Services—over 570 English, French, and multilingual video and audio signals via 68 satellite transponders
- Shaw MediaGlobal TV Network: 19 specialty networks, 11 television stations, more than 20 multimedia websites, four dedicated video-on-demand channels and a growing number of mobile applications

Telephony

- Shaw Home Phone: phone service with more than a million customers

New Media

- Shaw Internet: ISP with 1.8 million subscribers

Other

- Shaw Tracking offers integrated on-board computing technology and wireless data solutions for the Canadian transportation, mobile workforce and logistics industries.

Rogers Communications Inc.

Publishing

- Rogers Publishing: 58 magazine brands, covering entertainment, news, business, fashion, and sports

continued

TABLE 9.2 (continued)

Television

- Rogers Cable: next-generation digital cable and internet services to 1.8 million households
- All the popular prime-time shows, access to hit shows, music videos, and movies on Rogers On Demand, digital quality picture and sound plus 27 time-shifting channels
- 24 TV stations, delivered on multiple screens

Radio

- 56 radio stations from coast to coast, catering to all Canada's musical tastes

Telephony

- Rogers Telecom: home telephony service and Rogers Wireless communications to 9 million Canadians

New Media

- Rogers Media: 93 websites and 124 partnership sites
- Rogers Hi-Speed Internet: broadband internet provider

Other

- Sports Entertainment Group: five major-league teams, multi-platform content, and major sports venues
- Home Services: monitoring, automation, and energy management solutions
- Mobile Commerce: electronic payment and loyalty program information
- Digital Services: Outrank™, Zoocasa™, Vicinity™, Blackiron™ help businesses attract and build customer loyalty

Postmedia Network Inc.

Publishing

- *Newspapers: 43 major dailies, including *National Post*; more than 100 community newspapers
- Magazines: Financial Post and Postmedia Network Regional Magazines, which includes 8 local magazines

New Media

- Websites: Canada.com, househunting.ca, celebrating.ca, remembering.ca driving.ca, faceoff.com
- Informant: media consultancy firm, which provides reliable news and social data, accurate analytics, and true insights that serve as trusted guides to Canada's best marketers and communicators

Advertising

- Flyer Force

BCE Inc.

Television

- 30 local news channels, led by CTV; 35 specialty channels; pay television
- Bell Satellite TV and Bell Fibe TV

Radio

- 106 licensed radio stations in 54 markets across Canada

Telephony

- Bell Home Phone: local and long distance
- Wireless through Bell Mobility, SOLO, and Virgin Mobile Canada

continued

TABLE 9.2 (continued)

New Media

- Bell High-Speed Internet and Bell Fibe Internet
- Connectivity, internet protocol broadband services and information and communications technology solutions, including cloud computing through Bell Business Markets
- In 2013, Bell Media's websites streamed nearly 1.3 billion videos, averaging 107 million video streams each month, on average 11.6 million unique visitors each month, serving up to 51 million hours of video and a grand total of over 5.4 billion page views during this period

*In October 2014, Postmedia agreed to purchase Quebecor's Sun Media newspapers for $316 million. The agreement remains subject to Competition Bureau approval.

Media companies are no longer confined to their previous industry *silos* because they now have a digital presence as well. For much of media history, it made sense to talk about various analog media forms—books, newspapers, radio, television, cinema—as distinct technologies belonging to separate industries. With computerization and the translation of all types of information into the common digital language of os and 1s, these media silos have broken down. The combination of digitization and computer networking has resulted in the integration of all media, enabling the immediate and global exchange of every kind of content (Gasher, 2013).

Implications of Private Media Ownership

For those who believe that communication in all its forms involves much more than satisfying markets, the appropriation by private enterprise of a greater and greater share of the mass communication sphere is of great concern. While economists argue that the free-market organization of cultural production is the most efficient means of giving consumers what they want, political economists maintain that the commercial organization of cultural production limits choice and discriminates between those members of the public who have disposable income to spend on advertised products and those who don't. This is particularly the case when corporate concentration limits the number of, and distinctions between, producers and distributors (see Mosco, 2009: 158–75).

In the realm of the mass media, private enterprise is seen as having two particular social benefits. First, it stimulates the provision of affordable goods and services for which consumers have expressed a need or desire through their purchasing decisions. Second, because advertising subsidizes the media, consumers are able to receive content either free or at minimal cost. These benefits, of course, are not as straightforward as they may seem. First of all, anticipating what consumers will buy is an inexact science, notwithstanding polls and focus groups. Consumers can make choices only among products and services already offered—supply to a large extent governs demand—and media managers have been frustrated time and again in trying to determine which new services will attract consumers. Media economists have demonstrated, for example, that most major Hollywood movies lose money, and the studios depend on their blockbuster hits to make up for their far more numerous flops (see Gomery, 2004). The same applies to television series; each new fall season introduces more losers than winners, shows that are cancelled after only a few weeks. Advertising, social media alerts, and other forms of publicity, of course, play a role in generating excitement and consumer demand around new films, TV shows, music recordings, and book releases, but consumer tastes remain very hard to anticipate.

9.7 ▶▶ ▶ ▶ ▶▶

FREE CONTENT

Media organizations remain economically viable when the revenues they generate from producing and distributing content at least match and, preferably, exceed the costs required to obtain the resources necessary for content production: labour, technology, capital, and materials. One of the new economic challenges for media organizations is how to pay for those resources when consumers expect to receive content for free. If once we had to pay for newspapers or magazines or recorded music or films, we can now find almost everything we want free on the web. How, then, can media companies afford to keep providing content that we increasingly expect not to have to pay for? As *Wired* magazine editor Chris Anderson argues in his book *Free: The Future of a Radical Price*, in the digital marketplace, "Free is almost always a choice." He adds, "Sooner or later, most producers in the digital realm will find themselves competing with Free" (Anderson, 2009: 72).

Free is not entirely new. We have always received over-the-air radio and television as well as community newspapers and some kinds of magazines without having to pay a subscription fee. The costs to those radio and TV stations and newspapers and magazines were covered by the advertising they could sell. They still work that way. One difference today is that almost all media content comes to us free over the internet, and advertisers are not yet willing to pay the same amount for online advertising as they have paid for advertising in the traditional media. As more and more of us opt for online content, radio and TV ratings and the circulation of hard-copy newspapers and magazines fall, as do the advertising rates they can charge, rendering the old-media model less and less viable. A second difference is that the range of content available for free online is limitless; every kind of media content is available, from countries all over the world, and in hundreds of languages. Our local radio, television, magazine, and newspaper providers are now competing with thousands of other content providers.

How is the provision of free media content economically sustainable?

Anderson maintains that providing media content free can be the basis of a successful business model, provided that it is matched with some form of payment. "Free may be the best price, but it can't be the only one" (Anderson, 2009: 240). He provides four models of free. The "three party" model is the most familiar to us; it works by having advertisers pay the costs of providing us with free

---

Second, it is not entirely accurate to say consumers receive some media programming free, thanks to advertising. Instead, consumers pay for it in a roundabout way. Even if we do not directly hand over any money to a radio station to listen to its programming, we pay for that programming nonetheless every time we buy an advertised product. Advertising costs, in other words, are built into the sale price of potato chips and breakfast cereal, so that a share of the money we spend on groceries, snacks, clothing, beer, gasoline, and cosmetics pays for media programming.

Media economists also argue that we pay with our time—we literally pay attention—whenever we consume media services and that time and attention is what advertisers seek. The key point to understanding how commercial media work within the economic system is that to generate profits, managers of commercial media seek to attract audiences to their programming to sell those audiences to advertisers. Communications theorist Dallas Smythe (1994: 270–1) famously pointed out that what advertisers buy is not simply air time or newspaper space, but "the services of audiences with predictable specifications who will pay attention in predictable numbers and at particular times to particular means of communications." Through increasingly sophisticated audience-measurement techniques, media managers collect data on their audiences—not only the size of the audience is determined, but also demographic factors such as income, education, age, and sex—and sell advertisers access to the kinds of audiences that will be interested in

content. The "direct cross-subsidy" model works by combining free services with pay services. For example, your wireless provider may give you a free cellphone, but only if you buy a subscription to its telephone service. The "freemium" model works by offering customers a free basic service while charging others for a premium or enhanced service. This is the model used by some online newspapers and magazines, which offer some of their articles free, but charge a subscription fee for access to exclusive content and to archived editions. Finally, there is what Anderson calls the "non-monetary" model. In this case, the media organization benefits from the time we spend or the attention we pay to a particular website. Google, for example, collects data every time we use its search engine, data that ultimately improves its PageRank algorithm, and that ultimately increases the value of Google Search to advertisers (Anderson, 2009: 23–9).

The idea of making money by giving away content may be counterintuitive, but consider the example of the alternative rock band Radiohead. In 2007, Radiohead released its seventh album, *In Rainbows*, as a digital download, asking people to name their own price. While some people downloaded it without paying anything, the average price paid online was US $6, and the band made more money from the digital downloads than from the total sales of its previous album. When *In Rainbows* was released on CD, it sold another 3 million

copies worldwide, making it the band's most commercially successful album. Radiohead's subsequent concert tour, its biggest ever, sold 1.2 million tickets, bringing in yet more money (Anderson, 2009: 153–4). More recently, artists have teamed up with corporations to provide their albums free to customers of those corporations; Jay Z contracted with Samsung for the free release of his album *Magna Carta Holy Grail* (Smith, 2013) and U2 provided their *Songs of Innocence* album free to iTunes subscribers (Cook, 2014).

The media economy today is driven by a shift from scarcity to abundance of all kinds of media content; where once we had a choice between a finite number of radio stations, television channels, newspapers, magazines, books, recorded music, and films, we are now faced with an infinite array of media products and services from all over the world. This abundance is driven in part by the increasing cheapness of computer processing power, digital storage, and bandwidth (Anderson, 2009: 77). But if the supply of content has grown, demand, which is governed by how much time we can spend consuming media, has not kept pace, intensifying the competition among content suppliers (Anderson, 2009: 140–2). In the online world, Anderson argues, attention and reputation are the currencies most in demand (2009: 238). Content providers vie for our limited amount of attention, often relying on their reputation—their brand—to attract that attention.

buying their product or service. Mass media content, therefore, is merely "an inducement (gift, bribe or 'free lunch') to recruit potential members of the audience and to maintain their loyal attention." Smythe writes that "the free lunch consists of materials which whet the audience members' appetite and thus (1) attract and keep them attending to the programme, newspaper or magazine, and (2) cultivate a mood conducive to favourable reaction to the explicit and implicit advertisers' messages" (1994: 270–1).

The explosion of free media sites on the internet has necessitated new thinking about how to pay for the production and distribution of media content, as we discuss in Box 9.7.

Private ownership of the communications media raises four particular concerns. The first

is that private enterprise casts cultural production as commercial enterprise, whereby the goal of communication becomes the generation of profit. This form of organization imposes commercial constraints on communication. Communication as a commercial enterprise creates pressures to maximize entertainment value and to minimize difficulty and complexity, and to provide communication in an advertising- or consumption-friendly environment. In the medium of television, for example, competing programs are only a click of the remote away. Programming that is difficult, challenging, or slow-paced may have trouble holding the attention of audiences, and it could be hard for broadcasters to support. This includes newscasts, which, according to the expectations of commercial enterprise, need to maximize ratings in a competitive environment, even if that means sacrificing the quality and integrity of their journalism.

A second concern is that the increasing convergence of media properties reinforces the profit motive and moves owners further and further from their core areas of business. That is, conglomerates are in business to make money rather than to make movies or newspapers or books or video games. The goal of the conglomerate is to serve shareholders and paying customers only—not society at large. By privileging the profit motive above all else, the creation of conglomerates weakens the owners' commitment to core areas of business; media properties may become a lesser priority within the conglomerate than, for example, its real estate holdings. Managers can revise the conglomerate's mandate, or abandon media initiatives altogether for more lucrative industries.

Related to this is a third concern. The broader a conglomerate's reach becomes, the more businesses it is involved in, the greater the chance for a conflict of interest between its media business and its other holdings. Critical themes (e.g., environmentalism, labour practices, poverty) in newspaper and magazine stories, TV and film documentaries, or radio programs could threaten the earnings or community standing of the conglomerate's other holdings. In such cases, the conglomerate's media properties will feel pressure to avoid certain subject areas, depriving the public of a full airing of important social issues or confining their discussion within safe parameters. The issue of climate change, for example, raises serious questions about capitalism as an economic system (see Klein, 2014).

Finally, the trend toward corporate concentration has reduced substantially our sources of information at precisely the point in history when our dependence on communications media for our knowledge of the world has increased. The plethora of TV and radio channels, websites, books, magazines, newspapers, music recordings, and videos available to us is largely illusory; it disguises the fact that many of these media are the products of a mere handful of large corporations, and that others (e.g., websites) are primarily distribution channels for other media, rather than generators of original content. If we are to take seriously our role as citizens in democratic society, we should be encouraging the greatest variety of information sources possible, as well as an increase in distinct media channels for us to express ourselves. Taken together, these trends of private ownership have reduced our sources of information and narrowed the range of what can be said and how it can be expressed.

New Labour Issues

The transformations we have been discussing have had a huge impact on media workers. Media work is increasingly precarious and flexible. The Canadian Media Guild, a trade union representing 6,000 media workers, has estimated that 10,000 Canadian media jobs were lost between 2008 and 2013 through a combination of layoffs and buyouts (Wong, 2013). An increasing amount of the work that used to be produced by full-time, salaried workers is contracted out to temporary workers or freelancers at rates that are much lower than those paid to full-time employees and that do not include benefits. Freelance journalists, in fact, are paid rates that have not changed in 30 years, even though their work may be used on a number of platforms and even archived for future sales (Cohen, 2012). Some of this media work, too, has been handed to unpaid interns (see McKnight and Nursall, 2014); Canada's journalism, communications, and film schools are full of students eager to break into the industry through internships and other volunteer arrangements, altering dramatically the supply–demand relationship in labour markets.

For those media workers who remain, their jobs are characterized by increasing flexibility. This can mean a number of things: hiring and releasing workers as production demands shift, rendering jobs more temporary; adjusting employees' hours as immediate production demands rise and fall (see Dyer-Witheford and de Peuter, 2006); dividing labour processes into separate tasks carried out in distinct locales, often internationally (see Christopherson, 2006); combining previously distinct tasks, typically using digital technologies and software applications; and requiring workers to repurpose their work for several media platforms.

Related to the point made about internships and other volunteer work above, the generation of content by users is becoming a form of unpaid apprenticeship for some aspiring media workers (see Shepherd, 2013). Musicians, videographers, and writers post material to social media sites hoping to gain a following and perhaps follow the path of discovery laid by Justin Bieber. In a case study of four such Montreal apprentices, Tamara Shepherd defined the labour behind such user-generated content as "a non-remunerated training ground" driven by "the promise of notoriety that begets autonomous future employment" (2013: 41). Most user-generated content is posted to, and becomes the property of, commercial digital platforms, creating value for corporations out of this free labour. And unlike apprenticeships for electricians, plumbers, or carpenters, such media apprenticeships are completely unorganized and beyond the scope of cultural-policy mechanisms (Shepherd, 2013: 42).

If the field of user-generated content is rife with the potential for exploitation, the provision of this free content, some of it of excellent quality, also drives down the value of the work performed by those trying to make a respectable living in the cultural industries. While labour organizations have suffered membership losses with layoffs, buyouts, and contract work (e.g., Quebecor hired back just 62 of the 253 unionized *Journal de Montréal* workers the company locked out because of a contract dispute between 2009 and 2011), the deterioration of working conditions in the cultural industries may enhance trade unions' raison d'être in the long run. Over-extended workers in the video-game industry are looking to organize (Dyer-Witheford and de Peuter, 2006: 612) and the unions themselves

are combating the power of converged media corporations by converging themselves (Mosco and McKercher, 2006). In the United States, the International Typographic Union (ITU), The Newspaper Guild (TNG), and the National Association of Broadcast Employees and Technicians (NABET) joined the Communications Workers of America (CWA); the CWA represents a number of CBC's English-language workers. In Canada, the Communications, Energy and Paperworkers Union of Canada (CEP) merged with the Canadian units of ITU, TNG, and NABET, to represent workers across the spectrum of communications industries (Dyer-Witheford and de Peuter, 2006: 736). The CEP subsequently merged in 2013 with the Canadian Auto Workers to form Unifor, Canada's largest private-sector union, representing 305,000 workers (Unifor, 2014).

Media Democratization

The barriers to media ownership and participation have decreased considerably with digitization and the greater accessibility of a range of communication technologies, from personal computers to digital cameras and sound recorders (see Gillmor, 2004; Shirky, 2008). **Media democratization** implies greater involvement by citizens in the production and distribution of all kinds of media content. We have already made reference to user-generated content, but democratization would include structured initiatives such as the establishment of organizations dedicated to expanding public participation and broadening media perspectives, especially in the areas of news and current affairs.

The idea of democratizing the media has a history dating back at least to the 1960s and '70s, when cooperative radio stations, film and video collectives, and alternative or "underground" newspapers were established. In the 1960s, for example, the NFB launched its Challenge for Change program, putting film cameras in the hands of citizens to tell their own stories. And in the 1970s, Canada's Native Communication

Program helped establish a number of Aboriginal newspapers (Skinner, 2012: 37). Recently, however, the relative accessibility of the internet, the inadequacies of both public and private forms of ownership described above, and the hyper-commercialism that has accompanied globalization have combined to reinvigorate movements for media reform and the establishment of **alternative media** organizations.

Proposals for reforming the existing media include the following: imposing limits on ownership concentration, and especially cross-media ownership; amending the Competition Act to account for diversity in the expression of news and ideas; legislating a code of professional practice or a code of ethics for media organizations; restructuring provincial press councils and/or establishing a national media commission; and enacting right-of-reply legislation, which would permit editorial redress for persons misrepresented in the media (Skinner, 2004: 16–17). David Skinner argues that "these reforms would help ensure some diversity in corporate news voices, provide journalists some independence from their corporate employers and provide some checks on the relationship between the media and the public" (2004: 18). Reform initiatives, however, leave standing the fundamental structures of public and private media institutions.

Alternative media initiatives, on the other hand, pursue communication and cultural production to broaden public debate, to construct community, to advocate for social justice and to challenge concentrated media power (see Kozolanka et al., 2012). Kozolanka et al. note that "these media occupy contested and shifting terrain, and that the news and ideas they contain are not marginal in any larger social sense, but indicate sustained efforts for more democratic media and society as one and the same" (2012: 2). Among the media organizations serving these goals are campus and community radio stations, community television channels, magazines such as *Spacing*, *Briarpatch*, *Canadian Dimension*, *This Magazine*, and *The Tyee* (online only), as well as the online newspaper *The Dominion* (Skinner, 2012: 37–43). The challenge for alternative media organizations and their corporate cousins is to achieve economic sustainability. As David Skinner notes, "For the most part, these media have developed out of a concern for the expression of a particular set of ideas and values, and consideration of a business model has generally taken a back seat to this goal" (2012: 26). Alternative media organizations tend to be small and enjoy few economies of scale, and those who work for them often do so for little or no pay. The size and demographic profile of their audiences is often unknown, making it hard to generate advertising and subscription sales, and their ideological content can limit their appeal to advertisers (Skinner, 2012: 26).

▶ SUMMARY

There is no natural or inevitable way to organize mass communication. The media are social institutions structured in various ways according to their technological characteristics, the resources they draw upon, and the socio-political context in which they operate. But if all media organizations have something in common, it is that they participate in the economy by generating revenues for media owners, providing communication services to their audiences, advertising goods and services, and providing employment.

The mass media in Canada are owned both privately and publicly, but all operate in a mixed economy. No media industry in Canada is governed exclusively by free-market economics. Even newspaper publishing, which comes closest to an exclusively private enterprise, is subject to federal-government regulations regarding ownership intended to protect newspapers from foreign takeover and competition. Nor is any media organization in Canada immune to the demands of the marketplace; even the publicly owned CBC must pay attention to ratings and advertising revenues.

The critical difference between public and private forms of media ownership pertains to their bottom lines. Public ownership is devoted to providing communication as a public service, to employ the mass media for social and/or national goals. Private ownership is devoted to providing communication for the profit of media owners. These distinctions are fundamental because they speak to the role communication is assigned in Canadian society. The economistic view perceives communication, first and foremost, as commercial enterprise, subjecting all forms of cultural production to commercial criteria of supply and demand. The culturalist view regards cultural products as much more than commodities to be exchanged in the marketplace—they are expressions of a culture as a way of life and as a system of beliefs and values, and expressions of ideas and images that help a culture to imagine itself and to articulate its priorities. As private enterprise has encroached on more and more areas of mass communication in Canadian society, concerns have been raised over the commercialization of cultural production, conglomerate ownership of media organizations, conflicts of interest between media companies and other businesses owned by the same parent, and corporate concentration.

Moves to democratize the media have assumed two forms: *media reform*, which seeks to find ways to diversify and render existing media organizations more accountable; and *alternative media*, or the establishing of new independent media outlets dedicated to serving defined communities.

 KEY TERMS

advertising, p. 240
alternative media, p. 266
branding, p. 253
capital, p. 243
capitalism, p. 249
chain ownership, p. 258
commodity, p. 242
conglomerate ownership, p. 249
convergence, p. 258
corporate concentration, p. 250
economism, p. 246

labour, p. 240
market, p. 240
market externalities, p. 246
market failure, p. 246
mass marketing, p. 242
means of production, p. 249
media democratization, p. 265
private ownership, p. 249
public ownership, p.254
resources, p. 243
vertical integration, p. 258

 RELATED WEBSITES

Broadcast Dialogue: www.broadcastdialogue.com
Broadcast Dialogue offers a directory and contact information for all Canadian radio and television stations, as well as news from the broadcasting industry.

Newspapers Canada: www.newspaperscanada.ca
You will find a wealth of industry news and ownership information here.

Quebecor: www.quebecor.com
This site provides a detailed look at one of Canada's largest media companies, which has been a champion of media convergence.

 FURTHER READINGS

Aleander, Alison, James Owers, Rod Carveth, C. Ann Hollifield, and Albert N. Greco, eds. 2004. *Media Economics: Theory and Practice*, 3rd ed. Mahwah, NJ and London: Lawrence Erlbaum Associates. This collection addresses the economic specificities of the various cultural industries, from movies to newspapers.

Heilbroner, Robert L. 1980. *The Worldly Philosophers: The Lives, Times, and Ideas of the Great Economic Thinkers*. New York: Simon & Schuster. This very readable reference guide covers history's leading economic theorists.

Kozolanka, Kirsten, Patricia Mazeppa, and David Skinner, eds. 2012. *Alternative Media in Canada*. Vancouver: University of British Columbia Press. This collection of essays provides a thorough assessment of the move to create a media sector that forms a true alternative to the dominant corporate media.

Mosco, Vincent. 2009. *The Political Economy of Communication: Rethinking and Renewal*, 2nd ed. Los Angeles: Sage. Mosco's theoretical work applies contemporary political-economic thought to communication and cultural industries.

▶ STUDY QUESTIONS

1. What important changes have taken place to the media economy in recent years?
2. What resources do media organizations draw upon?
3. What is the rationale for state intervention in the cultural economy?
4. What are *market externalities* and how are they pertinent to the discussion of media economics? Cite an example of a positive externality and a negative externality.
5. What is advertising's role in the economy at large and in the media economy in particular?
6. What are the principal distinctions between public and private forms of ownership?
7. Name three forms that private ownership of the media can assume.
8. What is media convergence and what does it imply for media content?
9. How do media "sell audiences to advertisers"?
10. What is media democratization and what forms can it take?

Journalists as Content Producers

> The arts of rhetoric can serve either democracy or self-interested factions.
> Journalism is one of those arts. — Stephen J.A. Ward

Opening Questions

- What does it mean to say that news stories, like other kinds of media content, are produced or constructed? Why is this important?

- How is *networked journalism* different from the pipeline model of news production?

- Why is it important to understand journalism as a practice of representation?

- How do news stories produce meaning?

- What are the ideals that govern journalism as a practice of knowledge production?

- What economic challenges does journalism face as it becomes increasingly digital and networked?

Introduction

Content producers are central to mass communications. We often hear media analysts declare, in these changing economic and technological times, that "content is king." Radio hosts, magazine photographers, web designers, television producers, film editors, and songwriters all have vastly different job descriptions and work environments, but they all manufacture or produce media content. The stories and images we see and hear, whether based on fact or fiction, are never presented simply or "naturally," but are instead highly constructed by people with particular sets of technical and aesthetic skills, organized within a specific production environment, and guided by some combination of ideals, ideologies, conventions, regulations, and institutional demands. These stories and images, in other words, are products of mediation. Mediation involves a series of choices about what content to create—how, for what purpose, and for whom, regardless of whether those choices are made consciously or unconsciously. User-generated content entails the same kinds of choices, even if those choices are less structured, and even if users are less aware of, or attentive to, the various contextual parameters within which they are operating.

In this chapter, we posit journalism as a particular practice of content production, and an especially interesting one given the new ways it is evolving in our time, the new openings being created for people to participate in the production and circulation of news and commentary, the new opportunities for people to take up discussion of news stories and events, and the challenges this presents to the mainstream or commercial news industry. We have seen movements devoted to new journalism, public or civic journalism, alternative journalism, advocacy journalism, citizen journalism, peace journalism, and global journalism. But regardless of its form, journalism is a particular kind of content and journalists operate within a specific environment, guided by a set of ideals, storytelling conventions, and audience expectations that distinguish this practice from other kinds of content production. And the majority of original news reporting—whether we eventually receive it via social media channels like Twitter or Facebook, have it sent to us through RSS feeds, or find it on the site of a news aggregator like Google News—is still produced by journalists who work for legacy news organizations, those who attend the meetings, conduct the interviews, do the original research, and craft the original story (see Charles, 2014: 48–50; Dahlgren, 2013: 160).

Journalism is an especially suitable communications form for this chapter because we might not normally think of it as being manufactured or produced; some reporters still claim they simply mirror or reflect reality—that they simply report what happened. After all, journalism's self-appointed mission is to provide us with transparent accounts of newsworthy people, institutions, events, and trends, along with informed analysis. In its simplest definition, journalism provides the public with factual information and informed commentary about current events by addressing the most basic questions of who, what, when, where, why, and how. But as we will see, it is in all cases a manufactured product.

Journalism provides the public with factual information and informed commentary about current events by addressing the most basic questions of who, what, when, where, why, and how. But it is in all cases a manufactured product. *The Daily Show with Jon Stewart*, while a comedy show, irreverently and closely analyzed the ways news was presented to the public, ironically making a comedian a nationally trusted source of news.

Source: Brendan Smialowski/AFP/Getty Images.

News as Content Production

Like all forms of content, news is produced and, much like other mass media forms, news is produced and presented in story form. News items are typically referred to as *stories*, and, like all stories, they consist of characters, conflicts between characters, temporal and geographical settings, and narratives that take us from a beginning to an end—even if, for example, a story is serialized through subsequent editions, newscasts, and digitalized versions. News production has implications for how we think about news and for the role journalism plays in society. News stories, while based on actual events and real people, never simply mirror reality, as some journalists would contend. A mirror, after all, shows us only what is placed before it, nothing more and nothing less, and in the proportions presented to it; the person holding the mirror may have control over where to point it, but the depiction the mirror offers is always a simple,

direct, and unorganized reflection. The mirror metaphor and the associated notion of reflection do not adequately describe the role of journalists as content producers.

Nor is news simply gathered. Such a conception of journalism underestimates the degree of selection that goes into producing a news report and the extent to which events must meet the producer's understanding of "newsworthiness." Each day, journalists face an infinite number of events from which to fashion their news stories. They receive far more invitations to press conferences than they could possibly cover and more press releases than they could ever use. Even those individuals who simply redistribute news through social media or submit photos or video clips to news organizations operate from some sense of what they think is important and worthy of peoples' attention.

Journalists make choices about what to cover based on what they perceive to have "news value," what fits within their organization's

Source: © Pavlo Padufalov.

▌ All news stories are told from someone's perspective.

10.1 ▶▶▶▶▶▶

NETWORKED JOURNALISM

What do we mean by "journalism" in a period when the production and distribution of news, commentary, analysis, and correction is conducted not only by those who self-identify as journalists and work for a recognized news organization, but also by ordinary citizens, hobbyists, bloggers with particular interests, community groups, and advocates of every stripe? Journalism is both a practice (reporting and commenting upon current affairs) and an institution (the production and distribution system within which reporting occurs). If for most of the twentieth century, journalism was the bailiwick of professional reporters and editors working for legacy news organizations, that changed with the interactivity and accessibility of digital media. Communications scholar Peter Dahlgren sees journalism as "gradually becoming more interactive, collaborative, diverse, partisan, and immediate," and he describes online journalism as a "sprawling domain . . . comprised of mainstream online media, alternative journalism sites, the blogosphere, social media, individual and group productions, including efforts by social movements and other activists and groups of every imaginable persuasion—political, religious, and lifestyle advocates, hobbyists, and much more" (2013: 159–60). C.W. Anderson et al. put it this way: "We are living through a shock of inclusion, where the former audience is becoming increasingly intertwined with all aspects of news, as sources who can go public on their own, as groups that can both create and comb through data in ways the professionals can't, as disseminators, syndicators and users of the news" (2012: 80). If Dahlgren insists that mainstream reporting remains the predominant source of news and user-generated journalism largely operates "symbiotically," the result is that "facts and opinions, debates, gossip, nonsense, misinformation, the insightful, the deceptive, the poetic, are all mixed together, scrambling the traditional boundaries between journalism and non-journalism" (2013: 160).

Breaking down this dichotomy between what Dahlgren calls "mainstream journalism" and "participatory journalism," current scholarship perceives journalism today—both as a practice and as an institution—as *networked* rather than as a simple "pipeline" between news media and audiences (see Anderson, 2013; Anderson et al., 2012; Sheller, 2014; Archetti, 2014; Benkler, 2011; Clark and Van Slyke, 2011). Journalism, in other words, is the product of the perpetual and dialogic interactions among information sources of all kinds, news providers of all kinds, and news consumers who can tap into a vast array of information sources. Professional journalists, for example, draw on story leads and information from their traditional sources (experts, actors in their field, news releases, news conferences) as well as from other news providers (websites, social media sites, blogs, and audience feedback). Bloggers contribute to this network by drawing on mainstream news reporting, other blogs, websites, social media sites, their followers' comments, and their own expertise. News consumers, similarly, develop an understanding of a news event from whatever combination of information sources they frequent; increasingly, this means gleaning information and analysis from a variety of traditional and non-traditional media—what Sheller calls "source promiscuity" (2014: 8). News consumers, too, can make their own contributions to this journalism network.

Journalism scholar C.W. Anderson perceives journalism today as "a socio-material property of messy networks," characterized by open participation (Anderson, 2013: 1010). Anderson maintains that "we need to think about networks of journalistic expertise, with both human agents and non-human objects networked together in complex strands of material practice and knowledge production" (2013: 1021). Sources of news, such as experts as well as expertise and occupational groups, should be seen as "networked properties rather than jurisdictional conflicts or substantive possessions" (2013: 1021). Anderson writes, "By looking at 'newswork as network,' we can better factor in the cultural residue of a particular profession that constrains both its mental worldview and its available repertoire of action" (2013: 1021).

While *networked journalism* is a useful concept, it risks conflating the significant disparities between simpler forms of information production (e.g., content based on personal observation, recycled material, off-the-cuff analysis) and much more sophisticated and labour-intensive material (e.g., investigative reporting, expert document or data analysis, conflict reporting). The concept can, in other words, overlook or trivialize the skill

Pipeline model
- Largely one-way flow with media/journalists as gatekeepers

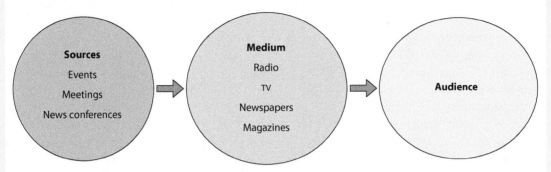

Network model
- Completely interactive, multi-dimensional flow of news, information, and commentary
- Gatekeeping role of news media mitigated

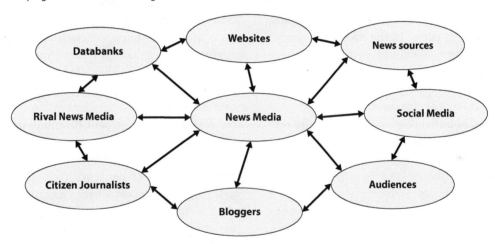

FIGURE 10.1 Networked Journalism

With an increasing number of opportunities to participate in the production of news—for ordinary citizens, bloggers, advocacy groups, citizen journalists, as well as professional journalists—journalism has become *networked*, the product of a complex web of interactions outlined here.

set, experience, work effort, resources, commitment, even moral and physical courage, required to produce professional-grade journalism. In a study of citizen journalism practices in local UK newspapers, Lily Canter distinguished between "low-level" and "high-level" categories of reporting. Low-level reporting was deemed to be the field of non-professionals, comprising such things as community events, charity events, "bottom-tier"

council meetings, and self-interest news. High-level reporting was seen as best done by professionals and included court cases, investigative reporting, major events and breaking news (2013: 1100). Similarly, Anderson et al. see journalists as being displaced rather than replaced in the news ecosystem, moving higher up the editorial food chain where the emphasis is on their skills of **verification** and interpretation (2012: 22).

particular areas of coverage (politics, business, sports, crime, the arts) and what they believe will interest their audience. Deciding what is news is a subjective operation, involving journalists in a complex, consultative, and sometimes hotly contested, process of selection. While news judgment is most often exercised intuitively by journalists under time pressure in the field, based on their experience and expertise (see Schultz, 2007), media scholars have identified a number of criteria that render some events news and others not news. Melvin Mencher (2006: 58–65), for example, identifies seven determinants of newsworthiness: *timeliness* (events that are immediate or recent); *impact* (events that affect many people); *prominence* (events involving well-known people, places, or institutions); *proximity* (events that are geographically, culturally, or "emotionally close" to the audience); *conflict* (events pitting two sides against one another); *peculiarity* (events that deviate from the everyday); and *currency* (long-simmering events that suddenly emerge as objects of attention).

Clearly, Mencher's **news values** require producers of news to exercise subjective judgment about what is new, what is important, what the target audience should know or care about. News is not an account of mundane activities, but a digest of extraordinary, unusual, significant or unexpected events. To cite a simple example, normal rush-hour traffic volume on a local urban freeway is not news, while a seven-car pileup that kills three people and closes several lanes of the freeway for a number of hours is definitely news. This process of selection has compelled some theorists to perceive journalists—especially editors and news directors—as gatekeepers, people who sift through a huge number of events and decide which will be covered and which stories will be circulated. But **gatekeeping** is only a partial explanation of the news-production process, applicable only to some stages of selection. A newspaper assignment editor, for example, chooses among an assortment of scheduled daily press conferences, meetings, and speeches and decides which will be staffed by a reporter and

which will not. This, admittedly, is a form of gatekeeping. Similarly, wire editors will sort through hundreds of wire-service stories from around the world each day to select those to be considered for publication. This, too, is gatekeeping.

Gatekeeping accounts for the question of *what* the news organization will cover, but it leaves aside the equally important issue of *how* an event will be covered. It ignores, for example, the extent to which wire-service stories are revised by editors and the different *play*—length and prominence—they receive from one news organization to the next. The same news item may occupy the first two-and-a-half minutes of the six o'clock news on one channel, complete with interviews and illustrative footage, and warrant only 15 seconds of the anchor's narration on another channel. Same event; different news stories. Newspapers, websites, and news aggregators, too, assign relative importance to news stories by how they play them—whether prominently or buried under mounds of other content. Again, the same event may receive completely different treatment from one news provider to the next.

The gatekeeping metaphor also ignores the creative nature of content production. Every news organization establishes a brand: an identity for its audience and its advertisers through the style of journalism it practises (e.g., serious and thorough, entertaining and concise). Developing and maintaining that identity is achieved by establishing a certain kind of editorial presence through the assignment of resources and the shaping of content. Tabloid newspapers like the *Toronto Sun* and *Le Journal de Montréal*, for example, pay a considerable amount of attention to crime stories, covering the police beat and the courthouse quite heavily. Their news stories are relatively short and written in a lively and provocative style, and their pages are filled with bold headlines and lots of photographs. Tabloids are typically populist newspapers, devoted to what they perceive to be the interests of the everyday person. More sober broadsheets like *The Globe and Mail* and *Le Devoir*, on the other hand, pay much more attention to political, foreign-affairs, and cultural reporting. They tend to feature much longer and in-depth stories. These newspapers are interested in very different kinds of stories and news presentations, catering to what they perceive to be a more discriminating audience and aspiring to be read by society's opinion leaders; they define news differently. This idea of branding is especially applicable in today's crowded mediascape, in what has been termed an "attention economy" (as we discussed in Chapter 9). Examining how any news organization's editorial style is created opens up the selection process to many more factors than the notion of gatekeeping can accommodate. The gatekeeping metaphor, nonetheless, does draw our attention to what gets left out of the selection process.

A useful exercise for the student of mass communication is to examine the content of a favoured news provider and consider the ways in which that news provider puts together a particular package of news for a target audience. What topics does it cover, first of all? Is it specialized in one or a few topics (e.g., politics, business) or does it offer a broad range of subject matter? Then, how does it cover those topics? What kind of language does it use? What aspects of the story does it highlight? Whose voices and images are included? What references does it make to other events, people, or institutions? To what extent does it feature its own original reporting and commentary? How much material has been sourced elsewhere? The answers to these questions provide clues about what kind of audience the news provider aims to build, who is included in that audience and who is excluded, underscoring the dialogic relationship between media and audiences.

In this vein, a more precise way to think of journalists as content producers is through the metaphor of the frame. Through words, images, sounds, and story themes, journalists "frame" reality. If we think of the blank page or the blank screen as an empty frame, it is journalists who decide how to fill that frame, by inserting into the frame particular stories, visuals, and graphics

and by leaving out much more material. They decide not only which events to include in the news frame, but also how to depict those events and what prominence to assign the story; what aspects or angle of the story to emphasize; whose voices are heard; what meanings they encourage audiences to take away from the story. It is useful to remind ourselves that every element of the news story, the news page, the news broadcast, the news site, has been put there—at the expense of other content.

The metaphor of the frame implies, first of all, that there are limits to what a news organization can properly present as news. These limits are defined by such practical considerations as the size of the "news hole" (the space or time available), the costs involved in producing the coverage (does it involve travel and hotel accommodation?), and the availability of reporting staff or other sources of information. Even the producers of online news sites, with much more capacity for content, make decisions about what to include and exclude, and which content to feature prominently on their home page. These limits are also governed by the more subjective criteria of an event's news value and how well it suits the news organization's particular areas of coverage, as we touched on above. We would expect a news provider specializing in arts coverage to send its own reporter to the Toronto International Film Festival or the Juno Awards rather than rely on the Canadian Press wire service, just as we would expect a news organization specializing in sports to send its own reporter to the Stanley Cup final, regardless of which teams are playing.

News coverage is also shaped by a given news organization's particular political stance, whether or not this position is ever explicitly stated. Think about how news organizations may react differently, even if the distinctions are subtle, in their coverage of labour–management disputes, same-sex marriage legislation, cuts in social spending, or environmental issues. In her groundbreaking study of news practices, *Making News: A Study in the Construction of Reality*, media scholar Gaye Tuchman (1978: 1) used the frame metaphor to

10.2 ▶▶▶▶▶▶

PUSHING AND PULLING

Until recently, it has been left to news providers to determine what to offer news consumers, through an imprecise calculation of what editors and producers think audiences want to know and need to know and what kinds of content will attract audiences that advertisers will want to reach. Legacy media like newspapers, magazines, and radio and television broadcasters are examples of push technologies, media that push content toward audience members, calculating that their supply will satisfy audience demand (see Sheller, 2014). Such media organizations, of course, track media consumption as best they can through surveys and ratings systems and manage content decisions accordingly, but they maintain ultimate control over what content is supplied.

The interactive capacities of digital technologies have shifted the supply–demand balance in a number of ways, and they can be understood as pull technologies. From the industry perspective, media organizations can track precisely audiences' consumption habits and tailor their content to audience demand. The websites of news providers, for example, often list the most popular stories, either as most viewed, most downloaded, or most shared. More significantly, though, news consumers no longer need to rely on push technologies; they can *pull* whatever kinds of news content they prefer, whenever and wherever they want, either by searching it out, subscribing to RSS services, or by customizing their news aggregator or mobile-phone app. If you want to know who is leading the Tour de France or whether the ceasefire between Israel and Gaza is holding, you don't need to wait for the next newscast or breaking-news bulletin.

This erodes somewhat the power of commercial news organizations by breaking their monopoly hold on news production, opening them up to competition not only from other commercial news providers worldwide, but also from an assortment of news aggregators, alternative news sites, digital independents, bloggers, even the principal actors in the news themselves (government departments, think tanks, university researchers, non-governmental organizations, advocacy groups, and so on) who can address audiences directly. It has changed dramatically how we consume news; no longer are we confined to the packages that news organizations provide for us because we can pull individual stories from numerous news and information providers.

In this way, some part of the gatekeeping function has been transferred to news consumers. Commercial news organizations, who want to maintain their hold on audiences, are now having to rethink the balance between giving people what news audiences indicate they want and giving people what news their editors believe audiences need. This change strikes at the heart of the question, *What is journalism for?* Relatedly, it speaks to concerns about journalism's standing as a democratic communications system. What are the implications for notions of citizenship and community if we get only the news we want—whether by push or by pull? Can we have a healthy democracy or any sense of local community without a shared body of knowledge about current affairs? Without sharing in this process of communication? This is what journalism scholar Ejvind Hansen terms news providers' "critical mediating function." Hansen writes, "If we lose the unifying aspect of the mass media, politics may devolve into a conflict of special interests that cannot even agree on a common framework for issues, much less on a structure ranking issues according to some criteria of relevance" (2012: 687). The "common," Hansen argues, "is that which has no clear proprietor or which is . . . owned by everybody" (2012: 688).

emphasize the necessarily restricted view of the world journalism provides:

Like any frame that delineates a world, the news frame may be considered problematic. The view through a window depends upon whether the window is large or small, has many panes or few, whether the glass is opaque or clear, whether the window faces a street or a backyard. The unfolding scene also depends upon where one stands, far or near, craning one's neck to the side, or gazing straight ahead, eyes parallel to the wall in which the window is encased.

No news organization can cover every event from every possible angle. Therefore, what stories it includes and excludes can reveal a great deal about the news judgment it applies when producing its news package. This judgment is exercised subjectively; it is not uncommon, in a newsroom production environment that brings together a diverse mix of individuals, for reporters and editors to disagree, sometimes vehemently, about whether an event is newsworthy at all—or if it is, how it should be covered and how it should be played.

As we have suggested, this practice of **framing** occurs within a production environment shaped by a number of factors: the ideals that distinguish journalism from other kinds of content production; the use of language—what combination of textual, aural, and visual—and the shaping of news reports into stories that give news events meaning; the specific sociopolitical culture in which news stories are produced; the laws and regulations that govern journalism; the economics of news production; and the technological infrastructure available to journalists.

As demonstrated by this *Toronto Star* advertisement, individual media organizations, as well as individual journalists, can tell vastly different stories about the very same event.

Ideals of Journalism

If news is constructed, it is also subject to particular ideals that distinguish journalism from other forms of storytelling—and that distinguish journalism as it is practised in Western democracies like Canada from the way it might be practised elsewhere. We can be justifiably skeptical about how well journalists and the news organizations they work for live up to the ideals of their profession. Ideals, after all, are lofty principles, even standards for perfection, but they do provide the yardsticks by which critics, practitioners, and audiences alike evaluate performance. These ideals form a kind of gold standard for what "good journalism" is, and help to distinguish journalism from other communication practices.

Journalism as we know it in Canada has a fundamental guiding ideal: the quest for truth. This quest is idealistic because the truth is not always accessible to us as fallible human beings, and certainly not readily accessible within the constraints placed on most journalists. Even the most conscientious, hard-working, and ethical journalists face time constraints, but journalists are also constrained by access—to people, to documents, to events—and by their own limits of expertise and analytical skill. The seemingly simple task of reporting on what happened—during a meeting, during a battle, during a public demonstration—is also always inflected with people's perception, interpretation, and pre-conceived ideas. Increasingly, we recognize that there is usually more than one truth at play;

we might agree on a basic set of facts, but how those facts are made meaningful can produce many truths. Nonetheless, journalism derives its authority from providing the public with credible accounts of current affairs. Credibility is the currency that the news media trade in, and no news organization wants to be perceived as lacking in credibility (see Box 10.3).

The performance of journalism's truth-seeking function is related to a second ideal: serving democracy. Truth-seeking is the foundation for **freedom of the press**, a fundamental freedom for all democracies that can be traced back to the Enlightenment (see Box 10.4) and that is explicitly noted in Canada's Charter of Rights and Freedoms (Section 2[b]). Journalism is tasked with the production and circulation of information and ideas for the benefit of all, extending the basic democratic right of freedom of expression

10.3 ▶▶▶▶▶▶

LOSING CREDIBILITY

The proper functioning of democratic society depends on a number of institutions providing its citizens with information that is factual, accurate, verifiable, trustworthy, and credible: government (through agencies such as Statistics Canada), the legal system (courts, police), the academy (through both research and teaching), the medical system (from doctors to researchers), and journalism. Factual information forms the basis of every kind of decision-making process. But all of these institutions have lost some measure of public trust, or credibility, in recent times, and for a variety of reasons.

Our trust in journalism has been eroded by its increasing commercialization, corporatization, and concentration (as we discussed in Chapter 9); by our increased understanding of how news is produced; as well as by breaches in both individual and institutional performance, whether it be through sensationalism, sloppiness,

or the compromises brought to bear when a news provider becomes too closely aligned with a particular political ideology or the businesses that pay its bills (e.g., advertisers, owners). The erosion of public trust is a serious threat, as media theorist Roger Silverstone argues, "For the media to be viable they have to be trusted by their addressees" (2007: 124). Once that trust is lost, Silverstone maintains, it is almost impossible to restore.

Bill Kovach and Tom Rosenstiel have described journalism as a "discipline of verification" as opposed to a "discipline of assertion." They write, "In the end, the discipline of verification is what separates journalism from entertainment, propaganda, fiction, or art" (2001: 71).

Methods of verification have taken on renewed importance in an age when both individuals and institutions have greater tools with which to misinform, deceive, or slant the information they contribute to news providers, whether through press releases, commissioned studies, or political announcements. Even the accounts of well-meaning citizen journalists require verification. And, of course, news consumers have greater capacity to do their own fact-checking (see Silverman, 2007).

granted to all individuals into the realm of the mass media. In their appraisal of the state of contemporary journalism, Kovach and Rosenstiel insisted that "[t]he primary purpose of journalism is to provide citizens with the information they need to be free and self-governing" (2001: 17). The renowned communication theorist James Carey declared that "journalism as a practice is unthinkable except in the context of democracy; in fact, journalism is usefully understood as another name for democracy" (Carey, 1997: 332).

A number of scholars have critiqued this normative definition of journalism as a democratic practice. Journalism historian Michael Schudson puts the argument this way: "There is no doubting . . . the importance of the press to a democracy. But the press by itself is not democracy and does not create democracy" (2003: 198). The political scientist Anne-Marie Gingras (2006) concurs, citing a serious misunderstanding in the relationship between the media and democracy, based on what she terms three "confusions." First, while freedom of expression is an essential condition for the functioning of democracy, it is not sufficient in and of itself, because it does not guarantee political representation of the broad spectrum of society, nor does it establish the mechanisms necessary for a true dialogue between civil society and the state. Second, freedom of expression does not speak to the quality—specifically, the veracity—of media messages. Third, communication does not guarantee harmony or consensus (Gingras, 2006: 3-4). The media, Gingras argues, are caught in a conflict between their commercial interests and their political responsibilities; producing quality information does not ensure commercial success, nor does commercial success necessarily result in quality information (2006: 8). For her part, communications theorist Beate Josephi (2012) turns the relationship between journalism and democracy on its head; journalism, she argues, can be practised without a supporting democratic political system. Instead, she notes that the prerequisites for what we normally think of as good journalism are conditions of freedom of expression and relative journalistic autonomy, citing as examples instances of credible news coverage in non-democratic countries in Asia—where two thirds of newspapers are produced—and the

10.4 ▶▶ ▶ ▶ ▶▶

JOHN MILTON'S *AREOPAGITICA*

One of the earliest and most forceful arguments for freedom of the press came in a speech to the English Parliament in 1644. In John Milton's speech, titled *Areopagitica*,* he objected to England's Licensing Order, by which publishing was restricted to government-licensed printers and written works had to be pre-approved before printing (read the full speech here: www.gutenberg.org/files/608/608-h/608-h.htm). Milton's appeal was unsuccessful—the Licensing Order remained in place until 1692—but his speech remains a classic Enlightenment text and his reasoning informs free-speech arguments to the present day.

If *Areopagitica* reflects Enlightenment thinking, it also appealed to the Christian sensibilities of Milton's audience. For example, Milton argued that God gave humankind free will, the capacity to choose between good and evil. "He that can apprehend and consider vice with all her baits and seeming pleasures, and yet abstain, and yet distinguish, and yet prefer that which is truly better, he is the true warfaring Christian." He questioned the practicalities of assigning fallible beings the responsibility for licensing, and argued that knowledge and truth emerge precisely through the process of reading and discussion. "Where there is much desire to learn, there of necessity will be much arguing, much writing, many opinions; for opinion in good men is but knowledge in the making."

*The full title is *Areopagitica: A Speech for the Liberty of Unlicensed Printing to the Parliament of England*.

Middle East, which is the main operating base of Al Jazeera (Josephi, 2012: 484–6).

The struggle for freedom of the press is ongoing and journalists are at the forefront of efforts to extend public **access to information** in both formal and informal ways, as we discuss in Box 10.5.

Journalists are often highly dependent on official sources and their own contacts for information, and the news media's role as **fourth estate** grants journalists the moral authority to gain access to the people and institutions that populate their reportage: politicians, bureaucrats, police officers, community leaders, celebrities, Parliament, the court system, the stock exchange, and so on. These people and institutions have had to be pressured to accept as legitimate journalists those representatives of the

many new news organizations that have sprung up online.

As we discussed in Chapter 3, the term *fourth estate*, which refers to the role the news media play in the governing of a democratic society, originated with journalists' struggle to gain access to the proceedings of the British Parliament in the late eighteenth and early nineteenth centuries. This was a recognition of the place of journalism in representing citizens as a kind of watchdog over their governors.

The news media today fulfill the role of the fourth estate by reporting on legislative debates and other government business, and by pressuring governments to increase access to information. All legislatures in Canada have press galleries populated by reporters, and journalists also regularly attend the public meetings of

---

10.5 ▶▶▶▶▶▶

FREEDOM OF THE PRESS

Constitutional guarantees and universal declarations are important, but they define freedom of the press in largely abstract terms. The real, concrete meaning of freedom of the press is derived from its daily exercise by those journalists who push at the boundaries of what can be screened, aired, and published.

Journalists exercise freedom of the press when they report what is truly new and important to the public interest; when they broaden the range of debate; when they expand the horizons of what can be reported, imagined, revealed, and criticized. Journalists also exercise freedom of the press when they hold their own news organizations to the standards and ideals of their journalistic calling, especially when that news organization may have to pay a political or economic price for its reportage.

Freedom of the press would be meaningless as a human right if journalists never exposed scandal; if they never revealed information that

government officials preferred not to divulge; if they never quoted critics of powerful people and powerful institutions; if they never drew attention to hypocrisy, greed, or arrogance—if, in other words, they never gave anyone cause to restrict press freedoms.

The right to freedom of the press is exerted not only in exceptional, headline-grabbing cases—for example, the Pentagon Papers, the Watergate scandal, the spying activities of the Communications Security Establishment of Canada or the National Security Agency in the United States (see Greenwald, 2014)—but also on a daily basis, in countless small ways. Journalists are giving meaning to freedom of the press every time they reveal more than their sources are willing to share with the public, every time they undermine the propaganda disseminated by corporate and political communications officers, every time they introduce factual evidence to accompany decision-makers' opinions.

To exercise freedom of the press, then, is to give it concrete value, when it means discomforting news sources, antagonizing public officials, prompting court challenges, even irritating fellow journalists and the members of the public they seek to serve.

municipal governments. Of all the coverage the news media provide, political reportage is considered to be the most closely related to journalism's role in democratic society: providing citizens with the information they need to be free and self-governing (see Kovach and Rosenstiel, 2001). If the original notion of the fourth estate was to be a watchdog over our governors, it has been expanded to include watching over all institutions of power, including the corporate sector. But, as with the other core journalistic values we have discussed, the fourth estate ideal is subject to critique. While the news media can serve as watchdogs on power, they can serve equally as lapdogs when they report uncritically on governments and corporations.

This notion of the news media as a fourth estate is connected to journalistic independence. Ideally, journalists are independent agents in service to the public, concerned only with the public good and beyond the influence of powerful private interests. This is, of course, a fantasy. For one thing, journalists are subjective beings with their own values and beliefs, and they are not above serving their own ideological or political interests, whether consciously or unconsciously. Even the most conscientious and self-reflexive journalist is not immune to the influences that can be brought to bear by the political and/or commercial agenda of the reporter's own news organization; by the public relations industry that serves governments, corporations, and other organizations; and by the motivations of the actors in the story who supply information and commentary, often for their own purposes. Our mainstream news organizations are not at all independent from either corporate Canada or political Canada, but have instead become closely intertwined with these institutions of power. A principal raison d'être of the alternative news providers that have emerged in recent years is precisely to reassert journalistic independence from political and economic power.

Perhaps the most contentious ideal of journalism is *objectivity*. Given all that we know about the communications media and how they work, it

has become commonplace to assert that there is no such thing as objectivity. This is, however, an unsatisfactory response, given that we have some expectation of objectivity not only from journalism, but from other institutions as well: for example, the legal system, the research community, and the medical system. Too often, objectivity is thought of as an absolute; in other words, a claim is either completely 100 percent objective, or it is not at all. But if freedom was defined this way—as absolute freedom—we would say that there is no such thing as freedom either. Both terms are best understood as relative; by objectivity, that is, we are really talking about *relative objectivity*.

It is important to discuss objectivity because it remains one of journalism's core values, at least as far as mainstream journalism is concerned. Journalists are supposed to report objectively, which is typically understood to mean separating clearly the reporting of verifiable facts from the assertion of values and opinions. In a conventional news report, facts are typically declared in the reporter's voice and values are attributed to others, whether as direct quotations or as paraphrased statements. The convention in newspapers is to distinguish physically news reports from commentaries—columns, editorials, letters to the editor, op-ed submissions—by placing them on clearly identified pages. News providers operating on other platforms usually apply similarly transparent measures to distinguish for their audiences facts and values.

Separating facts from values or opinions is much easier said than done, of course, which is why many people reject the notion of objectivity altogether. For one thing, as we noted above, journalism involves selection, which immediately brings into play a number of subjective judgments: *What is news? Why is it newsworthy? What angle to the story should be pursued? Who should be interviewed? What does this news event mean to the public?* For example, the verifiable facts of the 2014 Ebola outbreak in West Africa produced a range of different news frames. Second, as we discuss in the next section, the use of language to describe news events unavoidably attributes meaning to those events. And news, by definition, is what is perceived by journalists to be important or significant to the public interest; that is the first meaning given to any story, and it is further amplified by the amount and the type of coverage the story is granted.

Rather than reject objectivity altogether, there are more sophisticated ways to think about it. We summarize two approaches: the *critical realism* of communications scholars Robert A. Hackett and Yuezhi Zhao (1998) and the *pragmatic objectivity* of the ethicist and former journalist Stephen J.A. Ward (2004).

Hackett and Zhao reject the traditional *positivist* model of objectivity, which perceives truth as the relatively simple product of direct observation and accurate recording. The positivist model asserts that all that stands between reality and journalistic accounts of that reality is good reporting practice, an assertion that fails to account adequately for the mediating presence of the journalist, the language she employs, and the socialization she has undergone (1998: 109–66). Hackett and Zhao, however, also reject the postmodern position, which dismisses objectivity as unattainable because the real world cannot be perceived directly without the mediation of conventional concepts, theories, ideologies, and values, without the mediation of language (in all its forms), and, often, without the mediation of people describing the world on our behalf.

Instead, their critical realist approach to objectivity acknowledges the limitations of both positivism and postmodernism, but nonetheless insists that the real world is accessible, knowable, and describable. Coming to know the truth about the world, they maintain, is a never-ending process, with knowledge constantly produced and revised, subject to the mediation of our categories, concepts, values, and conventions, and emerging only as a result of "the interactive or dialectical to and fro between subject and object, concepts and reality" (Hackett and Zhao, 1998: 129). In other words, if knowledge about the real world cannot be taken at face value through direct observation, and if knowledge production is always subject to various layers of mediation, knowledge and truth can nonetheless emerge through careful and reflexive investigation. "The world is knowable—but not at first sight" (Hackett and Zhao, 1998: 130).

Ward, too, rejects what he calls "traditional objectivity" because it operates from dualisms of fact/value and truth/interpretation, which "distort our understanding of how we know, interpret and value" (2004: 261). He traces traditional objectivity to the nineteenth century, when reporters began to present themselves to the public as passive recorders of news events, echoing the mirror metaphor we discussed above (2004: 262). Instead, Ward's redefinition of objectivity as *pragmatic objectivity* is a more reflective and practical approach with an emphasis on process. "The aim of a theory of pragmatic objectivity is to find a place for objectivity in a world where fact, value, theory, and practical interests intertwine inextricably" (2004: 263).

Ward insists, first of all, that the pursuit of truth is always a work in progress, producing "tentative results" subject to challenge and revision. He notes, secondly, that all forms of inquiry—whether in journalism, or in other truth-seeking occupations such as law and the sciences—are based on interpretation. The inquirer is never passive, but "an active, purpose-driven agent in a social setting" (2004: 264–5). Finally, these acts of interpretation are "holistic" in the sense that they are based on larger systems of knowledge or conceptual schemes. When, for example, the sun appears red at sunset, we understand that it hasn't changed colour during the day, but that its light is being refracted through Earth's atmosphere (2004: 272). Acts of interpretation are also "ubiquitous" in that we are constantly interpreting "because we have no direct, cognitive contact with reality." Ward writes, "Even our seemingly direct perceptions of objects are the result of much processing of stimuli by our perceptual system. The mind must interpret the stimuli according to our categories, beliefs, and expectations" (2004: 273). Ward describes objectivity as "a fallible, context-bound, holistic method of testing interpretations. We judge an interpretation to be objective if it has good support, according to the best available standards of a conceptual system" (2004: 280).

To adopt Ward's "objective stance," then, requires those pursuing truths to adopt "four dispositions": open rationality, or the willingness to meet the demand to make logical assertions, to face facts, and to provide proper evidence for interpretations; partial transcendence, or the willingness to revise interpretations; disinterested truth, or the ability to reflect critically on interpretations; and intellectual integrity, or the willingness to be honest in producing interpretations (2004: 281–2). In their specific environment, journalists must pursue truths in the face of conflicting rhetoric, manipulative information sources, unconfirmed reports, powerful employers, limited resources, a lack of specialized subject knowledge, and deadlines (2004: 290–2).

Though daunting, this pursuit is essential, Ward argues, because of journalism's place in the "infosphere," a sphere he places alongside the biosphere and the social sphere. "[Journalism] generates information and opinion that become part of a system of social discussion that determines public policy. News is not just facts for individuals—it is material for the politics of citizens" (2004: 289).

Some journalists prefer to substitute the values of balance and fairness as a means of dodging the objectivity question, but these substitutes are highly flawed. Balance typically means presenting both sides of the story, a common practice in mainstream news reports. Think of the number of times a news program has featured commentators from two opposing sides of an issue. Balance,

Source: Photo by Richard Sambrook.

The rise of citizen journalism adds further complication to the contested notion of journalistic objectivity. What are the implications for Ward's "objective stance" when even mainstream news organizations are incorporating in their reports photographs and videos from citizens at the front lines of news events?

though, makes a number of presumptions that cannot be sustained. For one thing, there are many more than two sides to a story, and limiting the presentation to two often means choosing the most polarized positions, leaving aside more moderate views, and rendering the two polarized positions irreconcilable; this is one of the contentions of the peace journalism movement (see Lynch and McGoldrick, 2005). For another, the concept of balance can create the impression that the two views presented in a story are equally valid. News coverage of climate change, for example, often creates the impression that there is a serious debate about whether climate change exists by giving voice to both scientists and those who dispute their claims, granting comparable weight to both sides' positions. By refusing to discriminate among opinions, journalists do not bring us closer to the truth.

Similarly, fairness is a poor substitute for objectivity. Fairness is most often exercised in journalism by providing people with an opinion a fair hearing. Those opinions, however, may not be fair to the truth, as in the climate change example above. Both balance and fairness render journalists mere stenographers, absolving them of their responsibility for verification or discrimination between viewpoints.

Journalism as a Textual Practice

It should be clear at this point that journalists do not simply mirror or reflect the world in their news reports, but instead they produce or construct stories about the events they believe are most newsworthy. And, as the saying goes, no story tells the full story, no picture gives the whole picture. News stories are told through the medium of language, that is, a range of symbolic systems: written or spoken words, images, sounds, symbols, gestures, even colours. News stories are texts; rather than faithful reproductions of the world, they are highly constructed representations or depictions of the world

through language. Cultural theorist Stuart Hall (2013: 2) defines **representation** as "the production of meaning through language." In other words, journalists *represent* the objects of their reportage. As we discussed in Chapter 4, to represent is to make present, or depict, or symbolize, through language(s): in this case, through news photos, audio clips, television reports, newspaper articles, multimedia packages, and so on. In so doing, journalists unavoidably give those objects meaning.

At the simplest level, deciding to cover an event as news in the first place defines it as important, significant, relevant, and/or interesting. A second level of meaning pertains to precisely how the story is covered. How, for instance, should the story be framed? Why is it newsworthy? Is it good news or bad news, positive or negative, a natural disaster or a human-made tragedy? Is it a business story, a consumer affairs story, or a labour story? Is it worth prominent and extensive treatment or is it simply a news brief? Finally, what words are chosen to label the event? What images are selected to depict the event and its principal actors? Whose voices are heard? As Dahlgren notes, "Language use is . . . always already implicated in social horizons, pre-understandings, and power relations; ideologically charged discourses can shape the meanings of reported events, intentionally or not" (2013: 166–7). He adds, "News narratives are not just vehicles for content, they have an epistemic dimension as well; narratives comprise ways of knowing and relating to the world, offering different horizons and experiences" (2013: 168).

If language is the medium through which meaning is produced, how does the process work? The Swiss linguist Ferdinand de Saussure demonstrated that language works to produce meaning in the relationship between a **signifier**—an utterance of language (e.g., a word, an image, a symbol, a gesture, a sound)—and a **signified**—the image in our heads that is created when we see or hear a specific language utterance. While we normally do this unthinkingly, this is precisely the process we engage in when we acquire language skills as an infant, and what we might do if we later decide to acquire a second or third language. To cite a simple example, when we hear or see the word *tree* (the signifier), we picture in our minds a woody, leafy plant (the signified), even if we may not know which specific tree is being referred to. The signifiers *arbre*, *Baum*, or *coeden*, on the other hand, mean nothing to us unless we understand French, German, or Welsh.

If this seems straightforward enough, the process quickly becomes more complicated—even contentious—when we read or hear everyday words like *family* or *marriage*. What do these words mean? What do they not mean? For some of us, *family* denotes a nuclear family; for others, an extended family. We might exclude from that association other kinds of family: same-sex parents with an adopted child; unmarried parents with children, and so on. When journalists use the word *family*, then, what exactly do they mean, and what do they not mean? Similarly, what do we think of when we see the word *marriage*? What kinds of couplings does this include and exclude? Can two people of the same sex be married? Can two people who have been living together for years without having any kind of official wedding ceremony or marriage licence be considered married? The very definition of marriage is frequently the subject of news stories. In Quebec news reports, the term *Québécois* can have an inclusive meaning (all residents of Quebec) or an exclusive meaning (French-Canadian residents of Quebec). The distinction is significant, particularly during media discussions about Quebec sovereignty and nationhood. Even simple terms like *we* and *us* can have particular meanings when news reports pertain to immigration. Journalists' use of these terms can promote particular understandings depending on the larger context of the news story in question, thus privileging certain definitions.

Let's consider the flip side of this process. Journalists typically begin with the signified—the event, person, or institution they are covering—and need to assign the object of their coverage signifiers or language descriptors. Thus, they choose

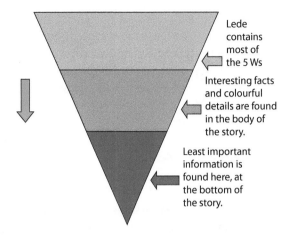

FIGURE 10.2 News Story Structure

News stories tend to follow a formulaic and hierarchical story structure known as *the inverted pyramid*. As the diagram illustrates, a story written in this manner puts the most essential information in the first few paragraphs, with less important details and comment further down. The lead, or introduction, provides *who, what, when,* and *where* information. Subsequent paragraphs seek to provide answers to the *how* and *why* questions.

Source: Newspapers Canada.

language to label and describe what they are covering, and those labels have meaning. Think about the ways in which journalists describe demonstrators at a protest, for example. Are they portrayed as engaged citizens exercising their democratic rights or as rabble-rousers and troublemakers? Which demonstrators are chosen to illustrate the event in news photographs: the peaceful, conservatively dressed marchers, or violent protestors breaking plate-glass windows and confronting police? The same demonstrators, and the same demonstration, can be made to mean, through news stories and images, a range of things.

While some journalists may make these choices deliberately, these meanings more often are produced unconsciously by journalists who are simply following news conventions (e.g., the violent demonstrator makes a more compelling photo than the peaceful marcher) or by subscribing to what they perceive to be their audience's common-sense viewpoint (e.g., a labour–management dispute as a disruptive inconvenience to the public). Regardless of whether we can establish intent, journalists' subjectivity and conventional notions of news reporting once again come into play.

The point here is that journalists are implicated in this process of *meaning production* in three specific ways:

- Journalists decide what is news.
- Journalists attach relative importance to news events.
- Journalists interpret those events through the language choices that constitute their coverage.

This production of meaning is significant because, as communications scholar Tony Bennett (1996: 296) observed, "The power which the media derive from their reality-defining capability is attributable to the service they perform in making us the indirect witnesses to events of which we have no first-hand knowledge or experience."

Source: The Canadian Press/Jake Wright.

A news photograph of a demonstration captures only a fragment of the entire event at a precise moment in time. But it nonetheless becomes the picture of that event for the news consumer. Think about which type of demonstrator is shown in this news photograph, how the person is depicted, and how this image shapes our understanding of the larger event.

Journalism as a Sociocultural Institution

Journalism is a sociocultural institution in the sense that it both informs and is informed by the society and culture in which it is practised. As a social institution journalism is integrated politically because, in a democratic society such as Canada, it assumes the role of serving democracy through its fact-finding mission. Journalism is integrated economically because it is an industry in and of itself, the news media are a key advertising vehicle, and the structure of news organizations within a large-scale news industry is consistent with the larger economic organization of Canadian society where predominantly corporate and commercial enterprises comprise and determine the nation's economy.

Journalism is also cultural because journalists produce texts that describe the communities in which we live, privilege certain community values and behaviours, define issues of central importance and situate our community within the larger world. News reportage identifies society's central institutions of power and its most influential players; news reports are often about those institutions—governments, the courts, the police, schools, businesses—and the people who run them—politicians, lawyers and judges, police officers, educators, business leaders.

Through the media we are presented with a picture of our community, its members, and their central preoccupations. The media also offer value judgments about right and wrong, legitimate and illegitimate, whether concerning how we behave, what we wear, how we drive, what we eat and drink, or what political beliefs we hold. Similarly, news coverage draws boundaries around *here* and *there*, and determines what is considered important and relevant to a particular community of people (Gasher, 2015). In this way, journalism makes distinctions between community insiders and community outsiders, establishing a sense of *us* and *them*. As communications scholar John Hartley (1992: 207) has argued, the news "includes stories on a daily basis which enable

10.6 ▶▶ ▶ ▶ ▶ ▶

STATUS OF WOMEN IN THE NEWS MEDIA

A comprehensive global study by the International Women's Media Foundation (2011) found there are equal numbers of men and women working for news media companies in Canada, but women are under-represented in the highest levels of media management and their average salaries are lower than men's in most occupational categories. The IWMF surveyed 11 Canadian news companies—five newspapers, three television stations, and three radio stations—and collected data on close to 14,000 employees (IWMF, 2011: 159).

The study determined that women accounted for approximately half of the workers in junior-level (54.8 percent) and senior-level (45.5 percent) professional positions, categories that include writers, editors, anchors, directors, producers, researchers, reporters, and correspondents. Women occupied half of the middle-management positions (senior editors, chiefs of correspondents, design directors, creative directors, senior human resources, and finance staff) and 55.1 percent of senior-management positions (news directors, editors-in-chief, managing editors, executive editors, human resource directors, bureau chiefs, administrative directors). Women hit the glass ceiling, though, at the top level of management (publishers, chief executive officers, chief financial officers), accounting for 39.4 percent, and governance positions (members of governing boards), where they accounted for 26.3 percent. Women predominated in sales, finance, and administrative positions (61.7 percent), but were under-represented in production and design (23.6 percent) and technical professional jobs (13.1 percent) (IWMF, 2011: 160).

With respect to salary, the IWMF study found that men tended to earn more than women in top-level management; senior-level management; middle management; senior- and junior-level professional positions; and in sales, finance, and administration. Most of the positions occupied by women in the news industry were full-time, regular jobs (IWMF, 2011: 161).

everyone to recognize a larger unity or community than their own immediate contacts, and to identify with the news outlet as 'our' storyteller." The boundaries between those defined as us and them are not coterminous with any formal political boundaries or citizenship but can be drawn from any number of bases: for example, gender, race, class, or ethnicity. News media, then, according to Hartley, not only help to define and constitute communities, but in doing so they also draw boundary lines that divide communities into domains of us and them.

Providing a picture of our community—who constitutes that community, what its history is, what its most pressing issues are, and what its norms and values are—is a complex task for journalists. There is always a gap between the reality of community life as we experience it and the constructed reality the news media provide us—that is, between the material world and the news world. Nonetheless, in mass societies such as Canada, where most of us live in large and diverse metropolitan areas, journalism remains a key component of what the political theorist Jürgen Habermas (1996: 55) termed the **public sphere**:

By "public sphere" we mean first of all a domain of our social life in which such a thing as public opinion can be formed. Access to the public sphere is open in principle to all citizens. A portion of the public sphere is constituted in every conversation in which private persons come together to form a public. They are then acting neither as business or professional people conducting their private affairs, nor as legal consociates subject to the legal regulations of a state bureaucracy and obligated to obedience. Citizens act as a public when they deal with matters of general interest without being subject to coercion; thus with the guarantee that they may assemble and unite freely, and express and publicize their opinions freely. When the public is large, this kind of communication requires certain means of dissemination and influence; today, newspapers and periodicals, radio and television are the media of the public sphere.

Habermas traces the emergence of an idealized public sphere to the eighteenth century, a period in the development of democracy when private persons gathered as peers in salons, cafés, and pubs to consider and discuss the issues of the day and come to some determination about them—that is, to form public opinion. This public sphere mediated between society and the state in the sense that it provided a forum for private citizens without formal political power to come together and influence political authority through rational argument. The newspapers of the day became "the vehicles and guides of public opinion" (Habermas, 1996: 58). Habermas regrets that the public sphere in contemporary society no longer operates on the basis of rational argument among private citizens coming together as equals, but has become instead "a field for competition among interests in the cruder form of forcible confrontation" (1996: 59). If the media provide some space for citizens to speak—increasingly so in the digital era—the focus of news coverage is almost exclusively on what are termed *opinion leaders*: politicians, business people, administrators, pollsters, public-relations spokespeople, researchers, intellectuals, and other assorted experts and officials. These people are not speaking for themselves or impartially, but usually on behalf of society's most powerful vested interests. This, again, explains the potential significance of alternative journalism forms, such as blogs and citizen journalism sites, that seek to restore citizens' voices to the mediascape, by relating opinions and points of view we don't

normally hear and by giving voice to people not often provided the opportunity to speak through mainstream media.

The news media's role in the public sphere is significant, given the extent to which we depend on the media for knowledge about our world. When, as citizens, we consider current events like Russian aggression on Ukraine's borders, Central American gang violence, or the relative risks of shipping oil by pipeline or railway, we typically rely on the news media for our knowledge of these issues, and it is through the media that responses to these issues are proposed to us by opinion leaders.

The media serve, too, as **socializing institutions** for all kinds of public attitudes about race, ethnicity, immigration, gender roles, the aged, youth culture, and so on, not only in news reports, of course, but also in advertisements, films, music videos, and television programs. It is through media representations that we are offered pictures of our society and the people who comprise our community. Because these pictures are representations, they are reductive and selective, and they often have an idealized or normative dimension, suggesting *this is the way we should look*. It is through the media that we "meet" the fellow community members and community leaders with whom we have no actual personal contact.

Roger Silverstone sees the media as constituting an environment and emphasizes "the significance of the media for our orientation in the world. . . . The media are both context and contextualized. They both construct a world, and are constructed by that world" (Silverstone, 2007: 6). What he calls the "mediapolis" is a significant moral space where we confront, and make judgments about, others:

> [The media] orient the reader and viewer to a world that embodies the primary values of the society that produces them, notwithstanding the inevitable differences and contradictions within and between societies in such matters. They inscribe judgements of good and evil, of

benevolence and malevolence, both in the narratives of global and national reporting, as well in the dramatization of fiction. There is in all of these frameworks a narrative of us and them, of origins and futures, of boundaries and the articulation of difference, without which our culture, indeed any culture, could not survive. (Silverstone, 2007: 62)

Journalism, like all media forms, is both text and context, a site upon which beliefs and values are developed and communicated, and where they can be reinforced or challenged. Journalists, in this sense, are social actors heavily implicated in this process.

Journalism is often described as a profession, even though, unlike the medical and legal professions, it has no independent regulatory body and requires no mandatory formal training. Anyone who practises journalism, whether as a freelancer, a blogger, or a staff member of a news organization, is a journalist. Unfortunately, we have no current data on who Canadian journalists are—the most recent study reports data collected in 2004 (see Miller, 2005/2006)—and the task of gathering this information has become ever more complicated as the mainstream media reduce the size of their newsrooms through layoffs and buyouts and contract out more work, and as a vast array of citizen journalists and alternative media groups devoted to news and commentary emerge. That said, there is widespread concern that journalism continues to be an exclusive occupation and that the newsrooms responsible for producing the bulk of our original reporting fall far short of reflecting the makeup of the Canadian population.

In the state-regulated broadcasting sphere, inclusivity is a prominent theme of the Broadcasting Act (1991). Section 3(d)(iii) of the Act declares that the Canadian broadcasting system should

through its programming and the employment opportunities arising out of its

operations, serve the needs and interests, and reflect the circumstances and aspirations, of Canadian men, women and children, including equal rights, the linguistic duality and multicultural and multiracial nature of Canadian society and the special place of aboriginal peoples within that society. (Canada, 1991)

Inclusivity is an important issue in a period of globalization and in a country as diverse as Canada, and newsmaking should bear some resemblance to the composition of Canadian society, both in the content generated and in the people employed. Clearly, who reports the news has implications for what gets covered, how, and to whom news reports are addressed (see Nielsen, 2009).

As we noted earlier, there is considerable room for interpretation in judging the news value and the appropriate presentation of a particular event or issue. Therefore, journalists' life experiences—their assumptions, their biases, their prejudices, their values—affect their reportage. In a report to the Canadian Race Relations Foundation, researchers Frances Henry and Carol Tator (2000: 169) concluded that journalists' "own sense of social location, experiences, values and world views, as well as the interests and positionality of publishers and newspaper owners, act as an invisible filter to screen out alternative viewpoints and perspectives." A relatively young reporting staff, for example, may be less aware of, and less sensitive to, issues that pertain to an aging Canadian population, such as the future of the Canada Pension Plan or the costs of prescription drugs. A predominantly male newsroom may be less receptive to issues of particular relevance to women, such as child care, reproductive rights, and sexism, and may be prone to patriarchal views of certain issues that especially involve women, such as sexual assault, spousal abuse, and pay equity (see Goodyear-Grant, 2013; Kimmel and Holler, 2011; Gidengil and Everitt, 2011; and Poindexter et al., 2008).

Henry and Tator argue that the media are particularly important sources for information about Canada's visible minority communities. But because only a minority of Canadian journalists are non-white and because Canadians of colour are rarely interviewed by journalists unless the news item directly concerns race, minority men and women are largely invisible in Canadian news coverage. This invisibility "communicates the message that they are not full participants in Canadian society" (Henry and Tator 2000: 52). Communications research has repeatedly determined that when people of colour are visible in news reportage, they are often depicted in negative and stereotypical ways. Henry et al. write, "A pervasive theme of both news and [dramatic] programming is the portrayal of people of colour as 'the outsiders within,' reinforcing the 'we–they' mindset" (2000: 296–310). People of colour lack access to the media to make their voices heard. Journalism educator John Miller (1998: 137) has argued that this also results in "blind spots" in news coverage: "If few women or visible minorities are in positions where they can determine what newspapers cover and how, issues affecting them are probably not going to receive proper attention or get on the agenda for public debate."

The point is not to turn the news media into organs of advocacy for the disenfranchised. Instead, Kovach and Rosenstiel (2001: 108) explain, "The ultimate goal of newsroom diversity is to create an intellectually mixed environment where everyone holds firm to the idea of journalistic independence. Together their various experiences blend to create a reporting richer than what they would create alone. And in the end that leads to a richer, fuller view of the world for the public."

Legal Parameters Governing Journalism

Freedom of the press is one of the most fundamental rights of a democratic society, and journalism in Canada is practised in a free-press environment. Section 2 of the 1982 Canadian Charter of Rights and Freedoms protects both freedom of expression and freedom of the press under the heading "Fundamental Freedoms":

2. Everyone has the following fundamental freedoms:
   (a) freedom of conscience and religion;
   (b) freedom of thought, belief, opinion and expression, including freedom of the press and other media of communication;
   (c) freedom of peaceful assembly; and
   (d) freedom of association.

The Canadian constitution is careful to extend the historical right of freedom of the press to all other media. As the journalism educator and former journalist Dean Jobb points out, "Books, plays, television documentaries, websites, videos, DVDs, Internet chat groups, online magazines, social-networking sites, new forms of media technology yet to be invented—whatever the medium, Canadians are free to publish and disseminate images and ideas" (Jobb, 2011: 59), subject only to the "reasonable limits" of a free and democratic society, as Section 1 of the Charter notes. Section 2(b) interprets freedom of expression quite broadly, including, for example, commercial advertising and union members' right to express grievances through peaceful picketing during management–labour disputes (Jobb, 2011: 60).

This does not mean, however, that this freedom is absolute, that journalists are free to report whatever they want. Press freedom in Canada is constrained by laws that ensure journalists' freedoms do not compromise the security of the state or the freedoms of other Canadian citizens. And it remains the subject of legal dispute as to whether journalists enjoy a special status, distinct from the freedom of expression enjoyed by all Canadian citizens (Jobb, 2011: 61–3). The courts have determined that broadcast journalists remain subject to the licensing conditions and other regulations applied by the Canadian Radio-television and Telecommunications Commission, as we outlined in Chapters 7 and 8.

Freedom of the press is a core right of all modern democratic states. But this tenet of liberal democracy is not interpreted exactly the same way by all democracies, compelling journalists to work within both national and international legal and policy frameworks. At the international level, Article 19 of the Universal Declaration of Human Rights (United Nations, 1948) provides the ethical foundation. It states,

> para. 1: Everyone shall have the right to hold opinions without interference.

> para. 2: Everyone shall have the right to freedom of expression; this right shall include freedom to seek, receive and impart information and ideas of all kinds, regardless of frontiers, either orally, in writing or in print, in the form of art, or through any other media of his/her choice.

> para. 3: The exercise of the right provided for in para. 2 of this article carries with it special duties and responsibilities. It may therefore be subject to certain restrictions, but these shall only be such as are provided by law and are necessary for the respect of the rights or reputation of others or for the protection of national security or of public order or of public health or morals.

Article 12 of the declaration also addresses infringement of privacy and attacks on honour and reputation: "Everyone has the right of protection of the law against such interference and attack." These two rights, free speech and the right to privacy, always exist in tension with one another. Journalists may have rights, but they also have legal obligations and ethical responsibilities.

While enjoying freedom of the press, Canadian journalists are also subject to national and international law, and they are compelled to subscribe to a variety of ethical codes that address the business of news production. These codes serve as guidelines rather than regulations, and while they may indeed encourage responsible journalism, their primary goal is to ward off legislative intervention.

In addition to the codes of ethics and regulatory bodies that guide Canadian newsmakers to provide fair and accurate reporting (see McCarten, 2013; Ward, 2014), particular Canadian laws aid or constrain the newsmaking process. These statutes are designed to protect the public interest and cover areas like access to information, defamation, privacy, and contempt of court.

Access-to-information laws have recently been enacted in North America as a way of extending the right to freedom of information. The basic principle holds that, in the name of democracy, most government information should be available to the people. Exceptions should be rare and are justified only when public access to information might pose a risk to national security, the privacy of individuals, or the confidentiality of certain political discussions (e.g., the advice of public servants to cabinet ministers). The federal government and all the provincial and territorial governments have access to information legislation, which outlines what kinds of government information are subject to scrutiny and how journalists and ordinary citizens can obtain access (see Jobb, 2011: 191–5).

Access-to-information laws are important to journalists and the general public for two reasons. First, governments are ravenous collectors of information and have considerable data at their disposal, ranging from budget and expenditure documents to tax returns and detailed census statistics. This information is required by journalists to ensure a full understanding of the social, political, and economic issues they cover. Journalists, for example, comprise one of the groups affected negatively by the federal Conservative government's 2010 decision to abandon the mandatory long-form census; census information is invaluable to anyone—journalists, researchers, policy analysts, local governments—interested in a detailed and comprehensive portrait of the

Canadian population. Second, much of a government's daily work and decision-making occurs outside of public meetings. In order for journalists to monitor government activities and report them to Canadians, they need to know what happens beyond public forums. Again, this access to information is required to report on and evaluate government performance.

While freedom-of-expression laws define the positive foundation of journalism, restraint laws define the negative constraints within which journalists must operate. For example, **defamation** (more commonly known as *libel*) is the publication or broadcast of a statement that is both false and damaging to a person's or organization's reputation (Jobb, 2011: 91). This includes the posting of material online. Jobb writes, "Reputation is a precious thing and, like anything else of value, it can be lost, stolen, or destroyed. Defamation . . . is a form of tort law that gives everyone the right to protect their good name from being sullied by the unjustified allegations or criticisms of others" (2011: 90). He insists that defamation law guards reputations as well as good journalism, because "common law and provincial defamation statutes offer defences that protect news stories and commentary that are factually correct, balanced, and fair" (2011: 90). Truth and fair comment, in other words, are defences against an accusation of defamation (2011: 109–15).

There remains some concern among journalists, however, about what is called **libel chill**, prompted by the threat of a costly and time-consuming defamation suit from an individual or organization seeking to ward off public criticism. Good journalism may be the best defence against a defamation suit, but it can be prohibitively costly to go through a long court procedure, and the onus remains on the journalist or news organization to prove that the published or broadcast statement constitutes truthful and/or fair comment. Quebec passed a law in 2009 to prevent such abuse of the legal system (Jobb, 2011: 135).

Among the greatest legal restraints faced by Canadian journalists concerns coverage of criminal and civil court cases. The large and complex category of **contempt of court** ensures the integrity of the court system and brings into play the constitutional right of the accused to a fair trial. Citing the 1967 case of *Hébert v. Québec*, Jobb defines contempt of court as "any conduct that tends to bring the authority and administration of the law into disrespect or disregard" or tends to "interfere with or to prejudice those involved in a court case" (2011: 241). Among the most common restrictions imposed on journalists are publication bans, which prohibit the identification of victims of sex-related crimes or of witnesses to those crimes who are under the age of 18 (Jobb, 2011: 281) and which shield the identity of youth offenders and any victims or witnesses under the age of 18 (Jobb, 2011: 299–301).The Supreme Court of Canada ruled in May 2010 that journalists do not have a constitutional right to protect the identity of their information sources during police investigations, but the Supreme Court agreed that some sources may warrant protection on a case-by-case basis (MacCharles, 2010). The decision upheld a 2001 judgment against editors of the *National Post*, forcing them to release a document received by reporter Andrew McIntosh, who was investigating the role of then prime minister Jean Chrétien in the Shawinigate affair.

Clearly, there is no simple, or universal, definition of freedom of the press. In Canada, freedom of the press is defined in the context of existing laws and judicial interpretations of constitutional guarantees informed by legal precedents.

Economics of News Production

As we discussed at length in Chapter 9, the economics of media production have changed dramatically in the era of convergence as media silos have broken down; as media markets have expanded their borders; as consumers are inundated with free online content; as paid subscriptions of all kinds become a tougher sell; as advertisers abandon the legacy media for cheaper digital platforms; as new competitors appear; and as converged and concentrated media companies put renewed emphasis on cost-cutting to offset reduced revenues. We are in a period when news organizations are searching for new economic models because the old ones—based on some combination of paid subscription, paid advertising, and government funding—appear to be collapsing beneath them. It is far too premature to declare the death of the news industry, or even the newspaper industry, but significant changes clearly are in store (see Edge, 2014).

While it is tempting to blame digital media for the economic challenges legacy news organizations face, a growing number of scholars insists that the news industry's problems began in the 1970s—two decades prior to the advent of World Wide Web—as news organizations became part of concentrated corporations (see Compton, 2010; McChesney and Nichols, 2009; Cooper, 2011; and Edge, 2014). Mark Cooper states bluntly, "Quality journalism was undermined by the commercial corporate business model that sought to squeeze high rates of profit out of highly concentrated markets by pressuring variable costs—reporters—to produce more with less. As the quality of the product declined, so too did the value of the business" (2011: 320). Cooper's analysis tracked a "massive underinvestment in journalism" starting in 1970. Between 1970 and 2000, he found, news organizations' net advertising revenues grew, but these monies were not reinvested in journalism (2011: 329–30). James Compton argues that the corporatization of the news industry in Canada since the 1970s has resulted in intensified competition for mobile capital investment, increasing sensitivity to stockholders, and imposes flexibility on news workers (2010: 592). This translates into pressures to further commercialize by shaping content to target the most attractive audience markets, compelling journalists to supply content to several media platforms, while at the same time reducing costs, whether that means paying down accumulated debt and/or reducing payroll, including the number of reporters and editors in newsrooms.

Exacerbating this decades-old trend, the networked environment in which journalism functions today creates more competition for audiences and revenues, whether those revenues come from advertising or subscription. On the one hand, it is a multimedia form of competition for audiences; newspapers no longer compete only with other newspapers, but with all media—other newspapers, yes, but also magazines, radio, television, and new digital news providers—on digital platforms. On the other hand, this multimedia competition largely erases the physical boundaries of conventional news markets; while there remains a strong appetite for local or regional news coverage, local media now compete with brand-name national and international players in the general news category, as well as with specialty media in areas such as business and sports, as content is gradually "unbundled" from the omnibus news packages of the legacy media (see Anderson et al., 2012: 8).

With all media now sharing the same digital newsstand, the value of a news organization's reputation becomes more important than ever. Marquee news providers like the BBC and *The New York Times* become the go-to sources for international news and analysis, while smaller players seek their own niche, the kind of news package that allows them to compete for audiences' attention. Anderson et al. explain: "So many sources of news are now available that any publication with a reputation for accuracy, probity or rigor has an advantage over the run-of-the-mill competition" (2012: 97).

The competition for advertising is similarly double-edged. News organizations in the same market continue to compete for advertising, but what is new is that an increasing amount of advertising is moving to digital platforms. This has had a negative impact on the news industry because digital advertising revenues do not come close to replacing advertising revenues on legacy platforms, and a significant portion of digital advertising goes to non-journalism sites like Craigslist, Yahoo, Facebook, and Google. This is a particularly vexing problem for the newspaper industry, as papers are maintaining their readership numbers by offering both print and digital options, but revenues are not keeping pace. A study by the World Association of Newspapers (2014) notes that while digital advertising revenues worldwide increased by 47 percent between 2009 and 2014, they did not make up for the 13 percent decline in print advertising over the same period. Digital advertising for newspapers "remains a relatively small part of overall internet advertising. Much of internet advertising revenue goes to only a handful of companies, and most of it goes to Google." Globally, the World Association reports, 93 percent of all newspaper revenues are generated by the print edition. This general trend applies to Canada as well, where print revenues remain "the foundation of the business" even as digital revenues rise (Hamilton, 2012). The dilemma for newspaper companies is that the printing and physical distribution of newspapers accounts for about half of their production costs; but it is the print edition of the newspaper that continues to pay the bills.

One attempt by the industry to meet the challenges of this new economy is a shift in audience address. This has happened gradually, but has intensified as news organizations respond to the increased competition of convergence by chasing markets rather than publics. If news organizations once felt compelled to address a general audience as part of some sense of public service, the trend instead is toward targeting those readers, listeners, and viewers most attractive to advertisers. This can mean increased emphasis on coverage of topics like business and sports, as well as a shift in how stories are told. News stories about labour–management disputes, for example, are told from the perspective of business and consumers rather than from the perspective of the affected workers. News stories about topics like poverty and homelessness speak to an affluent middle class rather than to the poor themselves, and they define poverty and homelessness as problems from their audience's perspective (see Nielsen, 2009; Jackson et al., 2011). An illuminating exercise is to read through

the travel or style section of the Saturday edition of *The Globe and Mail* and ask yourself who the stories are speaking to.

The economic uncertainty of today's news industry has a profound impact on both the working conditions and the resources available to journalists, whether they work for commercial news organizations or online start-ups; whether they are permanent employees, contract workers, or freelancers; or whether they are entering the job market straight out of school. Journalism is first and foremost a product of human labour. A story idea, the research behind it, the interviews that inform it, and the final presentation of the news item itself all require skilled labour. As Anderson et al. describe it,

> Getting key bits of descriptive information out of eyewitnesses, aggressively challenging the verbal responses of a seasoned government bureaucrat, knowing exactly where to find a key document, or navigating the routines and idiosyncrasies of complex modern organizations is a non-trivial intellectual endeavor, and a public good to boot. In many instances, the most important aspects of individual journalistic work remain what they've always been at their best: interviewing, making direct observations and analyzing individual documents. (2012: 23)

Not to mention crafting this information into a concise and compelling story package.

When Canadian newsrooms downsize, laying off or buying out the contracts of reporters, editors, and photographers, there is a qualitative impact on the journalism those newsrooms produce. The reporters who remain are squeezed to produce more content—often filing several stories per day, with less time and effort spent on each—and to provide updates to online and mobile platforms and promotional feeds to social media networks. Such pressures result in fewer opportunities for enterprise reporting; more single-source reports; more stories based primarily on news releases, news conferences, and official announcements; stories that are inadequately researched or fact-checked; and more stories produced by journalists who have little experience or knowledge of the topics they cover. As news organizations downsize their newsrooms, more journalists work on short-term contracts or try to survive on freelance rates that have not increased since the 1980s (see Cohen, 2012).

Among these pressures, journalists are being asked to play a more active role in building audiences to sell to advertisers. The notion of journalistic independence used to mean, in part, maintaining a clear separation between the editorial and the business sides of news organizations, particularly at newspapers. This so-called wall was never completely impenetrable; the travel and automotive sections of newspapers have always had everything to do with selling ads and very little to do with journalism, and newspapers large and small have often featured **advertorials**, or promotional material thinly disguised as a news story (usually with a different typeface and identified by the advertorial label). But the wall between the advertising and editorial departments is crumbling. Even the most reputable newspapers now allow advertisements on their front pages, and editors are often asked to team up with salespeople in planning distinct content sections around special events: major sporting events, cultural festivals, trade shows, and so on. The latest steps in this direction are called **brand journalism** and **native advertising**, in which journalists are being recruited to produce content that becomes a deliberate hybrid between journalism and promotion (see Box 10.7).

10.7 ▶▶▶▶▶▶

THE MARRIAGE BETWEEN JOURNALISM AND MARKETING

Two recent trends are bringing journalism and marketing together. Brand journalism consists of stories produced by journalists and paid for by companies or associations seeking to draw attention to their sphere of activity, if not directly to specific products or services. Typically, they are published in a magazine or posted to a website owned by the brand sponsor. Examples include articles about automobile travel and maintenance in *CAA Magazine*, articles about food and drink in the appropriately named *Food and Drink*, a glossy produced by the Liquor Control Board of Ontario, and blog posts and DIY videos posted on the Home Depot website (Basen, 2012; Ostrikoff, 2013). Journalist Ira Basen writes, "Brand journalism is storytelling meant to draw readers to a company's field of expertise, without laying on the hard sell. . . . The stories may be fairly and accurately reported by respected journalists . . .

but the fundamental aim remains marketing. It is always more about the brand than the journalism: It's not an attempt to ferret out the truth between opposing narratives" (Basen, 2012: F1).

Native advertising is a form of sponsored content published in newspapers and magazines, similar to what used to be called advertorials. They are articles constructed as news stories with the difference that they carry a label identifying them as sponsored content and are typically set in a different typeface than the neighbouring news stories. Native advertising generates revenue for the news organization and allows advertisers to better integrate their messages by avoiding the "ad ghetto" (Basen, 2012). "The essence of native advertising is that content that originates from a brand should be given the same prominence on the page or the screen as editorial content." A number of newspapers and magazines respected for their journalism have entered the native advertising market: *The New York Times*, *The Washington Post*, *The Economist*, and *The Globe and Mail*. The *Globe* launched its native advertising initiative in April 2014; the content is produced by freelancers under the direction of the advertising department, and the resultant articles carry "sponsored content" labels and set against a yellow background to distinguish them from news stories (Baluja, 2014b).

As we have suggested throughout this chapter, news stories are selective representations of the universe of daily events going on around us. Both the stories that are told and how they are told owe something to the prevailing values that define newsworthiness, the particular content needs and budget of the news organization, and the beliefs and ideas that tend to predominate in society (see Figure 10.3). In any consideration of the question, *What is news?*, a number of factors are at play. Jaap van Ginneken (1998: 60–3) has usefully identified five categories of "values" that are promoted widely and continuously and, hence, tend to predominate in the news coverage of the Western democracies:

1. The economic values of free enterprise and a free market.
2. The social values of individualism and social mobility.
3. The political values of pragmatism and moderation.
4. The lifestyle values of materialism and autonomy.
5. The ideological values that the West's point of view is based on scientific reason, while the views expressed in developing and non-Western countries are based on dogma.

These values, van Ginneken asserts, are widely shared among Western journalists, with the result being that they are taken for granted and through news media discourse become "naturalized." As these perceptions are subscribed to, particularly by those in power, they form a society's "dominant ideology." Alternative views, such as the belief in the necessity of market regulation or the balancing of individual with collective rights are thereby positioned as deviant or "unnatural."

The Future of Journalism

No one can tell us exactly what journalism as a practice or as an institution will look like 10 years from now—although there is no shortage

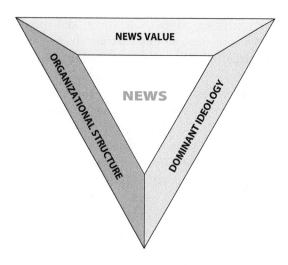

FIGURE 10.3 Defining the News

News can be seen as a product of the complex tension among the factors that inform news value; the economic, time, and space constraints of organizational structure; and the beliefs that comprise the dominant ideology in society.

of people who claim to be able to see the future (see Anderson et al., 2012; Shirky, 2008; Rettberg, 2008; Gillmor, 2004). Will legacy news organizations evolve and survive? If so, which ones? Will newspapers continue to print and deliver hard copies, or will they close up their printing plants and go completely digital? Will digital start-ups assume a more significant share of the original reporting that is the foundation of journalism? Which of those start-ups will establish a viable business model and be able to pay journalists fairly for their work? What will the journalism these news organizations produce look like? Will all news outlets become multi-platform? Will we see increasing topic specialization and the continued treatment of audiences as markets?

All of these unanswered questions mean it is an exciting time to be studying media because we can watch these developments as they take place, possibly even participate in them. But we have to temper our wishful thinking—for a digital revolution, a new golden age of journalism, or at least a corporate media comeuppance—with careful analysis of what is going on. Journalism is restructuring,

10.8 ▶▶▶▶▶

JOURNALISM WITHOUT JOURNALISTS?

The newsrooms of Canadian news organizations have been hard hit by the news industry's economic uncertainty. The Canadian Media Guild, a trade union representing 6,000 media workers, has estimated that 10,000 Canadian media jobs were lost between 2008 and 2013 through a combination of layoffs and buyouts (Wong, 2013). Sun Media, then Canada's largest newspaper publisher, added 200 to that number in December 2013, including 50 editorial positions (Quebecor, 2013). And the trend continued in 2014, as the *National Post* cut 7 positions and *The Globe and Mail* eliminated 9 in January (Baluja, 2014a). Postmedia announced 5 layoffs from its Parliament Hill bureau in March, along with the buyouts of 7 editorial staff at the *Ottawa Citizen* and 5 at the *Montreal Gazette* (Baluja, 2014a). In April, the CBC cut 657 positions as part of its strategy to cope with a $130-million budget shortfall, which is expected to lead to more job cuts—between 1,000 and 1,500 people—by 2020 (Kane, 2014; Bradshaw, 2014a), and Global News laid off 55 people as part of a reduction of 400 jobs throughout Shaw Media. The Star Media Group shut down the free print editions of *Metro* in Saskatoon, Regina, and London, Ontario, resulting in 25 layoffs in July (Dobby, 2014). And in August 2014, CTV cut 7 contract positions associated with its flagship newsmagazine show *W5* (Baluja, 2014c).

creating new conditions for the production of news. What will those new conditions be?

Alternatives to mainstream journalism have existed since at least the 1960s: campus radio stations and newspapers, non-profit community radio, community-access television, documentary film cooperatives, "underground" or alternative weekly newspapers (see Skinner, 2010: 225–31). These media tell different stories and adopt distinct storytelling styles. But there has been a veritable explosion of news providers and distributors since the mid-1990s. Perceiving a need for other approaches to journalism, they initially capitalized on the accessibility and distributive powers of the internet, and more recently have taken advantage of increasingly ubiquitous hand-held communication devices, resulting in what Natalie Fenton (2010) calls "the expansion of the locus of news production." This new media ecology includes social networking sites as both research resources (e.g., Twitter, Facebook, WikiLeaks) and circulation sites (e.g., Twitter, Facebook, YouTube). Although the bulk of the hard work, and most of the best journalism, still is produced by mainstream news organizations, it seems clear that the future of journalism will be digital and will include many more "born-digital" news providers.

The traditional news media were among the first to jump on the internet bandwagon in the mid-1990s, and they continue to evolve their online presence and attract significant audiences, even if they have been slow to invest resources in their digital operations (see Box 10.9). But the ease of use and affordability of digital technology, the accessibility of the internet, and the increasing media production skills of more and more people have combined to lower dramatically the barriers to entry to journalism, spawning thousands of new participants in the fields of news production, distribution, and commentary. Some, like The Tyee (thetyee.ca), Rabble (rabble.ca), The Dominion (www.dominionpaper.ca), and The Real News Network (therealnews.com), seek to provide independent and original news reporting and commentary. Many other sites aggregate news from other providers (e.g., canadanewsdesk.com, national newswatch.com) or house the personal blogs of professional and amateur commentators on every topic under the sun (e.g.,www.blogscanada.ca).

Clearly, some trends appear to have staying power. Anderson et al. (2012) outline what they

10.9 ▶▶ ▶ ▶ ▶▶

MULTIPLYING PLATFORMS

Clear signs that news organizations are abandoning the silo-media approach came with announcements in 2014 that the newspaper publisher Postmedia and the radio and television broadcaster CBC were adopting their own respective full-fledged multi-platform strategies. Postmedia revealed its "four-platform strategy" in May, an approach that began at the *Ottawa Citizen*, to be followed a few months later at its sister paper, the *Montreal Gazette*. Based on survey research that determined each platform attracts a distinct readership, the strategy involves tailoring content to each platform. The *Citizen*, for example, will feature more graphics and information boxes, with an emphasis on context and analysis and a focus on local news coverage, including Parliament Hill. The *Citizen* website will specialize in breaking news and the smartphone app will have a constantly updated news feed with "short and snappy" stories aimed at a younger audience. The *Citizen*'s iPad edition will be published each day at 6 P.M. as a "digital magazine," featuring interactive graphics, animation, and embedded audio and video (Duffy, 2014).

The CBC, which began radio broadcasting in the 1930s, television broadcasting in the 1950s, and was among the first Canadian news organizations to embrace the World Wide Web in the 1990s, announced its "digital-first" approach in June 2014 as part of a five-year plan to shift resources from its traditional broadcasting services into a new stream of mobile content. The plan calls for the production of more content tailored specifically for mobile devices. Among the consequences will be the reduction of some local television suppertime newscasts from 90 minutes to 30, more production through external partnerships, and a projected loss of between 1,000 and 1,500 jobs by 2020 (Bradshaw, 2014a). Journalist James Bradshaw writes, "It is an effort to transfer the broadcaster from a television and radio powerhouse to a leaner, more nimble organization that targets smartphone and tablets first to find readers, viewers and listeners wherever they are" (2014a).

call the new "post-industrial journalism" as consisting of the **unbundling** or specialization of content (what they call "expert journalism"); increased forging of partnerships with other information providers (e.g., WikiLeaks, foundations, university research centres); increased use of publicly available data; increased reliance on crowds and computer programs for data collection and analysis; and greater collaboration in general between journalists and members of the public, experts in all fields, and technology. From the perspective of news consumers, it would seem clear that mobility is part of this future; we will access news when and where we want it. If newspapers and magazines were the original mobile media (Sheller, 2014), media content of all kinds is now delivered to our hand-held devices and the tendency is to access news on numerous devices, depending on what news we want, and when and where we want it. A 10-country survey by the Reuters Institute for the Study of Journalism (Newman and Levy, 2014) found a significant move away from single-device access to news. Thirty-nine percent of survey respondents used at least two devices to access news, while 12 percent used three or more. Computers were the most common access point, followed by smartphones and tablets (Newman and Levy, 2014: 9). A trend to monitor in the future is the tendency of those who access news via smartphones to rely on fewer news sources than those using computers or tablets. Fifty-five percent of UK respondents said they accessed only one news source when using their smartphone (Newman and Levy, 2014: 11).

As intriguing as these new possibilities are, a central issue remains the question of resources. How sustainable is the sphere of digital start-ups, alternative media, and citizen journalism initiatives? As we emphasized above, journalism is produced by people with a skill set for obtaining newsworthy information, making sense of it, and relating it to audiences in a concise and compelling manner. Such journalists tend to work best when they have the support of a reputable and well-resourced news organization, which allows them appropriate amounts of time and funding for their work, editorial assistance, and legal support (if required), not to mention a regular paycheque.

As we discussed in Chapter 6, new media technologies do not have lives of their own. They are embedded in a context informed by history, politics, economics, and culture. As David Sholle (2002: 9) puts it, "If we are really to assess the 'newness' of digital technologies, we must look beyond these technical elements themselves to changes that connect them to changes in social relations, values, goals, and modes of thinking." Natalie Fenton maintains that the most

significant characteristics of digital technologies—speed, space, multiplicity, polycentrality, interaction, and participation—must be evaluated in terms of their actual application. Speed refers to the immediacy of digital technologies and space refers to their expanded geographical reach in a global network. But in actual newsroom application, speed can have a negative impact on journalism when reporters are required to file constantly to keep websites current, preventing them from further developing stories and verifying information. And in the context of smaller news staffs filing stories more frequently, this can confine reporters to their desks, reducing the number of journalists working outside the newsroom and thus shrinking the geographical reach of their reporting. *Multiplicity* and *polycentrality* refer to the increasing number of news providers and the many-to-many dissemination of information. But as a

10.10 ▶▶▶▶▶

CANADIANS DON'T WANT TO PAY FOR ONLINE NEWS

The widespread and free provision of online news and commentary has been a serious challenge for commercial news organizations, which typically pay for the costs of their original news production through a combination of subscription fees and advertising. These legacy media are responsible for the most significant and popular online news sites, but their attempts to charge subscription fees and erect paywalls for their electronic editions have largely failed, and they do not attract the levels of advertising their printed editions used to command. Some newspapers, like *The Globe and Mail*, *The Times* of London, *The Wall Street Journal*, *The New York Times*, and Montreal's *Le Devoir*, continue to charge visitors to their sites for access to at least some portions of their news packages.

The Canadian Media Research Consortium reported in a March 2011 survey that most Canadians reject the idea of paying for online news. The study noted that 92 percent of survey respondents said they would seek another free site if their favourite news sites started charging for content. Eighty-one percent said they would not pay to read their favourite online news site (Canadian Media Research Consortium, 2011).

These attitudes may change, of course, particularly if more and more of the quality and specialty news organizations retreat behind paywalls and comparable information cannot be found free of charge. After all, Canadians quickly got used to paying for drinking water when they were sold on the idea that bottled water was superior in purity and taste to freely available tap water.

A 2014 survey of news consumption habits in 10 countries, in fact, found increasing numbers of people willing to pay for online subscriptions to news sites: 47 percent of respondents in France, 63 percent in the United Kingdom, 68 percent in the United States, and 75 percent in Denmark (Newman and Levy, 2014).

number of studies indicate, this mostly results in the same stories told the same way on more news sites. Finally, Fenton argues, the benefits of interactivity and greater participation have been much exaggerated (Fenton, 2010: 559–64). She maintains that "many of the positive claims for new media reside in a small set of extraordinary examples and rest largely on the potential of new media alone to re-invigorate democracy rather than a consideration of technology in an economic, cultural, and technological context" (Fenton, 2010: 561).

 ## SUMMARY

It is easy to forget how much productive activity can go into media content, and this is particularly the case with journalism, which seeks to present news events as unobtrusively as possible. News is constructed or produced within a specific context, and it is informed by professional ideals, the nature of its textual forms, the sociocultural particularities of the diverse communities that journalism serves, the restrictions of Canada's legal system, the economic imperatives of news production, and the emergence of a networked and more competitive mediascape.

As a form of storytelling, journalism is based on real people and real events. But rather than mirroring reality, as is often suggested, the news media instead frame reality, selecting particular events, people, and aspects of a story as newsworthy, while excluding many others. News texts unavoidably attribute meaning to events, which is a significant matter when we depend on the media for so much of our knowledge of an increasingly interconnected world.

Journalism shares some of the characteristics of other forms of storytelling, but it is distinguished by the following features: its guiding ideals of truth-seeking, independence, and objectivity; the ethical and legal rights and obligations of the practice in a free-press environment; and the institutional context of news production. Freedom of the press, one of the linchpins of news reporting, does not mean that journalists are free to report whatever they choose. Such constraints as privacy and defamation law keep news producers in line with accepted notions of integrity.

Similarly, most original news production is conducted by media organizations that need to sell audiences to advertisers. The economics of news production is changing dramatically, and all news providers—commercial news organizations as well as digital start-ups—are searching for new and viable business models. This has become the principal concern facing journalism in Canada today.

The most exciting development in journalism, of course, is the emergence of new news providers, and new multi-platform initiatives by legacy news organizations. This ongoing experiment is creating new openings in the mediascape and new answers to the questions of what journalism is for and what role it is to play in contemporary society. To what extent will journalism be just another form of commodity production and to what extent can it live up to the ideal of being a central component of a democratic communications system?

 ## KEY TERMS

access to information, p. 280
advertorials, p. 295
brand journalism, p. 285
contempt of court, p. 292
defamation, p. 292
fourth estate, p. 280

framing, p. 277
freedom of the press, p. 278
gatekeeping, p. 274
libel chill, p. 292
mediation, p. 270
native advertising, p. 295

RELATED WEBSITES

Canadian Association of Journalists: www.caj.ca
The CAJ is a national organization of journalists, which both advocates on behalf of Canadian journalists and promotes excellence in journalism. The site contains news pertaining to journalism as well as a calendar of upcoming talks and meetings across the country.

Canadian Journalism Foundation: www.cjf-fjc.ca
The mission of this non-profit foundation is to promote and reward excellence in journalism. It contains news of interest to journalists as well as a calendar of events and programs it sponsors across Canada.

Canadian Journalism Project: j-source.ca and projetj.ca
A joint initiative by journalism educators across Canada, this comprehensive site brings together a wealth of news, commentary, and reference information about journalism and journalism education in Canada. The CJP has English- and French-language sites.

Media Magazine: www.caj.ca/media-magazine-archives
Published twice a year by the Canadian Association of Journalists, the magazine contains news and feature articles pertaining to the practice of journalism in Canada.

Fédération professionnelle des journalistes du Québec: www.fpjq.org
This association of Quebec journalists publishes a very good French-language magazine, *Le 30*, and holds a conference each fall addressing the practice of journalism and the theoretical issues facing the news industry.

 FURTHER READINGS

Anderson, C.W., Emily Bell, and Clay Shirky. 2012, November. *Post-Industrial Journalism: Adapting to the Present*. New York: Tow Center for Digital Journalism. This study provides a good look at the ongoing transformation of journalism and while it delves into prognostication, the research is based on current trends.

Jobb, Dean. 2011. *Media Law for Canadian Journalists*, 2nd ed. Toronto: Emond Montgomery Publications. This is a current and comprehensive guide to the legal environment in which Canadian journalists operate.

McChesney, Robert W., and Victor Pickard, eds. 2011. *Will the Last Reporter Please Turn Out the Lights: The Collapse of Journalism and What Can Be Done to Fix It*. New York and London: The New Press. This collection of essays by scholars, journalists, and activists addresses the current crisis in journalism and proposes ways to both salvage and improve the institution.

Silverstone, Roger. 2007. *Media and Morality: On the Rise of the Mediapolis*. Cambridge: Polity Press. This thought-provoking study posits the media as a contemporary social space in which we come to moral judgments about sameness and difference.

Stuart, Allan, ed. 2010. *The Routledge Companion to News and Journalism*. London and New York: Routledge. This comprehensive treatment of journalism covers a broad range of topics in both classic texts and new studies.

STUDY QUESTIONS

1. In what ways are news stories highly constructed?

2. Why does it matter that news stories are constructed?

3. What is the problem with the mirror metaphor as it is applied to journalism?

4. What challenges do journalists confront in trying to produce truthful, fact-based news stories?

5. What is the critical realist approach to objectivity? What is pragmatic objectivity?

6. How does the language of a news story produce meaning?

7. In what ways does journalism act as a socializing institution?

8. Why does it matter who journalists are, in terms of their age, sex, race, ethnicity, education level, and so on?

9. Freedom of the press in Canada is not an absolute right. What are some of the legal limits on this constitutional guarantee?

10. We have described journalism in this chapter as "networked." What does this mean and what is the danger in perceiving journalism in this way?

11. What is the greatest challenge facing both legacy media and newly established news organizations?

IV

An Evolving Communications World

11 Globalization

The local is increasingly lived under the shadow of the global.
— Stephen Coleman and Karen Ross

Opening Questions

- What do we mean by globalization?
- How does globalization affect the ways we communicate?
- In what ways can the media be perceived as agents of globalization?

- How does globalization shape the international flows of communication goods and services?
- How does globalization affect our sense of community, our sense of place?

Introduction

As we signalled in Chapter 1, and as has been evident throughout the book, Canadians' communication practices, government policy formation, and the activities of our cultural industries are in no way confined by municipal, provincial, or national borders. In an era of globalization, national communication systems can be seen as subsystems within a much larger and increasingly integrated global communication system, influenced and shaped by extra-national social, political, and economic currents, as well as by the everyday practices of media users, whether they are downloading music or video, accessing social networking sites, or reading news from abroad. In fact, we could say that the development of new information technologies has been very much part of the global reorganization of the capitalist economy since the mid-1970s. In this chapter, we examine globalization in broad terms and consider what globalization means for how each of us lives and communicates.

The activities and institutions we have described under the heading of "mass communication in Canada" are not, and never have been, exclusively Canadian. In television, radio, magazines, and on the web, foreign, particularly American, media abound in Canada. Similarly, Canadians' communicative practices—letters, telephone calls, emails, magazines, newspapers, books, music recordings, television programming, films, web surfing—have always been tied into international circulation. Federal and provincial cultural policy always has been informed both by universal covenants (e.g., freedom of expression, the sharing of the radio broadcast spectrum) and by the policies of neighbouring legal and political jurisdictions. Canadian media institutions were established and have continued to evolve in the context of other national media (particularly those of the United States). What distinguishes the current epoch is that the reach and speed of the mass media have increased so dramatically that borders, which in the past partially shielded one nation's communications

system from those of other nations, have become increasingly porous. Distance is less an impediment to communication, and the distinctions between "here" and "there" are increasingly fuzzy. Globalization has altered our **media geography**, shifting dramatically the parameters of the world in which we live and in which we engage in communicative activities.

Many are tempted to look at technological innovation as the principal, if not sole, determinant of this global integration. But, as we have discussed in previous chapters, if technology has played an undeniably significant role in enabling global communications, so, too, have communication law and cultural policy, trade liberalization, and changing social and cultural conditions. Building on our discussion in Chapter 2, in this chapter, we explain at length what globalization means, describe the ways in which the mass media serve as agents of globalization, and document briefly the general patterns of global information and communication flows. We follow with a discussion of how theorists have come to understand the importance and impact of globalization, and then focus on policy debates surrounding the New World Information and Communication Order in the 1980s and the World Summit on the Information Society in the 2000s. Finally, we consider how our globalized communicative activities have affected our sense of place.

Defining Terms

While the term *globalization* is often used to refer to the world's increased economic interdependence—formalized by the **World Trade Organization** (WTO), the **North American Free Trade Agreement** (NAFTA), and the ASEAN Free Trade Area—we define globalization as "the set of processes by which social, cultural, political, and economic relations extend further than ever before, with greater frequency, immediacy, and facility." More specifically, globalization refers to the increased **mobility** of people, capital, commodities, information, and images associated with the post-industrial stage of capitalism; with the development of increasingly rapid and far-ranging communication and transportation technologies; and with people's improved—though far from universal or equitable—access to these technologies. Simply put, globalization means we are more closely integrated with the rest of the world than ever before, even if these connections have significant gaps and are not shared equally by all Canadians, let alone by all citizens of the world. Globalization affects each one of us, even if it does so in different ways. The central questions explored here are how globalization changes the world in which we live and how this process influences the way Canadians communicate, how Canadian media companies participate in global networks, and how Canadian governments draft communications and cultural policy.

In economic terms, globalization means that many of us work for companies with operations in a number of countries around the world and that we consume products and services in a global marketplace. When we shop, we buy clothes made in China, wine made in Chile, and furniture made in Sweden. When we go out to eat, we choose among Chinese, Japanese, Thai, French, Italian, Lebanese, and Indian foods. The specific job we do may be part of a production process organized as a transnational assembly line, coordinated from a distant head office, and the product or service we offer likely is destined for export markets. Thomas Friedman (2005: 414–38) cites the example of Dell Computers, whose just-in-time production process includes designers, parts suppliers, and assembly stations in six countries. Those countries, their business leaders, and especially their workers compete with other governments, investors, and workers from all over the world to attract and/or maintain local economic activity. Globalization also means that Canadian media producers and distributors participate in an increasingly global marketplace.

In the political arena, globalization means that governments are increasingly implicated in events that occur well beyond their own borders, whether through international governing bodies

like the United Nations or on their own initiative. Whether the misfortune is famine, disease, war, or natural disaster, political leaders feel increasingly compelled to aid countries many of us cannot easily locate on a map. Canada, for example, was one of a number of Western countries compelled to act diplomatically and militarily in 2014 when Russia sought to repatriate Crimea and eastern Ukraine, in part because Canada has a significant Ukrainian population. Globalization has added further layers of supranational governance which means that Canadian communications and cultural policy must respect a growing list of international covenants.

In the social sphere, globalization means that friendships and family ties extend around the world and that our neighbours come from half a dozen different countries, speak different languages, wear different clothes and worship within different religions. This means that, on a personal level, we are increasingly implicated in world affairs, in large part through our leisure and consumption activities, including media consumption. During the men's 2014 World Cup in Brazil, the English, Brazilian, and Italian teams were followed as closely in Toronto, Montreal, and Vancouver as they were in London, Rio de Janeiro, and Rome.

In the cultural sphere, globalization means that some Hollywood movies are as popular in Tokyo and Madrid as they are in Los Angeles. It also means that we come into contact with more and more cultures through social media links, vacation travel and foreign-language acquisition. The internet connects us to a global newsstand, and to online radio stations and podcasts from places we've never been. What we consider to be Canadian art and cultural performance are increasingly infused by an array of international influences. Indeed, many of Canada's leading writers and performers have their roots in the Philippines, the Caribbean, Egypt, India, and Sri Lanka. Similarly, people around the world consume Canadian cultural exports, from films and television programs to popular music; Alice Munro won the Nobel Prize for Literature in

11.1 ▶▶▶▶▶▶

CANADA'S CHANGING FACE

It should be clear by now that serving Canada, with its vast geography and its scattered population, is one of the greatest challenges facing media organizations, whether their content is music, news, or dramatic entertainment. But that task is even more formidable in an era of globalization when the Canadian population is more diverse than at any time in its history, meaning media audiences may affiliate with any number of communities. The 2011 census conducted by Statistics Canada reported a Canadian population of about 33 million people who claimed more than 200 ethnic origins (Statistics Canada, 2011a, b). Diversity, of course, consists of much more than ethnicity; difference can be based on skin colour, maternal language, religious belief, sexual orientation, as well as on age, sex, education, and income levels.

Immigrants to Canada accounted for 20.6 percent of the population in 2011, the highest proportion of foreign-born among G8 countries. The largest share of recent immigrants—arriving between 2006 and 2011—came from Asia: 13.1 percent from the Philippines, 10.5 percent from China, and 10.4 percent from India. Most recent immigrants (62.5 percent) settled in Toronto, Vancouver, or Montreal. Forty-six percent of Toronto's population is foreign-born, followed by Calgary at 26.2 percent, and Ottawa–Gatineau at 19.4 percent (Statistics Canada, 2011a, b).

Close to one in five Canadians (19.1 percent) self-identify as belonging to a visible minority group, and visible minorities accounted for 78 percent of immigrants to Canada between 2006 and 2011. The three largest visible-minority groups are South Asians (25 percent of visible minorities), Chinese, and blacks (Statistics Canada, 2011a, b).

Two-thirds of Canadians self-identify as Christians (Roman Catholics are the largest group of Christians at 38.7 percent), while 23.9 percent of Canadians claim no religious affiliation. Just 3.2 percent of Canadians are Muslim (Statistics Canada, 2011a, b).

Canada's changing demographic profile is of great significance for media organizations, especially when media managers try to imagine, and ultimately serve, their target audiences. How do they account for such differences of background, language, religion, culture, belief, and life experience? This is a matter of great concern because, as Henry et al. (2000: 296) note, the media "are major transmitters of society's cultural standards, myths, values, roles, and images." Because racial-minority communities tend to be marginalized in mainstream society at large, "many white people rely almost entirely on media for their information about minorities and the issues that concern their communities" (Henry et al., 2000: 296). This applies to all media forms because they all participate in the practice of representing, or offering us a depiction of, Canadian society, through advertising, music, art, video games, films, news reports, blogs, and television dramas and sitcoms.

One response to Canada's increasing diversity has been the establishment of media dedicated to serving these distinct communities. The National Ethnic Press and Media Council of Canada, for example, boasts 530 members whose newspapers publish in English, French, Hindi, Punjabi, Tamil, Greek, Portuguese, Urdu, and Persian among other languages (www.nepmcc.ca). Canada has a national television network serving the Aboriginal population—the Aboriginal Peoples Television Network—and newspapers devoted to the gay and lesbian population (e.g., Pink Triangle Press, *Xtra*).

A second response—albeit much slower—has been the conscious attempt by mainstream media organizations to diversify their staffs, to normalize the depiction of Canadian society as multicultural, multi-racial, multi-faith, and so on. We still have a long way to go in this regard.

Diversity, however it is defined, is a particularly important issue for Canadians, because the communications media have been assigned such a central role in creating a sense of national community, a theme that permeates federal cultural policy. The media are a principal source of images of our country, our fellow Canadians, our place in the larger world, and they play, therefore, a central role in our understanding of who we are as a society. As a socializing institution, the media of mass communication either can continue to exclude people of colour and exacerbate racism and xenophobia, or they can become more inclusive, reflecting Canada's changing demographic profile and facilitating this ongoing social transformation.

What we consider to be Canadian art and cultural performance are increasingly infused by an array of international influences. Similarly, people around the world consume Canadian cultural exports; Alice Munro won the Nobel Prize for Literature in 2013 for an oeuvre of short stories set primarily in small-town southwestern Ontario.

2013 for an oeuvre of short stories set primarily in small-town southwestern Ontario.

In the environmental sphere, we are increasingly aware that how we use natural resources—air, water, land, minerals, plants, fish—in one corner of the world has significant implications for the rest of the planet. Debates over the Kyoto Accord and the subsequent Copenhagen Protocol, each of these an international agreement addressing climate change, symbolize both the difficulty and importance of collective struggles to come to terms with how we are degrading the global environment. In 2013, for example, rock-music legend Neil Young drew attention to the environmental impact—locally and globally—of bituminous sands development in northern Alberta with his cross-Canada Honour the Treaties Tour. In March 2011, when a massive earthquake and subsequent tsunami in northeast Japan caused meltdowns at the Fukushima Daiichi nuclear facility, countries around the world were compelled to examine their own commitments to nuclear energy and safety; Canada and the United States monitored potential nuclear fallout on their west coasts. Diseases, too,

travel globally and quickly. In 2014, Health Canada reported a significant increase in cases of measles in five Canadian provinces, relating the cases to travel to countries such as the Philippines and the Netherlands.

The term *globalization* can be misleading, however, if it implies that all significant social relations now occur on a global scale. Clearly, this is not so. For one thing, we do not all share in the mobility that globalization affords. Second, different aspects of our lives operate at local, regional, provincial, and/or national scales. What globalization more properly refers to is an intensified relationship between social activity on local and global scales (Massey and Jess, 1995: 226). Once predominantly local, face-to-face, and immediate, social interactions now commonly stretch beyond the borders of our local community so that "less and less of these relations are contained within the place itself" (Massey, 1992: 6–7). These trends have only increased in the 20 years since this definition was crafted. While we still talk to our neighbours when we meet them on the street, we also communicate regularly with friends, relatives, and associates—by email, social media, Skype—at the other end of the country and on the other side of the world. Globalization has altered dramatically the nature of human mobility as our travels, whether for business, school, or pleasure, carry us farther and farther afield, expanding the bounds within which most of us live.

Many of the features of globalization are not new. In fact, some theorists argue that the process of globalization is as old as humankind itself (see Lule, 2012: 22–3). International migration, for instance, is not new, nor is the mobility of investment capital or the global circulation of cultural products. What is new about globalization is its intensity: the expanded reach, facility, and immediacy of contemporary social interactions. The migration of people, whether

11.2 ▶▶▶▶▶

INDIGENOUS BROADCASTING

The World Indigenous Television Broadcasters Network was established in 2008 "to retain and grow indigenous languages and cultures" by providing an international forum, support and program exchange network for indigenous cultural producers who often work in minority languages, and serve minority populations in their home jurisdictions. Canada's Aboriginal Peoples Television Network was a founding member, joining broadcasters from Australia, Hawaii, Ireland, New Zealand, Norway, Scotland, South Africa and Taiwan.

regional, intra-national, or international—whether voluntary or forced—has become a more common experience, and many of those who migrate return frequently to their countries of origin. Two decades ago, Russell King (1995: 7) noted, "Nowadays, in the western world, only a minority of people are born, live their entire lives and die in the same rural community or urban neighbourhood." There is a greater circulation today of people seeking to improve their lives, whether they are refugees fleeing intolerable conditions, youths seeking educational and employment opportunities away from home, or what King calls "executive nomads" conducting business in markets around the globe.

Investment capital, too, has become increasingly mobile as companies seek business opportunities wherever they can be found and flee from regions deemed uncompetitive or hostile to free enterprise. Regions of the world are seen primarily as markets—sales markets, resource markets, labour markets—and corporate executives demonstrate less and less loyalty to their traditional places of business. American automakers, for instance, do not need to confine their operations to the Detroit area if cars and trucks can be made more cheaply with comparable quality standards in Canada or Mexico. Similarly, if Hollywood producers seek to reduce costs, they can film in places like Canada or Australia that may offer advantages in terms of currency exchange rates, labour costs, subsidies, and regulatory conditions. Recent Hollywood films shot at least partly in Canada include *Godzilla*, *The Bourne Legacy*, and the Twilight saga (*New Moon*, *Eclipse*, and both parts of *Breaking Dawn*). Companies and their business activities are less rooted to their "home" bases; they seek greater productivity and improved access to international markets wherever these advantages can be found.

Nowhere has capital been more successful at penetrating world markets than in the cultural sphere. The geographer Warwick Murray (2006: 232) cites six factors explaining this: the emergence of new global technological infrastructures; a rise in the velocity of cross-border cultural exchanges; the rise of Western culture as the central driver of global cultural interaction; the rise of transnational corporations in the culture industries; the rise of business culture as the main driver of cultural exchange; and a shift in the geography of cultural exchanges. David Morley and Kevin Robins (1995: 1–11) refer to a "new media order" in which the overriding logic of media corporations is to get their product to the largest possible number of consumers. The internet and mobile, hand-held technologies have expanded the range, the speed, and the possibilities of media distribution networks considerably, by reducing distribution costs, opening up markets wherever people have access to wired or wireless networks, and lowering the barriers to entry for new media producers.

Media images also serve as a reminder of how far our social interactions stretch, the extent to which those relations are technologically mediated, and the implications of such mediation. Morley and Robins (1995: 141) argue,

The screen is a powerful metaphor for our times: it symbolizes how we exist in the world, our contradictory condition of engagement and disengagement. Increasingly, we confront moral issues through the screen, and the screen confronts us with increasing numbers of moral dilemmas. At the same time, however, it screens us from those dilemmas. It is through the screen that we disavow or deny our human implication in moral realities.

Consider, for example, the stark images that television and internet news channels screen for us daily and what this means for our experience of the people, places, and events depicted.

The screen metaphor also applies to globalization itself, the processes of which filter out large segments of the population. This is a point easily ignored by those of us with easy, cheap, 24/7 access to communication technologies. We can assume that everyone enjoys these advantages. Globalization's impact, in fact, is decidedly uneven, dividing people along class lines, in particular. While relatively wealthy, educated urban dwellers have considerable access to the fruits of globalization, those with less mobility and more immediate priorities—food, clean water, shelter, personal safety—are largely excluded, wherever they are in the world. Think of how often we have walked past a homeless person begging in the street while we are using our smartphone.

Not all of us are in a position to reap the benefits of global interconnectivity because we don't all enjoy the same degree of mobility, even in a country like Canada. In fact, many Canadians have been hit hard by the new-found fluidity of investment capital—when, for example, sawmills are closed in British Columbia and automotive manufacturers leave Quebec and Ontario because their owners can simply shut down, pack up, and move in search of more hospitable investment climates. In such instances, those who control global capital are the only true "global citizens." As Zygmunt Bauman (1998: 2) states, "Globalization divides as much as it unites; it divides as it unites—the causes of division being identical with those which promote the uniformity of the globe." Corporations are increasingly free from the spatial constraints of nation-states. Their mobility creates a disconnect between their economic power and any sense of community obligation, whether local, regional, or national (Bauman, 1998: 8–9). Thus, some people, such as the major shareholders of transnational corporations, are full participants in, and major beneficiaries of, globalization processes, while a great many others are denied the benefits. Indeed, if many people are implicated at all, it is as casualties of the economic instability that globalization has created, not as beneficiaries of the wealth that it has created.

Mass Media as Agents of Globalization

Sophisticated and accessible transportation and communication technologies are enablers of globalization. As we saw in Chapters 1 and 2, transportation and communication networks have the ability to "bind space," to bring people and places closer together. They enable people to maintain close contact in spite of their physical separation. Airline connections between major cities allow business leaders and politicians to fly to a meeting in another city and to return home in time for dinner. Frequent email or text messaging connects friends and colleagues in remote locations, minimizing the implications of their actual separation.

In business, organizations need no longer be based on **Fordism**, in which assembly-line operations take place in a single, all-encompassing factory. The particular activities involved in the assembly of a product can now be dispersed globally to take advantage of cheap labour, ready supplies of resources, and/or lax regulatory environments. Alternatively, the production process can be moved closer to markets to minimize distribution costs. Through telephone contact, email, text messaging, and video-conferencing, managers can maintain two-way communication with remote operations, disseminating instructions to submanagers and receiving from them regular progress reports.

Since the end of World War II, globalization has prompted a new layer of international governance to coordinate the increasing number of integrated spheres of activity. Initially this meant the creation of the United Nations in 1945, which addresses military, economic, health, education, and cultural affairs between states. Today, the list of international governing agencies includes the North Atlantic Treaty Organization, the World Trade Organization, the Association of Southeast Asian Nations, Asia–Pacific Economic Cooperation, the African Union, the Group of Seven, the Latin American Integration Association (LAIA), the European Union, and many others.

The flip side of this international cooperation is international interference in cases where states' interests conflict. Globalization means that national governments no longer enjoy uncontested **sovereignty** within their own borders. This has significant policy implications when issues such as Canadian-content regulations, proposed quotas for cinema screens, subsidization of cultural production, enforcement of online hate-speech laws, or enforcement of copyright laws are raised. Countries can choose to ignore international law—something of which China has been accused with respect to international copyright agreements—or they can exert their political and economic might to derail legislation. The United States uses this latter tactic with any country's attempt to protect its domestic film industry against Hollywood's dominance of commercial theatre screens.

The mass media play four specific roles in the globalization process. First, they are the media of encounter, putting us in touch with one another, whether via mail, telephone, email, text messaging, social media, and so on. Second, they are the media of governance, enabling the centralized administration of vast spaces and dispersed places, whether by governments, businesses, or non-profit service organizations. Third, they situate us within the world, offering us a regular picture of where we are, who we are, and how we relate to other people and places in the world. Fourth, they constitute a globalized business in

and of themselves, conducting trade in information and entertainment products. Taken together, these roles alter fundamentally the geographical parameters within which we live our lives.

While face-to-face interaction remains integral to interpersonal relations in even the most globalized of environments—on the street, in the park, at work, at school—**proximity** no longer constricts our social interactions. Communications technologies like the cellular telephone and personal computer bind social spaces and enable people to maintain contact across distance, rendering the communications industry "a primary channel of social interaction" (Jackson et al., 2011: 56). This is particularly so as these technologies have become more sophisticated, more accessible in terms of cost, ease of use, and availability, and as these media have entered the private sphere of the home. The high speed of technologically mediated conversations approximates face-to-face communication. Such media enable us to conduct social relations over great distances, and their increasing sophistication minimizes—though does not eliminate entirely—the obstacles inherent to physical separation. There are perhaps no better examples of this than social networking sites like Facebook, LinkedIn, and Twitter, which enable friends, relatives, acquaintances, and colleagues to keep in touch across distance and over time. Often, of course, these media complement face-to-face interactions.

At the same time, as communication theorist Harold Innis points out, communications media enable the centralized governance of a political community on the scale of the modern nation-state and the centralized administration of a transnational corporation that spans the globe. Both national forms of governance and global forms of capitalism require efficient means of communication to establish a coherent agenda, to disseminate instructions and information, to monitor the activities of remote departments, and to receive reports from local managers or governors in the field. This relationship is one of power, in which an authoritative body exercises control over social space and social order (see

Drache, 1995: xlv–xlvi), but it is also increasingly a two-way relationship in which citizens or workers can use the same media to react or respond to these attempts at control. If a country as large and diverse as Canada is difficult to govern, its governance would be virtually impossible without modern communication and transportation technologies.

The scale on which governments and organizations function today can also, paradoxically, isolate nearby regions and peoples, if they are not deemed integral to the networks of governance or of commerce, or if they don't have a population base large enough to constitute either an important political constituency or a viable market (see Castells, 1999, 2001). On a global scale, Murray (2006: 225) notes that Tahiti is one of the most physically remote islands on earth, but remains culturally connected to the industrial West, whereas the Solomon Islands and Papua New Guinea are much closer to Western nations but much more culturally isolated. The cities of Tehran, Baghdad, and Kinshasa are similarly isolated because they are bypassed by global cultural flows. Even in Canada, isolation can occur when transportation companies cut service to some cities and towns because those routes are deemed not economically viable. When, for example, Via Rail in 2012 cut from six to three the number of trips its passenger trains make between Montreal and Halifax, it increased the isolation of people along the route who are dependent upon that connection. Similarly, when Bearskin Airlines made cuts to services on its northern Ontario routes in 2014, it in effect increased the distances between population centres like Sault Ste. Marie, North Bay, Thunder Bay, and Timmins, forcing travellers between these places to choose between much slower bus, train, or automobile travel, or not travelling at all.

The mass media also provide us with a sense of place and identity.

They represent to us who we are, where we live, how we are connected to one another, and how we differ from other peoples and places. These depictions contain value judgments, sometimes expressed explicitly, but more often inferred. Media scholar Roger Silverstone describes media work as "boundary work"; the media draw "macro" boundaries of national and linguistic cultures, but they also draw "micro" boundaries, "work which involves the continuous inscriptions of difference in any and every media text and discourse." This is "their primary cultural role: the endless, endless, endless playing with difference and sameness" (Silverstone, 2007: 19). Advertisements often seek to portray "typical" Canadians engaged in "normal" Canadian activities, offering us a definition of what typical and normal *Canadian-ness* is and suggesting what we look and act like. This is a key theme in, for example, Tim Hortons' corporate branding. Consider, too, the portrayal of the family in Canadian Tire commercials, the representation of Canadian males in Molson beer ads, or the gender roles assigned to men and women in commercials for any number of household cleaning products.

Finally, as we discussed in Chapter 2, the media have become a central constituent of globalization in what is called the *information age* or the **network society**. This means, first,

Advertisements often seek to portray "typical" Canadians engaged in "normal" Canadian activities, offering us a definition of what typical and normal Canadian-ness is and suggesting what we look and act like. What does this Canadian Tire ad convey about "typical" Canadians?

that the cultural industries are conducting a greater proportion of global trade by serving as the conduits for the exchange of information and entertainment commodities, including trade in hardware, such as computers, television sets, and sound systems, and in cultural products, such as books, magazines, DVDs, as well as music and video downloads. Instead of trading these goods and services regionally or nationally, they are increasingly traded on an international or global scale; the world is their market. Jack Lule (2012: 69) notes "the media are themselves now huge transnational global corporations that help drive globalization even as they embody globalization." Second, information and ideas are becoming increasingly important to an economy that now depends on innovation in all industrial sectors. Ideas that can lead to new product development, greater productivity, and the expansion of markets have become essential to maintaining growth in a capitalist economy. Even before the turn of the millennium, then corporate management guru Peter Drucker (1993: 8) maintained that the "basic economic resource" in today's economy is no longer investment capital, or natural resources, or labour, but knowledge. "Value is now created by 'productivity' and 'innovation,' both applications of knowledge to work."

The economic role that the mass media play has considerable implications for how we define communication as *commodity* or as *cultural form* (see Chapters 2 and 9), for who gets to speak (on both the individual and the collective levels), and for what kinds of messages become privileged. As Edward Herman and Robert McChesney (1997: 9) state,

> We regard the primary effect of the globalization process . . . to be the implantation of the commercial model of communication, its extension to broadcasting and the "new media," and its gradual intensification under the force of competition and bottom-line pressures. The commercial model has its own internal logic and, being privately owned and relying on

advertiser support, tends to erode the public sphere and to create a "culture of entertainment" that is incompatible with a democratic order. Media outputs are commodified and designed to serve market ends, not citizenship needs.

By making information an exploitable resource, the democratic ideal of free speech and freely circulating information has been transformed—at least in many sectors—into media proprietors' freedom to exploit world markets with that speech and with that information. This transformation has created the network that benefits the global entertainment and information industries.

This problem is offset somewhat by the emergence of individuals and public-service organizations seeking to employ the same communication technologies for quite different purposes—perhaps to combat economic globalization or militarism, to support environmental or human-rights measures, or simply to create their own cultural products. The question, Dave Sholle (2002: 3) points out, is whether new media technologies "will be an agent of freedom or an instrument of control." Lawrence Lessig (2008: 29–33) notes that the twentieth century was the first time in history that popular culture had become professionalized, creating a stark separation between artists and audiences, what he refers to as a "read-only culture." Digital technologies have reintroduced a more participatory "RW culture" in which people have the ability to create their own art, music, or film, whether it is completely original or based on an artifact of popular culture (e.g., a mash-up, sampling, remix, compilation). YouTube, for instance, features countless examples of such homemade videos. Consumers of media also become producers, or what are sometimes called *prosumers*.

In a more political vein, the same technologies enable the emergence of alternative media organizations; they are alternative in the sense that they present a non-commercial media model that emphasizes "the promotion of public dialogue, the exchange of ideas, and the promotion of social action" (Skinner, 2010: 222). Such media include newspapers (the *Georgia Straight* in Vancouver, *The Coast* in Halifax, *Le Mouton Noir* in Rimouski), magazines (*This Magazine*, *Canadian Dimension*, *Briarpatch*), radio (Radio Centre-Ville in Montreal, Vancouver Co-operative Radio), television (iChannel, Working TV), and, of course, the internet (Rabble.ca, TheTyee.ca).

Global Information Trade

Like other aspects of globalization, the cultural sphere is witnessing the expansion and intensification of a trend that already has a substantial history. This history reveals that international cultural exchanges have always been uneven, with a few sources of communication serving many destinations. This asymmetry intensified dramatically in the second half of the twentieth century as trade flows became increasingly concentrated; 20 countries account for 75 percent of international trade in merchandise and fifteen countries account for 65 percent of the international trade in services (Murray, 2006: 107–9). Murray argues that such economic flows form a "global triad," comprised of the European Union, the United States, and East and Southeast Asia (2006: 110–1). He adds, however, that when we look closer at the global economy, "we see that most investment and trade actually takes place between specialized industrial spaces. These clusters of economic activity increasingly define the global economy and imply even greater spatial concentration of activity than national macro-economic figures suggest" (2006: 110–2).

Terhi Rantanen (1997) points out that a handful of European news agencies—Havas, Reuters, Wolff—began to dominate global news coverage in the mid-nineteenth century and the development of the telegraph and submarine telegraph cables during those years meant that, for the first time, information could reliably travel faster than people. As Herman and McChesney (1997: 12) note in this regard,

From the beginning, global news services have been oriented to the needs and interests of the wealthy nations which provide their revenues. These news agencies were, in effect, the global media until well into the twentieth century, and even after the dawn of broadcasting their importance for global journalism was unsurpassed. Indeed, it was their near monopoly control over international news that stimulated much of the resistance to the existing global media regime by Third World nations in the 1970s.

Herman and McChesney (1997: 13–4) describe the film industry as "the first media industry to serve a truly global market." By 1914, barely 20 years after the advent of the motion picture, the United States had captured 85 percent of the world film audience, and by 1925, US films accounted for 90 percent of film revenues in the United Kingdom, Canada, Australia, New Zealand, and Argentina, and over 70 percent of revenues in France, Brazil, and the Scandinavian countries. Hollywood's hegemony in the film world continues to the present day.

Such developments have been criticized as instances of media imperialism—the exploitation of global media markets to build political, economic, and ideological empires of influence and control. If what used to be called media imperialism is now usually described more palatably as *media globalization*, concerns nevertheless remain that the mass communication sphere has come to be dominated by the world's largest media companies, the majority of them based in Western Europe and North America. The resources of these large, global media companies (e.g., Bertelsmann, Gannett, CBS, British Sky Broadcasting, Liberty Media, News Corporation, Viacom, Time Warner, Disney, Comcast) give them tremendous advantages over smaller, independent producers in terms of their ability to hire skilled professionals (including stars), the aesthetic quality of their productions, the power of their corporate brands, their access to distribution networks, and their ability to advertise and promote their products worldwide (see McChesney, 2003). Their use of digital platforms has only enhanced their ability to penetrate global markets. Global spending on media and entertainment was US $1.45 trillion in 2012, the largest chunk of that for broadband services. Three regions, Asia Pacific, North America, and Western Europe, accounted for 88 percent of that spending (McKinsey and Company, 2013: 4–5).

The point is that the interdependence inherent in globalization is rarely symmetrical. The decidedly uneven flow of information and entertainment products creates a situation in which a few countries, and relatively few companies, produce and profit from the vast majority of media content, leaving most of the world, to a great extent, voiceless. As we address later in this chapter, the United States has since the 1940s adopted an aggressive

posture in promoting the uninhibited flow of information and entertainment products worldwide. As shown in Table 11.1, Hollywood films dominate box offices around the world. Any issue of *Weekly Variety* indicates that theatre screens throughout the world have become a global market for the same Hollywood films we see in North America, although in some countries, such as France and Japan, audiences support indigenous films. Table 11.2, on the other hand, shows that the international popular music scene is somewhat more diverse, even if the bulk of music flows from transnational media companies based in the West, and particularly the United States and United Kingdom (see Murray, 2006: 252–8).

Public broadcasting systems, which operate on a public-service model, are under siege in Canada and around the world. In spite of increasing demands on CBC/Radio-Canada, the public

TABLE 11.1
Top Three Films at the Box Office, Selected Countries, April 2015

Germany	*Interstellar*	USA/UK/Canada
	Die Mannschaft	Germany
	Dumb and Dumber To	USA
France	*Furious 7*	USA/Japan
	Pourquoi j'ai pas mangé mon père	France/Italy/China/Belgium
	Home	USA
Italy	*Furious 7*	USA/Japan
	Mia madre	Italy/France
	Se dio vuole	Italy
Finland	*Furious 7*	USA/Japan
	The Divergent Series: Insurgent	USA
	Reunion	USA
Australia	*Furious 7*	USA/Japan
	Cinderella	USA/UK
	Home	USA
Ecuador	*Furious 7*	USA/Japan
	Paul Blart: Mall Cop 2	USA
	Run All Night	USA
China	*Furious 7*	USA/Japan
	Wan Wu Sheng Zhang	China
	Wolf Warrior	China

Source: Box Office Mojo (www.boxofficemofo.com).

TABLE 11.2
Top Five Music Singles, Selected Countries, April 2015

Country	Single	Origin
Austria	"See You Again"/Wiz Khalifa, Charlie Puth	USA
	"Are You with Me"/Lost Frequencies	Belgium
	"Cheerleader"/OMI	Jamaica
	"Don't Worry"/Madcon, Ray Dalton	Norway/USA
	"Fourfiveseconds"/Rihanna, Kanye West, Paul McCartney	USA/UK
United Kingdom	"See You Again"/Wiz Khalifa, Charlie Puth	USA
	"Cheerleader"/OMI	Jamaica
	"Hold My Hand"/Jess Glynne	UK
	"Can't Stop Playing"/Dr Kucho!, Gregor Salto	Spain/Netherlands
	"King"/Years and Years	UK
Denmark	"See You Again"/Wiz Khalifa, Charlie Puth	USA
	"Lean On"/Major Lazer, featuring MO, DJ Snake	USA/France
	"Fourfiveseconds"/Rihanna, Kanye West, Paul McCartney	USA/UK
	"Stole the Show"/Kygo	Norway
	"Love Me Like You Do"/Ellie Goulding	UK
Spain	"The Nights"/Avicii	Sweden
	"Love Me Like You Do"/Ellie Goulding	UK
	"Fourfiveseconds"/Rihanna, Kanye West, Paul McCartney	USA/UK
	"Cheerleader"/OMI	Jamaica
	"Elastic Heart"/Sia	Australia
New Zealand	"See You Again"/Wiz Khalifa, Charlie Puth	USA
	"Bloodstream"/Ed Sheeran, Rudimental	UK
	"Lean On"/Major Lazer, featuring MO, DJ Snake	USA/France
	"Lay Me Down"/Sam Smith	UK
	"Thinking Out Loud"/Ed Sheeran	UK

Source: Music Charts and Box-Office Ratings (allcharts.org).

broadcaster has had its parliamentary appropriation reduced repeatedly since the early 1990s, the most recent of which was a $115-million cut in 2012. In April 2014, the CBC announced 657 job cuts and its decision to abandon the broadcasting of professional sports in anticipation of a $130 million revenue shortfall in 2014–2015. A significant blow was its loss in 2014 of National Hockey League broadcast rights, and the accompanying advertising revenues, to the private broadcaster Rogers (Houpt, 2014; Taylor, 2014).

Even the venerable BBC, which has come to symbolize the best of public broadcasting, has adopted commercial strategies in some aspects of its operation. The BBC launched its BBC World Service Television as a global commercial venture in 1991, seeking "to capitalize upon the BBC brand name, considered [at that time] to be the second most famous in the world after that of Coca-Cola." In 1996, the BBC established joint ventures with two US corporations to create commercial TV channels for world markets. Herman and McChesney (1997: 46–7) write, "It is clear that the BBC has decided that its survival depends more upon locating a niche in the global media market than in generating political support for public service broadcasting." BBC Worldwide is the commercial arm of the BBC, generating profits of £156 million in 2012–2013 through its channels, content production, digital media, sales and distribution, magazines, and licensing to seven international markets in North America, Asia, Latin America, Western Europe, Australia, and New Zealand (BBC Worldwide, 2014).

What has emerged is a tiered global media market, dominated by US-based companies, which can capitalize on the competitive advantage of having "by far the largest and most lucrative indigenous market to use as a testing ground and to yield economies of scale" (Herman and McChesney, 1997: 52). In recent decades, for example, Canada became an important site of Hollywood film and television production, as US film companies took advantage of the lower Canadian dollar and comparable technical expertise of crews north of the border (see Elmer and Gasher, 2005; Gasher, 2002; Pendakur, 1998). The Hollywood animation industry has similarly taken advantage of the cheap yet stable labour markets of India, South Korea, Australia, Taiwan, and the Philippines for the time-consuming and labour-intensive execution of animation projects originally conceived in Los Angeles (Breen, 2005; Lent, 1998).

The large, transnational media companies are particularly interested in the world's most affluent audiences, because these audiences have the money to spend on advertised products and services. This means, for example, that the poorest half of India's billion people are irrelevant to the global media market and all of sub-Saharan Africa has been written off. The global media are most interested in markets in North America, Latin America, Europe, and Asia.

That said, the global media market does see some two-way traffic. The Globo and Televisa television networks in Brazil, for example, have succeeded in capturing a respectable share of Brazil's domestic market, and their telenovela productions are major exports. Globo is Latin America's largest broadcaster and the world's second-largest commercial television network (based on annual revenue). TV Globo International, a premium television service, has more than 700,000 clients worldwide; its recent telenovela *Brazil Avenue* was sold to 125 countries (Hopewell, 2014).

Canada, too, has begun to tap export markets in both the film and television industries, and it has quickly become the world's third-largest

video-games producer, behind Japan and the United States (CTV News, 2013). A renaissance in Canadian feature-film production since the mid-1980s means that directors like David Cronenberg (*Crash*, *ExistenZ*, *A History of Violence*, *Maps to the Stars*), Atom Egoyan (*Ararat*, *The Sweet Hereafter*, *Where the Truth Lies*, *Chloe*, *The Captive*), Deepa Mehta (*Fire*, *Earth*, *Water*, *Midnight's Children*), Denys Arcand (*Decline of the American Empire*, *The Barbarian Invasions*), François Girard (*Thirty-Two Short Films about Glenn Gould*, *The Red Violin*), Denis Villeneuve (*Maelstrom*, *Polytechnique*, *Prisoners*, *Enemy*), and Xavier Dolan (*J'ai tué ma mère*, *Mommy*) have made names for themselves in international film markets. For the first time in 2014, three Canadian feature films, by Cronenberg, Dolan, and Egoyan, were part of the Palme d'Or competition at the Cannes Film Festival. And Canada has become one of the world's leading exporters of television programming in the episodic, children's, and animation categories, with $454 million in export sales in fiscal 2012–2013 (CMPA, 2013: 9). The police drama *Flashpoint*, which ran on CTV for five seasons, has been sold to 100 territories globally (Wong, 2014). Among other exports are *Bitten*, *Remedy*, *Orphan Black*, *Continuum*, *Lost Girls*, and the Emmy-nominated *Degrassi: The Next Generation* (CMPA, 2013: 40–1; Wong, 2014).

All of this commercial activity, of course, both opens up and limits the circulation of communications goods. What digital technology on the one hand enables is access to a greater variety of both commercial and independently produced cultural products and services. Chris Anderson (2006), the editor-in-chief of *Wired* magazine, talks about the *long-tail* phenomenon, which allows companies to increase their inventory of books, films, and music as digitization reduces the costs of storage; iTunes, for example, can afford to offer older, more obscure, or less popular music because the costs of storing digital recordings for the handful of customers who might want to download them is minimal. Unlike the fast-disappearing local music store, which has only so much room on its display racks and

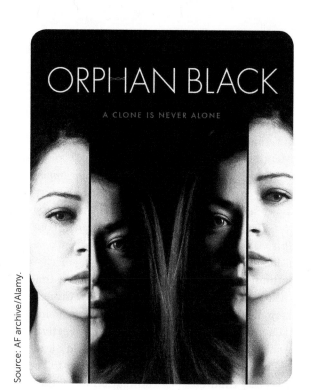

The award-winning *Orphan Black*, a Canadian science-fiction television series starring Canadian actress Tatiana Maslany, has won accolades and fans in Canada, the United States, and the United Kingdom.

so can't carry the same range of CDs, iTunes has a storage capacity that is almost limitless. Digital technology also allows budding musicians to distribute their music directly to listeners, via their own websites, through social media, and/or their own YouTube channel.

That said, it is still all about markets; to sustain the production of a diverse array of cultural materials, content producers need to be compensated. The corporate structuring of the media privileges the production and distribution of the most commercially viable products and services. We recall the comment from cultural theorist Raymond Williams (1989: 88), who underlined the commercial constraints on freedom of expression under capitalism, "where you can say that at times freedom in our kind of society amounts to the freedom to say anything you wish, provided you can say it profitably." The corporate structuring of communication also grants media companies the power to inhibit, even prohibit, the production and circulation of products or services with limited appeal, or products that are critical or threatening in some way (see Box 11.3).

11.3 ▶▶▶ ▶▶ ▶▶

WALLED GARDENS

The much-lauded Apple Inc. provides an example of a corporation that, while introducing a range of innovative computer products and services (e.g., Apple Watch, iTunes, iPhone, iPad, iCloud, Genius Bars) has also constructed an enclosed Apple universe, the kind of *walled garden* that the internet was supposed to eradicate. Apple will sell you the iPad, but it also runs the only stores that sell the software for it. As *Newsweek* explained it, "Instead of making a one-time sale, each iPad sold becomes a recurring revenue stream for Apple" (Lyons, 2010: 49). The iPad runs its own

microprocessor, so that means it will run Apple's Safari web browser only, and it won't play videos created in Adobe Flash software. This forces iPad users to buy their videos from iTunes, and those videos will run only on Apple devices. Other companies are following this same path: Kindle users have to buy their e-books through Amazon, and Microsoft has its own Zune Marketplace for downloads to its Zune music player (Lyons, 2010: 49–50). If Apple's walled garden keeps customers in, it can also keep undesirables out. Apple rejected a proposed iPhone application called NewsToons from Pulitzer Prize–winning editorial cartoonist Mark Fiore because his cartoons ridiculed public figures—corporate policy is to refuse all content deemed by the company to be obscene, pornographic, or defamatory (Trudel, 2010). Thereby, Apple's market dominance grants it a censoring power.

Theories of Globalization

There is a growing body of theoretical work on globalization, by historians, economists, political scientists, geographers, philosophers, sociologists and communications scholars, some celebratory, some critical. In a survey of the major thinkers, Andrew Jones (2010: 11–5) identifies three areas of consensus on globalization and three points of dispute. Theorists agree, first of all, that globalization is part of a long history of societal integration (dating at least as far back as the Roman Empire), that the contemporary period of globalization (since the 1950s) is qualitatively different from previous periods, and that globalization has a complex impact on nation-states. There is disagreement among theorists, however, on whether globalization constitutes a coherent system or whether it consists of several independent processes, whether it is ultimately positive or negative, and what the key drivers behind it are.

The predominant account of globalization to date has been **world systems theory**, as articulated by Immanuel Wallerstein (1974, 2007). Wallerstein's theory posits globalization as an economic phenomenon and, as the name of his theory suggests, he sees it as systemic. He argues that even though humans have engaged in trade for thousands of years (see Bernstein, 2008), a European, capitalist "world economy" emerged in the late fifteenth and early sixteenth centuries. This extra-national economy involved long-distance trade that forged links between Europe and parts of Africa, Asia, and what came to be known as the West Indies and North and South America (Wallerstein, 1974: 15–20). World systems theory focuses on the relationship between nation-states—the world system—rather than on nation-states themselves, and demarcates three zones in the integrated world economy: the core states, characterized by industrialization and the rise of a merchant class; the periphery, comprised of state economies based on resource extraction; and a semi-periphery, made up of in-between states whose economies share some characteristics of both the core and periphery (Wallerstein, 1974: 100–27). Wallerstein suggests that "the size of a world-economy is a function of the state of technology, and in particular of the possibilities of transport and communication within its bounds. Since this is a constantly changing phenomenon, not always for the better, the boundaries of a world-economy are ever fluid" (Wallerstein, 1974: 349). He proposes that capitalism requires a world system (2007: 24) because its participants seek constantly to expand markets and to exploit the most favourable labour markets, regulatory regimes and infrastructure, access to resources, and access to investment capital and government support.

The world system's asymmetry, particularly with regard to trade in cultural materials, drew the attention of communication scholars in the post–World War II period—this led to the development of two closely related theories: *media imperialism* and *cultural dependency*. Oliver Boyd-Barrett (1977: 117–8) used the term *media imperialism* to characterize the unidirectional nature of international media flows from a small number of source countries. More formally, he defined media imperialism as "the process whereby the ownership, structure, distribution or content of the media in any one country are singly or together subject to substantial external pressures from the media interests of any other country or countries without proportionate reciprocation of influence by the country so affected." Media imperialism research grew out of a larger struggle for decolonization in the aftermath of World War II (Mosco, 1996: 75–6).

Cultural dependency is a less deterministic means of characterizing cultural trade imbalances than is media imperialism. Whereas *imperialism* implies "the act of territorial annexation for the purpose of formal political control," Boyd-Barrett (1996: 174–84) maintains that cultural dependency suggests "de facto control" and refers to "a complex of processes" to which the mass media contribute "to an as yet unspecified extent."

While both approaches contributed a great deal to documenting communication flows within the world economy and drew attention to an obvious problem, neither theory offered a sufficiently complex explanation of the power dynamics behind international cultural trade, nor did they provide satisfactory descriptions of the impact of such asymmetrical exchanges. The media imperialism thesis tends to be too crudely applied, embodying elements of the effects theory that we discussed in Chapter 5 and, thereby, assuming too neat a relationship between the all-powerful source countries and their helpless colonies.

Ted Magder (1993) qualifies the media imperialism thesis by underlining four points: the imperial centre is rarely omnipotent; the target nation is rarely defenceless; certain actors within the target nation may stand to benefit from media imperialism; and the effects of media imperialism are often unintended and unpredictable. According to Magder, "It is not enough to document the internationalization of culture in its various forms; rather, the limits, conflicts, and contradictions of media imperialism must also be evaluated" (Magder, 1993: xx).

While slightly more nuanced, the cultural dependency thesis shared a number of the shortcomings of the media imperialism thesis. Like media imperialism, Vincent Mosco (1996: 125–6) argues, the concept of cultural dependency created homogeneous portraits of both the source and the target countries. It concentrated almost exclusively on the role of external forces and overlooked "the contribution made by local forces and relations of production, including the indigenous class structure." Cultural dependency also portrayed transnational capitalism as rendering the target state powerless. Like media imperialism, cultural dependency did not adequately account for how audiences in the target countries used or interpreted media messages that originate elsewhere. Current research seeks to account for the heterogeneity of national cultures, the specificity of particular industries and corporate practices, and varying reception practices—how cultural products are actually used by audiences, including the extent to which people become active

producers themselves through citizen journalism, mash-ups, sampling, and homemade videos (see Lessig, 2008).

Nonetheless, the clear asymmetry of globalization remains an important issue for researchers who study cultural policy and the political economy of communication from a range of perspectives. And it is particularly pertinent to the Canadian case, as we discussed in previous chapters. Canada's relatively small, dispersed population as well as its shared majority language and shared border with the United States have made it an easy target for the US media powerhouse; a central motive behind Canadian public policy for more than a century has been the promotion and protection of distinct and independent cultural production in all areas.

A New Media Ecology

Anthony Giddens (1990, 1999) studies globalization through the lens of sociology. He argues that globalization has transformed our sense of time and space, "disembedding" social relations from their local contexts and restructuring them across "indefinite spans of time-space" (Giddens, 1990: 21; see also Jones, 2010: 39). He writes, "In the modern era, the level of time–space distanciation is much higher than in any previous period, and the relations between local and distant social forms and events become correspondingly 'stretched'" (Giddens, 1990: 64). This "stretching process" is what we mean by globalization. He defines globalization as "the intensification of worldwide social relations which link distant localities in such a way that local happenings are shaped by events occurring miles away and vice versa. This is a dialectical process because such local happenings may move in an obverse direction from the very distanciated relationships that shape them" (1990: 64). Departing from Wallerstein's exclusive focus on economics, Giddens provides a four-dimensional model of globalization with the world capitalist economy, the world military order, the nation-state system, and the international division of labour serving as its component parts. The media serve as the "global extension of the institutions of modernity" (Giddens, 1990: 70–1).

Manuel Castells has proposed another way of looking at the contemporary world that places communication technologies at the centre of global economic—and by extension, social and political—interactions. Castells describes a "network society" that, as its name suggests, is a networked, or interconnected, world, which is less international than internodal, placing major global cities, rather than nations, at the centre of its analysis.

Castells argues that the internet has allowed people to forge a new kind of sociability—"networked individualism" (Castells, 2001: 127–9)—and a new global geography—"a space of flows" (2001: 207–8). Communications technologies form the "unifying thread" that links globalizing processes, so that the "space of flows" creates "a distributed network with clusters around nodes and hubs" (Jones, 2010: 55–9). This interconnected world, then, has considerable implications for the inclusion and exclusion of people and places from the network of global **information flows**. Internet use, he notes, is highly concentrated within a network of "metropolitan nodes" (Castells, 2001: 228), which become the new dominant hubs of economics, politics, and culture. According to Castells, "The internet networks provide global, free communication that becomes essential for everything. But the infrastructure of the networks can be owned, access to them can be controlled, and their uses can be biased, if not monopolized, by commercial, ideological, and political interests" (2001: 277). For this reason, Castells places a new onus on democratic governments to ensure political representation, participatory democracy, consensus building, and effective public policy (2001: 278–9).

Saskia Sassen (1998: xxv) sees in this network society "a new economic geography of centrality" in which certain global cities concentrate economic and political power and become "command centers in a global economy." If Sassen agrees with Castells that this new geography is produced by the internet's most prominent and active users (1998: xxvii), she is nonetheless concerned with the conflict that necessarily ensues between "placeboundedness"—those peoples, activities, and institutions bound to a specific place, often in support of the network infrastructure—and "virtualization"—those peoples, activities, and institutions capable of exploiting Castells's virtual space of information flows (1998: 201–2).

The political economist Vincent Mosco describes the process of overcoming the constraints of space and time as **spatialization**, and he attributes to communication a principal role as an enabling mechanism. He cautions that the global commercial economy does not annihilate space, but transforms it "by restructuring the spatial relationships among people, goods, and messages. In the process of restructuring, capitalism transforms itself" (Mosco, 2009: 157) by becoming increasingly mobile and, following Castells, by clustering together certain communicative activities in "agglomeration" zones (2009: 169). One of the oldest and clearest examples of such spatial agglomeration is Hollywood, which clusters together companies and workers devoted to film and television production, from the writers, actors, and directors to the specialists in editing, lighting, set design and construction, and costume design.

Clearly, what has emerged in the context of globalization is a new media ecology. James Carey has argued that the internet "should be understood as the first instance of a global communication system," displacing a national system that came into existence in the late nineteenth century with the development of, initially, telegraphy and railroad transportation, and later, national magazines, newspapers, radio, and television (Carey, 1998: 28). He suggests that we are witnessing the emergence of a "new media ecology, which transforms the structural relations among older media such [as] print and broadcast and integrates them to a new center around the defining technologies of computer and satellite" (1998: 34).

Carey underscores the point here that this new media ecology requires a cultural level to complement its global infrastructure, an imagining and an articulation of community on a global scale, enabled, but not automatically produced, by communications or transportation technologies alone.

All this is not to say that national (or provincial or municipal) boundaries are obsolete. They may be more porous, but the governments within those boundaries remain primarily responsible for creating the economic, political, and cultural conditions for globalization's various activities. National governments establish the supporting infrastructure; laws; policies; incentives; and health, education, and safety standards that businesses—including those in the cultural industries—require. Similarly, governments determine through policy measures what communication is for, and determine and protect the freedoms citizens enjoy in engaging in communications activities. Nation-states are also the representatives of their citizens' interests in international forums.

The main point we want to establish in this section is that the social conditions in which we live are changing and that technologies and processes of communication are at the heart of these changes.

New World Information and Communication Order

Cees Hamelink (1994: 23–8) observes that two features of international communication emerged in the last half of the twentieth century: the expansion of the global communication system and tensions in the system across both east–west and north–south axes. East–west tensions (i.e., Cold War tensions between the totalitarian Eastern Bloc led by the Soviet Union and the Western democracies led by the United States) were most prominent in the 1950s and '60s. North–south tensions (i.e., tensions between affluent, industrialized nations of the northern hemisphere and the post-colonial Global South countries of the southern hemisphere) arose in the 1970s as the Global South took advantage of its new-found voice in the General Assembly of

the United Nations, and they remain pertinent today. A number of United Nations initiatives led to a proposed New World Information and Communications Order (NWICO), which sought compromise between the US advocacy of the free flow of information and the Global South desire for a balanced flow.

The US push for the free-flow doctrine began during World War II when the American newspaper industry campaigned for the freedom of news gathering; in June 1944, the American Society of Newspaper Editors adopted resolutions demanding "unrestricted communications for news throughout the world." In 1948, the United Nations held a conference on freedom of information in Geneva.

At this stage, the free-flow doctrine met its stiffest opposition from the Soviet Union, which insisted on the regulation of information flows and complained that the Americans' freedom-of-information position endorsed, in fact, the freedom of a few commercial communication monopolies. Nevertheless, the free-flow doctrine was largely endorsed by the United Nations, and Article 19 of the 1948 Universal Declaration on Human Rights states, "Everyone has the right to freedom of opinion and expression; this right includes freedom to hold opinions without interference and to seek, receive and impart information and ideas through any media regardless of frontiers" (Hamelink, 1994: 152–5).

The issue of communication flows was revisited at the behest of Global South countries in the 1970s, when it became clear that the free-flow doctrine was a recipe for Western cultural hegemony, as the Soviets had anticipated. Starting in the mid-1960s, communications satellites became a key element in the emerging global media system. Because they offered a means to set up a national telecommunications system without a massive investment in land lines and equipment, countries were quick to see their advantage. But satellites also presented possible problems for developing countries. As Herman and McChesney note, the development and launching of geostationary and geosynchronous communication

11.4 ▶▶ ▶ ▶▶

THE DECLINING INVESTMENT IN INTERNATIONAL NEWS

International news coverage is an important source of information about the world we live in. In a period of globalization, when the people, places, and institutions that constitute our world are more closely connected than ever before, and when polls indicate a strong public appetite for foreign news coverage (Canadian Media Research Consortium, 2009), news organizations are decreasing their investment in international coverage. The principal reason is cost-cutting; the maintenance of foreign news bureaus is expensive—costing an estimated $200,000 to $300,000 per correspondent annually—and news organizations are opting to buy their international news from wire services like the Associated Press, Reuters, and Agence France-Presse rather than to produce it themselves. Because these news agencies serve clients all over the world, they deliver a homogenized form of reporting that perceives issues through the lens of their home countries (the United States, the United Kingdom, and France, respectively) and can ignore the specific needs of Canadian readers (Bielsa, 2008; Brown, 2009: 30).

Most Canadian newspapers do not have any foreign correspondents and the major television networks are cutting back. Typically, news organizations rely for most of their international coverage on the major international news agencies and only occasionally send one of their own reporters to cover a particularly dramatic story. This *parachute journalism* was the strategy employed by a number of Canadian newspapers and television networks, who flew journalists to Haiti to cover the aftermath of the January 2010 earthquake there; the same strategy was used during the high-profile August 2015 trial in Cairo of Canadian journalist Mohamed Fahmy and two other reporters. In spite of the best efforts of the individuals involved, parachute journalism means reporters have little background knowledge of the issues they are covering, usually do not speak the local language, have few local contacts and so are more reliant than normal upon official sources who can then determine the news agenda and define stories from their own perspective, based on their own interests (see Macdonald, 2008). Most metropolitan daily newspapers devote more of their travel budgets to sports coverage than to foreign news coverage.

A study of the international news coverage of Canada's three self-described "national" newspapers—*The Globe and Mail*, the *National Post*, and *Le Devoir*—revealed that 25 percent of their stories were filed from abroad, but there were important qualifiers: the United States accounted for 40 percent of all international coverage, 25 percent of international coverage concerned professional sport, and most international coverage came from five countries (the United States, the United Kingdom, France, Iraq, and Germany). These newspapers portrayed a highly circumscribed world, with the continents of Africa and South America almost wholly absent. Eighty percent of the international coverage in *The Globe and Mail* came from wire services, as did 89 percent in *Le Devoir*. Only 6 percent of the *National Post*'s stories had foreign place lines (see Gasher, 2007).

Canadian readerships interested in international news events can, of course, search for coverage online. But much of that coverage is supplied by the same few news agencies and provides no Canadian perspective.

satellites in the 1960s and '70s "fanned the flames of concern about global media."

Satellites held out the promise of making it possible for Third World [now called Global South] nations to leapfrog out of their quagmire into a radically more advanced media system, but at the same time satellites posed the threat of transnational commercial broadcasters eventually controlling global communication, bypassing any domestic authority with broadcasts directly to Third World homes. (Herman and McChesney, 1997: 23)

The major global institutions addressing communication issues at the time—the United Nations, the UN Educational, Scientific and Cultural Organization (UNESCO), and the International Telecommunications Union—all included majorities of Global South countries and sympathetic totalitarian states. The impetus for a renewed debate on international communication came from the 90-member movement of the Non-Aligned Nations.

The international debate at that time focused on three points, as it still does to some extent. First, historically, communication services together with evolved information technologies have allowed dominant states to exploit their political and economic power. Through historical patterns and enabling technology, such as communication satellites, these dominant states have assumed a presence in the cultures and ideologies of less dominant states. That presence, whether it comes from being the principal source of foreign news or from beaming satellite signals into another country, is strongly felt by developing nations, just as it is in Canada.

Second, the economies of scale in information production and distribution threaten to reinforce this dominance. It takes considerable capital and infrastructure to engage in the mass production, circulation, and promotion of cultural products, which is why so many countries struggle to establish viable film industries. And any attempt to counteract a worsening situation must avoid feeding into the hands of repressive governments that would curtail freedom of expression and information circulation.

Third, a few transnational corporations have mobilized technology as a vehicle for the exploitation of markets rather than as a means of serving the cultural, social, and political needs of nations. In other words, the large corporations have seized the opportunity to develop and use communication technologies, but they have employed those technologies primarily to exploit the value of audiences to advertisers rather than to provide information, education, and entertainment to these audiences for their own benefit or for the benefit of the larger cultural whole.

11.5 ▶▶▶▶▶

AL JAZEERA ENGLISH

Amid substantial controversy, the world's first English-language global news network came to Canada in 2010 and represents a significant step in the internationalization of Canadian television news. After having received regulatory approval as a digital cable channel from the CRTC in November 2009, Al Jazeera English reached an agreement with the Canadian distributors BCE, Rogers Communications, and Videotron to be offered to their cable and satellite television subscribers as of May 2010. Previously, Al Jazeera English has been available only via the internet (Krashinsky, 2010c).

Al Jazeera English was founded in 2006 as a sister network to the Qatar-based Al Jazeera Arabic. It has 60 news bureaus on 6 continents and is seen in 250 million households in 130 countries. Al Jazeera English is headquartered in Doha, Qatar, and has broadcast centres in Doha, Kuala Lumpur, London, and Washington (Al Jazeera English, 2014).

Pressure from the Global South compelled the United Nations to broaden the concept of free flow to include "the free and balanced flow of information." International debate over the design of a New World Information and Communication Order coalesced around the final report of the 16-member International Commission for the Study of Communication Problems (the MacBride Commission), established by UNESCO in December 1977 (UNESCO, 1980).

The MacBride Commission advocated "free, open and balanced communications" and concluded that "the utmost importance should be given to eliminating imbalances and disparities in communication and its structures, and particularly in information flows. Developing countries need to reduce their dependence and claim a new, more just and more equitable order in the field of communication" (UNESCO, 1980: 253–68). The

MacBride Commission's conclusions were based on "the firm conviction that communication is a basic individual right, as well as a collective one required by all communities and nations. Freedom of information—and, more specifically the right to seek, receive, and impart information—is a fundamental human right; indeed, a prerequisite for many others" (UNESCO, 1980: 253).

Recognizing that leaving the development of communication systems solely to market forces serves to block access to them for particular groups of people and ideas, the MacBride Commission pointed to an essential conflict between the commercialization and the democratization of communication. Consequently, the MacBride Commission clearly favoured a movement for democratization, which would include respect for national sovereignty in areas of cultural policy and recognition that the "educational and informational use of communication should be given equal priority with entertainment." The report stated, "Every country should develop its communication patterns in accordance with its own conditions, needs and traditions, thus strengthening its integrity, independence and self-reliance" (UNESCO, 1980: 254).

The MacBride Report also criticized the striking disparities between the technological capacities of different nations, and described the right to communicate as fundamental to democracy: "Communication needs in a democratic society should be met by the extension of specific rights, such as the right to be informed, the right to inform, the right to privacy, the right to participate in public communication—all elements of a new concept, the right to communicate" (UNESCO, 1980: 265).

From NWICO to WSIS

The MacBride Report proved to be a better manifesto on the democratization of communication than a blueprint for restructuring international communication exchanges. Even though UNESCO adopted its key principles—eliminating global media imbalances and having communication

serve national development goals—the NWICO was poorly received in the West "because it gave governments, and not markets, ultimate authority over the nature of a society's media" (Herman and McChesney, 1997: 24–6). The NWICO was seen by its opponents as a curb on media freedom, argues communications scholar Kaarle Nordenstreng, "while in reality the concept was designed to widen and deepen the freedom of information by increasing its balance and diversity on a global scale" (Nordenstreng, 2012: 37).

Western countries in the 1980s, led by the United States under Ronald Reagan and the United Kingdom under Margaret Thatcher, chose the more aggressive path of pursuing liberalized global trade. In the face of concerns over the ways NWICO reforms would affect their media industries, the United States and United Kingdom pulled out of UNESCO in 1985, severely undermining the organization's budget and making the recommended reforms impossible (Nordenstreng, 2012: 34). As Nordenstreng describes it, the United States adopted its own version of a "new world order" consisting of neo-liberalism and US exceptionalism (2012: 35). Even Canada, which was one of the affluent industrialized nations identified by the MacBride Commission as being dominated by cultural imports, began to pursue the neo-liberal agenda of free trade and budget cutbacks in the 1980s under the Progressive Conservative government of Brian Mulroney. Very little changed in Canadian government policy after Jean Chrétien's Liberals assumed power in 1993, and the pattern continued under both Paul Martin's Liberals and Stephen Harper's Conservatives. Such issues as deficit reduction and freer trade continue to dominate the political agenda and the ministers of industry, international trade, and finance enjoy as much influence over cultural policy as the minister with the culture portfolio, if not even more (see Gasher, 1995).

International bodies like the World Trade Organization (originally, the General Agreement on Tariffs and Trade) have become more important to the major cultural producers than the United Nations, and the rules of the game for international communications have been written in such treaties as the North American Free Trade Agreement (NAFTA) and the Treaty on European Union. Herman and McChesney (1997: 30–1) write, "The political design of all these regional and global trade agreements has been to remove decision-making powers from local and national legislatures in favor of impersonal market forces and/or supranational bureaucracies remote from popular control." NAFTA, for example, "requires that government agencies operate on a strictly commercial basis, and it explicitly removes the possibility that governments can take on any new functions."

The New World Information and Communication Order, in other words, was almost immediately supplanted by what Herman and McChesney (1997: 35) call the "new global corporate ideology." As the communications media have become increasingly implicated in the global economy, media policy is governed more and more by international financial and trade regimes, such as the International Monetary Fund and the World Trade Organization.

Nonetheless, as Mosco (2009: 178) puts it, the struggle continues to be to "build a more democratic process grounded in genuinely global governance." New concerns for the Global South arose in the 1990s with the emergence of digital information networks, the creation and expansion of cyberspace, issues pertaining to internet governance, and the financing of digital activities (Masmoudi, 2012: 25). The International Telecommunications Union (ITU) launched the World Summit on the Information Society (WSIS, 2010), which took the form of international conferences bringing together scholars, civil society groups, governments, and policy experts in Geneva in 2003 and Tunis in 2005. The Geneva conference laid out a 67-point declaration of principles and an action plan, and the Tunis conference addressed the financial implementation of the action plan, including the creation of the Digital Solidarity Fund.

The Geneva declaration privileges an understanding of information as a resource for the promotion of freedom, equality, peace, and democracy, rather than simply as a consumer product, and its main target was the digital divide between those peoples, organizations, and nations in the world with the ready access and the skills to take full advantage of communications technologies and those who lack that access and those skills. The WSIS meetings had been preceded by the 1984 Maitland Report and the UN's 2000 statement of Millennium Development Goals. The principal concern of the Maitland Report, produced by an independent ITU commission, was "the expansion of telecommunication networks and reducing the technology gap between the rich and the poor, later labelled the 'digital divide'" (Mansell, 2012: 125–6).

Three decades later, the digital divide between the information-rich and the information-poor remains a central concern. According to 2014 ITU figures, 78 percent of the population of developed countries is online compared to only 32 percent in developing countries. Internet-user penetration is 19 percent in Africa compared to the world average of 40 percent. There is a comparable gulf in penetration rates for mobile devices, with 84 percent penetration in the developed world and 21 percent in the developing world (ITU, 2014). The cost of access to information and communication technologies is "inversely proportional to the economic wealth of a territory." For example, broadband access costs an average of $28 per month in developed countries and $190 per month in developing countries (Nicey, 2012: 166–7). Even more than access to digital networks, though, communications scholar Jérémie Nicey argues that computer literacy needs to be seen as a basic human right. "UNESCO and other institutions now stress a priority that is even greater than access to information and knowledge: 'information literacy'" (2012: 172). (See Box 11.6 for more about the digital divide.)

The international news agencies that were implicated in originating global information disparities continue to play a role in the digital divide. The world's three major wire services, Associated Press, Reuters, and Agence France-Presse, have used the internet to reinforce their dominance and have developed audio-visual services to supply international all-news television networks like CNN, BBC, and Al Jazeera (Laville and Palmer, 2012: 179–84). This dominance is enhanced by a general withdrawal from international news coverage by newspapers and national television networks (see Box 11.4 on page 323).

The Geneva declaration expressed the desire to create an information society "where everyone can create, access, utilize and share information and knowledge, enabling individuals, communities and peoples to achieve their full potential in promoting their sustainable development and improving their quality of life." Among its specific principles were freedom of opinion and expression; greater access to technology; greater access to information and better information and knowledge sharing; and the need to address media imbalances due to "infrastructure, technical resources and the development of human skills" (WSIS, 2010).

Sadly, though, as Robert Savio (2012: 237) argues, what has emerged instead is a "New Information Market Order" characterized by corporate concentration and commercialization.

Changing Notions of Place

A number of scholars have attributed to the communications media a significant role in how we imagine, define, understand, and experience place. The philosopher Charles Taylor (2005: 23) refers to this as the "social imaginary," which he defines as "the ways people imagine their social existence, how they fit together with others, how things go on between them and their fellows, the expectations that are normally met, and the deeper normative notions and images that underlie these expectations." The widespread commercialization of cultural production, communication, and information exchange, and the

Source: © IMNATURE/iStockphoto.

Appadurai argues that the world we live in today is characterized by a new role for the imagination of social life; globalization comprises distinct processes rather than a coherent system. How could Appadurai's five 'scapes appear in a crowded subway car?

11.6 ▶▶ ▶ ▶ ▶▷

THE DIGITAL DIVIDE

The digital divide refers to the gap between the information-rich and the information-poor, and can be measured on both a global scale—between the regions and countries of the world—and on a national scale—between individuals based on where they live, their access to digital networks, and demographic characteristics like household income, education level, age, and sex. The existence of this divide is a clear reminder that not everyone, even in our own communities, enjoys the same access to digital communication technologies. Given the importance of information and connectivity in modern society, the digital divide represents a measure of inequality that can have a serious impact on quality of life.

Jan A.G.M. van Dijk (2005: 15) captures the significance of the digital divide and at the same time explains why, as a negative feedback loop, it persists and worsens:

1. Categorical inequalities in society produce an unequal distribution of resources.
2. An unequal distribution of resources causes unequal access to digital technologies.

3. Unequal access to digital technologies also depends on the characteristics of these technologies.
4. Unequal access to digital technologies brings about unequal participation in society.
5. Unequal participation in society reinforces categorical inequalities and unequal distribution of resources.

At stake here is full participation in, or exclusion from, contemporary society. The digital divide also provides a measure of the economic health of nations and peoples.

Van Dijk (2012: 196) describes four types of access to computer networks: motivation; material or physical access; digital skills; and usage. Motivation affects individuals' decision "to purchase a computer and network connection, to learn the requisite skills, and to use the interesting applications" (2012: 197). Motivation can be influenced by a person's available time, by affordability, by need, and by a person's inclination to learn and use the internet (2012: 198). Material and physical access refer to the affordability and availability of computer hardware and network connections, whether in the home or in a public place. Van Dijk notes that the material access divide between haves and have-nots is decreasing in developed countries like Canada, but widening in developing countries (2012: 198–9). Digital skills are "the collection of skills

extent to which we rely on these media for our communicative activities, raise a number of questions about the relationship between communication and culture. The perpetual flows of people, capital, goods, services, and images that characterize globalization carry significant implications for how we experience and imagine place, how we define community, and how we constitute identity. Media globalization, Jack Lule (2013: 50) writes, "affected the 'imagination' of the world, allowing people to imagine a world, a different world from where they were, but a world perhaps accessible and reachable."

The social anthropologist Arjun Appadurai (1996) argues that the world we live in today is characterized by a new role for the imagination of social life and he perceives globalization as comprising distinct processes rather than a coherent system. The imagination, for Appadurai, is a "social practice" and he proposes five "'scapes" that create fundamental "disjunctures" between economics, culture, and politics (1996: 31–3). The *ethnoscape* is the "landscape of persons who constitute the shifting world in which we live." *Technoscapes* are formed by the global configuration of technology. *Finanscapes* are "the disposition of global capital." **Mediascapes** are "image-centered" and "narrative accounts of strips of reality." Finally, *ideascapes* are "concatenations of images" that reflect dominant ideologies and counter-ideologies (1996: 33–6). These five 'scapes form the "building blocks" of our needed to operate computers and the internet, to search and collect information in them, to communicate with them, and to use them for one's own purposes" (2012: 199). Usage, finally, refers to the need, opportunity, obligation, time, and effort that govern whether those with other kinds of access actually use computer networking (2012: 201–2).

International Telecommunications Union figures for 2014 showed that the world's developed countries had internet penetration rates of 78 percent compared to 32 percent in the developing world. The divide was even more pronounced in the fastest-growing market segment, mobile broadband subscriptions, where the penetration rate in the developed countries was 84 percent compared to 21 percent in the developing world (ITU, 2014).

These figures vary dramatically, of course, among sectors of the population within these countries.

Even if Canadians are among the best-connected people in the world, clear and persistent distinctions in internet usage remain, depending on income and educational levels, age, and community size. The Canadian Internet Use Survey conducted by Statistics Canada in 2012 found that, overall, 83 percent of Canadian households had internet access, up from 79 percent in 2010. This ranged from a low of 77 percent in New Brunswick to a high of 86 percent in both Alberta and British Columbia. Among households with internet access, 97 percent had a high-speed connection. Access figures ranged based on income, however: 98 percent of households with income of $94,000 or more had internet access, compared to 58 percent of households with income of $30,000 or less. Similarly, only 28 percent of Canadians 65 and over in the lowest income quartile used the internet, compared to 95 percent aged 16 to 24 in the same income category (Statistics Canada, 2013).

TABLE 11.3
Internet Penetration Rates

Country	Penetration (percentage of population)
Iceland	97.1
Norway	96.9
Canada	83.0
United States	78.3
China	45.6
Russia	44.3
Brazil	42.2
South Africa	13.9
Mali	2.9
Chad	1.9
Burundi	1.7

Source: Internet World Stats, 2012.

"imagined worlds, that is, the multiple worlds that are constituted by the historically situated imaginations of persons and groups spread around the globe" (1996: 33; see also Appadurai, 1990; Jones, 2010: 209–26).

These contending 'scapes have profound implications for how we situate ourselves in the world, for how we relate to our own immediate community and other parts and peoples of the world. Doreen Massey (1991: 24) asks, "How, in the face of all this movement and intermixing, can we retain any sense of a local place and its particularity?" Globalization has intensified struggles over the meaning of place. This is particularly the case in countries like Canada, whose citizens tend to be more familiar with cultural imports than with the ideas and expressions of their own artists and intellectuals. This struggle also owes something to Canada's policy of multiculturalism, as Canada—urban Canada, especially—becomes a mixing ground for peoples of diverse backgrounds, beliefs, and traditions. If the literary critic Northrop Frye famously framed the Canadian identity question as "Where is here?" we can follow that question with one that is intimately related: *Who are we?* It is through our communications media that we seek answers to these questions.

Benedict Anderson defined the nation as "an imagined political community" and depicted eighteenth-century newspapers and novels as implicated in the projects of nation building and nationalism. The nation, he wrote, "is imagined because the members of even the smallest nation will never know most of their fellow-members, meet them, or even hear of them, yet in the minds of each lives the image of their communion" (Anderson, 1983: 15). He described the novel and the newspaper as new forms of imagining, which provided the technical means to produce in people a sense of "nation-ness." If novels created a "sociological landscape" through the depiction of simultaneous events tying together a population of imagined characters (Anderson, 1983: 35–6), newspapers presented news stories whose sharing of the news cycle—their "calendrical coincidence"—and whose juxtaposition on the newspaper page created connections among them (1983: 37–8). The short shelf life of the newspaper—its "obsolescence"—in turn created "an extraordinary mass ceremony: the almost precisely simultaneous consumption ('imagining') of the newspaper-as-fiction" (1983: 39).

In a similar vein, John Hartley (1992, 1996) maintains that publics are created by institutions and discourses, arguing that "the media are simultaneously creative and participatory. They create a picture of the public, but it goes live, as it were, only when people participate in its creation, not least by turning themselves into the audience" (1992: 4). Audiences, thereby, are "discursive productions" (Hartley, 1996: 67). But Hartley points out that media can exclude as well as include, creating divisions between those who belong and those who don't. Communities, that is, are largely defined by their distinction from other communities and by specific membership criteria. Newspapers, for example, speak to a particular audience of readers, so that "news includes stories on a daily basis which enable everyone to recognize a larger unity or community than their own immediate contacts, and to identify with the news outlet as 'our' storyteller" (Hartley, 1992: 207). The news, Hartley argues, is organized around strategies of inclusion and exclusion from our community, creating domains of *We-dom* and *They-dom*, dividing people into "us" and "them." The boundaries of We-dom and They-dom are not

coterminous with any formal political boundaries, but they can be drawn from any number of bases: not only citizenship, but also gender, race, class, ethnicity, sexual orientation, and so on (Hartley, 1992: 207). News media, then, not only help to define and constitute communities, but in doing so also draw boundary lines that divide communities into domains of us and them (see Box 11.7).

As noted above, the various flows we associate with globalization are not new. What globalization has done, however, has been both to increase the traffic—human, material, electronic—across some borders and to reconfigure others. So, for example, the Canada–United States Free Trade Agreement was an attempt to facilitate trade across the border dividing the two countries. Although the legal boundary remains, the meaning of the border has changed, at least as far as trade relations are concerned. The signing in December 2001 of the Smart Border Declaration between Canada and the United States, whereby the latest communications technology was to be used to create a more secure shared border in the wake of the 9/11 attacks on New York and Washington, DC, means that the very term *border* has taken on a changed and less Canadian-determined meaning for the foreseeable future. This applies to cultural exchanges as well; it has become more difficult for Canada to preserve some space within its own market for indigenous cultural products. Technologies like the internet ignore terrestrial boundaries altogether.

The heightened permeability of borders has been met, among some, by the desire for a more rooted, or more secure, sense of place. Gillian Rose (1995: 88–116) notes that place has been a privileged component of identity formation. "Identity is how we make sense of ourselves, and geographers, anthropologists and sociologists, among others, have argued that the meanings given to a place may be so strong that they become a central part of the identity of people experiencing them." Places, and the experiences we associate with places, both as individuals and as members of a group, inform memory and our sense of belonging. This sense of belonging is critical to understanding the relationship between identity and a particular locale. "One way in which identity is connected to a particular place is by a feeling that you belong to that place." We might, therefore, detect a very different sense of belonging between native residents of a place and migrants. Migrants such as refugees and exiles, who have not moved of their own free will, may feel little sense of belonging to their new place of residence.

Culture is another means by which identities of place are constructed and sustained. Stuart Hall argues that we tend to imagine cultures as "placed" in two ways. First, we associate place with a specific location where social relationships have developed over time. Second, place "establishes symbolic boundaries around a culture, marking off those who belong from those who do not."

11.7 ▶▶ ▶ ▶ ▶▶

REASONABLE ACCOMMODATION

The diverse makeup of Canada's population is often celebrated, but at other times it can be perceived as a source of conflict with, even a threat to, what we believe to be the Canadian way of life, our customs, norms, and values. This diversity raises the age-old, but always complex, identity question: *Who are we as a people?* And it can evoke a range of emotional responses, sometimes xenophobic or bigoted, but at other times serious and legitimate. These issues tend to get played out in the news media in sensational and simplistic ways, rendering difference a problem to be solved.

The question of *reasonable accommodation* has been raised most noticeably in Quebec. Given the province's own concerns about its status within Canada as an identifiably distinct society, Quebec has long been uneasy about the Canadian Multiculturalism Act (1988), particularly what multiculturalism means for the status of Quebec's francophone population (Karim, 2009: 704). The aim of Québécois to be recognized as constituting a nation or a people conflicts with Canada's official status as a multicultural country.

A number of specific controversies in 2006 and 2007 prompted the Quebec government to establish the Consultation Commission on Accommodation Practices Related to Cultural Differences (better known as the Bouchard–Taylor Commission). The controversies included: a 2006 Supreme Court of Canada decision defending the right of a Sikh student from Quebec to wear a kirpan to school; a decision by a Montreal YMCA to frost its windows at the request of a neighbouring synagogue whose members objected to the sight of women exercising; a decision by Canada's chief electoral officer to permit Muslim women to wear a niqab or burka while voting; a *Journal de Montréal* poll in which 59 percent of Quebecers self-identified as racist; the 2007 decision by the Quebec town of Hérouxville (population 1,300) to adopt a "code of living," which banned, among other things, the stoning of women and female circumcision.

The Bouchard–Taylor Commission was mandated to review accommodation practices in Quebec, analyze the issues, conduct extensive consultations with citizens and provide recommendations to the Quebec government to "ensure that accommodation practices conform to Quebec's values as a pluralistic, democratic, egalitarian society" (Bouchard–Taylor Commission, 2008: 17). Hearings were conducted throughout the province in the fall of 2007 and the commissioners, Gérard Bouchard and Charles Taylor, produced a report with 37 recommendations in May 2008.

The minority Parti Québécois government introduced Bill 60 in 2013, outlining a controversial Charter of Values that affirmed the secular character of the Quebec state but at the same time banned the wearing of conspicuous religious symbols by public-sector workers, including teachers and daycare employees. The bill was perceived as an example of wedge politics and it died on the order paper when the PQ government was defeated in the April 2014 provincial election (see *Montreal Gazette*, 2014: "More Wedge Politics from the PQ Government").

Physical settlement, continuity of occupation, the long-lasting effects on ways of life arising from the shaping influence of location and physical environment, coupled with the idea that these cultural influences have been exercised amongst a population which is settled and deeply interrelated through marriage and kinship relations, are meanings which we closely associate with the idea of culture and which provide powerful ways of conceptualizing what "culture" is, how it works, and how it is transmitted and preserved. (Hall, 1995: 177–86)

At the same time, Hall explains, "There is a strong tendency to 'landscape' cultural identities, to give them an imagined place or 'home,' whose characteristics echo or mirror the characteristics of the identity in question."

The widespread migration of peoples so prevalent in our time—more than 20 percent of Canada's population in 2011 were immigrants (Statistics Canada, 2011a)—brings together people with very different roots, histories, traditions, and values. In some instances these differences are embraced. But at other times they can be perceived as threatening to our sense of community, of place, of culture, of identity; consider the proposal by the Parti Québécois in 2013 to introduce a Charter of Values, which would have prohibited Quebec public employees from wearing visible symbols of their religious affiliation. Again, much of our engagement with our community takes place through the media, and our understandings of Canadian histories, traditions, and values not only come from news reports but from music, film, television, and printed sources (e.g., books, magazines). It is through various media that we often first meet those who are different from ourselves, and where our initial understandings of those people originate.

If one impact of globalization has been to call into question the notion of "place" as the basis for identity and/or culture, postmodernism and improved networks of transportation and communication facilitate the imagination of communities based on gender, race, ethnicity, sexual orientation, social class, and so on. Proximity, in other words, is not a necessary element of identity formation. If culture and identity are not confined to a particular place, it follows that any one place is not confined to a single culture or identity—hence the Quebec conundrum of interculturalism and of its being a distinct society. This issue of identity formation has precipitated localized struggles over immigration and language, as well as over urban development, architecture, and foreign investment. Mike Featherstone (1996: 66) remarks that "cultural differences once maintained between places now exist within them. . . . [For example,] the unwillingness of migrants to passively inculcate the dominant cultural mythology of the nation or locality raises issues of multiculturalism and the fragmentation of identity." Massey argues, "The way in which we define 'places,' and the particular character of individual places, can be important in issues varying from battles over development and construction to questions of which social groups have rights to live where" (1995: 48).

The conventional container of identity and culture that has come under greatest challenge from the reimagining of community prompted by globalization has been the nation-state. Questions of citizenship and questions of identity have been increasingly dissociated (Morley and Robins, 1995: 19). The emergence of trade blocs in Europe, Asia, and North America plus the prevalence of both international and subnational cultural networks have undermined the primacy of the nation-state in contemporary imaginings of community, identity, and culture.

We should not overreact to these changes, however. Canadians still have democratically elected national, provincial, and municipal governments, which, as we discussed in Chapters 7 and 8, continue to pass laws and pursue policies that form the basic framework within which media organizations operate in Canada. These laws and policies are responses to pressures from both the global economy and local cultures. Laws like the Broadcasting, Telecommunications, and Income Tax Acts, the funding programs of Telefilm Canada and the Canada Council, and cultural institutions like the Canadian Broadcasting Corporation remain pre-eminent in structuring cultural production in Canada. No media industry is untouched by them. Globalization alters the context in which mass communication takes place, but local conditions of cultural production remain both pertinent and central to the ways in which it is undertaken.

▶ SUMMARY

We hear the term *globalization* used all the time, such that we can be unclear about its precise meaning and unaware of the implications this has on our lives, and particularly on how we communicate.

This chapter began with an extended definition of globalization and showed how it is not simply an economic phenomenon, but an intensification of social relations across time and space that touches every aspect of our lives, from how we shop to what we see on our television and computer screens. We then outlined four roles the communication media play in the globalization process: as media of encounter; as media of governance; as media situating us within the world; and as a globalized business in and of themselves. We subsequently reviewed the predominant theories to explain international communication flows and their implications, beginning with Immanuel Wallerstein's world systems theory, touching briefly on media imperialism and cultural dependency, and concluding with Manuel Castells's notion of the *network society* and Vincent Mosco's discussion of *spatialization*.

On this conceptual groundwork, we traced the history of international communication exchanges, concentrating particularly on the period from the 1940s to the present. We discussed the doctrine of *free flow* promoted by the United States and then we explained the rise, and subsequent downfall, of the New World Information and Communication Order, whose proponents sought to alleviate communication imbalances between national communities in the 1970s and to promote the "right to communicate" as a fundamental human right. Instead, the 1980s and '90s were characterized by further trade liberalization and the reinforcement of the commercial view of communication as commodity exchange. We summarized briefly the 2003 and 2005 conferences of the World Summit on the Information Society as the latest coordinated efforts to democratize communication on a global scale.

We concluded the chapter with a discussion of the impact of globalization on how we think about *place*, *community*, and *identity*, given the importance of communication and cultural exchange to our sense of belonging, and we expanded on Castells's ideas about the new forms of sociability and the new global geography that characterize our time.

▶ KEY TERMS

cultural dependency, p. 319
Fordism, p. 310
information flows, p. 321
media geography, p. 305
media imperialism, p. 314
mediascape, p. 328
mobility, p. 305

network society, p. 312
North American Free Trade Agreement, p. 305
proximity, p. 311
sovereignty, p. 311
spatialization, p. 321
world systems theory, p. 319
World Trade Organization, p. 305

RELATED WEBSITES ─────────────────────────────

European Union: http://europa.eu/index_en.htm
The official site of the European Union includes an institutional overview, regular news dispatches, and official report.

International Telecommunications Union: www.itu.int
The ITU is an international organization through which governments and private corporations coordinate telecommunications networks and services.

UNESCO: www.unesco.org/
The principal objective of the United Nations Educational, Scientific and Cultural Organization is to contribute to global peace and security by promoting international collaboration through education, science, culture, and communication.

World Summit on the Information Society (WSIS): www.itu.int/wsis/index.html
Taking the form of two international conferences, the WSIS is a coordinated effort to democratize the institutions of mass communication and to eradicate communicative inequalities between peoples and nation-states.

World Trade Organization: www.wto.org
The WTO governs trade between nations and seeks to promote trade liberalization throughout the world.

 FURTHER READINGS ─────────────────────────────

Bauman, Zygmunt. 1998. *Globalization: The Human Consequences*. New York: Columbia University Press. This book looks at globalization from a critical and human perspective, considering its political, social, and economic implications on people's daily lives.

Castells, Manuel. 2001. *The Internet Galaxy: Reflections on the Internet, Business, and Society*. Oxford: Oxford University Press. Written by one of the foremost contemporary theorists on international communications networks, this book examines the internet from a number of perspectives, including its history and how it affects the way people work, consume media, and interact socially.

Frau-Meigs, Divina, Jérémie Nicey, Michael Palmer, Julia Pohle and Patricio Tupper (eds). 2012. *From NWICO to WSIS: 30 Years of Communication Geopolitics*. Bristol, UK: Intellect. The essays in this collection trace key communication policy issues from the time of the MacBride Commission to the present.

Held, David, and Anthony McGrew, eds. 2003. *The Global Transformations Reader: An Introduction to the Globalization Debate*. Cambridge, UK: Polity Press. This is a comprehensive reader with concise chapters from leading scholars covering every aspect of globalization, from its economics to its political, social and cultural implications.

Jones, Andrew. 2010. *Globalization: Key Thinkers*. Cambridge, UK: Polity Press. As its title suggests, this book summarizes the arguments of globalization's principal theorists, contextualizes their ideas, and provides succinct analysis of each of their positions.

Morley, David, and Kevin Robins. 1995. *Spaces of Identity: Global Media, Electronic Landscapes and Cultural Boundaries*. London: Routledge. This is a provocative look at how the globalization of communication has undermined and altered conventional notions of national and cultural belonging. The ideas proposed in this book remain current.

Raboy, Marc, and Jeremey Shtern, eds. 2010. *Media Divides: Communication Rights and the Right to Communicate in Canada*. Vancouver/Toronto: UBC Press. This book contains a number of important essays that follow up on the work of the MacBride Commission and WSIS in the Canadian context.

Taylor, Charles. 2005. *Modern Social Imaginaries*. Durham and London: Duke University Press. An accessible philosophical study of the way we imagine our world and constitute identity in a period of significant political, economic, and social upheaval—a period of "multiple modernities."

UNESCO. 1980. *Many Voices, One World: Report by the International Commission for the Study of*

Communication Problems (MacBride Commission). Paris: UNESCO. The controversial MacBride Report was critical of the free-flow doctrine promoted by the United States and proposed measures to ensure more equitable and balanced communication flows between nations.

Wallerstein, Immanuel. 2007. *World-Systems Analysis: An Introduction*. Durham and London: Duke University Press. This is an up-to-date introduction to world systems theory, which describes the emergence of an extra-national economy involving long-distance trade links between Europe and parts of Africa, Asia, and what came to be known as the West Indies and North and South America.

▶ STUDY QUESTIONS

1. The term *globalization* is often used to mean economic globalization. Besides economics, what other globalizing forces affect the communications sphere?
2. In what ways do the mass media act as agents of globalization?
3. Is media globalization the same as media imperialism? Why or why not?
4. What is the argument in support of the free flow of communication? What is the basis for criticism of this position?
5. What was the MacBride Commission's position on international communication flows?
6. What is the World Summit on the Information Society?
7. What is world systems theory?
8. What does Manuel Castells mean by *a space of flows*?
9. How is globalization liberating? How is it confining?

12 Mass Communication in a Digital Age

> Where is the knowledge we have lost in information? — T.S. Eliot

Opening Questions

- What does it mean to approach the study of media and communication from a critical perspective?

- What are some of the key theoretical perspectives in communication studies?

- What is the role of public policy in the media and communication industries?

- What are some of the problems of thinking of media and communication in simply economic terms?

- What are the key issues facing media in Canada today?

Introduction

Communication media pervade practically all facets of our lives. They encompass traditional media—film, books, magazines, television and radio broadcasting, newspapers, telecommunications—as well as an increasing range of new electronic information and communications technologies. With computers, tablets, iPads, internet-based media, smartphones, and new emerging technologies like the Apple watch, communications media are shifting how we understand our world and our place within it.

We began our study of media and communication by considering the shifting nature of communication technology, reflecting on how media and communication systems are central to the functioning and operation of society, and examining how they orient our understanding of the world and our actions within it. We considered the broad history of media, and the ways they have been implicated in political, economic, and social development. We looked at a wide range of media theories, considered the different perspectives they provide on the broad processes of communication—particularly encoding and decoding—and weighed the different accents they put on the importance of structure and agency. We also examined the formal institutions of communication and the influence that professional values have on their operation, and considered the role of larger social forces, such as politics and economics, in shaping the development and character of these activities.

As we have seen, the influence exerted by these media ranges across all dimensions of society: politics, economics, education, culture, the family, and individual lives. The media also have an enormous impact on our worldview and our frame of reference on events. But, as we have seen, media are incomplete and imperfect tools for understanding our world. To study the dynamics of media, as we have been doing in this book, is to attempt to understand the dynamics of representation and the ways in which it informs our understandings of the world and our place within it.

This final chapter summarizes the various ideas and perspectives on media and communication that we have examined, and points the way to future study and directions of growth and development of the field.

The Shifting Character of Media

Media are central to how we understand culture and society and share in them. In this context, we have approached the study of media and communications from a *critical perspective*. That is, we have been considering how media are implicated in our knowledge and understanding of the world.

Our discussion of oral, literate, and electronic forms of communication introduced how media of communication can influence social form and structure. Our discussion of oral communication, for instance, illustrated that media shape the production and transmission of knowledge. An examination of written or literate communication shows how media can shrink social distance and shift relations of political power. Digital electronic communication does all this and more. It can have both binding and fragmenting effects as barriers to constructing relationships across space collapse. While many digital divides continue to cause inequalities both at home and internationally, the electronic media overall contribute to shrinking social, political, economic, and geographic distances. Who will reap the majority of the benefits from these changes remains to be seen.

But as we have discussed, technology is not the sole defining feature of media systems. While specific types of media might have particular propensities, media systems are the product of a much larger set of political, economic, social, and cultural forces. Broadly speaking, in the context of Western societies, contemporary media reflect cultural forms and social practices engendered by the shift from feudal to industrial society, and the migrations and divisions of labour that characterized that shift. Moreover, in a large industrial nation such as Canada, the media are complexly woven into the social and cultural fabric. The unique characteristics of Canada, such as its large land mass, a small population spread primarily along the border with the United States, its regionalism, two official languages, and multiculturalism, have all laid their stamp on the structure and character of the Canadian media.

Rising from these circumstances, media both orient and animate social life. On the one hand, they reflect the larger set of social and cultural values that frame our lives. On the other hand, we come to know our society—its institutions, organizations, relationships—and the ideas, values, beliefs, and art forms that comprise our culture largely through media and our engagement with them. Set in this context, some of the questions we have considered are the following: Does it matter who owns the media? How does advertising influence what we see in the media? What role do the media play in the economy? In globalization? In the construction of our tastes and desires and personal identity? Does it matter if Canadian media are dominated by foreign, mainly US, media products? Are television sitcoms, shows promoting celebrities, and other seemingly innocuous programs simply entertainment, or do they play other roles in our lives? In other words, whose or what interests do media serve, and what role do they play in creating and maintaining social relationships, particularly relations of wealth and power?

In considering these questions we have seen that communications technology is currently a key site of social change and struggle, as a range of social interests fight for position in the shifting social landscape. Some might shy away from terms like *social struggle*. Neo-liberal critics might prefer "new, open, more competitive markets" or, as those of a more idealist bent might put it, a "new chance for democracy." But a social struggle it is.

Because they are embedded in a larger set of social and political circumstances, changes in our media systems signal much broader social change. In the current environment, we are not merely throwing out a bunch of old machines and bringing in some new, sleek, quieter, more effective ones. Rather, we are setting in motion the revision and reformation of the jobs associated with those machines. We are encouraging the reorganization and perhaps the re-establishment of associated organizations and institutions. We are opening up for reconsideration the foundations of **public policy** governing those activities and institutions. And we are recasting the dimensions of the economy, the location of labour, and the role of the consumer. In some ways, we are also recasting notions of citizenship.

Practices and institutions of mass communication are currently being undermined by the fragmentation of media markets and the rise of a sophisticated, publicly accessible transmission system—the internet. Internet television, radio, and podcasting, for example, can circumvent the state and commercial apparatus controlling mass broadcasting. Independent recording labels and bands who sell their music via the internet have been able to get around the control of the recording industry giants, such as Sony, EMI, Universal, and Warner. Consider as well open-source software, which is a concerted effort on the part of digital labourers to undermine the centralized production and market domination by a handful of companies such as Microsoft. News production, once generally the purview of large media corporations, is being taken up by bloggers, citizen journalists, and a host of small and financially tenuous news producers (see Box 12.1). Similarly, social media sites like Facebook, Twitter, Instagram, and Tumblr offer an increasing range of new forms of social interaction. These are but a few examples in the growing range of interactive communications.

At the same time, the shifting structure and character of media industries is raising a host of new political, economic, and cultural issues. Over-the-top program distributors like Netflix, Google, and Apple TV are circumventing regulations, undermining the viability of Canadian screen industries, and raising new concerns about cultural sovereignty. Traditional jobs in journalism and the media are becoming increasingly

12.1

THE MEDIA CO-OP

One of the most innovative online media organizations in Canada is The Media Co-op (www.mediacoop.ca), which has a number of independent newspapers under its umbrella (e.g., *The Dominion* [www.dominionpaper.ca], which arose out of efforts to establish an alternative national journalistic voice, and has been published monthly in both print and online editions since May 2003 by a network of independent journalists across Canada). The Media Co-op is federally incorporated and has three types of members—readers, journalists, and editors—all with their own respective interests and roles in the organization.

In an effort to promote a more horizontal relationship between readers and the news organization, reader members are invited to participate in decision-making in terms of both developing story ideas and administrative issues. Journalist members are the main-story contributors, and the editors do the administrative work for the organization. While some of the published material is contributed by volunteers, the cooperative pays contributors wherever possible, in both cash and exchange. The organizational goal is to set up local media cooperatives across the country that produce news at both the local and national levels. At present, there are local cooperatives in Halifax, Toronto, and Vancouver, and more are said to be on the way. Each of these organizations has its own website for local news as well. Despite the ongoing struggle of raising money and developing resources, the co-operative has been steadily growing for over 11 years.

precarious. There is a growing digital divide both domestically and internationally, and multiplying concerns over privacy as both industry and government strive to more closely track our activities.

The foundations of this change from mass distribution of centrally produced media products to mass communication by and through an expanding range of people and institutions can be understood by recalling the definitions introduced in Chapter 1:

- Mass communication is the centralized production and dissemination of mass information and entertainment.
- Mass communication is the decentralized production and wide accessibility of information and entertainment by means of public access to the internet.
- Mass communication is the interactive exchange of information (or messages or intelligence) to a number of recipients.

As we have seen, the latter two meanings of the term *mass communication* are relatively new. The processes they describe are not new:

decentralized, widespread production of content describes early newspapers and small literary magazines; widespread person-to-person communication by means of the postal system is very old; and the telegraph and telephone have been with us since 1846 and 1876, respectively. What is new in the case of widespread production of cultural products is vastly increased ease of access and interaction. The greater variation of media text, sound, and image, together with the capacity for immediate transmission, storage, and manipulation, greatly extends the capabilities of traditional media. The social challenge new media present is how they might be put to work in the broader public interest rather than the interest of large private corporations—particularly foreign corporations with little to no concern for issues of Canadian sovereignty.

Communication and Democracy

Developments in communication media may interact with the fundamentals of democracy, particularly in terms of how ownership and control of media may enable or constrain the range of ideas and perspectives found in those media.

The history of this interaction can be traced back at least to the printing press in the mid-fifteenth century, which at first was controlled by the state or governing elite. But as the potential of communications technology for undermining and shifting the bases for political power became apparent, struggles over its control ensued. First, in the case of religion, in sixteenth century Europe, Protestants such as Martin Luther sought to undermine the social control held by the Catholic Church. Later, governments sought to control the press and the flow of ideas that might stem from it. And in the twentieth century, the corporate control of media became a central question of concern. Should media organizations be free to use their potential power to advance their biases in favour of business, certain political parties, and specific policies (such as free commercial speech)? Or should they act in a more constrained fashion, as self-aware institutions with a privileged position in society and, consequently, a responsibility to act for the social good of all, for a larger public interest? These questions exemplify how communication interacts with notions of democracy.

We saw in Chapter 3 that the social responsibility thesis, particularly in Canada, has provided a backdrop against which media performance in this regard might be measured—at least until the late twentieth century—not only in the press but also in the founding of broadcasting and specifically through the creation of a national public broadcasting service. Even more than the press, broadcasting was seen as a potential harbinger of greater social coherence, public expression, and responsibility in the media, offering enlightenment to individuals and encouraging the pursuit of democratic ideals. Drawing on Canada's tradition of governmental or public enterprise, the CBC gave the state the chance to finance a medium of communication on behalf of the people and the nation itself that would counterbalance the commercial media, which are often

financed 80 percent or more through advertising by the business sector.

At the international level, the efforts of UNESCO—beginning in the 1970s and carrying through to the 2000s—to extend the ideals of public communication through a new world order were founded on a similar idea of social responsibility. Dubbed "fair flows of information" rather than "free flows" (where the strongest in the market were free to dominate), the New World Information and Communications Order was championed by UNESCO in the 1980s as the possible impact and potential of new communications technology was becoming apparent. In large part, however, these efforts were squelched by the United States and the United Kingdom when they withdrew their support for UNESCO. The desire of these two countries to maintain their predominance as exporters of information, entertainment, and ideology to the world overrode any sense either had of social justice or of the value of celebrating diversity on a worldwide scale. Canadian policy was mostly set against this kind of imperialism and, with the help of favourable government policy, this country built up cultural industries capable of carrying Canadian creative content to domestic audiences in the face of the dominance of US media products in Canadian markets. More recently, given the ongoing advantages enjoyed by US and other foreign media producers, pressures have mounted to revisit current Canadian regulation that allows for more open markets. Critics have been raising questions as to the continued ability of Canadian perspectives to maintain their place in the Canadian mediascape.

In the digital age, because of the opportunities new media present for expanding public participation in formerly cloistered venues of decision-making, the question is perhaps how quickly and extensively large corporations will move to consolidate their predominance and, hence, their control of changing media and media markets. This is already happening in terms of concentration of ownership of traditional media; the vertical integration of content producers, such as television networks and newspapers, with the telecommunications companies that provide access to the internet; and corporate consolidation and control of web-based media organizations such as Google, Facebook, and Netflix. In the face of this ongoing consolidation, media policy becomes a particularly important vehicle for ensuring public participation and representation in both the development of new media and, perhaps more importantly, issues of governance in general. As illustrated in Box 12.2, "Advocating for Change," struggles to help ensure that the media are responsible to the greater public interest have a long history in Canada and continue today.

Content and Audiences

When we study communication, especially content, we are generally studying practices or processes of representation—that is, the act of putting ideas into words, paintings, sculpture, film, plays, television programs, websites, podcasts, or any other medium of communication. In this context, communication, or the making of meaning, is an active process that requires specific engagement at the levels of both encoding and decoding.

In the study of communication, the importance of a statement is not limited to whether it predicts events, can be refuted by others, or generates other interesting hypotheses—all standards used in science. The focus is on how an act of communication represents or reconstructs something, and what gives a particular representation its force or its ability to persuade. Whatever makes a particular novel, painting, or film more popular or revered than another—or perhaps even a novel more powerful than a film—cannot be satisfactorily discussed by reference to the relative truth of each communication. Such media and individual works are discussed by communication scholars in terms of their rhetorical force or in terms of the nature or style of their representation.

Communication researchers use a range of analytical perspectives to wrestle content into some meaningful framework so that they might better understand how it is generated and how it frames our understanding of the world. Each theoretical perspective provides a particular point of view on understanding content. And different perspectives can be deployed as the situation demands. From a critical theoretical perspective, however, our task is not to understand variables affecting communication in an effort to attain seemingly perfect communication, as a mathematical model might lead us to do in another field of study. Indeed, as we have seen, because everybody approaches the act of communication with different histories and assumptions, such an ideal is impossible. Our task is instead to understand the social processes involved in the creation and transmission of meaning.

In approaching this task, we can focus, for example, on the agency of the individual producers: on the life and intent of the author and the dynamics involved in the publication of a particular media text. Working from another direction, we can consider the ways in which larger social structures and processes impose limits and pressures on the media and media messages. Like structuralists and semioticians, we can consider how both the organizational dimensions of a story and the signifiers deployed refer back to a larger set of social circumstances and ideas, how the sign system is itself part of a larger set of social processes and circumstances, or, following the lead of the post-structuralists, we can delve into the particularities of the meaning system that has been created by audience members in the act of interpretation.

Similarly, political economy offers insight into how politics and economics give form to media content. From this perspective, we can examine the production of content in terms of the interests of the producers and those paying for production, as well as the impact on content of government regulation, professional codes and values, and, especially, the profit motive. This perspective provides an account of why certain

12.2 ▶▶ ▶▶ ▶▶

ADVOCATING FOR CHANGE

Efforts by citizens' groups to encourage the development of comprehensive media and tele-communications systems have a long history in Canada—sometimes to encourage the growth of public ownership and/or Canadian-owned industry; other times to mitigate the effects of market forces on the cost and character of services and products. Precedents go back at least to the early decades of the twentieth century and the fight by citizens of the Prairie provinces of Alberta, Saskatchewan, and Manitoba to establish public ownership of telephone systems (Babe, 1990: 102–11). As distinctions were drawn between content and carriage during that period, however, telecommunication and media regulation began to develop largely independently of each other (Babe, 1990: 202–07). In that process—driven by values such as the need for an informed citizenship, access to a diversity of media, and cultural sovereignty—media regulation took on a higher public profile.

In this regard, federal government inquiries and commissions have often played an important role in animating public debate around media. In 1929, for instance, the government struck the first major inquiry into media: the Royal Commission on Radio the Broadcasting (Aird Report). The struggle for public broadcasting developed out of this inquiry, with the Canadian Radio League using it as a springboard to develop a broad public campaign that led to the institution of the Canadian Radio Broadcasting Commission—the predecessor to today's Canadian Broadcasting Corporation—in 1932.

As media industries expanded through the middle part of the twentieth century, government sponsored inquiries continued to play an important role in highlighting and bringing forward issues concerning their growth and development. Pressures to increase profits encouraged escalating concentration of ownership, which took a toll on content. The overall number of reporters and editorial voices declined as newspapers and broadcast newsrooms shared stories and other material across the chain, and owners took increasing liberties in shaping stories and other editorial content.

Source: openmedia.ca.

Openmedia.ca is just one of many citizen groups advocating for an open internet and other pro-internet policies.

Public outcries spawned several inquiries through the 1970s and '80s, including the 1970 Special Senate Committee Report on the Mass Media and the 1980 Royal Commission on Newspapers (Canada, 1971; Canada, 1981). These investigations provided forums for expressing public discontent on the state of these industries and, rising from those concerns, pressure from activists helped shape the development of alternatives to corporate media, such as community television and radio (cf. Goldberg, 1990; Girard, 1992; Hackett and Carroll, 2006: 167-8). However, in terms of large corporate media, few of the recommendations of these inquiries were ever acted upon (Skinner et al., 2005: 56–64).

Following changes in regulations that had been designed to keep newspaper, broadcasting, and telecommunications companies separate, a series of cross-media ownership deals were struck in 2000 that radically altered the Canadian mediascape. This was the first round of corporate consolidation designed to reap the supposed economic benefits of technological convergence. However, layoffs and corporate tinkering with editorial policy followed, prompting public calls for a federal inquiry into the effects of these mergers. And, in the mid-2000s, more public inquiries were conducted to look into the impact of concentration of ownership on the media, particularly news and editorial content.

Today, organizations such as Friends of Canadian Broadcasting (www.friends.ca), Open Media (www.openmedia.ca), and the Canadian Internet Policy and Public Interest Clinic (cippic.ca) continue to lobby governments and advocate on broadcasting and telecommunications issues on behalf of the public.

kinds of content are produced and disseminated and other kinds are not.

At quite a different level again, organizational analysis provides insight into how the characteristics of specific organizations—such as whether an organization is mandate-driven or profit-oriented—impinge on media content. We can also gain an understanding of content through analyzing the characteristics of particular media forms, such as news stories, ads, soap operas, documentaries, and music videos: how ads are constructed to draw us in; how news presentation privileges the news anchor or one of the protagonists in a story; how investigative television can present a convincing veracity where there may be none at all; and how soap operas captivate audience members in their presentations of fictional characters. Each of these perspectives contributes to the richness of our understanding of both referents (signifieds) and the symbols (signifiers) used to represent them.

With the overall understanding these various perspectives make possible, we can then extend our understanding of the nature and roles of the media in society. We can understand, for example, how the media are separate from, yet intrinsic to, society. We can appreciate the role they play in incorporating content from subcultures, making it part of the culture as a whole, or how they can reject as legitimate perfectly normal styles of living that are a part of any culture. We can also gain a sense of how autonomous the media are in their capacity to create their own realities, what their inherent shortcomings are, and, by extension, why we might need mechanisms that help ensure they cannot entrap us in a world of their own construction.

But the encoding or construction of media messages is only one side of the equation. Decoding, or how they are received, is another. Thus, we have also considered how audience members engage with the media—what they take from the media and how.

The first principle in understanding content–audience interaction is recognizing that it is an active process. Even when distracted, audience members are meaning-generating entities. That is, they filter information and entertainment through their own histories and understandings of the world, through established opinions and knowledge, and through situational variables—fatigue, their assessment of the presentation, other pressing concerns of the day, their anticipation of certain events, their position in the workforce, and so on. Similarly, the media are active generators of meaning insofar as they create programs targeted at certain audiences, with certain intensities, designed to engage audience members in a certain fashion.

Early studies of audiences perceived them as relatively passive, and the media as having direct effects on human behaviour and attitudes. While evidence for this latter notion is controversial at best, the argument that media serve some sort of agenda-setting function, or that they work to cultivate particular conceptions or attitudes, has gained some credibility among researchers. From this perspective, media don't so much tell people *what to think* as they do *what to think about*. Another perspective drawn from early effects research that we considered was uses and gratifications research, which analyzes the uses to which audience members put media content and the satisfaction and reward audience members feel they derive from media content.

Working from a different starting point, we also considered theories that focus on the ways that the media position audiences to reproduce dominant social ideas and values. Marxist perspectives on media, for instance, illustrate how they often serve to promote the ideas and values associated with capitalism, while the Frankfurt School's examination of the industrialization of the production of information and entertainment illustrates how economics structures cultural form in general.

In the face of these critiques, researchers of British cultural studies strove to better understand the complexity of the dynamics between media and audiences. Working with youth subcultures and social movements, their emphasis was on audience members as active agents and the numerous ways different groups of people engaged with media content. Working from yet another direction, feminist research illustrates how media and practices of communication contribute to social inequalities in terms of sex and gender.

Industry-based research approaches audiences from another direction, as commodities to be sold to advertisers. Such a perspective emphasizes quite different variables. At a first level, the number of people in the audience is of central importance. Then come their age, education, gender, income level, location, and so forth, followed by a consideration of how these elements are indicative of certain characteristics, such as specific attitudes; consumption patterns of particular products; and the time they spend listening, reading, and/or watching. Such information is valuable for the business of buying, selling, renting, and accessing audiences, and is also valuable in understanding general patterns in society.

The media and audiences tend to engage each other in diverse ways, and the resulting interaction creates many social issues. The various starting points and perspectives we use to gain insight into what audiences make of content reflect that diversity. In simple terms, media content, such as hate speech, may serve as an igniting spark for anti-social behaviour—a good reason for us to be concerned about content generation and how media might contribute to anti-social behaviour. But media content may also inspire lifelong ambition, grand humanitarian gestures, respect for individual freedom, social plurality, cultural values, and the building of community. This positive spark is even more important to understand.

As interactive public communication systems become more common in society, it is increasingly important to understand how media systems and content frame and animate social life.

The Social Dimensions of Media and Communication

Having acquired some understanding of the character and history of media, as well as some of the key perspectives on their content and interaction with audiences, we can turn to some of the larger social dimensions of media and communications: (1) policy, or, more comprehensively speaking, law and policy; (2) ownership and control of communication institutions; (3) the role and actions of professionals; and (4) information and communication technology and globalization.

Public Policy

Policy creates a framework for how these factors play themselves out. It provides a set of rules and regulations governing the way information and media products are created and consumed. For instance, the Broadcasting Act describes the roles and responsibilities of the various elements of the broadcasting system, helping ensure that Canadian ideas and perspectives are represented in Canadian media content. Copyright legislation works to develop markets for media products and other forms of intellectual property. Privacy legislation works to protect the rights of individuals. Advertising regulations frame the kinds of claims advertisers can make and the kinds of products they may advertise. Libel laws structure the way journalists and news organizations operate. And income tax policies encourage advertisers to spend their ad dollars with Canadian media outlets and ensure Canadian ownership of newspapers.

Creating a Place for Canada

At a more basic level, policy also creates opportunities for Canadian media producers. As we have seen, the market is itself a form of regulation, and left to its own devices favours some interests over others. Because of the economies of scale involved, it is simply much cheaper for Canadian broadcasters to buy foreign programming than it is to produce their own. Thus, particularly in English Canada, without Canadian-content regulations, there would be even more US programming on television than there is now.

Similarly, as we have seen, prior to the enactment of content regulations for radio in the 1970s, less than 5 percent of the music played on domestic radio stations was Canadian. This was not because Canadians did not make good music, but because of the marketing and publicity spilling over from US markets into Canada, as well as other factors. It was simply more lucrative for Canadian radio owners to play American music. As well, there is not the same market in the States for Canadian cultural materials as there is in Canada for US products. Again, this is not because Canadian products are somehow of inferior quality but the result of simple economics. American producers supply more than enough product to meet demand in their home markets and—due to economies of scale—it is cheaper to use that product than purchase Canadian content. These economics necessitate some form of regulation if Canadian media products are going to find space on the shelves in their home markets. The situation is somewhat different in Quebec, where a range of cultural factors allow homegrown products to compete successfully with foreign fare.

In short, public policy shapes the ground—particularly the economic ground—on which media products are created and, in turn, influences the character of those products and the ways they represent the world.

Ownership

A long-standing focus in Canadian media policy has been concerned with forms of **ownership**, and the interests of owners are seen to have significant effects on the content and character of media. In the face of cheap US media products, Canadian ownership and content regulations have been used to create an economics of Canadian production and to prevent Canadian media companies and markets from becoming simple extensions of their American cousins. In the broadcasting, cable, and telecommunications industries, legislation imposes limits on foreign ownership. In the newspaper industry, tax policy ensures that newspapers stay in Canadian hands.

At the same time, however, as we saw in Chapter 7, a number of public inquiries have voiced concern about how the economic forces underlying private ownership lead to escalating concentration of ownership and a narrowing range of voices and perspectives in the media. Consequently, issues of ownership in Canada have been framed by various government regulations that, on the one hand, have tried to keep the ownership of Canadian media in Canadian hands, and, on the other hand, have wrestled with the drawbacks and supposed benefits of allowing for large, privately owned media companies to get a foothold in the industry. As a result, no media industry in Canada is governed exclusively by **free-market economics**; the industries are constrained by a multitude of regulations and, in some cases, reflect a complex mixture of public and private enterprise.

The central difference between public and private forms of ownership pertains to the mandate or purposes that guide their operations. In contradistinction to privately owned media that foreground the profit motive, public and community media are mandated to serve broad social purposes. As laid out in the 1991 Broadcasting Act, Section 3.1(l), for instance, the CBC is to "provide radio and television services incorporating a wide range of programming that informs, enlightens and entertains." Just as the CBC did in the development of television, in the face of shifting technologies today, it has moved to develop a range of web-based services. Chief among these are an increasing number of television programs that can be downloaded from its website (www.cbc.ca); CBC Music, an online site that provides over 50 radio streams; ICI Musique, a French-language streaming service; and CBC Radio 3, an online radio service devoted to new and emerging independent Canadian music.

Community media also are expected to fulfill social goals. For instance, while the mandate of community television stations is not enunciated in legislation, in its 2010 Community Television Policy the CRTC specifies that "the role of the community [television] channel should be primarily of a public service nature, facilitating self-expression through free and open access by members of the community" (CRTC, 2010a). Similarly, but set at the organizational level, the

12.3 ▶▶▶▶▶▶

NATIONAL CAMPUS AND COMMUNITY RADIO ASSOCIATION/ASSOCIATION NATIONALE DES RADIOS ÉTUDIANTES ET COMMUNAUTAIRES (NCRA/ANREC)

Broadcasting in over 60 languages, member stations of the NCRA/ANREC employ over 180 full-time staff and 5,900 volunteers, who work an estimated 21,000 hours per week. Community radio is about volunteerism, social engagement, independent music, learning by doing, community capacity building, citizen journalism, and more. Here's a quick sketch of the NCRA:

- total watts of broadcasting power: 85,882
- staff: 182.5 (full-time equivalent)
- volunteer force: 5,992 working an estimated 21,000 hours per week

Source: www.ncra.ca/about-cc-radio.

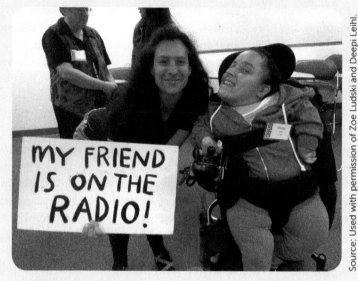

Source: Used with permission of Zoe Ludski and Deepi Leihl.

On the left is NCRA volunteer Cousin Awd, host of CJMP's *42 Fish* in Powell River, BC, meeting with Vancouver-based CITR volunteer news reporter Deepi Leihl at the National Community Radio Conference hosted by CFUV in Victoria.

Statement of Principles of the National Campus and Community Radio Association/Association Nationale des Radios Étudiantes et Communautaires (NCRA/ANREC), which represents 80 campus and community stations across the country, notes "that mainstream media fails to recognize or in many instances reinforces social and economic inequities that oppress women and minority groups of our society" and commits members to "providing alternative radio to an audience that is recognized as being diverse in ethnicity, culture, gender, sexual orientation, age, and physical and mental ability" (NCRA, 1987).

Still, private ownership is the dominant ownership form within the media system and, in the face of ongoing pressure to tie the expansion of Canadian media to the profit motive, to what degree a larger set of public purposes might be maintained within the system is in question.

One of the central features of Canadian media policy has been to protect the revenues of Canadian media producers in order to ensure that they are profitable enough to invest in production. Yet, as we have seen, particularly in the broadcasting sector, it has always been a struggle to get the big private corporations to invest in quality Canadian programs, and changes in technology are working to narrow the range of private corporations at work within the Canadian mediascape.

With the digitization of information, communication systems that were once capable of carrying only one type of message can now carry a range of signals. Telephone, cable, and satellite systems all can be used to transmit television, telephone, and computer data. Webcasting is poised to supplant traditional television and radio broadcasting, and traditional newspaper and periodical delivery as well. And information-based products, like news and advertising, once destined for one medium, are now tailored for use across a range of media. Spurred by this technological convergence, companies in what were once separate industries, like newspapers and television or cable television and telecommunication, are vying to break into each others' markets and fuelling corporate convergence—in other words, concentration of ownership.

With companies trying to capture cost savings by forging new economies of scale and scope, recent trends toward concentration of ownership have raised particular concerns. Some of the important *synergies*—as the efficiencies gleaned from consolidation are sometimes called—sought by these corporations are reduced labour requirements; cross-promotion of media products; larger and more flexible advertising markets; the *repurposing* of content created for use in one medium for use in another; the integration of executive and administrative functions; and vastly increased barriers to entry for would-be competitors. Consequently, concentration is seen as narrowing the range of perspectives and distinct voices available in the media, while new editorial policies and sanctions evolving through these changes are raising fears for editorial independence.

Bu as we have seen, while the internet presents many new opportunities for producing and distributing media content, it is not the fountain of alternatives to traditional media that some pundits claim. High-quality media content is expensive to produce. Most of the news found on the internet comes from professional organizations, and most blogs and posts simply republish or comment upon it.

Professionalism

Professionalism governs communications and cultural production in its own way. Cultural producers are not, strictly speaking, "professionals" in the same manner that lawyers and doctors are. Law and medicine require accredited formal training, permission to practise from recognized licensing bodies, and are subject to their own specialized regulatory authorities. But cultural producers nonetheless derive a sense of professionalism from their specialized skills, their practice-specific codes of ethics, recognized sets of qualitative conventions, and, above all, the conviction that their work is an essential contribution to *culture* in the fullest sense of the term. Like other kinds of professionals, cultural producers owe some allegiance to their employer or their client and they remain subject to laws particular to the communications field, such as those pertaining to libel, copyright, privacy, and access to information. But their professionalism means that cultural producers are especially responsible to uphold and advance the recognized standards of their practice and to earn the respect of their peers.

Cultural producers' sense of professionalism is tied very closely to the Enlightenment ideals of freedom of speech, freedom of expression, and freedom of the press, of questioning and challenging received wisdom and other forms of authority. They promote the notion that mass communication, which, in all its manifestations,

Many students do internships as a way to get experience in the field and on-the-job training. The Canadian Intern Association (www.intern association.ca) advocates against the exploitation of interns and aims to improve the internship experience for both interns and employers.

Source: © Steve Debenport/iStockphoto.

is a key element of a democratic society. While we might attribute these ideals most readily to journalists, most cultural producers might make the claim that their communicative activities serve the cultural, political, social, and/or economic goals of society.

This sense of professionalism, though, is being eroded. Employers are increasingly treating cultural producers simply as workers like any others—replaceable parts in the assembly line of production, subject to layoffs and buyouts, relegated to contract work, compelled to emphasize quantitative efficiencies over qualitative merits. Newsrooms are shrinking across all platforms, television dramas share prime time with reality formats, radio hosts are replaced by computerized music programming, and freelance magazine writers work for the same rates they were being paid 30 years ago. The government policies that promote cultural production in Canada, as we described in Chapters 7 and 8, do little to protect cultural producers within their own industries.

Faced with fragmenting audiences and shrinking revenues, media corporations are laying off full-time employees and turning to contract workers or freelancers who are generally paid less, have little if any job security, and few benefits. For people trying to get their first job in media, unpaid internships have become a seemingly necessary rite of passage. But paid employment often remains elusive for many and, recently, governments have begun to crack down on internships that they perceive to be illegal and exploitive (CTV, 2014b). At the same time, labour unions such as the Canadian Media Guild (cmg-freelance.ca) have been working to help improve working conditions for this new army of part-time workers through providing a range of supports, such as mentoring, training, and helping improve working conditions.

Information and Communications Technology and Globalization

Technology does not exist in a vacuum or as a social force on its own. While different theoretical perspectives on technology afford both its developers and adopters differing levels of agency, as we have seen, technology is the product of a complex set of political, economic, and social forces that work to shape and configure its development. Policy also helps to set the context for technology. Whether in terms of government aid for research and development, licensing that allows organizations to offer particular technological services (e.g., cellphones, cable or satellite TV), tax incentives that encourage individuals or organizations to adopt particular technologies (or ownership mandates), policy can play a number of important roles in technological development. In communication, policy issues, such as who can use what technology for what purpose, who can control that technology, and how that control can be exploited, are critical.

Because technology encompasses machines, techniques, and social institutions, it has a substantial impact on the structure and functioning of society as a transformative agent, an agent of change that may bring both negative and positive consequences. And while we often think of information and communications technology (ICT) in terms of content, such as film, video, television, or music, one of the most dramatic changes it might be implicated in is a shift in the locus of control: the greater the ability to communicate, the further the control system can be from the phenomenon being controlled. As the history of communication illustrates, communication developments have often led to increased centralization of control. Whether in terms of the centralization of political control, as in the case of the railway and communications technology enabling early Canadian governments to exert east–west control over the northern territory of North America, or in the case of the centralization of economic control, as today's transnational corporations harness information technology to coordinate supply and demand in global markets (media markets and others), ICT is often a key vehicle for addressing problems of spatialization.

ICTs are not the first set of technologies that have been seen as reshaping society (see Box 12.4), but the social changes arising from

Source: Scott Greene, *Channel Babel*, oil on canvas, 1998. Courtesy of the artist and Catherine Clark Gallery, San Francisco, California, USA.

Communication and accompanying media pervade our lives in modern society. The power of both the world-wide transmission of messages and the transformation that digital communication offers is the foundation for the remaking/reordering of society.

the widespread implementation of ICTs are far-reaching, and they are central to the industrial restructuring taking place both at home and abroad.

The global economy is not a new development and there has been strong global trade for over 500 years. But since the mid-1970s economic recession and the lure of cheap labour have fuelled international trade agreements and the investment of manufacturing capital in places like Southeast Asia, China, northern Mexico, and the American Sunbelt. To combat this competition, companies remaining in traditional industrial centres restructured, reducing staff and adopting labour-saving technologies.

Through facilitating the movement of capital and goods, ICT has been important in facilitating

this shift in labour processes, providing a vital link between the newly industrialized countries where these goods are now produced and the markets in old industrialized centres, such as North America and Western Europe, where they are consumed. ICT also has been central to the reorganization of industry in these old industrial centres, where it has been used to centralize control over operations, amalgamate responsibilities and functions, and more closely monitor and coordinate employees as companies have restructured to confront new global competitors.

As the information economy has taken form, ever-growing types of information commodities, both products and services, have been created. Changes in copyright legislation, for instance, provide legal sanctions against the

12.4 ▶▶▶▶▶▶

KONDRATIEV WAVES: TRACKING TECHNOLOGICAL CHANGE

Nikolai Kondratiev hypothesized that economies expand and contract with the introduction of new technologies. According to this theory, the waves or cycles last approximately 50 years and there have been five such waves since about 1800, based on (1) steam power; (2) the railway; (3) electrical and chemical engineering; (4) petrochemicals and automobiles; and (5) the current cycle of information technology, with its basis on the microchip and digitization.

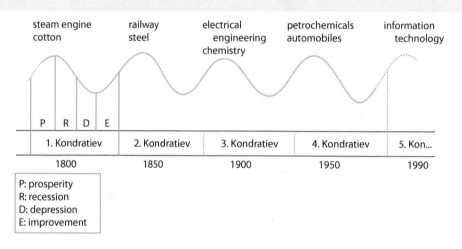

FIGURE 12.1   Kondratiev Wave

Source: Nikolai Kondratiev, *The Major Economic Cycles* (1925).

unauthorized copying of computer software, video and sound recordings, television programs, and other forms of data, and these changes have been instrumental in developing and expanding multi-million dollar markets for these products. Similarly, sanctions against photocopying for other than personal use and royalties on public photocopiers and blank CDs have created new revenue streams for media companies and creators. Twenty-five years ago, professors often copied class readings and other course materials and handed them out to students for the cost of the copying. Today, such behaviour might be subject to heavy fines or even imprisonment.

The television universe available via cable, satellite, and the internet also has expanded dramatically, as has the cost. Video games have become big business. Education, a necessarily information-based activity, has become increasingly commercialized and responsible to market forces. The internet has given rise to an expanding range of new web-based businesses and services, and access to the internet itself has become an increasingly costly service. With a whole new set of mobile telecommunications and internet-based services and products soon to hit the market, the information economy is proceeding apace.

Issues and Policy Trends

In the shifting field of communication, various new issues are rising and old concerns are taking new form.

Over-the-Top Video

As we illustrated in Chapter 8, online or *over-the-top* (OTT) video delivery services such as Netflix, Google TV, and Apple TV threaten to overwhelm the Canadian television system. Because the CRTC has previously ruled that that it would not regulate Internet content, these services lie outside of the regulatory system. Consequently, without the obligation to contribute to the production of Canadian programming, or even to ensure that Canadian programs are available on their systems, they sidestep the regulations that literally make Canadian television possible.

In the face a number of issues confronting broadcasting regulation, including the growing influence of these services, the CRTC held a public hearing in the fall of 2014 called "Let's Talk TV" (www.crtc.gc.ca/eng/talktv-parlonstele.htm). A wide range of organizations and individuals responded to the CRTC's call for comments—including TV, cable and satellite companies, program producers, media workers unions, advocacy organizations, as well as thousands of individual Canadians. Hundreds travelled to the CRTC headquarters in Hull, Quebec, to speak at the hearing. While they attended the hearing, both Netflix and Google refused to disclose key information to the CRTC regarding the number of Canadians subscribing to their services. And, as a result of that intransigence, the CRTC removed their testimony from the public record (Bradshaw, 2014b).

As this book goes to press, the CRTC has yet to respond to the issues and concerns raised at the hearing. While some people argue that it is impossible to regulate the internet, and that we should finally surrender to the logic of the market, as we have seen in previous chapters, new technologies have long threatened to overwhelm the Canadian broadcasting system with foreign programming. And, with varying degrees of success, regulators have found ways to meet with those challenges.

In 1932, for instance, as a flood of US radio signals threatened to smother the nascent Canadian radio broadcasting system, the Canadian Radio Broadcasting Commission was put into place to help counter that threat. In 1952, with US television signals rolling across the border and attracting Canadian audiences, the CBC and the government mounted a feverish campaign to build a Canadian television system. And in the mid-1960s, when cable TV was set to overwhelm the adolescent Canadian system with popular US channels, the 1968 Broadcasting Act made cable companies responsible to the broad social purposes of broadcasting and a series of regulations like simultaneous substitution helped make the industry a responsible player within the system. In the 1980s, and again in the early 1990s, signals from US satellite broadcasters sent regulators scrambling to find ways to keep Canadians tuned in to the system. Scores of new pay-TV channels and a boost to the Canadian production industry was the response to that crisis.

In the face of all these technological threats to the domestic mediascape, regulators were able to forge a system that delivered Canadian perspectives to Canadian viewers. As its many critics point out, the current regulatory system is not perfect. And if history is to be our guide, any regulatory solutions to the current problems facing the system will inevitably be temporary and fleeting. To surrender to the latest technology, however, might well lead to the representation of Canadian ideas and values being overwhelmed by foreign programming on the growing range of screens watched by Canadian audiences. Solutions to these concerns, such as geo-blocking, do exist. Whether the CRTC and/or the federal government choose to exercise these options remains to be seen.

Foreign Ownership

Increasing foreign ownership of Canadian media is also a developing issue. The current Conservative federal government and its allies argue that increasing foreign ownership in the telecommunications sector will boost investment in the industry and result in lower mobile telephone prices and better services. Critics, however, point out a number of problems with this plan. First, given the growing cross-media ownership between telecommunications and broadcasting companies, allowing foreign ownership of telecommunications will inevitably lead to foreign ownership of broadcasting and a decline in investment in Canadian media production. Second, they argue that there is no incentive for foreign companies to invest in providing services in areas that present little return, such as in rural communities and the Far North—the areas most in need of investment to bridge digital divides. And third, there is concern that regulators are less able to exert control over foreign-owned companies than over their domestic counterparts. How this issue plays out could affect Canadian control over the long-term development of both the telecommunications and broadcasting fields.

Digital Divides

At another level, **digital divides** at the local, regional, national, and global levels threaten to split the information society into a world of *haves* and *have-nots*. Without computers and high-speed access to the internet, or the knowledge of how to use these technologies effectively, many people are excluded from the political, economic, and social benefits enabled by these technologies. As acquiring information increasingly hinges on the ability to pay for it, it is difficult for schools, universities, and public libraries to keep up with the rising cost. Consequently, the quality of education and general availability of information are being reduced and those people and organizations that cannot pay for it are in danger of being deprived of these crucial communications resources. (As Jennifer Pybus points out, there is also an important divide between circulating personal information on the internet and understanding the implications that information may have on our lives. See Box 12.5, "Digital Literacy.")

There are also many places on earth outside of the wired world and, thereby, outside the reach of information technology. In Canada, rural areas with small populations such as in the Prairies and the North don't present the economies of scale to make it profitable for large corporations to invest in communications infrastructure and to supply services. Such areas, then, are sometimes left outside of the digital world. Similarly, in many areas of the Global South, people simply cannot afford to buy into the communications transformation taking place.

Privacy

Privacy, too, is of rising concern. As social life is increasingly mediated by ICT, information about our activities is being monitored and collected by numerous organizations and government agencies. The unauthorized use of this information threatens our privacy in a number of ways. In the workplace, ICT can be used to monitor email and telephone conversations, or to count keystrokes and attempt to measure the volume of work undertaken by employees. (Charles Frederick Taylor, the originator of scientific management in the workplace in the early twentieth century, would be pleased!) Insurance companies purchase health and accident records in an attempt to assess the potential risk of applicants, sometimes denying coverage on this basis. Law-enforcement agencies are considering ways to use the information contained in databases to identify potential criminal suspects. And in both Canada and the United States, there is ongoing debate between law-enforcement agencies and public-interest groups over the right of government agencies to monitor electronic conversations and data flow.

These concerns are compounded by the fact that both personal information and important social, legal, and economic information is often stored and processed outside of the country. Private corporations, governments, universities, libraries, and the legal and engineering professions all sometimes use data services and networks outside of Canada to process and store personal tax, credit, and medical data, as well as

12.5 ▶▶▶▶▶▶

DATA LITERACY

By Jennifer Pybus

Data literacy is an emergent field that seeks to empower people to critically understand the dynamic flows and processes related to our steadily growing digital footprint, while providing tools to actively engage with the data we collectively generate. Currently, we produce more than 2.5 billion gigabytes daily with estimates of a 2,000 percent increase by 2020 (Tucker, 2013). Yet, the value generated from this data primarily benefits social media platforms, analytics firms and corporations. Similarly, security agencies are accumulating, collating, cross-checking, and analyzing user-generated data for their purposes. In the face of this growing imbalance between those who produce data and those who produce value from it, data literacy strives to create new forms of digital literacies, such as privacy literacies, information literacies, code literacies, algorithmic literacies, database literacies and so forth.

The foundations for data literacy are based on the developments in the digital humanities. Scholars in this discipline are considered data literate if they are able to access, assess, convert, manipulate, summarize, and (re)present large datasets (Schield, 2004). Data literacy, as such, is a precondition for research, demanding a clear understanding of the relationships between the people and things it represents, as well as the complex digital environments within which it is applied and utilized (Prado and Marzal, 2013). The challenge for the everyday user is to develop aspects of these highly specialized skills to engage with their own data that circulates amidst various digital platforms. Part of data literacy must then be to help the non-technical user engage with those platforms at the level of code, algorithms and databases. For instance, Kevin Driscoll (2012) has introduced the idea of "code literacy" in the context of understanding the circulation of a user's Twitter.

In addition, data literacy would benefit from building on the rich paradigm of media literacy, which examines the social, political, and economic conditions that govern the media's influence on our everyday lives. Rather than focus on mediated texts, representations, and discourses, however, data literacy is predicated on what Mayer-Shoenberger and Cukier refer to as *datafication* (2013). In this regard, data literacy looks to the dynamic ways in which a user's cultural practices and sociality become quantified, not only on various social media platforms—wherein user-generated content is used to generate advertising revenue—but equally by considering the privacy agreements that govern information-sharing practices on browsers and mobile applications. Data literacy can then extend media literacy by focusing our attention on the circumstances that allow a user's data to be circulated, shared, stored, recalled and re-used within highly proprietary digitalized environments.

Moving forward, a comprehensive approach to media literacy needs to include a consideration of data literacy so that users can initiate and demand more transparency, autonomy and control over their own data and, thereby, their own lives.

—Jennifer Pybus is a lecturer at the Winchester School of Art, University of Southampton.

educational materials and information on natural resources and other matters of national import. Because this trans-border data flow places the information outside of the reach of national laws and regulation, it raises a host of issues for both Canadian sovereignty and the economy, and it leaves Canadians vulnerable to a host of potential problems, including trade sanctions, bankruptcies, and theft.

Concern over these infringements on personal privacy centres on the issue of self-determination (see Box 12.6). As private corporations and governments increase their abilities to monitor and control individual action, personal freedom is reduced to a series of choices that are predetermined by forces outside of the individual's knowledge and control. As the ongoing debate over the federal government's decision to discontinue

12.6

PRIVACY: KEEPING OUR PRIVATE LIVES PRIVATE

As our lives become increasingly mediated by electronic technologies, information regarding our activities is being monitored and stored in massive databases. Every time you visit a medical facility, fill out an application, use a credit or debit card, give out your social insurance number, or even sit down at a computer, chances are that information about that activity is being monitored and recorded. These records reveal much about ourselves and are often used by organizations to exert economic and political control over our lives.

Sometimes, breaches in privacy can take on particularly sinister tones. Take, for instance, the case of Sean Bruyea, a 1991 Gulf War veteran and leading advocate for wounded Canadian veterans and their families. A story in the *Toronto Star* on 18 November 2010 reported that Bruyea launched a lawsuit against the federal government after learning that sensitive medical documents were accessed and passed around "by hundreds of federal bureaucrats, including policy-makers," in an effort to discredit him and his lobbying efforts. The story detailed how "Bruyea alleged bureaucrats wanted to use his medical records, particularly psychiatric reports, to 'falsely portray me and my advocacy to help other veterans as merely a manifestation of an unstable mind.'" Canada's privacy commissioner, Jennifer Stoddart, had "ruled that Bruyea's case was 'alarming' and the treatment of his personal information was 'entirely inappropriate.'" The lawsuit resulted in a settlement and apology from Veterans Affairs Minister Jean-Pierre Blackburn (Cheadle, 2010). Since that time, Bruyea has gone on to become a staunch advocate for veteran's rights. (See his website: www.seanbruyea.com.)

At a time when our every online move can be monitored and information about us is almost always stored electronically, Sean Bruyea's case reminds us that breaches in privacy can provide others unwarranted power and control over our lives.

Statistics Canada's long-form census illustrates, however, comprehensive information about the population as a whole is also critical to intelligent social planning and efficient government (*The Globe and Mail*, 2010). Consequently, information collection and tracking is a double-edged sword.

Other Issues

In the midst of ongoing technological change, there are also a number of other issues facing regulators. As convergence accelerates, for instance, the CRTC is faced with trying to improve the overall coherence of the regulatory framework and there are discussions around merging the Broadcasting and Telecommunications Acts. A concern here is what might happen to the cultural objectives of broadcasting should such a merger take place.

Protecting access to the internet is also an ongoing concern, and net neutrality and throttling continue to be issues for the CRTC. To contend with ongoing ownership consolidation and rapid technological change, the CRTC is also asking Parliament for greater powers, particularly in terms of being able to issue fines to companies that do not comply with regulations. While the CRTC has the power to suspend an intransigent company's licence, it is loath to do so, as such action might cause serious problems for the customers of those companies if they were to unexpectedly shut down. Consequently, the CRTC is looking for more flexible means of discipline.

Shifting Economic Currents

The changing media environment is not only animating change in the realm of public policy, but, as some critics argue, it is also shifting the economics of media production.

The Long Tail

Popularized by Chris Anderson, editor-in-chief of *Wired* magazine, in a book of the same title, the **long-tail** phenomenon refers to what appears to be a change in the economics of media production brought on by the electronic storage and distribution of media productions.

The book begins with a bow in the direction of blockbuster hits, which, as Anderson points out, are the foundation of massive media and entertainment industries. Hits rule, he says, and, thus, the factors that are fundamental to making hits also rule: centralized production, celebrities, huge production budgets, massive marketing campaigns, restricted distribution systems, and formulas that attract members of the mass public, who are seeking entertainment. Everyone makes money when a hit comes along. An author such as J.K. Rowling earned a substantial amount of money when each new title in the Harry Potter series was published—sharing in the economic windfall were her agent; her publishers around the world; the designers; the editors; the warehouse staff; the booksellers; the filmmakers; the lawyers who draw up the movie rights, toy rights, and product rights; the actors; and the theatre owners. In fact, everyone benefits financially—right down to the babysitter who fills in because the usual sitter who must go and see the latest movie adaptation.

So lucrative are hits that the entire industry is hooked on finding the next blockbuster. Potential sales channel and determine retail opportunities, whether space on a bookshelf, music store shelf, or magazine rack, screen time in a movie theatre, or a time slot or playlist on television or radio. To gain exposure, a product must fit an established category that sells. In books, such categories are mysteries, biography, romance, politics, self-help; on TV they are drama, reality TV, news, current events, game shows, and sports. Once comfortably slotted into a consumer category, the product must perform in comparison with established norms—it must sell at a certain pace from the opening days of its availability or else it vanishes unsold from the mainstream marketplace.

Cultural markets work in such a manner because the distribution and display system is both costly and highly competitive. Hits are the high flyers, but for the normal to slow sellers, it is a dog-eat-dog world; sales monitored week by week tell the tale of what products will survive and which will vanish. If it a product isn't selling as quickly as retailers think it should be, away it goes and a new version takes its place.

The point Anderson makes in his book, however, is that distribution/display costs are much more forgiving in the online world. Once digital copies of a piece of music, a book, a film, or a game are uploaded into an online inventory, they can stay available indefinitely at a very low cost, perhaps selling only a few copies each year. Figure 12.2 is taken from an online essay of Anderson's, published under a Creative Commons licence, which illustrates this point (www.changethis.com/manifesto/show/10.LongTail). It depicts a typical *long-tail* distribution and describes the different sales and availability at Walmart (a "bricks-and-mortar" chain) and Rhapsody (an online distributor): Walmart carries 39,000 titles; Rhapsody well over 200,000. At the left-hand side of the graph are the hits and other bestsellers, with the vertical axis representing the number, or frequency, of sales. Moving to the right, we see the pattern of sales for those titles that are not bestsellers.

As the curve suggests, most surprisingly, a high percentage of the products available on the right side of the curve are accessed by consumers. In other words, a significant number of sales come from this extended inventory. Similar data patterns were reported by Ecast, a digital jukebox company. At one point, the company noted that 98 percent of the 10,000 albums that were available sold at least one track every three months. In other words, when a vendor has very low display/distribution costs, and item costs are low but access is easy, consumers choose widely rather than focusing their choices solely on hits. The same pattern is reported by Apple with its iTunes service.

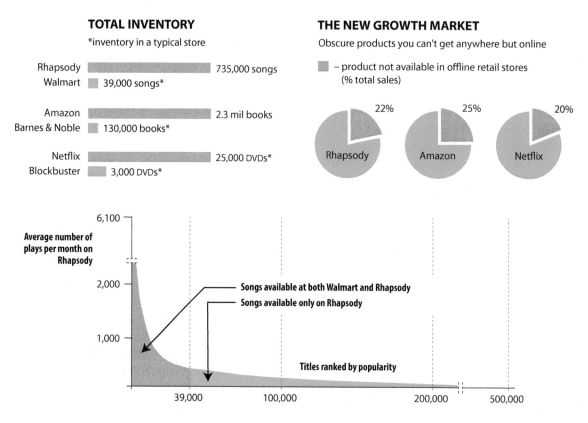

FIGURE 12.2 Anatomy of the Long Tail

Online services carry far more inventory than traditional retailers. Rhapsody, for example, offers 19 times as many songs as Walmart's stock of 39,000 tunes. The appetite for Rhapsody's more obscure tunes (charted in dark blue) makes up the so-called long tail. Meanwhile, even as consumers flock to mainstream books, music, and films (bottom), there is a real demand for niche fare found only online.

The pie graphs in Figure 12.2 indicate that the sales of music not carried by Walmart and other major music stores are not trivial. They account for 20 to 25 percent of the profit for an online retailer like Amazon. True, they may represent as much as 90 percent of inventory, but when the cost of holding and managing the inventory is reduced to close to zero, as it can be with digital products and computerized control, there is a viable business.

Online services carry far more inventory than traditional retailers. In Anderson's example, for instance, Rhapsody offers 19 times as many songs as Walmart's stock of 39,000 tunes. The appetite for Rhapsody's more obscure tunes (charted in dark blue) makes up the so-called long tail.

The selection enabled by this kind of inventory provides online retailers a distinct advantage over bricks-and-mortar ones. Moreover, having such an expanded inventory provides more sales opportunities, as consumers purchasing a copy of a currently popular song, film, or book can be automatically directed to similar products found in the long tail. As the automated message one receives after making an online purchase reads, "Customers interested in (insert popular song, book, film title you purchased here) were also interested in (insert long-tail title here)."

At the same time, low cost and easy access combine in this universe of expanded choice to produce exploratory behaviour. Such exploration by large numbers of people produces sales of all kinds of products. In the light of this shifting filed of consumer choice, Anderson says we need to understand that the economics of online retailing allow for a fundamentally more inclusive and diverse set of choices than one governed by scarce and expensive retail display space. What impact the long tail may have on the market for Canadian media products remains to be seen. In the meantime, however, it demonstrates that, even in a seemingly open market, supply and performance are not produced by simple consumer demand but rather by the structure of the system of production, distribution, and retailing.

Is More Choice a Bad Choice?

While the seemingly ever-growing number of media choices would appear to be a bonanza for consumers as Napoli (2011) illustrates, in terms of broadcast media in particular, it can have negative impacts on the range and quality of products available. There are at least two dimensions to this concern.

First, is the fact that while there may be a large number of channels and networks available, many of them have very small audiences. As Napoli points out (2011: 67), while "the average television household in the United States receives over 120 channels . . . (but) 90 percent . . . have audience shares under one percent." Obviously, the fact that these channels have small audiences means that they have very little, if any, money to devote to original production.

Second, this problem is compounded by the fact that as audiences for such channels shrink, their programming budgets seem to shrink disproportionately faster. Napoli goes on to states,

> industry data indicate that as the potential audience for a cable network shrinks, the amount of money spent on programming shrinks even more. Thus, for instance, networks such as Discovery, Nickelodeon, and MTV, which have more than 90 million subscribers, spend roughly 250

million dollars on programming. When we consider cable networks with roughly half that many subscribers (such as Bloomberg, Nicktoons, and National Geographic), the annual programming budget drops to roughly 35 million dollars. And when we cut the potential audience in half yet again (for networks such as Boomerang or the Anime Network, which have only 20–25 million subscribers), annual programming budgets drop to roughly 12 million dollars. (2011: 67–8)

In other words, it would appear that the economies of scale created by their larger audiences enable large networks to spend more per audience member on programming than networks capturing smaller audiences.

The net effect of these phenomena is that many stations or networks have little money to spend on original programming. Consequently, they employ a range of strategies to fill their program schedules. For instance, one common strategy is to repeat programs in different time slots, perhaps scheduling the same program at more than one time in the day or more than one day a week. Another common strategy, one particularly favoured by companies that own more than one channel or network, is to *repurpose* programs from one channel to another. In other words, they simply use the same programming on different channels or, more recently, on different platforms. Broadcasters holding the rights to sports programs are increasingly employing this strategy as they move to broadcast games on a range of different types of screens, such as television, tablets, or mobile devices. A third option that has become quite common is to schedule reruns of old programs where the broadcast rights cost a small fraction of creating or acquiring new programs. A recent example of this strategy was found on Zoomer TV, where they regularly schedule programs from the 1970s and '80s, such as *Columbo* and *Murder She Wrote*.

If, as Bruce Springsteen noted in his 1992 song, there were "57 channels (and nothin' on)," with over 150 channels today, there may be even less.

A "Free" Market for Cultural Products?

Is the unfettered market the best way to produce and consume social resources? As a society, we don't seem to think so in terms of big issues like health care, education, and the environment. In fact, leaving such important social resources to a simple calculus of commercialism would necessarily lead to greater social inequity and environmental devastation as the market sorted between the services and activities that were the most profitable and those people that could afford to pay to access them. In other words, particularly in terms of education and health care, we would end up with fewer options and fewer people being able to access them—in short, greater ignorance and illness. In terms of the environment, such a rationale would allow natural resources to be put to the purposes commanding the highest price, with little regard to the interests of the people or other flora and fauna that depend on the natural world for their survival. Global warming and the wholesale devastation of forests, fish, and other wildlife species are clear evidence of where this path leads.

By the same token, in the context of ICT and the media it encompasses, should our perspectives, knowledge, and understandings of the world be subject to a purely economic rationale? Historically, as we discussed in Chapter 7, the Canadian public and policy-makers have answered with a resounding "No." For over a century, governments and others have recognized the need for regulation if Canadians are to enjoy fair and affordable access to communications services and media as well as cultural content that represents the breadth of Canadian perspectives. Common-carriage regulation in telecommunications, the founding of the CBC, ownership regulations, Canadian-content regulations, production funds, and numerous other regulatory initiatives have been put into place to help ensure these purposes are met.

Yet over the last several decades, a pattern has emerged of cutting back on various forms of media regulation in favour of leaving business to market forces alone. Cuts to the CBC's budget, a gradual loosening of ownership regulations, including those governing foreign ownership and concentration, a winnowing of support for community and Aboriginal broadcasting, and the CRTC's reluctance to regulate the internet all exemplify this trend.

Although the internet is often touted as the solution to the traditional problems plaguing our media systems, left to simple market economics, the internet holds little promise for increasing the range of media products and perspectives available to us. For film and television products, the internet does nothing to address the economic advantages conferred by economies of scale, and just as our television, movie, and computer screens are now dominated by US products, so, too, will they probably continue to be as the internet takes on a greater role in the distribution of such products. Although bloggers, citizen journalists, and a number of web-based news sites seem to have increased the range of news available to us, quality news production requires a high degree of knowledge and skill on the part of the people producing it and, because of this expense, most internet news sites act as aggregators rather than producers of original news reports. Bloggers tend to offer little more than opinions gleaned from professionally produced news. At the same time, and perhaps most importantly, cross-media companies that count newspapers, broadcast, and web-based media among their holdings have business strategies that hinge upon repurposing media content generated for use in one medium for use in another. Consequently, whichever medium we turn to for news, the content is virtually the same.

The Cultural Commodity?

Compounding these problems is the fact that, as commodities, information and cultural products have quite different economic characteristics than other products such as soap, clothes, or cars. As Canadian lawyer Peter Grant and journalist Chris Wood point out in their book, *Blockbusters and Trade Wars: Popular Culture in a Globalized World* (2004), laws fundamental to economic thinking do not apply in the same way to information and cultural production. Rather, information and cultural products display a number of anomalies, or different economic characteristics, from other types of commodities:

- *Anomaly 1:* Cultural products such as TV programs, movies, and music are not consumed in the sense that they are not destroyed in our use of them. Your listening to music does not deprive the next person from listening to the same music on the same CD. The market for cultural products behaves differently from normal commodities markets.
- *Anomaly 2:* The relationship between first-copy costs and run-on costs is dramatically different in cultural production than in the production of other commodities. In other words, the cost of making the "first copy" of a cultural product—such as a film, a television program, a concert, a novel, or a textbook—is enormous compared to the cost of subsequent copies. For instance, reportedly the budget for the film *The Hobbit: The Desolation of Smaug* was $225 million—that, then, is the cost of the "first copy." Making an electronic copy of the film, however, costs little more than the cost of download or a CD (a few cents). Compare that dynamic to theatrical performances where the players must gather each night to put on the play; or manufacturing automobiles, where each "copy" requires a substantial outlay in parts and labour. For the cost of a cultural product to be the same as other kinds of commodities, the creation of each CD would require an artist to record anew. Similarly, for normal economic laws to hold, concert-goers would each suck out a little of the sound so that with a maximum audience there would be no sound left over.

For books, the implications of consumption would be that as each page was read (perhaps not by the first, but let's say by the fiftieth reader) the print would disappear and by the end, the book would collapse into dust.

- *Anomaly 3:* Consumption patterns of cultural products and services are also different. Certain cultural products—blockbusters—command a major share of the market while others don't come close to earning back their costs of creation. For instance, as few as one in ten feature films make big profits, three to five may break even, and the others lose money. Moreover, reduced pricing is rarely successful in persuading a person to watch an unpopular movie, read a bad book, or listen to a dull, tedious piece of music.
- *Anomaly 4:* Hidden consumer subsidies in the form of advertising or grants (by governments or those with a vested interest) can make cultural commodities available at a much lower price than their cost of production (e.g., magazines, newspapers) or, at times, even "free" to consumers (e.g., TV or). Indeed, those with a vested interest can buy their way into cultural products—such as product placement in movies—so that the cultural consumer inadvertently consumes images that cause him or her to associate a product with a certain social dynamic (e.g., Apple laptops and powerful people).
- *Anomaly 5:* The appeal of any particularly cultural good is not readily predictable, a characteristic that is captured by Grant and Wood with the phrases "Nobody knows" (whether a cultural product will succeed in the marketplace) and "All hits are flukes." With normal commodities, most manage to capture some share of the market at some price.

These anomalies illustrate the fact that cultural products are quite different from standard industrial commodities. They call into question the appropriateness of applying standard economic theory to cultural products and underline the importance of regulations to help nurture and support the economic development of cultural industries at the local, regional and national levels.

One other particularly important anomaly rests on the fact that information is not value-neutral. Economic analysis generally assumes that similar commodities are substitutable for one another. For instance, all things being equal, a stove from the United States is seen to be as good as one from Peru; or clothes made in China are as good as those made in Montreal. While there are a number of problems with this assumption, a key concern when applying this idea to media and information products is that the information such products contain is not value-neutral.

As we have seen, Canadians often seem to know more about US politics, history, and culture than about their own. In this regard, media and information products reflect particular ideas and attitudes, and those ideas provide specific ways of approaching and thinking about the world.

Do imported educational materials, for example, incorporate Canadian values of diversity, tolerance, and common purpose, or are they underwritten by notions of competitive individualism that place the interests of the individual over the community at large? Do reports and studies authored elsewhere in the world and used by Canadian governments and industry to formulate policy and investment decisions take into account local and/or national environmental and community concerns, or are they simply based on abstract global economics?

As the lives of Canadians are spun in an ever-growing global web of dependencies, it is in our interest to consider carefully how media and information products are shaping our understanding of the world. The degree to which distinctive Canadian ideas and values are nurtured and carried into the future may, at least in part, hinge on the future of media regulation and its ability to keep those ideas circulating in our media.

 SUMMARY

In this book, we have examined the nature of communication in contemporary Canadian society. This final chapter has echoed the major themes, issues, and ideas treated in the preceding chapters. We have also gone beyond the analysis provided in the preceding chapters and discussed some of the directions in which the development of media and communications technology appear to be headed and the issues that these developments raise.

 KEY TERMS

free market, p. 345
horizontal relationship, p. 339
long tail, p. 355
ownership, p. 345

policy, p. 344
privacy, p. 352
public interest, p. 339
UNESCO, p. 350

 RELATED WEBSITES

Canadian Association of Community Television Users and Stations (CACTUS): cactus.independentmedia.ca
Canada's association of independent community television stations.

Kondratiev Waves: www.kondratieffwavecycle.com/kondratieff-wave
A site devoted to discussion of the Kondratiev wave phenomenon.

National Campus and Community Radio
Association: www.ncra.ca
One of Canada's largest alternative media organizations.

CRTC, "Let's Talk TV": www.crtc.gc.ca/eng/
talktv-parlonstele.htm
A website archiving all the materials from their
September 2014 "Let's Talk TV" hearings.

The Long Tail: www.longtail.com/about.html
A website that discusses the theory and application
of the idea of the long tail.

 STUDY QUESTIONS ————————————————————————

1. Is the world being transformed by the internet,
   or will the internet soon be largely captured
   by corporate interests such that its democratic
   potential will be lost?
2. Are the media alone a solid foundation for
   democracy?
3. While the media industries look at audiences in one manner, scholars tend to view
   them in another. Are these two approaches
   reconcilable?
4. Name and discuss three key issues facing
   media today.
5. Name three ways that media products differ
   from other kinds of commodities.

Selling Soap: Is Dove's "Campaign for Real Beauty" the Real Deal?

By Nicole Cohen

You could say that advertising is soap's dirty little secret. It started during the colonization of North America, when European settlers pushed Aboriginal populations off the land that is now Canada and the United States. According to Andrea Smith, who wrote *Conquest: Sexual Violence and American Indian Genocide*, in order to justify the elimination of indigenous people, settlers had to construct Aboriginal bodies as "dirty" and "impure." An advertisement for Proctor & Gamble's Ivory Soap helped popularize the myth of the "dirty native." The ad read,

> We were once factious, fierce and wild,
> In peaceful arts unreconciled
> Our blankets smeared with grease and
>   stains
> From buffalo meat and settlers' veins.
> Through summer's dust and heat
>   content,
> From moon to moon unwashed we went,
> But IVORY SOAP came like a ray
> Of light across our darkened way
> And now we're civil, kind and good
> And keep the laws as people should,
> We wear our linen, lawn and lace
> As well as folks with paler face
> And now I take, where'er we go,
> This cake of IVORY SOAP to show
> What civilized my squaw and me
> And made us clean and fair to see.

The ad suggested that Ivory Soap "civilized" Aboriginal people, while furthering the colonists'

racist ideas about them being dirty and uncivilized. In the mid-nineteenth century, soap companies Pears, Lever, Proctor & Gamble, and Kirk's continued to market their soap as a way to achieve "whiteness," which was associated in these ads with being gentle, soft, and civilized.

Unsurprisingly, soap advertising was also used to tell women how to behave, promoting traditional gender roles. A 1937 Palmolive ad shows an image of a bride and groom on their honeymoon and advised the woman that "romance comes to girls who guard against dry, lifeless . . . middle age skin," reminding the happy bride that her marriage was dependent on her preserving her youthful, soft skin. Soap ads directed at women have since made their message a little less blatant, relying instead on visual signifiers that reinforce the notion that women are expected to stay thin, soft, supple and flawless. Then, in October 2004, one company changed its tune. Dove, which makes soap and other beauty products, launched its global Campaign for Real Beauty to appeal to folks tired of seeing unrealistic representations of women used in advertising, and to spread a feel-good message based on watered-down feminist notions of empowerment.

Dove launched its Campaign For Real Beauty through images. It set up a photography exhibit in a shopping mall, for which 58 female photographers submitted an image they thought captured female beauty—a group of teenagers carefully applying makeup, a woman standing in the shadows wearing a burka, a girl having her "before" photo taken at summer weight-loss camp, old women, young women, women from around the world. The exhibit was designed to spark a conversation about the representation and meaning of beauty, which, on the surface, it did well: it showed women of different shapes and sizes doing all sorts of activities in front of various backdrops. Every woman who viewed the exhibit could likely identify with at least one of the images.

The "Wall of Sentiments" featured quotes from viewers. "I love that the photographs capture the real essence of beauty and not what the media throws at us day after day," wrote one visitor. "Thank you for showing that true beauty is not just a small waist and large breasts, it's something that comes from within," wrote another.

While viewers could walk out of the exhibit filled with positive feelings about women and beauty, the message was not without a sales pitch: at the exit, a Dove employee was handing out samples in a blue-and-white box that read, "Beauty has nothing to do with perfection and everything to do with care."

Dove is a major brand owned by Unilever, a multinational corporation that sells food, home, and beauty products, with profits in the billions of dollars. That Dove's marketing push focused on "real" beauty is a clever twist on traditional advertising approaches: it has brought the company loads of free publicity as newspaper writers buzz about seeing "real women"—as opposed to modelling agency ideals—being promoted as beautiful.

And it seems that Dove's commitment to "real" beauty is more than skin deep—the company has set up the Dove Self-Esteem Fund to support programs that boost young women's self-image. It also made a donation, at the time of the mall exhibit, to the National Eating Disorder Information Centre (NEDIC), an organization concerned with the sociocultural factors that can influence disordered eating, including the damaging messages of beauty and fashion ads.

Dove even commissioned a study that surveyed 3,300 girls and women aged 15 to 64 in Brazil, Canada, China, Germany, Italy, Japan, Mexico, Saudi Arabia, the UK, and the US to "explore self-esteem and the impact of beauty ideals on both women's and girls' lives." It's impressive coming from an industry that's usually only interested in what shade of red gets women most excited.

The report found that 90 per cent of women want to change something about their physical appearance, usually their weight. Sixty-seven per cent said their negative body image prevented them from participating in "life-engaging" activities such as going to school or speaking out on issues they care about. Enraging stuff; and Dove has based its confidence-boosting efforts on this information.

Still—and product pitches at the end of thoughtful photo exhibits are an obvious reminder of this—it's difficult to believe that Dove's efforts are entirely altruistic. After all, they're doing this to sell soap. And when you take a deeper look at the brand, underlying corporate contradictions begin to emerge. Dove's parent company, Unilever, also owns the Slim Fast meal-replacement milkshake brand, which encourages people to skip meals to lose weight. Then there is Fair and Lovely, a skin-lightening cream marketed heavily in India, which capitalizes on privileged notions and imagery of Western beauty. Finally, there is the male fragrance Axe, another member of the Unilever family whose advertising campaigns feature ultra-thin, hyper-sexualized women uncontrollably lusting after a guy wearing Axe.

You will likely never see a Dove model in an Axe ad. The print-ad component of the Dove campaign has featured the faces and bodies of real women (read: not models) on billboards around the world, selling the idea that this is a brand that cares about the kind of beauty that comes from within. A visit to www.campaignforrealbeauty.ca greets you with "For too long, beauty has been defined by narrow, stifling stereotypes. . . . We believe real beauty comes in many shapes, sizes and ages." A series of billboard advertisements featured women with so-called flaws, images that don't represent traditional signifiers of female beauty: "Ugly spots or beauty spots?" asked the ad featuring a freckled woman. "Wrinkled or wonderful?" asked another.

Many people were impressed that ads were finally featuring women who look less like femmebots and more like themselves. After all, feminist researchers and academics have been critiquing advertising's unrealistic and objectified vision of women for years. As Salon.com writer Rebecca Traister put it, Dove's campaign was "a little ray of sanity in this anorexic world."

So what happens when an advertisement for beauty products exposes the tricks-of-the-trade other advertising companies use to sell similar products? Does the positive representation in the Dove campaign counter all the negative representation women and girls are faced with in advertisements? Do these images really break from the traditional "code" of beauty product marketing? Do they signify alternative ideas about what makes a woman beautiful? And, finally, can a business that exists solely to make money sincerely promote social change? How excited should we get over a campaign like Dove's—no matter how socially conscious it appears to be—when at the end of the day, the goal is to move product? If there is one thing that can be said about the images in Dove's campaign, it's that they really have us thinking about the power of images.

Nicole Cohen is an assistant professor at the Institute of Communication, Culture, Information and Technology at the University of Toronto–Mississauga. She is also the co-founder and former co-editor of *Shameless*, a magazine for young women and trans youth. This article first appeared in *Shameless*.

APPENDIX B

Canada's Impact on the Global Children's Television Industry

By Natalie Coulter

The logo for Nickelodeon is instantly recognizable; it's the ubiquitous green splat. But, what is not recognized is that the green splat had its origins in Canada. When Nickeodeon was being launched in the early 1980s and the network was searching for children's television shows to fill up its schedule, there was not much content being produced at the time. Where they found content was in Canada; shows such as Sharon, Lois and Bram's *Elephant Show* and *Today's Special* provided the backbone of Nickelodeon's programming slate. Nickelodeon's breakthrough hit was a little Canadian show produced in Ottawa by CJOH called *You Can't Do That on Television*. One of the signature moments of the show was "sliming" during which a green bucket of slime was dumped on a character's head. The show was such a critical component of Nickelodeon's schedule that the slime was incorporated into the logo.

This lost history of how Canadian children's and youth television shows have been central to global children's media corporations is a story that needs to be told. As Canadians, we are unaware of the long history and global reputation of the Canadian children's television industry. University students often tell me that they do not watch Canadian television, but when I ask them what shows they watched as children, they list off a whole ream of shows that are Canadian: *Franklin and Friends* (1997–2003), *Caillou* (1997–2006), *Fred Penner's Place* (1985–1997), the various generations of the Degrassi franchise, *Mr Dressup* (1967–1996), and *Babar* (1989–1991). But like most Canadians, they fail to recognize these shows as Canadian.

The children and youth television industry in Canada is large. Currently, there are over 110 children's media production companies in Canada, including 9 Story Entertainment, Sinking Ship Entertainment, Thunderbird Films, Epitome Pictures, and Télé-Québec. Canadian children have their own television stations, including Treehouse and YTV. Many other stations such as the CBC and TVO have long-running interstitial programming like Kids' CBC (2003–current), TVO's *The Space* (1994–current), and *Gisèle's Big Backyard* (1998–current). This industry sector creates roughly 2,500 production jobs and 3,900 spin-off jobs, with export revenues of over $100 million on top of its domestic production revenues of over $300 million (YMA, 2009). There are many post-secondary programs on children's media, including the children's entertainment program offered at Centennial College in Toronto, and Sheridan College in Oakville, Ontario, is considered to be one of the top schools in North America for animation training. Perhaps most tellingly, *Kidscreen*, the top trade publication for the global children's entertainment industry, is produced in Toronto, demonstrating the depth of cultural capital here in Canada. *Kidscreen* magazine is published eight times a year and reaches 15,000 industry decision-makers around the world. The publication's annual industry conference, the Kidscreen Summit, is held in New York and is attended by over 1,600 delegates from 46 countries.

Canada is internationally renowned for its children's content. It has a reputation for producing quality children's television that is exported around the globe. For example, Nelvana's *Franklin and Friends*, which started off as a book series by Kids Can Press in 1986, has sold 65 million books in more than 24 languages and as a television show it has been broadcast in over 160 countries. And Canadian children's media have been a mainstay of the major children's networks. For years, *Road to Avonlea* (1990–1996), for example, was a staple of the Disney Channel and available to over 150 export markets (Kotsopoulos, 2004). Canada was such a leader in the industry in the 1990s that popular culture critics Geoff Pevere and Greig Dymond declared, "In the world of children's entertainment, Canada is something approaching its own Hollywood: it enjoys world renown and near-global market saturation. It is looked up to and envied, and it has been far more often challenged than surpassed" (1996: 116).

Today Canada still has an international reputation. Take Nelvana, for example, a production company located in Toronto, started by two graduates of York University, now a subsidiary of Corus Entertainment. Nelvana's content is shown in over 160 countries and it has received over 70 major international awards. In 2013, its show *Bubble Guppies*, which is broadcast by Treehouse and on Nickelodeon, won a Daytime Emmy Award. One of Nelvana's major properties, *Franklin and Friends*, currently has a deal with China's national broadcaster Chinese Central Television (CCTV) to air the show to over 400 million households providing many opportunities for lucrative merchandising deals. In 2014, Nelvana signed a deal with the Cartoon Network Latin America for 78 half-hours of original programming for three shows: *Mr Young*, *Scaredy Squirrel*, and *Detentionaire*.

Children's and youth shows are unique as the only genre defined by its audience, not its program content. In Canada, the CRTC has defined children's programming as that which is targeted at persons aged 2 to 11, and youth programming as being targeted at the 12 to 17 age group. The CRTC has an interest in supporting this genre as the Broadcasting Act clearly states in Article 3(d)(iii) that the "Canadian Broadcasting system should, through its programming and the employment opportunities arising out of its operations, serve the needs and interests, and reflect the circumstances and aspirations, of Canadian men, women and children" (in this case, "children" refers to a legal definition of anyone under the age of 18).

There are some serious economic and cultural implications to the fact that we as Canadians have little knowledge of the richness and history of this industry, one of them being that we do not defend the industry in times of economic pressures. Currently, the industry is facing huge struggles in how it is being funded and supported by governments. If there is little financial support for producing original programming in Canada, then the Canadian networks will start to fill up their schedule with cheaper American content. CBC, for example, is currently cutting back its children's programming, including the long-running interstitial *Kids' Canada*, which features puppets representing parts of Canada, such as the Kensington Market yam called Mamma Yamma and Saumon de Champlain, the Québécois salmon who teaches French words to the show's hosts. We have to ask ourselves as Canadians where this leaves us as Canadians if the major media content our children consume loses its Canadian references.

Natalie Coulter is an assistant professor in the Department of Communication Studies at York University in Toronto.

APPENDIX C
Two Opposing Views on Journalism Today

Journalism Has Entered a Golden Age

By Henry Blodget
Business Insider (www.businessinsider.com),
13 August 2013

CNN host Brian Stelter was kind enough to have me on his show *Reliable Sources* over the weekend. In response to one question, I said that journalism has entered a "golden age."

Judging from the Twitter reaction, many of Brian's viewers agreed.

One viewer, however, a former print journalist, called this assertion "absurd."

It's true that "golden age for journalism" is not usually the first thing that you hear when you go to conferences and listen to panels of middle-aged newspaper people talk about the state of the newspaper business.

But I wasn't talking about the newspaper business.

I was talking about journalism.

And what I was suggesting is that—far from the picture of unremitting gloom occasionally painted by newspaper folks—journalism is now in better shape than it has ever been.

Consider:

- The world is vastly better informed than ever before. Yes, there have been high-profile examples of "iconic" news organizations cutting back or shutting down, but there has also been a mind-boggling explosion of other news and information sources over the same period, including Facebook, Twitter, blogs, Bloomberg LP, Google, WikiLeaks, thousands of digital news and information sites, YouTube, and the installation of cameras, audio recording devices, and instant publishing tools in the pockets of nearly 2 billion people worldwide. Meanwhile, the vast majority of traditional news organizations, including TV, radio, magazines, and even most newspapers, still exist, and many are thriving. The standard by which the health of journalism should be judged is the degree to which important facts are being unearthed and shared and important stories are being told. And even the most diehard newspaper fan would admit that, these days, more people around the world are being informed about more important facts than ever before.

- More great journalism is being produced today than ever before. There are thousands upon thousands of successful professional news organizations in the world, and they employ hundreds of thousands of professional journalists. In addition, anyone in the world with an internet connection can now create journalism—and lots of them do. You don't need a printing press to create and distribute journalism anymore. You don't need a broadcast network or a radio station. All you need are your eyes, ears, nose, and storytelling and digital publishing tools, the latter of which are included for free on every smartphone. If anyone anywhere publishes an important fact or tells an important story, people will find it and share it. And it will get the attention it deserves.

- Every journalist on earth can now reach nearly every human on earth—directly and instantly. On the internet, everything is a click away. What's more, on the internet, all stories can be stored permanently and viewed from anywhere, anytime. Compare that to the world of 20 years ago, when news had to be distributed on paper or broadcast over ephemeral airwaves, and news consumers had to either lay their hands on a newspaper or magazine or plop themselves (at the appropriate time) in front of a radio or TV.

- The struggles of the traditional news business have been greatly exaggerated. Despite all the hand-wringing about the hardship in the newspaper business, the world's overall news-gathering and publishing capacity has been radically increased over the past decade. Even within professional journalism, the overall picture is healthy. Yes, some newspapers and magazines have closed. Yes, others are cutting back. But the TV news business is still growing, and many newspapers and magazines are hanging in there. And, importantly, the growth of professional digital news organizations is exploding.

- Digital news organizations now employ a whole new generation of talented journalists, and these organizations are getting better, more comprehensive, and more sustainable by the day. In the early years of the cable news business, the capabilities of networks like CNN were a mere fraction of what they are today. Today's native digital news organizations are already producing excellent journalism, and their talent, reach, and resources are continually increasing. Over the next few decades, vast new global news brands will be built that take full advantage of the capabilities of this new medium. And they will produce journalism that is more comprehensive, faster, more efficient, and more effectively distributed than ever before.

- The proliferation of mobile gadgets has made it possible to consume news anywhere 24 hours a day. As recently as 20 years ago, news consumption was limited to morning and evening papers and TV and radio broadcasts. For most of the past two decades, meanwhile, this consumption was largely limited to anywhere you had a tethered internet connection. Now, you can get your news anywhere, anytime, in the palm of your hand. Just as important, you can immediately share it.

- Today's journalism now offers a full range of storytelling formats: No longer are journalists limited to text when telling their stories, or to an occasional picture, or to broadcast "packages" produced with audio and video. Today's journalists can use whatever storytelling tools and formats will best communicate their stories, and they can mix and match them in whatever way is most efficient and effective.

- There are no longer any time or space limits for any story. Stories in print or broadcast are constrained by physical time and space, regardless of the merit of the material. Digital stories aren't. If the best story length for a reader is just a link to another website, today's journalists can publish a link. If the best story for the reader is a book-length investigative article, the journalist can write one of those. If the best story for the reader is a short or long video, or audio snippet, the journalists can produce those. Each story can be exactly as long or short as it needs to be.

- There are no space or topic constraints for the broader publication. In the physical world, publications have to be either general (newspapers or broadcast news networks) or specialized (focused magazines or networks). In the digital medium, there is no such limitation. A fully developed digital news network can (and will) be both extraordinarily broad and extraordinarily deep.

- Publications can now take advantage of many different forms of distribution. We still have paper, airwave, and cable distribution. And we also now have digital distribution, which is vastly more flexible, cheaper, and ubiquitous. With digital, content can roam free:

There's no all-powerful "gatekeeper" who can control information, set the terms of the conversation, and capture an outsize share of influence and profitability. And digital publications can build many different sources of distribution within the medium, including direct, search, social, and referrals, thus further reducing dependence on "distributors."

- There is now more media accuracy and "consensus knowledge" than ever before. Yes, social media and news organizations still get things wrong. But that's nothing new. And thanks to the 2 billion fact-checkers who use the internet every day, all information can be instantly and publicly challenged, debated, debunked, and sometimes even corrected by the source publication faster than ever. And the subjects of journalism can respond to stories directly, without the need of an intermediary.
- It is easier than ever before for talented aspiring professional journalists to start practising their trade. Think you might want to be a journalist? Then start being one! All you need is a laptop, a cellphone (camera), a blog, and a few social media accounts. Once you demonstrate that you are good at unearthing facts, sharing images, and telling stories readers like, you'll be off to the races.

I could go on.

But you get the picture.

The business of journalism is changing, certainly, especially at newspapers. You can't have change without loss. And loss is often painful and disruptive.

But journalism itself is entering a new golden age.

And, contrary to the assertions of some newspaper owners, even the journalism business is going to be okay.

In fact, when some of today's upstart digital news organizations have matured, and the transformation of the newspaper business is complete, the journalism business is not just going to be okay. It's going to be excellent.

All we have to do is get through this tumultuous transition period.

In the meantime, journalism itself has never been in better shape.

The Golden Age of Journalism? You've Got to Be Kidding

By Paul Benedetti and James R. Compton
J-Source.ca—The Canadian Journalism Project,
4 April 2014

It's official: journalism has entered a golden age. Or at least that's the proposition currently circulating as a popular meme among some journalistic prognosticators. The idea gained steam after Henry Blodget proclaimed it in a column for *Business Insider* in August 2013. His piece was picked up, commented upon, tweeted about and generally positively bandied about the web, eventually getting the nod from *New York Times* media columnist David Carr.

Too bad Blodget's piece is nonsense; a string of unsupported claims, clichés, exaggerations and half-baked ideas that don't hold up to even the mildest scrutiny. It's a repetitive piece, so we won't bother to debunk every point, but let's look at the central claims he makes for why we are living in "the golden age of journalism."

Blodget says the "world is vastly better informed than ever before" thanks to an information explosion. Witness "Facebook, Twitter, blogs, Bloomberg LP, Google, WikiLeaks, thousands of digital news and information sites."

This claim to universal enlightenment is deeply puzzling. Try saying Iraq has weapons of mass destruction five times in a row really fast. Did that jog any memories? Too long ago? Can't remember that far back? How about in 2008 when the legalized Ponzi scheme we call the housing bubble burst, fuelling a global recession? These are two of the most important stories of our lifetime and the news media failed miserably.

As for how well informed Americans are, a poll in 2006 found that three years after the US-led invasion of Iraq, 50 per cent of respondents said they still believed Iraq had weapons of mass destruction when the US invaded. A 2010 Harris Poll found that 24 per cent of Republicans thought President Obama may be the anti-Christ. Almost 60 per cent thought he was a Muslim and 67 per cent thought he was a socialist. All these ideas are demonstrably false or crazy. Good news, though: when the liberal-leaning Public Policy Polling posed the anti-Christ question in 2013, the number of Republicans who said yes had dropped to 20 per cent, while only 6 per cent of Democrats agreed. See, this internet thing must really be working!

Blodget claims that "more people around the world are being informed about more important facts than ever before." Really? It's not easy to judge what's happening in the entire world, but let's look at the state of a wealthy, first-world nation like the United States. A recent Pew study found that both cable news and local TV news are providing less news and more commentary, opinion, weather, and sports. Across the board in all media, fewer resources are devoted to reporting with noticeable results. The survey found that "nearly a third (31 per cent) of US adults have deserted a news outlet because it no longer provides the news and information they had grown accustomed to receiving . . . noticing erosion in quality of coverage even more than diminishing quantity. Fully 61 per cent said they noticed that stories were less complete compared with 24 per cent who said they noticed fewer stories overall."

Some golden age.

Blodget then claims that "more great journalism is being produced today than ever before." More great journalism? By whose standards and what measurement? When these claims are put to the test, they fail. The 2013 Pew report found news stories and comprehensive coverage were being replaced by more "filler" content. The report states,

In local TV, our special content report reveals, sports, weather and traffic now account on average for 40% of the content produced on the newscasts studied while story lengths shrink. On CNN, the cable channel that has branded itself around deep reporting, produced story packages were cut nearly in half from 2007 to 2012. . . . This adds up to a news industry that is more undermanned and unprepared to uncover stories, dig deep into emerging ones or to question information put into its hands.

Virtually every survey or study of journalism has pointed to a decline in investigative reporting. Today, audiences are at the mercy of politicians, corporations, and marketers whose claims go unchecked and unchallenged. Today, journalists are outnumbered by public-relations workers by more than three to one.

But no worries—Blodget then tells us that the decline in mainstream reporters is balanced by a kind of reserve army of citizen journalists telling stories all over the word. He writes, "all you need are your eyes, ears, nose, and story-telling and digital publishing tools, the latter of which are included for free on every smartphone. . . . Anyone in the world with an internet connection can now create journalism."

Really? That's like saying anyone with Microsoft Word can write a good novel or anyone with Photoshop can make art. We fully acknowledge how the widespread distribution of smartphones and other forms of digital audio–video technology has brought profound changes to the coverage of spot news, such as political protests. But these are changes in the scale of modern visibility, not in the nature of the craft.

Journalism is not about technology, it's about reporting. The foundation of journalism is reporting. This fact seems to get trampled in the rush to connect access to a computer and the internet with the reporting and the production of news stories. Reporting is work. And good reporting requires skill, experience, and resources. We are not making the now tired, and unhelpful, distinction between professionals and amateurs. We are drawing your attention to the necessary labour of reporting. Journalists do reporting. And where are the journalists?

The facts here are clear: newsrooms across North America have been gutted. The American Society of Newspaper Editors reported in 2011 that 41,500 men and women worked in daily newspaper newsrooms. That's down from 55,000 in 2007. Over those three-plus years, that's a loss of 13,500 jobs, a 25 per cent decline. In Canada, the picture is about the same. In the past five years, media job losses reached about 10,000, according to Canadian Media Guild. New media enthusiasts may cheer the slow death of legacy media outlets, but the decline translates into less news and current affairs for readers and viewers. As Pew says, "signs of the shrinking reporting power are documented throughout this year's [2013] report."

Blodget celebrates connectivity, boasting that "every journalist on earth can now reach nearly every human on earth—directly and instantly. On the internet, everything is a click away."

This argument reminds us of the old joke:

First guy: "The food at this restaurant is terrible."

Second guy: "Yeah, but there's lots of it."

This is another iteration of the more-communication-leads-to-better-communication fallacy. Techno-enthusiasts often make the logical error of mistaking what people can do with what people actually do. We'll ignore for the moment that less than 16 per cent of Africans have internet access. Even with better access for everyone, one needs to examine the kind of political information that is being accessed. It turns out, according to years of Pew Center data and other scholarly research, that the internet has not overturned the power of corporate media. A small number of elite websites and bloggers attract the most attention.

Matthew Hindman, in *The Myth of Digital Democracy*, reports that "political traffic is a tiny portion of web usage." "The link structure of the web limits the content that citizens see." "Much search engine use is shallow." "Even in the digital world, some content is expensive to produce."

As a result, Hindman concludes that a "power law" distribution predominates in which a relatively small number of political websites—often the same companies laying off reporters—get the vast majority of traffic. "Instead of the 'inevitable' fragmentation of online media," writes Hindman, "audiences on the web are actually more concentrated on the top ten or twenty outlets than are traditional media like newspapers and magazines."

Conclusion: Hyperlinks are not giant slayers.

Blodget acknowledges the cutbacks in traditional newsrooms, but is optimistic because "the growth of professional digital news organizations is exploding." It certainly is true, as reported by Pew, that there has been a recent surge of venture capital investment in online news organizations. Vice, HuffPo, and BuzzFeed have all enjoyed significant growth. And eBay founder Pierre Omidyar's newly launched First Look Media has attracted venerable journalistic stars such as Glenn Greenwald.

But Pew also reports that the 30 big digital outlets have created roughly 3,000 new jobs, or 102 jobs per outlet. This remains a drop in the proverbial bucket compared to the slashing of newsroom budgets over the past decade.

And what are digital news organizations? This can be an interesting and, as usual, blurry phrase. Yes, there are more content aggregators, list makers, link machines, portals to other data, and re-users and recyclers of other people's content. This accounts for the bulk of HuffPo's output. Along with their investments in news reporting, HuffPo, Vice and BuzzFeed have proven to be masters of "clickbait." This is the emerging digital business model.

And so, Blodget's claims pile up, one upon the other until we get to this: "over the next few decades, vast new global news brands will be built that take full advantage of the capabilities of this new medium. And they will produce journalism that is more comprehensive, faster, more efficient, and more effectively distributed than ever before."

This is a straight prediction with no evidence to back up such a rosy view of the future. In fact, most nascent news start-ups fail. Others are hanging on for dear life. Few employ more than a handful of editorial people, if any. Many run on volunteer labour despite being for-profit start-ups. Others pander to the lowest common denominator and pay a pittance to writers churning out piecework for these traffic-driven content farms. Meanwhile, venerable news organizations such as *The Guardian*, which employs hard-working reporters and editors breaking investigative blockbusters, would not exist but for a charitable trust and are still bleeding millions a year (about 40 million pounds last year to be exact). What "vast new global news brands" is Blodget talking about?

We agree with the sobering conclusion of noted scholar and activist Robert McChesney. Available evidence suggests that "the internet does not alleviate the tensions between commercialism and journalism; it magnifies them."

And now we come to Blodget's biggest claim: that the golden age of journalism has ushered in a new era of accuracy and knowledge for the masses. He writes,: "There is now more media accuracy and 'consensus knowledge' than ever before . . . thanks to the 2 billion fact-checkers who use the internet every day, all information can be instantly and publicly challenged, debated, debunked, and sometimes even corrected by the source publication faster than ever."

This "wisdom of the crowd" thesis suggests that large groups of people will correct errors and mistakes, acting as a kind of real-time crucible for truth. There's no doubt that universal access and instantaneous feedback have meant that journalists' feet are now more often held to the fire. Mistakes are noticed and commented upon and media organizations have been forced to deal with those much more openly and transparently—or risk censure. (Witness the recent Margaret Wente plagiarism debacle at *The Globe and Mail*.)

But the notion that this crowd correcting leads to a higher degree of overall accuracy and a much more informed public is unsupported. Ironically, this universal access to information and this supposed self-correcting system has resulted in a constant tsunami of responses, commentary, and opinion that all but drowns out the slow, but necessary, work of checking validity claims against verifiable facts. We are now awash in extremism, conspiracy theories, fringe ideas, irrational beliefs, and propaganda—all presented and disseminated in this grand gatekeeper-free zone. There are smart people posting smart stuff online, but they are often drowned out by the vile, the crazies, the racists, the extremists, and the deranged.

In fact, it was accelerated crowd-sourced reporting that led to innocent people being identified online in the manhunt for the Boston Marathon bombers in April 2013. Saying the media eventually got it right is to defend bad reporting.

Let's look for a moment at the single-most important challenge facing humankind today—climate change. Despite Blodget's claim of a modern zenith of "media accuracy and consensus knowledge," Pew Research found that only 33 per cent of Americans thought global warming was a "very serious" problem and only 42 per cent agreed that it was caused mostly by human activity. Ubiquity of information does not translate into an informed public.

We apologize for the polemical nature of this article, but we view it as a kind of antidote to the widespread, uncritical promotion of these ideas. They have become so pervasive that the proposition of a new "golden age of journalism" has even made its way into journalism schools themselves. To be clear, we are both involved in the education of future journalists and have a deep, powerful belief in the necessity and power of good journalism in democratic society. It's clear to us that to cut through this propaganda about a new "emergent" journalism, one has to focus on the necessary work of reporting. Then, and only then, can we distinguish between what is craft and what is promotion.

We do, in fact, see some signs of optimism in this time of great upheaval. We are cautiously optimistic about recent investments in news organizations in both the United States and the United Kingdom. And we recognize that very good work is still being done by both public and private news organizations from CBC Radio to *The New York Times* to *The Guardian* and non-profits such as *ProPublica*. The latest Pew Report on the State of the Media offers glimmers of hope in some rather dark times.

But, we are a long, long way from any kind of "golden age of journalism." And, we believe that the circulation of this idea is not merely baseless promotion, but it is insidious in two ways: 1) it masks the very real colonization of a once proudly skeptical profession with promotional hucksterism, and 2) it reinforces a false notion that all is well.

We are extremely troubled by a number of issues undermining the notion of journalism as a public good. The rampant economic rationalization of newsrooms, whether broadcast, print, or digital, has eroded the independence of professional journalistic standards. The use of PR news subsidies, in the form of video news releases (VNR) is on the rise, as is so-called "native" content—a form of sponsored or custom "content," paid for by advertisers, produced by journalists, and presented as news. There is a continuing decline of original news reporting, particularly among local TV stations, which increasingly fill their broadcasts with weather and sports. And, of course, the continuing decline in full-time professional newsroom employment at newspapers, which still account for the vast majority of original reporting in Canada and the United States.

Perhaps most disturbing, we see a blurring of a necessary distinction between news as a public good and a promotional commodity. Moral entrepreneurs, such as Blodget, Jeff Jarvis, and Marc Andreessen, continue to sell the idea that we have entered a new world. Gone are the fetters of the old top-down model of news production. Today we are blessed with the freedom of the "link economy." All that is required is for people to embrace a new "entrepreneurial journalism." Laid-off reporters and journalism students struggling with heavy debt loads are being told to build their personal brands. Embrace the market and all will be well. It's up to you! This claim, as we have shown, is obviously false.

A few high-profile winners will be celebrated as a signal to others that they, too, can succeed if they work hard; but the vast majority of reporters will be left with the piecework of precarious employment. History has shown that the best journalism is the result of hard individual work and talent, yes, but with the collective support and resources of a well-funded newsroom that works hard to protect the integrity of the craft. The best newsrooms didn't always succeed, but they always endeavoured to separate journalism from the profane interests of owners and advertisers. Today's hucksters are preaching the opposite.

Glossary

access to information Related to the concept of freedom of information, it refers to the principle that information collected by governments belongs to the Crown and citizens must appeal to governments for access to this information; this is the operating principle in Canada. In the United States, *freedom of information* is the more appropriate term because information collected by governments belongs to the people.

advertising Media content designed to promote broad awareness of a product, service, program, or organization. Typically, media space or time is purchased for advertising, and it thus serves as an important revenue source for media companies. However, advertising can also appear in unconventional, non-media spaces—such as bathroom walls and the floors of subway stations, or anywhere that it can attract attention.

advertorials Promotional articles in magazines and newspapers thinly disguised as news stories, usually printed in a different typeface and identified by the advertorial label. As the name suggests, they are a cross between advertisements and editorial material.

affiliate An independently owned radio or television station associated with either a private or public network of stations; a station not owned by the network.

agenda-setting function The process by which priorities are established; it usually refers to elite actors or media owners and managers using their influence to shape society's priorities.

allocative control The kind of control over media operations exercised by people at the uppermost levels of management—publishers, station managers, chief executives, shareholders, directors—who assign resources of labour and capital to a media organization and determine the organization's overall mandate; it is control over the structural and philosophical context in which media content is produced.

alternative media Organizations that pursue communication and cultural production in ways alternative to, or distinct from, private, commercial, or state-owned media. Typically, alternative media seek to broaden public debate, construct community, advocate for social justice, and challenge concentrated media power.

Areopagitica An essay written by John Milton in 1644 to oppose press licensing in England, expressing faith in the power of truth to prevail through free inquiry and discussion. It remains a foundational document in the libertarian theory of the press and informs discussions of freedom of the press to this day.

audience fragmentation The breakup of traditional television audiences because of the proliferation of TV channels in the last 25–30 years; the increasing draw of the internet has also further fragmented the audience.

backbone providers Organizations that develop communications infrastructure and make it available to users, typically as a business. Telephone and cable companies are examples of backbone providers.

bandwidth The frequency range within which signals are broadcast, typically measured in hertz; with respect to the internet, data transmission rates, the amount of data transferable over a given channel in a given amount of time.

barriers to entry An economic term that refers to the impediments one must overcome—e.g., raising investment capital, purchasing equipment or technology, finding a market niche, finding labour expertise—to enter into a new business enterprise.

Berne Convention The basis of international copyright law, which requires, among other things, that foreign authors be treated in the same way as domestic authors and that there be a minimum number of years of protection for a copyrighted work.

Birmingham School The media scholars at Birmingham University in the United Kingdom who developed the Marxist-derived, critical school of thought that became cultural studies.

bits Binary digits, that is, zeros or ones; the basis for the information-carrying capability of most computing systems. A byte is eight bits.

blogs, blogging Usually personal commentaries made public via the web on topics of interest to the author or website owner; the word *blog* is a contraction of *web* and *log*, as in keeping a log or record of activities. Blogs customarily include text, images, and sound, often including material lifted from other sites, and can be opened for others to make comments as well. Blogging is the activity of creating a blog.

bourgeoisie A new land-owning class that emerged during the Enlightenment with the development of capitalism; this class generally controlled the means of production.

branding The creation of an identity for a company or a specific product that generates clear and positive associations among consumers.

brand journalism A recent trend seeing newspaper and magazine stories being produced by journalists and paid for by companies or associations seeking to draw attention to their sphere of activity, if not directly to specific products or services.

British cultural studies An approach to social analysis that began in the 1950s and was led by scholars Richard Hoggart, Raymond Williams, and Stuart Hall; it extended a Marxist class analysis to include race, gender, and other elements of cultural history, and asserted the legitimacy of popular culture forms as objects of study.

Broadcasting Act (1991) Federal legislation governing all forms of broadcasting in Canada.

broadsheets Full-sized newspapers (as opposed to half-sized tabloids) that tend to be targeted at middle-class or elite readers; this newspaper form generally has much more text and relatively fewer photos than the tabloid format typically displays.

Canadian content A legal definition of material that either has been developed by Canadians and/or contains Canadian information; in broadcasting, filmmaking, and publishing, Canadian content is defined by reference to a specific set of production criteria, rather than content per se, designed to encourage the production of Canadian cultural materials by Canadians.

Canadian Radio League A lobby group founded in 1930 by Graham Spry and Alan Plaunt to lead a campaign to support the Aird Commission's central recommendation of a national public radio system for Canada.

Canadian Radio-television and Telecommunications Commission (CRTC) The federal agency that enforces the rules and regulations for broadcasters and telecommunications companies in Canada, as set out in the 1993 Telecommunications Act.

capital Funds invested, or available to be invested, for the express purpose of generating profits; not to be confused with money proper.

capitalism An economic system based on the private ownership of the means of production and the clear separation of capital—owners of the means of production engaged in the pursuit of profit—and labourers, who satisfy their material needs (e.g., food, shelter, clothing) by exchanging their work for a wage.

carriage A policy term designed to distinguish between the simple dissemination or transmission of communication (as in telephone service provided by telephone companies) and the production or selection of content; in regulation, this distinction is drawn in order to differentiate between carriage and content activities (e.g., distinguishing between the carriage and content-production or content-selection activities of a television network).

closure Refers to the fixing of a given technology into a socially recognized object, producing a kind of *black box*: an artifact or way of doing things that comes to be seen as natural, inevitable, or most logical. Closure prevents us from considering the historical process that led to a given technological form, and it hinders us from considering the technology's social origins and possible alternative forms and uses.

collective rights Rights accruing to groups of people or communities that are meant to privilege the collectivity over individuals; language laws in Quebec, for example, are designed to protect and promote the language of the French-speaking majority; Canadian content rules on radio and television are similarly meant to protect and promote the cultural expression of the Canadian community.

commercial media Media outlets organized to produce profits for their owners through the sale of content and/or advertising; regardless of what kind of content the outlet produces, a primary goal of a commercial institution is to produce regular profits. Their objectives and purpose are different from those of not-for-profit (e.g., the Aboriginal Peoples Television Network), community (e.g., community radio and television), and public (e.g., the CBC) media.

commodities Goods sold in the marketplace valued primarily for the earnings they can generate through market exchange.

common carriage Telecommunications services provided to all members of the public at equitable rates; a common carrier is in the business of providing carriage services rather than content.

communication The act of transmitting and exchanging information and meaning through any form of language. While communication typically refers to exchanges through verbal, written, and electronic forms of transmission, clothing, gesture, and architecture, among many others, are also forms of communication.

communications policy Policy regime laid down by international regulatory bodies and national and regional governments to ensure that media serve not only their owners and content creators, but individual citizens and society as a whole.

compression The process of encoding information using as few *bits* as possible, thereby saving disk space and needed transmission *bandwidth*. The MP3 and zip file formats are compressed file formats. In certain cases, compression results in a loss of *fidelity* (referred to as *lossy compression*).

concentration of ownership (or corporate concentration) The consolidation of ownership of a number of media organizations by relatively few large corporations. There are a number of different types or forms of media concentration, such as horizontal or chain ownership, *vertical integration*, and cross-media ownership.

conglomerate ownership A company that contains within it many companies carrying on a variety of businesses not necessarily related to one another: a media conglomerate does the majority of its business in the media; a general or non-media conglomerate has its foundation in non-media firms.

connotative meaning Implicit, suggesting, implying; a connotation is an implied meaning; in communication theory, words and messages are said to have connotative as well as *denotative* (or explicit) meanings.

conservative A political stance oriented to preserving current conditions and power structures rather than adapting to, embracing, or instigating changed, often more egalitarian, conditions.

consortium A group, usually of institutions, gathered together for a common purpose, such as marketing or lobbying policy-makers.

constructivism A point of view arguing that technology is constructed by members of society and shaped by social forces, giving it both a technical and a social logic.

contempt of court A ruling by which a court of law determines that a person or an organization has disobeyed or contravened the authority of the court.

content analysis A quantitative research method that establishes units of analysis—specified ideas, phrases, sentences, column inches, placement, accompanying illustrations, categories of spokespersons quoted or cited—and counts them to try

and analyze the meaning or perspective of a particular communication, such as a newspaper article or television news story.

contract carrier A company that provides *carriage* to a private client, usually a firm, to transmit or communicate signals, but does not offer the same service on equitable terms to others; the opposite of *common carriage*.

convergence Generally, bringing together once separate communication technologies, such as telephone, broadcasting, computers, and sound and video recording, into one technological platform (e.g., the internet). The key to this technological convergence is the digitization of media content such that it can be translated into a common format. Similarly, concentration of ownership is sometimes referred to as *corporate convergence*, as media companies combine the resources and content of two or more different media properties to realize cost savings in content production and cross-promotional opportunities.

copyright The exclusive right to reproduce a work requiring intellectual labour; this right belongs to the author and constitutes (1) a property right, which may be assigned to others, and (2) a moral right, which may not be assigned but may be waived.

Copyright Act Legal framework governing the right to reproduce a published work.

corporate concentration An economic term used to describe a particular industry ownership pattern, whereby ownership of the participating companies is concentrated in only a few hands.

critical theory Generally, theoretical perspectives that focus on the ways in which wealth and power are unequally distributed in society.

cross-ownership Ownership of two or more different media in the same market—for instance, newspapers and radio stations.

Crown corporations Canadian businesses owned by the federal or one of the provincial governments, but operating at arm's length from government as individual corporations.

cultivation analysis An examination of content for the way in which it may encourage or cultivate a positive attitude in the audience member toward a particular person or perspective.

cultural dependency A relationship in which one country comes to rely on the media products of stronger, exporting countries to satisfy the cultural and entertainment needs of its population.

cultural imperialism The ways in which one culture imposes ideas and values on another culture, with the effect of undermining the cultural values of the recipient; media and cultural products are a primary vehicle for such imposition.

cultural industries Groups of companies that employ large-scale, industrial methods to produce cultural products.

culturalist The perception of complex phenomena and institutions in terms of their cultural impact and cultural characteristics; such a view foregrounds and privileges the cultural aspect of issues.

cultural sovereignty The capacity of a state or group to govern cultural activity (i.e., form policy, establish laws and conventions) independent of interference from other governments or groups.

culture As Raymond Williams points out, it is "one of the two or three most complicated words in the English language" (Williams, 1958: 87). In this book, it is used to indicate a "particular way of life, whether of a people, a group, or humanity in general." From this perspective, culture includes "knowledge, belief, art, morals, law, custom, and any other capabilities acquired by man as a member of society" (Thompson, 1990: 128).

database A collection of records or information stored in a computer in a systematic, structured way so that a computer program can consult it to answer queries.

data mining The compilation and analysis of data usually collected as part of a financial transaction and aimed at revealing patterns that are useful for a third party to know.

decoding Interpreting or meaning-making—for example, to interpret or make meaning from an advertisement, television program, or film, one must decode the signs and symbols used to construct those media texts.

defamation Injuring a person's good reputation by means of insults, or interference with the course of justice.

demographic (1) Used as an adjective, related to the statistical study of populations through the identification of characteristics of a given population (e.g., age, sex, education, income level); (2) used as a noun, it describes a specific group that may be identified through such analysis.

denotative meaning Explicit, literal meaning of a communication; in communication theory, words and messages are said to have both denotative and *connotative* meanings.

deregulation The process by which the state gradually withdraws from regulating particular spheres of activity and allowing freer market activity. The term is, however, something of a misnomer because market forces are also a form of regulation, producing simply an alternative form of governance. For this reason, some commentators prefer the term *reregulation*.

deskilling The simplification of complex tasks into components that are readily mastered by workers, who often are working in conjunction with sophisticated machines.

determinism A point of view that sees technology as operating according to an inexorable logic that is inherent in the technology itself.

determinist illusion The notion of inevitability in the form and function of a particular piece of technology, as in, it was bound to develop in the way it did because it is such a perfect device for its current function.

digital A universal code that reduces sounds and images to a series of 0s and 1s; digitization allows the easy transfer of communications from one medium to another, enabling convergence.

digital divide The (increasing) difference in the development and use of information and communication technology between rich and poor countries, and between the haves and have-nots within a society.

digitization The process by which all forms of information—textual, visual, aural—are translated into a common computer language of 0s and 1s, so that content produced originally for one digital platform can be used on all other platforms.

discourse analysis In popular usage, all forms of text and talk; in communication studies, text and talk about a particular topic or field of activity.

disintermediation The elimination of those involved in between the creator and the final consumer—that is, the elimination of intermediaries, such as publishers, libraries, record companies, and film distributors.

dominant ideology The set of ideas most commonly used to explain events in a given society; conventional wisdom or conventional explanations of phenomena that are taken by most people as unchallenged assumptions.

economies of scale Efficiencies in costs that can be achieved via repetition of some aspects of the production and distribution processes—for example, the reduction of the per-unit cost of printing 10,000 copies of a book once the presses have been set up, as opposed to printing just 1,000 copies.

economism The reduction of complex phenomena and institutions to their economic characteristics;

such a view foregrounds and privileges economic values to the exclusion of political, cultural, or other social considerations.

effects The direct results of the media influencing human behaviour.

elite The few who are considered superior or more powerful in society or within a particular group in society.

encoding Placing meaning in a particular code; for instance, language, digital signals, song.

encryption The process of obscuring information to make it unreadable without special (decoding or decryption) knowledge.

Enlightenment An early-eighteenth-century change in Western European worldview distinguished by an intellectual approach based on a scientific and rational perspective on the world, a fundamental shift in worldview that championed science over religion, justice over the abuse of power, and a social contract that specified individual rights and freedoms over the absolutist rule of monarchs and popes.

false needs As described in Leiss et al. (2005: 83–7), the continuous bombardment of flashy and seductive advertisements are seen as fuelling an increasing array of "needs": goods and services that people do not really require and that drive a lifestyle characterized by an escalating frenzy of consumption.

fee-for-carriage The compensation television networks receive for the use of their signals by cable and satellite distributors.

feminist research A perspective that is critical of the character of modern societies for the male domination of women (patriarchy) that has led to profound human inequalities and injustices.

fidelity In sound and electronic engineering, the signal-to-noise ratio, or the accuracy of electronic systems in reproducing the input signal—the higher the fidelity, the lower the noise in comparison to the signal.

file sharing The practice of freely exchanging digital files through computer networks, most commonly referring to the exchange of music and video downloads through the internet.

Fordism The concentration of production on a single site modelled after Henry Ford's automobile assembly lines, whereby raw materials are turned into standardized finished products as part of a single, multi-faceted mass-production process.

formative research Research undertaken, usually by means of focus groups, to obtain reactions to television programs and films as they are being made.

fourth estate The media; refers to the role of the media in watching over the other powerful institutions in society.

frame/framing Both a noun and a verb drawing attention to the boundaries a picture, story, or other means of communication places on that to which it refers; these boundaries tend to limit the range of interpretation by audiences or privilege particular readings.

Frankfurt School A school of thought led by the German intellectuals Max Horkheimer, Theodor Adorno, and Herbert Marcuse, who argued, among other things, that cultural life in modern times has been profoundly changed by the detrimental impact of capitalist methods of mass production.

freedom of information The principle by which information collected by governments belongs to the people rather than the state. This is the operating principle in the United States.

freedom of speech The right of any individual to speak freely on matters of concern without fear of retribution; this freedom is not absolute, but subject to certain legal limits.

freedom of the press (1) The freedom of the press and other media to exercise the right to free speech, usually in the name of the public good; (2) the freedom of press and other media owners to pursue market interests unhindered by the state; this freedom is not absolute, but subject to certain legal limits.

free flow of information The doctrine that advocates the rights of producers to sell information to anyone anywhere, and, conversely, the right of any individual to choose to receive any information from any source.

free market (economy/theory) The general approach to commerce, positing that a free market is the most efficient way of creating and allocating social resources.

frequency allocation The assignment by the International Telecommunications Union of frequency bands within the earth's electromagnetic spectrum for use by specific communications services, such as radio, television, and emergency communications.

gatekeeping The control of access to media publication or broadcast that determines what gains access according to the identity or character of the media outlet.

geostationary An orbit situated directly over the equator in which objects (i.e., satellites) rotating around the earth remain in a fixed location relative to the earth.

geosynchronous An orbit twice the distance of geo-stationary orbit, which similarly allows for objects to remain in a fixed position relative to the earth.

globalization The processes by which social, political, and economic relations extend further than ever before, with greater frequency, immediacy, and facility.

global village A metaphor introduced by Marshall McLuhan that captures the sense in which the possibility of instantaneous communication makes societies seem closer together.

hegemony In simple terms, the social process through which the existing relations of social power are made to appear natural and legitimate.

horizontal integration The combination of a group of companies owned by the same company and operating in the same business but occupying different markets—also known as chain ownership; horizontal integration allows for economies of scale through the streamlining of common needs and business practices.

horizontal relationship A unique arrangement between readers and a news organization, where reader members are invited to participate in decision-making in terms of both developing story ideas and administrative issues. Journalist members are the primary story contributors and the editors do the administrative work for the organization. While some of the published material is contributed by volunteers, such a cooperative pays contributors wherever possible, in both cash and exchange.

human agency The notion that human beings control their behaviour through purposive action; humans have subjectivity.

icon A sign that looks like the object it describes. Maps and photographs are both icons.

ICT Information and communication technology.

ideology A coherent set of social values, beliefs, and meanings; in Marxist terms, it is a critical concept that refers particularly to dominant or ruling-class values, beliefs, and meanings—what came to be called the dominant ideology.

index A sign related to the object it represents. Smoke is an index of fire and a sneeze is an index of a cold, allergy, or irritant.

individual rights Rights that accrue to the individual and that, in the first instance, favour the individual (usually over the community); individual rights include those dealing with free speech and privacy.

Industrial Revolution The application of growing scientific knowledge to production and industry that began to dominate in the late eighteenth century in Western Europe.

infant industries New (typically local) industries seeking to gain a foothold in a market already populated by established and dominant industries.

information flows Patterns of circulation of information commodities or products—for example, movies, magazines, television programs; a summary concept describing the imports and exports of goods, specifically information and entertainment products.

information society A society in which the production, distribution, and consumption of information take on growing and significant political, economic, and social importance.

instrumentalism A philosophical position whereby an adherent of this approach perceives technology as a value-neutral tool that can shorten the path to natural ends or, alternatively, social goals; technology here is simply a means to an end and can be used for whatever purpose we choose. Technology from an instrumentalist perspective is simply a tool for our use.

intellectual property The set of rights that accrue to an author by virtue of the work expended in the creation of a literary, dramatic, artistic, or musical work; the owned expressions of intellectual work derived from copyright law; intellectual property carries two sets of rights—moral rights and property rights.

interactivity As a descriptor of media, the inclusion of user-created content as part of what is presented to the audience. While it may be claimed that such devices as letters to the editor are an interactive element of newspapers and magazines, they are placed in separate sections from the content produced by the publication itself. Interactivity is strongest when the boundary between the content producers and the audience is least. To use a theatrical analogy, in strongly interactive media the boundary between the stage and audience vanishes.

International Telecommunications Union A United Nations agency that coordinates standards and regulations for international information and communication technologies.

intertextuality Refers to the idea that the meaning we make of one text depends on the meanings we have drawn from other sets of signs we have encountered.

invisible hand The notion proposed by Adam Smith that the marketplace generally works in the best interests of society by encouraging individuals to pursue their own self-interest and economic opportunity; refers to the self-regulation of a market economy.

labour The human resources necessary to produce and distribute communications. This can include people working individually on their own creative products (e.g., novels, websites) and those working within an industrial production setting (e.g., large media companies). The category includes those directly involved in media production (e.g., writers, actors, photographers) and those in supporting roles (e.g., truck drivers, press operators).

legislation Acts, statutes, and laws passed either by Canada's federal Parliament or by provincial/territorial governments.

libel (1) A published written statement that does damage to the good reputation of a person; in France and the United States, libel can express true facts, while in the United Kingdom and derivative systems, truth is an absolute defence against an accusation of libel; (2) any false or insulting statement.

libel chill The threat, real or imagined, and under which authors and publishers live, that they will be accused of libel and need to expend considerable sums of money to defend themselves, especially when publishing controversial or critical material about powerful people and institutions; this threat often leads to self-censorship as a form of protection.

liberalism A political philosophy in which society is seen as composed of individuals (as opposed to social classes or definable communities) and that advocates the liberty of individuals as the primary social goal.

libertarian theory A political philosophy that views the sole purpose of the state as enforcing individuals' rights.

lingua franca The primary or common language in a society where numerous languages are spoken.

long tail Concept introduced by Chris Anderson of *Wired* magazine, whereby the distribution/display costs are much more forgiving in the online world. Because of very low costs for display and distribution, and because item costs are low but access is easy, consumers choose widely rather than focusing their choices solely on hits.

market Generally, any arena in which sellers of goods and services are brought together with potential consumers of those goods and services. Today, buyers and sellers can be brought together virtually (e.g., through e-commerce) or physically (e.g., in a shopping mall). The term can also be used to refer to a specific market, meaning either a particular place (Calgary) or a specific group of consumers (luxury home buyers).

market externalities The costs and benefits of economic activity that are not accounted for by (i.e., are external to) the immediate economic transaction between buyer and seller.

market failure The inability of the free market to reflect the true value of (or provide) a good or service, for example, a work of art, which may be sold for a small sum during the life of the artist but for increasingly greater sums after the artist's lifetime.

Marxist analysis An approach to studying society that derives from the writings of Karl Marx, who emphasized class as a fundamental dividing element in society, separating and placing in conflict the interests of workers (the class that sells its labour for wages) from capitalists (the class that owns and controls the means of production).

mash-up Any kind of media product—website, song, video—that consists of content brought together from other sources.

mass audience A convenient shorthand term for the great numbers of people who constitute the mass entertainment audience; rather than being conceived as homogeneous, vulnerable, and passive, the mass audience is better thought of as a great number of individuals of heterogeneous backgrounds who use the media for a great variety of purposes.

mass communication Historically, a term used to describe communication to a large undifferentiated group. More recently, the term has also been used to describe communication between a large number of individuals.

mass culture A culture or way of life that is largely constructed through mass media and industrial production. In this context, people are often seen as being relatively easily manipulated by the media and satisfied by cheap industrial goods.

mass marketing A term that includes a number of practices associated with the large-scale promotion and sale of goods or services. These practices include surveys of actual and potential customers, analyses of ratings, circulation and/or attendance data, advertising of all kinds, other forms of publicity, and promotional campaigns.

mass media Newspapers, magazines, film, television, radio, advertising, book publishing, the internet, and popular music.

means of production The mechanism or process by which we satisfy our material needs for food, clothing, and shelter, and thus ensure our survival.

media democratization A movement seeking to democratize media organizations through public or cooperative ownership, and by opening these organizations' decision-making processes to broad public participation.

media geography The physical space that any given media organization occupies and seeks to serve. For example, a national television network occupies and serves audiences and advertisers within a given country.

media imperialism The use of the media to build empires of influence and control.

media silos In a converged, multi-platform media environment, specific media platforms (e.g., radio, television, newspapers, magazines) that are not converged.

medium Any vehicle that conveys information; plural: *media*.

mobility A characteristic that refers to the relative portability or transportability of people, cultural products, investment capital, organizations, etc.

models As in computer models, a pattern, plan, representation, or description designed to show the structure or workings of an object, system, or concept.

monopoly Exclusive control over the supply of a particular product for a specified market; a market in which consumers have a single source for a product or service.

monopoly capitalism A form of capitalism that encourages greater and greater concentration of ownership, resulting in monopolies and, thus, negating market competition.

moral rights The set of rights associated with intellectual property that are deemed to be the creator's by virtue of a work being created—they are most often associated with the integrity of the work; moral rights may be held or waived but not assigned to any other person; moral rights are distinct from *property rights* and not considered to be material.

multiplier effects Indirect economic activity that results from a particular industry. Movie theatres, for example, generate economic activity for popcorn sellers, parking lots, gas stations, and restaurants.

narrowcasting Used in contrast to *broadcasting* to describe media (largely radio and television) services targeted at a small or niche audience with very specific characteristics.

nation-state A sovereign political unit that exercises political control over a territory and is composed of people who identify themselves as part of the nation, often sharing linguistic, historical, and ethnic heritage.

native advertising A form of sponsored content published in newspapers and magazines (similar to *advertorials*). Native advertising consists of articles constructed as news stories, with the difference being that they carry a label identifying them as sponsored content and are typically set in a different typeface than the neighbouring articles.

net neutrality Internet service providers (ISPs) treating all content and applications equally, without degrading or prioritizing service based on their source, ownership, or destination.

network Generally, a group of individuals or organizations that share and/or distribute information (e.g., a social network, computer network); a group of television or radio stations that share programming so that distribution is extended to a broader area. Network stations are usually, but not necessarily, owned by the same company.

network neutrality A characteristic of communication systems that refers to the network's capacity for transferring data without regard to the form or nature of data being transferred.

network society Taken from the work of Manuel Castells, a description of contemporary society as bound together less by physical location than by globalized social, communication, and economic networks.

new media Technologies, practices, and institutions designed to encourage public participation in information creation, production, and exchange (i.e., communication) on a mass scale by means of either increased access to production facilities (decentralized production) or through *interactivity*. They are usually, but not always, digital media.

news values The criteria journalists apply to determine whether a particular person or event is newsworthy, and the extent to which the person or event merits news coverage.

non-governmental organizations Non-profit citizens' organizations independent of governments; NGOs are designed to provide a social or political service on a regional, national, or international basis.

North American Free Trade Agreement A trilateral trade pact signed by Canada, Mexico, and the United States; it came into effect in January 1994.

objectivity The relatively impartial or unbiased perception of reality. A controversial but nonetheless core value of journalism that seeks to separate opinion from fact.

open-source software The production and development of software that allows users and others to see source code and thereby make adjustments to it to suit their needs.

operational control The kind of control over media organizations exercised by editors and producers who are responsible for day-to-day production decisions; these managers determine how best to employ the labour and capital resources assigned to them by upper management, who exercise *allocative control*.

packets The sending of blocks of data, such as symbols, characters, or numbers, using variable time intervals separating the transmission of the blocks in discrete recognizable sequences, each with addressing and error-checking information attached.

peer-to-peer system A form of communications network in which there is no central control point. The internet was developed as a peer-to-peer system, arranged like a web, in which points on the network are redundantly interconnected; the route by which any particular piece of information travels is guided by software rather than by the physical connections, and all points on the internet are designed to be equals or peers.

people meter Electronic device that allows audience members to record their media-consumption habits.

phishing A form of online fraud in which computer users are deceived into providing sensitive personal information. Typically, computer users are sent an email from someone posing as a legitimate service—e.g., a bank, the government, a telephone company—requesting username and password information. That information is then used for an illegal purpose, such as theft.

piracy Theft of intellectual property—often of works by persons in one country by persons based in another country that does not recognize the laws of the first country.

politics The social process whereby people make collective decisions. This definition includes formal processes of government; but it also includes a much wider range of activities that frame and animate formal government policies and activities, as well as informal discussions of social norms and values. From this perspective, politics is a key element in many aspects of social life. Whenever we are discussing or otherwise are engaged with issues of collective concern with other members of society, be it in a large or small group, or simply with just one other person, we are engaging in politics.

political economy The study of the ways in which politics and economics enable and constrain the allocation, production, distribution, and consumption of social resources.

polysemic The idea that a sign may have many meanings. Depending on the context, an image of an apple might be interpreted as knowledge, as a computer company, or simply as fruit.

postmodernism A contemporary philosophical perspective that questions whether there can be any objective truth and views reality as a largely ever-shifting social construct.

primary definers Terms used to define the important elements of a news story; also used to designate those people who are first to assert a meaning to news events; primary definitions tend to be difficult to change.

privacy The right of people to protect certain aspects of their personal lives from the media. Such rights do not exist in Britain in any formal way and they are weak in the United States.

private ownership Ownership by individuals or corporations, including of publicly traded companies, as opposed to *public ownership*.

privatization The transfer of publicly owned enterprises into the hands of private individuals or corporations.

probes As used by Marshall McLuhan, probes were new, original, seemingly profound ideas that may or may not have much foundation; by calling his pronouncements *probes*, McLuhan was indicating that such ideas were works in progress.

product placement The insertion of identifiable commercial products into the content of entertainment or information media for the purpose of promoting awareness of them.

property rights The rights pertaining to the ownership of property; intellectual property rights pertain to the ownership and material benefit one may gain from *intellectual property*.

proximity The degree of closeness, which can be physical, cultural, or emotional closeness.

public interest The investment that a national group or other polity has in preserving or developing the best of its values and ideals.

public ownership Ownership by arm's-length government agencies (e.g., the CBC) or by groups of individuals (e.g., cooperatives), which members of the public can join for a token membership fee. Public ownership contrasts with commercial or *private ownership* of commercial companies, some of which are publicly traded and therefore called, in business circles, *public companies*.

public policy The set of rules, laws, and practices that govern the operation of communication sectors.

public service An orientation, usually of public sector, volunteer, or cooperative institutions and associations, that places the interests of society above the interests of individuals or specific groups.

public sphere A place or space where people can meet to discuss and debate issues and ideas of common concern.

pull technologies Media forms that allow people to seek out—or *pull* out—content from a seemingly infinite array of options found within a seemingly unlimited range of sources. The internet is an example of a pull technology, with an emphasis on user demand.

push technologies Media forms that present—or *push* toward—audience members a limited range of content options within a finite number of sources. Conventional television, for example, offers the viewer a number of programs from which to select at a given time from a relatively limited array of channels. The emphasis on push technologies is with the supply on offer.

reach The percentage of audience members who tune into a broadcast program at least once during a specified time period.

reception analysis A research method that investigates how and in what context audiences consume media products.

regionalism A political ideology that emphasizes a primary identification or affiliation with a particular region. In Canada, for example, some people may identify themselves as westerners or Quebecers first, and as Canadians second.

regulations Rules that address the details and practical applications of pieces of legislation. The authority to make regulations related to a particular government act is assigned within the act itself; regulations have the full force of law.

re-intermediation Refers to the reintroduction of intermediaries in digital communications, resulting from the emergence and growth of corporate aggregators. The filtering and sorting capacities of these services counter the initial trend of the internet, meant to allow users direct, or unmediated, access to online content.

Renaissance A cultural movement between the fourteenth and seventeenth centuries in Western Europe that highlighted a return to classical forms of learning and knowledge.

representation The production or construction of ideas or images in a communicative form; the depiction through language of an idea, event, person, or institution.

resources The elements necessary for media production—specifically, time, labour (workers), technology (hardware, software), capital (money to invest), and physical materials (paper, plastics, metals, and so on).

rhetoric A persuasive form of communication; a research method in which communications are studied as examples of persuasive speech.

right to communicate The expansion of the notions of *freedom of expression*, *freedom of speech*, and *freedom of the press* to include the right to be informed, the right to inform, the right to *privacy*, and the right to participate in public communication.

royal commissions High-level inquiries established by government to investigate problems of significant public concern and recommend solutions. Members are appointed by the governor-in-council and have the power to subpoena witnesses and request documents. They are more ambitious undertakings than task forces and have a higher profile, but they are limited to making recommendations to government, which it may or may not heed.

royalty payments A percentage of receipts received by copyright owners from those who trade in intellectual property.

satellite footprints The terrestrial areas covered by specific satellite signals.

scientific management The study and implementation of methods to maximize the efficiency of workers' contributions to production processes. It is sometimes called *Taylorism*, after Frederick Winslow Taylor, who in the early twentieth century conducted time and motion studies to break down work-related tasks into their component parts and determine the most efficient means of organizing such tasks. Scientific management was ideally suited to industrialized, mass-production processes that combined workers and machinery in various forms of assembly line.

semiotics The study of signs and sign systems and the ways in which they create meaning.

share The percentage of the average audience that tunes into a program or channel over any specified time period.

sign (1) A physical form (a word, gesture, even an object like a rose) used in communication to refer to something else (an object, a feeling) and recognized as such; (2) the totality of associations, thoughts, understandings, or meanings brought about by the use of symbols in reference to an object, person, phenomenon, or idea.

signified The mental concept of what is referred to—for instance, an object as we think of it when we hear a word (e.g., the image of table when we hear the word *table*).

signifier The physical form of the *sign*—for instance, symbols such as words.

socializing institutions Those institutions in society, such as the education system, the media, and the family, through which social norms and values are communicated—they can be reinforced or contested.

socially contingent A point of view emphasizing that technology arises and takes a particular form reflecting the dynamics of the society in which it emerges.

social responsibility theory The notion that the media have a responsibility to make a positive contribution to society and that they occupy a privileged position of which they should be aware.

social theory Generally, it is a representation of the social world—a set of ideas about how the world is organized and functions.

society A general term for the larger set of institutions and relationships that contextualize the ways in which a relatively large group of people live.

socio-technical ensemble A term coined by Wiebe Bijker to describe a technical apparatus to reflect the fact that built into all commonly used technology are both social dynamics and technical feasibility (and history).

sovereignty The quality of independence, typically referring to the ability of nations to self-govern.

space bias An idea advanced by Harold Innis, which notes the tendency of certain communication systems and societies to privilege the extension of ideas over space or distance as opposed to time or history.

spatialization The process of overcoming the constraints of space and time, typically applied to organizations such as media companies.

spectrum allocation The process by which governments assign radio and television frequencies to over-the-air broadcasting stations.

streaming The process by which audiovisual communications—e.g., music, all types of radio and television programming, films—are delivered over digital platforms.

structuralism A method and theory that emphasizes how the formal elements of a linguistic or

social system limit or determine the agency of the individuals that use that system.

substantivism A point of view that sees technology as operating according to its own inexorable logic, and that this logic is at the expense of human concerns and hence humanity.

summative research Research that measures the effectiveness of a program after its completion.

symbol A sign that bears no direct resemblance to what it signifies, such as words. Thus, symbolic production is the systematic communication of ideas and images through language.

syndicated Material sold by an organization for simultaneous publication or transmission in a variety of places—for instance, a newspaper column or comic strip in various papers or a television sitcom on different networks.

tabloids Half-size newspapers convenient for reading in limited space that often provide bare-bones stories. Tabloids often engage in yellow journalism—that is, the prying into the private and personal lives of the rich and famous in order to uncover scandal.

task forces Bodies of inquiry, whose members are appointed by the governor-in-council, assigned to investigate a particular problem on behalf of government. They differ from royal commissions in that their objects of inquiry are typically less significant, they operate with smaller budgets, their reports are less extensive and typically reflect the government's point of view, and they do not have to be made public.

technological convergence The capacity of a variety of seemingly different technological devices to perform the same task.

technological determinism The notion that technology is an autonomous and powerful driving force in structuring society or elements of society.

technological hubris A form of human conceit. A position whereby a person perceives technology as contributing inherently to progress—a naive position that ignores or downplays technology's limits or its potential downsides.

technological imperative The notion that technological developments provide form and direction to social development.

technology From the Greek *techne*, meaning "art, craft, or skill." From this perspective, technology is considered to be more than simply tools, gadgets, or devices. It is devices or machines *plus* the knowledge or understanding of their use or operation—that is, an understanding of how they fit into a larger set of social circumstances or way of life.

technology transfer The transfer of a particular technology from one society to another.

Telecommunications Act The legal statute passed by Parliament governing "the emission, transmission or reception of intelligence by any wire, cable, radio, optical or other electromagnetic system, or by any similar technical system."

time bias An idea advanced by Harold Innis, which notes the tendency of certain communication systems and societies to privilege the extension of ideas over time or history as opposed to space or distance.

topsight The electronic recording and collection of online transactions for the purpose of creating a body of data that can provide a big picture of online activity and subsequently be mined for valuable information.

Toronto School (of communication theory) Harold Innis and Marshall McLuhan lived and worked in Toronto—as such, the Toronto School is said to be composed of scholars who base(d) their research on the ideas of Innis and McLuhan.

trade liberalization The process by which trade in goods and services between national and subnational jurisdictions is gradually freed from various forms of government regulation.

unbundling The breaking up of the content packages assembled by legacy media, such as radio, television, magazines, and newspapers. New media technologies allow users to access individual articles and programs from the websites or apps of legacy media organizations themselves or through social media.

UNESCO The United Nations Education, Scientific and Cultural Organization, a specialized agency of the United Nations.

Universal Declaration of Human Rights Global declaration of basic rights adopted by United Nations General Assembly in 1948, Article 19 of which is specific to freedom of opinion and expression.

Unix A computer operating system (trademarked UNIX) originally developed in the early 1970s by a group of AT&T employees at Bell Labs and made available to government and academic institutions, thereby becoming—in practice at least—an open system available for widespread and free use. Linux and Mac OS X are operating systems derived from Unix.

uses and gratification research (U&G) A theory of media focusing on how audience members use the media—for instance, for information, for entertainment, for conversation—and what satisfaction they derive from media.

verification The process whereby a claim or a statement is authenticated as truthful or factual.

vertical integration A group of companies linked by common ownership that exist in a supply–demand relation to one another, such as a sound recording company and a radio network.

viewing time The number of hours spent viewing, expressed over the course of a day, week, or longer period of time.

virtual reality Computer generated environments that can simulate places and situations in the real world.

Web 2.0 The extension of web applications though the addition of new communication and interaction options that replace static informational sites with social media applications that allow people to discuss, collaborate, or otherwise interact.

WIPO copyright treaty One of 23 international treaties administered by the United Nations agency, the World Intellectual Property Organization. WIPO was created in 1967 to encourage creative activity and to promote the protection of intellectual property throughout the world. As of 2007, 183 countries were members of WIPO.

wireless spectrum Consists of electromagnetic and radiation frequency bands used by wireless communications services.

world systems theory A theory articulated by Immanuel Wallerstein that focuses on the relationship between nation-states in a global economic system. The theory categorized nations as core, peripheral, and semi-peripheral states depending on the role they play in the international economic system.

World Trade Organization An intergovernmental body that governs trade and is committed to reducing trade barriers between member nations.

References

Aboriginal Peoples Television Network (APTN). 2014. "About." Retrieved 7 November 2014 from www.aptn.ca.

Abramson, Bram Dov, and Marc Raboy. 1999. "Policy globalization and the 'information society': A view from Canada." *Telecommunications Policy*, 23: 775–91.

Adorno, T., and M. Horkheimer. 1972. *Dialectic of Enlightenment*. New York: Herder and Herder.

———. 1977 [1947]. "The culture industry." In *Mass Communication and Society*, J. Curran, M. Gurevitch, and J. Woollacott, eds. London: Edward Arnold.

Advertising Standards Canada. 2010. "Broadcasting Code for Advertising to Children." Accessed 4 November 2010 at www.adstadards.com.

Advertising Standards Council (ASC). 2014. "About us." Retrieved 7 November 2014 from www.adstandards.com.

Alasuutari, Pertti, ed. 1999. *Rethinking the Media Audience*. Thousand Oaks, CA: Sage.

Al Jazeera English. 2014. "About us." Accessed 9 May 2014 at http://www.aljazeera.com/aboutus/2010/11/20101110131438787482.html.

Allan, Stuart, ed. 2010. *The Routledge Companion to News and Journalism*. London and New York: Routledge.

American Gaming Association. 2010. "Industry information: Fact sheets: Industry issues." Retrieved 9 August 2010 at www.americangaming.org/Industry/factsheets/issues_detail.cfv?id=17.

Ananny, M. 2011 (14 April). "The curious connection between apps for gay men and sex offenders." *The Atlantic*. Retrieved 11 March 2013 from www.theatlantic.com/technology/archive/2011/04/the-curious-connection-between-apps-for-gay-men-and-sex-offenders/237340.

Anderson, Benedict. 1983. *Imagined Communities: Reflections on the Origin and Spread of Nationalism*. London: Verso.

Anderson, Chris. 2006. *The Long Tail: Why the Future of Business Is Selling Less of More*. New York: Hyperion.

———. 2009. *Free: The Future of a Radical Price*. New York: Hyperion.

Anderson, C.W. 2013. "What aggregators do: Towards a networked concept of journalistic expertise in the digital age." *Journalism*, 14, no. 8: 1008–23.

———, Emily Bell, and Clay Shirky. 2012 (November). *Post-Industrial Journalism: Adapting to the Present*. New York: Tow Center for Digital Journalism.

Anderson, Robert, Richard Gruneau, and Paul Heyer, eds. 1996. *TVTV: The Television Revolution: The Debate*. Vancouver: Canadian Journal of Communication.

Anderssen, Erin. 2014 (2 October). "Big data is watching you. Has online spying gone too far?" Accessed at www.theglobeandmail.com/life/relationships/big-data-is-watching-you-has-online-spying-gone-too-far/article20894498/?page=all.

Ang, Ien. 1985. *Watching Dallas*. London: Methuen.

———. 1991. *Desperately Seeking the Audience*. London: Routledge.

———. 1996. "Dallas between reality and fiction." In *The Communication Theory Reader*, Paul Cobley, ed. London and New York: Routledge.

———, and Joke Hermes. 1991. "Gender and/in media consumption." In *Mass/Media and Society*, James Curran and Michael Gurevitch, eds. London: Edward Arnold, 307–28.

Appadurai, Arjun. (1990). "Disjuncture and difference in the global cultural economy." *Theory, Culture and Society* 7: 295–310.

———. (1996). Modernity at Large: *Cultural Dimensions of Globalization*. Minneapolis: University of Minnesota Press.

Archetti, Cristina. 2014. "Journalism and the city: Redefining the spaces of foreign correspondence." *Journalism Studies*. Retrieved 5 August 2014 from dx.doi.org/10.1080/1461670X.2014.894354.

Armstrong, Robert. 2010. *Broadcasting Policy in Canada*. Toronto: University of Toronto Press.

Armstrong, Sarah. 2000. "Magazines, cultural policy and globalization: The forced retreat of the state?" *Canadian Public Policy*, XXVI no. 3: 369–85.

Arnott, Peter D. 1989. *Public and Performance in Greek Theatre*, London: Routledge.

Asquith, Kyle, and Alison Hearn. 2012. "Promotional prime time: 'Advertainment,' internal network promotion, and the future of Canadian television." *Canadian Journal of Communication*, 37, no. 2. Retrieved 4 August 2014 from www.cjc-online.ca/index.php/journal/article/view/2494.

Association of Research Libraries. 2010. "Copyright and intellectual property policies." Retrieved 25 October 2010 from www.arl.org/pp/ppcopyright/copyresources/copytimeline.shtml.

Attallah, Paul, and Leslie Regan Shade, eds. 2006. *Mediascapes: New Patterns in Canadian Communication*, 2nd ed. Don Mills, ON: Nelson.

Babe, Robert E. 1979. *Canadian Broadcasting Structure, Performance and Regulation*. Ottawa: Economic Council of Canada.

———. 1988. "Emergence and development of Canadian communication: Dispelling the myths." In *Communication Canada*, R. Lorimer and D.C. Wilson, eds. Toronto: Kagan and Woo.

———. 1990. *Telecommunications in Canada*. Toronto: University of Toronto Press.

Baeker, Greg. 2002. "Sharpening the lens: Recent research on cultural policy, cultural diversity, and social cohesion." *Canadian Journal of Communication*, 27: 179–96.

Bagdikian, Ben H. 1990. *The Media Monopoly*. Boston: Beacon Press.

Baltruschat, Doris. 2009. "Reality TV Formats: The Case of *Canadian Idol*." *Canadian Journal of Communication*, vol 34, no. 1. Retrieved 6 August 2014 from www.cjc-online. ca/index.php/journal/article/view/2032.

Baluja, Tamara. 2014a (13 January). "Updated: Layoffs announced at Postmedia and *The Globe and Mail*." J-Source.ca.

———. 2014b (16 April). "*Globe* launches pilot native advertising project." J-Source.ca.

———. 2014c (15 August). "CTV cuts W5 episodes and staff." J-Source.ca.

Baril, Hélène. 2003 (9 May). "Quebec engranger des profits de Star Académie." *La Presse*, D1.

Barker, Chris. 2012. *Cultural Studies: Theory and Practice*. Thousand Oaks, CA: Sage Publications.

Barney, Darin. 2005. *Communication Technology*. Vancouver: University of British Columbia Press.

Barthes, Roland. 1968. *Elements of Semiology*, A. Lavers and C. Smith, trans. New York: Hill and Wang.

———. 1972. *Mythologies*. London: Jonathan Cape.

———. 1977a. *Image–Music–Text*. London: Fontana.

———. 1977b. "The death of the author." In Barthes, 1977a: 142–9.

Basen, Ira. 2013 (12 September). "Going native: The death of journalism or the way of the future?" J-Source.ca.

———. 2012 (4 August). "Is that an ad or a news story—and does it matter which?" *The Globe and Mail*, F1.

Bashevkin, Sylvia. 1988. "Does public opinion matter? The adoption of federal royal commission and task force recommendations on the national question, 1951–1987." *Canadian Public Administration* 31, no. 1 (Fall): 390–407.

Baudrillard, Jean. 1995. *Simulacra and Simulation*, Sheila Glaser, trans. Ann Arbor, MI: University of Michigan Press.

Bauman, Zygmunt. 1998. *Globalization: The Human Consequences*. New York: Columbia University Press.

Baym, Nancy. 2000. *Tune In, Log On: Soaps, Fandom, and Online Community*. Thousand Oaks, CA: Sage.

BBC Worldwide. 2014. "About us." Accessed 25 April 2014 www.bbcworldwide.com/about-us.aspx.

Bell, Daniel. 1976. *The Coming of Post-Industrial Society*. New York: Basic Books.

Benkler, Yochai. 2006. *The Wealth of Networks*. New Haven, CT: Yale University Press.

———. 2011. "Giving the networked public sphere time to develop." In *Will the Last Reporter Please Turn Out the Lights: The Collapse of Journalism and What Can Be Done to Fix It*, Robert W. McChesney, and Victor Pickard, eds. New York and London: The New Press, 225–37.

Bennett, Tony. 1996. "Media, 'reality,' signification." In *Culture, Society and the Media*, Michael Gurevitch, Tony Bennett, James Curran, and Janet Woollacott, eds. London and New York: Routledge, 287–308.

——— and Janet Woollacott. 1987. *Bond and Beyond: The Political Career of a Popular Hero*. New York: Methuen.

Bergen, Bob. 2002. *Exposing the Boss: A Study in Canadian Journalism Ethics*. Calgary: Sheldon Chumir Foundation. Accessed at www.chumirethicsfoundation.calgary._ ab.ca/downloads/mediafellows/bergenbob/bergenbob index.html.

Berger, Peter, and Thomas Luckmann. 1966. *Social Construction of Reality: A Treatise on the Sociology of Knowledge*. New York: Doubleday.

Bermejo, Fernando. 2011. "The evolution of audience labor: Appropriating online activities. In Park, et al., 67–82.

Bernstein, William J. 2008. *A Splendid Exchange: How Trade Shaped the World*. New York: Grove Press.

Best, Steven, and Douglas Kellner. 1997. *The Postmodern Turn*. New York: Guilford Press.

Bielsa, Esperança. 2008. "The pivotal role of news agencies in the context of globalization: A historical approach." *Global Networks* 8, no. 3: 347–66.

Bijker, Wiebe. 1993. "Do not despair: There is life after constructivism." *Science, Technology & Human Values* 18: 113–38.

Bird, Roger, ed. 1988. *Documents of Canadian Broadcasting*. Ottawa: Carleton University Press.

Black, Edwin. 2001. *IBM and the Holocaust: The Strategic Alliance between Nazi Germany and America's Most Powerful Corporation*. New York: Crown Books.

Blanchfield, Mike, and Jim Bronskill. 2010 (6 June). "Documents expose Harper's obsession with control," *Toronto Star*. Retrieved 16 July 2014 from www.thestar.com/ news/canada/2010/06/06/documents_expose_harpers_ obsession_with_control.html.

Blok, Andersw and Torben Elgaard Jensen. 2011. Bruno Latour: *Hybrid Thoughts in a Hybrid World*. New York: Routledge.

Blumler, Jay, and Elihu Katz, eds. 1974. *The Uses of Mass Communications: Current Perspectives on Gratifications Research*. Beverly Hills, CA: Sage.

Boggs, Jeff. 2012. "Book publishing: Dying one Chapter(s) at a time?" In *Cultural Industries.ca: Making Sense of Canadian Media in the Digital Age*, Ira Wagman and Peter Urquhart, eds. Toronto: James Lorimer, 94–109.

Bouchard–Taylor Commission. 2008. *Building the Future: A Time for Reconciliation*. Accessed 25 July 2010 at www. accommodements.qc.ca/documentation/rapports/ rapport-final-integral-en.pdf.

Bowker, G., and S.L. Star. 1999. *Sorting Things Out: Classification and Its Consequences*. Cambridge, MA: MIT Press.

Boyd-Barrett, Oliver. 1977. "Media imperialism: Towards an international framework for the analysis of media systems." In *Mass Communication and Society*, James Curran, Michael Gurevitch, and Janet Woollacott, eds. London: Edward Arnold.

———. 1996. "Cultural dependency and the mass media." In *Culture, Society and the Media,* Michael Gurevitch, Tony Bennett, James Curran, and Janet Woollacott, eds. London and New York: Routledge.

Bradley, Dale. 2010. "Balance or betrayal: Copyright reform and the right to culture in the digital age." In Shade, 2010: 356–71.

Bradshaw, James. 2014a (26 June). "CBC plans massive staff cuts as it shifts to mobile-first strategy." *The Globe and Mail.* Retrieved 18 August 2014 from J-source.ca.

———. 2014b (6 September). "Five major factors in the CRTC hearing on Canadian TV choice." *The Globe and Mail.* Retrieved 4 November 2014 from www.theglobe andmail.com.

Braverman, Harry. 1974. *Labor and Monopoly Capital: The Degradation of Work in the Twentieth Century.* New York: Monthly Review Press.

Brean, Joseph. 2014 (28 January). "Privacy chief calls for surveillance limits; Controls on CSEC." *The National Post,* A4.

Breen, Marcus. 2005. "Off-shore pot o' gold: The political economy of the Australian film industry." In *Contracting Out Hollywood: Runaway Productions and Foreign Location Shooting,* Greg Elmer and Mike Gasher, eds. Lanham, MD: Rowman & Littlefield, 69–91.

Brethour, Patrick. 2002 (25 April). "Media convergence strategy praised." *The Globe and Mail,* B2.

Bright, David. 2002. "The West wants in: Regionalism, class and *Labour/Le Travail,* 1976–2002." *Labour/Le Travail,* no. 50 (Fall). Accessed 24 October 2010 at www.history cooperative.org/journals/llt/50/bright.html.

Brown, Kimberley. 2009. "Do foreign correspondents matter?" *Media* 14, 1.

Brownell, Claire. 2014 (7 October). "Postmedia scoops up Quebecor's Sun chain." *Montreal Gazette,* B1.

Bruns, Axel. (2008). *Blogs, Wikipedia, Second Life, and Beyond: From Production to Produsage.* New York: Peter Lang.

Bryant, Randal, E., Randy H. Katz, and Edward D. Lazowska. 2008. "Big-data computing: Creating revolutionary breakthroughs in commerce, science, and society." *Computing Community Consortium.* Available at www.cra.org/ccc/files/docs/init/Big_Data.pdf.

Bryce, J. 1987. "Family time and TV use." In *Natural Audiences,* T. Lindlof, ed. Norwood, NJ: Ablex, 121–38.

Buckler, Grant. 2009 (8 June). "Putting limits on who can view online video: How it works and why it's done." CBC News. Accessed 9 October 2010 at www.cbc.ca/technology/story/2009/02/04/f-tech-goblocking.html#ixzz13IRvzlJ2.

Budinsky, Jennifer, and Susan Bryant. 2013 (June). "'It's not easy being green': The greenwashing of environmental discourses in advertising." *Canadian Journal of Communication* 38, no. 2: 207–26.

Burkell, Jacquelyn. 2010. "What is 'new media' anyway?" In Shade, 2010.

Butalia, Urvashi. 1994. "The issues at stake: An Indian perspective on copyright." In *Copyright and Development: Inequality in the Information Age,* Philip G. Altbach, ed. Chestnut Hill, MD: Bellagio Publishing Network.

Canada. 1929a. Order-in-Council 2108. *Canada Gazette,* 19 January, 2306.

———. 1929b. *Report of the Royal Commission on Radio Broadcasting* (Aird Commission). Ottawa: F.A. Acland.

———. 1951. *Report of the Royal Commission on National Development in the Arts, Letters and Sciences, 1949–1951* (Massey–Lévesque Commission). Ottawa: Edmond Cloutier.

———. 1957. *Report of the Royal Commission on Broadcasting* (Fowler Commission). Ottawa: Edmond Cloutier.

———. 1968a. Department of Industry, Trade and Commerce. *Report on Book Publishing* (Ernst and Ernst). Ottawa: Department of Industry, Trade and Commerce.

———. 1968b. Minister of Industry. *White Paper on a Domestic Satellite Communications System for Canada.* Ottawa: Queen's Printer.

———. 1969. *Report of the Task Force on Government Information.* Ottawa: Supply and Services.

———. 1971. *Mass Media, vol. 1: The Uncertain Mirror: Report of the Special Senate Committee on the Mass Media* (Davey Committee). Ottawa: Information Canada.

———. 1977a. Department of the Secretary of State. *The Publishing Industry in Canada.* Ottawa: Ministry of Supply and Services.

———. 1977b. Department of the Secretary of State. *The Film Industry in Canada.* Ottawa: Minister of Supply and Services.

———. 1978a. Department of the Secretary of State. *English Educational Publishing in Canada.* Hull, QC: Minister of Supply and Services.

———. 1978b. Department of the Secretary of State. *French Educational Publishing in Canada.* Hull, QC: Minister of Supply and Services.

———. 1981. *Report of the Royal Commission on Newspapers* (Kent Commission). Ottawa: Minister of Supply and Services.

———. 1982a. *Report of the Federal Cultural Policy Review Committee* (Applebaum–Hébert Committee). Ottawa: Minister of Supply and Services Canada.

———. 1982b. Federal Cultural Policy Review Committee. *Summary of Briefs and Hearings.* Ottawa: Minister of Supply and Services Canada.

———. 1984. *The National Film and Video Policy.* Ottawa: Minister of Supply and Services.

———. 1985. Canadian Multiculturalism Act. R.S. 1983 c. 24. At www.pch.gc.ca/multi/html/act.html.

———. 1985. *Report of the Film Industry Task Force.* Ottawa: Minister of Supply and Services.

———. 1986. Minister of Communications. *Report of the Task Force on Broadcasting Policy* (Caplan–Sauvageau Task Force). Ottawa: Minister of Supply and Services.

———. 1987. Department of Communications. *Vital Links: Canadian Cultural Industries.* Ottawa: Minister of Supply and Services.

———. 1988. *Canadian Voices: Canadian Choices—A New Broadcasting Policy for Canada.* Ottawa: Supply and Services Canada.

———. 1991. Broadcasting Act. At www.crtc.gc.ca/_ENG/LEGAL/BROAD_E.HTM.

———. 1993. Telecommunications Act. At www.crtc.gc.ca/ENG/LEGAL/TELECOME.HTM.

———. 1996a. *Information Highway Advisory Council Report.* At strategis.ic.gc.ca/SSG/ih01015e.html.

———. 1996b. Mandate Review Committee: CBC, NFB, Telefilm. *Making Our Voices Heard.* Ottawa: Minister of Supply and Services.

———. 1999. *Report of the Feature Film Advisory Committee.* Ottawa: Ministry of Canadian Heritage.

———. 2000. *From Script to Screen.* Ottawa: Department of Canadian Heritage.

———. 2002 (March). *Canadian Content in the 21st Century: A Discussion Paper about Canadian Content in Film and Television Productions.* Ottawa: Department of Canadian Heritage.

———. 2003 (June). *Our Cultural Sovereignty: The Second Century of Canadian Broadcasting.* Report of the Standing Committee on Canadian Heritage. Ottawa: Communication Canada Publishing. Available at www.parl.gc.ca/InfoComDoc/37/2/HERI/Studies/Reports/herirp02-e.htm.

———. 2006a (June). *Final Report on the Canadian News Media*, vol. 1. Standing Senate Committee on Transport and Communications. Ottawa: Senate Committees Directorate.

———. 2006b. *Final Report of the Telecommunications Policy Review Panel.* Ottawa: Industry Canada.

———. 2006c. *Report of the Events Relating to Maher Arar: Analysis and Recommendations.* Commission of Inquiry into the Actions of Canadian Officials in Relation to Maher Arar. Ottawa: Government of Canada.

———. 2008 (19 November). Department of Canadian Heritage. "Canadian culture online strategic statement." Accessed 11 November 2010 at www.pch.gc.ca/pgm/pcce-ccop/sttmnt-eng.cfm.

———. 2010a. Department of Canadian Heritage. "The Canadian music industry: 2008 economic profile." Accessed 1 November 2010 at www.pch.gc.ca/pgm/fmusc-cmusf/pubs/prfl_08/index-eng.cfm.

———. 2010b (July). Department of Canadian Heritage. "Investing in the future of Canadian books: Review of the revised foreign investment policy in book publishing and distributing." Accessed 1 November 2010 at www.pch.gc.ca/eng/1276620365197/1278337615182.

———. 2010c. Department of Canadian Heritage. "Canada Book Fund." Accessed 1 November 2010 at www.pch.gc.ca/eng/1268182505843/1268255450528.

———. 2010d. Department of Canadian Heritage. "Canada Periodical Fund." Accessed 10 November 2010 at www.pch.gc.ca/eng/1268240166828.

———. 2010e. Digital Economy Consultation. Accessed 9 August 2010 at www.digitaleconomy.gc.ca.

———. 2014a. Department of Canadian Heritage. *Book Distribution and Bill 51 in Quebec.* Retrieved 30 October 2014 from www.pch.gc.ca/eng/1372789992292/1372790043461#h2.

———. 2014b. Department of Canadian Heritage. *Canada Book Fund.* Retrieved 28 October 2014 from www.pch.gc.ca/eng/1268182505843.

———. 2014c. Department of Canadian Heritage. *Canadian Periodical Fund.* Retrieved 30 October 2014 from www.pch.gc.ca/eng/1268240166828.

———. 2014d. Department of Canadian Heritage. *Canadian Arts Presentation Fund.* Retrieved 31 October 2014 from www.pch.gc.ca/eng/1267553110077.

———. 2014e. *Digital Canada 150.* Retrieved 14 October 2014 from: www.ic.gc.ca/eic/site/028.nsf/eng/00576.html#item3.

Canada Council. 2014 (6 October). "Canada Council for the Arts releases annual report, highlights funding for the arts and creativity across Canada." News release retrieved 28 October 2014 from www.canadacouncil.ca.

Canada Post. 2009. *Annual Report.* Retrieved 10 November 2010 at www.canadapost.ca.

———. 2014. *Annual Report, 2013.* Retrieved 26 October 2014 from www.canadapost.ca.

Canadian Broadcast Standards Council (CBSC). 2014. "About us." Retrieved 7 November 2014 from www.cbsc.ca.

Canadian Film and Television Production Association (CFTPA). 2009. *Profile 2009: An Economic Report on the Canadian Film and Television Production Industry.* Accessed 1 November 2010 at www.cftpa.ca.

Canadian Media Directors' Council. 2010. *Media Digest 09/10.* Toronto: *Marketing Magazine.*

Canadian Media Fund (CMF). n/d. "Funding streams." Retrieved 20 November 2014 from www.cmf-fmc.ca/funding-programs/overview.

Canadian Media Research Consortium. 2009. *The State of the Media in Canada: A Work in Progress.* Accessed 13 July 2010 at www.cmrcccrm.ca/documents/SOM_Canada_0702.pdf.

———. 2011 (29 March). "Canadian consumers unwilling to pay for news online." Accessed 30 Mar. 2011 at www.mediaresearch.ca.

Canadian Newspaper Association. 2009. "Daily newspaper paid circulation data." Accessed 18 October 2010 at www.cna-acj.ca/en/daily-newspaper-paid-circulation-data.

Canadian Press. 1993 (1 March). "Ontario's A-G orders probe into news coverage in case of serial-rape suspect." *Vancouver Sun*, A7.

———. 1999 (1 May). "CRTC cuts CKVL's license over complaints about host." *Montreal Gazette*, C5.

Canadian Wireless Telecommunications Association (CWTA). 2010 (July). "Wireless communications: A strong signal for a stronger Canada." Accessed 8 November 2010 at www.cwta.ca.

Canter, Lily. 2013. "The source, the resource and the collaborator: The role of citizen journalism in local UK newspapers." *Journalism*, 14 no. 8: 1091–109.

Carey, James. W. 1997. "Afterword: The culture in question." In *James Carey: A Critical Reader*, Eve Stryker Munson and Catherine A. Warren, eds. Minneapolis and London: University of Minnesota Press, 308–39.

———. 1989. "Technology and ideology: The case of the telegraph." In *Communication and Culture: Essays on Media and Society*. Boston: Unwin and Hyman.

———. 1998. "The internet and the end of the national communication system: Uncertain predictions of an uncertain future." *Journalism and Mass Communication Quarterly* 75, no. 1: 28–34.

Castells, Manuel. 1996. *The Rise of the Network Society*. New York: Blackwell.

———. 1999. *End of Millennium*. Oxford: Blackwell.

———. 2001. *The Internet Galaxy: Reflections on the Internet, Business, and Society*. Oxford: Oxford University Press.

———. (2009/13) *Communication Power*. Oxford: Oxford University Press.

CBC. 1977. *The Press and the Prime Minister: A Story of Unrequited Love*. television documentary directed and produced by George Robertson. Toronto.

———. 1999a. *CBC/Radio-Canada Annual Report, 1998–99*. Ottawa.

———. 1999b (9 April). "It's Time to Talk about the CBC. . . . Your Voice Matters." Press release.

———. 2003 (1 December). "Response to Broadcasting Notice 2003–54." Accessed at www.cbc.radio-canada.ca/submissions/crtc/2003/BPN_CRTC_2003-54_CBCSRC28 1103_e.pdf.

———. 2009. *CBC/Radio-Canada Annual Report*. Toronto. Accessed at www.cbc.radio-canada.ca/annualreports/2008-2009/index.shtml.

———. 2012. *Annual Report 2011–2012*. Retrieved 15 September 2014 from www.cbc.radio-canada.ca/site/annual-reports/2011-2012/pdf/cbc-rc-annual-report-2011-2012.pdf.

CBC News. 2008 (11 October). "Ex-hacker 'Mafiaboy' tells all in memoir." Accessed 18 November 2010 at www.cbc.ca.

———. 2009 (31 July). "Moore restructuring Canada Music Fund." Accessed 4 November 2010 at www.cbc.ca.

———. 2011 (14 September). "Greenpeace 'genius' turns media spectacle into action." Retrieved 18 June 2014 from www.cbc.ca/news/canada/greenpeace-genius-turns-media-spectacle-into-action-1.1086409.

———. 2013 (8 April). *Arctic Air* season finale takes the second screen experience to new heights. Accessed 24 April 2014 at www.cbc.ca/mediacentre/arctic-air-season-finale-takes-the-second-screen-experience-to-new-heights.html.

Centre for Contemporary Cultural Studies. 1982. *The Empire Fights Back: Racism in Britain in the 1970s*. London: Hutchinson.

Ceruzzi, P.E. 1998. *A History of Modern Computing*. Cambridge, MA: MIT Press.

Chadwick, Andrew. 2013. *The Hybrid Media System: Politics and Power*. New York: Oxford University Press.

Chapman, Glen. 2010 (16 May). "YouTube serving up to 2 billion videos daily." Agence France-Presse. Accessed 13 August 2010 at www.google.com/hostednews/afp/article/ALeqM5jK4sI9GfUTCKAkVGhDzpJ1ACZm9Q.

Charland, Maurice. 1986. "Technological nationalism." *Canadian Journal of Political and Social Theory* 10, no. 1: 196–220.

Charles, Alec. 2014. "The abuse of power: Savile, Leveson, and the internet." In *The End of Journalism 2.0: Industry, Technology and Politics*, Alex Charles, ed. Oxford, UK: Peter Lang, 1–52.

Cheadle, Bruce. 2010. "Veterans advocate Sean Bruyea settles privacy suit with Ottawa." *Toronto Star*, Accessed 18 November 2010 at www.thestar.com/article/892818--veterans-advocate-sean-bruyea-settles-privacy-suit-with-ottawa.

Cherry, Paul. 1998 (11 April). "'A bad day,' photographers say." *Montreal Gazette*, A4.

Christopherson, Susan. 2006 (September). "Behind the scenes: How transnational firms are constructing a new international division of labor in media work." *Geoforum* 37, no. 5: 739–51.

Chung, Emily. 2013 (21 October). "Muzzling of federal scientists widespread, survey suggests." Retrieved 21 November 2013 from www.cbc.ca/news/technology/muzzling-of-federal-scientists-widespread-survey-suggests-1.2128859.

Clark, Jessica, and Tracy Van Slyke. 2011. "How journalists must operate in a new networked media environment." In *Will the Last Reporter Please Turn Out the Lights: The Collapse of Journalism and What Can Be Done to Fix It*, Robert W. McChesney and Victor Pickard, eds. New York and London: The New Press, 238–48.

CMPA (Canadian Media Production Association) and AQPM (l'Association québécoise de la production médiatique). 2013. *Profile 2013: Economic Report on the Screen-based Media Production Industry in Canada*. Retrieved 1 October 2014 from www.cmpa.ca/industry-information/profile.

Cohen, Nicole. 2008. "The valorization of surveillance: Towards a political economy of Facebook." *Democratic Communique* 22, no. 1: 5–32.

———. 2012 (12 September). "How much do freelance journalists make?" J-Source.ca.

Coleman, Stephen, and Karen Ross. 2010. *The Media and the Public: "Them" and "Us" in Media Discourse*. Chichester, UK: Wiley-Blackwell.

Collett, Peter, and Roger Lamb. 1986. *Watching Families Watching TV*. Report to the Independent Broadcasting Authority. London.

Collins, Richard. 1992. *Satellite Television in Western Europe*, rev. ed. London: John Libbey Academia Research Monograph 1.

Commission on Freedom of the Press. 1947. *A Free and Responsible Press*. Chicago: University of Chicago Press.

Communications Security Establishment Canada (CSEC). 2014. "What we do and why we do it." Accessed 23 June 2014 http://www.cse-cst.gc.ca/home-accueil/inside-interieur/what-nos-eng.html.

Compton, James R. 2010. "Newspapers, labor and the flux of economic uncertainty." In *The Routledge Companion to News and Journalism*, Stuart Allan, ed. London and New York: Routledge.

comScore. 2010 (March). "Canada: Digital year in review 2010." Accessed 25 March 2011 at www.comscore.com/Press_Events/Presentations_Whitepapers/2011/2010_Canada_Digital_Year_in_Review.

Cook, James. 2014 (11 September). "Apple's forced 'gift' of U2's new album has iTunes users freaking out." *Financial Post*. Retrieved 15 September 2014 from business.financialpost.com/2014/09/11/apples-forced-gift-of-u2s-new-album-has-itunes-users-freaking-out.

Cool, Julie. 2010 (29 July). "Wage gap between women and men." Library of Parliament Background Paper. Retrieved 3 October 2014 from www.parl.gc.ca/content/lop/researchpublications/2010-30-e.pdf.

Cooper, Mark. 2011. "The future of journalism: Addressing pervasive market failure with public policy." In *Will the Last Reporter Please Turn Out the Lights: The Collapse of Journalism and What Can Be Done to Fix It*, Robert W. McChesney and Victor Pickard, eds. New York and London: The New Press, 320–39.

Copyright Board of Canada. 2014 (16 May). "Fact sheet." Retrieved 31 October 2014 from www.cb-cda.gov.ca.

Cormier, Ryan. 2014 (10 April). "Ex-soldier jailed for online sex crimes." *Edmonton Journal*, A4.

Coulter, Natalie. 2014. "From the top drawer to the bottom line: The commodification of children's cultures." In *Mediascapes: New Patterns in Canadian Communication*, Leslie Regan Shade, ed. Don Mills, ON: Nelson Education, 409–26.

Cox, Kirwan. 1980. "Hollywood's empire in Canada." In *Self-Portrait: Essays on the Canadian and Quebec Cinemas*, Pierre Véronneau and Piers Handling, eds. Ottawa: Canadian Film Institute.

Cox, M., and Ellsworth, D. 1997. *Application-Controlled Demand Paging for Out-of-Core Visualization* (No. NAS-97-010). Moffett Field, CA: NASA Ames Research Center, pp. 1–5. Retrieved from www.nas.nasa.gov/assets/pdf/techreports/1997/nas-97-010.pdf.

Crawford, Michael G. 1990. *The Journalist's Legal Guide*, 2nd ed. Toronto: Carswell.

Crawford, Trish. 2013 (4 December). "Ticket sales slump while fundraising up at TSO." *Toronto Star*, E1.

Croteau, David, and William Hoynes. 2003. *Media/Society*, 3rd ed. Thousand Oaks, CA: Pine Forge.

———. 2014. *Media/Society: Industries, Images, and Audiences*. 5th ed. Los Angeles: Sage.

Crow, Barbara, Michael Longford, and Kim Sawchuk, eds. 2010. *The Wireless Spectrum: The Politics, Practices and Poetics of Mobile Media*. Toronto: University of Toronto Press.

CRTC (Canadian Radio-television and Telecommunications Commission) 1999 (25 February). "The means may be changing but the goals remain constant." Speech by Wayne Charman to the 1999 Broadcasting and Program Distribution Summit. Accessed at www.crtc.gc.ca/_ENG/NEWS/SPEECHES/1999/S990225.htm.

———. 2000 (24 November). "CRTC approves new digital pay and specialty television services—more choice for consumers." Press release. Accessed 24 November 2000 at www.crtc.gc.ca/ENG/NEWS/_RELEASES/2000/R001124-2.htm.

———. 2001 (2 August). "CRTC renews CTV and Global's licences—more quality programming and services." Press release. Accessed at www.crtc.gc.ca/ENG/NEWS/_RELEASES/2001/R010802.htm.

———. 2009a. *CRTC Monitoring Report, 2009*. Accessed 25 July 2010 at www.crtc.gc.ca/eng/publications/reports/policymonitoring/2009/cmr.htm.

———. 2009b (8 June). Speech accessed 10 November 2010 at www.crtc.gc.ca/eng/com200/2009/s090608.htm.

———. 2010a. Broadcasting Regulatory Policy CRTC 2010–622. Accessed at www.crtc.gc.ca/eng/archive/2010/2010-622.htm.

———. 2010b. Broadcasting Notice of Consultation CRTC 2010–783. Accessed 19 November 2010 at www.crtc.gc.ca/eng/archive/2010/2010-783.htm.

———. 2010c. *Navigating Convergence: Charting Canadian Communications Change and Regulatory Implications*. Ottawa. Accessed 13 October 2011 at www.crtc.gc.ca/eng/publications/reports/rp1002.htm.

———. 2010d. *Communications Monitoring Report 2010*, July. Accessed 27 October 2010 at www.crtc.gc.ca.

———. 2010e (February). *Navigating Convergence: Charting Canadian Communications Change and Regulatory Implications*. Retrieved 7 November 2014 from www.crtc.ca.

———. 2011 (March). "CRTC forum: Shaping regulatory approaches for the future." Ottawa. Retrieved 15 April 2011 from www.crtc.gc.ca/eng/publications/reports/rp110324.htm.

———. 2013 (September). *CRTC Communications Monitoring Report*. Retrieved 15 August 2013 from www.crtc.gc.ca.

———. 2015 (12 March). "Let's Talk TV: CRTC announces measures to support the creation of content made by Canadians for Canadian and global audiences." News Release. Accessed 12 November 2015 http://news.gc.ca/web/article-en.do?nid=947269.

———. 2014a (January). *Let's Talk TV: A Report on Comments Received during Phase I*. Retrieved 4 November 2014 from www.crtc.gc.ca.

———. 2014b (24 April). *Broadcasting Notice of Consulation CRTC 2014-190*. Retrieved 4 November 2014 from www.crtc.gc.ca.

CTV. 2014a. "About CTV." Retrieved 15 September 2014 from www.ctv.ca/About/Corporate-Info/About.aspx.

CTV News. 2013 (27 October). "Canada's growing video game industry pumps $2.3B into economy." Retrieved 25 April 2014 from http://www.ctvnews.ca/sci-tech/canada-s-growing-video-game-industry-pumps-2-3b-into-economy-1.1516104.

———. 2014 (27 March). "No more unpaid internships: Ontario warns well-known magazines, other sectors." Accessed 27 September 2014 at toronto.ctvnews.ca/no-more-unpaid-internships-ontario-warns-well-known-magazines-other-sectors-1.1749571.

Curran, James. 1990. "The new revisionism in mass communication research: A reappraisal." *European Journal of Communication* 5, no. 2–3: 135–64.

Curtis, Liz. 1984. *Ireland, the Propaganda War: The Media and the "Battle for Hearts and Minds."* London: Pluto Press.

Dahlberg, Lincoln and Eugenia Siapera, eds. 2007. *Radical Democracy and the Internet: Integrating Theory and Practice.* New York: Palgrave Macmillan.

Dahlgren, Peter. 2013. "Online journalism and civic cosmopolitanism: Professional vs. participatory ideals." *Journalism Studies*, 14, no. 2: 156–71.

Dale, Stephen. 1996. *McLuhan's Children: The Greenpeace Message and the Media.* Toronto: Between the Lines.

Darnton, Robert. 1982. *The Literary Underground of the Old Regime.* Cambridge, MA: Harvard University Press.

Daschuk, James. 2013 (19 July). "When Canada used hunger to clear the West," *The Globe and Mail.* Retrieved 15 July 2014 from www.theglobeandmail.com/globe-debate/when-canada-used-hunger-to-clear-the-west/article13316877.

Datamonitor. 2009. *Global Media: Industry Profile.* Accessed 15 July 2010 at www.datamonitor.com.

Day, Richard J.F. 2005. *Gramsci Is Dead: Anarchist Currents in the New Social Movements.* Toronto: Between the Lines.

Dayal, G. 2012 (9 September). "The algorithmic copyright cops: Streaming video's robotic overlords." Retrieved 15 March 2013 from www.wired.com/threatlevel/2012/09/streaming-videos-robotic-overlords-algorithmic-copyright-cops.

de Beauvoir, Simone. 1957 [1949]. *The Second Sex*, H.M. Parshley, trans. and ed. New York: Knopf.

DeFleur, Melvin L., and Sandra Ball-Rokeach. 1989. *Theories of Mass Communication*, 5th ed. New York: Longman.

de Kerckhove, Derrick. 1995. *The Skin of Culture: Investigating the New Electronic Reality.* Toronto: Somerville House.

de la Haye, Yves. 1980. *Marx and Engels on the Means of Communication (The Movement of Commodities, People, Information and Capital).* New York: International General.

Demers, David. 1999. "Corporate newspaper bashing: Is it justified?" *Newspaper Research Journal* 20, no. 1: 83–97.

Derrida, Jacques. 1981. *Positions.* London: Althone.

Desbarats, Peter. 1990. *Guide to Canadian News Media.* Toronto: Harcourt Brace.

Digital Readership. 2014 (7 April). "Digital readership on the rise: PMB." *Masthead.* Retrieved 28 October 2014 from http://www.mastheadonline.com/news/digital_readership_on_the_rise_pmb/.

Dizard, Wilson P. 1985. *The Coming Information Age: An Overview of Technology, Economics and Politics.* New York: Longman.

Dobby, Christine. 2014 (10 July). "Postmedia records loss as ad revenue continues to drop." *The Globe and Mail.* Retrieved 18 August 2014 from J-source.ca.

Drache, Daniel. 1995. "Celebrating Innis: The man, the legacy and our future." In *Staples, Markets and Cultural Change: Selected Essays*, Daniel Drache, ed. Montreal and Kingston: McGill-Queen's University Press.

Drezner, Daniel, and Henry Farrell. 2004. "The power and politics of blogs." Paper presented at the annual meeting of the American Political Science Association. Accessed at www.utsc.utoronto.ca//farrel/blogpaperfinal.pdf.

Driscoll, Kevin. 2012. "From punched cards to 'Big Data': A social history of database populism." *Communication +1*, 1(Article 4). Available at scholarworks.umass.edu/cpo/vol1/iss1/4.

Drucker, Peter F. 1993. *Post-Capitalist Society.* New York: HarperCollins.

Druick, Zoë, and Aspa Kotsopoulos. 2008. *Programming Reality: Perspectives on English-Canadian Television.* Waterloo, ON: Wilfrid Laurier University Press.

Dubinsky, Lon. 1996. "Periodical publishing." In *The Cultural Industries in Canada: Problems, Policies and Prospects*, Michael Dorland, ed. Toronto: James Lorimer.

Dubrowski, Wojtek. 2008 (16 December). "Quebecor's Sun Media to cut 600 jobs." *Ottawa Citizen*, 3.

Duffy, Andrew. 2014 (20 May). "Meet the new, four-platform *Citizen*." *Ottawa Citizen*. Retrieved 26 August 2014 from www.ottawacitizen.com.

Durham Peters, John. 1999. *Speaking into the Air: A History of the Idea of Communication.* Chicago: University of Chicago Press.

Dutrisac, Robert. 2002 (6 September). "Concentration de la presse—Québec demandera à l'industrie de s'autorégle-menter." *Le Devoir*, A3.

Dyer-Witheford, Nick. 1999. *Cyber-Marx: Cycles and Circuits of Struggle in High Technology Capitalism.* Champaign, IL: University of Illinois Press.

———, and Greig S. de Peuter. 2006. "'EA spouse' and the crisis of video game labour: Enjoyment, exclusion, exploitation and exodus. *Canadian Journal of Communication*, 31: 599–617.

Eagleton, Terry. 2007. *Ideology: An Introduction.* London: Verso.

Eaman, Ross Allan. 1994. *Channels of Influence: CBC Audience Research and the Canadian Public.* Toronto: University of Toronto Press.

Eastwood, Joel. 2004 (18 March). "Recording industry earns more from fan videos than from official music videos." *Toronto Star.* Accessed 24 April 2014 at www.thestar.com/entertainment/music/2014/03/18/recording_industry_earns_more_from_fan_videos_than_from_official_music_videos.html.

Ebner, D. 2009 (3 August). "Toronto scores points in the video game sector." *The Globe and Mail.* Accessed 19 October 2014 at www.theglobeandmail.com.

Eco, Umberto. 1982. "Narrative structure in Fleming." In *Popular Culture Past and Present*, B. Waites et al., eds. Milton Keynes, UK: Open University Press.

———. 1986. "The multiplication of the media." In *Eco's Travels in Hyperreality*. New York: Harcourt Brace Jovanovich, 148–69.

Edge, Marc. 2014. *Greatly Exaggerated: The Myth of the Death of Newspapers*. Vancouver: New Star Books.

Èdinova. 2008. *The Diffusion and Distribution of French-Language Books in Canada*. Montreal: Èdinova.

Edwardson, Ryan. 2008. *Canadian Content: Culture and the Quest for Nationhood*. Toronto: University of Toronto Press.

Eisenstein, Elizabeth. 1979. *The Printing Press as an Agent of Change*, 2 vols. New York: Cambridge University Press.

———. 1983. *The Printing Revolution in Early Modern Europe*. Cambridge: Cambridge University Press.

El Akkad, Omar. 2011. "Canadians' internet usage nearly double the worldwide average." *The Globe and Mail*. Retrieved 9 March 2011 from www.theglobeandmail.com/news/technology/canadians-internet-usage-nearly-double-the-worldwide-average/article1934508.

——— and Jacquie McNish. 2010 (18 November). "A regulatory nightmare: Facebook and its goal of a less private web." *The Globe and Mail*, A16.

Ellul, Jacques. 1964. *The Technological Society*. New York: Knopf.

Elmer, Greg. 2004. *Profiling Machines: Mapping the Personal Information Economy*. Cambridge, Mass: The MIT Press.

———, and Mike Gasher, eds. 2005. *Contracting Out Hollywood: Runaway Productions and Foreign Location Shooting*. Lanham, MD: Rowman & Littlefield.

———, Ganaele Langlois, and Fenwick McKelvie. 2014. "The permanent campaign online: Platforms, actors, and issue-objects." In *Publicity and the Canadian State*, Kirsten Kozolanka, ed. Toronto: University of Toronto Press. 240–61.

Ericson, Richard V., Patricia M. Baranek, and Janet B.L. Chan. 1989. *Negotiating Control: A Study of News Sources*. Toronto: University of Toronto Press.

Esslin, Martin. 1980 (October). "The exploding stage." CBC Radio, *Ideas*.

Everett-Green, Robert. 2010 (27 October). "COC uses cash infusion despite selling out every show." *The Globe and Mail*, R4.

Facebook, 2014. "What are lookalike audiences?" Retrieved 7 October 2014 from www.facebook.com/help/164749007013531.

Faguy, Steve. 2014a (20 February). "Could Videotron become a national wireless company? Maybe." Retrieved 7 November 2014 from www.fagstein.com.

———. 2014b (12 August). "Cooperation, not acquisition, might be better option for Quebecor." Retrieved 7 November 2014 from www.fagstein.com.

———. 2014c (4 September). "CRTC hearings: A consumer's primer on the issues to be debated." *Montreal Gazette*. Retrieved 4 November 2014 from www.montrealgazette.com.

Fairclough, Norman. 2010. *Critical Discourse Analysis: The Critical Study of Language*. New York: Routledge.

Featherstone, Mike. 1996. "Localism, globalism, and cultural identity." In *Global/Local: Cultural Production and the Transnational Imaginary*, Rob Wilson and Wimal Dissanayake, eds. Durham, NC: Duke University Press.

Fédération professionelle des journalistes du Québec. 2010 (11 October). "La FPJQ appuie la tenue d'une commission parlementaire sur le conflit au *Journal de Montréal*." Accessed 18 October 2010 at www.fpjq.org.

Feenberg, Andrew. 1999. *Questioning Technology*. New York: Routledge.

Felczak, Michael. 2006. "Online publishing, technical representation, and the politics of code: The case of CJC-Online." Unpublished paper.

Fekete, Jason. 2013 (10 October). "Spy agency meets industry regularly; CSEC says its foreign intelligence activities follow Canadian law." *The Edmonton Journal*, A15.

Fenton, Natalie. 2010. "News in the digital age." In Allan, 2010, 557–67.

Fessenden, Helen. 1974. *Fessenden: Builder of Tomorrows*. New York: Arno Press.

Filion, Michel. 1996. "Radio." In *The Cultural Industries in Canada: Problems, Policies and Prospects*, Michael Dorland, ed. Toronto: James Lorimer.

Fiske, John. 1987. *Television Culture*. London: Routledge.

———. 1989a. *Reading the Popular*. Boston: Unwin Hyman.

———. 1989b. *Understanding Popular Culture*. Boston: Unwin Hyman.

———. 1989c. "Moments of television: Neither the text nor the audience." In *Remote Control*, Ellen Seiter et al., eds. London: Routledge.

Fletcher, Fred. 1981. *The Newspaper and Public Affairs*, vol. 7. Research Publications for the Royal Commission on Newspapers. Ottawa: Supply and Services.

Flew, Terry, and Richard Smith. 2014. *New Media: An Introduction*, 2nd Canadian ed. Don Mills, ON: Oxford University Press.

Foot, Richard. 1999 (3 May). "Court orders magazine to stop writing about abortion." *National Post*, A4.

Fornas, J., U. Lindberg, and O. Sernhede. 1988. *Under Rocken*. Stockholm: Symposium.

Forsey, Eugene A. 2006. "Order-in-council." *The Canadian Encyclopedia*. Retrieved 25 November 2014 from www.thecanadianencyclopedia.ca.

Foucault, Michel. 1980. *The History of Sexuality*. Robert Hurley, trans. New York: Vintage Books.

———. 1988. *Madness and Civilization: A History of Insanity in the Age of Reason*. Richard Howard, trans. New York: Vintage Books.

———. 1995 [1979]. *Discipline and Punish: The Birth of the Prison*. Alan Sheridan, trans. New York: Vintage Books.

Fowler, Robert. 2014 (4 October). "We've got to get nasty, or get the hell out." *The Globe and Mail*. Kindle edition.

Franklin, Sarah, C. Lury, and J. Stacey. 1992. "Feminism and cultural studies." In *Culture and Power*, Paddy Scannell et al., eds. London: Sage.

Franklin, Ursula. 1996. *The Real World of Technology*. Concord, ON: House of Anansi Press.

Frau-Meigs, Divina, Jérémie Nicey, Michael Palmer, Julia Pohle, and Patricio Tupper eds. *From NWICO to WSIS: 30 Years of Communication Geopolitics*. Bristol, UK: Intellect.

Friedan, Betty. 1963. *The Feminine Mystique*. New York: Norton.

Friedman, Thomas L. 2005. *The World Is Flat: A Brief History of the Twenty-First Century*. New York: Farrar, Straus & Giroux.

Friend, David. 2010 (17 December). "Sun papers publisher to cut 600 jobs across Canada." *Saint John Telegraph-Journal*, B5.

Frith, Simon. 1988. "The industrialization of popular music." In *Popular Music and Communication*, James Lull, ed. Newbury Park, CA: Sage, 53–77.

Fuchs, Christian. 2009. "Information and communication technologies and society: A contribution to the critique of the political economy of the internet." *European Journal of Communication* 24, no. 1:. 69–87.

Gajjala, Radhika, and Yeon Ju Oh, eds. 2012. *CyberFeminism 2.0*. New York: Peter Lang.

Gans, Herbert. 1979. *Deciding What's News: A Study of CBS Evening News, NBC Nightly News, Newsweek, and Time*. New York: Pantheon Books.

Garfinkel, Harold. 1984. *Studies in Ethnomethodology*. Cambridge: Polity Press.

Gasher, Mike. 1988. "Free trade and the Canadian film industry." *Canadian Dimension* (November): 31–4.

———. 1992. "The myth of meritocracy: Ignoring the political economy of the Canadian film industry." *Canadian Journal of Communication* 17, no. 2: 371–8.

———. 1995. "Culture lag: The liberal record." *Point of View* 26 (Winter): 22–4.

———. 1997. "From sacred cows to white elephants: Cultural policy under siege." *Canadian Issues* 19: 13–29.

———. 1998. "Invoking public support for public broadcasting: The Aird Commission revisited, *Canadian Journal of Communication* 23: 189–216.

———. 2002. *Hollywood North: The Feature Film Industry in British Columbia*. Vancouver: University of British Columbia Press.

———. 2007. "The view from here: A news-flow study of the on-line editions of Canada's national newspapers." *Journalism Studies* 8, no. 2: 299–319.

———. 2010. "From the business of journalism to journalism as business: 1990 to the present." In *The New Journalist*, Paul Benedetti, Kim Kierans, and Tim Currie, eds. Toronto: Emond Montgomery, 63–76.

———. 2013. "Media convergence." *The Canadian Encyclopedia*. Accessed at www.thecanadianencyclopedia.ca/en/article/media-convergence.

———. 2015. "Geographies of the news." In *Mediated Geographies/Geographies of Media*, Susan Mains, Julie Cupples, and Chris Lukinbeal, eds. New York: Springer.

Geddes, John. 2010 (21 January). "Voice of fire: Are we over this yet?" *Maclean's*. Accessed 3 August 2010 at www2.macleans.ca/2010/01/21/are-we-over-this-yet.

Geist, Michael. 2006 (31 July). "Libel case key for internet free speech." *Toronto Star*, D3.

———. 2012 (10 November). "What the new copyright law means for you. *Toronto Star*. Retrieved 10 November 2014 from www.thestar.com.

———. 2014 (29 July). "What the recording industry isn't saying about the Canada's internet streaming royalties." Retrieved 31 October 2014 from www.michaelgeist.ca.

Gendreau, Bianca. 2000. "Moving the mail." In *Special Delivery: Canada's Postal Heritage*, Francine Brousseau, ed. Fredericton, New Brunswick, and Hull, Quebec: Goose Lane Editions and Canadian Museum of Civilization, 125–39.

Geraghty, Christine. 1991. *Women and Soap Opera: A Study of Prime-Time Soaps*. Cambridge: Polity Press.

Gerbner, George. 1969. "Towards 'cultural indicators': The analysis of mass-mediated public message systems." *AV Communication Review* 17, no. 2: 137–48.

———. 1977. *Trends in Network Drama and Viewer Conceptions of Social Reality, 1967–1976*. Philadelphia: Annenburg School of Communications, University of Pennsylvania.

Giddens, Anthony. 1984. *The Constitution of Society: An Outline of a Theory of Structuration*. Berkeley, CA: University of California Press.

———. 1990. *The Consequences of Modernity*. Cambridge, UK: Polity Press.

———. 1999. *Runaway World: How Globalization is Reshaping Our Lives*. London: Profile Books.

Gidengil, Elisabeth, and Joanna Everitt. 2011. "Unconventional politicians: Gender and media coverage of Canadian leaders' debates, 1993, 1997, 2000." In *The Gendered Society Reader*, Michael S. Kimmel, Amy Aronson, and Amy Kaler, eds. Don Mills, ON: Oxford University Press, 304–17.

Gilder, George F. 1991. "Into the telecosm." *Harvard Business Review* (March/April): 150–61.

Gillespie, T. 2014. "The relevance of algorithms." In *Media Technologies*, T. Gillespie, P. Boczkowski, and K. Foot, eds. Cambridge, MA: MIT Press, 167–94. Retrieved from www.tarletongillespie.org/essays/Gillespie%20-%20The%20Relevance%20of%20Algorithms.pdf.

Gillmor, Don. 2004. *We the Media: Grassroots Journalism by the People, for the People*. Sebastopol, CA: O'Reilly.

Gingras, Anne-Marie. 2006. *Médias et Démocratie: Le Grand Malentendu*, deuxième édition. Québec: Presses de l'Université du Québec.

Girard, Bruce, ed. 1992. *A Passion for Radio: Radio Waves and Community*. Montreal: Black Rose Books.

Glaser, Mark. 2010. "Citizen journalism: Widening world views, extending democracy." In Allan, 2010: 578–90.

Glasgow Media Group. 1976. *Bad News*. Boston: Routledge & Kegan Paul.

Gleick, James. 2011. *The Information: A History, a Theory, a Flood*. New York: Pantheon Books.

Globe and Mail, The. 2002 (19 August). "When violating rights becomes the routine." A12.

———. 2010 (21 July). "Canada's long form census debate." Retrieved 25 November 2010 at www.theglobeandmail.com/news/politics/canadas-long-form-census-debate/article1647591.

———. 2014 (27 September). "Thinking outside the idiot box." Editorial. Kindle edition.

Globerman, Steven. 1983. *Cultural Regulation in Canada*. Montreal: Institute for Research on Public Policy.

Goffman, Erving. 1959. *The Presentation of Self in Everyday Life*. Harmondsworth, UK: Penguin.

Goffey, A. 2008. "Algorithm." In *Software Studies: A Lexicon*, M. Fuller, ed. Cambridge: MIT Press, 15–20.

Goggin, Gerard. 2011. "Telephone media: An old story." In Park, et al. , 231–49.

Goldberg, Kim. 1990. *The Barefoot Channel: Community Television as a Tool for Social Change*. Vancouver: New Star Books.

Gomery, Douglas. 2004. "The economics of Hollywood: Money and media." In *Media Economics: Theory and Practice*, 3rd ed., Alison Aleander, James Owers, Rod Carveth, C. Ann Hollifield, and Albert N. Greco, eds. Mahwah, NJ, and London: Lawrence Erlbaum Associates.

Gooderham, M. 2010 (10 January). "Career satisfaction—and a life." *The Globe and Mail*. Accessed 19 October 2014 at www.theglobeandmail.com.

Goody, J.R. 1977. *The Domestication of the Savage Mind*. Cambridge, UK: Cambridge University Press.

Goodyear-Grant, Elizabeth. 2013. *Gendered News: Media Coverage and Electoral Politics in Canada*. Vancouver: University of British Columbia Press.

Google. 2014. "How content ID works—YouTube help." Retrieved 24 March 2014 from support.google.com/youtube/answer/2797370?hl=en.

Gouglas, Sean, Jason Della Rocca, Jennifer Jenson, Kevin Kee, Geoffrey Rockwell, Jonathan Schaeffer, Bart Simon, and Ron Wakkary. 2010. "Computer games and Canada's digital economy: The role of universities in promoting innovation." Report to the Social Science Humanities Research Council. Knowledge Synthesis Grants on Canada's Digital Economy.

Grant, George. 1969. *Technology and Empire*. Toronto: Anansi.

Grant, Peter S., and Chris Wood. 2004. *Blockbusters and Trade Wars: Popular Culture in a Globalized World*. Vancouver: Douglas & McIntyre.

Grant, Tavia 2013 (4 October). "Canadian income data 'is garbage' without census, experts say." *The Globe and Mail*. Retrieved 17 June 2014 from www.theglobeandmail.com/report-on-business/economy/without-census-data-on-canadian-income-garbage-experts/article14701515.

Gray, Ann. 1999. "Audience and reception research in retrospect: The trouble with audiences." In *Alasuutari, Rethinking the Media Audience*: 22–37.

Greenwald, Glenn. 2014. *No Place to Hide: Edward Snowden, the NSA, and the U.S. Surveillance State*. Toronto: McClelland & Stewart.

Grofman, Bernard, Alexander H. Trechsel, and Mark Franklin eds. 2014. *The Internet and Democracy in Global Perspective: Voters, Candidates, Parties and Social Movements*. Cham: Springer.

Grossberg, Lawrence, Ellen Wartella, D. Charles Whitney, and J. Macgregor Wise. 2006. *MediaMaking: Mass Media in Popular Culture*, 2nd ed. Thousand Oaks, CA: Sage.

Gunster, Shane. 2004. *Capitalizing on Culture*. Toronto: University of Toronto Press.

———. 2011. "Covering Copenhagen: Climate politics in B.C. media." *Canadian Journal of Communication*, vol. 36, no. 3. Retrieved 6 August 2014 from www.cjc-online.ca/index.php/journal/article/view/2367.

Gutstein, Donald. 2009. *Not a Conspiracy Theory*. Toronto: Key Porter Books.

Habermas, Jürgen. 1989. *The Structural Transformation of the Public Sphere: An Inquiry into a Category of Bourgeois Society*. Cambridge: Polity Press.

———. 1996. "The public sphere." In *Media Studies: A Reader*, Paul Marris and Sue Thornham, eds. Edinburgh: Edinburgh University Press, 55–9.

Hackett, Robert A., and Yuezhi Zhao. 1998. *Sustaining Democracy? Journalism and the Politics of Objectivity*. Toronto: Garamond Press.

———, and Richard Gruneau. 2000. *The Missing News: Filters and Blindspots in Canada's Press*. Ottawa and Aurora, ON: Canadian Centre for Policy Alternatives and Garamond Press.

———, and William F. Carroll. 2006. *Remaking Media: The Struggle to Democratize Public Communication*. New York: Routledge.

Hager, Mike. 2014 (14 April). "RCMP lay charges in Todd case." *Calgary Herald*, A15.

Hall, Edward T. 1980. *The Silent Language*. Westport, CT: Greenwood Press.

Hall, Stuart. 1980. "Encoding/decoding." In *Culture, Media, Language*, Hall et al., eds.

———. 1993. "Encoding/decoding." In *The Cultural Studies Reader*, Simon During, ed. London: Routledge.

———. 1995. "New cultures for old." In *A Place in the World?*, Massey and Jess, eds.

———. 1997. "The work of representation." In *Representation: Cultural Representations and Signifying Practices*, Hall, ed. London: Sage.

———. 2013. "The work of representation." In *Representation*, 2nd ed., Stuart Hall, Jessica Evans, and Sean Nixon, eds. Milton Keynes, UK: The Open University, 1–47.

——— et al. 1978. *Policing the Crisis: Mugging, the State and Law and Order*. London: Macmillan.

———, Dorothy Hobson, Andrew Love, and Paul Willis, eds. 1980. *Culture, Media, Language: Working Papers in Cultural Studies*. London: Hutchinson.

Hamelink, Cees J. 1994. *The Politics of World Communication*. London: Sage.

———. 1995. "Information imbalance across the globe." In *Questioning the Media: A Critical Introduction*, Ali Monhmmedi, ed. Thousand Oaks, CA: Sage, 293–307.

Hamilton, Anita. 2013 (22 April). "It's getting harder to make money on YouTube." *Bloomberg Businessweek*. Retrieved 8 October 2014 from www.businessweek.com/

articles/2013-04-22/its-getting-harder-to-make-money-on-youtube.

Hamilton, Gordon. 2012 (11 May). "Printed word still drives revenues: Publishers weigh in on digital versus print debate." *Vancouver Sun*, E2.

Handbook on Audience Research. 1987. London: British Broadcasting Corporation.

Handfield, Catherine. 2010 (12 October). "Journal de Montréal: Les syndiqués rejettent l'offre patronale." Accessed 18 October 2010 at lapresseaffaires.cyber presse.ca.

Hanitzsch, Thomas. 2007. "Deconstructing journalism culture: Toward a universal theory." *Communication Theory* 17: 367–85.

Hansen, Ejvind. 2012. "Aporias of digital journalism." *Journalism* 14, no. 5: 678–94.

Haraway, Donna. 1991. "A cyborg manifesto: Science, technology, and socialist-feminism in the late twentieth century." In *Simians, Cyborgs and Women: The Reinvention of Nature*. New York: Routledge, 149–81

Hardin, Herschel. 1974. *A Nation Unaware*. Vancouver: Douglas & McIntyre.

Hartley, John. 1987. "Invisible fictions." *Textual Practice* 1, no. 2: 121–38.

———. 1992. *The Politics of Pictures: The Creation of the Public in the Age of Popular Media*. London and New York: Routledge.

———. 1996. *Popular Reality: Journalism, Modernity, Popular Culture*. London: Arnold.

Havelock, Eric. 1976. *Origins of Western Literacy*. Toronto: OISE Press.

Hebdige, Dick. 1979. *Subculture: The Meaning of Style*. London: Methuen.

Heflet, Miguel. 2009 (6 October). "YouTube eases the way to more revenue." *The New York Times*. Accessed 4 August 2010 at www.nytimes.com/2009/10/07/technology/internet/07youtube.html.

Heilbroner, Robert L. 1980. *The Worldly Philosophers: The Lives, Times, and Ideas of the Great Economic Thinkers*. New York: Simon & Schuster.

Henry, Frances, and Carol Tator. 2000 (March). *Racist Discourse in Canada's English Print Media*. Toronto: Canadian Race Relations Foundation.

———, ———, Winston Mattis, and Tim Rees. 2000. *The Colour of Democracy: Racism in Canadian Society*. Toronto: Harcourt Brace.

Herman, Edward S., and Noam Chomsky. 2002. *Manufacturing Consent: The Political Economy of the Mass Media*. New York: Pantheon Books.

——— and Robert W. McChesney. 1997. *The Global Media: The New Missionaries of Global Capitalism*. Washington: Cassell.

Hermes, Joke. 2006. "Feminism and the politics of method." In *Questions of Method in Cultural Studies,* Mimi White and James Schwoch, eds. Oxford: Blackwell, 154–74.

Hester, Al. 1974. "International news agencies." In *Mass Communications: A World View*, Alan Wells, ed. Palo Alto, CA: Mayfield Publishing.

Heyer, Paul. 2003. "America under attack 1: *The War of the Worlds*, Orson Welles, and 'media sense'" *Canadian Journal of Communication* 28, no. 2 (2003): 149–65. Available online at www.cjc-online.ca/index.php/journal/article/view/1356/1421.

Hickling Arthurs Low Corp. 2009 (25 March). *Canada's Entertainment Software Industry: The Opportunities and Challenges of a Growing Industry*. Accessed 12 November 2010 at www.theesa.ca/facts-and-research/research.php.

Hindman, Matthew. 2008. *The Myth of Digital Democracy*. Princeton, NJ: Princeton University Press.

Hirji, Faiza. 2014. "The colour of difference: Race diversity and journalism in Canada." In *Mediascapes: New Patterns in Canadian Communication*, 4th ed., Leslie Regan Shade, ed. Don Mills, ON: Nelson, 390–408.

Hirst, Martin, John Harrison, and Patricia Mazepa. 2014. *Communication and New Media: From Broadcast to Narrowcast*, Canadian Edition. Don Mills, ON: Oxford University Press.

Hobson, D. 1980. "Housewives and the mass media." In Hall et al., 1980.

———. 1982. *Crossroads: The Drama of Soap Opera*. London: Methuen.

Hogg, Chris. 2006 (12 January). "Taiwan breeds green-glowing pigs." BBC *News*. Accessed at news.bbc.co.uk/2/hi/asia-pacific/4605202.stm.

Hoggart, Richard. 1992 [1957]. *The Uses of Literacy*. New Brunswick, NJ: Transaction.

Holmes, Nancy. 2008 (September). *Canada's Federal Privacy Laws*. Ottawa: Library of Parliament. Retrieved 18 June 2014 from http://www.parl.gc.ca/Content/LOP/researchpublications/prb0744-e.pdf.

Hopewell, John. 2014 (27 January). "Brazilian TV giant innovates in services, sales, shows." *Variety*. Retrieved 25 April 2014 from http://variety.com/2014/tv/global/globo-unveils-newsource-movies-new-tv-fiction-1201072733/

Houpt, Simon. 2014 (4 October). "It's time to be honest: Netflix is parasitic." *The Globe and Mail*, R6.

Industry Canada. 2009 (August). "Canadian ICT sector profile." Retrieved 12 November 2010 from www.ic.gc.ca/eic/site/ict-tic.nsf/eng/h_ito7229.html.

———. 2013 (March). "Canadian ICT sector profile." Retrieved 9 November 2014 from www.ic.gc.ca.

———. 2014 (5 November). "Strengthening Canada's digital economy and increasing high-speed internet access." News release retrieved 10 November 2014 from www.ic.gc.ca.

Infantry, Ashante. 2013 (1 October). "CBC wades gently into on-air commercials." *Toronto Star*. Retrieved 15 September 2014 from www.thestar.com/business/tech_news/2013/10/01/cbc_wades_gently_into_onair_commercials.html.

Infopresse. 2010. "Télévision." In *Médias: Guide annuel des médias*. Montreal: Éditions Infopresse, 42.

Information Highway Advisory Council. 1997. *Preparing Canada for a Digital World: Final Report*. Ottawa: Industry Canada.

Innis, Harold. 1950. *Empire and Communications*. Toronto: Oxford University Press.

———. 1951. *The Bias of Communication*. Toronto: University of Toronto Press.

Interactive Advertising Bureau of Canada. 2014 (17 September). *Canadian Internet Advertising Revenue Survey*. Accessed 19 September 2014 from www.iabcanada.com.

Intergovernmental Panel on Climate Change (IPCC). 2014. *Climate Change 2014 Synthesis Report*. IPCC: Geneva.

International Telecommunications Union (ITU). 2014. "The World in 2014: ICT facts and figures." Accessed 9 May 2014 http://www.itu.int/en/ITU-D/Statistics/Documents/facts/ICTFactsFigures2014-e.pdf.

International Women's Media Foundation (IWMF). 2011. *Global Report on the Status of Women in the News Media*. Washington: International Women's Media Foundation.

Ives, Nat. 2010. "Mounting web woes pummel newspapers." *Advertising Age* 81, 26: 6.

Iype, Mark. 2010 (5 July). "CP news service to privatize." *Vancouver Sun*, B2.

Jackson, John, Greg Nielsen, and Yon Hsu. 2011. *Mediated Society: A Critical Sociology of Media*. Don Mills, ON: Oxford University Press.

Jay, Martin. 1974. *The Dialectical Imagination*. London: Routledge.

Jeffrey, Liss. 1994. "Rethinking audiences for cultural industries: Implications for Canadian research." *Canadian Journal of Communication* 19, 3–4: 495–522.

Jenkins, Henry. 1992. *Textual Poachers: Television Fans and Participatory Culture*. New York: Routledge.

———. 2006. *Convergence Culture: Where Old and New Media Collide*. New York: New York University Press.

Jensen, Klaus Bruhn. 1990. "The politics of polysemy: Television news, everyday consciousness and political action." *Media, Culture and Society* 12, no. 1: 57–77.

Jhally, Sut. 1997. *Advertising and the End of the World* (video). Media Education Foundation.

Jiwani, Yasmin. 2010. "Rac(e)ing the nation: Media and minorities." In Shade, 2010: 271–86.

Jobb, Dean. 2011. *Media Law for Canadian Journalists*, 2nd ed. Toronto: Emond Montgomery Publications.

Johnston, Russell. 2010. "Advertising in Canada." In Shade, 2010: 104–20.

Jones, Andrew. 2010. *Globalization: Key Thinkers*. Cambridge, UK: Polity Press.

Josephi, Beate. 2012. "How much democracy does journalism need?" *Journalism* 14, no. 4: 474–89.

Kamenetz, A. 2013 (7 November). "Why video games succeed where the movie and music industries fail." *Fast Company*. Accessed 19 October 2014 at www.fastcompany.com.

Kane, Laura. 2014 (13 August). "CBC lays off veteran sportscasters Steve Armitage and Mark Lee." Canadian Press. Retrieved 18 August 2014 from J-source.ca.

Karim, Karim H. 2009. "Commentary: Pundits, pachyderms, and pluralism: The never-ending debate on multiculturalism." *Canadian Journal of Communication* 34: 701–10.

Katz, Elihu, and Paul Lazarsfeld. 1955. *Personal Influence: The Part Played by People in the Flow of Mass Communications*. New York: Free Press.

Kehaulani Goo, Sara. 2006 (7 October). "Ready for its close-up." *Washington Post*. Accessed 4 August 2010 at www.washingtonpost.com/wpdyn/content/article/2006/10/06/AR2006100600660.html.

Khakoo, Salza. 2006. "Colour TV." *Ryerson Review of Journalism* (Spring). Accessed at www.rrj.ca/issue/2006/spring/624.

Kidd, Terry, and Irene Chen. 2008. *Social Information Technology: Connecting Society and Cultural Issues*. Hershey, PA: Information Science Reference.

Kimmel, Michael S., and Jacqueline Holler, eds. 2011. *The Gendered Society*. Don Mills, ON: Oxford University Press.

King, Russell. 1995. "Migrations, globalization and place." In Massey and Jess, 1995.

Klein, Naomi. 2014. *This Changes Everything: Capitalism vs. the Climate*. Toronto: Knopf Canada.

Kleinman, Alexis. 2012 (19 December). "12 items Walmart considers more dangerous than assault weapons." *Huffington Post*. Retrieved 3 October 2014 from www.huffingtonpost.com/2012/12/18/walmart-banned-products_n_2324382.html.

Kotsopoulos, Patsy. 2004. "The nostalgic appeal of a popular place: Female fans interpreting *Road to Avonlea*." *Canadian Children's Literature* (Spring): 113–4.

Kovach, Bill, and Tom Rosenstiel. 2001. *The Elements of Journalism: What Newspeople Should Know and the Public Should Expect*. New York: Crown.

Kozolanka, Kirsten, ed. 2014. *Publicity and the Canadian State*. Toronto: University of Toronto Press.

———, Patricia Mazeppa, and David Skinner. 2012. "Considering alternative media in Canada: Structure, participation, activism." In *Alternative Media in Canada*, Kirsten Kozolanka, Patricia Mazeppa, and David Skinner, eds. Vancouver: University of British Columbia Press, 1–22.

Krashinsky, Susan. 2010a. "CRTC favours broadcasters in TV shakeup," *The Globe and Mail*, 23 March, A1.

———. 2010b (18 November). "Cineplex to unveil movie download service." *The Globe and Mail*, B10.

———. 2010c (5 May). "Al Jazeera English to launch in Canada." *The Globe and Mail*, B8.

———. 2014 (15 August). "Brought to you buy . . . Blurring the lines between news and ads." *The Globe and Mail*, B6.

Krippendorf, Klaus. 2004. *Content Analysis: An Introduction to Its Methodology*. Thousand Oaks, CA: Sage.

Kristeva, Julia. 1969. "Le mot, le dialogue et le roman." In *Sèmiòtikè: Recherches pour une sémanalyse*. Paris: Editions du Seuil.

Kücklich, J. 2005. "Precarious playbour: Modders and the digital games industry." *Fibreculture Journal* 5. Accessed 18 October 2014 at journal.fibreculture.org.

Ladurantaye, Steve. 2010 (11 September). "Bell ushers in new era with CTV deal." *The Globe and Mail*, 1, 18.

LaGuardia, Robert. 1977. *From Ma Perkins to Mary Hartman: The Illustrated History of Soap Opera*. New York: Ballantine Books.

Lam, H-L, D. H. Boteler, B. Burlton, and J. Evans. 2012 (October). "Anik-E1 and E2 satellite failures of January 1994 revisited." *Space Weather* 10, no. 10. Retrieved 23 June 2014 from: DOI: 10.1029/2012SW000811.

Larrain, Jorge. 1979. *The Concept of Ideology*. London: Hutchinson.

———. 1983. *Marxism and Ideology*. London: Macmillan.

Laville, Camille, and Michael Palmer. 2012. "The international news agencies (and their TV/multimedia sites): The defence of their traditional lead in international news production." In Frau-Meigs, et al., 175–85.

Law Central Alberta. n.d. "Statutes and Regulations (Federal)." Retrieved 12 November 2015 from http://www.lawcentralalberta.ca/en/know/laws-canada/statutes-regulations-federal.

Law Central Canada. n.d. "Statutes and regulations." Retrieved 1 November 2014 from www.lawcentralcanada.ca/CanadianLaw/Cstatutes.aspx.

Law, J., and M. Callon. 1988. "Engineering and sociology in a military aircraft project: A network analysis of technological change." *Social Problems* 35, 3: 285.

Learmonth, Michael. 2010. "Can YouTube rake in Google-size revenue?" *Advertising Age* 81, 5: 1–19.

Leblanc, Jean-André. 1990. "Pour s'arranger avec les gars des vues, l'industrie du cinéma et de la video au Canada 1982–1984." In *Les Industries de la Culture et de la Communication au Québec et au Canada,* Gaëtan Tremblay, ed. Sillery, QC: Les Presses de l'Université du Québec.

Leblanc, Daniel, and Tu Thanh Ha. 2014 (16 April). "RCMP charge teen in relation to Heartbleed bug attack on CRA." *The Globe and Mail.* Retrieved 23 June 2014 from http://www.theglobeandmail.com/news/national/rcmp-charge-teen-in-relation-to-alleged-heartbleed-bug-theft/article18041007/.

Lee, Richard E. 2003. *The Life and Times of Cultural Studies.* Durham, NC: Duke University Press.

Leiss, William, Stephen Kline, and Sut Jhally. 1990. *Social Communication in Advertising: Persons, Products and Images of Well-Being,* 2nd ed. Scarborough, ON: Nelson Canada.

———, ———, ———, and Jaqueline Botterill. 2005. *Social Communication in Advertising,* 3rd ed. New York: Routledge.

Lent, John A. 1998. "The animation industry and its offshore factories." In *Global Productions: Labor in the Making of the "Information Society".* Gerald Sussman and John A. Lent, eds. Cresskill, NJ: Hampton Press.

Lessig, Lawrence. 2001. *The Future of Ideas: The Fate of the Commons in a Connected World.* New York: Random House.

———. 2008. *Remix: Making Art and Commerce Thrive in the Hybrid Economy.* New York: Penguin.

Lévi-Strauss, Claude. 1969. *The Raw and the Cooked.* London: Jonathan Cape.

Lewis, Michael. 2014 (17 September). "'We're here to stay,' Wind Mobile says." *Toronto Star,* B1.

Lievrouw, Leah. 2011. *Alternative Media and Activist New Media.* Malden, MA: Polity Press.

Litt, Paul. 1992. *The Muses, the Masses, and the Massey Commission.* Toronto: University of Toronto Press.

Lord, A.B. 1964. *The Singer of Tales.* Cambridge, MA: Harvard University Press.

Lorimer, Rowland. 2002. "Mass communication: Some redefinitional notes." *Canadian Journal of Communication* 27, 1: 63–72.

———. 2012. *Ultra Libris: Policy, Technology, and the Creative Economy of Book Publishing in Canada.* Toronto: ECW Press.

Lule, Jack. 2012. *Globalization and Media: Global Village of Babel.* Lanham, MD: Rowman and Littlefield.

Lumpkin, John J. 2003 (22 May). "US officials examine the quality of information war planners had before invasion." Accessed at www.sfgate.com/cgi-bin/article._cgi?f=/news/archive/2003/05/22/national1251EDT0637.DTL.

Lynch, Jake, and Annabel McGoldrick. 2005. *Peace Journalism.* Stroud, UK: Hawthorn Press.

Lyons, Daniel. 2010 (5 April). "Think really different." *Newsweek*: 47–51.

McCarten, James, ed. 2013. *The Canadian Press Stylebook: A Guide for Writers and Editors,* 17th ed. Toronto: The Canadian Press.

McCarthy, Shawn. (Feb. 10, 2012). "Ottawa's new anti-terrorism strategy lists eco-extremists as threats." *The Globe and Mail.* Retrieved 1 October 2014 from www.theglobeandmail.com/news/politics/ottawas-new-anti-terrorism-strategy-lists-eco-extremists-as-threats/article533522.

———. 2015 (17 February). "Anti-petroleum movement a growing security threat to Canada, RCMP say." *The Globe and Mail.* Retrieved 5 March 2015 from www.theglobeandmail.com/news/politics/anti-petroleum-movement-a-growing-security-threat-to-canada-rcmp-say/article23019252.

MacCharles, Tonda. 2010 (8 May). "No right to shield sources, court rules." *Toronto Star,* 4.

———. 2014 (13 June). "Police need warrant to get internet customers' identities, Supreme Court rules." *The Toronto Star.* Retrieved 24 June 2014 from http://www.thestar.com/news/canada/2014/06/13/police_need_warrant_to_get_internet_customers_identities_supreme_court_rules.html.McChesney, Robert W. 1997. *Corporate Media and the Threat to Democracy.* New York: Seven Stories Press.

———. 1998. "The political economy of global communication." In *Capitalism and the Information Age: The Political Economy of the Global Communication Revolution,* Robert W. McChesney, Ellen Meiksins Wood, and John Bellamy Foster, eds. New York: Monthly Review Press.

———. 2003. "The new global media." In *The Global Transformations Reader: An Introduction to the Globalization Debate,* David Held and Anthony McGrew, eds. Cambridge: Polity Press, 260–8.

———. 2013. *Digital Disconnect: How Capitalism Is Turning the Internet against Democracy.* New York: The New Press.

———, and John Nichols. 2009. *The Death and Life of American Journalism.* New York: Nation Books.

McDiarmid, Jessica. 2013 (28 November). "Canada let US spy at G20, report says: Documents released by Snowden show Ottawa allowed surveillance in 2010," *The Toronto Star*, A3.

MacDonald, Gayle. 2007 (24 November). "Wanted: Cancon everywhere." *The Globe and Mail*, R13.

Macdonald, Isabel. 2008. "'Parachute journalism' in Haiti: Media sourcing in the 2003–2004 political crisis." *Canadian Journal of Communication*, 33: 213–32.McGuigan, Jim. 1992. *Cultural Populism*. London: Routledge.

McGuigan, Lee, and Vincent Manzerolle, eds. 2014. *The Audience Commodity in the Digital Age*. New York: Peter Lang.

McInturff, Kate. 2014 (1 May). "Where are all the women on Canada's 100 top CEOs list?" Canadian Centre for Policy Alternatives. Retrieved 3 October 2014 from www.huffingtonpost.ca/kate-mcinturff/canada-100-top-ceos_b_454681.

McKelvey, F. 2010. "Ends and ways: The algorithmic politics of network neutrality." *Global Media Journal*, Canadian ed., 3(1), 51–73.

McKenna, Barrie. 2014 (7 October). "Mail delivered directly to your door—only $20 a month." *The Globe and Mail*, B1, B11.

McKercher, Catherine. 2002. *Newsworkers Unite: Labor, Convergence, and North American Newspapers*. Lanham, MD: Rowman & Littlefield.

McKnight, Zoe, and Kim Nursall. 2014 (28 March). "Province cracks whip on unpaid internships." *Toronto Star*, A16.

McLuhan, Marshall. 1962. *The Gutenberg Galaxy: The Making of Typographic Man*. Toronto: University of Toronto Press.

———. 1964. *Understanding Media: The Extensions of Man*. Toronto: McGraw-Hill.

McQuail, Denis. 2000. *McQuail's Mass Communication Theory*, 4th ed. Thousand Oaks, CA: Sage.

———. 2010. *McQuail's Mass Communication Theory*, 6th ed. Thousand Oaks, CA: Sage.

Magazines Canada. 2005 (17 October). "A taxing question." Retrieved 31 October 2014 from www.magazinescanada.ca.

———. 2013a. *Digital Factbook 2013*. Accessed 1 May 2014 at www.magazinescanada.ca/uploads/File/AdServices/FactBooks/2013/DigitalMagazineFactBook2013FinalEng.pdf

———. 2013b. *Magazine Trends 2012*. Retrieved 27 October 2014 from https://www.magazinescanada.ca/uploads/File/AdServices/Research/Trends/Trends2012EngJun2013.pdf.

Magder, Ted. 1985. "A featureless film policy: Culture and the Canadian state." *Studies in Political Economy* 16: 81–109.

———. 1993. *Canada's Hollywood: The Canadian State and Feature Films*. Toronto: University of Toronto Press.

Mah, Bill. 2010 (23 September). "Netflix launches in Canada." *Calgary Herald*, C1.

Maimona, M. 2013 (31 May). "Made in Canada video games industry contributes $2.3 billion to country's GDP." *Financial Post*. Accessed 19 October 2014 at business.financialpost.com.

Malik, S. 1989. "Television and rural India." *Media, Culture and Society* 11, 4: 459–84.

Mansell, Robin. 2012. "ICTs, discourse and knowledge societies: Implications for policy and ractice." In Frau-Meigs, et al., 123–39.

Marcuse, Herbert. 1963 [1954]. *Reason and Revolution: Hegel and the Rise of Social Theory*. New York: Humanities Press.

———. 1964. *One-Dimensional Man: Studies in the Ideology of Advanced Industrial Society*. Boston: Beacon Press.

Marshall, P. David. 2004. *New Media Cultures*. New York: Arnold.

Martin, Robert, and Stuart Adam. 1991. *A Source-Book of Canadian Media Law*. Ottawa: Carleton University Press.

Marvin, Carolyn. 1988. *When Old Technologies Were New: Thinking about Electric Communication in the Late Nineteenth Century*. New York: Oxford University Press.

Masmoudi, Mustapha. 2012. "Correlations between NWICO and information society: Reflections of a NWICO actor." In Frau-Meigs, et al., 17–28.

Massey, Doreen. 1991. "A global sense of place." *Marxism Today* (June): 24–9.

———. 1992. "A place called home?" *New Formations* 17: 3–15.

———. 1995. "The conceptualization of place." In Massey and Jess. 1995.

———, and Pat Jess, eds. 1995. *A Place in the World? Cultures and Globalization*. New York: Oxford University Press.

———, and ———. 1995. "Places and cultures in an uneven world." In Massey and Jess, 1995.

Masthead. 2010 (21 January). "Canadian Periodical Fund: Winners and losers." Accessed 11 November 2010 at www.mastheadonline.com/news.

———. 2014a (7 April). "Digital readership on the rise: PMB." *Masthead*. Retrieved 28 October 2014 from www.mastheadonline.com.

———. 2014b (7 April). "Ontario Labour Ministry cracks down on unpaid internships." Retrieved 28 October 2014 from www.mastheadonline.com.

Mayeda, Andrew, and David Akin. 2008 (24 September). "PM slams Quebec arts community: Protests over cuts fail to 'resonate with ordinary people.'" *National Post*, A4.

Mayer-Schönberger, Viktor, and Kenneth Cukier. 2013. *Big Data: A Revolution That Will Transform How We Live, Work, and Think*. Boston: Eamon Dolan/Houghton Mifflin Harcourt.

Media Awareness Network. 2010. "Ethnic media in Canada." Accessed 26 July 2010 at www.media-awareness.ca.

Mediacaster Magazine. 2011. "TV or not TV?" Retrieved 25 March at www.mediacastermagazine.com/issues/story.aspx?aid=1000405845.

Media Education Foundation. 2010. *Killing Us Softly IV* (video). Northhampton., MA.

Media Technology Monitor. 2014 (18 June). *Media Technology Adoption, Spring 2014: Analysis of the English-Language Market*. (rep.).

Mencher, Melvin. 2006. *News Reporting and Writing*, 10th ed. New York: McGraw-Hill.

Meyers, Marian. 1997. "News of battering." In *Social Meanings of News: A Text-Reader*, Dan Berkowitz, ed. Thousand Oaks, CA: Sage.

Meyrowitz, Joshua. 1985. *No Sense of Place: The Impact of Electronic Media on Social Behavior*. New York: Oxford University Press.

———. 1994. "Medium theory." In *Communication Theory Today*, David Crowley and David Mitchell, eds. Stanford, CA: Stanford University Press, 50–7.

Mezei, Jean-François. 2009 (30 March). "An analysis of telecom decision *CRTC* 2008–108." Available at www.vaxination.ca/crtc/2008_108_analysis1.pdf.

Milberry, Kate. 2012. "Freeing the net: Online mobilizations in defense of democracy." In *Alternative Media in Canada*, Kirsten Kozolanka, Patricia Mazepa, and David Skinner, eds. Vancouver: University of British Columbia Press.

Miller, John. 1998. *Yesterday's News: Why Canada's Daily Newspapers Are Failing Us*. Halifax: Fernwood.

———, and Caron Court. 2004. "Who's telling the news? Race and gender representation in Canada's daily newsrooms." Accessed at www.diversitywatch.ryerson.ca/home_miller_2004report.htm.

———. 2005/2006. "Who's telling the news? Racial representation among news gatherers in Canada's daily newsrooms. *International Journal of Diversity in Organisations, Communities and Nations* 5, no. 4: 133–42.

Miller, Toby. 2010 (June 2). "Why do so many First World academics think cultural imperialism is old hat when so many other people don't?" Lecture, Canadian Communication Association, Montreal.

Mills, Sara. 2004. *Discourse*. New York: Routledge.

Mitchell, D. 1988. "Culture as political discourse in Canada." In *Communication Canada*, Rowland Lorimer and D.C. Wilson, eds. Toronto: Kagan and Woo.

Mitrovica, Andrew. 2006–2007. "Hear no evil, write no lies." *The Walrus* 3, 10: 37–43.

Modleski, Tania. 1984. *Loving with a Vengeance: Mass-Produced Fantasies for Women*. London: Methuen.

Moll, Marita, and Leslie Regan Shade, eds. 2004. *Seeking Convergence in Policy and Practice*. Ottawa: Canadian Centre for Policy Alternatives.

———. 2008. *For Sale to the Highest Bidder: Telecom Policy in Canada*. Canadian Centre for Policy. Retrieved 5 August 2014 from www.policyalternatives.ca/sites/default/files/uploads/publications/National_Office_Pubs/2008/For_Sale_To_The_Highest_Bidder_contents_intro.pdf.

———. 2011. *The Internet Tree: The State of Telecom Policy in Canada 3.0*. Canadian Centre for Policy Alternatives. Retrieved 5 August 2014 from www.policyalternatives.ca/sites/default/files/uploads/publications/National%20Office/2011/06/Internet_Tree_0.pdf.

More wedge politics. 2014 (26 February). "More wedge politics from the PQ government," *The Gazette*, A20.

Morley David. 1980. *The "Nationwide" Audience: Structure and Decoding*. British Film Institute Television Monographs, 11. London: BFI.

———. 1986. *Family Television: Cultural Power and Domestic Leisure*. London: Comedia.

———, and Kevin Robins. 1995. *Spaces of Identity: Global Media, Electronic Landscapes and Cultural Boundaries*. London: Routledge.

Morris, Peter. 1978. *Embattled Shadows: A History of Canadian Cinema, 1895–1939*. Montreal and Kingston: McGill-Queen's University Press.

Mosco, Vincent. 1996. *The Political Economy of Communication: Rethinking and Renewal*. London: Sage.

———. 1998. "Militant particularism: Beta testing a new society." Accessed 31 May 2011 at www.mip.at/attachments/362.

———. 2009. *The Political Economy of Communication*, 2nd ed. London: Sage.

———, and Catherine McKercher. 2006. "Convergence bites back: Labour struggles in the Canadian communications industry." *Canadian Journal of Communication* 31: 733–51.

Mulvey, Laura. 1975. "Visual pleasure and narrative cinema." *Screen* 16, no. 3: 6–18.

Murdock, Graham. 1990. "Large corporations and the control of the communications industries." In *Culture, Society and the Media*, Michael Gurevitch, Tony Bennett, James Curran, and Jane Woollacott, eds. Toronto: Methuen.

Murphy, Rex. 2010 (19 March). "A government gone viral." *National Post*, A16.

Murray, Catherine. 2007. "The Media." In *Policy Analysis in Canada: State of the Art*, Laurent Dobuzinskis, Michael Howlett, and David Laycock, eds. Toronto: University of Toronto Press, 525–50.

———. 2010. "Audience-making: Issues in Canadian audience studies." In Shade, 2010, 83–103.

Murray, Laura. 2005. "Bill 60 and copyright in Canada: Opportunities lost and found." *Canadian Journal of Communication* 30, no. 4: 649–54.

Murray, Stuart. 2012. "Nous sommes avenir / à venir: The voice of the we yet to come." *Canadian Journal of Communication* 37: 495–97.

Murray, Susan, and Laurie Ouellette. 2004. *Reality TV: Remaking Television Culture*. New York: New York University Press.

Murray, Warwick. 2006. *The Geographies of Globalization*. London: Routledge.

Music Canada. 2012 (12 April). *Economic Impact Analysis of the Sound Recording Industry in Canada*. Retrieved 31 October 2014 from www.musiccanada.com.

———. 2013. *Music Canada Statistics 2013*. Retrieved 31 October 2014 from www.musiccanada.com.

———. 2014. *Tariff 8 Q & A*. Retrieved 31 October 2014 from www.musiccanada.com.

Napoli, Philip. 2011. *Audience Evolution*. New York: Columbia University Press.

Nash, Knowlton. 1994. *The Microphone Wars: A History of Triumph and Betrayal at the CBC*. Toronto: McClelland & Stewart.

National Campus and Community Radio Association (NCRA). 1987. "The NCRA statement of principles." Accessed 29 July 2004 at www.ncra.ca/business/NCRA Statement.html.

Negroponte, Nicholas. 1995. *Being Digital*. New York: Knopf.

Nesbitt-Larking, Paul. 2007. *Politics and the Media: Canadian Perspectives*, 2nd ed. Peterborough, ON: Broadview Press.

Newman, Nic, and David A.L. Levy, eds. 2014. *Reuters Institute Digital News Report, 2014*. Oxford, UK: Reuters Institute for the Study of Journalism.

NewMedia TrendWatch. 2010. Canada, June. Accessed 11 November 2010 at www.newmediatrendwatch.com/markets-by-country/11-long-haul/45-canada.

Nicey, Jérémie. 2012. "The notion of access to information and knowledge: Challenges and divides, sectors and limits." In Frau-Meigs, et al., 163–74.

Nielsen, Greg. 2009. "Framing dialogue on immigration in *The New York Times*." *Aether: Journal of Media Geography* 4: 22–42. Accessed at 130.166.124.2/~aether/volume_04.html.

Nordenstreng. Kaarle. 2012. "The history of NWICO and its lessons." In Frau-Meigs, et al., 29–40.

Nordicity. 2013. *Canada's Video Game Industry in 2013: Final Report*. Ottawa: Nordicity.

O'Brian, Amy. 2006 (9 September). "Will this man save the music biz? Vancouver's Terry McBride, who manages a clutch of superstars, found success by learning to ignore his critics." *Vancouver Sun*, F3.

Olson, David R., ed. 1980. *The Social Foundations of Language and Thought*. New York: Norton.

Ong, Walter. 1982. *Orality and Literacy: The Technologizing of the Word*. London: Methuen.

Ontario Arts Council. 2014. *2012–2013 Grants History*. Retrieved 29 October 2014 from www.arts.on.ca.

Ontario Media Development Corporation. 2008 (30 September). *A Strategic Study of the Magazine Industry in Ontario*. Accessed 10 November 2010 at www.omdc.on.ca.

———. 2010. *Industry Profile: Book Publishing*. Retrieved 1 November 2010 from www.omdc.on.ca.

———. 2014. *Industry Profiles: Book Publishing*. Retrieved 29 October 2014 from www.omdc.on.ca.

Oreskovic, Alexei. 2014. "Exclusive: Facebook to expand video ads to seven countries outside U.S." Reuters. Accessed 21 May 2014 at www.reuters.com/article/2014/05/20/us-facebook-video-idUSBREA4J0LR20140520.

Ó Siochrú, Seán. 2010. "Implementing communication rights." In Raboy and Shtern, 2010.

Osler, Andrew M. 1993. *News: The Evolution of Journalism in Canada*. Toronto: Copp Clark Pitman.

Osnos, Peter. 2009. "What's a fair share in the age of Google?" *Columbia Journalism Review* 48, no. 2: 25–8.

Ostrikoff, Lisa. 2013 (31 January). "Farewell 'push' marketing, hello brand journalism." *The Globe and Mail*. Retrieved 26 August 2014 from www.theglobeandmail.com.

O'Sullivan, T., J. Hartley, D. Saunders, and J. Fiske. 1983. *Key Concepts in Communication*. Toronto: Methuen.

Paré, Daniel J. 2012. "Télécommunications: Plus ça change, plus c'est la même chose?" In *Cultural Industries.ca: Making Sense of Canadian Media in the Digital Age*, Ira Wagman and Peter Urquhart, eds. Toronto: James Lorimer, 110–28.

Park, David W., Nicholas W. Jankowski, and Steve Jones eds. *The Long History of New Media*. New York: Peter Lang.

Patel, Fay, Prahalad Sooknanan, Giselle Rampersad and Anuradha Mundkur. 2012. *Information Technology, Development, and Social Change*. New York: Routledge.

Paterson, Chris A. 2001. "Media imperialism revisited: The global public sphere and the news agency agenda." In *News in a Globalized Society*, Stig Hjarvard, ed. Göteborg: Nordicom.

———. 2005. "News agency dominance in international news on the internet." In Skinner et al., 2005: 145–63.

Payzant, Geoffrey. 1984. *Glenn Gould: Music and Mind*. Toronto: Key Porter.

Peers, Frank. 1969. *The Politics of Canadian Broadcasting, 1920–1951*. Toronto: University of Toronto Press.

———. 1979. *The Public Eye*. Toronto: University of Toronto Press.

Pegg, Mark. 1983. *Broadcasting and Society 1918–1939*. London: Croom Helm.

Pendakur, Manjunath. 1990. *Canadian Dreams and American Control: The Political Economy of the Canadian Film Industry*. Toronto: Garamond Press.

———. 1998. "Hollywood North: Film and TV production in Canada." In *Global Productions: Labor in the Making of the "Information Society,"* Gerald Sussman and John A. Lent, eds. Cresskill, NJ: Hampton Press.

Pevere, Geoff, and Greig Dymond. 1996. *Mondo Canuck: A Canadian Pop Culture Odyssey*. Scarborough, ON: Prentice Hall.

Pew Research Center, Project for Excellence in Journalism. 2010 (11 January). *How News Happens: A Study of the News Ecosystem of One American City*. Accessed 6 October 2010 at www.journalism.org/analysis_report/how_news_happens.

Picard, Robert G. 1989. *Media Economics: Concepts and Issues*. Newbury Park, CA: Sage.

PIPA/Knowledge Network. 2003. "Study finds widespread misperceptions on Iraq highly related to support for war." Accessed at www.pipa.org/OnlineReports/Iraq/IraqMedia_Oct03/IraqMedia_Oct03_pr.pdf.

Plato. 1973. *Phaedrus*. Walter Hamilton, trans. Toronto: Penguin.

Poindexter, Paula, Sharon Meraz, and Amy Schmitz Weiss, eds. 2008. *Women, Men, and News: Divided and Disconnected in the News Media Landscape*. New York and London: Routledge.

Prado, Javier Calzada, and Miguel Angel Marzal. 2013. "Incorporating data literacy into information literacy programs: Core competencies and contents." *Libri* 63, no. 2: 123–34.

Press, Andrea L. 2000. "Recent developments in feminist communication theory." In *Mass Media and Society*, James Curran and Michael Gurevitch, eds. New York: Oxford University Press, 2–43.

——— and Sonia Livingstone. 2006. "Taking audience research into the age of new media: Old problems and new challenges." In *Cultural Studies and Methodological*

Issues, Mimi White, James Schwoch, and Dilip Goanker, eds. London: Blackwell, 175–200.

Print Measurement Bureau (PMB). 1998. *PMB 98 Readership Volume.* Toronto: PMB.

———. 2006. *PMB 98 Readership Volume.* Toronto: PMB.

———. 2009. *PMB 2009 Readership Volume.* Toronto: PMB.

———. n.d. "Introducing PMB." Accessed at www.pmb.ca.

Pritchard, David, and Florian Sauvageau. 1999. *Les journalistes canadiens: Un portrait de fin de siècle.* Quebec: Les Presses de l'Université Laval.

Professional Writers Association of Canada. 2014. *What to Pay a Writer.* Retrieved 30 October 2014 from www.writers.ca/index.php/component/content/article/80-pwac-resources/76-pwac-resource-what-to-pay-a-writer.

"Properties." Retrieved 3 August 2010 at www.ctv.ca/properties.

Propp, Vladimir. 1970. *Morphology of the Folktale.* Austin: University of Texas Press.

Quebec. 2010. "L'information au Québec: Un intérêt public." Québec: Groupe de travail sur le journalisme et l'avenir de l'information au Québec.

Quebecor. 2010. "Quebecor at a glance." Accessed 3 August 2010 at www.quebecor.com.

———. 2013 (4 December). "Sun Media continues implementation of its restructuring and optimization plan." News release retrieved 18 August 2014 from J-source.ca.

Quill, Greg. 2009 (22 October). "CBC revamps news flagships." *Toronto Star,* A24.

Raboy, Marc. 1990. *Missed Opportunities: The Story of Canada's Broadcasting Policy.* Montreal and Kingston: McGill-Queen's University Press.

———. 1995a. *Accès inégal: les canaux d'influence en radiodiffusion.* Sainte-Foy, QC: Les Presses de l'Université du Québec.

———. 1995b. "The role of public consultation in shaping the Canadian broadcasting system." *Canadian Journal of Political Science* 28, 3: 455–77.

———, and Jeremy Shtern, eds. 2010. *Media Divides: Communication Rights and the Right to Communicate in Canada.* Vancouver: University of British Columbia Press.

Radway, Janice. 1984. *Reading the Romance: Women, Patriarchy, and Popular Literature.* Chapel Hill, NC: University of North Carolina Press.

Rantanen, Terhi. 1997. "The globalization of electronic news in the 19th century." *Media, Culture and Society* 19, 4: 605–20.

Renzetti, Elizabeth. 2014 (17 October). "When Iggy Pop can't make a living off his art, what chance do the rest of us have?" *The Globe and Mail.* Retrieved 18 October 2014 from www.theglobeandmail.com.

Resnick, Philip. 2000. *The Politics of Resentment: British Columbia Regionalism and Canadian Unity.* Vancouver: University of British Columbia Press.

Re:Sound. 2014 (5 August). *Tariff 8 Fact Sheet.* Retrieved 31 October 2014 from www.resound.ca.

Rettberg, Jill Walker. 2008. *Blogging.* Cambridge: Polity Press.

Reuters. 2013 (8 April). "77 percent of people use their computers while watching TV: Survey." *Huffington Post.*

Accessed 1 October 2014. Available at www.huffingtonpost.com/2013/04/09/tv-multitasking_n_3040012.html.

Rever, Judi. 1995 (4 February). "France faces off with Rambo." *The Globe and Mail,* C3.

Reynolds, Bill. 2002 (3 August). "Why your local radio station sounds like this (white bread)." *The Globe and Mail,* R1, R5.

Rheingold, Howard. 2003. *Smart Mobs: The Next Social Revolution.* Cambridge, MA: Perseus.

———. 2008. "Mobile media and political action." In *Handbook of Mobile Communication Studies,* James E. Katz, ed. New York: Springer, 225–39.

Rice-Barker, Leo. 1996 (6 May). "Victor victorious." *Playback,* 1, 5: 14.

Richer, Jules. 1999. "La presse québécoise en plein marasme: Chantal Hébert sonne l'alarme." *Le 30* 23, 3 (March): 11–13.

Richter, Solina, Kathy Kovacs Burns, Yuping Mao, Jean Chaw-Kant, Moira Calder, Shirley Mogale, Lyla Goin, and Kerry Schnell. 2011. "Homelessness coverage in major Canadian newspapers, 1987–2007." *Canadian Journal of Communication* 36, no. 4. Retrieved 6 August 2014 from www.cjc-online.ca/index.php/journal/article/view/2417.

Rideout, Vanda, and Andrew Reddick. 2001. "Multimedia policy for Canada and the United States: Industrial development as public interest." In *Continental Order? Integrating North America for Cybercapitalism,* Vincent Mosco and Dan Schiller, eds. Lanham, MD: Rowman & Littlefield.

Rose, Gillian. 1995. "Place and identity: A sense of place." In Massey and Jess, 1995.

Rose, Jonathan. 2014. "Taming the untameable? Constraints and limits on government advertising." In *Publicity and the Canadian State,* Kirsten Kozolanka, ed. Toronto: University of Toronto Press, 132–50.

———, and Simon Kiss. 2006. "Boundaries blurred: The mass media and politics in a hyper media age." In *Mediascapes: New Patterns in Canadian Communication,* 2nd ed., Paul Attallah and Leslie Regan Shade, eds. Don Mills, ON: Nelson, 332–45.

Rosenberg, Ross. 2010. "Sexual addictions: An introduction." Accessed 9 August 2010 at www.rosenbergtherapist.com.

Rosengren, K.E., and S. Windahl. 1989. *Media Matters: TV Use in Childhood and Adolescence.* Norwood, NJ: Ablex.

Roth, Lorna. 1996. "Cultural and racial diversity in Canadian broadcast journalism." In *Deadlines and Diversity: Journalism Ethics in a Changing World,* Valerie Alia, Brian Brennan, and Barry Hoffmaster, eds. Halifax: Fernwood.

———. 1998. "The delicate acts of 'colour balancing': Multiculturalism and Canadian television broadcasting policies and practices." *Canadian Journal of Communication* 23: 487–505.

———. 2005. *Something New in the Air: The Story of First Peoples Television Broadcasting in Canada.* Montreal and Kingston: McGill-Queen's University Press.

Rotstein, Abraham. 1988. "The use and misuse of economics in cultural policy." In *Communication Canada: Issues in Broadcasting and New Technologies,* Rowland Lorimer and D.C. Wilson, eds. Toronto: Kagan and Woo.

Ruddock, Andy. 2007. *Investigating Audiences*. London: Sage.

Ruggles, Myles. 2005. *Automating Interaction: Formal and Informal Knowledge in the Digital Network Economy*. Cresskill, NJ: Hampton Press.

Rutherford, Donald. 1992. *Dictionary of Economics*. London: Routledge.

Rutherford, Paul. 1990. *When Television Was Young: Primetime Canada*. Toronto: University of Toronto Press.

Sarikakis, Katharine, and Leslie Regan Shade. 2008. *Feminist Interventions in International Communications*. Lanham, MD: Rowman & Littlefield.

Sassen, Saskia. 1998. *Globalization and Its Discontents*. New York: New Press.

Saussure, Ferdinand de. 1974. *Course in General Linguistics*. London: Fontana.

Savage, Philip. 2014. "Audiences are key." In *Mediascapes: New Patterns in Canadian Communication*, 4th ed., Leslie Regan Shade, ed. Don Mills, ON: Nelson Education, 127–49.

Savio, Robert. 2012. "From New International Information Order to New Information Market Order. In Frau-Meigs, et al., 233–37.

Sawchuk, Kim. 2014. "Beyond the f-word: A constellation of feminist concepts for media researchers." In *Mediascapes: New Patterns in Canadian Communication*, Leslie Regan Shade, ed. Don Mills, ON: Nelson Education, 59–80.

Scannell, Paddy. 1988. "Radio times: The temporal arrangements of broadcasting in the modern world." In *Television and Its Audiences: International Research Perspectives*, P. Drummond and R. Paterson, eds. London: BFI.

———, and D. Cardiff. 1991. *A Social History of Broadcasting: Serving the Nation 1922–1939, vol. 1*. Oxford: Blackwell.

Schield, Milo. 2004. "Information literacy, statistical literacy and data literacy." *ISASIST Quarterly* 28, no. 2/3: 6–11.

Schlesinger, Philip. 1978. *Putting "Reality" Together: BBC News*. London: Constable.

———. 1983. *Televising "Terrorism": Political Violence in Popular Culture*. London: Comedia.

Schudson, Michael. 1978. *Discovering the News: A Social History of American Newspapers*. New York: Basic Books.

———. 2003. *The Sociology of News*. New York: W.W. Norton & Co.

Schulman, Mark. 1990. "Control mechanisms inside the media." In *Questioning the Media: A Critical Introduction*, John Downing, Ali Mohammadi, and Annebelle Sreberny-Mohammadi, eds. Newbury Park, CA: Sage.

Schulman, Norma. 1993. "Conditions of their own making: An intellectual history of the Centre for Contemporary Cultural Studies at the University of Birmingham." *Canadian Journal of Communication* 18, no. 1: 51–74.

Schulte, Stephanie Ricker. 2011. "Cutting the cord and 'crying socialist wolf': Unwiring the public and producing the third place. In Park, et al., 37–54.

Schultz, Ida. 2007. "The journalistic gut feeling: Journalistic doxa, news habitus and orthodox news values." *Journalism Practice* 1, no.2: 190–207.

Schumacher, E.F. 1973. *Small Is Beautiful: Economics as If People Mattered*. New York: Harper & Row.

Seigenthaler, Katherine. 1989 (12 September). "Hot singer, cool reception: Singer says disc jockeys don't play her records—they say they do, but . . ." *Chicago Tribune*. Retrieved 7 October 2014 from articles.chicagotribune.com/1989-09-12/features/8901120337_1_country-music-airplay-lang.

Seiter, Ellen, Hans Borchers, Gabrielle Kreutzner, and Eva-Maria Warth, eds. 1989. *Remote Control: Television, Audiences, and Cultural Power*. London: Routledge.

Shade, Leslie Regan. 2005. "Aspergate: Concentration, convergence, and censorship in Canadian media." In Skinner et al., 2005: 101–16.

———, ed. 2010. *Mediascapes: New Patterns in Canadian Communication*, 3rd ed. Don Mills, ON: Nelson Education.

———, ed. 2014. *Mediascapes: New Patterns in Canadian Communication*. Don Mills, ON: Nelson Education.

Shannon, Claude E., and Warren Weaver. 1949. *The Mathematical Theory of Communication*. Urbana, IL: University of Illinois Press.

Shea, Albert A. 1952. *Culture in Canada: A Study of the Findings of the Royal Commission on National Development in the Arts, Letters and Sciences (1949–1951)*. Toronto: Core.

Sheller, Mimi. 2014. "News now: Interface, ambience, flow, and the disruptive spatio-temporalities of mobile news media." *Journalism Studies*. Retrieved 5 August 2014 from dx.doi.org/10.1080.1461670X.2014.890324.

Shepherd, Tamara. 2013. "Young Canadians' apprenticeship labour in user-generated content." *Canadian Journal of Communication* 38: 35–55.

Shiach, Morag, ed. 1999. *Feminism and Cultural Studies*. London: Oxford University Press.

Shirky, Clay. 2008. *Here Comes Everybody: The Power of Organizing without Organizations*. New York: Penguin Press.

———. 2010. *Cognitive Surplus: Creativity and Generosity in a Connected Age*. New York: Penguin Press.

Sholle, David. 2002. "Disorganizing the 'new technology.'" In *Critical Perspectives on the Internet*, Greg Elmer, ed. Lanham, MD: Rowman & Littlefield, 3–26.

Signorielli, Nancy, and Michael Morgan, eds. 1990. *Cultivation Analysis*. Beverly Hills, CA: Sage.

Silverman, Craig. 2007. *Regret the Error: How Media Mistakes Pollute the Press and Imperil Free Speech*. New York: Sterling.

Silverman, Kaja. 1983. *The Subject of Semiotics*. New York: Oxford University Press.

Silverstone, R. 1981. *The Message of Television: Myth and Narrative in Contemporary Culture*. London: Heinemann Educational Books.

———. 2007. *Media and Morality: On the Rise of the Mediapolis*. Cambridge: Polity Press.

———. 1999. *Why Study the Media?* Thousand Oaks, CA: Sage.

Sinclair, Gerri, Julie Zilber, and Ed Hargrave. 2008 (March). *Regulating Content on the Internet: A New Technological Perspective*. Ottawa: Industry Canada.

Skinner, David. 2004. "Reform or alternatives? Limits and pressures on changing the Canadian mediascape." *Democratic Communiqué* 19 (Spring): 13–36.

———. 2010. "Minding the growing gaps: Alternative media in Canada." In Shade, 2010: 221–36.

———. 2012. "Sustaining independent and alternative media." In *Alternative Media in Canada*, Kirsten Kozolanka, Patricia Mazeppa, and David Skinner, eds. Vancouver: University of British Columbia Press, 25–45.

———. 2013 (28 August). "How best to lower cost of wireless? Stronger government regulation." *Winnipeg Free Press*. Retrieved 18 November 2014 from www.winnipegfreepress.com/opinion/analysis/stronger-government-regulation-how-best-to-lower-cost-of-wireless-221438811.html.

———, James Compton, and Mike Gasher, eds. 2005. *Converging Media, Diverging Politics: A Political Economy of News Media in the United States and Canada*. Lanham, MD: Lexington Books.

Slack, Jennifer Daryl, and J. Macgregor Wise. 2007. *Culture and Technology: A Primer*. New York: Peter Lang.

Smith, Adam. 1937 [1776]. *An Inquiry into the Nature and Causes of the Wealth of Nations*. New York: Modern Library.

Smith, Elaine. 2014 (May 5). "Racial bias 'entrenched' in Canadian advertising: Asian = technocrat, black = blue collar, researchers find." *U of T News*. Available at news.utoronto.ca/racial-bias-canadian-advertising.

Smith, Gavin John David. 2009. "Empowered watchers or disempowered workers? The ambiguities of power within technologies of security." In *Technologies of (In)security: The Surveillance of Everyday Life*. Katja Franko Aas, Helene Oppen Gunhus, and Heidi Mork Lommel eds. New York: Routledge-Cavendish.

Smith, Kevin. 2013 (24 June). "The Samsung app that lets you get Jay-Z's new album for free is available right now." Business Insider. Retrieved 15 September 2014 from www.businessinsider.com/jay-z-magna-carta-holy-grail-android-app-2013-6.

Smythe, Dallas. 1977. "Communications: Blindspot of Western Marxism." *Canadian Journal of Political and Social Theory* 1: 1–27.

———. 1981. "Communications: Blindspot of economics." In *Culture, Communication and Dependency: The Tradition of H.A. Innis*, William H. Melody, Liora R. Salter, and Paul Heyer, eds. Norwood, NJ: Ablex.

———. 1994. *Counterclockwise: Perspectives on Communication*, Thomas Guback, ed. Boulder, CO: Westview Press.

Société de développement des entreprises culturelles (SODEC). 2010. "Livres." Accessed 10 November 2010 at www.sodec.gouv.qc.ca/fr/programme/route/livre.

SODEC (Société de développement des entreprises culturelles). 2014. *Livres*. Retrieved 29 October 2014 from www.sodec.gouv.qc.ca.

Sontag, Susan. 1999. "On photography." In *Communication in History: Technology, Culture and Society*, David Crowley and Paul Heyer, eds. Don Mills, ON: Longman, 174–7.

Sotiron, Minko. 1997. *From Politics to Profit: The Commercialization of Daily Newspapers, 1890–1920*. Montreal and Kingston: McGill-Queen's University Press.

Spangler, Todd. 2013 (11 December). "Google video site to net $1.96 billion in advertising revenue this year, according to eMarketer." *Variety*. Accessed 25 April 2014 at variety.com/2013/digital/news/youtube-to-gross-5-6-billion-in-ad-revenue-in-2013-report-1200944416.

Spry, Graham. 1931. "Canada's broadcasting issue." In *Canadian Forum* (April).

Standing Senate Committee on Transportation and Communication. 2010. *Plan for a Digital Canada*. Accessed at www.planpouruncanadanumerique.com/index.php?option=com_content&view=article&id=1&Itemid=10&lang=en.

Stanford, Jim. 2008. *Economics for Everyone: A Short Guide to the Economics of Capitalism*. Black Point, NS: Fernwood.

Starr, Paul. 2004. *The Creation of the Media: Political Origins of Modern Communications*. New York: Basic Books.

Statistics Canada. 1997. *Recent Cultural Statistics (Highlights from Canada's Culture, Heritage and Identity: A Statistical Perspective)*. Accessed at www.pch.gc.ca/culture/library/statscan/stats_e.htm.

———. 1998a. "Focus on culture." *Quarterly Bulletin from the Culture Statistics Program* (Winter). Catalogue no. 87–004–XPB.

———. 1998b. "Hitting a high note: Canadian recording artists in 1998." *Quarterly Bulletin from the Culture Statistics Program* 14, 2. Accessed at www.statcan.ca/english/ads/87-004-XPB/pdf/fcdart.pdf.

———. 2001. *Overview: Access to and Use of Information Communication Technology*. Catalogue no. 56–505–XIE. Ottawa: Minister of Industry, March.

———. 2003. *Immigration and Visible Minorities*. Accessed at www12.statcan.ca/english/census01/products/highlight/Ethnicity/Index.cfm?Lang+E.

———. 2005 (14 June). "More magazines, higher profit." Accessed at www.statcan.ca/english/freepub/11-002-XIE/2005/06/16505/16505_02.htm.

———. 2006 (15 August). "Canadian internet use survey." *The Daily*. Accessed at www.statcan.ca/Daily/English/060815/d060815b.htm.

———. 2009. *Canada Year Book 2009*. Ottawa: Statistics Canada, 155–66.

———. 2010 (10 May). "Canadian internet use survey." Accessed 28 July 2010 at www.statcan.gc.ca/daily-quotidien/100510/dq100510a-eng.htm.

———. 2011a. *Immigration and Ethnocultural Diversity in Canada: National Household Survey, 2011*. Catalogue no. 99-010-X2011001. Ottawa: Statistics Canada.

———. 2011b. "2011 National household survey: Immigration, place of birth, citizenship, ethnic origin, visible minorities, language and religion." Accessed 6 May 2014 at http://www.statcan.gc.ca/daily-quotidien/130508/dq130508-eng.pdf.

———. 2013. "Households with home internet access." Accessed 6 May 2014 at www.statcan.gc.ca/daily-quotidien/131116/t131126d001-eng.htm.

———. 2014a. *Radio Broadcasting Industry 2013*. Catalogue no, 56-208-X, June. Ottawa: Minister of Industry.

———. 2014b. *Television Broadcasting Industries 2013*. Catalogue no. 56-207-X, July. Ottawa: Minister of Industry.

———. 2014c. *Book Publishers 2012*. Catalogue no. 87F0004X. Ottawa: Minister of Industry.

———. 2014d. *Periodical Publishing 2011*. Catalogue no. 87F0005X. Ottawa: Minister of Industry.

Steel, Emily. 2010 (15 July). "Google wins Omnicom as ally." *Wall Street Journal*. Accessed 12 August 2010 at www.wsj.com/articles/SB10001424052748704746804575367401477982456.

Steeves, Valerie. 2010. "Privacy in a networked world." In Shade, 2010: 341–55.

Storey, J. 1993. *Cultural Theory and Popular Culture*. London: Harvester Wheatsheaf.

Sullivan, John L. 2013. *Media Audiences: Effects, Users, Institutions, and Power*. Thousand Oaks, CA: Sage Publications.

Sutel, Seth. 2000 (11 January). "New media marries old." *Montreal Gazette*, F1, F4.

Tarkka, Minna. 2011. "Labours of location: Acting in the pervasive media space." In *The Wireless Spectrum: The Politics, Practices, and Poetics of Mobile Media*. Barbara Crow, Michael Longford, and Kim Sawchuk eds. Toronto: University of Toronto Press, 131–45.

Taylor, Charles. 2005. *Modern Social Imaginaries*. Durham, NC: Duke University Press.

Taylor, Kate. 2014 (12 April). "What should it be? Folio: CBC." *The Globe and Mail*. (Kindle edition).

Taylor, Frederick Winslow. 1997 [1911]. *The Principles of Scientific Management*. Mineola, NY: Dover Publications.

Taylor, Gregory. 2013. *Shut Off: The Canadian Digital Television Transition*. Montreal and Kingston: McGill-Queen's University Press.

Taylor, Lesley Ciarula. 2011 (8 March). "Canadian scientists crack code for tracing anonymous emails." *Toronto Star*. Accessed at www.thestar.com/news/canada/2011/03/08/canadian_scientists_crack_code_for_tracing_anonymous_emails.html.

Thompson, Edward P. 1980 [1963]. *The Making of the English Working Class*. Harmondsworth, UK: Penguin.

Thompson, John B. 1990. *Ideology and Modern Culture: Critical Social Theory in the Era of Mass Communication*. Stanford, CA: Stanford University Press.

———. 1995. *The Media and Modernity*. Stanford, CA: Stanford University Press.

———. 1999. "The trade in news." In *Communication in History: Technology, Culture and Society, David Crowley and Paul Heyer, eds*. Don Mills, ON: Longman, 118–22.

Thomson Reuters. 2009. "About us." Accessed 15 December 2009 at www.thomsonreuters.com.

Thorne, Stephen. 2005 (4 September). "Court rejects radio station's case against CRTC." *St John's Telegram*, A11.

Tiessen, Paul. 1993. "From literary modernism to the Tantramar Marshes: Anticipating McLuhan in British and Canadian media theory and practice." *Canadian Journal of Communication* 18, no. 4: 451–68.

Trotman, Andrew, and Christopher Williams. 2014 (23 April). "Facebook profits triple as half of internet world now uses website." *The Telegraph*. Accessed 25 April 2014 at www.telegraph.co.uk/finance/newsbysector/mediatechnologyandtelecoms/digital-media/10783576/Facebook-profits-triple-as-half-of-internet-world-now-uses-website.html.

Trudel, Jonathan. 2010. "Steve Jobs n'est pas le sauveur." *Trente* 34, no. 6 (juin): 5.

Tuchman, Gaye. 1978. *Making News: A Study in the Construction of Reality*. New York: Free Press.

Tucker, Patrick. 2013 (7 May). "Has big data made anonymity impossible?" *MIT Technology Review*. Accessed at www.technologyreview.com/news/514351/has-big-data-made-anonymity-impossible.

Turkle, Sherry. 1995. *Life on the Screen: Identity in the Age of the Internet*. New York: Simon & Schuster.

Turner, Graeme. 1990. *British Cultural Studies: An Introduction*. London: Routledge.

Turner-Riggs Strategic Marketing Communications. 2007. *The Book Retail Sector in Canada, Sept*. Vancouver: Turner-Riggs Strategic Marketing Communications.

———. 2008. *Book Distribution in Canada's English-Language Market, May*. Vancouver: Turner-Riggs Strategic Marketing Communications.

UNESCO. 1980. *Many Voices, One World: Report by the International Commission for the Study of Communication Problems* (MacBride Commission). Paris: Unipub.

UNESCO Institute for Statistics. 2005. *International Flows of Selected Goods and Services, 1994–2003*. Accessed 14 July 2010 at www.uis.unesco.org/template/pdf/cscl/IntlFlows_EN.pdf.

Unifor. 2014. "About Unifor." Accessed 22 September 2014 from www.unifor.org/en/about-unifor.

United Nations. 1948. *Universal Declaration of Human Rights*. Accessed at www.unhchr.ch/udhr/lang/eng.htm.

Vaidhyanathan, Siva. 2001. *Copyrights and Copywrongs: The Rise of Intellectual Property and How It Threatens Creativity*. New York: New York University Press.

van Dijk, Jan A.G.M. 2005. *The Deepening Divide: Inequality in the Information Society*. Thousand Oaks, CA: Sage.

———. 2012. *The Network Society*, 3rd ed. London: Sage.

van Dijk, Teun A. 1985. *Handbook of Discourse Analysis*, 4 vols. London: Academic Press.

———. 1997. *Discourse as Structure and Process*. Thousand Oaks, CA: Sage.

van Ginneken, Jaap. 1998. *Understanding Global News: A Critical Introduction*. London: Sage.

Van Schewick, B. 2010. *Internet Architecture and Innovation*. Cambridge, MA: The MIT Press.

Vipond, Mary. 1992. *Listening In: The First Decade of Canadian Broadcasting, 1922–1932*. Montreal and Kingston: McGill-Queen's University Press.

———. 2000. *The Mass Media in Canada*, 3rd ed. Toronto: James Lorimer.

———. 2011. *The Mass Media in Canada: Who Decides What We Read, Watch, & Hear?* 4th ed. Toronto: James Lorimer.

Wagman, Ira, and Peter Urquhart. 2012. *E Cultural Industries.ca: Making Sense of Canadian Media in the Digital Age*. Toronto: James Lorimer.

Wakefield, Jane. 2010 (19 March). "World wakes up to digital divide." *BBC News*. Accessed 2 August 2010 at news.bbc.co.uk/2/hi/technology/8568681.stm.

Wallerstein, Immanuel. 1974. *The Modern World-System: Capitalist Agriculture and the Origins of the European World-Economy in the Sixteenth Century*. New York: Academic Press.

———. 2007. *World-Systems Analysis: An Introduction*. Durham, NC: Duke University Press.

Ward, Stephen J.A. 2004. *The Invention of Journalism Ethics: The Path to Objectivity and Beyond*. Montreal and Kingston: McGill-Queen's University Press.

———. 2014. "Ethics resources." *Media Morals*. Retrieved 26 August 2014 from mediamorals.org/ethics-resources/.

Warnica, Richard. 2005 (28 October). "Cultural diversity: Canada's UN victory." *The Tyee*. Accessed at www.thetyee.ca/News/2005/10/28/CanadaUNVictory.

Waters, Richard. 2010 (22 January). "Exclusive: YouTube profits 'coming this year,'" *Financial Times* techblog. Accessed 4 August 2010 at blogs.ft.com/techblog/2010/01/exclusive-youtube-profits-coming-this-year.

Watters, Haydn. 2015 (18 June). "C-51, controversial anti-terrorism bill, is now law. So, what changes?" Retrieved 30 July 2015 from www.cbc.ca/news/politics/c-51-controversial-anti-terrorism-bill-is-now-law-so-what-changes-1.3108608.

Weir, Ernest Austin. 1965. *The Struggle for National Broadcasting in Canada*. Toronto: McClelland & Stewart.

Wikström, Patrik. 2009. *The Music Industry: Music in the Cloud*. Cambridge: Polity Press.

Wilkinson, Alec. 2006 (31 July). "The lobsterman: Solving a mystery off the Maine coast." *New Yorker*: 56–65.

Williams, Carol T. 1992. *It's Time for My Story: Soap Opera Sources, Structure and Response*. London: Praeger.

Williams, Raymond. 1958. *Culture and Society: 1780–1950*. New York: Columbia University Press.

———. 1976. *Key Words: A Vocabulary of Culture and Society*. London: Fontana.

———. 1974. *Television: Technology and Cultural Form*. Glasgow: Fontana Collins.

———. 1989. *Resources of Hope: Culture, Democracy, Socialism*, Robin Gable, ed. London: Verso.

Williamson, Judith. 1978. *Decoding Advertisements: Ideology and Meaning in Advertising*. London: Boyars.

Willis, Andrew, Susan Krashinsky, and Grant Robertson. 2010 (12 May). "New life for CanWest papers, but debt remains." *The Globe and Mail*, B1.

Willis, John. 2000. "The colonial era: Bringing the post to North America." In *Special Delivery: Canada's Postal Heritage*, Francine Brousseau, ed. Fredericton, NB, and Hull, QC: Goose Lane Editions and Canadian Museum of Civilization, 35–46.

Willis, Paul. 1977. *Learning to Labor*. New York: Columbia University Press.

Wilson, Kevin G. 2002 (18 May). "The rise and fall of Teleglobe." *Montreal Gazette*, B5.

Wingfield, Nick. 2014 (15 October). "Feminist critics of video games facing threats in 'GamerGate' campaign." *The New York Times*. Retrieved 2 March 2015 from www.nytimes.com/2014/10/16/technology/gamergate-women-video-game-threats-anita-sarkeesian.html?_r=0.

Winner, Langdon. 1977. *Autonomous Technology: Technics-out-of-Control as a Theme in Political Thought*. Cambridge, MA: MIT Press.

Winseck, Dwayne. 1998. *Reconvergence*. Cresskill, NJ: Hampton Press.

———. 2010. "Financialization and the 'crisis of the media': The rise and fall of (some) media conglomerates in Canada." *Canadian Journal of Communication* 35: 365–93.

———, and Jin, Dal Yong. 2012. *The Political Economies of Media: The Transformation of the Global Media Industries*. New York: Bloomsbury Academic.

Withers, Edward, and Robert S. Brown. 1995. "The broadcast audience: A sociological perspective." In *Communications in Canadian Society*, Benjamin D. Singer, ed. Don Mills, ON: Nelson, 89–121.

Wober, J. Mallory, and Barrie Gunter. 1986. "Television audience research at Britain's Independent Broadcasting Authority, 1974–1984." *Journal of Broadcasting and Electronic Media* 30, 1: 15–31.

Women's Studies Group. 1978. *Women Take Issue: Aspects of Women's Subordination*. Birmingham: Centre for Cultural Studies.

Wong, Jan. 2013 (19 November). "Canadian Media Guild data shows 10,000 job losses in past five years." Retrieved 18 August 2014 from J-Source.ca.

Wong, Tony. 2014 (19 April). "TV shows like *Orphan Black* signal rise of the Canadian showrunner." *The Toronto Star*. Retrieved 25 April 2014 from http://www.thestar.com/entertainment/television/2014/04/19/tv_shows_like_orphan_black_signal_rise_of_the_canadian_show runner.html.

Wood, Ellen Meiksins. 2002. *The Origin of Capitalism: A Longer View*. London: Verso.

Woodcock, George. 1985. *Strange Bedfellows: The State and the Arts in Canada*. Vancouver: Douglas & McIntyre.

World Association of Newspapers. 2008 (2 June). "World press trends: Newspapers are a growth business." Accessed 18 October 2010 at www.wan-press.org/article17377.html.

———. 2010 (4 August). "World press trends: Advertising revenues to increase, circulation relatively stable." Accessed 18 October 2010 at www.wan-press.org/article18612.html?var_recherche=2009+circulation.

———. 2014 (9 June). "World press trends: Print and digital together increasing newspaper audiences." News release. Paris and Darmstadt, Germany: World Association of Newspapers.

WSIS (World Summit on the Information Society). 2010. Accessed 23 June 2010 at www.itu.int/wsis/index.html.

YMA (Youth Media Alliance). 2009. "The case for kids programming." Accessed 19 June 2014 from www.ymamj.org/pdf/thecase2009.pdf.

York, Geoffrey. 2002 (5 October). "Great firewall of China stifles dissent on the net." *The Globe and Mail*, A14.

Ze, David Wei. 1995. "Printing as an agent of social stability during the Sung dynasty." Doctoral dissertation, Simon Fraser University.

Zelizer, Barbie. 2010. "Journalists as interpretive communities, revisited." In Allan, 2010: 181–90.